UNITY IN DIVERSITY

*Italian Communism and
the Communist World*

CENTER FOR INTERNATIONAL STUDIES
MASSACHUSETTS INSTITUTE OF TECHNOLOGY

Studies in International Communism

UNITY IN DIVERSITY

*Italian Communism and
the Communist World*

Donald L. M. Blackmer

THE M.I.T. PRESS
Massachusetts Institute of Technology
Cambridge, Massachusetts, and London, England

Copyright © 1968 by
The Massachusetts Institute of Technology

Set in Linotype Baskerville and printed by
The Heffernan Press Inc., Worcester, Massachusetts
Bound in the United States of America by
The Riverside Press, Cambridge, Massachusetts

Library of Congress catalog card number: 67-27339

In memory of
Alexander G. Korol

PREFACE

Research on nonruling Communist parties has often, in my view, failed to convey a sensitive appreciation of the domestic environment in which a given party must operate. This is particularly difficult, if only for reasons of space and emphasis, in a book such as mine whose main focus is not domestic issues, but the evolution of a party's policies and attitudes with respect to international Communist affairs. Yet one cannot evade the responsibility of trying to understand the causal link between a party's domestic interests and actions and its behavior on the international scene.

For me, much of the fascination of this study has been in the effort to perceive the effects on the Italian party of the interaction between external events—above all, the crises of de-Stalinization and the Sino-Soviet split—and the potent political and economic pressures operating on the party at home. Although I have tried to view the problem from the perspective of Rome rather than Moscow, I cannot pretend to that combination of intensive training in both Communist and Italian affairs that is ideally to be desired. My background is in Soviet studies, and it was from that vantage point that I first began to take an interest in the increasingly self-assertive role the Italian party was assuming in the Communist world.

It seems likely that in future studies of the Italian party the relative emphasis on domestic and international aspects will have to be reversed. In the last few years the Italian party has passed through what may well prove to have been an irrevocable qualitative transformation of its relations with the Communist world. In 1956, with Stalin's shadow still reaching long over the Communist world, the central issue before the party was the nature of its ties with the Soviet Union. This issue is of course not finally resolved: the dialectical slogan "unity in diversity" expresses well the permanent tension between the party's desire for autonomy and its simultaneous need to uphold the values of proletarian internationalism.

But the question for the next decade is not this. It is whether the party can successfully adapt to the changing realities of Italian life,

preserving or enhancing its share of power in that society without
at the same time giving up the essential attributes of organization
and ideology that make a Communist party different from any
other.

It would be redundant to venture additional comment at this
point. Some further discussion of the book's purposes and perspectives is to be found in the opening pages of the first chapter, and
the Epilogue contains a few reflections about the present condition
and future prospects of Italian communism, along with a review of
relevant recent events.

There remains only the pleasant duty of counting up my many
blessings. My greatest debt is to my colleagues in the Department of
Political Science and the Center for International Studies, M.I.T.,
and especially to Max F. Millikan, whose wisdom and generosity
have meant much to me personally over the past decade and who is
largely responsible for making the Center the stimulating place it
is. I owe a great deal to the energy and imagination of William E.
Griffith, director of the Center's research program on international
communism. During the past half-dozen years Professor Griffith and
his staff have built up a collection and filing system of current materials on Communist affairs that is probably unsurpassed in university circles for its combination of accessibility and wide-ranging
coverage. Without these files—available, incidentally, to any scholar
desiring to use them—my research task would have been far more
difficult. This program is being supported by a generous grant to
M.I.T. by the Ford Foundation for research and teaching in international affairs; my own research time to work on this book was
financed from this source.

I am grateful to Professor Joseph LaPalombara of Yale for his
enthusiastic support at an early stage of the research and for his
help, along with that of Dr. Gloria Pirzio Ammassari, in making
the arrangements for a brief but extremely helpful round of interviews in Rome in the summer of 1964. The anonymity of those with
whom I talked during those weeks will be preserved, but I cannot
fail to record with appreciation the invariable openness and courtesy with which I was received, by Communists as well as observers
of the Communist scene.

Many friends and colleagues were kind enough to read and com-
ment on all or parts of the manuscript. For this I want particularly
to thank Kevin Devlin, Giorgio Galli, William Griffith, Richard
Hatch, Ernst Halperin, Nathan Leites, Daniel Lerner, Renato
Mieli, Alessandro Pizzorno, Lucian Pye, Robin Remington, Sidney
Tarrow, and Joan Urban. Special thanks go to my parents for their

discerning observations on the manuscript, merely one among their countless manifestations of support over the years. I have a particular debt to Professor Merle Fainsod of Harvard, not only for his advice and encouragement as supervisor of the dissertation on which this book is based, but for the high standards set by his personal example as teacher and research scholar.

A particular word of gratitude is due to those who provide the indispensable supporting services offered by the Center and administered so cheerfully and capably by James Dorsey, Mary Burns, Kathleen Gallery, and their associates. The Center's Librarian, Patricia Carey, was unfailingly resourceful in mobilizing an unending flow of books and journals from the most diverse sources. Martha Gillmor, then the Center's editor, sharpened my prose and deftly reduced a longer manuscript to more readable dimensions. Jean P. S. Clark saved me more than a few unfortunate slips by devoting to the proofs the passion for accuracy of detail and expression that is her trademark. To Virginia Jackson my thanks for her long and careful labors with the index. I am grateful, finally, for the superior secretarial assistance of two charming young ladies, Diane Cook and Sally Lewis, and for the outstanding accuracy and intelligence applied by Mrs. Eileen Smith to the typing of two drafts of the manuscript.

My last and greatest debt is to my wife Joan, and to Steve, Alex, and Kate. This book owes much to them, but nothing so irreplaceable as the compelling proof their presence and personalities provide that life is indeed full of richer things.

Cambridge, Massachusetts   DONALD L. M. BLACKMER
September 1967

CONTENTS

CHAPTER ONE

PERSPECTIVES ON THE
ITALIAN COMMUNIST PARTY

For more than twenty years the Partito Comunista Italiano (PCI) has been one of the largest, politically most influential, and intellectually most lively of the nonruling Communist parties. Yet until recently little scholarly interest has been directed its way. Of the several reasons why this should have been so, perhaps the most telling was the widely held conviction that the PCI, like other Communist parties, was to be regarded essentially as an agent of the Soviet Union, its actions prompted less by the realities of Italian life than by the will of those who care for the interests of the Kremlin.

Acting on this not unreasonable though limited assumption, American students of Communist affairs turned their attention to the USSR itself and to other parties in power, for the most part extending their horizon to the nonruling parties only as one aspect of the study of Soviet foreign relations. The French party, having an important auxiliary role to play in Soviet foreign policy, evoked a certain interest, whereas Italy's lesser international status virtually assured the relative neglect of its Communist party.[1]

The PCI has not been similarly ignored by Italian observers, whose interest has naturally focused on matters of domestic strategy and operations. But Italian writing on the PCI has generally been distinguished by the strong polemical quality so evident in all aspects of Italian political life; the party has tended to be either attacked from a right-wing perspective as the most sinister threat to the values of a bourgeois, capitalist, and above all Catholic society, or berated by those on the non-Communist left as a traitor to the real interests of the working class, a massive and cynical obstruction

[1] On the French party see especially Marshall D. Shulman, *Stalin's Foreign Policy Reappraised* (Cambridge, Mass.: Harvard University Press, 1963), and Alfred J. Rieber, *Stalin and the French Communist Party: 1941–1947* (New York: Columbia University Press, 1962).

to desperately needed social and economic reforms.[2] Whichever the angle of vision, both Italian and other Western observers have agreed that the PCI's failure to make constructive contributions to Italian life since the Resistance and the immediate postwar years has been directly related to its subservience to Soviet interests.

The collapse of both the myth and the reality of monolithic communism that began to be revealed so plainly in 1956 gave rise to a changed outlook on the PCI. Non-Italian students of Communist affairs in particular, more interested in the Italian party as a participant in the international Communist movement than as a domestic political force, have fastened upon every sign of change in its relations with the USSR. The PCI has attracted attention primarily during such dramatic and emotion-laden periods as those following the Twentieth and Twenty-Second Soviet party Congresses, and they have accordingly tended to place particular weight on what they interpret as the party's conscious and active efforts to free itself from previously tight Soviet control. Richard Lowenthal, for example, has written that beginning in 1956 the Italian Communists "grasped the chance of greater polycentric autonomy implied in the weakening of Soviet authority. They welcomed it all the more eagerly because they hoped that visible proof of their independence would remove the principal obstacle to winning a share of power along the 'peaceful road.' "[3] Since that time, he adds, after their failure to react autonomously to the Hungarian crisis, they "have been waiting for their chance to become *really* independent."

Such an image of a party eagerly grasping at every opportunity to widen its freedom of action has not generally been shared by Italian observers. Although not denying, especially after 1963, that the quality of relations between the Italian and Soviet parties has somehow changed, they have stressed the aspects of continuity, the signs that the PCI has retained its ultimate and necessary dependence on the USSR. Giorgio Galli, for example, in one of the few studies of the Italian party available in English, contends that the PCI has virtually never assumed positions opposed to those of

[2] As an example of the former, see Angelo Perego, *Dottrina e prassi del partito comunista italiano* (Rome: Società Grafica Romana, [1961]). The latter can be illustrated by the Trotskyist perspective of Livio Maitan, *Teoria e politica comunista nel dopoguerra* (Milan: Schwarz, 1959). See also Giorgio Galli, *La sinistra italiana nel dopoguerra* (Bologna: Il Mulino, 1958), for an analysis of the 1945–1958 period, in which the PCI is presented as a conservative instrument for maintaining the status quo in Italy.

[3] "The Prospects for Pluralistic Communism" in Milorad M. Drachkovitch, ed., *Marxism in the Modern World* (Stanford: Stanford University Press, 1965), p. 263.

the USSR. Apparent divergences are explained as a calculated device:

A division of labor exists between the CPSU and the PCI: the second anticipates sometimes, as a *ballon d'essai,* positions which the first cannot yet publicly assume. Until October 1963 no single important position of the PCI that appeared to differ from the current Soviet line was not followed within a short time by a similar policy statement by the CPSU.[4]

While recognizing that a change had occurred during 1963 as a result of the Sino-Soviet dispute and the decline of Soviet authority, Galli and others have emphasized not the PCI's growing independence, but the caution and reticence with which it has acted: the party, despite its "considerable international prestige, has done remarkably little to safeguard its own interests; it assumed a new attitude only after realizing that not only the Poles but even the Rumanians were showing greater independence and dynamism."[5] All in all, the Italian stance is seen as a grudging and partial concession to the minimal requirements of political reality:

The positions of the PCI, which sometimes seem the most advanced of any party in the international Communist movement, are in reality as pro-Soviet as they possibly can be within the context of its location in the West and of Italian reality and of the leeway Moscow is willing to allow it.[6]

Each of these viewpoints stresses certain dimensions of the PCI's complex political profile and underplays others. The one approach, while usefully highlighting the enduring relevance of the Italian party's links with the Soviet Union and the pressures of domestic politics, seems reluctant to recognize both the extent of recent change and the significance of earlier clashes of interest. The other approach nicely grasps the historic significance for the Communist movement of what has occurred but somewhat slights the domestic factors and overplays the degree to which the Italian party has, since 1956, been actively seeking ways to enhance its bargaining power and its "real" independence from Soviet control.

The point of these comments is not to criticize one or another outlook but to introduce and illustrate the central question with

---

[4] "Italian Communism" in William E. Griffith, ed., *Communism in Europe: Continuity, Change, and the Sino-Soviet Dispute,* Vol. 1 (Cambridge, Mass.: The M.I.T. Press, 1964), pp. 302–383, at p. 303. Galli's essay was originally drafted before October 1963, then modified to take the events of that period into account. The author maintained, however, that his interpretation of the relationship did not require basic revision in the light of the PCI's response to the Sino-Soviet dispute in the summer and fall of 1963; see p. 379.

[5] *Ibid.,* p. 381.

[6] *Ibid.,* p. 303.

which this study deals: what has been the relationship of the Italian party with the Communist movement, and with the Soviet Union in particular, during a period of years when both international communism and Italian society were undergoing deep and in some respects dramatic change?

The differences in outlook derive partly, perhaps primarily, from the different contexts in which the Italian party has been viewed. Looked at from the standpoint of the international Communist movement, the PCI, in comparison with other nonruling parties, may often appear outspoken and even daring, an articulate advocate of more autonomous and decentralized relationships among the parties and of more flexible and cooperative policies with respect to non-Communist social and political forces. From the perspective of the Italian political scene, it may seem conservative and timid in its attitudes toward the Soviet Union and the Communist movement, capable of expressing ideological or political dissent only partially and by indirection, and thus failing to fulfill in fact its pretensions to be a truly independent national party of the Italian left.

Interpretation is complicated by other problems of perspective, not the least of which is the necessity, on most occasions, of referring to "the Italian Communist party" as though it were a monolithic organization with a readily definable set of goals and responses. It is in reality a complex political organism made up of individuals and informal coalitions whose interests and purposes are often not in harmony. When one attempts to interpret the party's intentions at any given moment, as must implicitly or explicitly be done in developing general hypotheses about its relationship with the Communist movement, it is difficult not to simplify its internal processes. What "the party" wants is not to be neatly summed up as what Palmiro Togliatti or Luigi Longo wants, still less as what may be desired by those on the party's left or right wing. Leadership in the PCI is a complex business of reconciling conflicting goals and instincts in order to arrive at policies at least minimally acceptable to all influential groups. The contrast, for example, between what for simplicity's sake we tend to label as "the party's attitude" toward the Soviet Union in 1956 and in 1961 was in good part determined by the reduced influence of the pro-Soviet conservative wing of the party in the latter year.

The shifting balance of forces within the party relates in turn to another crucial set of factors: the changing quality of Italian society and its impact on Communist behavior. The PCI's basic announced strategy of a peaceful, reformist, and parliamentary transition to socialism has been consistently upheld ever since Togliatti returned to Italy in 1944 to take over active direction of the party. These gradualist pronouncements notwithstanding, many Communists were unable for years after the war's end to renounce the vision of a violent revolutionary upheaval assisted in some way by the Soviet Union. Italy's political stability and dynamic economic growth, together with the moderation of Soviet policy, eventually rendered this perspective untenable. It became increasingly necessary, therefore, for the party to take seriously its own pretensions to be working out a distinctively Italian road to socialism. Younger generations of Communists in particular, less deeply affected by the prestige of the Soviet Union and better attuned to the realities of Italian life, began to urge the party to assume an increasingly autonomous position.

The researcher's problem, more easily stated than resolved, is somehow to combine these several perspectives. In order to comprehend the PCI's position in the world of international communism one should take into account all important aspects of its domestic situation, and vice versa. But one cannot, unhappily, do both things at the same time and do them equally well. I have been concerned primarily and in some detail with the PCI in its international role. Domestic factors, including the party's internal politics, have been introduced only to the extent—by no means negligible—that an understanding of its behavior within the Communist movement has seemed to require. My main purpose has been to throw some light on the policies and "personality" of one of the most interesting and yet most neglected of Communist parties, while at the same time offering a case study in the transformation of the international Communist movement during a peculiarly fascinating and decisive phase of its history.

In essence, my view of the PCI has been of a party attempting to reconcile conflicting values—one could loosely call them nationalist and internationalist values—in the face of a series of events largely outside its control. Between 1956 and my arbitrary but convenient end point of Togliatti's death in the summer of 1964, three main forces impinged upon the Italian Communist party. First, the related and acute crises of de-Stalinization and upheaval in Eastern Europe heightened the tensions between old and younger generations of Italian Communists and forced the leadership to confront the whole perilous question of the party's attitude toward the Soviet Union and toward freedom and democracy in socialist society. Second, there was the slower and deeper evolution of Italian political and economic life that created an endemic crisis in the party's alliance system and induced it to move more decisively along the reformist road already implicit in its actions during the early postwar years. Finally, there came the Sino-Soviet split and the accompanying decline of Soviet authority, encouraging the party to take up a more independent position and to rely increasingly on its own ideological and political resources. The cumulative effect of these interacting sets of developments has been to push the PCI into a more assertive and autonomous role in the international movement.

Each of these external forces has resulted from historical processes over which the party has had rather little influence. It could and did attempt to intervene at various points in both domestic and international Communist affairs, but in no case has it had the inherent strength to play a decisive part. The party has, therefore, despite the impression of responsible activism it has sought to convey, for the most part been reacting and adapting to circumstances rather than consciously and successfully manipulating events in pursuit of certain clear goals. At every stage the party leadership has tried to protect its essential interests by balancing the pressures coming from within the party, from the Italian political scene, from the realities of economic and social life, and from the Soviet Union and the international movement as a whole. In so doing, the PCI has sought to enhance its strength at home by revising its ideology and action to keep pace with the evolution of Italian society, while at the same time remaining true to deeply ingrained but increasingly tenuous principles of international proletarian solidarity.

The PCI in Historical Perspective

To understand why the Italian Communist party responded as it did to the forces at work upon it requires a brief excursion into its past. In the party's first two decades, it existed as a largely ineffectual and wholly dependent outpost of the international Communist movement; during the postwar period, it had a dramatic rise to a position of political strength in Italy and of considerable potential influence within the ranks of international communism. Nevertheless, despite its notable electoral successes, the party failed to capitalize fully on the tremendous opportunities that appeared to be open to it in the years just after the war. This failure, linked as it was in the minds of many to the PCI's subordination to Soviet priorities, helped create the preconditions for the changes that would begin to be realized during and after the pivotal year of 1956. And perhaps most important of all, a selective look at the early history of the Italian party enables one to perceive something of the personality and political style of Palmiro Togliatti, that subtle but tough intellectual-bureaucrat who dominated the party's life for nearly forty years.

The PCI was formed in early 1921, when a group of radical Socialists seceded from the Italian Socialist party (PSI) at its Seventeenth Congress in Livorno. Rejecting both the reformist spirit of many Socialist leaders and the romantic radicalism of much of the rank and file, the dissidents were determined to create an efficient and tightly organized working-class party affiliated to Moscow's Third International. For more than two decades the party would lead a highly precarious and frustrating existence, squeezed between the increasingly effective repressions of the Fascist police, who made it virtually impossible to launch and sustain organized political activities, and the importunate demands of Comintern officials who knew little and cared less about the real conditions of Italian life.[7]

Until the end of 1926 the party remained legal, at which time, along with other parties, it was outlawed and driven underground. From then until 1934 the PCI concentrated its domestic activities on covert propaganda and on efforts to stimulate labor disturbances and other shows of resistance to Mussolini's regime. Supported by funds and technical assistance from Moscow transmitted through headquarters established first in Switzerland, then in Paris, the PCI's operations were more widespread and effective than those of any other group.[8] The party's active cadres were few, however, and its efforts took a tremendous toll.[9] Layer after layer of party organizers and activists were rounded up and sent off to Fascist jails, especially beginning in November 1926, when Antonio Gramsci, Umberto Terracini, and other leading figures were arrested. Virtually all those who would emerge at the war's end in leading party positions spent some part of the 1930's in confinement.

The prime exceptions to the rule were the men directing the party's fortunes from abroad, chief among whom was Palmiro

[7] The only general history of the PCI yet published is Giorgio Galli, *Storia del Partito comunista italiano* (Milan: Schwarz, 1958), on which this summary review has necessarily relied for many questions of fact.

[8] "Indeed, over the entire period of the dictatorship there can be little doubt that the PCI's work of propaganda, organization, and reorganization was on a broader scale than that of *Giustizia e Libertà* or any of the other active groups. . . ." Charles F. Delzell, *Mussolini's Enemies: The Italian Anti-Fascist Resistance* (Princeton: Princeton University Press, 1961), p. 110.

[9] After 1926, active membership probably did not rise above 3,000, although higher figures were claimed. See Delzell, *Mussolini's Enemies*, p. 126, and Aldo Garosci, "The Italian Communist Party," in Mario Einaudi, Jean-Marie Domenach, and Aldo Garosci, *Communism in Western Europe* (Ithaca: Cornell University Press, 1951), p. 174.

Togliatti, a close associate of Gramsci since their student and early revolutionary days in Turin. Serving as the PCI's representative at Comintern headquarters in Moscow at the time of Gramsci's arrest, Togliatti was designated by the Russians to take command of the party. Until his death nearly four decades later he remained its chief, first as a little-known exile, then, after 1944, as one of Italy's most respected and feared public figures, the undisputed leader of the largest Communist party in the West.

The explanation for the PCI's relatively active role in the anti-Fascist movement is probably to be found less in the special heroism or patriotism of its members than in the simple fact that it was being continually spurred on from abroad. The party's strategy and tactics during those years were determined not by the facts of the Italian situation so much as by the pressing requirements of Soviet domestic and foreign policy. The Soviet turn to the left in 1928, for example, obliged the PCI to abandon earlier efforts to construct an anti-Fascist front of democratic forces and to turn loudly against the alleged "social fascism" of the social democrats. Similarly in 1934, when Soviet priorities were reversed following Hitler's rise to power, the Italian party quickly followed the French in instituting a policy of popular front alliances with other anti-Fascist parties. That neither tactic made a noticeable dent on the situation can hardly be blamed on either the Comintern or the PCI itself: the conditions of Fascist dictatorship were not such as to have permitted effective resistance from within.

It should not be supposed that the rather feeble record of tangible accomplishment meant that these years were being wasted. Despite Fascist persecution—indeed in large measure because of it—the party's organization was being tested and tempered in combat. A small but reliable group of top- and middle-level leaders was receiving a baptism of fire under the most difficult of circumstances, in which a high premium was placed on personal physical and moral toughness, on organizational talents, and on unquestioning obedience to authority. The party's successes both in the Resistance movement and in its organizational work after the fighting had ceased must certainly be traced back to the experience gained under the trying circumstances of underground life.

To this tangible legacy must be added the enormous political credit deriving from the PCI's role and reputation as the principal organized force in the anti-Fascist movement. This would later prove of inestimable value not only among the working class but also, and even more significantly, among Italian intellectuals. Ugo La Malfa has well described how, during the "sad and desperate

period" in Italian life after 1929 when democracy appeared bank-
rupt, many young Italian intellectuals grasped eagerly at the Communist explanation that the bourgeoisie, in a last-ditch defense of
their class interests, had sold themselves to fascism.[10] Their faith in
democracy gone, such men as Giorgio Amendola, Emilio Sereni, and
Eugenio Reale, an impressive group of young intellectuals from
Naples, were won over to the party most clearly identified at home
and abroad with the fight against fascism.

The prominent role played by such leading Communists as
Giuseppe Di Vittorio and Luigi Longo in the Spanish Civil War
strongly reinforced this image.[11] The payoff came a few years later
when the military and organizational training the Communists had
received in Spain, as well as in Italy itself, enabled them to play a
dominant role in the partisan movement in the North and to
emerge at the war's end with the enormous political and moral
credit of having materially helped Italy redeem herself from the
humiliations of the previous two decades.

TOGLIATTI AND THE COMINTERN. Important as were the PCI's
credentials as a leading participant in the national struggle against
fascism, the early history of Italian communism cannot be read in
exclusively or even predominantly domestic terms. The party did
manage to sink roots into Italian soil which would enable it, better
than any other Western Communist party, to become and remain
an effective mass organization, but it was a good deal more than
just a national force. Some part of its strength, and of its weakness
as well, derived from its status as a section of the Communist International, a loyal and disciplined ally of the great Socialist father-
land.[12]

There was from the start never the least doubt about this. Those
who left the Socialist party in 1921 to form the PCI did so in explicit
fulfillment of one of the central criteria for membership laid down
by the Communist International, the need to split parties Moscow

10 "Il dramma di una generazione," La Voce repubblicana, June 21, 1956, in
Il 1956: La crisi del comunismo e la via della democrazia (Bologna: Il Mulino,
1957), p. 49.

11 In Stuart Hughes' estimation, it was the Civil War that first gave the Com-
munists a position of supremacy in the anti-Fascist movement: "By the ruthless
use of the superior organization and material means at their disposal, the
Communists had squeezed out or suppressed their rivals." H. Stuart Hughes,
The United States and Italy (rev. ed.; Cambridge, Mass.: Harvard University
Press, 1965), p. 106.

12 No adequate study of the PCI's role in the Comintern has yet appeared.
I am much indebted to Joan Barth Urban for showing me several chapters of
her manuscript on "Moscow and the Italian Communist Party: 1926–1945."

chose to regard as reformist. The Italian Communist party, therefore, was "born through the direct intervention of the Communist
International, which was already dominated by the overpowering
weight of the effective power and myth of the Russian revolution."[13]
The first and only major shift in the party's top leadership, which
occurred during the mid-1920's, was similarly a reflection of Soviet
interests. When the USSR, having for the time being abandoned
hope of revolution in Europe, adopted a tactic of united action
with the Socialists, the new line was only grudgingly accepted by
Amedeo Bordiga, the PCI's insurrection-minded leader. Antonio
Gramsci won the leadership job from Bordiga by demonstrating not
only his adherence to the substance of Soviet policy (which Tasca on
the party's right wing also supported) but his acceptance of the
basic principle that the Comintern's authority was to be unconditionally recognized.[14]

Loyalty to the Comintern was adopted as a first principle by
Palmiro Togliatti as well. Early in 1926, shortly before Gramsci's
arrest, Togliatti had in fact found it necessary to remind his mentor
of the PCI's inevitable subordination to the demands of the Soviet
state and party. In reply to a worried letter from Gramsci, disturbed
by Stalin's evident willingness to wreck the unity of the Bolshevik
party by imposing stiff disciplinary measures against Trotsky and
other oppositionists, Togliatti brusquely dismissed the complaint,
insisting on the impossibility of meddling in Soviet affairs and on
the need for absolute trust in the actions of the Soviet leadership.[15]

One of the PCI's leading intellectuals, commenting on this episode
years later in a revealing and partially critical commemorative article on the first anniversary of Togliatti's death, observed that
while Togliatti always believed Gramsci's particular virtue to lie
in his great intuition and moral strength, he claimed for himself the
special role of political realist.[16] The characterization is an apt one.
Togliatti's ability to sense and to follow the prudent, realistic course
even when personal preference would have led him another way
was demonstrated time and again throughout his long career.

[13] Garosci, "The Italian Communist Party," in Einaudi et al., Communism in
Western Europe, p. 159.

[14] For this interpretation see Giorgio Galli, "La formazione del gruppo dirigente del PCI: (1923–1924)," Tempi moderni, New Series, No. 8 (January–March
1962), pp. 94–106.

[15] The exchange was published only in 1964: "1926: sulla rottura nel gruppo
dirigente del partito bolscevico," Rinascita, May 30, 1964, pp. 17–20. See Chapter
Ten for further comment on the publication of this exchange.

[16] Rossana Rossanda, "Unità politica e scelte culturali," Il Contemporaneo,
No. 8 (August 1965), p. 19; supplement to Rinascita, August 28, 1965.

By late 1926 the dictates of political realism had already begun to conflict with Togliatti's personal sense of how affairs ought to be managed in the Comintern and in the Soviet state itself. It was not a question of sympathizing with Trotsky's leftist domestic and foreign policies, for Togliatti was then and would remain by inclination a Communist of the right, associated more closely in spirit with Bukharin than with any other leading Soviet figure. To support the Stalin-Bukharin coalition of 1925–1927 was the natural thing for Togliatti to do. He was even then, however, coming to share some of the concerns Gramsci had expressed over the course the Soviet political struggle seemed to be taking.

Ignazio Silone has described an episode at a Comintern Executive Committee meeting in May 1927 at which the assembled delegates were asked to approve a resolution violently condemning a document Trotsky had addressed to the Soviet Politburo. Silone, with the support of Togliatti and the French and Swiss representatives, declined on grounds of principle to endorse the resolution unless he were first shown the Trotsky document, but the Soviets insisted on keeping it to themselves. Despite the "indignant, angry protests" of the other delegates, the dissenters stood by their position. The two Italians then drafted a letter to the Soviet comrades, promptly withdrawn on Bukharin's advice, attempting to explain that whereas the historical pre-eminence of the Russians gave them certain rights, these could not be imposed "in a mechanical and authoritarian way."[17] Gramsci's letter to Togliatti of only a few months before had tried to make exactly the same point: "But unity and discipline in this case cannot be mechanical and coerced."[18]

Togliatti would express such views openly, and at some risk to his own position, on one further occasion, the Comintern's Sixth Congress in the summer of 1928. It had by then become clear that Stalin was aiming to break with Bukharin and to shift Soviet policies and those of the Comintern decisively to the left. In this context, with another bitter factional struggle shaping up, Togliatti chose to deliver himself of a plea for an end to "organizational measures" as a solution to factional disputes within parties:

These forms of struggle can take on the force of an internal logic that can lead, even against our will, to the splitting and the atomization of the leadership forces of a party. We cannot close our eyes to the fact that

17 Ignazio Silone in Richard Crossman, ed., *The God That Failed* (New York: Harper & Row, 1963), pp. 108–112. See also the confirming remarks by the Swiss delegate to the meeting, Jules Humbert-Droz, "Le contraddizioni della politica sovietica," *Tempo presente*, I, 4 (July 1956), p. 280.
18 *Rinascita*, May 30, 1964, p. 19.

such phenomena exist today in some of our sections. We must face up to the danger before it has caused us graver damage.[19]

These episodes reveal an important dimension of Togliatti's political style. Although entirely capable of decisive and ruthless action when the chips were down, he was instinctively a man of moderation and compromise. Consistently opposed to sharp ruptures, he preferred to believe that unity could be preserved without either destroying one of the contending factions or establishing by superior force a purely artificial consensus. He was clearly worried by the course events were taking as Stalin consolidated his rule, in the Soviet Union and in the Comintern as well.[20] But being both a realist and a dedicated Communist, Togliatti would set aside his personal convictions if they happened to clash with the higher demands of the movement to which he was irrevocably committed. Not for him the hopeless gesture of resistance to forces beyond his control; this was but the foolish conceit of the intellectual, proud to display his moral integrity. Not for him, either, the sterile act of resigning from the party, as Silone and many others were to do. Silone has recorded Togliatti's own explanation of his choice in the difficult years of the late 1920's:

The present state of the International, he said in brief, was neither satisfactory nor agreeable. But all our good intentions were powerless to change it; objective historical conditions were involved and must be taken into account. The forms of the Proletarian Revolution were not arbitrary. If they did not accord with our preferences, so much the worse for us. And besides, what alternative remained? Other Communists who had broken with the Party, how had they ended up? Consider, he said, the appalling condition of Social Democracy.[21]

After his speech to the Sixth Comintern Congress, Togliatti accepted the inevitable and submitted to Stalinist discipline. The next years were not easy for him or for his party. As Togliatti

[19] "Il discorso di Ercoli al VI Congresso del Internazionale," *ibid.*, July 11, 1964, pp. 15–20, at p. 20. In an introductory note the speech is described as one "of discussion and open resistance to left extremist positions." Because it was so out of key with the prevailing tendency toward the left, in the context of Stalin's campaign against Bukharin, the speech was "received rather badly" by the Congress; on the pretext of insufficient time, Togliatti was not allowed to finish delivering his remarks. For recent debate over Togliatti's role at the Sixth Congress, see Giuseppe Berti, "Negli scritti di Grieco diciott' anni di vita del PCI," *ibid.*, June 18, 1966, pp. 21–23, and Luigi Amadesi, "Lo scontro al VI Congresso del Comintern," *ibid.*, September 3, 1966, pp. 22–23.

[20] For an interesting indication of Togliatti's reaction to the takeover of the Comintern by Stalinist bureaucrats, see the commemorative article by the Austrian Communist Ernst Fischer, "Un debito di gratitudine," *Il Contemporaneo*, No. 8 (August 1965), p. 9; supplement to *Rinascita*, August 28, 1965.

[21] Crossman, *The God That Failed*, p. 112.

personally was under suspicion for his association with the now discredited Bukharin, so the PCI as a whole came under fire for "rightist deviations" in policy and organizational matters. The Comintern berated the Italians for not having undertaken a vigorous offensive in Italy to capitalize on the presumed rising revolutionary tide and for having failed to repudiate early and decisively enough the PCI's rightist faction led by Tasca. At Moscow's insistence, therefore, purges were carried out within the top leadership, and the party's clandestine organization was reactivated, despite the exceedingly discouraging conditions then prevailing in Italy.

By 1934 the worst had passed, as Hitler's rise to power induced an about-face in Soviet foreign policy. The struggle for peace rather than revolution became the order of the day, and Communist parties everywhere developed their own versions of the popular front, the alliance of democratic forces against the Fascist menace. Popular front politics being far more in Togliatti's style than the radicalism of the previous years, he stepped forward at the Seventh Comintern Congress in 1935 along with the Bulgarian Dimitrov as a leading spokesman of the new line. For the next dozen years, despite some further Comintern criticism in 1938 for revisionist deviations, PCI policies appeared to be basically in harmony with those of Moscow. With the Spanish Civil War and the wartime Resistance movement in Northern Italy, the PCI entered into the heroic phase of its history. At last the party could turn all its energies outward into effective action against the Fascist enemy. And this time it managed to end up on the winning side, acquiring along the way the political and moral credit that would transform it almost overnight from a small exile organization into a powerful party of the masses.

THE POSTWAR YEARS. By the late spring of 1945, with Mussolini dead and the Resistance movement triumphant, "Italy was gripped by a strong revolutionary tide."[22] Especially to those Communists and other leftists who had fought in the partisan armies, the moment for a thorough political and social upheaval seemed at hand. But the revolution did not occur, in part because the Communist leadership did not wish it to.[23]

When Palmiro Togliatti returned to Italy in March 1944 after eighteen years abroad as an agent of the Communist International

[22] Delzell, *Mussolini's Enemies*, p. 554.
[23] For the broader context in which the conservative forces reasserted themselves over the leftist tide, see Delzell, *Mussolini's Enemies*, pp. 554–576, and Hughes, *The United States and Italy*, pp. 133–170. For the PCI's response to the situation, see Galli, *Storia del Partito*, pp. 235–280.

he had set out to reassure one and all that the Italian Communist party had not the least idea of attempting a proletarian revolution. The PCI was to be a national not a class party, open to all men and women of democratic persuasion whatever their religious beliefs or social status. Its avowed policy was to collaborate with all anti-Fascist forces, Socialist and Catholic alike, so as to bring the war to a speedy conclusion and begin building a new and democratic Italy.

Though such a policy of moderation was undoubtedly congenial to a man of Togliatti's political instincts, it was by no means only a reflection of his personal style. The balance of forces in Italy, occupied as it then was by Allied armies, was anything but favorable to insurrection by a Communist minority. Fully as important, Soviet interests were clearly opposed to Communist adventurism in Western Europe; Stalin had his eyes fixed on prizes nearer home, which might slip from his grasp if the West were prematurely aroused. Italy was to be American and British territory.

The PCI was, therefore, for all these reasons, the very model of reasonableness, seeking in every way possible to establish its claims to a share in governmental power. The Communist leaders helped write the Constitution of the Italian Republic, contenting themselves with incorporating broad statements of democratic objectives rather than specific economic and social reforms of a socialist character. Perhaps most clearly indicative of their compromising attitude, and of their acute awareness that Catholic hostility was the special and powerful barrier to communism in Italy, was the decision to abandon the anticlerical traditions of the Italian left and to vote in the Constituent Assembly to include the 1929 Lateran Pacts in the new Constitution, thereby perpetuating the Church's special status in the Italian system. The party made major efforts to collaborate with other political forces in the nongovernmental spheres as well, especially in the critical field of organized labor; a unified Italian General Confederation of Labor (CGIL) was established with power shared by Communist, Socialist, and Catholic labor leaders.

An effective strategy of penetration required the party to develop and demonstrate political and organizational strength by expanding its membership and its electorate and by exerting influence at critical points in the society. The PCI had emerged from the war already a mass party, claiming over 1.7 million members by the time of its Fifth Congress at the end of 1945.[24] The party's ranks

24 Galli, *ibid.*, p. 269.

would continue to grow for the next five years, then hold steady at a figure of more than 2 million for another five years before beginning to decline. This extraordinary membership (at its peak about 900,000 greater than the Christian Democrats) was effectively organized into an extensive network of sections and cells that made the party's presence felt in every corner of the country, especially in the industrial North and the largely agricultural "red belt" of Central Italy, where old socialist traditions plus the PCI's organizational work in the Resistance gave the left particular strength.

In the first postwar elections in June 1946 the PCI and the PSI together gained nearly 40 per cent of the vote, acquiring control separately or together over many towns and provinces in Northern and Central Italy. For the Socialists, who outpolled the Communists in 1946, this first election proved to be the high-water mark. Their electoral fortunes declined after Giuseppe Saragat led a group of right-wing Socialists out of the party in 1947 in protest against its alliance with the Communists. The PCI, on the contrary, increased its share of the vote in every subsequent national election, largely by consolidating its already strong position in Central Italy and by more than doubling its vote in the South and the islands. By the general election of 1953 the PCI's total of 22.6 per cent of the vote was well distributed over the country as a whole.

Saragat's secession from the PSI was an unmistakable sign that the postwar honeymoon had ended. In response to the political imperatives of the cold war, Togliatti's efforts to establish the PCI's credentials as a moderate, democratic, reformist party quickly collapsed. In May 1947 the Communist party was excluded from De Gasperi's government, and the years of Christian Democratic (DC) monopoly began. In September of that year the Cominform held its founding meeting, the French and Italian parties being assigned their part in neutralizing the newly aroused capitalist West. The PCI was subjected to scathing criticism (on Soviet orders, but at the hands of the then leftist Yugoslavs) for the failure of its conservative line, symbolized by its inability to prevent or even mount an effective protest against its exclusion from the government. The PCI's conservative policy had been endorsed and probably inspired by the Soviets, but the Italians may have played their part rather too convincingly for Moscow's taste. Now that the international situation had radically shifted, the PCI's proclivity to reformist parliamentary tactics had to give way to more aggressive actions designed to weaken Italian participation in the new American alliance.

Togliatti could not help but respond in some fashion to the external pressures for a more radical line. With the world rapidly being split into hostile camps, there could be no question as to his party's position. Any Communist leader who had failed to conform at such a time would certainly have had to confront a Soviet-backed challenge to his authority. And despite Togliatti's great prestige, there were many party officials and ordinary members, frustrated and disillusioned by the collapse of their revolutionary hopes, who would have enthusiastically welcomed a more radically minded leadership. In response to these pressures the party's propaganda and action temporarily assumed a harsher, more militant tone, especially during the fall and winter of 1947 when a campaign of general strikes and other mass demonstrations was undertaken in the major industrial centers.[25]

But cold war conditions imposed severe difficulties. The elections of April 1948, conducted by the Christian Democrats and the Vatican in the shadow of the Czech coup as a virtual crusade against atheistic communism, resulted in a sharp defeat for the left. The PCI-PSI Popular Front gathered only 31 per cent of the vote, while the Christian Democrats, strongly supported by the Southern peasantry and the urban middle class, advanced from the 35 per cent of two years before to their all-time high of 48 per cent. A further setback occurred a few months later when the Christian Democrats and Social Democrats quit the Communist-dominated CGIL and set up rival trade union federations under their own control. Defending Soviet coexistence policy many years later, the Italian party recalled those difficult years:

The facts have in reality shown all the obstacles that the cold war created for the people's struggle. In the capitalist countries the cold war gave force and vigor to the more reactionary and aggressive groups. It was one of the basic cohesive elements of the coalition of all the conservative forces in defense of the bourgeois order, a coalition led by these groups with the support and open intervention of the great imperialist powers. The cold war helped to aggravate and harden deep divisions and wounds among the popular masses.[26]

Despite the PCI's inability to escape the damaging consequences of the Soviet confrontation with the West, Togliatti had no inten-

[25] W. Hilton-Young, *The Italian Left: A Short History of Political Socialism in Italy* (London: Longmans, Green, 1949), p. 200, describes the Communist disorders as being of a new type: ". . . it was a carefully controlled technique which sought to excite the greatest possible alarm while inflicting the fewest possible casualties and provoking the least possible reprisal."

[26] "Per una nuova avanzata e per l'unità del movimento comunista internazionale," *L'Unità*, October 26, 1963, p. 3.

tion of turning back from the fundamental course on which he had set his party. He saw no viable alternative to the strategy of gradually increasing the PCI's strength on a national basis, moving out from its base of influence among the industrial and agricultural proletariat of the North and Center into the Southern peasantry and, if possible, sections of the urban middle class as well. As he would remark years later, "a purely working-class or Socialist alternative would be a grave error, isolating the proletariat from the masses of the working and middle class in a country where the proletariat is still weak, even numerically."[27] An intransigent policy relying heavily on the disruptive strength of organized labor would only alienate nonproletarian groups and draw the battle lines more sharply between the minority Marxist parties and the rest of a Catholic nation subject to the political influence of the Church. Decisive proof of the party's unwillingness to risk a direct confrontation with the government came in July 1948, when Togliatti was gravely wounded in an assassination attempt. Communist workers in Genoa, Turin, Milan, and other Northern cities staged a partly spontaneous general strike that might well have grown into a full-fledged insurrection had not the party leadership succeeded in restraining the rank and file.[28]

Following the setbacks of 1947–1948, the PCI attempted to reconcile its conflicting revolutionary and conciliatory instincts by settling into a pattern of behavior that combined loud verbal demands for reform with a minimum of effective action to achieve them. It seemed to some observers that the party had in effect reconciled itself to the status quo, accepting the benefits accruing to a large and permanent opposition party in the Italian parliamentary system and no longer even thinking seriously of overthrowing the existing balance of power. Giorgio Galli, writing from the perspective of 1958, concluded that "the PCI cooperates under the present system of parliamentary democracy not for the purpose of proposing a positive political alternative to the majority forces, or of pushing progressive innovations and reforms, but merely for the purpose of preserving the system itself, the institutional forms of which afford the Communists enough of a share of power to satisfy them."[29]

27 *Ibid.*, October 6, 1961.
28 For a detailed analysis of this episode and of the entire 1945–1948 period see Galli, *La sinistra italiana nel dopoguerra.*
29 "The Italian CP: Conservatism in Disguise," *Problems of Communism,* VIII, 3 (May–June 1959), p. 32. See also his earlier article, "The Italian CP, Part II: The Road toward a Dilemma, 1945–56," *ibid.,* V, 3 (May–June 1956), pp. 41–45.

Right or wrong as an interpretation of the leadership's intentions, the same impression was gradually sinking into the consciousness of many of the party's members and supporters. By the early 1950's signs of an incipient crisis had begun to emerge, especially in the industrial centers that constituted one of the party's greatest points of strength. The elections of June 1953, although in over-all terms a considerable victory for the PCI (its total increased by about one million votes over 1948, or from 19 per cent to 22.6 per cent of the electorate), showed a decline in some Northern industrial areas. Although party membership reached a peak of 2,145,317 in 1954 before beginning a virtually uninterrupted decline over the next decade, this aggregate figure concealed a steady shift away from the Northern areas. Whereas in 1946 about 54 per cent of the PCI membership had been in the North, by 1961 the figure had dropped to about 30 per cent; during the same period the percentage in the South and the islands had risen from 25 per cent to 46 per cent.[30]

Even more telling was the steady weakening of the CGIL's competitive position with the non-Communist labor unions. Effective discriminatory policies of the employers against Communist workers and their union, as well as the CGIL's own failure to adapt its bargaining strategy to the rapidly changing structure of Italian industry, had weakened its ability to protect the interests of its most important constituency. A growing loss of confidence in the CGIL was beginning to be reflected in trade union elections in the factories during 1954, and in the spring of the following year the CGIL suffered a particularly stinging defeat at the Fiat plants in Turin.[31]

To many dedicated Communists of different ranks and social origins, the party appeared to have reached something of a dead end. Underneath the official optimism there was a sense of frustration deriving from the party's evident inability to act either as an effective instrument for an eventual revolutionary overthrow or as an influential force for gradual transformation of the existing social order. The patrimony of energy, idealism, and organizational strength acquired during and just after the war was wasting away through disuse. To some of its adherents the party appeared to be losing a clear sense of what it was and where it was going, gradually

[30] For these and other useful membership data on the PCI I am indebted to a draft of Part Two of the study on "Patterns of Political Participation in Italy" prepared by a research group at the Carlo Cattaneo Research Institute in Bologna. A summary version of the findings will be published in English by the Twentieth Century Fund, followed by Italian publication of the full study in several volumes.

[31] See Chapter Eight.

relinquishing even the capacity for effective resistance to the conservative coalition of industrialists, landowners, and churchmen that dominated the Christian Democratic party and the nation as a whole.

Many, including probably a solid majority of party officialdom at all levels, arrived without great inner travail at a disciplined and passive acceptance of the situation. Persuaded by the leadership that the domestic and international balance of forces was not such as to permit an insurrection, and in any case instinctively skeptical of the idea of a peaceful, parliamentary road to socialism, they were reduced to the alternative of relying on the expectation of assistance from abroad. As Bernard Morris observed in 1956 about the European Communist parties: "They wait for what may never come, that is, the Soviet army. And it is precisely because the Western European Communist parties know their own ultimate weakness that their spirit and activity must often fade and falter."[32] Togliatti and his associates in the PCI leadership, however much they lectured against the crude belief of the so-called "sectarians" that the PCI could come to power only through direct Soviet military aid, were themselves infected by the passive frame of mind labeled *attesismo*. They too were waiting, not in expectation of the Red Army itself, perhaps, but in hopes of the favorable international environment that only Soviet power could create and that alone could decisively shift the balance of power within Italy itself.

There were dissenters, however. Some, sharing the conviction of the sectarians that routine activities in trade unions and cooperatives, in parliament, and in local governments would not lead to socialism in their time, called for more radical action. They declined to believe the semiofficial line put forward within the privacy of the party that Togliatti's strategy reflected Soviet instructions to avoid a direct assault on the capitalist enemy in Italy. Open expression of these leftist attitudes came in 1954 in the wake of one of the PCI's most notorious defections, that of Giulio Seniga, who had been a close collaborator of party Secretary Pietro Secchia and was particularly close to ex-partisan and worker groups in the North. Seniga and a small group of associates launched a journal, *Azione comunista,* in which they directly attacked Togliatti and called for an end to the "temporizing and capitulationist policy of the PCI and the CGIL."[33]

[32] Bernard S. Morris, "Some Perspectives on the Nature and Role of the Western European Communist Parties," *The Review of Politics,* XVIII, 2 (April 1956), p. 166.
[33] See Galli, *Storia del Partito,* pp. 337–341, for excerpts from the open letter in which Seniga stated his case.

The right wing, equally dissatisfied, felt that the party was pursuing its declared strategy only halfheartedly, without serious and sustained effort to focus its vast potential resources toward solution of the problems facing the working class. Especially among the skilled workers and party intellectuals of the North, frustration was mounting at the failure to undertake the detailed research into the conditions of factory life and the changing nature of industrial technology that would be required to devise effective means of mobilizing the workers in defense of their interests. Genuinely believing in the possibility of a distinctively Italian road to socialism, they could see no evidence that the party was moving in that direction.

The frustration began to lead to a heretical conclusion—that the root of the difficulty lay in the PCI's dependence on the USSR. This painful verdict was reached as early as 1950 by Valdo Magnani, a prominent figure in the party, personally close to Togliatti and then serving in the Secretariat of the Reggio Emilio federation. Together with Aldo Cucchi, a leader of the Italian Resistance, Magnani found the courage to point openly to the diminishing effectiveness and increasing isolation of the PCI, attributing its decline to an underestimation of the strength of the Italian working class and to the political error of assuming that "the great day of victory" could be won only with the help of Soviet bayonets.[34]

Magnani's crisis of faith was unusual in that it came relatively soon after the war and was provoked above all by the deep sympathies for Yugoslavia aroused during his wartime association with the Yugoslav partisans. Tito's stubborn and successful resistance to Stalin's excommunication contrasted favorably in his eyes with Togliatti's apparently comfortable acceptance of Soviet priorities.[35]

[34] Valdo Magnani and Aldo Cucchi, *Crisi di una generazione* (Florence: La Nuova Italia, 1952), p. 82. The book recounts their introduction to the Communist party during the heroic anti-Fascist period when virtue appeared exclusively on the side of the Communists and the Soviet Union, and their growing disillusionment in the postwar years as the PCI seemed to become bureaucratic and unresponsive to working-class needs. Italian interests, they insisted, had to begin to take precedence over those of the USSR in determining the party's course. An earlier book by the same authors, *Dichiarazioni e documenti* (Bologna: Tip. Luigi Parma, 1951), contains the official documents pertaining to their break with the party.

[35] Magnani was expelled from the party as an unprincipled traitor who had maintained contact with "Titoist elements, provocateurs of betrayal, [and] agents of warmongering imperialist forces. . . ." *Ibid.*, pp. 22–24, quoted in Galli, *Storia del Partito*, p. 309. He rejoined the party more than a decade later, shortly after the Soviet Twenty-Second party Congress, when Tito had been restored to the fold and Togliatti had set the PCI on a more independent course.

But if the particular circumstances were distinctive, the Magnani episode was nevertheless revealing of a frame of mind actually or latently present in many another comrade. Confidence in the Italian party was so closely linked to confidence in Stalin and the Soviet Union that a blow to Soviet prestige became a blow to the PCI as well. The strength of this proposition would not be fully revealed until the spring of 1956, when the shocking revelations Khrushchev had made about Stalin at the Twentieth CPSU Congress began to enter into the consciousness of Italian Communists. It is at this point, therefore, that our story begins.

CHAPTER TWO

DEATH OF THE HERO

For the PCI, as for other Communist parties, Khrushchev's rude destruction of the Stalin myth at the Twentieth Congress of the Soviet party proved to be of decisive importance. The shock effects of that event, when combined with other domestic and international factors, provided the political and psychological basis for a gradual restructuring of the PCI's relations with the Soviet Union and for an equally slow and partial revitalization of the party's domestic program.

But none of this was immediately evident. The message Togliatti brought back from Moscow was an optimistic one, exuding confidence in the present strength and potential of the Soviet Union, the Communist movement as a whole, and the Italian party in particular. In taking this line he was not merely dutifully reiterating the official mood and content of the Congress. The results of that gathering did in fact appear almost ideally suited to the strategic and tactical requirements of Italian communism as Togliatti saw them.

Togliatti's report to the PCI Central Committee following his return to Rome shows how he intended to turn to his party's advantage the various key proclamations of the Congress. Three interrelated themes were woven into the speech: first, the basic transformation of the international environment resulting from the continued decay of imperialism and the mounting strength of the socialist world, united in a solid system of socialist states; second, the consequent need to change the old pattern of relationships between the Soviet Union and other states and parties in the international movement; and finally, the rapidly growing economic strength and democratization of the USSR itself.

With respect to the first point, Togliatti echoed enthusiastically the Soviet contention that the possibility of avoiding war was now greatly enhanced. Both the changed relation of forces between the socialist and imperialist countries and the nature of modern weapons had made peaceful coexistence a thoroughly realistic, indeed necessary, strategy. Togliatti observed that a similar line had been developed at the Seventh Comintern Congress, on which occasion Togliatti himself had presented the major speech. Just as the peace campaign inaugurated then had succeeded in mobilizing the masses against the Fascist menace, he argued, so could people today be united against the threat of atomic war. Conditions were indeed far more favorable, for the subjective factor—the peace forces—had now been reinforced by a critically important objective factor, the undermining of the economic bases of imperialism. Nevertheless, although war was no longer fatally inevitable, it could not be ruled out. Imperialist ruling circles were responsible for the cold war, for military blocs, for the arms race; no guarantee could be given that they would respond rationally by accepting the changed balance of forces.[1]

Togliatti's wholehearted acceptance of the Soviet line of peace and détente, a strategy practiced for some time but now given full articulation and ideological support at the highest level, was not surprising. The PCI had been hurt by the repressive measures of Italian government and industry during the years of the cold war; the high level of international tension had served to unite and strengthen the party's opponents, giving them a potent weapon against the Communists. A peace line, on the other hand, suited the party's domestic alliance strategy, particularly because it offered one of the most effective modes of entry into the Catholic camp. Peace campaigns have been a stock in trade of Communist strategy in Western Europe, as much in times of cold war as of international détente, but the outstretched hand of the Italian Communist was likely to be taken more seriously if the Soviet Communist appeared to be doing the same.

A second theme discussed at some length concerned the new "system of socialist states," the creation of which was to be regarded as "the most important new element in the contemporary situation."[2] Its very existence, proclaimed Togliatti, was proof that socialism had triumphed securely over the worst efforts of its enemies to destroy it, when it was weak and isolated. In those early years, when the Soviet Union was the only socialist state and encircled by menacing imperialist powers, it was "historically necessary" for Moscow to play the commanding role in the Communist movement. But now circumstances had changed, and "the states

---

[1] "Il XX Congresso del PCUS" in Palmiro Togliatti, *Problemi del movimento operaio internazionale, 1956–1961* (Rome: Editori Riuniti, 1962), pp. 27–72, at pp. 46–52; originally in *L'Unità*, March 15, 1956.

[2] *Ibid.*, p. 29.

that are marching along the road to socialism are free states, independent, sovereign, fully autonomous." This new autonomy was
most clearly expressed, Togliatti added, in the right to follow an
independent economic path, to develop the various branches of
the economy at a tempo suited to the particular situation. The
Soviet economic model, in short, no longer possessed its obligatory
character. In all this Togliatti was following the line set forth by
Khrushchev at the Congress, reflecting Soviet hopes that economic
differentiation in Eastern Europe could strengthen the economic
position of the various countries and their internal political stability
without diluting the essence of Soviet political control.

While thus echoing Moscow's line on the "people's democracies,"
Togliatti was rather more interested to explore the wider international implications of the idea of "different roads to socialism,"
and to reassess the Soviet Union's guiding role:

> Today we must recognize—and I believe it would be incorrect for us not
> to do so—that this position is, at least, in process of modification. The
> experience which the Soviet comrades have had remains a basic one. It is
> necessary to study it deeply, to know how to evaluate it, to appreciate all
> its decisive elements, for it remains a guide to all those who wish to go
> toward socialism. However it is no longer the only experience. Other
> experiences are being accumulated by the work of other movements, other
> parties, other peoples.[3]

After referring to the examples of the Eastern European countries,
China, and Yugoslavia, Togliatti added

> It is inevitable that these experiences of ours, these novelties introduced
> by us, should serve, if not yet as a guide, at least as something for other
> parties to study. It was not for nothing, while we were at the Twentieth
> Congress, that comrades from other parties all over the world, from Asia
> to South America, came to consult with us so as to understand better this
> Italian fact, which is something new in the international socialist and
> workers' movement.[4]

This was perhaps the only note in Togliatti's speech which might
have caused a raised eyebrow or two, especially in Moscow and in
Paris. But could it not be excused as a pardonable touch of local
pride, intended to bolster the morale of the party and provide a
theme for the coming electoral campaign? In an election speech
ten days later Giorgio Amendola asserted: "Today we have had the
satisfaction of seeing the Congress of the CPSU confirm our original
national experience, which constitutes an example of international

3 *Ibid.,* pp. 58–59.
4 *Ibid.,* p. 60.

significance."[5] Certainly no grave significance should be read into Togliatti's remark, nor into his effort to include the nonruling parties under the implications of the "many roads to socialism" slogan, intended by the Russians to pertain primarily to the states where Communist parties were in power. All the same, the touch of pretension in the remark cannot be entirely overlooked, for it would be heard again, and in louder tones.

The third major theme of Togliatti's report concerned the USSR itself. He dwelt on the real and presumed triumphs of the Soviet economy, acknowledging certain "defects and errors" in agriculture and other fields, but proclaiming that the introduction of new methods of management had now assured that these mistakes would be permanently overcome. He insisted, too, that despite some taints of bureaucratism, Soviet democracy had proven its worth: the system of soviets was "the great creation of the October Revolution," the means by which "the democratic content of socialist society manifests itself and penetrates down to the most elementary cell of Soviet society. . . ."[6]

In summary, then, the central policy themes of the Twentieth Congress—peaceful coexistence, different roads to socialism, Soviet economic and international victories—all appeared to reinforce Togliatti's Italian strategy. In its main outlines he saw the Congress as setting the seal on a decisive and positive shift in the Soviet approach to international affairs and to relations among Communist states and parties. There was still, however, the question of Stalin, which had unexpectedly and in a disquieting fashion been introduced publicly in the speeches of Mikoyan and others and privately in Khrushchev's dramatic speech of denunciation.

The Stalin issue was a particularly sensitive question for Togliatti, one he had done his best to avoid ever since it had first been broached by the Soviet leaders in 1953 in the privacy of a Cominform gathering. But it could hardly be ignored entirely at the Central Committee session, so Togliatti introduced the topic cautiously:

> The question is grave and difficult. It should be examined by us with the deepest sense of responsibility, not only because of what Stalin has represented in the international workers' and socialist movement and thus for the fact that the criticisms touch upon still vivid emotions, but because it is not in anyone's interest that these criticisms should become the battle charger of the usual champions of anticommunism. . . .

---

5 *L'Unità*, March 26, 1956.
6 "Il XX Congresso del PCUS" in Togliatti, *Problemi del movimento*, p. 39.

None of us believes that it is possible to erase Stalin from history. None of us believes that it is possible to annul of destroy that which he was in the Russian Revolution and the international movement, that which he represented in the life and fate of the Soviet state. . . . Stalin was and remains a great figure for our whole movement. . . .

Stalin was a great Marxist thinker. In his writings he often achieved a profound unity of analysis and a clarity of expression such as not many are able to approach. . . .[7]

To be sure, he added, Stalin was not always correct in his judgments, particularly in his view that the class struggle would grow sharper in socialist society even after the exploiting classes had been destroyed. This thesis, as the Soviets had already acknowledged, was "exaggerated, false," and had led to unnecessary and unwarranted persecutions. Nevertheless, Stalin held that belief "in good faith—I repeat, in perfect good faith. . . ."[8] The Soviet leaders, he asserted, could not dodge the responsibility of criticizing Stalin in order to restore the proper norms of party life and Soviet legality, and their having done so should be regarded as an example of great courage. They should now make the criticism more precise through a new analysis of the history of the party and of Soviet society, to which the PCI should make its own serious and reasoned contribution. But he added

We know how many Communists suffered and died in our countries with that name on their lips. . . . We know that entire armies of our partisans went into battle with that name. We must understand and make others understand that that name means, first of all and above all, faith in our cause, certainty that our cause is just, uncontrollable faith in our victory.[9]

These words of praise stand in striking contrast to the treatment Stalin had received at the Congress itself, where not a single Soviet leader had found occasion to mention him with favor. The contrast is particularly noteworthy since Togliatti was almost certainly aware of the substance of Khrushchev's secret speech, delivered on the last day of the Congress. Although foreign Communists had been barred from the session, Togliatti had been in Moscow at the time and, with the network of informants undoubtedly available to someone of his stature and experience, could hardly have failed to be kept informed. Many observers, including Giuseppe Boffa, the Moscow correspondent for *L'Unità,* reported that rumors of the contents of Khrushchev's speech had begun to circulate almost immediately,

7 *Ibid.,* p. 65.
8 *Ibid.,* p. 66.
9 *Ibid.,* p. 70.

even before being discussed in party meetings around the country.[10] Fabrizio Onofri, then a member of the PCI Central Committee, has written categorically that "he was already aware of the 'secret report' but took care not to say a word about it."[11]

Why should Togliatti have chosen to stand up against the anti-Stalin tide? He had no way of knowing, for one thing, how long the current was likely to run in that direction. A struggle for power was evidently under way among the Soviet leaders, and it seemed reasonable to suppose that Khrushchev's bold initiative might lead to a successful comeback attempt by the more orthodox forces. He would naturally have assumed, moreover, that the question of Stalin's role, packed with political dynamite as it was, would be handled with the greatest of caution. All of Stalin's former associates, including Khrushchev himself, seemed to have more at stake than anyone else in keeping the issue out of the public eye.

The uncertainty of the Soviet situation alone, then, might have led Togliatti to try to project a balanced image of Stalin, free of both the eulogistic extremes of the past and the harsh accusations of the secret speech. Togliatti's handling of the issue was not primarily determined, however, by his estimate of the state of affairs in Moscow. Far more important to him was the situation within his own party, which also called for a cautious and balanced treatment of the question.

The PCI and Stalin

The problem of Stalin for the Italian party needs to be viewed in historical perspective. A significant political fact during the crisis of 1956 was the powerful sense of identification, bordering on idolatry, with Stalin and with the Soviet Union, that most ordinary party members had acquired by the war's end. From its founding until the outbreak of the war the PCI had been a small, illegal group, its headquarters outside the country and its operations in Italy limited and largely ineffectual. The war and especially the period of armed resistance to the Germans after Mussolini's collapse created the conditions for a massive increase in the party's appeal, its numbers, and its strength.

[10] Giuseppe Boffa, *Inside the Khrushchev Era*, trans. Carl Marzani (New York: Marzani & Munsell, 1959), p. 37.
[11] Fabrizio Onofri, *Classe operaia e partito* (Bari: Editori Laterza, 1957), pp. 106–107. Renato Mieli, a former Communist then in regular contact with Togliatti as an official of the Central Committee's foreign section, has confirmed to me Togliatti's knowledge of the secret speech.

The party's drawing power resulted not only from its effectiveness in organizing and leading the Resistance, in which it was by no means alone, but also from the special prestige acquired through its association with the Soviet Union, the country that had borne the brunt of Hitler's offensive. This link with the USSR gave the PCI the aura of an international power, the prestige of being something different and more to be reckoned with than other Italian parties.

This psychology operated particularly effectively among the working class and among those intellectuals of bourgeois origin whose repulsion to fascism and disillusionment with the liberal response to it had led them to the ideology of socialism. In addition to the appeal of its socialist principles, the PCI and the Soviet Union appeared also to epitomize efficiency, toughness, and organizational skill, to combine clarity of principles with a powerful orientation to action. Liberalism and Catholicism, the competing ideologies, were tainted by compromise with fascism or ineffectualness in fighting it; they represented the old and tired prewar world, not the glorious new society that could and must be constructed on the ruins of the old.

A typical explanation of the mood which led many to join the party in those years has been given by Fabrizio Onofri, who was to resign in 1956, bitterly disillusioned:

My antifascism took on a definite Communist coloration after the Soviet Union was invaded by Hitler: I then felt that the outcome of our struggle was tightly linked to victory in the armed struggle that the Soviet people was waging in defense of its land. The vast Ukrainian plains, the prairies and steppes covered by the Red partisans on horseback, and the villages defended one by one by the Red Army against the Nazi invader, all these became linked together in a single great field of battle with the narrow dimensions of our own conspiracy. Everyone knows what Stalingrad represented then for the liberation struggle in the entire world.[12]

It was not only the war but the social and economic achievements of the USSR, as glorified in Communist propaganda, that attracted thousands of workers and intellectuals disillusioned by the economic bankruptcy of prewar capitalism. As Giorgio Galli has expressed it in his history of the PCI:

The myth of October, the figure of Stalin, the five-year plans, the electric power stations pushing up like mushrooms, the army that pulverized the proud armies of Hitler: all this exercised a real fascination, outside Soviet borders, for the intellectuals who see the broad outlines of an epic event, for the popular masses who hear about the might of a country that proclaims itself socialist, that has eliminated injustice and exploitation, that is the beacon of all the oppressed, the sword behind all demands. The intellectuals who have no Marxist training or who know such a system of thought or political economy only superficially, the masses who have neither the time nor the means to understand or to probe deeply, all feel for the USSR an instinctive admiration.[13]

The myth of the Soviet Union and of Stalin, its chief symbol, thus became a political factor for the leaders of the PCI to reckon with, a profound source of strength for them and for the party as long as it remained inviolate, a potential threat to the party's morale and unity and to their own security should the idol fall. There is no need to quote at length from the innumerable paeans of praise bestowed by official PCI literature on the USSR and on Stalin in careful cultivation of the myth, but one sample may serve as a stimulus to the imagination. This specimen of party prose is taken from Luigi Longo's tribute to Stalin:

Stalin is dead . . . his titanic work, his genius, his life have for more than three decades astonished the world and won for his person the gratitude and the infinite care of the peoples. A third of humanity, eight hundred million people, thanks above all to his guidance and his example, have once and for all eliminated the exploitation of man by man, have been liberated from all servitude and have taken their destiny firmly into their own hands. . . .
The name of Stalin has been for so many years, for all of us, the beloved name of master, of teacher, and of leader, for so many years an incentive and comfort in the fight, an assurance of victory. . . .
We have the good fortune of having a great leader: Comrade Togliatti, the great pupil and friend of Stalin. Under his guidance we will know how to confront victoriously the tasks that await us, we will know how to fulfill all the commandments left us by Stalin.[14]

It is pointless to speculate on the proportions of cynicism, sentiment, and routine Communist rhetoric in such a declaration. What matters is that party members, intellectuals and workers alike, tended to take such talk seriously. In sharp contrast to those who had actually experienced life under Communist regimes, Italian Communists were able to retain their faith in the official myths. In the spring of 1956 a Polish Communist asked an Italian professor in astonishment how it could possibly be that "Italian Communists have idolized Stalin for so long if no one has forced them to do so."[15] Stalin and the Soviet Union were virtually inseparable, and faith in Stalin was part of what Adam Ulam has called "the emotional

---

[13] *Storia del Partito*, pp. 258–259.
[14] "Gloria a Stalin," *Rinascita*, X, 2 (February 1953), pp. 65–68.
[15] Gustavo Herling, "Il disgelo letterario a Mosca e a Varsavia," *Tempo presente*, I, 3 (June 1956), p. 191.

Russophilia that became ingrained in every Communist" during the prewar years.[16] Among Italians, sheltered from the realities of Communist life, the faith survived somewhat longer than elsewhere.

Such sentiments were not the exclusive property of the party rank and file. The leaders of the party themselves, cynical as they doubtless were in the manipulation of the Stalin myth and aware as many of them must have been of the "defects" in Stalin's character, were not wholly immune to the mystique surrounding his name. They had dedicated their lives to the Communist enterprise for which Stalin had become the symbol. To deny him would be to deny the cause. This same mechanism had been seen to work in the Soviet Union itself in the terrible years of the purges, when loyal party members went to their death or into political oblivion at Stalin's hands without losing faith in him and in the cause he personified. The circumstances were different in Italy, and the analogy far from complete, but the PCI's leaders can be credited with a degree of genuine loyalty to the person of Stalin and the work he had accomplished. Specific errors, even gross violations of justice, could be thrust aside by pride in the achievements of the Revolution and by confidence in still greater things to come. To some extent, and in varying degree, the leaders of the party shared the typical militant's need to believe in Stalin and his works.

The leadership had even more compelling reasons for continuing to proclaim loyalty to Stalin after his death. Politically they had been closely linked with him for their entire career. Togliatti himself had been known for over a quarter century as one of Stalin's men and was as vulnerable as anyone in the Communist world outside the Soviet Union to attacks on the master's reputation. Since 1926, when he had found himself unexpectedly holding the reins of his party, Togliatti's career had been that of a leading international Communist functionary, fully loyal (after his brief period of identification with Bukharin) to the General Secretary of the CPSU. Moving from one assignment to another in Moscow, France, Spain, and elsewhere, he had become in some sense more a European or an international Communist than an Italian. Only in 1944, upon his return to Italy, did the image of Togliatti as the man from Moscow begin to be replaced by a national identification.

But it would be wrong to suppose that this image was negative or harmful for him. Within the party, and within the working class as a whole, Togliatti's association with the Soviet Union and with

16 Adam B. Ulam, "Titoism," in Drachkovitch, *Marxism in the Modern World*, p. 140.

Stalin personally were important political assets that he assiduously cultivated.[17] The PCI's official farewell salute to Stalin, for example, closed with this appeal:

The Italian Communists unite in the name of Stalin, around their party, around their Central Committee, and around comrade Palmiro Togliatti, the man who, in the school of Stalin, has done the most for the national and social liberation of our country. They call upon all Italians to rally in ever greater numbers to their banner, symbol of the highest ideals of humanity, ideals to which Stalin consecrated all his prodigious and legendary existence.[18]

Thus Togliatti's personal authority and prestige, and to a lesser extent those of his colleagues in the leadership, were rendered legitimate by their association with Stalin. Charges, actual or latent, of undemocratic practices within the party, of excessive dominance by the *apparat*, could easily be shunted aside by references to the Soviet model, to the heritage of Lenin and Stalin alike.

In the three years preceding the Twentieth Congress, the PCI's refusal to confront the issue of Stalin, even in the face of Soviet pressure to do so, demonstrates its extreme sensitivity for Togliatti. Revealing information on this score comes from Giulio Seniga, a former Communist official who served for years as private secretary to Pietro Secchia, one of the old-time militants and until 1955 Vice-Secretary General of the PCI along with Luigi Longo. In July 1954, having concluded that the PCI under Togliatti's leadership had irrevocably lost its revolutionary spirit and capacity for action, Seniga abandoned the party to create one of the small splinter groups that have periodically, and without much effect, formed on the fringes of the Italian workers' movement.[19] Seniga subsequently published information and documents that throw revealing light on the PCI's relations with the Soviet leaders in 1953 and 1954.[20] Of particular interest is his account, based on a

[17] The importance of this point is perhaps best shown by the fact that Stalin was most revered in precisely those north central regions of Italy where the PCI was most powerful in terms of membership, votes, and control of local governments, trade unions, and cooperatives. See, for example, Gianluigi Degli Esposti, *Bologna PCI* (Bologna: Il Mulino, 1966), p. 106: "If there is one place in Europe where the cult of Stalin's personality was most carefully cultivated at the popular level it is certainly Bologna."

[18] *L'Unità*, March 8, 1953.

[19] For a survey of these various dissident Communist groups, see Enzo Tiberti, "The Italian Ex-Communists," *Problems of Communism*, VIII, 1 (January–February 1959), pp. 52–56.

[20] Giulio Seniga, *Togliatti e Stalin: Contributo alla biografia del segretario del PCI* (Milan: Sugar editore, 1961). The reliability of Seniga's documentation on these points has not, to my knowledge, been publicly challenged. He is by no means an unbiased observer, however, and his accuracy on other matters

verbatim transcript copied by Secchia, of a secret gathering of the Cominform parties and of the Chinese held in Moscow in mid-July of 1953, immediately following Beria's removal.[21]

The meeting—or rather series of meetings, for the satellite parties, the Chinese, and the French and Italians were dealt with in three separate sessions—was presided over jointly by Malenkov, Molotov, and Khrushchev, united briefly in their anti-Beria alliance. In addition to offering their well-known explanations of the Beria affair, which apparently aroused open skepticism on Secchia's part,[22] the Soviet leaders for the first time criticized Stalin's policies and methods of leadership, both within the party and with respect to the economic life of the USSR and the satellites. Attributing the errors and mistakes to the aberration of the "personality cult," they proclaimed that henceforth the principle of collective leadership would be respected, in the Soviet Union and in Communist parties elsewhere. "You too must change," they are said to have told their Communist colleagues, and instructions were given to reprint certain articles on the personality cult that had appeared in *Pravda* and *Kommunist* in May.[23]

Togliatti published the articles as directed, but aside from this formal gesture of compliance did nothing else to transmit the Soviet position to his party. Indeed, he and Secchia apparently informed only Longo and D'Onofrio of the situation, leaving the Central Committee and even the *Direzione* (roughly equivalent to the Soviet Presidium or Politburo) largely in the dark.[24] The PCI's official response to the Cominform meeting was in effect conveyed in Secchia's *Rinascita* article, "Lessons of the Beria Case," which repeated in full the Soviet line on Beria's infamous activities as an agent of imperialism but gave only the barest hint of criticism of Stalin, saying that "the individual decisions of a Communist leader, even if he is great, a strong personality, are almost always one-sided." The "defects of collective leadership," as well as the machinations of the enemies of socialism, were said to have helped make possible Beria's criminal activities but were dealt with solely in this context.[25]

---

leaves much to be desired. The source of his information, Secchia, had long been at odds with Togliatti and was soon to be removed from the party Secretariat.

21 *Ibid.*, pp. 34–35 and 39–42.

22 *Ibid.*, p. 35. When Secchia expressed some doubts about Beria's role as imperialist agent since 1919, Molotov is reported to have retorted brusquely: "We are telling you these things ourselves, and that ought to be enough."

23 *Ibid.*, p. 43.

24 *Ibid.*

25 "Insegnamento del caso Beria," *Rinascita*, X, 7 (July 1953), pp. 393–397, at p. 396.

This effort to submerge the question of the personality cult in a wave of vituperation against Beria was partly vitiated by publication of the Soviet articles just mentioned. These stirred up discussion within the party and resulted in at least one troubled letter to the *Direzione* from a group of comrades in Florence who asked whether "there is not a contrast between what we are doing in Italy in regard to certain leaders and what the articles in *Pravda* and *Kommunist* are denouncing, . . . whether it is not hero-worship to talk about the great Stalin, or the leader Togliatti. . . ."[26] These were the sorts of questions Togliatti did not want to hear, even if it could be assumed they were posed in good faith rather than as an attack on the methods of party rule. An answer was required, and Edoardo D'Onofrio, a member of the Secretariat and one of the more extreme Stalinists in the leadership, was assigned to give it.[27]

His speech was a masterpiece of diversion. Dissociating the entire question of the "collective leadership" from Stalin and from the Beria affair, D'Onofrio insisted that these problems had in fact arisen not recently, but as long ago as the Nineteenth Congress where important steps had been taken toward their solution—thus by implication assigning to Stalin himself the responsibility for the campaign on behalf of collective leadership and internal party democracy begun in 1952. D'Onofrio suggested that those who had written the questioning letter had missed the essential point of the Soviet discussions by failing to understand that the criticisms were not of any great leader or his actions, but of the "writers, historians, and lecturers" who had fallen into the idealist deviation of portraying "the ideas and actions of great men as determining factors of social and historical evolution."[28]

With this, responsibility was shifted from Stalin to his Soviet admirers, from Togliatti to *L'Unità*, which was pronounced guilty of errors of ideological judgment that the Cominform itself, as D'Onofrio observed, had a few months previously found it necessary to point out. Criticism was diverted to other quarters as well, especially to the middle and lower cadres of the PCI, where the "growth of personal tendencies" could be observed among the leaders of federations or sections of the party. Although the central leadership had sometimes unwittingly encouraged this abuse of

26 "Democrazia interna e direzione collegiale," *Orientamenti di lavoro e di lotta* (Rome, 1953), quoted in Seniga, *Togliatti e Stalin*, p. 44.

27 A summary version of the speech, delivered first in Florence and repeated in Rome and Bologna, was published in two installments: "Il problema della direzione collegiale nel P.C.I.," *Rinascita*, X, 11 (November 1953), pp. 628–632, and "Il problema della direzione collettive nel P.C. dell' U.S.," *ibid.*, X, 10 (October 1953), pp. 566–568.

28 *Ibid.*, X, 11 (November 1953), pp. 628–629.

authority by supporting the local comrades too vigorously, the fault lay essentially with the latter.

Lest this be misunderstood, D'Onofrio ended with a strong warning against an equally serious tendency of some "would-be leaders" to turn the party into a discussion group and avoid taking decisive, even though sometimes necessarily unilateral, action. In this way, Togliatti and his associates in the Secretariat came close to denying the very existence of a "Stalin problem" and maintained that in any event, whatever Soviet difficulties may have been, they had only superficial relevance for the Italian party.

Stalin Dethroned

With this background in mind it will be easier to follow and interpret the sequence of events in the months following the Twentieth Congress. At first things went smoothly. During the Central Committee debate in March 1956, most of the speakers followed the lead given by Togliatti's report on the Congress, amplifying on one or another of the positive themes enunciated by the Soviet leaders. The only sign of controversy appeared in the remarks of Umberto Terracini, who departed from the script and chose to discuss "the personality cult and the reverberations that the criticism formulated at the Twentieth Congress has had among all Communist militants."[29]

Terracini, one of the party's most prominent and independent-minded personalities since the earliest days, called for a more serious analysis of the errors of the Soviet past. He suggested, according to L'Unità's deliberately vague account, that the errors stemmed from a "convergence of responsibility" which "nourished" the personality cult. Serious self-criticism was required, he said, intimating that not only the present Soviet leaders but Togliatti as well had to accept some responsibility for Stalin's errors. Terracini is reported to have raised in his speech the extremely sensitive question of what had happened to the Hungarian Communist leader Bela Kun and to the entire leadership of the Polish party, which vanished after the party's dissolution by the Comintern in 1937. The degree of Togliatti's complicity in these infamous episodes in his capacity as member of the Comintern Secretariat was a favorite subject for speculation in informed Italian Communist circles. Potentially, at least, these cases hung over his head in rather the same way that the Leningrad affair hung over Malenkov's, as a symbol of involvement

29 L'Unità, March 16, 1956.

in Stalin's crimes.[30] Togliatti responded to this attack in his concluding speech with the confident remark that "self-criticism was not
lacking; but it was the self-criticism of a party that presents a balance
of victory and that has already positively resolved the very problem
of restoring collective leadership and internal democracy: self-
criticism of a method in order to establish an opposite method."[31]

That Togliatti's attempt to restrain this discussion was destined
for trouble became evident almost immediately. On March 17 the
Italian press seized upon a report published the day before in the
United States purporting to reveal the gist of Khrushchev's secret
speech at the Congress. The Communists quickly found themselves
at the center of what *Rinascita* called a "vast polemic" and an
"unprecedented national debate" provoked by the party's enemies.[32]
L'Unità did not mention the published summary of the Khrushchev
speech, preferring instead to attack the "bourgeois press" more
generally for its distortions of Soviet reality, and warning its
readers against crediting the lies and slanders of the enemy.[33] But
the party did now take the step of confirming that the Khrushchev
speech had in fact taken place.[34] This news was accompanied, however, by a warning that the speech, which was reported to have dealt
with the "merits" as well as the "errors" of Stalin, was still "an
internal affair" of the Soviet party, even though it was now being
widely communicated even to nonparty Soviet citizens. The article
cautioned further that the contents of the speech as described in
the Western press appeared in some (unspecified) ways to be false
and distorted.

Internal as well as external pressures were forcing the PCI leadership to confront the Stalin issue openly. The party had been thrown
into sudden turmoil. Local party meetings, previously routine and
apathetic, suddenly turned into agitated discussion forums that the
cadres found difficult to control. They themselves, like the rank and
file, did not know quite what to believe. Were the allegations to be
taken seriously or not? Many found it easier to believe, and Boffa's

---

[30] That Togliatti had been stung by Terracini's remarks is suggested by his
sharp reply to a letter complaining about *L'Unità*'s "brutal synthesis of Terracini's speech, which was the most significant" given at the Central Committee
session: "Terracini's speech could not help but be abridged, because he had
very little to say." Quoted in Antonio Ghirelli, "Il punto del dissenso," *Il Ponte*,
XII, 12 (December 1956), p. 2084. For a balanced discussion of Togliatti's role
in the Hungarian and Polish affairs see Renato Mieli, *Togliatti 1937* (Milan:
Rizzoli editore, 1964), *passim*.

[31] *L'Unità*, March 16, 1956.

[32] "Politica italiana," *Rinascita*, XIII, 3 (March 1956), p. 195.

[33] See especially Ingrao's editorial, *L'Unità*, March 21, 1956.

[34] Through Boffa's dispatch from Moscow, *L'Unità*, March 18, 1956.

serene reporting from Moscow did not discourage the belief, that the whole affair was just another of those bourgeois plots, a vicious international campaign designed to throw smoke in the eyes of the Italian electorate. Those who found it difficult to take refuge in outright denial were deeply disturbed by the threat to that which had until then been sacred. As Aldo Natoli, Secretary of the Roman federation, subsequently observed,

Once the first surprise had been overcome and the sudden feelings of agitation had waned, the criticism of Stalin remained for the overwhelming majority of comrades like a sort of "foreign body." They had not succeeded in grasping with conviction its connection with the great, new political perspectives opened up to the USSR and to the international workers' movement. The criticism at that time (still before the "secret" report of Khrushchev was known) appeared like a summary liquidation, not sufficiently motivated and, for that reason, anything but persuasive, besides being offensive to the ideal and sentimental patrimony of the party and of the workers' and democratic movement.[35]

The most serious and widespread repercussions were felt among the intellectuals, both because of their own latent doubts about the party and because they were able to sense more fully the potential significance of all that had happened in Moscow for the Communist movement in Italy and elsewhere. But for the moment they too were primarily concerned to put the Stalin question in proper perspective. A representative sample of the prevailing mood of uncertainty appears in a letter sent to the party's cultural journal *Il Contemporaneo* in the middle of March by Antonio Ghirelli, a Communist journalist in his early thirties.[36]

Ghirelli made several criticisms of the Twentieth Congress, but his primary concern was over the unilateral treatment of Stalin. It was, he felt, unfair of the present Soviet leadership to ignore Stalin's great ideological contributions to their own policy line and especially unjust for them to demolish the Stalin cult they had themselves done so much to nurture. The leaders of the PCI, he added, had to accept a share of responsibility for the situation. Despite Togliatti's tremendous qualities and achievements—which Ghirelli lauded "even at the cost of passing for the last Mohican of the personality cult"—the PCI's leaders had undeniably helped to

35 "Il dibattito sul XX Congresso nella Federazione de Roma," *Rinascita*, XIII, 5–6 (May–June 1956), p. 318.
36 Ghirelli, *Il Ponte*, XII, 12, pp. 2075–2091. Ghirelli's letter was not published by *Il Contemporaneo*. The editors of this journal had just announced that its pages were being opened for a debate on the relations between culture and politics and on the role of Marxist intellectuals in Italy. See *Il Contemporaneo*, March 17, 1956, p. 1, and subsequent issues.

stimulate the cult of Stalin. Ghirelli was also disturbed by the ease with which Togliatti had been willing to accept the errors attributed to Stalin in the conduct of the war:

This is not a matter of sentimentalism. . . . Stalin's war is for all of us the war of liberation of humanity; and if there were great errors, all right, we want to know fully and mercilessly what they were. But if they were small, marginal, almost inevitable like the errors of Caesar, of Napoleon, of Frederick the Great, well then—allow me to say it frankly—then *they should have kept quiet.* Because the cult of the dead is not like the cult of personality: it is something really sacred.[37]

In its emotional tone and sometimes confused reasoning, Ghirelli's letter reflected the mood of many in the party. If, as all would have preferred to believe, Stalin's faults were only the inescapable mistakes of a great statesman, then there was no excuse for destroying his reputation. But if they were serious, then the leaders of the Communist world were equally at fault for keeping party members in ignorance and failing to make courageous criticisms at a time when they might have done some good. What makes Ghirelli's letter of particular interest is that we have Togliatti's reply, sent not to Ghirelli personally but to his party cell, where it was read aloud. Ghirelli published the exchange some time later, when he had left the party.

Perhaps the most interesting aspect of the reply is its conciliatory and reasoned tone, a world removed from the angry and harsh mood which would dominate his reactions, public and private, only a few weeks later. He found nothing to object to in the complaint that Stalin's ideological contributions had been overlooked by Khrushchev at the Congress. This, he explained, resulted from the Soviet habit of concentrating on only one aspect of things at a time without introducing qualifying factors that might weaken an argument; by way of illustration he cited the Soviet Encyclopedia, which contains "unilateral negative judgments that by our lights not only deal inadequately with the subject but are even counterproductive." By contrast, Italians "always prefer to weave motifs together—positive, negative, historical—and the total picture that results is always in this respect richer. . . . I can understand, however, that at times our polemics are incomprehensible to the Soviet comrades." Togliatti also agreed with Ghirelli that Soviet criticism of Stalin did not seem well balanced. In their place, he would have been more self-critical and would have stressed more heavily the historical cir-

37 Ghirelli, *Il Ponte,* XII, 12, p. 2082.

cumstances and "the great positive contribution made by Stalin to the party, to Russia, to the entire world."[38]

The exchange is instructive. On the substance of the Stalin issue, Togliatti was consistent with his Central Committee speech, but he was prepared, in a private communication, to be somewhat more candid about his differences with the Soviet leaders. Not until the secret speech had been published three months later would he publicly express these reservations. His reply constituted tacit approval of reasonably open discussions within the party. But by declining to publish Ghirelli's letter, Togliatti made it clear that these sensitive questions were not to be raised in public.

In allowing debate within the party, Togliatti was only bowing before an accomplished fact. That the issue could not be kept under wraps became clear at a meeting of the PCI's parliamentary group toward the end of March. Togliatti opened the debate on that occasion by sticking tenaciously to much of his earlier position: the Congress was right to criticize Stalin's errors and defects, especially since most of them had already been corrected; it was impossible for anyone "to negate or destroy the greatness of Stalin and of the work he achieved." On one tactical question, however, Togliatti was forced to concede: the unrest within the party and the conditions of Italian political life now obliged the PCI to "reason and argue fully," to debate the issue openly in a way the Soviet leaders were for obvious reasons not required to do.[39]

The discussion that followed showed that it was within the party's own ranks that reasoning and argument were most needed. For the first time, the unmistakable conflicts that had begun to rock the party began to emerge publicly. The orientation of each of the speakers could be judged from those issues he chose to confront, and those he chose to ignore. The most striking contribution was again that of Umberto Terracini, who this time more clearly than before used the Twentieth Congress as a springboard for criticisms of the PCI itself.

Terracini urged two main points: first, the PCI must not merely repeat mechanically the slogan of the Italian road to socialism but must elaborate upon it theoretically and translate it into action; second, the party must eliminate the causes and consequences of Stalinism in its midst, the "bureaucratisms and dogmatisms" especially in the cultural field.[40] It appears that this speech, like his earlier one, was far more outspoken and critical than is conveyed by

[38] *Ibid.,* pp. 2082–2084.
[39] *L'Unità,* March 23, 1956.
[40] *Ibid.,* March 29, 1956.

the official summary version. It caused what the PCI monthly journal termed "scandalistic speculation" in the non-Communist press to the effect that Terracini, one of the oldest and most respected of the PCI leaders, was directly challenging Togliatti for the leadership.[41] The mere fact that *L'Unità* let a week go by before publishing its third and final installment on the senators' meeting, and then pushed it back from the first to the third page, suggests behind-the-scenes resistance to giving it any publicity at all. Togliatti was protesting too much when he declared during an interview that as a result of the debate on Stalin "there has not arisen in any way, nor do I believe that there can arise, an internal problem in our party."[42]

A few days later, the party *Direzione* agreed to put at least a temporary end to the debate in order to prepare for the local elections to be held in May. A resolution was issued asserting that the party, strengthened and stimulated by its great debate, would now go forward to even greater triumphs.[43] This theme also dominated the deliberations of the National Council, the convocation of which brought together for two days in April the members of the Central Committee, the Central Control Commission, and the secretaries of all the provincial federations, together with several hundred leading officials and other representatives of the party from all over the country. This massive show of strength was calculated to demonstrate to the party itself and to its electoral opponents that far from having been weakened by recent events, the party had emerged stronger, purified, and more united than ever.

The National Council session was an impressive demonstration of control and discipline. Discussion of Stalin and of the Twentieth Congress was kept to a minimum, and attention focused largely on purely national questions. Verbal counterattacks were directed at Giuseppe Saragat, Ugo La Malfa, and other non-Communist public figures who had dared propound the slanderous notion that the errors of Stalin indicated basic flaws or failures in the Soviet system. Symbolic of the leadership's successful insistence that internal criticism be set aside until after the election was Terracini's speech, dealing wholly with national issues and containing no trace of a reference to his earlier concerns; small wonder that *L'Unità* observed that he had been "warmly applauded," the only speaker noted to have been so received.[44]

41 "Politica italiana," *Rinascita*, XIII, 4 (April 1956), p. 259.
42 *L'Unità*, March 25, 1956.
43 *Ibid.*, March 31, 1956.
44 *Ibid.*, April 6, 1956.

Not all the delegates were pleased at the leadership's decision to suppress discussion of the issue that most concerned them, and many sent messages of protest to the chairman.[45] Giorgio Amendola, reflecting the discontent, departed from the pattern of dealing with domestic issues and made an impassioned plea for the need to break away from foreign tutelage and strike out boldly along the Italian road to socialism.[46] Although his speech stirred speculation in the press that he might be bidding to replace Togliatti as Secretary General, his aspirations almost certainly did not reach so far. He appeared to have been attempting to place himself at the head of the reformist wing of the party, gathering around him those who felt the need for introducing a new and more independent spirit into the party's affairs. Gian Carlo Pajetta, Amendola's colleague in the Secretariat, also appeared to be identifying himself with the "young Turks."

From about this time until well into June the PCI managed to keep critical discussion to a minimum, or at any rate out of public view. It was not possible to ignore the personality cult entirely, for the opposition press hammered away constantly at the issue, but discussion in the Communist press was for the most part conducted obliquely, by way of extensive reporting from the Soviet Union, China, and Eastern Europe. Major articles were given prominent treatment, for example the *People's Daily* piece "On the Historical Experience Concerning the Dictatorship of the Proletariat," as well as several Soviet discussions of collective leadership and the restoration of Leninist norms of party life. The central point was to demonstrate that whatever the problems of the past, the USSR had now turned a decisive corner: economic success, full restoration of political democracy, an active policy of coexistence, disarmament, and détente—these, not the shadows of Stalinism, were shown to characterize the Soviet Union and the entire Communist world.

The administrative elections held at the end of May were no triumph for the PCI, but neither were they the disaster many had feared. The general pattern around the country, with a few exceptions, was for moderate PCI losses as compared with 1953, but its percentage of the total vote dropped by less than 1 per cent. As expected, the Socialist party was the big gainer, apparently picking up votes from both left and right. Primarily because of the Socialist success, the combined vote of the three left-wing parties registered a significant increase and now totaled about 40 per cent of the vote,

45 Onofri, *Classe operaia*, p. 107.
46 *L'Unità*, April 6, 1956.

allowing the PCI to claim a general advance of the left.[47] This was in fact the most anyone in the PCI could reasonably have hoped for, given the difficulties within the party and the damaging publicity it had received over the Stalin issue. But the PCI was fortunate the elections took place when they did, for a week later the party was plunged into a turmoil before which the troubles of the previous three months paled into insignificance.

On June 4 *The New York Times* published what purported to be the full text of Khrushchev's secret speech. The document, immediately picked up by the Italian press and reproduced in full by two weekly journals, created a sensation in Italy. The next day *L'Unità* carried a three-paragraph note on the front page announcing that the U.S. State Department claimed to have received a text of the speech from confidential sources and did not guarantee its authenticity; as was known, the report had not been made public in the Soviet Union, although its contents had been discussed at party meetings. Then for six days, while the storm raged about the party's leaders, *L'Unità* remained silent. Not until June 13 was the speech mentioned again, this time in a note announcing the forthcoming publication of an important interview by Togliatti. This document, a written response to a series of questions addressed to Togliatti and other prominent figures by the monthly periodical *Nuovi argomenti,* was thus the first official word from the PCI after the appearance of the secret speech. Given advance publicity in *L'Unità* for several days, it was eagerly awaited by men of all political persuasions.

To be understood, Togliatti's interview must be placed in the context of the situation he confronted by the middle of June. Togliatti was being challenged on two fronts. One set of pressures arose from the Socialists and the left-of-center lay and Catholic forces, that is, from the PCI's actual or potential political allies. His other and more serious concern was with the party itself, for its strength and cohesion seemed seriously threatened by the crisis of faith through which many of its members were passing.

The Internal Crisis of the PCI

The publication of the Khrushchev secret report greatly aggravated the sense of despair and anger already felt by many Communists. It was bad enough that the rumors about Stalin should now be confirmed, surpassing the worst suspicions, but that the

---

[47] "I risultati elettorali," *Rinascita,* XIII, 5–6 (May–June 1956), pp. 265–275.

word should have been given by the enemy, with neither forewarning nor a word of official explanation or denial, was almost intolerable. The party faithful were now naked before the assault of their adversaries, and many were tormented by doubts.

Among the rank and file, bewilderment and frustration appear to have been the most common reactions. Traces of these emotions, no doubt watered down by the traditions of party discipline, found their way into the party's popular weekly magazine *Vie nuove*, which printed what purported to be excerpts from some of the debates in party sections and cells. Here is a typical comment by a worker:

The Twentieth Congress fell on our heads just a month before the elections and our opponents made a whole electoral campaign out of it. We were a bit quiet, and even when we spoke we didn't have the political arguments. Everybody was saying, as an employee put it to me, "what are you going to do now, now that you've lost your old man?" We were bitter and we weren't able to fight back, because after all we went off to fight in the mountains with that name, and now it isn't easy to get it out of our minds.[48]

It was the intellectuals who were by and large more deeply affected than the rest, for their attachment to the party often had an idealistic quality peculiarly susceptible to disillusionment. Of the days following publication of the secret speech, when his own crisis of faith was coming to a head, Fabrizio Onofri wrote:

I saw spreading over the countenance of my dearest friend the gray pallor of desperation; a deep, intense desperation, without surcease or escape, the same pallor that I felt rising on my own face, day after day. Everyone felt himself stricken unto death in the very heart of his being. It was as though a chasm had opened beneath us, within us. I have retained furious and desperate pages written at that time as the only escape from the political and moral death that was pressing on my soul.[49]

A similar sense of loss and disorientation is revealed in the mood of a younger Communist, evidently an intellectual in his middle thirties, as reported by a friend:

"We don't know any longer whether we are Communists or what," he said. He spoke without looking at me, with an absorbed air. "Stalin meant for all of us a lesson in force and in hardness. We were drunk with that hardness. Prague, the trials, Berlin, Korea. They weren't things that could embarrass us, we accepted them consciously, as a test. Likewise the faith in the Soviet Union, the deafness to the reasoning of the adversaries, the organized mythology. . . ."

[48] "Come si discute nelle cellule e nelle sezioni del p.c.," *Vie nuove*, June 28, 1956, p. 5.
[49] Onofri, *Classe operaia*, p. 107.

"If Togliatti had been less preoccupied with political necessity and more with our sentiments, he would have had to shout: we do not renounce Stalin, we do not renounce the best years of our lives. We will get used to it, but if we had to take the 'new course' really seriously, there would be nothing left but to make our excuses to the social democrats."[50]

But while the emotional sense of loss and betrayal was shared by virtually all within the party, except perhaps for those few among the older generation who had long since learned for themselves Stalin's true colors, there was no similar consensus as to what should be done. The collapse of the Stalin myth served to sharpen long-existing basic differences of orientation.

The instinctive response of the party conservatives, Stalinist in method and in policy as well as in emotional loyalty, was to deny or minimize the significance of Khrushchev's revelations, to hang on to whatever could be salvaged from the myth of Stalin's greatness and launch a counterattack against the slanders of the bourgeoisie. If Stalin made mistakes he should be criticized, yes, but his heroic contributions to the building of socialism in the face of imperialist determination to destroy the new socialist state must never be forgotten; whatever passing harm he may have done was justified by these circumstances and by the glorious victories of socialism in the USSR and throughout the world.

This attitude, widespread among the rank and file and among the cadres, especially at the middle and lower levels of the party, was expressed with greatest conviction and eloquence by one of the few party intellectuals to share this frame of mind. The speaker was Concetto Marchesi, a classics professor personally close to Togliatti and widely respected in the party; the occasion the Eighth Congress of the PCI in December 1956.

These revelations, which spread such unabridged joy in the enemy camp, excited surprise and grief among many Communists, especially among the most faithful of the working class. Among the, shall we say, intellectual Communists, there were some waverers, those most exposed to the agitated currents of thought. Others, incorrigible, remained firm. Among the incorrigible and less deluded Communists I counted myself. (Applause)
I have never supposed, comrades, that in countries where war and revolution and the genius of the leaders had beaten down autocratic, imperialist dominion, the well-being of the people and the reign of just men could immediately follow. Well-being of the people is a fruit that is slow to mature, especially if it is growing in the desert or is planted again in the ruins. And men are not born just but, if nature permits, they

50 Enzo Forcella, "Quaderno sotto chiave," Tempo presente, I, 5 (August 1956), p. 408.

become so in their individual and social relations through a succession of experiences, and thus also of uncertainties and errors.

. . . It is easy to understand, moreover, how the open criticisms and, immediately after, the sharp accusations against the work of a man who appeared to epitomize in his own person, through long and terrible years, the soul and the strength of the USSR, have nourished the fury of the capitalists' attack.

Later we will perhaps be able to see the situation more clearly, for we cannot all yet make out well the reasons why there has been felled in such a brusque and clamorous fashion one of the great builders of the USSR, around whom, living and dead, so many voices of praise have resounded; the man who, dying, left a Russia so mighty and powerful. . . . Tiberius, one of the great and infamous emperors of Rome found his implacable accuser in Cornelius Tacitus, the unparalleled historian of the principality. Stalin, less fortunate, found Nikita Khrushchev. It was perhaps not necessary, in order to cure our own ills, to add our own malediction to the unyielding hatred of the capitalists for the socialist regime. One can do much more with the work of the living than with condemnations of the dead. (*Applause*).[51]

That such things could be said and roundly applauded, despite the obvious and explicit disagreement of the party hierarchy, was telling confirmation of the powerful undercurrent of emotional resistance in the party to the dethroning of Stalin. Almost equally important was the widespread feeling, articulated so brilliantly by Marchesi, that as Stalin was a heroic figure, so his accusers—Nikita Khrushchev and the rest—were unsympathetic personages of the second rank.

The psychological need to rehabilitate Stalin was not shared by all in the party. Many, particularly among the intellectuals, saw that the only way out of the party's moral and political crisis was to face facts and move forward, not back. They knew it was naïve to suppose that the disasters of Stalinism could be explained solely in terms of a personal tyranny, imposed on an otherwise healthy political and social system. Could the new leaders, themselves deeply implicated in Stalin's crimes, be counted on to set things right? Judgment on the state of affairs in the Soviet Union could perhaps be reserved, for little more than questionable official claims was known about it, but whatever the facts and the prospects, was it not clear that the USSR could no longer be regarded as the model and mentor of Communist parties elsewhere?

Many of the intellectuals had for years been troubled by the evident stagnation of the PCI, by its inability to move forward ideologically and politically along the Italian road to socialism. The excitement and promise of the Resistance days and of the immediate

51 *VIII Congresso del Partito Comunista Italiano: atti e risoluzioni* (Rome: Editori Riuniti, 1957), pp. 137–138.

postwar years had dissolved in the monotonous and stultifying routine of daily activities. Idealism, energy, dedication, hope—all had been swallowed up in the bureaucratization of the party as it sought to play its frustrating and apparently perpetual role as principal member of the parliamentary opposition.

The shock of the Soviet events suddenly began to crystallize sentiments such as these which had long been vaguely and diffusely held by many of the party's intellectuals. And the revelations about Stalin began to suggest an explanation for the stagnation of the recent past. Was it not likely that the PCI's failure to move off dead center could be explained in part by its deference to Soviet interests, its attachment to the Soviet road to power? Could this not help explain the phenomenon long apparent in the party's actions and increasingly openly alluded to by the opprobrious label of *doppiezza*,[52] denoting the divergence between the party's claim to be following a distinctively Italian road to socialism and its failure to develop either a theory or a practical policy corresponding to that claim? Through this chain of reasoning the denigration of Stalin came to be linked in the minds of some articulate Communist intellectuals with the need for a thorough renovation of the party's ideology, its strategy, and its internal life.

Between July 1956 and the Eighth Congress the following December the PCI conducted the most extensive and open debate in its history on basic issues of strategy and of internal party life. The outcome of the debate, conducted under the dark shadow of the Polish and Hungarian events, was deeply disturbing to many dedicated Communists of reformist inclinations, who found they could no longer remain in the party's ranks. Despite their justified disillusionment, the debate nevertheless marked the start of an evolution that in less than a decade would move the party a long way toward the new, more independent strategy urged by the "renovators" of 1956.

These questions will be examined more fully in the next two

---

[52] No accurate English rendition can be given of the word *doppiezza*. "Duplicity" or "double dealing" suggest a conscious effort at deception, which misses the point. In any given instance, of course, the party leadership might set out to deceive its own followers or the outside world. *Doppiezza* has to do, however, not with particular acts of deception but with the fundamentally ambiguous position of the PCI in Italian society. Since the party has chosen to maintain its antidemocratic internal traditions, its ideological premises, and its revolutionary aspirations while at the same time making all the practical political compromises required of an active participant in the parliamentary system, it has been bound to follow a "double road," justifying its actions by two separate and incompatible standards of judgment. *Doppiezza* thus points to an inherent structural characteristic of the party, to a kind of institutionalized schizophrenia.

chapters, for they are critical to an understanding of the relation between the PCI's domestic situation and its international orientation. We need anticipate the later discussion only to state that through June 1956 Togliatti's response to the Stalin crisis seemed clearly to favor the reformist wing of the party. While always avowedly sympathetic to the "sentimental" attachments to the past of many party cadres and rank-and-file members, he was hoping to use the Stalin issue and the Twentieth Congress as a whole as a means of consolidating and reinvigorating his long-term strategy of alliances with "progressive forces" from the bourgeoisie as well as the working class. For this purpose he had to rely primarily on a younger generation of leaders dedicated to this strategy rather than on older and more conservative men who did not, and probably could not, fully appreciate the subtleties of his approach, with its rejection of a pure ideology of class and its implicit postponement of the great day of revolution.[53] He could not, however, afford to alienate the conservative backbone of the party, whose unquestioning loyalty and dedication were among its chief assets. To maintain the unity of the party was a prerequisite for any successful strategy.

Reactions of the Socialist Party

Togliatti's strategy obliged him to keep a close eye on the situation outside as well as within his party, so as to assess the effects of the Stalin crisis on other parties and on public opinion generally. His foremost concern was with the Socialists, since maintenance of a degree of solidarity and cooperation with the PSI had been a keystone of PCI strategy in all the postwar period. Under the circumstances of the mid-1950's, a definitive break with the PSI and its reunification with the Social Democrats in an anti-Communist front of reformist socialists would have been a near mortal blow to the strategy of the peaceful, parliamentary road to socialism. Fear of such an eventuality must have haunted Togliatti during the spring and summer of 1956. The PSI's success in the May elections seemed to suggest that they had at last begun to learn to profit from the Communist stagnation of recent years. The Stalin issue, although not regarded as a decisive influence on the election results, had played into Socialist hands, and the right wing of the PSI in particular had not hesitated to draw advantage from it.

53 Togliatti's intentions on this score had already been made clear well before the Twentieth Congress when he removed Pietro Secchia, leader of the conservative orientation, from the position of Vice-Secretary General. He would at the Eighth Congress decisively weaken this faction by removing from the Central Committee and *Direzione* others of its leading exponents.

The secret speech greatly accentuated the trend toward increasing disassociation of the Socialists from the PCI, a tendency in evidence since 1953. Nenni himself, tainted by long personal ties with Stalin and by close identification with the Soviet Union, and evidently also genuinely shocked by the Khrushchev speech, hastened to demonstrate an independent and critical attitude. In several major articles he made his views public. While avoiding a tone of hostility toward the USSR, he did not hesitate to express, in far stronger terms than those employed by the Communist leaders, his concern over the implications for Soviet society of the Stalin cult. He hammered away particularly at the absence of political liberty:

Now the whole problem of Soviet society boils down to the need for its internal democratization, for the circulation of ideas, in a word for political liberty, needs which have been suppressed in Soviet society for many years. . . . What is in question are not the titles of legitimacy of the Revolution but the institutions—from the party to the soviets—that the Revolution has forged in the fire of its experience. These institutions, instead of evolving toward forms which would increasingly adequately express the free political will of individual citizens and of the masses, have instead been progressively voided of their democratic content and their powers, have become sterile and suffocated in their functioning. In this way a formidable advance of social and economic forces has not been matched by an equal advance of political liberty.[54]

To this Nenni added the opinion that the Soviet leaders had thus far wholly failed to provide either a convincing analysis of the reasons for what he termed the "degeneration" of the Soviet system, or a set of remedies and guarantees against its recurrence. Unless the Soviet leaders were able to evaluate the phenomenon as something deeper than personal tyranny alone, and to take measures to modify the institutional forms and practices of the party and the state, a skeptical attitude would have to be taken about the future.

The views expressed in these articles represented Nenni's personal reactions to the denunciation of Stalin rather than, as might have been imagined, merely his official public attitude. Between June and October 1956 Nenni exchanged letters with Mikhail Suslov, the Soviet party secretary principally responsible for liaison with foreign parties; the letters were published by Nenni eight years later, at a time when he had completed his psychological and political journey from Soviet fellow traveler in matters of foreign policy

[54] "I 'vergognosi fatti' del rapporto segreto di Krusciov" in Pietro Nenni, *Le prospettive del socialismo dopo la destalinizzazione* (Turin: Einaudi editore, 1962), pp. 33–51, at pp. 46–47; originally in *Mondo Operaio*, June 1956.

to lukewarm supporter of the Western alliance.[55] The exchange is interesting not only for its confirmation of Nenni's views but particularly for its indication of the delicate position in which the Soviet leaders found themselves in dealing with his criticisms. It will be useful to compare the tone and substance of Suslov's response with the attitude assumed by Togliatti during the same period.

Nenni wrote Suslov toward the end of June (the letter reached Moscow on July 10), enclosing a copy of his *Mondo Operaio* article on the Twentieth Congress. Suslov's reaction was as follows:

Concerning your letter I must say that your article in *Mondo Operaio* surprised us and made us very sad, especially in view of the criticism which you have also expressed in your letter. This is due to the fact that your letter lists a number of positions which we believe to be wrong and with which we can in no way agree. Among these positions are first of all your statements about the degeneration of the Soviet State; about the suppression of democratic life in the party and in the State; about the transformation of the dictatorship of the proletariat into a party dictatorship and then into Stalin's dictatorship; about the absence of political freedom and of democratic content in the party, in the soviets, and in other State organs; and also about the crisis of the Soviet system and of the party which, according to you, started in Moscow with the Twentieth Congress. We believe that you unfortunately see—in this article—only the negative practical consequences of the cult of Stalin, and fail to see also the many-sided truly democratic life of our party and of our people, and the gigantic historic victories of socialism in the USSR, unless you avoid all this intentionally. However, this gives the article a unilateral and non-objective character.[56]

Suslov expressed particular regrets that Nenni had chosen to publish a second article going further "in a negative judgment on the Soviet regime" even after having seen the Central Committee resolution of June 30 which ought to have answered many of his questions. This second article had "contributed considerably to the resumption of bourgeois anti-Soviet propaganda," and the Soviet leaders had considered answering it publicly. They had refrained for the present, however, "because we fear that our intervention might raise further difficulties in the path of the union of the forces which fight for peace and for the interests of the workers."

I must say that we understand the difficulties that have arisen with regard to the activity of your party, as well as those the Italian Communist party must face, as a result of our work for the liquidation of the personality cult and of its consequences. Life itself will, however, confirm our certainty that our friends' difficulties are temporary, that they will be

55 *Mondo Operaio*, October 1964, pp. 2–6.
56 *Ibid.*, pp. 3–4.

successfully overcome, and that this will occur within a relatively short period. Later it will be possible to discuss everything more fully in a constructive way, so as to improve the effects of our common action.[57]

In concluding Suslov expressed the opinion that Nenni's stance resulted primarily from lack of knowledge of what had been happening in the Soviet Union in recent years and invited the Socialist leader to spend his vacation in the Soviet Union or to send a party delegation for consultation.

This attitude of patient forbearance in the face of provocation is revealing. It suggests the importance the Soviets attached to maintaining friendly relations with Nenni, leader of the only Socialist party in postwar Europe to have maintained its allegiance to the Soviet Revolution and rejected the lures of reformist social democracy. It also suggests full Soviet support for Togliatti's basic approach to the PSI during the crisis of de-Stalinization: the Soviet and Italian party leaders were in agreement on the need to go as far as possible in smoothing Nenni's ruffled feathers in hopes of continued effective collaboration in the years to come. As we shall see, however, such a consensus on objectives did not guarantee agreement on just how far compromise and conciliation should go.

In his articles Nenni was speaking to his Communist colleagues in Italy, and to the left wing of his own party, as well as to the Russians.[58] He wanted it understood that he was not going over to the openly anti-Communist position of the Social Democrats and the non-Marxist lay and Catholic left; the ideals and ideology of Marxism were still valid for him, as was the heritage of the October Revolution. The Soviet Union would have to break decisively with the Stalinist era, however, if it were to receive the continued support of Italian socialism. Furthermore, the PCI for its part would have to demonstrate a greater autonomy of judgment and action with respect to both the Stalinist past and the still uncertain Soviet future. Nenni's attitude seems to have been a blend of mild threat and strong encouragement designed to help the PCI overcome its crisis in such a way as to permit renewed and strengthened collaboration between the two mass workers' parties, a collaboration in which the weight of the Socialists would be expected steadily to increase. This attitude, born in the crisis of de-Stalinization, would

[57] *Ibid.*, p. 4.

[58] In a subsequent explanation of his attitude in 1956 Nenni is quoted as saying that "the aim we had in mind was to push the Communists in Moscow, but primarily in Rome, to take the decisive step, to shift criticism of what had happened from Stalin to the system." Eugenio Scalfari, "Li sto aspettando da quarant' anni," *L'Espresso*, November 1, 1964, p. 3.

not survive intact the shock of Hungary and the evolution of Italian politics in the years thereafter.

In 1956 a wide spectrum of attitudes toward the PCI and the USSR existed among other parties and party factions to the left of center; these attitudes were characterized by a greater or lesser degree of skepticism about the PCI's ability or desire to break away from Soviet tutelage and to become in reality the "party of a new type" proclaimed in its propaganda. The PCI's interest has been to soften the skeptics and encourage the optimists by making a convincing demonstration of its autonomy and of the implicitly revisionist character of its policies. The effectiveness of this endeavor has historically been constrained by the opposite necessity to demonstrate to the party faithful the retention of ties with the Communist movement led by the Soviet Union and the continued vigor of orthodox Marxist-Leninist ideas.

The latent conflict between these two demands could emerge at any moment when the Soviet Union found itself under serious attack, as in the spring of 1956. To the extent that the PCI has felt able to appeal to the nonparty audience, important for the longer run but not critical in a showdown, essentially the same themes have had to be used as when appealing to Nenni and his followers. The PCI has had to try to show itself capable of criticizing Soviet behavior and of responding to a situation in such a way as to appear to be Italians first, international Communists second.

In any full analysis of Italian Communist strategy, the PCI's efforts to attract support from, or at least not to alienate, groups to the right of the PSI would require serious and detailed treatment. Since our focus is on the PCI's relations with international communism rather than with the center-left forces in Italy, we can do little more than point occasionally to this aspect of the domestic scene.

Togliatti's Article in Nuovi Argomenti

The situation created by the Twentieth Congress and suddenly greatly exacerbated by the publication of the Khrushchev secret report required Togliatti to contend simultaneously with strong and conflicting pressures from left and right, from inside his party and without. To meet this crisis successfully would require a full measure of the Secretary General's much vaunted ability to say different things to different people. There was, perhaps, but one overriding message he could hope to convey to all: that the Communist party, despite the blows to which it was being subjected, remained calm, strong, and unshaken, faithful to its ideological heritage but capable of shaping out of an apparent crisis the materials for a new thrust forward on the Italian road to socialism. To get across this message he would have to confront more fully than before the delicate question of the causes and consequences of Stalinism. A convenient opportunity to do so was offered by the periodical *Nuovi argomenti,* whose editors invited Togliatti along with other prominent intellectuals and public figures to respond to a series of questions concerning the "personality cult."[59]

For the first time a leading Communist figure insisted seriously in print on the need to explain the phenomenon of Stalinism more adequately than the Soviets themselves had done. Togliatti faced up to the delicate question of the "coresponsibility for these errors of the whole political leadership group, including the comrades who have today taken the initiative both in denouncing and in correcting the harm which had previously been done and the consequences stemming from it."[60] He accepted Khrushchev's contention that it had been impossible in practice to remove Stalin from power because no one in the Soviet Union would have understood and accepted such a move, which would thus have compromised the safety of the Revolution and the state. But in Togliatti's view this fact, while it helped explain the difficulties faced by Stalin's colleagues, "at the same time complicates and aggravates the picture." If such a general consensus did exist, he remarked, one would be obliged to admit either that Stalin's errors were not known to the leading cadres of the country, or that they were not considered errors by these cadres and therefore by the public opinion which they controlled: "it seems much more correct to recognize that despite the errors he committed, Stalin had the support of the largest part of the country and above all of his leading cadres and of the masses as well."[61]

If this had been the case, he argued, then it was not possible to maintain that the "personality cult" of Stalin had been the basic cause of everything that happened.

The explanation can only be found through a careful investigation of the way in which the system characterized by Stalin's errors came about. Only thus will it be possible to understand how these errors were not only something personal, but entered deeply into the reality of Soviet life. . . .

[59] "L'Intervista a *Nuovi argomenti*" in Togliatti, *Problemi del movimento,* pp. 85–117; originally in *Nuovi argomenti,* No. 20 (May–June 1956). Although generally referred to rather misleadingly as an "interview," the article was a carefully conceived written reply to nine specific questions.

[60] *Ibid.,* p. 99.

[61] *Ibid.,* p. 101.

Here it is necessary to recognize, openly and unhesitatingly, that while the Twentieth Congress has made an enormous contribution to posing and solving many serious and new problems of the democratic and socialist movement, while it signals a crucial stage in the development of socialist society, it is not possible to regard as satisfactory the position that was taken at the Congress and is today being amply developed in the Soviet press concerning the errors of Stalin and the causes and conditions that made them possible.[62]

Deeper understanding of the problem, he continued, would be achieved only by means of a serious Marxist analysis of the historical evolution of the Soviet state and party. Such an analysis would have to take into account the objective contradictions of social development as well as Stalin's subjective errors, and it would demonstrate that

Stalin was at one and the same time the expression and the author of a situation, for the reason that he proved himself to be the most expert organizer and director of a bureaucratic-type *apparat* at the moment when it got the better of the democratic forms of life as well as because he gave a doctrinal justification of what was in reality an erroneous line, one on which his personal power was based, to the point of assuming degenerate forms.[63]

Togliatti himself suggested some of the elements in such a historical approach, stressing particularly the growth of a bureaucratic mentality in the state and party leadership which led to a sharp decline in the initiative of the masses and a tendency to view all obstacles and errors as a consequence of sabotage by the class enemy. It was up to the Soviet comrades themselves, Togliatti stressed, to develop this line of thought, for only they were in possession of the full facts.

This analysis was well calculated to meet the needs of Togliatti's two principal domestic pressure groups. To those within the PCI who retained in one degree or another their attachment to Stalin and all he stood for, Togliatti was saying reassuringly that the tragedy could not have been all Stalin's doing, that responsibility fell on other Soviet leaders and more broadly on the whole leadership class in the Soviet Union. But at the same time as he was delivering this message to his own party, and particularly to its conservative wing, he was also demonstrating to those Communists and Socialists of opposite convictions that he was fully capable of taking an independent stance vis-à-vis the Russians, that the days of automatic alignment with the Soviet position had passed away with Stalin himself.

62 *Ibid.*
63 *Ibid.*, p. 106.

The terms in which Togliatti called for a Marxist analysis of the causes of Stalinism were virtually identical to those employed by Nenni. Even non-Marxists capable of reflecting on the problem in nonpolemical tones were urging such a historical approach, with the difference, to be sure, that they put into question even the Leninist heritage of the party, whereas Togliatti urged only a restoration of Leninist norms. Nevertheless, despite the obvious limitations of his analysis, coming from a Communist party leader it was something new and seemed to give promise of a new psychology, a new independent spirit.

He could not, however, imply this new autonomy, avoid alienating the Stalin sympathizers within his party, and at the same time not offend Soviet sensibilities. Togliatti was apparently ready to risk the latter course in response to his urgent domestic needs. In developing his argument about the partial responsibility of the new leaders for Stalin's "errors," he went so far as to deliver a rebuke, mild but unmistakable, to the new Soviet rulers:

> The present Soviet leaders knew Stalin much better than we (I will perhaps have occasion to speak on another occasion of some contacts I had with him), and we must therefore believe them when they describe him in this way. We can only think, among ourselves, that since this was so, aside from the impossibility of making a timely change, as discussed above, they could at least have been more prudent in that public and solemn exaltation of this man's qualities to which they had accustomed us. It is true that today they are criticizing him, and this is to their great credit, but in this criticism a little of their own prestige is without doubt being lost.[64]

Those recalling the praise lavished on Stalin by Togliatti and his associates, who were hardly *that* ignorant of the real Stalin, must have reflected that the Soviet leaders were not the only ones to be sacrificing some of their prestige in the whole affair. But this was a consequence Togliatti could not hope to escape entirely, and his personal position would be strengthened to the extent that the burden of guilt could be shifted from Stalin personally, whose lieutenant Togliatti had been during the worst years of the tyranny, onto impersonal circumstances and onto Stalin's heirs.

The second major theme of Togliatti's analysis concerned the consequences for Soviet society of the Stalin cult. Implicit in his assertion that the causes were deeper and more complex than a mere personal aberration on Stalin's part was the belief that the Soviet system itself had in some degree been damaged. He handled this theme gingerly, prefacing his remarks with the warning that

64 *Ibid.*, p. 102.

if one tried to reduce the negative effects to a single general concept, "one runs the risk of excessive, arbitrary, and false generalizations" about Soviet reality. He then proceeded to lend halfhearted support to one such generalization, evidently with Pietro Nenni in mind:

> The least arbitrary of the generalizations is the one which sees in Stalin's errors the progressive imposition of personal power on collective entities which are democratic in their origin and nature and, as a result of this, the accumulation of phenomena of bureaucracy, of violation of legality, of stagnation, and also, partially, of degeneration at different points of the social organism.
> However, it must be said at once that this imposition was partial and probably had its most serious manifestations at the summit of the leading organs of the state and the party.[65]

Having ambiguously endorsed a hypothesis hinting at the possibility of partial "degeneration," Togliatti promptly backed away from a radical interpretation of it by denying that the fundamentals of Soviet society had been affected by the limited restrictions on democratic life: "I may be wrong," he maintained, "but in my opinion there are not to be foreseen today institutional changes in the USSR, nor should such changes be implied by the criticisms openly formulated at the Twentieth Congress."[66] Adoption of such formal institutional guarantees against abuse of personal authority as exist in bourgeois societies (e.g., independence of the judiciary, a multiparty system) would, he said, be ridiculous and impossible in the Soviet Union, where the foundations of real rather than purely formal democracy had been laid long ago. Nevertheless, certain basic changes in the Soviet system might be required:

> But while I believe it absurd to hold that the system should be destroyed in order to turn back, I nevertheless feel that modifications, even profound ones, can and will have to be introduced on the basis of the experience that has been acquired, the successes achieved in all fields, and the necessity to have more effective guarantees against errors such as Stalin's.[67]

In the absence of concrete specification of possible "profound modifications" of the system, aside from a laudatory reference to the economic decentralization he felt was then in progress, it is pointless to speculate on just what sort of reforms Togliatti was urging on the Soviet leadership. Even if he had had specific ideas on the subject, little would have been served by advancing them. His purpose was essentially to disassociate himself and the PCI from the Stalinist system by proclaiming the need for reform, while at

65 *Ibid.*, p. 89.
66 *Ibid.*, p. 90.
67 *Ibid.*, p. 94.

the same time maintaining his credentials as a Marxist-Leninist. Modifications, yes; institutional changes implying acceptance of bourgeois democratic forms, never.

In the final section of the interview Togliatti turned to the consequences of de-Stalinization for the international Communist movement. He described the historical evolution of the movement since World War I, when responsibility for centralized leadership naturally lay in Russian hands. Gradually the separate parties had become stronger and more independent, a state of affairs recognized at the Seventh Comintern Congress in 1935 where it had been decided that "decision-making and practical political action had to be the task of the individual parties, fully entrusted to their initiative and responsibility."[68] When, after the Second War, the Cominform had been founded, serious mistakes had been made in failing to recognize in practice the full autonomy of the parties.

Under present circumstances, with the Cominform dissolved and the principle of autonomy accepted by all, conditions were now once again such as to strengthen mutual trust and solidarity among the parties. There had definitely arisen, however, "not only the necessity but also the desire for an ever greater autonomy of judgment." The Soviet model could no longer be obligatory, neither for the countries already building socialism, nor for others where the Communists were not the leading party: "The whole system is becoming polycentric and in the Communist movement itself one cannot speak of a single guide but rather of progress being achieved by following paths that are often different."[69] We shall examine more closely in the next chapter some of the implications of this line of thought and of this particular statement, which has probably been more widely quoted by analysts of Communist affairs than anything else Togliatti ever wrote. It is necessary to pause at this juncture only to note that the repudiation of Stalin brought into question not only Soviet internal arrangements but also, and increasingly critically as time went on, Soviet relationships with other Communist parties and states.

Togliatti's *Nuovi argomenti* article has often been viewed in the West, especially in retrospect, as something akin to an Italian Communist declaration of independence from the Soviet Union. Its tone was unusually forthright; it was critical of Soviet leadership and of some aspects of the Soviet system; and it dared to speak openly of a "polycentric" system of international communism, a loosely defined concept, to be sure, but one which seemed to hint

68 *Ibid.*, p. 114.
69 *Ibid.*, p. 116.

strongly of aspirations toward national communism. Looking back from the vantage point of later years, at a time when Soviet authority within international communism had shown itself to be irrevocably compromised and when the movement was split apparently beyond repair, it is tempting to view Togliatti as a bold prophet or even as something of a rebel—at the very least as the forthright spokesman of a new and more liberal communism, respectful of democratic principles and national autonomy alike.

The temptation should be resisted. Togliatti had shown no previous inclination to thrust himself or his party into the limelight as a critic of the Soviet Union. The circumstantial evidence suggests that he moved only as far and as fast as he felt obliged to do in order to deal with pressing domestic political needs. The interview in *Nuovi argomenti* should be seen primarily as a skillful effort to respond to those pressures from within his own party and from sources outside that could not safely be ignored. Although he was talking *about* the Soviet Union and may well have anticipated a reaction from it, he was addressing himself to an Italian not a Soviet audience. Given the extreme sensitivity of his subject, this was in itself a significant fact. It was, however, as a Marxist might put it, a fact of objective rather than subjective importance. To the extent that Togliatti was a rebel, he was a rebel *malgré lui;* the role was less chosen than forced upon him by the nature of the circumstances.[70]

It would be mistaken, however, to suppose that for him the relationship of the PCI with the Soviet Union remained just as it had always been. The open Soviet denunciations of Stalin, implicitly throwing into question the merits of the Soviet system as well as of the great dictator himself, had created a wholly new situation. Earlier attitudes of unqualified and unreasoned support were no longer objectively possible for a politician trying to maintain the unity of his own party and to influence an electorate with open sources of information about the world.

---

[70] While I do not believe the evidence supports an image of Togliatti as a conscious rebel against Soviet authority, neither can I accept the interpretation of some Italian observers to the effect that his *Nuovi argomenti* interview represented essentially a miscalculation of Soviet intentions. Ignazio Silone, for example, viewed it simply as a mistaken effort to appear as a particularly zealous supporter of the anti-Stalin policy of the new Soviet leaders; "Invito a un esame di coscienza," *Tempo presente*, I, 9 (December 1956), p. 687. Giorgio Galli has written that Togliatti was led "into the error of diverging from a Soviet position" when he used the term polycentrism only because of "the confusion within the Communist bloc"; "Italian Communism" in Griffith, *Communism in Europe*, Vol. 1, p. 303. Such interpretations are based on the tacit prior assumption that since he necessarily gave first priority to not offending the Soviets, he could have differed from them only by miscalculation.

No elderly political leader, entrenched in his ways and irrevocably bound to his own past, could be expected to welcome an external shock that forced him to see and do things differently: Togliatti most certainly did not welcome de-Stalinization and was slow and reluctant to adapt to it. The very fact that he was obliged to do so, to modify his style and in effect repudiate parts of his past, could hardly have failed to stimulate some resentment against those who had placed him in that position. If true, this is a political and psychological fact of some importance in understanding the relations since 1956 of the Italian and the Soviet parties.

Definitive proof of such a contention would be difficult to obtain, though the logic of the situation and such bits of evidence as are available tend to confirm it. One might mention, first, the attitude to be expected of Togliatti and his colleagues that no visible candidate for the Soviet succession would be entirely capable of filling Stalin's shoes. Togliatti's own sense of his personal stature as one of the few remaining comrades-in-arms of the great leader would have contributed further to a general skepticism toward the new leadership. Some feeling of this is given by Seniga, writing of the Soviet request that Togliatti attend a secret Cominform meeting to be held in Prague in June 1954.

> In the meeting of the PCI Secretariat, Togliatti let it be understood that he had no desire to leave Italy. The other members of the Secretariat praised him and urged him to make his weight felt so that "they" (the Soviets) would take his personality properly into account. They were saying: "When Stalin was there, that was something to think about, but now Togliatti doesn't have to pick up and leave just because some Khrushchev or other gives him the nod," adding that "in any case after Stalin's death there are only two Communist personalities left, Togliatti and Rakosi."[71]

The PCI did in fact send another representative, D'Onofrio, the man who had been assigned the task a few months earlier of reinterpreting the personality cult so as to deprive it of its anti-Stalinist meaning.

This episode suggests that, in the upper echelons of the PCI, a distinctly disrespectful attitude had developed toward Nikita Khrushchev in particular among the Soviet contenders for Stalin's power. The ultimate outcome of the succession struggle was anything but evident during those years, and the Italians may have been placing their money elsewhere. Seniga observes that during 1953 and 1954 the Communist press in Italy invariably played up the activities of Molotov and Malenkov while largely ignoring

[71] Seniga, *Togliatti e Stalin*, p. 49.

Khrushchev;[72] the same can be said of the early months of 1956, when Malenkov and Bulganin received front-page treatment, the former in connection particularly with his trip to England.

Khrushchev may have been deprecated in part for his lack of personal dignity, for the image of the "buffoon" which caused many outside the Soviet Union, and quite possibly inside as well, to underestimate seriously his strength and talents. Beyond this, he may have been distrusted as a man who seemed inherently unpredictable and irresponsible, addicted to rash behavior likely to cause trouble for Communists forced to adjust after the fact to sudden changes in the Soviet line. Khrushchev's handling of the resumption of relations with Yugoslavia had given some grounds for this concern, which was then painfully confirmed by his secret speech at the Congress. The PCI leaders felt not only that he had gone further than was necessary or wise in his demolition of Stalin but that, whatever Khrushchev's domestic needs may have been, he had failed to consider the consequences of the speech for the West European parties. Above all, its publication by the enemy press, without prior warning or any other assistance in warding off the blow, had left Western Communists disoriented and defenseless.[73]

Although the ties that bound the PCI to the Soviet Union went well beyond the personal loyalties that Stalin managed to create through some combination of fear, respect, and ideological conviction, the personal element was nevertheless there, and its sudden removal is a fact of considerable psychological consequence, however difficult it may be to measure. Without Stalin's authority, international communism could never again be the same.

[72] *Ibid.,* p. 50.

[73] Seniga writes in retrospect that "Khrushchev, on whom the leaders of the PCI would never have bet a cent, and who by his public and clamorous revelations about Stalin and his disconcerting theatrical gestures had won for himself the hatred and the disesteem of the majority of the Italian comrades, had become the most powerful and most important man in the Communist world." *Ibid.,* p. 47.

CHAPTER THREE

THE CLAIMS OF
PROLETARIAN INTERNATIONALISM

The Central Committee met in Rome toward the end of June, a few days after Togliatti's interview had appeared, to continue the discussions that had begun three months before and that were now, after publication of Khrushchev's speech, raging ever more intensely within the party. For the most part those speakers who did not deal exclusively with domestic matters directed their attention to another and potentially even more serious aspect of the Soviet events—their implications for relationships among the Communist parties. As we have already observed, many of the more thoughtful members of the party had been led to wonder whether the party's failure to realize its earlier promise had not been caused in part by its close ties with the Soviet Union. Was it conceivable, they asked themselves, that Stalinist methods and policies had not negatively affected Soviet foreign policy and relations among the parties? The example of Yugoslavia showed that it had; the new Soviet leaders had conceded the point. How much of the past was being implicitly repudiated in the rehabilitation of Tito which had begun in 1955, and in the dissolution of the Cominform, announced without fanfare in April 1956? What did all these facts, together with the new official endorsement of the validity of different roads to socialism, imply for the future relations of Italian communism with Moscow?

Togliatti's interview had reaffirmed, though briefly, the value and necessity of historical ties with the USSR, but had pronounced that the world socialist movement had now inescapably become "polycentric," with all that this concept appeared to imply. In his speech of June 24 to the Central Committee Togliatti returned to the subject, this time dwelling more fully on the past and on his expectations for the future.[1]

[1] "La via italiana al socialismo" in Togliatti, *Problemi del movimento,* pp. 121–169; originally in *L'Unità,* June 26, 1956.

For the particular benefit of "the 'young' comrades . . . whose historical experience is more limited," Togliatti explained that the possibility of different paths of political development toward socialism had been explicitly recognized by Lenin and other early Soviet writers and, although partially forgotten under Stalin, had by no means been completely abandoned. Citing the examples of the popular front policy and the Spanish Civil War, in both of which he had been personally involved, he stated that the doctrine of the necessary diversity of paths of development now had to be much more fully elaborated and applied, in response to the fundamental changes that had occurred in the socialist, capitalist, and former colonial countries of the world. Although the Soviet Union "remains the first great historical model of conquest of power by the working class," its experience cannot provide "either a ready-made solution of all the problems which arise today in those countries already ruled by the working class and by Communist parties or, much less, a ready-made answer to the questions which arise where, instead, the Communist parties or parties oriented toward socialism are opposition parties moving in an environment completely different from that in which the vanguard of the Russian working class operated during and after the seizure of power."[2]

Togliatti went to some pains to set the record straight on the successes and errors of Soviet foreign policy in Europe since the Revolution, and hence on the validity of the Italian party's stance during this period. He asserted the essential correctness of the Soviet line in defense of democracy, insisting that the PCI's support of the USSR "was and continues to be our principal historical merit, in addition to the undeniable heroism of our militants during the Resistance and the war, which some people would like to have us believe was our only merit."[3] Thus reaffirming the value of his own and the party's past contributions to the internationalist cause, he attempted to show that it was precisely during those years of greatest adherence to "the inspiration and guidance" of the Soviet party that the Communist movement had first begun to develop its autonomy.

It is a lie that the Communist International contained only a group that gave orders and non-Russian Communists who obeyed. We shall have to recall these things also to the minds of comrades who do not know them because they have not lived them. Great disputes took place within the Communist International for years and years, accompanied, to be sure, by great discipline.[4]

2 *Ibid.*, p. 136.
3 *Ibid.*, p. 142.
4 *Ibid.*, p. 143.

As evidence he referred to various "errors" and "mutual misunderstandings" which had led the PCI to resist Soviet judgments and directives, in 1928–1931 and later. After the war the PCI had also objected, Togliatti revealed, to the establishment of the Cominform, an action that appeared to the Italians to be "substantially contrary" to the line of development implied by the dissolution of the Comintern. He recalled, finally, that as late as January 1951 he had declined to accept Stalin's proposal that he give up the leadership of the PCI in order to become Secretary General of the Cominform.[5] But all these differences, he was careful to add, "never broke our mutual solidarity and understanding." It was necessary, therefore, as the principle of autonomy came to be further developed and applied, that the party reaffirm and strengthen the spirit of proletarian internationalism, giving it a new and more solid substance rather than allowing it to deteriorate into an empty repetition of old formulas.

Returning to the idea of polycentrism, Togliatti once again pointed to the growth of "a complex, multiform movement" composed not of Communist parties alone but of socialist forces of various descriptions operating in a wide variety of circumstances. The structure of the Communist movement would have to change accordingly:

The experience acquired in the building of a socialist society in the USSR cannot contain directives for resolving all the questions that may arise today for us and for Communists of other countries, whether or not they are in power, and for all the avant-garde parties of the working class and the people.

Thus various points or centers of orientation and development are being created. There is coming into being what I called, in the interview you have read, a polycentric system, corresponding to the new situation, to the change in the structure of the world and in the structure of the workers' movements themselves, and to this system correspond also new forms of relationships among the Communist parties themselves. The solution that today probably most nearly corresponds to this new situation may be that of the full autonomy of the individual movements and Communist parties, and of bilateral relations between them, so as to establish complete mutual understanding and complete mutual trust, conditions necessary for collaboration and for giving unity to the Communist movement itself and to the entire progressive movement of the working class.[6]

Such a pattern of relations, he added, would not only help the various Communist parties understand each other better, but would also permit more fruitful contact between these parties and socialist

---

[5] *Ibid.*, pp. 144–145.
[6] *Ibid.*, pp. 136–137.

and social-democratic movements in the capitalist and under-developed countries. Greater autonomy of individual parties, in short, would allow each in its own way to pursue alliances with non-Communist forces, just as the PCI had done with the Italian Socialists, thus endowing the entire movement with a flexibility and breadth of appeal it had largely forfeited under Stalin's rigid control.

The significance of what Togliatti intended to convey by the idea of polycentrism can be determined far better in the light of his subsequent actions than by textual analysis alone, but a few pre-liminary observations can usefully be made.

There is no evidence, first of all, to suggest that Togliatti in-tended to propose a radical decentralization of the Communist movement or a sharp decline of Soviet authority. He was not trying to be disruptive, only to adapt to what he saw as an objectively new situation requiring new patterns of behavior, a situation that the Soviets themselves, moreover, seemed already to have tacitly ac-cepted. The term polycentrism appears to have been coined essen-tially as a way of describing a new state of affairs in the world at large, characterized by growing diversity within both imperialist and Communist alliance structures and with respect to the under-developed nations as well. As he saw it, this new fact of international life introduced the logical corollary of a greater need for inde-pendent analysis and action on the part of each of the Communist parties in response to the diversities in their circumstances: national roads to socialism were simply an intrinsic aspect of a polycentric world. Togliatti appears to have been trying to generalize about a new pattern of interparty relationships from his personal percep-tions of the world, from the needs of his party, and perhaps most importantly, from Khrushchev's own evident recognition that Com-munist relations would henceforth have to be placed on a new basis.

The PCI's attitude toward Yugoslavia and toward Khrushchev's Yugoslav policy is a revealing case in point. For a number of reasons the Italian party had been slow to reverse its anti-Tito position after Khrushchev announced the change of line to the Cominform in June of 1954. The PCI was quite prepared to continue capital-izing on Italian national antagonism toward Yugoslavia, summed up in the complex Trieste issue with its international ramifications. The PCI may also have been reluctant to switch positions on this issue, as on the Stalin question, because of the real possibility that neither Khrushchev's authority nor the policies with which he was personally closely identified would long survive. The major com-plication, however, lay within the party itself: the Trieste party organization, which had been given special autonomous status, was both pro-Stalinist and fiercely opposed to any rapprochement with Tito. The influence of Vittorio Vidali, leader of the Trieste organization, may have been sufficient to block any moves toward resumption of formal relations between the two parties.

Whatever the weight of these various factors, for nearly two years after the June 1954 Soviet announcement no public and official steps toward rapprochement were undertaken. However, *L'Unità* assigned a reporter to Yugoslavia, so that news from that country began once again to appear in the Communist press. Unofficial delegations of trade unionists and other nonparty groups also began to be exchanged during this period. Then at the end of May 1956, just after the Italian elections, Togliatti suddenly arrived in Belgrade, following Khrushchev by a year on the road to Canossa. After the meeting Togliatti acknowledged the mistaken judgments of the past along with the "useful contributions of the Yugoslav leaders to international détente and the fact that despite the difficulties of past years they have kept their country on the road of socialist development."[7] He appeared reticent about endorsing Yugoslav domestic arrangements, however, as is suggested by his remark, more hopeful than assured, that "naturally, the Yugoslav comrades are I think far from attributing today a universal and definitive value to their experience."[8]

The PCI's real enthusiasm was reserved for the farsighted statesmanship of the Soviet leaders and the long-term implications of the rapprochement with Tito. Immediately after his conversations with Togliatti, the Yugoslav leader left for an extended stay in the Soviet Union, an event hailed as a political landmark by the Italian Communist press. Gian Carlo Pajetta, the Secretariat member often assigned to represent the PCI in its negotiations with other Communist parties, wrote a glowing editorial in *L'Unità:*

> Soviet policy toward Yugoslavia today has a value which beyond any doubt transcends the recognition that a certain judgment and political act were erroneous. The present policy is a particular aspect of a larger vision of the relations between the workers' parties and socialist states and is based on an awareness of the strength of the socialist camp and a recognition of the maturity of the parties which are at the summit of revolutionary action. It is the practical consequence of the theoretical enunciation of national roads to socialism, of the ideological understanding of the historical peculiarity of democratic development in the various countries. . . .[9]

7 *L'Unità*, May 29, 1956.
8 *Ibid.*, June 3, 1956.
9 *Ibid.*, June 5, 1956.

The same evaluation was given by *L'Unità*'s Moscow correspondent when reporting the signing, on June 20, of the Soviet-Yugoslav state and party declarations. "For the first time," he wrote, "the diversity of 'roads to socialism' has found recognition and explicit application in an international document." The agreement should have "wide repercussions" by serving as a model and a precedent for others along similar lines.[10] Togliatti made this assessment official in his Central Committee speech two days later, terming the Soviet-Yugoslav accord "a model of what the new relations ought to be that are being established among the different sectors of the Communist movement."[11]

The idea of polycentrism should be viewed in reference to this sequence of events. Togliatti, unlike his colleague Thorez, personally welcomed the Soviet line—his hasty visit to Tito just before the latter's departure for Moscow is sufficient evidence in itself. In part at least, the term "polycentrism" may have been regarded by its author as an expression and confirmation of the new status quo implicit in Khrushchev's rapprochement with Tito. Both the form and the substance of the Soviet-Yugoslav declaration seemed amply to justify Togliatti's emphasis on the principles of bilateral relations and full autonomy of each party, as the key clause of the declaration suggests:

Believing that the paths of socialist development differ in various countries and conditions, that the wealth of forms of socialist development tends to strengthen socialism, and proceeding from the fact that any tendency to impose one set of views on the paths and forms of socialist development is alien to both, the two parties have agreed that the aforementioned cooperation between our parties is to be based on full freedom and equality, friendly criticism and comradely exchange of views on controversial questions.[12]

Given such justifications for Togliatti's position, did he consider his ideas about a polycentric Communist system to be merely a legitimate extension of what appeared to be the new Soviet policy, reflected most clearly in Khrushchev's dealing with Tito? This would go too far. Togliatti must have known that his stress on autonomy, bilateral relations, and decentralization was not likely to be greeted with enthusiasm in Moscow. It was one thing for the Soviets themselves to pronounce in favor of autonomy for the par-

---

10 *Ibid.*, June 22, 1956.

11 "La via italiana al socialismo" in Togliatti, *Problemi del movimento*, p. 138.

12 *Pravda*, June 21, 1956; quoted from Leo Gruliow, ed., *Current Soviet Policies—II: The Documentary Record of the 20th Communist Party Congress and Its Aftermath* (New York: Praeger, 1957), p. 229.

ties and to treat Tito as head of an equal, sovereign state; it was something else again for the leaders of other parties to assume that all this applied to them. Not much imagination was required to perceive that the Soviets wished to regard Yugoslavia as a special case, not as a model for relations with other Communist states and parties. Events in Poland and Hungary only a few weeks later would dramatically reveal the limits the Soviets wished to impose on the autonomy of their East European satellites.

More probably, Togliatti was attempting neither to oppose outright nor to align himself unconditionally with the Soviet Union. He had correctly perceived that relations within the Communist world could not be as before and welcomed the various signs that the Soviet leaders themselves appeared to have recognized this fact. But Soviet policy was in a state of flux, groping uncertainly for new modes of behavior while remaining rooted in many respects in the practices and mental habits of the past. Togliatti must have wanted to nudge the Soviets further along the path Khrushchev appeared to have chosen, interpreting the developments of recent months as though they constituted a firm new set of principles for the Communist movement. In so doing, he implicitly introduced some potentially significant departures from the old order of things.

Togliatti's stress on bilateral relations among Communist parties, for example, and his parallel rejection of centralized organizations such as the Comintern and the Cominform implied the real possibility of a decline in the Soviet party's ability to control and discipline the movement as effectively as in the past. In criticizing those past episodes when the PCI's perceptions and interests had been overridden by the unified weight of the international movement, he was tacitly asserting that his party should bargain directly with the Soviet Union in defense of its views, thus potentially, under the right set of circumstances, increasing its leverage. It seems paradoxical, given the unchallenged primacy of the USSR, but Soviet power stood to be diluted rather than enhanced in a system based primarily on bilateral relationships. Since the USSR had formally conceded the principles of equality and full autonomy, its superior strength and authority could most easily be brought to bear when exercised in the name of the movement as a whole. A system based on bilateral relations, furthermore, would enhance the possibility of communication and alliances among parties whose mutual interests ran counter to those of the USSR. If all parties were to develop direct ties rather than know each other largely only through their common link with the Soviet party, then a new and potentially disruptive element would be introduced into the Communist movement.

A second point of particular potential significance in Togliatti's discussion of the new polycentric socialist system was the link he established between autonomy of the parties and the ability of international communism to appeal to potential allies within what the Communists refer to as the broader international workers' movement. The Soviets had, at the Twentieth Congress and before, made plain their determination to work more vigorously and flexibly than in the past to influence forces ranging from the socialists and social democrats of Europe to the national bourgeoisies of the underdeveloped world. This strategy was perfectly suited to the PCI's needs, enabling it simultaneously to advance its own domestic purposes and to demonstrate its continued attachment to international Communist strategy.

Togliatti, in maintaining that this rightist strategy could most effectively be implemented by giving maximum autonomy to the individual parties, gave this argument a twist not intended by the Soviet leaders. The traditional assumption had been that Soviet interests were automatically those of the international movement as a whole. But now the order of priority seemed to become subtly and implicitly reversed: alliances that were good for the various parties would automatically be good for the Soviet Union, the leading force in the international Communist movement.

The Soviet party did not register public dissatisfaction with Togliatti's polycentrism formulation. (Their rebuke to him at the end of June concerned only his treatment of the Stalin issue.) It was not until late in 1960, when Togliatti again resurrected the term, that polycentrism would be explicitly and openly criticized by a number of parties, presumably with the full accord of the USSR. It is a curious footnote to history that the only Communist leader on record as having indicated to the PCI in 1956 his disapproval of the idea of polycentrism was Mao Tse-tung. Mao's criticism was expressed privately, during a talk in September 1956 with Davide Lajolo, then editor of the Milan *L'Unità* and head of a PCI delegation to the Chinese party Congress; Lajolo's summary of the talk was not published until August 1963, at a time when Sino-Soviet relations had taken a drastic turn for the worse.[13]

Mao began the conversation by objecting to Togliatti's complaints about the form of the Soviet denunciation of Stalin: the criticism was absolutely essential, the Soviet comrades showed great courage in making it, and no one had any right "to make a fuss because

13 "Mao dalla parte di Krusciov: Intervista di Davide Lajolo," *L'Europeo*, August 18, 1963, pp. 24–29.

some drops from that boiling pot fell on our heads and burnt us."
When Lajolo tried to explain that Togliatti had firmly supported
the Twentieth Congress and had been critical only to the extent
required by "the historical, cultural, and special traditions of Italy,"
Mao gave this sharp rejoinder:

> I do not consider that any of us has the right to introduce even the
> smallest critical note that might, however superficially, affect the unity
> of the socialist camp or suggest that we do not recognize the USSR as the
> center and guide of the whole revolutionary movement.
> No special conditions, in this or that country, can in any way justify a
> position contrasting with that of the Soviet Union. I completely disagree
> with Togliatti's proposal to create several centers of organization for
> Communist parties and countries. There can be no polycentrism that does
> not break the unity of the workers' movement. The only center must be
> Moscow, that is the CPSU, because it is the party of the October Revolu-
> tion, the party that first achieved socialism and is the only guide and
> center of attraction for all Communists.[14]

Mao added later on, requesting that his views be conveyed to
Togliatti, that "precisely because Stalin's errors have been correctly
denounced, there must be no talk of polycentrism, even though, in
one sense, it was the USSR that proposed this; in the same way, we
must continue to treat the CPSU as the guide party, even though
that party has itself suggested a different arrangement."[15]

The particular fascination of this report of Mao's views lies in
its glimpse of the Chinese leader as a strong backer of Khrushchev's
line on Stalin and a solicitous defender, *plus royaliste que le roi*,
of Soviet hegemony within the movement. But it is revealing from
our narrower perspective as well, for it suggests the concern that
any orthodox Communist leader would be likely to have felt over
the implications of Togliatti's ideas. From Togliatti's own perspective, however, if this was heresy, it was so only potentially and
implicitly. The germs may have been there, but it would take a
particular set of conditions for them to mature. In Togliatti's discourse, the claims of polycentrism were always balanced against

---

[14] *Ibid.*, p. 26. As will be discussed in Chapter Six, it is questionable that
Togliatti ever intended to propose the creation of "several centers of organization." Despite Mao's reproach to Togliatti, the PCI press appeared genuinely
respectful during this period toward the Chinese party's attitude to Stalin and
to the need for independent roads to socialism. See, for example, the favorable
comments made about the major Chinese statement, "More on the Historical
Experience of the Dictatorship of the Proletariat"; *L'Unità*, December 29, 1956,
and Maurizio Ferrara, "Ricerche e discussioni nel movimento operaio internazionale," *Rinascita*, XI, 4 (April 1956), p. 178.

[15] Lajolo, "Mao," *L'Europeo*, August 18, 1963, p. 27.

those of proletarian internationalism, against his sense of identification with an international movement of which the Soviet Union
was the undisputed leader and foremost power. This would soon be
clearly shown by his response to the succession of events in Eastern
Europe that rocked the Soviet empire to its foundations. The first
tremor was felt just four days after Togliatti's Central Committee
speech.

Togliatti Turns to the Left

On June 28, after several days of mounting tension, a large-scale
demonstration broke out against the authorities in Poznań, one of
Poland's largest industrial cities. Led by workers unable to obtain
redress for their grievances through legitimate channels, the uprising had to be put down by the army after various municipal
buildings, including the prison, the radio station, and party headquarters, had been seized by the demonstrators. The event itself
triggered an increasingly open and irreconcilable split within the
Polish leadership between a group advocating liberalization and
institutional reform and a faction favoring less substantial change
and continued close links with the Soviet Union. The Soviet leadership, alarmed by the seriousness of the uprising and fearing broader
consequences for the unity of the bloc, supported the conservative
faction and attempted over the succeeding months to insert itself
decisively into the internal political process in Poland.[16]

The Italian party wavered between two conflicting though not
mutually exclusive interpretations of the Poznań uprising. The first,
and as it turned out the dominant view, maintained that *agents
provocateurs,* probably inspired by a clandestine group aided by
foreign agents, had intervened during a meeting of honest workers,
taking advantage of certain legitimate grievances to incite the crowd
to violence.[17] But an on-the-spot report from Poznań by *L'Unità's*
Warsaw correspondent, Sansone, interpreted the event somewhat
differently, giving a sympathetic account of the workers' complaints
and placing responsibility for the origins of the crisis directly on
poor economic planning and the general inexperience of the young
socialist government. Sansone also referred to provocation, but gave
the term a rather calm and sociological flavor, pointing to recently
recruited and unstable elements among the working class rather

16 See Zbigniew K. Brzezinski, *The Soviet Bloc: Unity and Conflict* (rev.
ed.; Cambridge, Mass.: Harvard University Press, 1967), pp. 248–267.
17 *L'Unità*, June 29 and 30, 1956.

than to agents inspired from the outside.[18] If Sansone's report served to stir up latent doubts among the Communist faithful, already being subjected to a hostile barrage from the bourgeois press, then a declaration by Giuseppe Di Vittorio appearing the next day disoriented them further.

Di Vittorio, Italy's most popular and respected labor leader, a long-time Communist and Secretary General of the CGIL as well as President of the World Federation of Trade Unions, had found it impossible to accept at face value the PCI's official version of the uprising. He did not, in his statement, dispute the presence of *agents provocateurs*, maintaining that public buildings would not have been subjected to armed attack if the demands had been purely economic, but he did insist strongly that the *provocateurs* could easily have been isolated and rendered ineffectual if there had not existed a profound discontent among the workers. Did the Polish leaders, he asked, know of the existence and depth of the discontent, and if so what had they done to alleviate it? In a socialist country the workers could impose sacrifices on themselves for the sake of the future, but they were also entitled, through their unions, to determine the limits of these sacrifices. Even in a socialist country, he concluded, the unions "have the task of defending energetically the just demands of the workers, in relation to the demands of the general development of socialist society."[19]

Such a declaration, in conflict with the official Communist view and thus violating the traditional norms of party solidarity, must certainly have deeply offended the party hierarchy. That it was printed at all is testimony not only to Di Vittorio's prestige and seniority, but to the depth of his personal feeling on the issue and, even more important, to the force of his characteristic insistence on the need to preserve the unity of the CGIL and thus its potential appeal to the entire Italian working class. He undoubtedly argued that for the CGIL to swallow a party line that in effect endorsed the repression by force of a workers' demonstration in a Communist country would forever brand it as a tool of the PCI in the eyes of the workers, in particular those adhering to the CGIL's Socialist minority.

The official Soviet reaction to the Poznań events was strong and unambiguous. On June 30 the Soviet Central Committee adopted a resolution, "On Overcoming the Personality Cult and Its Consequences" (published in *Pravda* on July 2), which replied to the

[18] *Ibid.*, July 1, 1956.
[19] *Ibid.*, July 2, 1956.

criticisms and demands for clarification that had flooded in upon Moscow from Communist and socialist parties around the world after publication of the Khrushchev secret speech. But the Poznań revolt had broken out just as the Central Committee was meeting, and a few somber paragraphs of evaluation and warning were added at the end of the resolution. The Poznań uprising was attributed unequivocally to the renewed efforts of American monopolistic capital to revive the cold war and overthrow communism, a policy revealed in the Senate's recent appropriation of $25,000,000 for subversive activities under the cynical disguise of "encouraging freedom" behind the "iron curtain": "It is clear, for example, that the antipopular demonstrations in Poznań were financed from this source." The episode demonstrates "that there can be no complacency with regard to new machinations by the imperialist agents, who seek to penetrate the socialist countries in order to harm and undermine the working people's achievements."[20]

The language of this appeal for vigilance in the face of imperialist provocation and subversion was familiar to any Communist leader who had lived through the Stalin era. He knew that the Soviet party meant to be taken seriously when it spoke in such terms as these. But in case the force of the message should have been dulled by the Soviet "new look" in interparty relations symbolized by the Soviet-Yugoslav agreements then only a week old, the resolution was quite explicit about the responsibilities of the parties:

Under the new historical conditions such international working-class organizations as the Comintern and Cominform have ceased their activities. It does not follow from this, however, that international solidarity and the need for contacts among revolutionary fraternal parties adhering to positions of Marxism-Leninism have lost their significance. Today, when the forces of socialism and the influence of the ideas of socialism have grown immeasurably throughout the world, when differences in paths to socialism in various countries are becoming apparent, the Marxist parties of the working class should naturally preserve and strengthen their ideological unity and international fraternal solidarity in the struggle against the threat of a new war, in the struggle against the antipopular forces of monopoly capital which seek to suppress all revolutionary and progressive movements.[21]

In this and subsequent paragraphs the resolution thus conveyed the idea that recognition of national peculiarities in the road to socialism could in no wise be allowed to weaken the ideological and political bonds among the parties.

20 *Pravda*, July 2, 1956; quoted from *Current Digest of the Soviet Press* (hereafter cited as *CDSP*), VIII, 24, p. 8.
21 *Ibid.*

In addition to this message, addressed to all the Communist parties but particularly to the Poles and Yugoslavs, there was much in the June 30 resolution of particular interest to Togliatti and his party. The document was primarily intended as an answer to those foreign Communists who had insisted on the need for a fuller explanation of the causes and consequences of Stalin's misdeeds. The personality cult was attributed to the specific historical conditions of socialist development in the USSR and to the personal aberrations of Stalin, not to any presumed weaknesses in Soviet society:

But it would be a serious mistake to infer from the existence of the cult of an individual in the past that the social system in the USSR has changed somehow or to look for the sources of this cult in the nature of the Soviet social system. Both alternatives are absolutely wrong, for they do not accord with reality, they contradict the facts.[22]

After praising the approval given Soviet actions against the personality cult by the Chinese, French, and American parties, the resolution singled out Togliatti for criticism. His "detailed and interesting" interview in *Nuovi argomenti,* although containing "many very important and correct conclusions," was unfortunately incorrect on some points: "In particular, one cannot agree with the question raised by Comrade Togliatti as to whether Soviet society has not reached 'certain forms of degeneration.' There are no grounds whatever for this question." Togliatti's statement is "all the more incomprehensible," the resolution continued, since elsewhere in the interview he had correctly maintained that the essence of the socialist system had not been lost.[23]

Togliatti responded promptly to this unusually direct public criticism by means of a short statement appearing first in the Communist-controlled newspaper *Paese sera* on the afternoon of July 3, the day after the resolution had been printed in *Pravda.* Although the statement was by no means a complete capitulation, as it has sometimes been described, neither was it defiant. Togliatti began by saying that he had not yet read the resolution's full text, which may have been true but also could well have been a way of holding open the option of later modifying his response. He stated that "the document provides a contribution of extreme importance" for clarifying the questions aroused by the criticisms of Stalin and expressed the "unreserved approval" of the PCI of the actions thus far taken to overcome the consequences of the personality cult for

22 *Ibid.,* p. 6.
23 *Ibid.,* p. 7.

the USSR and the international movement. Regarding the consequences themselves, however, he was less compliant:

> As for my attitude at my well-known interview, perhaps the best thing
> to do now is to read carefully what I have written. In my opinion, and I
> have said so openly, the line followed by the Soviet comrades in the
> construction of a communist society was undoubtedly right; but within
> the general framework of this acknowledgment there may be differing
> opinions on the value and importance of the errors committed under
> Stalin's leadership, the violations of legality, the restrictions on democracy,
> and so on, over the economic and political development of the Soviet
> Union.
>
> I repeat that such differing opinions are possible, and a frank discussion
> on the matter cannot but prove useful for the development of our move-
> ment, because it corresponds to a higher degree of maturity and of mutual
> understanding and confidence.[24]

Although this exchange appeared limited to a difference of
opinion concerning a single point, the relationship of the personality cult to the Soviet system, it went deeper. In Soviet eyes
Togliatti's criticism must have seemed a more general breach of
faith and a violation of the first principle of proletarian internationalism, respect and assistance for the Soviet party and government. This is suggested rather more clearly in the *Pravda* editorial
on the resolution than in the document itself. The resolution simply
lamented the incorrectness of Togliatti's view; the editorial referred
to opinions linking the personality cult to the faults of the Soviet
system as "slanderous assertions" held by "the enemies of socialism."[25] Although Togliatti was not being accused of disloyalty, he
was being warned against toying with ideas that objectively gave aid
and comfort to the enemy. His reply, which declined to concede that
the Soviet resolution had dealt adequately with the historical problem of Stalin, must have given less than full satisfaction to the
Soviet comrades.

Togliatti had, however, already found a better and more convincing way of demonstrating his loyalty, one having the particular
merit of not requiring him to renounce publicly his ideas. He
published in *L'Unità* on July 3 a short but sharp editorial article
whose title alone, "The Presence of the Enemy," left no doubt by
its Stalinist overtones about the direction of his thought. The
burden of his message was simple and to the point: despite the
constantly growing strength of the Communist movement and the
impossibility of halting its forward march, the capitalist ruling
classes had not yet laid down their arms:

24 *L'Unità*, July 4, 1956.
25 *Pravda*, July 4, 1956.

The enemy does exist. He is strong, he is active, and he is without pity. He is still powerful outside our camp and does not lack strength and points of influence even within our camp. Woe betide us if we forget this. The events that have taken place at Poznań remind us of it, and remind us particularly strongly.

It is not with rifles and machine guns that the problems of labor . . . are posed and solved in a society that does not have any more capitalists to exploit human labor. But how many rifles and machine guns can be put to use by spending 125 million dollars a year, such as the budget of the American government sets aside to foment violence and provocation in countries that are no longer capitalist?

The enemy is, therefore, present. He was present at Poznań, in a way which is becoming increasingly clear. But he is present elsewhere as well, trying to make us deviate from our path, to sow confusion and defeatism, to slander reality, to prevent socialism from advancing by any means at his disposal, and to prevent Communists from being the main motive force in today's great movement of liberation of men from the chains of any kind of slavery.[26]

Why did Togliatti, who had up to this moment consistently shown an acute sensitivity to the political requirements of his situation, including particularly the need to avoid alienating the Socialist party, suddenly revert to a hard neo-Stalinist position on an issue of extreme sensitivity for the working class? Outside the party this position could not possibly win support. With this editorial he also effectively sacrificed his mediating stance between conflicting tendencies within the party and came down decisively in favor of the conservative wing.

Several factors appear to have contributed to Togliatti's move. By echoing the harsh language of the Soviet statement and accepting fully its neo-Stalinist interpretation of the Poznań riots, Togliatti could demonstrate to the Russians that the demands of proletarian internationalism still retained their compelling power. It is altogether plausible, moreover, that his own deepest instincts, conditioned by decades of viewing the world through Stalinist lenses, would in fact have led him to credit the interpretation of the Poznań riots as a provocation of the imperialists. And whatever his personal beliefs in the matter, for him to have taken issue with the explanation being offered at that moment by the Polish government itself would have been a politically irresponsible act, an almost inconceivable violation of the spirit of proletarian internationalism.

Togliatti may also have been motivated by internal party considerations, by the desire to redress the balance between the liberal

26 "La presenza del nemico" in Togliatti, *Problemi del movimento*, pp. 172–173; originally in *L'Unità*, July 3, 1956.

and the conservative factions. Right through the end of June Togliatti's words and actions had tended to favor the proponents of "renewal," with their insistence on a more independent Italian road. He may now have felt it important to avoid further antagonizing the militants, the hard core of the party's organizational strength. This group, already shaken by the Stalin crisis and further disoriented by the leadership's adherence to the softer line of the post-Congress period, could have become seriously disaffected if the party had in effect joined *Avanti!* in berating a socialist government for firing on the workers.

Such a vigorous reaffirmation of loyalty to the USSR, a vivid reminder to all that the traditional symbols and methods of class war were not being forgotten even while peaceful coexistence blossomed, was in fact well suited to serve a dual objective: to reassure both the Soviet leaders and the PCI's own hard core that Palmiro Togliatti still knew how to be a good disciple of Lenin and of Stalin. *Pravda* reprinted the editorial the next day, suggesting that the significance of his gesture had not been lost on Moscow.[27] The Soviet anathema was definitively lifted two weeks later when a *Pravda* lead article attacking the efforts of the imperialists to split the Communist movement made special favorable reference to Togliatti, quoting his endorsement of Soviet steps to overcome the consequences of the personality cult.[28]

It quickly became clear inside the party that a turning point had been reached. In June Togliatti had professed to see "nothing terrible or scandalous" in the strongly critical remarks made during a gathering of Communist intellectuals in Rome;[29] after the Poznań events, however, he took immediate steps to restrict the freedom of discussion, most clearly in what came to be known as the "Onofri case."

At the June meeting of the Central Committee, Fabrizio Onofri had been among those who chose to speak about Togliatti's interpretation of the personality cult, raising in particular the question of whether the PCI's domestic activities had not suffered as a result of its automatic identification with Soviet interests, especially as imposed through the Cominform. Dissatisfied both by the difficulty of expressing his views in the limited time allotted to him at the meeting and by what he termed *L'Unità's* "mutilation" of his remarks, Onofri decided to prepare an article for the PCI monthly

27 *Pravda*, July 4, 1956.
28 *Ibid.*, July 16, 1956; translation in *CDSP*, VIII, 29, p. 3.
29 "La via italiana al socialismo" in Togliatti, *Problemi del movimento*, p. 169.

developing his ideas more fully.[30] The article, highly critical of PCI policy and action in most of the postwar years, appeared during August (but in the July issue of *Rinascita*) under the title assigned by Togliatti, the journal's editor, "An Inadmissible Attack on the Policy of the Italian Communist Party"; it was accompanied by Togliatti's personal rebuttal.[31]

Onofri's analysis began with a question: why was it that at a time when the objective political situation, internationally and in Italy, favored the workers' movement, the PCI's influence over the situation had for some years steadily declined? This contradiction, he argued, stemmed from the party's effective abandonment early in 1947 of the basic slogan of the Italian road to socialism. Why had the slogan tacitly been dropped as a guide to policy even though it had continued to be formally proclaimed? It had sometimes been hinted, as, for example, by Amendola at the recent meeting of the National Council, that the fault lay in the party's having accepted for reasons of solidarity, rather than conviction, the political line of the Cominform. This was no doubt in one sense true, wrote Onofri, but it did not exhaust the question. The deeper fact was that in 1947 the PCI had accepted as its own the Cominform's evaluation of the international and domestic relationship of forces, an evaluation which had proven to be profoundly mistaken. By underestimating its own strength at home and the strength of the forces of socialism and peace on the international scene, the party had been led to adopt a defensive posture and implicitly to reject the possibility of moving forward on the democratic road to socialism. Onofri cited many instances of the PCI's failure to comprehend the real situation during the years since 1947, measured in terms both of the electoral and trade union struggle and of mistaken theoretical formulations. The net result, he insisted, was a party relying increasingly on sterile propaganda rather than concrete action to assist the working class, on repressive methods of bureaucratic control within the party, on the vain hope that revolution could be achieved only through a *coup d'état* or Soviet intervention rather than through the party's own actions in the daily political battle.

A far-reaching indictment indeed, to which Togliatti replied with a masterful combination of sarcasm, invective, and judicious selection of facts. More interesting than the substance of Togliatti's

---

[30] Onofri, *Classe operaia*, pp. 108–109.

[31] Fabrizio Onofri, "Un inammissibile attacco alla politica del Partito comunista italiano," *Rinascita*, XIII, 7 (July 1956), pp. 365–369; Palmiro Togliatti, "La realtà dei fatti e della nostra azione rintuzza l'irresponsabile disfattismo," *ibid.*, pp. 369–372.

rebuttal, however, is the fact that he allowed Onofri's piece to be published. If the attack was "inadmissible," why give it currency? Togliatti himself gave one answer to that question in a showdown meeting with Onofri in his office after reading the manuscript. As Onofri later reported it, Togliatti was in an angry mood, accusing him of factionalism and thus hinting at expulsion from the party. Togliatti said that if Onofri insisted, he was ready to publish the article for the positive effect he felt it would have on his position in the party. "You want to do political battle with the 'leftists,'" he told Onofri, "but in this way you are letting me recover them all, to group them tightly around the center of the party, to re-create that unity which the Twentieth Congress, because of the way in which its results were made known, has gravely compromised."[32]

Onofri asked for twenty-four hours in which to reflect before finally committing his article to publication, in the course of which he meditated upon Togliatti's reasons for wanting to print the article. Not, surely, to demonstrate that the internal party debate Togliatti had urged would really be free and open, for the promised rebuttal would destroy any illusions on that score.

Why then? Suddenly the other aspect of the question struck me clearly . . . Just in that month of July the Central Committee of the CPSU had replied [to the *Nuovi argomenti* interview] condemning explicitly the judgments of P. Togliatti: a totally new fact for the Italian Communist party, and one such as to shake further the already damaged prestige of its chief. . . . My article provided a providential occasion for P. Togliatti: to reply to the Soviets between the lines, addressing himself at the same time to the party in such a way as to draw it strongly around his own person, to galvanize it with a strong injection of "party patriotism," in sum, to make it appear that once again he, P. Togliatti, was the man around whom the unity and the defense of the Communist patrimony was secured. The reply to my article . . . was thus an indirect way of saying to the Soviets: my loyalty to your policy is beyond discussion; just let me demonstrate it in the most opportune way, better adapted to the present circumstances and the situation of my party.[33]

Onofri's analysis, as is natural in such an account of a traumatic personal experience, shows some tendency to exaggerate the importance of his own case among the events of those dramatic days. Nevertheless, his appraisal of Togliatti's response largely coincides with the interpretation offered above of Togliatti's reaction to Poznań. It was not Onofri's article but the upheaval at Poznań that was the turning point, providing Togliatti with a "providential occasion" to speak to the Russians and to his own party as well.

32 Onofri, *Classe operaia*, pp. 112–113.
33 *Ibid.*, pp. 114–115.

Onofri then offered Togliatti a convenient way of confirming his return to orthodoxy and of preventing any further "inadmissible attacks" by irresponsible intellectuals on the party's policies.

Whether the internal party situation or the Soviet position was the more significant is irrelevant. Under the circumstances Togliatti's effort to restore unity in the party under his firm guidance could best be accomplished by adopting a hard line and reaffirming loyalty to the USSR. But if the more prudent course appeared to lie with orthodoxy, Togliatti's choice was not without its risks. In taking the position he did, he was bound to alienate many within his party, especially those intellectuals who shared some of Onofri's concerns about the party and who feared and resented all that was implied by the resumption of Stalinist manners and methods. The Onofri case became, in fact, according to one account of those turbulent months, "the center of a bitter dispute, to some extent everywhere, but particularly in Rome":

The attack against this comrade was facilitated by his limited authority and by the absence of an organization behind him that upheld his ideas: nor was it enough of a counterweight to recall the numerous occasions on which Togliatti himself had shown his predilection for Onofri. The harsh treatment of this "case" was meant to set an example of the absolute limits of allowable discussion. For a minority of the party it was, on the contrary, an occasion on which to raise a clamorous demand for the principle of the fullest freedom of discussion, even on basic topics such as those raised by Onofri, especially since Khrushchev's revelations had demonstrated the damage done by silence and the lack of internal democracy.[34]

Letters of protest flooded into the editorial offices of *Rinascita,* including one drafted after a long meeting of Communists connected with the University of Rome, which defended not Onofri personally, nor his particular interpretation of the party's difficulties, but the right of any party member to express his opinions on such basic questions, however mistaken, without being attacked as a traitor to the cause.[35] The dissent in Rome came to a head in mid-September at a general assembly of the university Communists

[34] Giuliana D'Amelio, "La lotta politica del 1956 fra gli universitari e gli intellettuali comunisti di Roma," *Passato e presente,* No. 13 (January–February 1960), pp. 1704–1739, at p. 1713. This article, whose author was herself one of the dissident Communist student leaders, provides an excellent chronological account of the stages of the dispute between party officials and Communist intellectuals in Rome between the spring of 1956 and the Eighth Congress in December. Included are substantial excerpts from documents that have not been published elsewhere.

[35] *Ibid.,* pp. 1713–1716; Onofri, *Classe operaia,* p. 116. None of these letters were published.

presided over by Pietro Ingrao, then editor of *L'Unità*'s Rome edition, and other high officials of the party. The confrontation was a standoff: the intellectuals did not moderate their criticism in the face of Ingrao's effort to portray Togliatti as basically a determined advocate of renewal who happened to be confronted with an extremely delicate international situation; and the party authorities in their turn did not yield an inch on their refusal to publish the critical letter prepared by the university group earlier in the month.[36] If debate on basic issues of strategy and party life were to be permitted in advance of the upcoming party Congress, then it was imperative that the unwritten limits of permissible discussion be clearly understood. Criticism of specific aspects of the party's policies or actions would be permitted, but wide-ranging attacks like Onofri's, which threw into question the soundness of the party's entire postwar strategy and its links with international communism, had to be ruled out of bounds.

The party's organizational and ideological weapons appeared capable of dealing with the challenge presented by its intellectual critics, but Togliatti faced another kind of risk. The long-term strategy he had chosen for the party would require it to move, or appear to move, substantially to the right in matters of policy and relations with other parties. This strategy was being resisted by the party left, that is, by precisely those whom Togliatti was addressing when he adopted his hard-line response to Poznań and the Onofri case. To put over this longer term plan, to make it an actual rather than merely a verbal strategy, would require the backing of the liberal intellectuals and their supporters within the party. These were the people with the technical competence, the breadth of outlook, the easy access to non-Communist circles that an effective alliance strategy would demand. A sharp move to the left ran the risk of damaging beyond repair the prospects of promoting all that was meant by the democratic road to socialism. This was a risk Togliatti was willing to take, apparently confident of his ability to regulate the delicate balance between the two wings of his party.

The Impact of Poland and Hungary

Following Togliatti's turn to the left in July, efforts were made to re-create a somewhat more liberal atmosphere inside the party. Now that the limits of allowable criticism had been established, the pre-Congress discussions could safely be resumed. During the

36 D'Amelio, *Passato e presente*, No. 13, pp. 1718–1719.

summer and early fall a full page of articles and letters appeared two or three times weekly in *L'Unità* debating the party's most pressing issues—agricultural and cultural policy, trade union affairs, the Italian road to socialism, party democracy, relations with the Soviet Union. The leadership was hoping to ease internal tensions by means of a controlled debate which would, at the same time, communicate to the party faithful the positions to be presented and duly adopted at the Congress.

The change of mood was manifested also by an official display of sympathetic attitudes toward Yugoslavia, the chief example of the now officially sanctioned independent national roads to socialism. The party journal published a long article by Kardelj, the most revisionist of the Yugoslav leaders, on the leading role of the League of Communists,[37] and a top-level delegation under Longo's leadership was sent to Belgrade in the first half of October. Longo's public reports on the trip could hardly have been more satisfying to his hosts: he criticized the "bitter and unjust struggle" conducted by all those, including the Italians, who had failed to understand that Yugoslavia was indeed engaged in building socialism and acknowledged that the Yugoslav experience, along with that of the Soviet Union, China, and the people's democracies, constituted a precious patrimony for the Communist movement.[38]

The unusually warm and positive tenor of Longo's comments contrasts with the growing coolness being displayed by the Soviet Union during this period toward both Yugoslavia and Poland. The major *Pravda* editorial of July 16, affirming the original Soviet assessment of Poznań and warning of imperialist efforts to undermine the unity of the Communist movement, was followed by other public statements in the same vein on the need for ideological and political unity among the Communist states and parties.

The most pointed expression of Soviet concern, however, came in a secret circular letter sent to the satellite leaders in late August or early September. According to the summary later published in the *Manchester Guardian*, the document went straight to the heart of the matter:

> The Communist Party of the Soviet Union considers that it remains the directing party among all the Communist organizations of the world.
> Each Communist party is judged in the light of the more or less intimate relations which it has with the Soviet Communist Party, for the interests

[37] "Sulla funzione dirigente della Lega dei comunisti jugoslavi nella edificazione socialista," *Rinascita*, XIII, 7 (July 1956), pp. 356–361.

[38] *L'Unità*, October 26 and 29, 1956; "Vivo interesse e attento studio per le esperienze dei comunisti jugoslavi," *Rinascita*, XIII, 11 (November 1956), pp. 569–573.

of the Communist Party of the Soviet Union are closely tied in with those of the other sister parties. . . . It is in accordance with the theories of Lenin to respect national differences in the building of socialism and in the setting up of the popular democracy, on the condition that the principle mentioned above is not forgotten. A permanent collaboration of the different Communist parties will be possible only with those of them which keep strictly to the Marxist-Leninist doctrines.

Other proletarian parties must be led to collaborate with the Communist parties on the fundamental problems of the working class. Better and more frequent contacts will have to be established. However, it must be affirmed that socialism can be built only under the banner of internationalism, in close liaison with the socialist countries, and not under the banner of nationalism, without liaison with the socialist countries.[39]

The PCI made little effort during the summer and early fall to keep its followers informed about the increasingly delicate situations in Poland and Hungary and the mounting Soviet concern over them. Only occasional articles on the satellite countries appeared in the Italian daily Communist press, all in the usual laudatory style and echoing official Polish and Hungarian views. *L'Unità* did not mention the dramatic meeting of the Polish Central Committee, interrupted by the sudden and uninvited arrival of the top Soviet leaders, until after the Russians had already returned to Moscow and other Italian papers had given prominence to stories about Soviet pressures on the Poles. These reports for the first time mentioned attacks by *Pravda* on the "antisocialist" and "nationalistic" attitudes appearing in the Polish press.[40]

The Polish crisis provided a new source of tension between certain of the PCI intellectuals and the party bureaucracy, which tended to view Gomułka and his "new course" with considerable apprehension. In Rome, party officials "spoke deprecatingly about the movement of the Polish workers, while in other sectors of the party there reigned great enthusiasm, the words of Gomułka being read as an example of how, in Italy too, one had to break with the past and seek out a new road."[41] Togliatti himself, responding in the privacy of his office to the criticism of a delegation from Pesaro about the party's lack of solidarity with the Poles, did not disguise his lack of enthusiasm for the Polish experiment and for Gomułka

39 *Manchester Guardian*, October 19, 1956. Similar but less ample versions had appeared in other Western newspapers, including some in Italy. The Yugoslavs admitted the existence of the document as early as September 30 in *Borba* of that date, but Togliatti a month later referred to the version published in the United States as "an all too obvious falsification"; *L'Unità*, November 29, 1956.

40 *L'Unità*, October 21, 1956.

41 D'Amelio, *Passato e presente*, No. 13, p. 1719.

as an individual, although he allowed that there had been no acceptable alternative.[42]

Nothwithstanding these official concerns, *L'Unità* published extracts from Gomułka's address to the Polish Central Committee, including the following pointed rebuttal of the Soviet interpretation of the Poznań riots:

The workers of Poznań did not protest against the people's power, against socialism, when they went out into the street; they protested against the evil that was widespread in our social system and that also injured them painfully, against the distortion of the basic principle of socialism, which is their idea. It would be a great political naïveté to try to present the tragedy of Poznań as the work of imperialist agents and provocateurs.[43]

The statement was aimed at Gomułka's hard-line opponents in the Natolin group and at their Soviet supporters, but no sophisticated Italian reader could have failed to note that it directly contradicted Togliatti's "Presence of the Enemy" editorial and vindicated the stand taken by the PSI, by Di Vittorio, and by the intellectual stratum of the party. Publication of Gomułka's view might have seemed a tacit retraction of the earlier party line and a cautious endorsement of the Poles in their test of strength with the USSR, but whatever the paper's editor may have wished to convey, this was evidently not Togliatti's intent. On the very day Gomułka's speech appeared in *L'Unità*, Togliatti, expressing his concern over Polish "revisionism,"[44] rejected out of hand the demand presented by an "excited group" of party members in Rome for an official party stand in support of the Poles.

Nevertheless, Togliatti could not oppose Gomułka outright without revealing too blatant a contradiction in his position. After all, Gomułka and his colleagues were apparently struggling to put into effect, against Soviet opposition, the very lessons which Togliatti himself had insisted must be drawn from the Twentieth Congress and the repudiation of Stalin. To have attacked Gomułka's insistence on autonomy from the USSR, thorough economic reform, rejuvenation of the party's internal life, liberalization of Polish social and political conditions—this would have been to repudiate the essence of Togliatti's entire post-Congress position and to strain to the breaking point the willingness of socialists and of modern-

[42] Domenico Settembrini, "La polemica a Pesaro sui fatti di Ungheria e l'opinione di Togliatti sull' intervento Sovietico," *Passato e presente*, No. 13 (January–February 1960), p. 1745. Settembrini, who attended the meeting, reports that Togliatti was particularly suspicious of Gomułka's concessions to the Catholic Church.

[43] *L'Unita*, October 22, 1956.

[44] D'Amelio, *Passato e presente*, No. 13, p. 1720.

izers in the PCI to believe in the genuineness of the party's defense of democratic and autonomous roads to socialism.

The rapid and peaceful way in which the Polish crisis was resolved enabled the PCI to escape from its dilemma and adopt a cautiously liberal line without risk of affronting the Soviet Union. Once the USSR had, late on October 22, capitulated to Gomułka's basic demands, the threat of a confrontation between the traditional Stalinist principle of support to the USSR at all costs and the apparent Khrushchevian principle of autonomy no longer remained. The PCI was then able to assume a public stance of what might be termed a rather nervous optimism that everything would work out for the best. Ingrao's editorial of October 23 attempted to reassure the party militants that the Polish events in no sense represented a victory for reaction; the issue concerned only the mode and tempo of socialist construction, a process which had to be carried out under the banner of liberty and justice. But realizing the uncertainty and instability of the situation, the party tried to cover itself against a future change of line by warning that "the enemy is maneuvering" to take advantage of difficulties and that no one could afford to exclude the possibility that errors might be made by the new Polish leadership.[45]

The need to take a more explicit stand on Poland was avoided by the sudden eruption of a far more difficult and dangerous situation in Hungary that would stretch the party's resilience to its furthest limit. The outburst of violence in Budapest, requiring Soviet troops to control, was at first treated by the PCI as similar to the case of Poznań. It was maintained that a "counterrevolutionary putsch" had been staged by armed rebels in an effort to overthrow a regime struggling to correct the serious errors of the past. The PCI was "greatly distressed" that the unfortunate weakness of the government had compelled it to rely on Soviet military assistance, but the alternative had clearly been a restoration of fascism. In an evident effort to distinguish the Hungarian from the Polish situation, it was said that there would be time enough tomorrow to talk about the mode and tempo of socialist construction; the task today was to defend the revolution itself:

It is necessary to choose: either for the defense of the socialist revolution or for the white counterrevolution, for the old fascist and reactionary Hungary. . . . A third camp does not exist.[46]

A powerful wave of sympathy for the rebels and of protest against

45 *L'Unità*, October 23, 1956.
46 *Ibid.*, October 25, 1956.

Communist oppression quickly swept over Italy, as elsewhere in the West, leading the PCI gradually to modify its stance. As *Rinascita* later somewhat ruefully understated the case, the party's initial response to the Hungarian situation, based on "a paucity of detailed information, lent itself to accusations, retorts, and polemics of a strongly anti-Communist flavor."[47] During the next several days, the party gradually altered its line to acknowledge the popular character of the revolt and to assign principal responsibility for the tragedy not to Fascist reactionaries but to the previous Hungarian regime, whose criminal errors, incomprehensible reluctance to introduce the reforms necessitated by the Twentieth Congress, and consequent total loss of authority had allowed the situation to deteriorate so completely.

By October 30 Togliatti had reached the point of granting that the use of Soviet troops had "complicated things" and "should and perhaps could have been avoided," but he continued to imply that responsibility for this sad necessity rested with the Hungarian leaders, not the Soviets. He pointed out that it was, after all, the Soviet Union that had courageously insisted on the urgent need for reform in all the socialist countries. The errors of the past had to be openly recognized and corrected, but no Communist could allow himself to cross the line between sound criticism and "hasty and grotesque judgments according to which the people's and socialist regimes become something similar to fascism, and the Soviet Union something like an imperialist state." In the face of such difficult circumstances, he warned, Communists had to hold firm to a class perspective and not surrender to one-sided and sentimental emotions.[48]

In spite of such statements, it cannot quite be said, as most non-Communist Italian accounts have maintained, that Togliatti followed the Soviet line inflexibly during those tension-laden days.[49] As in the Poznań case, the Soviet leaders from the start placed primary and at times exclusive emphasis on the role of "a reactionary counterrevolutionary underground, well armed and thoroughly prepared for decisive action against the people's government, [which] had been organized with outside help."[50] The USSR held to this contention throughout the crisis, for it provided the necessary justification for Soviet military intervention. Even after the

[47] "Politica italiana," *Rinascita*, XIII, 11 (November 1956), p. 630.
[48] *L'Unità*, October 30, 1956.
[49] See, for example, Galli, *Storia del Partito*, pp. 354–355; Ghirelli, *Il Ponte*, XII, 12, p. 2087; and Ugo La Malfa, *La Voce repubblicana*, November 1, 1956.
[50] *Pravda*, October 28, 1956; quoted from *CDSP*, VIII, 41, p. 12.

withdrawal of Soviet troops by agreement with the Nagy government, the door had to be kept open against the possibility of their being needed once again.

The Soviet explanation was not, however, being accepted by all in the "socialist camp." As Togliatti would have known by the time he wrote his October 30 article, both the Poles and the new Hungarian Communist government itself had vigorously and explicitly rejected this view, which the Hungarian party newspaper went so far as to label erroneous, deplorable, and insulting to "the basic patriotic and democratic aims of the great popular uprising."[51] The PCI's second-stage interpretation of the revolt, then, plus its refusal to endorse the first Soviet military intervention, represented a conscious though cautious departure from the Soviet position. (The French party, by contrast, refused to make concessions and staunchly upheld the Soviet version of events.)

Several factors appear to account for this deviation. One may have been the fleeting hope that the Hungarian crisis could, in fact, be considered a reaction against Stalinism and against excessive Soviet control that would not lead to a repudiation of essential Communist principles. Such an interpretation was being given some substance not only by the Hungarian, Polish, and Yugoslav response, but also by the fact of Soviet military withdrawal from Budapest, which seemed to suggest a readiness to give the Nagy government the benefit of the doubt. In the confused circumstances of that dramatic week, when no one could be certain of the facts and when Soviet words and actions were ambiguous and even contradictory, the Italian position was understandable even from the standpoint of Communist orthodoxy.

But while uncertainties concerning the situation in Hungary and the ultimate Soviet reaction to it enabled the PCI to depart cautiously from the Soviet line without serious risk to its Communist credentials, the most relevant factors were closer to home. The PCI was mercilessly attacked by center and right-wing forces for its refusal to join in the chorus of outrage against Communist brutality. Subtle distinctions from the Soviet position, however, could hardly be expected to influence the reactions of its enemies on the right, who saw in the Hungarian events a sudden and unexpected second chance to score heavily against Italian communism.[52] The

51 *Trybuna Ludu*, October 28, 1956, in Paul E. Zinner, ed., *National Communism and Popular Revolt in Eastern Europe: A Selection of Documents on Events in Poland and Hungary, February–November, 1956* (New York: Columbia University Press, 1956), pp. 440–444; *Szabad Nep*, October 29, 1956, in *ibid.*, pp. 449–451.

52 See, for example, La Malfa, *La Voce repubblicana*, November 1, 1956, for a blistering indictment of Togliatti's article of October 30.

PCI's central concern, therefore, was not with such implacably hostile forces but rather with its erstwhile allies in the Socialist party and the waverers among its own membership. From both sources an unprecedented storm of opposition had suddenly arisen.

PRESSURE FROM THE SOCIALISTS. The full extent of the problem confronting the PCI during the Hungarian crisis cannot be appreciated without a review, necessarily superficial, of the issue that dominated Italian domestic politics during the summer and fall of 1956, that of socialist reunification. As we have seen, Khrushchev's secret speech had resulted in a rapid deterioration of the PCI's relations with its Socialist ally. The dogmatic Communist response to the Poznań riots put a further strain on the relationship, canceling the soothing effect of Togliatti's *Nuovi argomenti* interview. Unable to accept Togliatti's rigid defense of the "enemy agent" explanation of Poznań, the PSI had berated the Polish authorities for resorting to machine guns as a means of dealing with protesting workers.[53]

The chief political consequence of this growing divergence between the two parties, furthered by the PSI's simultaneous success in the May elections, had been the revival of serious negotiation toward overcoming the split that had in 1947 led to the creation of two separate socialist parties. Since the main cause of the split had been Saragat's rejection of the principle of close cooperation with the PCI and of loyalty to the USSR, Nenni's reaction to the events of 1956 almost automatically served to reopen the issue. Even before the Hungarian crisis erupted many observers had thought it possible that the Communists might be reaching the end of the line in Italy as a mass electoral force, and that the future of the Italian left might lie instead with a reunited socialist party having a working-class base and a Marxist ideology, but wholly free of Soviet control. These speculations were given a more concrete basis late in the summer when Nenni and Saragat had their much publicized meeting in Pralognan, promptly followed by intensive conversations in Rome in which a major role was played by the French Senator Pierre Commin, Vice Secretary of the Socialist International. The outcome of these talks, though inconclusive, was considered encouraging by both sides, and unification came to be regarded by all political circles as a virtual certainty. Only the timing, the form, and the precise political coloration of the new party seemed at issue, though factional intrigue within the two parties was recognized as a serious complicating condition.

The PCI was seriously concerned over what *Rinascita* termed

[53] *Avanti!,* June 30, 1956.

this "new fact" of Italian politics.[54] It was conceivable that Communist sympathizers in a reunified socialist party might manage to keep alive the special ties between the two parties, in which case unification might actually further the effort to promote a general European opening to the left; but more likely was the prospect that unification could be accomplished only on conditions distinctly disadvantageous to the PCI. Saragat, whose political identity had been created in the struggle to develop an Italian socialist party free of Communist influence, could be counted upon to try to give the merged party an anti-Communist and anti-Soviet flavor, incorporating it into the mainstream of European social democracy.

Some of the PCI leaders felt that the PCI could and must oppose unification outright, on the ground that it was likely to result in the betrayal of socialism by the PSI and the isolation of the Communists. Togliatti and others recognized the risks but evidently felt that the situation could be kept under control, that Nenni would be restrained from moving too far to the right both by his own ideological heritage and by the strength of the PSI's left-wing faction.[55] This latter view prevailed, and it was decided to give verbal support to unification, which in any event seemed assured, but at the same time to take steps to ensure continued collaboration with the Socialists.

Early in October Togliatti proposed, and Nenni accepted, a formal abrogation of the unity of action pact in effect between the two parties since 1947 and its replacement by a much looser agreement calling for regular consultation, with full respect for the autonomy of both parties.[56] This agreement appears to have genuinely aroused Saragat's apprehensions, although it may simply have provided him with a useful pretext for disrupting the negotiations. In any case, despite the PSI's repeated reassurances that the pact actually represented a significant weakening of its ties with the PCI, and that unification remained "an irreversible fact,"[57] Saragat attacked it bitterly, referring to it as "a stone thrown in the gears of socialist unity."[58] Whatever Togliatti's intention had been—whether to impede the unification process or merely to secure a minimal guarantee against its acquiring an anti-Communist flavor—the maneuver had been a success, for it served to remind forgetful Socialists of the gulf between their vision of the PCI and that of Saragat.

54 "Politica italiana," *Rinascita*, XIII, 8–9 (August–September 1956), p. 486.
55 *L'Unità*, September 10, 1956.
56 *Ibid.*, October 6, 1956.
57 *Avanti!*, October 6, 1956.
58 *La Giustizia*, October 6, 1956.

All the same, the setback caused by the PSI-PCI pact appeared only temporary, and unification was still generally considered a near certainty. It therefore remained critically important for the PCI to prevent relationships with the PSI from deteriorating to the point that an anti-Communist psychology could prevail. The upheavals in Eastern Europe thus had threatening implications for the PCI's domestic political position, for the two parties found themselves far apart.

While the Communist press was expressing its nervous concern over the Polish situation and attacking the Hungarian revolt as a counterrevolutionary putsch, *Avanti!* was applauding Gomułka and insisting that it was impossible to defend a proletarian revolution without the emotional and physical support of the workers. Nenni called for the withdrawal of Soviet troops ("Down with armies of repression! Down with armies of foreign intervention!"), and for the first time the Socialist party broke with the Communists on a major issue, joining a demonstration of sympathy for the Hungarian rebels organized in the Chamber of Deputies by the center and right-wing parties. Nenni and Saragat met and announced their substantial agreement on Hungary, thereby dramatizing the isolation of the Communist party.[59] Such manifestations of an emotional and political rift between the Socialists and the Communists would have been disturbing at any time, but they were particularly alarming at this precise moment, when it was particularly important to keep alive in the PSI a sense of its class position and its traditional solidarity with the PCI and the Soviet Union.

The concessions made by the party, particularly in Togliatti's article of October 30, certainly reflected in part the gravity and urgency of this situation. Even more critical, however, was the state of affairs within the Communist party itself.

CRISIS IN THE PARTY. The Hungarian rebellion touched off an intense but short-lived crisis in Communist circles. With discipline already weakened by the events of the spring, the sympathy and shame kindled by the fighting in Budapest could not so easily be cooled by considerations of political expediency. The strongest and most articulate objections to the PCI's original hard-line position came from the same intellectual and trade union circles that had been most affronted by de-Stalinization and Poznań. They saw in the "counterrevolutionary putsch" line yet another sign that the party leadership was still unwilling or unable to relinquish its dependence on Soviet authority.

[59] See *Avanti!*, October 20–28, 1956.

The students at the University of Rome were the first to protest. A brief resolution was sent on October 25 to *L'Unità, Paese sera,* and *Avanti!* (published only by the latter) expressing full support for the process of democratization then going forward in Hungary and Poland.[60] During the next three days a general assembly of the Communists at the University, composed of professors, assistants, and students, drew up and approved a strongly worded motion endorsing the fullest possible democratization of the socialist regimes and the irrevocable end of Stalinism, and attributing developments in Hungary and Poland to the failure to respect the principles of autonomy and equality essential to the discovery of genuinely national roads to socialism. The motion then explicitly refuted and called for revision of the essence of the party's official position on Hungary:

> To regard the movement of the insurgents *in its entirety* as a counterrevolutionary movement does not correspond to the truth, would be slanderous for Hungary, and can favor anti-Communist propaganda in Italy; in reality, it appears that we are dealing with a wave of anger stemming from economic difficulties, from love of liberty, and from national pride, along with which are mingled elements of precise reactionary intent.[61]

The intellectuals were emboldened in their protest by the decision of the CGIL Executive Committee to approve and publish a declaration expressing its deep sorrow for the bloodshed in Hungary, condemning the undemocratic methods of government that had caused the tragedy, and rejecting the Soviet military action: "The CGIL, faithful to the principle of the nonintervention of one state in the internal affairs of another, finds it deplorable that the intervention of foreign troops was requested and occurred in Hungary."[62]

The effect of this statement was all the greater since this was the first time in the CGIL's history that it had followed the Socialist rather than the Communist stand on an important issue. Then Giuseppe Di Vittorio himself issued a supplementary personal statement supporting the CGIL position. He stressed that the demands of the rebels were concerned wholly with issues of liberty and independence and had nothing to do with a return to fascist terrorism, as the PCI was maintaining; above all, he insisted, "they are mistaken who think that things can continue and go on as before in the socialist world."[63]

60 D'Amelio, *Passato e presente,* No. 13, p. 1721.
61 *Ibid.,* p. 1723.
62 *L'Unità,* October 28, 1956.
63 *Corriere della sera,* October 28, 1956. *L'Unità* did not publish his statement.

When rebuked by the party Secretariat for taking such a stand, Di Vittorio is said to have defended himself by pointing both to the irresistible pressures from the CGIL's rank and file and to the imperative need, if the CGIL wished to retain its Socialist minority and its hopes for trade union unity in Italy, of not sticking rigidly to the PCI line on this issue.[64] Togliatti rejected this, maintaining that the Socialist rank and file would tend to be sympathetic to a firm PCI position. Di Vittorio, he is reported to have said, "is a sentimentalist, not a politician!"[65]

Resistance was spreading rapidly within the party itself. Motions were passed by a number of party sections, particularly in Rome and Turin, taking objection to the party's stand, and private protest meetings were held by groups of intellectuals in a number of cities, who forwarded letters of dissent to the Secretariat. By October 29, according to one right-wing journalistic account,

A true and proper "revolt" is by this time spreading even within the PCI: trade unionists and parliamentarians, journalists, students, intellectuals, cells and sections—all are in opposition to the leadership concerning the Hungarian events. What have until now been rumors and murmurings are translating themselves into open declarations, public motions, and orders of the day, with an air almost of liberation, while the Secretariat of the PCI appears to be always behind the times and thrown into disarray by the Hungarian events.[66]

In Rome, a group of about one hundred Communist intellectuals signed a manifesto addressed to the PCI Central Committee which, when L'Unità refused to print it, promptly found its way into the non-Communist press and radio. Significantly, the manifesto did not confine itself only to supporting the Socialist and dissident Communist views on Hungary:

Our party has not yet formulated an open and consequential condemnation of Stalinism. For months the tendency has been to minimize the significance of the collapse of the Stalin cult and myth, to try to conceal from the party the crimes committed by and under this leader, defining them as "errors" or even "exaggerations." There has been no criticism of the system constructed on the basis of the personality cult such as was done in Comrade Gomułka's report to the Central Committee of the Polish United Workers' Party.[67]

Most disturbing of all, the manifesto expressed the urgent hope of a "profound renewal of the leading group of the party."

64 *Ibid.*, October 31, 1956.
65 Settembrini, *Passato e presente*, No. 13, p. 1746.
66 *Corriere della Sera*, October 30, 1956.
67 D'Amelio, *Passato e presente*, No. 13, p. 1726. The full text of the manifesto and the list of signers are included in this article.

The party leadership must have felt itself more directly and seriously challenged in the Hungarian crisis than over the Stalin issue. In the earlier case frustration and anger had been directed principally at the USSR and only secondarily at Togliatti, who had managed to protect himself by appearing to sympathize with many of the reactions of his fellow party members and by partially dissociating himself both from Stalin's crimes and from Khrushchev's attack on them. Now, however, his uncompromising attitude toward Poznań, his harsh treatment of critics, and his initial acceptance of the Soviet line on Hungary placed him in direct opposition to important and vocal sectors of the party. There was, indeed, enough talk of the need for a major shakeup in the party leadership that *L'Unità* felt it necessary to ridicule the rumor that Di Vittorio was about to replace Togliatti as Secretary General of the party.[68] It is most unlikely that any such direct attack on Togliatti's position was seriously contemplated by Di Vittorio or others in the *Direzione*, and the rumor was probably printed largely as a warning to the critics of the party's position on Hungary that their opposition, however honestly motivated it may have been, was objectively weakening the unity of the party.

The situation remained extremely tense during the last days of October. Manifestoes similar to that prepared in Rome appeared in other leading cities, including Palermo, Pisa, Turin, Mantua, and Perugia.[69] While stern warnings were issued against leaking party matters to the opposition press, the right to dissenting opinions within the party had to be recognized: "The *Direzione* believes it to be legitimate and not surprising that comrades are expressing their own critical judgments and preoccupations regarding the grave events."[70] Several of the signers of the Rome intellectuals' manifesto, undoubtedly under severe pressure from party officials, hastened to express their indignation at its release to the public; others insisted on the inaccuracy of press reports that they had signed the document.[71]

The seriousness of the situation stemmed essentially from the same basic cause as the crisis over Stalin. In both instances the party found itself caught in an inherently ambivalent position, halfway between the habitual impulses of its Stalinist days and the patterns appropriate to the new age of communism inaugurated by the Twentieth Congress. The delicate balance of modernizing and

68 *L'Unità*, October 30, 1956.
69 D'Amelio, *Passato e presente*, No. 13, p. 1728.
70 *L'Unità*, October 31, 1956.
71 *Ibid*.

traditional forces at all levels in the party, combined with the ambiguous nature of the Soviet response to the consequences of de-Stalinization and the divergences among the Communist states themselves, made it difficult for the PCI leaders to find a solid footing. They could not easily return to parroting the Soviet line as long as it appeared obviously to conflict with the new and more liberal image of world communism that the USSR itself had been endeavoring to create.

During the tense last week of October the party leaders temporized, modifying their position to assuage internal critics, but staying well this side of overt criticism of the Soviet Union or open sympathy for the new Hungarian government. Prudence would understandably dictate such a course. The terrible uncertainties of the Hungarian situation, whose outcome seemed less predictable every day, in itself required that definitive judgment be delayed.

THE CRISIS RESOLVED. By the first of November, however, the grounds for choice had begun to emerge. Communist reports from Hungary began to announce mass assassinations of Communists and to highlight the growing volume of exiles from the Horthy regime returning to Budapest. The themes of white terror and fascist restoration became increasingly dominant. Almost as significant was the Anglo-French military action in Egypt, which on November 1 took Hungary completely off the front page of *L'Unità*. Here at last was not only something to throw back at those who had been taunting the Communists for supporting a military intervention, but also a solid fact to lend some credibility to Soviet assertions that Hungary represented one phase of a larger imperialist plot against the socialist countries and their supporters in the underdeveloped world.

Togliatti may indeed have believed this to be true. "It may seem like a melodrama to you," he remarked to an unconvinced delegation of Communists from Pesaro, "but I believe that there is the strictest link between the Hungarian insurrection and the aggression in Egypt, that the first was fomented in order to prepare the second, because despite all the errors committed in Hungary, the revolt would not have assumed the dimensions of total subversion if there had not been American meddling in support of the internal reaction that exploited the party's crisis of faith in order to raise its head."[72]

A further new fact was the Soviet declaration of October 30 which, while it continued to call for vigilance before "the forces

---

[72] Settembrini, *Passato e presente*, No. 13, p. 1745.

of black reaction and counterrevolution," represented primarily an effort to restate "the principles of complete equality, of respect for territorial integrity, state independence and sovereignty, and of noninterference in one another's internal affairs" on which relations among socialist countries were said to be based.[73] The declaration for the first time gave some promise of tangible concessions to these principles, with its offer to review economic relations, to recall economic and military advisers, and to consider withdrawing its troops from any Warsaw Pact country, provided all member states agreed. The declaration was useful to the PCI, for it enabled the party to salute the positive promise of a Soviet new deal for Eastern Europe and, when added to the negative image being projected of an international imperialist conspiracy, to rally its members in support of the Communist cause.

This new phase was crystallized by a major resolution of the party *Direzione* published on November 3. At last the situation in Hungary appeared to justify a call to arms:

The first duty of any Communist, of every socialist, and of every democrat in this hour is to raise his voice against the reactionary wave which is sweeping over Hungary, against the white massacres, so that there may be averted the danger of fatal provocations emerging from the chaos in which the unlucky Hungarian nation finds itself today.[74]

Earlier judgments on the responsibility of the former Hungarian government for the conditions leading to the uprising were repeated, but the equivocation of the previous week concerning the legitimacy of the rebellion was gone. The declaration stated flatly:

Whenever political struggle or popular protest in socialist countries assumes the character of an armed insurrection, the road is inevitably open to provocation and reactionary adventure. Whatever may have been the sentiments and proposals of the masses and working strata who were led astray into revolt by the faults and errors of the past, at that moment the stakes became these: whether or not the capitalistic regime would be restored.[75]

Equivocation regarding the Soviet Union had also vanished. The party declared itself "absolutely in agreement" with the principles enunciated in the Soviet October 30 statement and reaffirmed its complete "solidarity and friendship with the USSR" as the "irreplaceable leader and decisive force" in the fight against imperialism. The first Soviet military intervention had taken place, said the declaration, because it had been requested and because the Hun-

[73] *Pravda*, October 31, 1956; quoted from *CDSP*, VIII, 40, pp. 10–11.
[74] *L'Unità*, November 3, 1956.
[75] *Ibid.*

garian government had proved itself incapable of guaranteeing the country against the menace of a reactionary restoration. Although Soviet troops had then been withdrawn by agreement with the government, one could not now ask the USSR to accept as a consequence the spread of anarchy and white terror and a threat to the peace in Europe. Here, in effect, was advance indication of the PCI's readiness to support decisive military action by the Soviet Union.

In this context, the second Soviet armed intervention was greeted with almost visible relief by Togliatti and his colleagues, both because it put an end to uncertainty about the Soviet response, and hence about the outcome in Hungary, and because it cut the ground out from under the dissenters inside the party. The outer limits of loyal disagreement could suddenly be defined with clarity, and further open challenge to the leadership became psychologically and politically impossible for anyone not prepared to leave the party. The atmosphere within the party was radically transformed: the liberals became deeply discouraged, realizing that they had lost their chance to push the party toward the reforms they favored, while the conservatives were triumphant, their faith in the USSR restored, their darkest suspicions about reformist brands of communism vindicated. As a party leader from Sicily later reported in a speech to the party Congress, the Soviet intervention brought out in many comrades "a certain pugnacious euphoria," expressed in such terms as "Stalin was right," and "They've finally understood that you can't be soft."[76]

The party leadership now leaned heavily on the theme of the indissoluble link between the struggle for a democratic, socialist society in Italy and the world struggle against imperialism:

Whoever separates these two aspects of the struggle and denies one or the other of them disarms the workers, obscures the real terms of the struggle, cancels out fundamental aspects of the experience the workers' movement has been elaborating during a century of battles, defeats, and victories.[77]

In subsequent speeches Togliatti returned to this theme, insisting that it was precisely the firm consciousness of international solidarity that gave the Communist his special stamp:

It is true, we are internationalists, and internationalism is an essential element of our political consciousness, of the action of our party. But proletarian internationalism does not consist only in a generic appeal to the

[76] Giuseppe Prestipino, *VIII Congresso*, p. 101.
[77] *L'Unità*, November 3, 1956.

organized forces of the parties and the working masses; when the working class takes power and organizes its own state, it must take all the necessary measures to organize and defend that state.

Proletarian internationalism must take account of the conditions in which the workers' movement finds itself in a particular situation. Today, there are socialist states, and we must understand international solidarity as solidarity also with all these states and with their governments. . . .[78]

The doctrine was simple and by no means new: when the chips are down and the socialist camp finds itself, for whatever good or bad reasons, at sword's point with its class enemies, dissent becomes an impermissible luxury. Togliatti asserted frankly that Communists could not accept as an absolute principle the nonintervention of one state in the affairs of another. Soviet intervention had been imperative, not only to prevent fascism from returning in Hungary but also to safeguard the peace; with Europe divided into two military blocs, a restoration of capitalism in Hungary could not help but create a grave threat to international security. "It is my opinion," he said, "that a protest should have been made against the USSR if, having been invited to intervene a second time, it had failed to do so—this time with all its force—to bar the road to white terror and crush fascism in the bud, in the name of that solidarity which ought to unite all peoples in defense of civilization, above all those already launched on the road to socialism."[79] One could not object, he observed in private, on the ground that workers had participated in the fighting; the Kronstadt revolt had long ago shown that the workers were not invariably right. Moreover, he is said to have added, "Beware of speaking ill of Soviet tanks: one day we may have need of them ourselves."[80]

The appeal for consolidation in the party's ranks was effective. By November 4, following a meeting with Togliatti,[81] Giuseppe Di Vittorio, the most prestigious among the dissenters, had made his retraction before the party by declaring that although he and others had not personally wholly agreed with the CGIL statement on Hungary, they had signed it as a necessary sacrifice on the altar of unity within the union.[82] He stressed his complete loyalty to the

[78] *Ibid.*, November 12, 1956. *Pravda* carried a long summary of the article the following day.
[79] *Ibid.*, November 6, 1956.
[80] Settembrini, *Passato e presente*, No. 13, p. 1745. Assuming it is authentic, a remark such as this last, implying a set of attitudes deeply at odds with that on which the strategy of an Italian road to socialism would have to be based, makes one aware of how difficult it must have been for someone of Togliatti's training to overcome his Stalinist instincts.
[81] *Ibid.*, p. 1748.
[82] *L'Unità*, November 5, 1956.

Soviet Union and the vital need for unity in the party, retaining from his earlier position only an insistence on the need for democratization and closer ties between socialist regimes and their citizens.

But other dissenters, less deeply committed to the principle of party unity and discipline, could not bring themselves to sacrifice their personal convictions. Since open opposition, however discreet, was becoming increasingly difficult, many resigned, including some of the party's most noted intellectuals. And although less easily seen and recorded, the frustration and anger of the intellectuals was shared by many working-class members of the party, especially by relatively skilled workers with a higher degree of education. They felt the same sense of moral outrage at Soviet repression of the Hungarian revolution, the same sharp awareness of the shallowness of the official explanations, the same resentment against the PCI's inability to free itself from dependence on the Soviet Union.[83] Hungary was not the only cause of disillusionment, but for many it provided the necessary emotional stimulus for the psychologically painful step of breaking with the party.

A BALANCE SHEET. As the intensity of the crisis within the party waned, the attacks from outside increased. Anti-Communist agitation, which had quieted down during the brief period when Soviet troops had withdrawn from Budapest, rose once again to fever pitch, with student and Fascist riots, demonstrations in the streets of Rome, and an emotional confrontation in the Chamber of Deputies. When Pietro Nenni and his fellow Socialists rose to their feet to join all but the Communists in a tribute to the fallen heroes of Budapest, they were met with angry shouted accusations of betrayal from the Communist side. The threat of being politically isolated, alienated from its Socialist ally and thus of its means of entry into a broader alliance system, appeared to be stronger at the end of 1956 than at any other moment in the party's history.

One should not suppose, however, that the party leaders had any real choice in their response to the second Soviet intervention. The risk of political isolation was a relatively long-term, not an immediate, problem; while it might gradually erode the effectiveness of the party's strategy for peaceful conquest of power, it was not likely to damage rapidly or irreparably the party's capacity for action. Far more intense and immediate were the threats first to the party's

---

[83] See Hadley Cantril, *The Politics of Despair* (New York: Collier Books, 1962), pp. 191–215, for an analysis of interviews with Italian and French Communists concerning the events in Hungary.

unity and internal discipline, and thus to the power and prestige of its leaders, and second, to the principle of international solidarity with the socialist world.

The party leaders could not openly have repudiated Soviet policy on an issue of such magnitude as Hungary, whatever their personal appraisal of its merits, without creating a virtual state of war between conservative and liberal party factions. In such a test of strength the conservatives would almost certainly have triumphed: their strength at all levels of the party apparatus together with the support they would have received from the Soviet party would almost surely have sufficed to overthrow any group standing on principles of independence from the USSR and a strictly national road to socialism. The conservatives would have had behind them not only control over the party machinery but unchallengeable ideological credentials as well. No reasonably prudent leader in such a situation would have dared alienate the militant core of his party, and prudence was Palmiro Togliatti's hallmark.

For Togliatti to have taken a neutral or an anti-Soviet stand in the Hungarian crisis would have been for him to violate one of the unassailable bedrock principles of the Communist movement, the principle of international proletarian solidarity, which through decades of Stalinist practice had come to mean unquestioning allegiance to the needs of the Soviet state in its struggle with imperialism. Such a principle would gradually, under later more favorable circumstances, come to be watered down and reinterpreted so as to lose much of its effective force, but in 1956, at a moment of acute crisis, it could not be abruptly repudiated without damaging severely the unity of the party and the authority of its leaders. At such a time, Togliatti's remarkable flexibility and political subtlety could not operate to advantage: the situation called rather for rigidity, for an application of the dogmatic instincts of a politician trained in Stalin's school.

During the early phases of the Hungarian revolt, when the battle appeared to be between a reforming Communist party struggling to break the bonds of Stalinism and a Soviet state fearful of losing its grip over a satellite neighbor, the principle of solidarity had been less compelling, and the PCI could afford to conciliate the pro-Hungarian sympathies of large parts of the Italian working class and intellectuals, in and out of the party. Even then, it could afford to do so only partially and hesitatingly, creating a situation of ambiguity and uncertainty deeply unsettling to an authoritarian party accustomed to strong guidance. When at last the Soviet Union intervened decisively in an apparent riposte to the aggressive efforts of the imperialist powers to subvert the socialist system, all ambiguity was removed. The party then had no choice but to show its true colors, whatever the immediate cost to its domestic political position.

Early in 1958, discussing the weakening of ties between the Communist and Socialist parties, Giorgio Amendola referred to the differences that had arisen over Hungary, explaining why it was that the party could not compromise basic principles for the sake of long-run political strategy:

> To suppose that the Communist party, so as not to "isolate itself" from other political forces on the left and from the Socialist party itself, ought to assume a certain attitude toward the problems of the international workers' movement, and thus end up by "isolating itself" from the other Communist parties, to suppose that in the face of events such as those in Hungary it ought to express judgments corresponding to those of the social democratic international, is to imagine that the Communist party is something other than what it has always been and has always affirmed itself to be; it means asking the party no longer to be itself. . . .[84]

The events in Eastern Europe, then, showed that the Italian Communist party, despite its efforts earlier in the year to fashion a new image, was still a disciplined and loyal supporter of the Soviet Union, the leader of the socialist world. It remained an open question, however, whether this was a permanent retreat from the new positions toward which Togliatti had seemed to be advancing after the impact of the Twentieth Congress and de-Stalinization.

The Italian party learned in 1956 the painful lesson that other parties such as the French had absorbed long before: that allegiance to the USSR could cause it a traumatic shock. The PCI had of course long since learned to live with the weight of official church and state hostility to communism and had suffered the consequences thereof, most notably in the elections of 1948 that ended its postwar surge. Still, the fact that it had between the wars been a small illegal party operating in exile had largely protected it from blows like the Nazi-Soviet pact, which severely shook a mass party such as the French. Its Soviet connection had, by and large, been a positive fact for the PCI, and the Soviet myth had accordingly been assiduously cultivated. Would it now, as some contemporary observers surmised, go the way of the PCF and resign itself to playing the role of a small and intransigent opposition, faithful to the ex-

---

84 "Cause e pericoli dell' allentamento dei legami unitari tra comunisti e socialisti," *Rinascita*, XV, 1 (January 1958), p. 16.

igencies of Soviet policy and effective at the polls, but without any serious prospect of attaining power peacefully by applying a political strategy responsive to the realities of Italian life?

This dilemma had always existed for the PCI, as for all Communist parties, but it took the events of 1956 to force the party to take seriously the need to define and pursue its own road. The Soviet model would not do: not only could it not be sold in Italy, as had been understood from the beginning, but it was now suddenly seen to be defective even in its own terms, and many in the party now viewed it with deep skepticism. Nevertheless, the Italian party was irrevocably a part of the international Communist system of which the Soviet Union remained the central force. For the PCI leadership the problem was one of reconciling the requirements imposed by effective political action in Italy with those imposed by the need to remain a member in good standing in its international club.

For reasons of history, ideology, and power, the alternative of cutting the PCI off from the international movement did not exist as a practical possibility. A nonruling party, deprived of the support of powerful nationalistic sentiments such as Tito enjoyed and dependent for its prestige partly on its international connections, could not under the circumstances of 1956 have taken such a step without virtually destroying itself. Later, when the unity of the Communist movement had been lost, such an alternative would become more feasible, though still highly unlikely. Togliatti's actions after 1956 unfolded within the relatively narrow range of possibilities this formulation implies. Subsequent chapters will attempt to show how this worked out in practice as the PCI adapted itself to the changing realities of international communism, of Europe, and of Italian society.

CHAPTER FOUR

REVISIONISTS, SECTARIANS, AND THE ITALIAN ROAD TO SOCIALISM

For a year or more after the outbreak of the Hungarian revolution, the Communist movement was in an open state of disarray. Each major party, to an extent unprecedented in the history of the movement, found it necessary during these months to define and defend its interests in a context of open controversy among the parties and of uncertainty as to the ultimate direction of Soviet policy. The necessity arose primarily from the blow to Soviet authority, still only dimly perceived but evident nonetheless, caused by the destruction of the Stalin myth, the revision of basic doctrinal principles, and the successful Polish challenge to Soviet power.

Some parties, including those of France and most of the East European satellites, fell back on their well-trained reflexes and tried to act almost as though nothing had happened. The Poles, urged on by the Yugoslavs, were determined to prove this hope illusory and by word and deed set out to show that the days of automatic conformity to Soviet-imposed solutions had gone for good. Insisting on giving real content to the theory of "national roads to socialism" and to the principle of equality in relations between Communist parties, they seemed at the end of 1956, in the Soviet view, to stand at the very brink of the heresy of "national communism." The Poles and Yugoslavs together threatened not only to weaken the solidarity of the Communist world but also, through their criticisms of the bureaucratic degeneration of the Soviet state and party and their relative cultural and economic liberalization, to question the very premises on which Soviet domestic power was built.

The Soviet leaders were themselves divided as to how these issues should be handled, the coalition around Molotov stressing the damage to Soviet domestic and international authority caused by past policies, the Khrushchev faction maintaining that the setbacks of 1956 and the stagnation of earlier years only reaffirmed the necessity for controlled change in both domestic and international spheres. In part because of this division within Soviet ranks, in part because of the underlying ambiguity of the Soviet Union's objective situation, which stimulated powerful pressures both for conservation and for change, Soviet leadership within the movement lacked force and assurance. Unable to take a firm and unequivocal position behind either the dogmatic or the revisionist extreme, the prime Soviet objective during this period was to achieve a pragmatic compromise that would restore the unity of the movement under Soviet leadership. If possible, the new unity should include the Yugoslavs; if not, as proved to be the case, they could go their own way.

For several months it appeared that the Chinese interest was very much the same. Their restrained criticism of Stalinism, their support for the realization of separate roads to socialism within the framework of classical Marxist-Leninist principles, their restrained and unpolemical attitude toward all parties, their repeated insistence on Soviet leadership of the socialist camp—all these seemed for a time to provide the guidelines for a workable compromise capable of restoring the unity of the movement. The illusion was short-lived. By the end of 1957 the Chinese party had taken a sharp turn to the left in both domestic and foreign policies, resulting in the formulation of strategic positions that were on certain critical points directly at odds with those of the USSR. At the November meeting in Moscow, where forty years of Soviet rule were being celebrated, the Chinese challenge was first clearly though still only partially articulated. The movement's unity was formally restored, though without Yugoslavia, through the preparation of a compromise declaration incorporating Chinese qualifications to the Soviet theses of peaceful coexistence, the avoidance of war, and the possibility of peaceful transition to socialism by parliamentary action.[1]

The primary purpose of this chapter will be to identify and explain the posture of the PCI at this important juncture in international Communist affairs. It is relevant first, however, to report briefly on the party's internal situation.

There were some interesting parallels in the two environments, for in both cases the party leadership was confronted with the need to take a position with respect to fairly clearly defined "sectarian" and "revisionist" tendencies. The polar positions represented by

[1] This period has been analyzed in detail by several writers. See especially Brzezinski, *The Soviet Bloc*, chaps. 10–15; Donald S. Zagoria, *The Sino-Soviet Conflict, 1956–1961* (Princeton: Princeton University Press, 1962), chaps. 1–2; Richard Lowenthal, *World Communism: The Disintegration of a Secular Faith* (New York: Oxford University Press, 1964), chaps. 2–4; Edward Crankshaw, *The New Cold War: Moscow v. Pekin* (Baltimore: Penguin, 1963), chaps. 6–7.

France, on the one hand, and by Yugoslavia and Poland on the other, were mirrored within the Italian party itself. Just as the Soviet Union, if it wished to retain the unity and effectiveness of the movement, could not support either of the two extremes unconditionally, so Togliatti, by the logic of his own and his party's position, was obliged to conciliate and equivocate, seeking to consolidate his control by manipulating the forces on both sides of the political center.

A Struggle on Two Fronts: Sectarianism and Revisionism in the Party

A full exploration of the PCI's internal tensions would ideally require careful sociological and psychological as well as political analysis. Here we cannot attempt more than a general sketch of the situation, concentrating on aspects relevant to the party's international posture and making frequent reference to the Eighth Congress of the party, held in Rome in December 1956, when the leadership defined its course in relation to conservative and liberal trends.

We are dealing here not with organized minorities but with general attitudinal tendencies. At no point did party discipline become so weak that distinct factions with clear alternative programs were able to crystallize. Those who did speak boldly were relatively few in number, though some were important enough to cause the party some embarrassment, and most of those who did so finished by resigning from the party. The leadership was not faced, therefore, with a "clear and present" threat to its authority.

The situation in 1956–1957 can best be regarded as only a more intense and more open manifestation of the tensions flowing from the PCI's fundamental strategic dilemma: how to move in the directions necessary to increase its prestige and influence in the circumstances of Italian life without at the same time losing the qualities that gave it special advantages and distinguished it so sharply from other participants in the political game. These often conflicting interests have been reflected through the years in a persistent tug of war between conservative and innovative forces in the party. The events of 1956 dramatized this struggle, creating a political context qualitatively different from that prevailing in the past.

THE SECTARIAN FRONT. A few words, first, about those whom the rest of the party liked to label "extremist sectarians." Often referred to as left-wing opponents because of their identification with a doctrinaire strategy of direct class conflict and with all the other classical ideological principles of the Stalinist era, it is more relevant to think of them, like their counterparts in the USSR itself, as Communist conservatives. Although intransigent in attitude and resentful of the constraints imposed on their activist instincts by the necessity to play a parliamentary game, their role was, in objective terms, a conservative rather than a revolutionary one: since the situation was anything but ripe for insurrection, the only strategy they could propose was to obstruct and to wait for things to grow worse, meanwhile maintaining the party's unity and revolutionary will through rhetoric and stubborn defense of sacred principles.

The traditionalists, represented at the summit by such prominent personalities of the prewar and early postwar years as Edoardo D'Onofrio, Pietro Secchia, Arturo Colombi, and Mauro Scoccimarro, remained in 1956 well entrenched at all levels of the party bureaucracy and received strong support from many of the older and more militant party members throughout the country. By and large their commitment to the party dated back to Fascist days, when they acquired through working in clandestine conditions or in exile a style of work and a habit of unconditional loyalty to the Soviet Union that could not later be shaken off. Their métier being revolutionary conspiracy and their preferred milieu the party itself, they were poorly equipped to carry out the gradualist strategy of reforms and political alliances that became the PCI's trademark in 1944. As disciplined Communists they might accept the necessity for *advocating* a peaceful, parliamentary road to socialism based on respect for the existing constitutional structure, but they neither genuinely believed in it as a serious possibility nor were capable of pretending convincingly enough to persuade others of its likelihood. Togliatti had already commented on this mentality as early as 1946:

> Whenever we delve into the minds of our comrades, we find the strangest conceptions of what communism should be, conceptions which are difficult to reconcile with our political line. Acceptance of this line [by party members] is often superficial or formal, or is justified by the same foolish characterizations as our opponents allege regarding us—"tactics," trickery, secret plans, and so forth.[2]

The root of the problem, at a rational level of analysis, was the unwillingness of the "sectarian comrades" to believe that the party could ever come to power without a violent revolutionary upheaval

2 Quoted by Giorgio Galli, "The Italian CP, Part II: The Road toward a Dilemma, 1945–56," *Problems of Communism*, V, 3 (May–June 1956), p. 43.

supported by Soviet military force, actual or potential. For them, the Leninist revolutionary model, as qualified by the East European experience, remained the only valid one: power would come through insurrection and at the point of Soviet bayonets. Although it was difficult, particularly after the Twentieth Congress, for the conservatives to do more than hint at this conviction while ostensibly accepting official contentions to the contrary, it is evident from the persistent criticisms of their opponents that their mental reservations were not shaken.[3] For another five years or more, until the influence of the conservative wing finally dwindled into insignificance, deploring reference would continue to be heard to those who still sat in passive expectation of the mythical "X-hour" of revolution.

The sectarian theory of revolution undoubtedly rested on the deeper psychological fact that the talents, training, and life experience of these militants were suited only to the strategy logically flowing from their particular revolutionary perspective. If revolution were to come by insurrection and outside intervention, the party's essential task was to maintain its hard-core strength among the working class, its classical ideological doctrines, its unquestioned allegiance to the Soviet Union. These were tasks the conservatives understood and had long since mastered; they knew how to arouse and discipline the workers, to capitalize on the inherent radicalism and consciousness of class still very much a part of the Italian scene.

But if the revolution were conceived as a gradual transition to socialism resulting from a long series of economic and social reforms, the task of the party militant was wholly different. He had to learn to operate outside the party's ranks and beyond the limits of the working class, to find and play upon issues capable of attracting the sympathy and collaboration of Catholics, progressive intellectuals, and middle-class groups. He must be open to others, ready to engage in debate and accept compromise, able gradually to break down the stereotyped image of the Communist militant and become accepted as a respected participant in local and national political life. More than anything else, perhaps, it was the inability of the old-line party bureaucrat to play this game convincingly that led him to oppose, silently but nonetheless effectively, the party's basic strategic line. The trouble with the "conformist Communist," according to one party spokesman, is that he simply divides the

---

[3] See, for example, the article by Arturo Colombi in *L'Unità*, July 28, 1956, and the rebuttal to it by Carlo Salinari, *ibid.*, August 22, 1956, and by Piero della Seta, *ibid.*, August 25, 1956.

world in two: "the Communist part, which is all and always good; the non-Communist part, which is all and always bad. From this comes the indiscriminate and deep attitude of scorn, of suspicion for others, which has been and remains the greatest difficulty of so many among us."[4]

Sectarianism in the PCI is best viewed as the equivalent of Stalinism in the Soviet party: as a narrow and intolerant bureaucratic mentality rather than a consistent and reasoned strategic view. It was hard to locate and destroy because it was so widespread and because it concealed itself behind a formal acceptance of the official line. Giorgio Amendola, then in charge of a party organization inherited shortly before from the old-guard leader Pietro Secchia, found it necessary at the Eighth Congress to assure his audience that the danger of sectarianism really did exist:

> But is this front of struggle against sectarian conservatism really there, or is it a nonexistent front? In the absence of open and impossible defense and of explicit though necessary self-criticisms, it would seem that even the traces of sectarianism have disappeared, that we find ourselves fighting only the phantoms of the past. And yet we know that it is not so, that the struggle must still go on against sectarianism as against any other form of opportunistic passiveness. . . .[5]

The sectarian mentality was certainly not just a phantom of the past even though few traces of it were displayed in the Congress debates, where the only open opposition to the Togliatti line came from the opposite pole. Despite the greater sensationalism and openness of the revisionist opposition, Togliatti felt it appropriate to designate the sectarian challenge as the more serious, in the sense that "extremist sectarianism is more deeply rooted in our ranks."[6] At the Eighth Congress, in fact, Togliatti took a big step in the process begun a year or so earlier of removing many of his former closest collaborators, now linked with the sectarian opposition, from positions of power: Scoccimarro and several others were shifted from the Central Committee to the Central Control Commission; Secchia, D'Onofrio, and Roveda were removed from the *Direzione*. By the Ninth Congress in early 1960 the purge had reached well into the middle and lower levels of the organization.

Because the party's campaign against sectarianism served many

---

4 Velio Spano, *L'Unità*, July 14, 1956.

5 *VIII Congresso*, p. 462.

6 "Togliatti's Report to the Congress" in *The Eighth Congress of the Italian Communist Party, 8–14 December 1956* (Rome: Foreign Section of the Italian Communist Party, [1957]), p. 220. Since this English translation of the main documents of the Congress is more readily available than the Italian version, citations will be given from this source where possible.

purposes other than the declared one, the dangers may have been intentionally magnified. Togliatti was engaged in political infighting as well as in defending a particular strategy when he removed from power those among the old guard capable of challenging his personal authority. His opponents, moreover, made ideal scapegoats for all the mistakes of the past. Togliatti, taking renovation of the party as his slogan, could and did pin on his own "antiparty group" and their supporters in the party apparatus responsibility for errors in carrying out what was a basically correct party line: "The party was not lacking in orientation; it lacked boldness and enthusiasm in carrying out this policy."[7] He could also associate himself with the strong current of demands for greater democracy in party affairs by regretting the rude behavior of those party officials who failed to grasp the need for greater participation by the rank and file.

Vigorous denunciation of the sectarian mentality, furthermore, was an excellent way to appeal both to party members with revisionist leanings and to socialist and other potential sympathizers outside the party's ranks. In 1956, with faith in the PCI's credentials as a democratic, constitutional party at a low ebb, a convenient and effective way to begin the long climb back toward respectability was to launch a strong attack against the party's "Stalinist" wing. It was a good tactic, for example, to denounce as "instrumentalists" those who chose to regard discussion with the Catholics "as something 'transitory,' as a preparatory stage for an absorption of the popular Catholic forces" rather than as a genuine effort to achieve unity of action with Catholic trade union and other organizations.[8]

The leadership's response was nevertheless bound to be ambivalent, simply because the conservatives held other attitudes, which, from the leadership's perspective, were positive—above all, their dedication to the Leninist concept of the party, to the discipline embodied in the principles of democratic centralism. At moments of crisis, this conviction provided resistance to those demanding liberalization, greater freedom of dissent, the creation of minority groups. Second, there was the conservatives' firm adherence to the principles of proletarian internationalism, to the doctrine and practice of Soviet leadership.

In the battle with the revisionists and others on the party's right wing, the sectarian presence was most useful. It was not accidental that so many of the old guard were shifted onto the party's Central Control Commission: losing their influence over questions of party

[7] Togliatti, *ibid.*, p. 219.
[8] Mario Pirani, "I cattolici nella marcia verso il socialismo," *Rinascita*, XIII, 7 (July 1956), p. 345.

strategy, where their views were increasingly out of joint with the times, they could yet continue to serve in the less conspicuous but still highly important role of preserving the party's basic heritage, its unity and organizational strength.

THE REVISIONIST FRONT.   Despite repeated assurances at the PCI's Eighth Congress that revisionism (or reformism, often used synonymously) was the lesser danger, it received the lion's share of attention. The reason was obvious: the only explicit dissent from the party line expressed during the pre-Congressional debate and at the Congress itself came from right-wing, reformist directions. The vocal nature of the opposition from the right was logical enough: the dissenters, for the most part intellectuals without a secure base of power in the party hierarchy, had, as their only weapons, ideas and the courage to articulate them. Most had long been disturbed at the growing gap between the party's pretensions and the reality of its actions, and they saw in the emotional and ideological shock of the Twentieth Congress and of Hungary the best and possibly the last chance to arouse the party to a full awareness of what the slogan of an independent course toward a socialist society really implied.

The reformist critics hammered away at three related themes: the economic, social, and political content of the party's strategy, its ties with the Communist world, and the character of its internal life. Many of the illustrations of these points will be drawn from the views of Antonio Giolitti, the most prominent among those to challenge and ultimately leave the Communist party in the wake of the 1956 upheaval. Giolitti, nephew of the famous liberal statesman, had made a brilliant career in the party as Resistance fighter, member of Parliament, and intellectual, and was secretary of the Communist parliamentary group at the time of his resignation in July 1957. While he was still in the party, Giolitti became the spokesman for revisionist thought after the publication in early 1957 of *Reform and Revolution*.[9] A full-length rebuttal was issued by Luigi Longo, who during these years consistently played the role of defender of the faith, and the world Communist press thereafter pointed to Giolitti as Exhibit A of Italian revisionism.[10]

As far as strategic issues went, the position of those labeled revisionists was in many respects difficult to distinguish from those

9 Antonio Giolitti, *Riforme e rivoluzione* (Turin: Einaudi editore, 1957).

10 Luigi Longo, *Revisionismo nuovo e antico* (Turin: Einaudi editore, 1957); see also Valentino Gerratana, "Old Revisionism in New Guise," *World Marxist Review*, I, 1 (September 1958), pp. 87–91.

among the leadership who thought of themselves as *rinnovatori*, proponents of "renewal." The two groups were united in denouncing passive sectarian resistance to the party's line of structural reform through parliamentary action, and Togliatti did his best to demonstrate his own dedication to renewal, conceding that an impression of *doppiezza* might have been fostered by the apparent gap between theory and practice.[11] The reformists, however, skeptical of Togliatti's intentions, would not grant that the root of the problem lay in resistance and incomprehension on the part of a conservative bureaucracy. It was in the analysis of the causes and the corresponding proposals for reform that the line between acceptable "renovator" and heretical "revisionist" came to be drawn.

Two areas of the party's program received particular attention. The reformists tended to put special emphasis on the need for careful and detailed analysis of the social and economic evolution of capitalism, using Marxist tools to grasp the nature of a system no longer what it was in Marx's day. Giolitti, for example, insisted on the necessity of taking centrally into account the technical and organizational advances that had led to increasing productivity and a strengthening of capitalism but that could, if correctly understood and manipulated, also create new possibilities of controlling the process for the benefit of the laboring classes: automation, nuclear energy, increasing monopolistic concentration and intervention in economic affairs, international economic cooperation. In his view the thesis of an automatic eventual collapse of capitalism had to be discarded, along with such corollaries as the tendency toward absolute and relative impoverishment of the proletariat: the road to revolution lay not through violent assault on a weakened capitalist system but through structural reforms of the economy made possible by the ultimate power of the working class as the nation's chief productive force.[12]

In themselves, these concepts were difficult for the PCI to refute in a reasoned way, for they were hardly more than an emphatic restatement of the party's official position. The PCI itself was upholding essentially the same principles when accused of revisionism by the French, and by 1962, in the Theses for its Tenth Congress, would go far toward incorporating them explicitly into its program. Nevertheless, because they were an intrinsic part of an analysis containing other far more dangerous doctrines, they had to be refuted. Thus Longo insisted that despite his denials, Giolitti had in fact fallen into the economic determinism of Bernstein,

11 Togliatti, *Eighth Congress*, pp. 216–219.
12 Giolitti, *Riforme e rivoluzione*, pp. 7–28.

accepting a reformist perspective that largely ignored the class struggle and the determining revolutionary role of the working class and its proletarian vanguard, the Communist party. Carry Giolitti's argument to its logical conclusion, Longo argued, and the workers would end up by identifying so fully with technical progress as to seal forever their subordination to the monopolies.[13]

A second and more serious criticism of the reformists concerned their attitude not to the acquisition of power but to its eventual exercise. Taking as a premise the peaceful road to power (which, they tended to argue, was not just the *possibility* acknowledged in the new Soviet doctrine but an absolute necessity in an advanced capitalist society), they attempted to dismiss the continued relevance of the dictatorship of the proletariat, a concept linked in their minds to the use of revolutionary violence. The rationale for throwing over this keystone principle of Leninist thought was not only, or even primarily, the newly legitimate theory of peaceful transition. The main impulse came, rather, from the shattering of the Stalin myth and the forceful demonstration that personal liberties and proletarian dictatorship seemed incompatible. The hegemony of the proletariat during the revolutionary period must be kept from degenerating into a one-party dictatorship by guarantees of individual liberty and freedom of thought, by full autonomy for trade unions and other organizations, and by political institutions ensuring pluralism and a division of power.[14]

Carlo Salinari, a prominent intellectual who stopped short of a break with the party, was strongly criticized for suggesting that many of the institutions and practices of bourgeois democracy had become part of "the patrimony of the socialist movement and must be defended and developed, unreservedly, as the cement of the alliance system that must lead us to socialism."[15] Giolitti was more specific in his speech to the Eighth Congress:

Therefore we can and must proclaim, without reservation or ambiguity, that democratic liberties, even in their institutional forms of separation of powers, formal guarantees, parliamentary representation, are not "bourgeois" but an indispensable element in building a socialist society in our country. . . . I believe that this imposes a re-examination in the light of Marxist principles and of historical experience of the Leninist theory of the conquest of power.[16]

13 Longo, *Revisionismo nuovo e antico*, pp. 11–17.
14 See Giolitti, *Riforme e rivoluzione*, pp. 29–41.
15 *L'Unità*, August 22, 1956; for the official rebuttal, see Luciano Romagnoli, *ibid.*, September 5, 1956.
16 *VIII Congresso*, p. 231.

To such dangerous notions as these, the party responded by reiterating the absolute necessity of a proletarian dictatorship (in a different form from the Soviet model, to be sure, but essential even in the absence of violent revolution) and by repeating the standard catechism about the distinctions between formal bourgeois democracy and the substantive democracy guaranteed by the very existence of a workers' state.[17]

It was above all their awareness of the gross defects of the Soviet system that led the reformists to such a strong insistence on an independent Italian path to socialism. Our party, Giolitti argued, should not only acknowledge the possibility that the Italian road *could* be different from the Soviet; we should insist that it could not possibly be otherwise. We should recognize openly the fact that crimes as well as errors have been committed and renounce forever "the blind fanaticism ready to sacrifice men to a mythical socialism. . . ."

We must refute this fanaticism in a preconceived and inflexible fashion, not only because of a legitimate and necessary revulsion of sentiments but because of the rational conviction that it is necessary to eliminate at its source the danger that blind faith in a man be reborn as blind faith in a myth: the myth of the party above all else, of socialism as a messianic coming, of the USSR as the perfect incarnation of socialism on earth.[18]

André Gide was right, he added, when he said that one day our eyes would open and we would ask ourselves how we could have kept them closed for so long; some loyal Communists have already begun to see the light, he implied, quoting Kardelj and Gomułka on the necessity of guaranteeing democracy in a socialist state.[19] In blindly accepting the Soviet state and party as the ideal incarnation of socialism, the reformists maintained, we have not only ignored the evil in that society, we have seriously retarded our own pursuit of a sound strategy and an ideology suited to the needs of contemporary Western society. We have accepted Marxist ideology as crystallized by Stalin as a universal truth, whereas, in Giolitti's words, "It ought now to be clear that not only Marxist historicism but also the whole of lay and modern thought rejects the concept and the term 'universal truth,' especially when it is used to designate certain generalizations deduced by scientific analysis and dialectical synthesis from specific historical, social, political, and economic experiences."[20]

[17] See, for one example of many along these lines, Longo, *Revisionismo nuovo e antico*, pp. 36–55. This topic was then, and remained for many years, one of the most frequent subjects of debate between the PCI and the Socialist party.
[18] Giolitti, *Riforme e rivoluzione*, pp. 48–49.
[19] *Ibid.*, pp. 49–50.
[20] *Ibid.*, p. 56.

The revisionist critique had one further closely related aspect of cardinal importance, in some respects the most sensitive of all from the standpoint of the leadership. Of the many ways in which un-questioning acceptance of the Soviet model had impeded the pursuit of an independent Italian road to socialism, the organization of party life seemed to them perhaps the most damaging. Lenin's conception of democratic centralism had been perfectly adapted to the needs of a party of professional revolutionaries struggling to overthrow Tsarist autocracy, but it was ill suited to a party in the PCI's circumstances.[21] Centralism in the execution of a single political line, yes, but not in thought and discussion at any stage: "The policy of the Italian road to socialism requires continual elaboration of the political line, continual adaptation of the or-ganization to the reality of the moment, and above all continual scientific research—and therefore criticism—that tests the theoret-ical presuppositions and anticipates by way of hypothesis the prac-tical results of political action."[22] Secret voting, free discussion, open minorities having the right to defend their positions in the hope of becoming majorities—all these must prevail in the PCI, the reform-ers argued, if it is to liberate itself fully from the past and develop a flexible, energetic strategy for the future.

Here was an issue close to the personal experience of every party activist; the intellectual shared with the ordinary worker a sense of resentment at the petty corporalism of the bureaucrat that stifled initiative from below and often reduced participation in party life to the minimum formalities. Many in the PCI and outside were hopeful, in the words of one observer in the spring of 1956, that "the crisis of Stalinism and the end of the personality cult and of the concept of the leader-State represent the catalyst that in its turn is creating a crisis in the bureaucratic and antidemocratic concept and practice that has up to now dominated the internal life of the Italian Communist party."[23]

Grievances against party despotism were potentially threatening to the leadership if only because they were so widespread, but they were not difficult to control. Because the chief target of the com-plaints was the middle- and lower-level bureaucrat, Togliatti and his colleagues in the Secretariat could safely adopt a sympathetic attitude, finding fault with a party official's paternalism and lack of respect for the rank and file, and with his undemocratic faith

21 *Ibid.*, p. 43.
22 *Ibid.*, p. 44.
23 Franco Ferrari, "Nell' attivo di Reggio Emilia," *Risorgimento socialista*, VI, 27 (July 1956), p. 4.

(reminiscent of the "personality cult") that the Center was the source of all wisdom.[24] One tangible concession was introduced—secret voting in election of the new Central Committee at the Congress—but the leadership insisted that what counted was not reform of the party statute but correct application of the basic Leninist principles of democratic centralism. The proposed reforms, particularly those concerning minority rights and the adoption of two slates of candidates at party elections, would lead straight to factionalism and thus destroy the party's unity and efficiency.

An important reason why the party was more worried by its revisionist than its sectarian opposition lay in the political alternatives open to each group. Splinter groups had emerged from time to time on the left, organized by former party members unable to reconcile their ideals and revolutionary instincts with Communist electoral tactics, but none had succeeded in becoming of more than nuisance value.[25] For those on the right, however, the Socialists or Social Democrats offered a natural ideological and political home, one in which the former Communist could uphold his Marxist persuasion and yet reject all he had found repugnant in the PCI. The ready availability of these alternatives was a constant source of pressure on the PCI leadership.

Togliatti's efforts at the Eighth Congress to quiet the restive reformists on the right did not succeed in preventing a large-scale exodus from the party, especially by dissident intellectuals. Much of this took place in full view of the public, with the non-Communist press doing its best to weave an atmosphere of crisis around the PCI. The first and probably most dramatic resignation was that of Eugenio Reale, PCI senator and former Italian ambassador to Warsaw as a member of the first postwar government; for Reale, long estranged from the party, the Hungarian revolution was the watershed, leading him to denounce in a non-Communist paper (after L'Unità had refused to publish his letter) the PCI's unconditional support for Soviet foreign policy interests.[26] Other

[24] See Pietro Ingrao, "La democrazia interna, l'unità e la politica dei comunisti," Rinascita, XIII, 5–6 (May–June 1956), pp. 315–318, for a typical expression of this argument.

[25] See Enzo Tiberti, "The Italian Ex-Communists," Problems of Communism, VIII, 1 (January–February 1959), pp. 53–54, for a review of the principal leftist splinter groups, including Seniga's group, Azione Comunista. For a report on the brief existence of Democrazia Comunista, an abortive effort in 1956 to organize leftist dissidents from the South, see "Tentative de dissidence communiste italienne," Est & Ouest, VIII, 149 (April 1–15, 1956), pp. 20–21.

[26] His letter appeared in Corriere d'Informazione, December 29, 1956; for a summary of the Reale case, including excerpts from the relevant documents, see "L'Affaire Eugenio Reale," Est & Ouest, IX, 166 (January 16–31, 1956), pp. 21–23.

resignations and expulsions followed, especially of professors, artists, editors, and writers in Rome, Turin, Milan, Naples, and elsewhere.[27] Fabrizio Onofri submitted his resignation in January; in July, it was Antonio Giolitti's turn.[28]

The same pattern was occurring at lower levels; by September 1957 the party acknowledged having lost more than 200,000 members, or about 10 per cent of its strength, during the preceding twelve months.[29] It would be wrong to attribute these losses exclusively to the immediate effects of the crisis of 1956, for a decline of substantial proportions had been registered since 1954 and would continue for another several years, but this in itself tends to confirm that the 1956 crisis reflected a deeper set of problems with which the party had not yet effectively begun to deal.

The Revisionist Front Abroad

TOGLIATTI AND TITO.   Ever since 1956 one of the most reliable single indicators of a party's general position within the Communist movement has been its attitude toward the Yugoslav comrades. Such was certainly the case in the confused months following the Hungarian revolution, one important byproduct of which was the collapse of Khrushchev's efforts to bring the Yugoslavs back into the socialist camp.

Public Soviet-Yugoslav controversy had been revived by Tito's well-known speech at Pula on November 11, as Soviet troops were completing their task of restoring order in Hungary. While acquiescing with ill grace to the second Soviet intervention in Hungary as a "bad" but "necessary" action in defense of a socialist regime, Tito unequivocally scored the first military action as a "fatal mistake" on the ground that it mistook a "justified revolt" against tyranny and mismanagement for a reactionary counterrevolution. Responsibility for the Hungarian tragedy, he maintained, lay not with fascism and imperialism, but with "hard-bitten Stalinist elements" who justified their refusal to accept the real significance of Stalin's fall from grace by the party's explanation of his "errors" as mere personal aberrations. "The cult of personality," Tito insisted, "is in fact the product of a system" whose roots lie in the bureaucratic apparatus and in mistaken methods of leadership.

27 *L'Unità,* January 26, 1957.

28 "Antonio Giolitti quitte le P.C. Italien," *Est & Ouest,* IX, 179 (September 16–30, 1957), pp. 14–16.

29 Giorgio Amendola, report to the Central Committee, *L'Unità,* September 27, 1957.

Tito believed that relations among socialist states and parties had undeniably improved, but that the USSR had unfortunately so far declined to apply to other countries the correct principles embodied in its recent agreement with Yugoslavia. Although the Soviets had ceased interfering in Polish affairs just in time to permit a peaceful solution of the October crisis, "I cannot say that this positive development in Poland, which is very similar to ours, has met with much joy in the remaining countries of the 'socialist camp.'" The polemical tone of the speech was particularly evident in Tito's disdainful reference to two Communist leaders who had sharply criticized Yugoslavia, Maurice Thorez and Enver Hoxha, as a "would-be professor of history" and a "would-be Marxist," respectively.[30]

Sharp rebuttals were promptly delivered by all the ruling parties, Poland excepted, and a polemical exchange began which was to last several months. The most serious issue was the increasingly explicit Yugoslav insistence on a policy of peaceful coexistence, defined as a neutral position somewhere between the socialist and capitalist systems and their opposed military blocs. Such a thesis, difficult enough for the Soviets to swallow even with respect to Yugoslavia, still very much on the fringes of the socialist system, could in no event be allowed to make headway elsewhere, notably in Poland, where similar tendencies were in evidence.

The PCI leadership, although not in full sympathy with Tito, was unwilling to join the chorus of criticism. Togliatti handled the Pula speech gingerly, observing that while the PCI accepted Tito's position on certain (unspecified) points, the Italian attitude on others was "more cautious, more prudent."[31] Another sign that the PCI objected more to Tito's intransigent tone than to the substance of his argument was Giuseppe Boffa's dispatch from Moscow, which stressed the "calm and responsible" flavor of the Soviet reply and, in obvious allusion to Molotov's recent resurgence, expressed concern that Tito's polemical manner might only encourage rigidity in Moscow.[32]

Togliatti's reluctance to become involved in the dispute was not unrelated to the fact that the PCI's Eighth Congress was about to get under way. This was hardly the moment to give publicity to views of Tito's which had a double potential for embarrassing the party leadership: they not only closely resembled those being ex-

30 *Borba,* November 16, 1956; quoted from Zinner, *National Communism,* pp. 516–541.
31 *L'Unità,* November 19, 1956.
32 *Ibid.,* November 24, 1956.

pressed by many disaffected PCI intellectuals but also bore a discernible family resemblance to Togliatti's own positions of a few months back. He had hinted at a possible degeneration of the Soviet system, and Tito now insisted on it; he had regretted the necessity of the first Soviet intervention in Hungary, and Tito now flatly condemned it. There was nothing to be gained by reminding the party of Togliatti's flirtation with such "revisionist" sentiments.

The PCI continued to display a friendly attitude toward Yugoslavia for many months thereafter. Right after the Congress the Yugoslav delegation toured Northern Italy for ten days, under the PCI's auspices. The communiqué issued after talks between the two delegations in Rome noted certain unspecified differences of view on particular questions but suggested that this fact only confirmed the value of open and sincere bilateral exchanges of opinion.[33] Official Yugoslav comment on the discussions tended to be rather more enthusiastic in tone, stressing the common goals and ideals of the two parties and the particular realism and value of the PCI's position in support of bilateral relationships as the principal mode of contact between parties.[34] During the subsequent months of increasing Soviet-Yugoslav tension, L'Unità continued to report, without editorial comment, the major polemical exchanges between the two parties, including the sharp rejoinder to foreign minister Popović's speech in late February asserting his government's insistence on adhering to a neutralist foreign policy.[35]

The Italian party's continued unwillingness to participate in the controversy was demonstrated indirectly but unmistakably in mid-March by the publication, a week after Pravda's strong rebuttal of Popović, of a lengthy interview with Kardelj, the man regarded by Moscow as the most dangerous source of Yugoslav revisionism.[36] On the same day Togliatti and Longo made public a telegram of condolence they had sent Tito on the death of Mosha Pijade in which warm reference was made to the restoration of friendly relations between the two parties.[37]

These apparently trivial but nonetheless meaningful gestures of sympathy for Yugoslavia contributed to developing a favorable image that was further reinforced through a series of eight articles by Maurizio Ferrara, one of the party's most skilled and reliable

33 Ibid., December 25, 1956.
34 Borba, December 28, 1956, as reported in L'Unità, December 30, 1956.
35 Pravda, March 11, 1957; translation in CDSP, IX, 12, pp. 7–8.
36 L'Unità, March 17, 1957. For an explicit Soviet rebuttal of Kardelj's views on class struggle, proletarian internationalism, and other basic issues see Pravda, December 18, 1956; translation in CDSP, VIII, 51, p. 11.
37 L'Unità, March 17, 1957.

journalists. After a month's tour in Yugoslavia, Ferrara concluded his series with a sympathetic evaluation of that country's experience as unquestionably both original and socialist in character. Although raising objections to certain trends of thought—especially the tendency to give universal value to the Yugoslav road to socialism and to apply the diplomatic principles of peaceful coexistence to international socialist relations—Ferrara gave the Yugoslavs the benefit of the doubt by suggesting that these views represented primarily the opinions of certain young people rather than official sentiments.[38] The same reservations were expressed more strongly and more authoritatively in an article by Luigi Longo the following month describing the results of a study conference at the Gramsci Institute in Rome between a group of Italian and Yugoslav specialists, but Longo continued to affirm the great value of the Yugoslav experience in building socialism.[39]

That the PCI was during these months assuming a maverick attitude toward Yugoslavia was explicitly acknowledged in the course of discussions held in Moscow in July 1957 between a visiting Italian delegation and a group of Soviet officials. Longo, head of the delegation, found it advisable to explain the PCI's special friendship with the Yugoslavs in the context of a discussion as to why the Italian road to socialism could not be classed as a deviation toward "national communism":

We Italians are considered by other Communist parties as "the best friends" of the Yugoslav comrades. We have had various contacts with these comrades. We recognize and appreciate their socialist efforts, even though we retain some doubt and some reservations about the efficacy of certain of the instruments they have created for the socialist guidance of the economy and about the correctness of their positions relative to the socialist camp and the analysis of the capitalist world. Our relations with the Yugoslav comrades are in sum fraternal, Communist relations, with a reciprocal exchange of experiences and of criticism.[40]

As these illustrations suggest, the PCI's posture toward the Yugoslavs was cautious. The Italians were, in part, guaranteeing themselves against any future outcome of the still fluid situation by expressing both concern and respect toward Yugoslavia. When the conflict proved to be irreconcilable, as became evident after the November 1957 Moscow meeting, the PCI would at last become openly critical. It does not, all the same, do justice to the Italian

[38] *Ibid.*, April 23, 1957.
[39] "Aspetti della costruzione socialista in Jugoslavia. Un dibattito all' Istituto Gramsci," *Rinascita*, XIV, 5 (May 1957), pp. 240–245.
[40] *Problemi e realtà dell'URSS: Relazione sul viaggio della delegazione del PCI nell'Unione Sovietica* (Rome: Editori Riuniti, 1958), p. 70.

position to attribute it entirely to an opportunistic desire to perch on the middle of the fence. Differences of emphasis are crucial in the Byzantine niceties of relations among Communist parties, and the PCI's relatively positive tone toward the Yugoslavs put it out of step with the majority of parties, as Longo's comment confirms. The Italians plainly felt it in their interest to see Yugoslavia's rapprochement with the Communist movement consolidated, and throughout 1957 they exerted what small influence they had to that end.

There are good reasons why this should have been so. Yugoslavia was, as the PCI itself had loudly proclaimed in June, widely viewed as a test case of the genuineness of Soviet acceptance of the principle of national roads to socialism. If the Yugoslavs were not to be allowed to build a socialist society in their own way, free of Soviet interference, then the PCI's claims not to be bound by the Soviet model could in turn hardly be taken seriously. Many Italian Socialists in particular had fixed an attentive eye on Yugoslav affairs, hoping to find ideological and practical guidelines for the construction of a socialist society free of Stalinist degeneration and Soviet domination alike. The PCI's interest in revitalizing its traditional alliance with the Socialists would not be served if Tito were once again to be clamorously drummed out of the Communist brotherhood, confronting the Italian party with the unenviable choice of either joining the pack, and thereby tarnishing the image of the *via italiana*, or of isolating itself from the rest of the movement.

Also important to the Italian party was what the Yugoslavs appeared to represent for the structure and operating style of the Communist movement. Togliatti's notion of polycentrism, while ambiguously and vaguely expressed, bore some considerable resemblance to Tito's understanding of the international environment and to the correspondingly appropriate pattern of relationships in the Communist world. The two leaders appeared to agree that the monolithic unity of old could not and should not be restored, that it was inevitably giving way to a pattern of "unity in diversity" requiring tolerance of divergent opinions and practices, within the framework of a shared ideology and a common international outlook.

In the Italian view, this conception would stand a chance of being realized only if the parties proved able to overcome their standard reflex of publicly attacking those whom they believed had gone astray. The preconditions of monolithic unity had disappeared along with Stalin, and a new form of unity required a wholly different *style* as well as a new substance of international Communist relations. Differences of opinion and interest should be recognized and fully discussed in private, in a spirit of mutual understanding and compromise, while formal public relationships should be correct and cordial. The Italians were hoping, in short, to overcome precisely the same "Stalinist" mode of dealing with disagreements among the parties as it was fighting in its attacks on "the residues of sectarianism" within the PCI itself.[41]

The Italian hope of substituting reasoned discussion for polemical debate was to prove no more than wishful thinking. Tolerance is an appropriate attitude in politics only when fundamental interests do not appear to be threatened, which was not the case on either the Soviet or the Yugoslav side. The coherence of their ideological and political position in the Communist world required the Yugoslavs to insist on questions of principle, to clarify rather than obscure their differences with the Soviets and with the conservative segment of the movement. The Italians thus found the Yugoslav polemical style fully as disturbing as that of the parties on the other end of the ideological spectrum. We need not be concerned, said Amendola, by the fact that controversy exists, "but we can be disturbed by its bitter tone, by the simplistic nature of certain positions such as the division made by Comrade Tito between Stalinist and non-Stalinist parties."[42]

The fact of the matter was that the Yugoslav interest in defending national independence and the doctrinal premises on which this interest was based conflicted directly with the goal of restoring full unity to the movement, which as things stood was possible only on terms disadvantageous to Yugoslavia. The convergence of the long-run interests of the two parties in a more loosely organized and less disciplined movement came to be of smaller significance than the difference in the degree of their commitment to the goal: the Yugoslavs insisted on complete ideological and political autonomy, the Italians only preferred it, and that within the context of a unified movement. The PCI, unlike the Yugoslav party, was not prepared to go it alone.

A final factor that helps explain the Italian attitude toward the Yugoslavs in early 1957 relates to the internal Soviet political situation. Both Togliatti and Tito must have been aware that a

---

[41] A decade later, commenting on Togliatti's Eighth Congress reference to sectarianism as being "more deeply rooted in our ranks," Alessandro Natta would point out explicitly that Togliatti was not referring to the Italian party alone; "Togliatti e il partito," *Rinascita*, January 22, 1966, p. 4.

[42] *L'Unità*, November 26, 1956.

fierce struggle for power was in progress in the USSR and that the Soviet position toward Yugoslavia would be a prime element in the struggle. Following the Poznań riots Khrushchev had been in retreat, as was evident from Molotov's appointment as Minister of State Control in November and from the economic reforms introduced at the December session of the Central Committee.[43] The anti-Yugoslav campaign of those months was certainly related to the general upsurge of conservative influence in the Soviet leadership: Molotov must have been aching for revenge for the humiliation of his removal as Foreign Minister the previous June on the very day when Marshal Tito arrived on his triumphal visit to the Soviet Union. It was hardly accidental, furthermore, that the anti-Yugoslav campaign suddenly declined toward the beginning of March—immediately following Khrushchev's sudden victory at the Central Committee plenum of mid-February.[44]

In this context, Togliatti's demonstrations of sympathy for Tito can be read as a gesture of support for Khrushchev, the Soviet leader particularly and personally identified as the agent of rapprochement with Yugoslavia and the author of the Twentieth Congress line. The Yugoslavs, to be sure, had far more at stake than the Italians in the resolution of the power struggle, and Tito's actions during 1957 were more directly conditioned by this circumstance than were Togliatti's.[45] There was, moreover, a tactical difference between the two parties on this point resulting from the basic discrepancy in their strategic positions mentioned above. The Italians were concerned that Tito's outspokenness, his blunt challenge to the "Stalinists" in the Soviet Union and elsewhere, would only result in weakening Khrushchev's position or in forcing him onto more conservative ground. Here was another basis for Togliatti's feeling that differences among Communist parties should be played down, not magnified. At the Eighth Congress, in explicit reference to the Yugoslavs, he said: "We consider as dangerous, untrue, and erroneous the attempt to divide the Communist movement into two parts, as though there existed one part opposed in principle to the decisions of the Twentieth Congress and the conclusions that must be drawn from them."[46]

THE PCI AND THE POLISH ROAD TO SOCIALISM. In the unsettled circumstances of 1956 and 1957, the Polish party occupied a posi-

[43] See R. Conquest, *Power and Policy in the U.S.S.R.: The Study of Soviet Dynastics* (New York: St. Martin's Press, 1961), chap. 12, for a detailed analysis.

[44] Brzezinski, *The Soviet Bloc*, p. 284.

[45] See especially Lowenthal, *World Communism*, pp. 85–98, for an analysis of Tito's vacillations toward Khrushchev during this period.

[46] Togliatti, *Eighth Congress*, p. 174.

tion in the Communist movement even more sensitive than that of Yugoslavia. Poland's successful defiance of the Soviets in October had stretched to the outer limits the autonomy permissible to a Communist state and party without cutting itself off from the movement; the doctrine of independent roads to socialism appeared here to be receiving a decisive test. Yugoslav independence was an accomplished fact; the Polish challenge represented something new in international communism.[47]

Togliatti's hasty endorsement of the Soviet position on Poland after the Poznań riots had aroused the deep opposition of many within the party, becoming something of a symbol of Togliatti's retreat from the advanced positions of the spring. When the Poles themselves had reversed field and rejected the Soviet line, Togliatti had been left in the uncomfortable position of appearing to denounce precisely the courageous and innovating reform spirit he had earlier insisted was required to overcome the disastrous legacies of Stalin. While remaining cautiously noncommittal in public, Togliatti had privately indicated his reservations about Gomułka and his policies.[48]

The Poles, for their part, must certainly have been offended by Togliatti's attitude, recalling as it did the conformity to Soviet positions that had been Togliatti's trademark as Deputy Secretary General of the Comintern. It is difficult, in the absence of direct evidence, to speak with confidence about the personal and political antagonisms that may have been lingering on within the Communist movement from Comintern days, but it would be surprising if the Polish Communists, and Władysław Gomułka in particular, had not harbored resentments against Togliatti for his association with the Comintern's dissolution of the Polish party in 1938 and the liquidation of much of its top leadership. One of the few inside views of the Communist international scene, Eugenio Reale's documented report on the founding of the Cominform, hints at the existence of ill-feeling between Gomułka and Togliatti stemming from this episode.[49]

[47] See Adam Bromke, *Poland's Politics: Idealism vs. Realism* (Cambridge, Mass.: Harvard University Press, 1967), pp. 122–136, for a convenient summary of Polish-Soviet relations in 1956–1957.

[48] See Chapter Three.

[49] Eugenio Reale, *Nascità del Cominform* (Milan: Mondadori, 1958), pp. 21–22. Indirect supporting evidence can be seen in Togliatti's major article on the international movement following the Twenty-Second Congress in 1961, at a moment when Polish-Italian differences had been overcome and the Poles were almost alone in greeting with enthusiasm the PCI's renewed commitment to a liberalization of Communist ideology and practice. In discussing the successes and failures of the Comintern, Togliatti made his apologies to Gomułka by pointedly referring to the dissolution of the Polish party as "a mistaken and catastrophic decision";

Despite the underlying tensions generated by such factors, the PCI was nevertheless bound by the logic of its general position to support Gomułka's actions, provided they did not go so far as to threaten fundamental Soviet interests and disrupt Communist unity. Togliatti, wishing to project the image of a "liberal" though disciplined Communist standing in the advance guard of the anti-Stalinist ranks, naturally preferred to avoid being contrasted unfavorably with Gomułka, who appeared to epitomize in actions as well as words the new spirit of post-Stalin communism. Gomułka's stubborn and successful resistance to Soviet interference in Polish domestic affairs had given a hard political meaning to the doctrine of independent roads to socialism on which the Italian political line was grounded.

The PCI therefore tended to give a generally positive appraisal of the Polish regime. In the first authoritative review of the Polish scene after the Hungarian revolution, Velio Spano, then director of the Central Committee's foreign affairs section as well as a member of the *Direzione,* wrote in summary that "the evaluation that should be given of the present Polish situation is clearly positive. I firmly believe that the Polish comrades, in the crisis that tormented their party and their country, chose the only possible road, and I am equally convinced that that road is correct."[50] He conceded that excesses are inevitable at such moments of crisis, and that generalizations involving ideological concessions alien to Marxist-Leninist thought had cropped up in the Polish press. But Spano then added:

> It would all the same be a grave error to throw hastily into the same sack and to condemn *en bloc* as harmful and inspired by the enemy those positions which open the road to verifiable deviations and other positions which, although they break through acquired mental habits and preconceived notions, actually reflect a healthy desire to sharpen the weapons of Marxism-Leninism on the hard stone of changing reality. It seems to me that *Pravda* has fallen into this error in that correspondent's report, mistaken in so many aspects and in any case inopportune, in which it judged by the same measure and lumped together in the same condemnation an article by Florczak and one by Putrament.[51]

This unusually direct refutation of a quasi-official Soviet pronouncement was probably more an indication of the PCI's opposi-

---

"Diversita e unità nel movimento operaio e comunista internazionale," *Rinascita,* XVIII, 12 (December 1961), p. 909. See Mieli, *Togliatti 1937,* pp. 15–38, for a review of the limited evidence concerning Togliatti's responsibility for this event. As for Polish attitudes in 1956–1957, Dr. Ernst Halperin, who was then residing in Poland, has confirmed to me from his personal experience the existence among Polish party officials of antagonistic sentiments toward Togliatti and the PCI.

50 "Contributo a un giudizio sugli avvenimenti della Polonia," *L'Unità,* November 27, 1956.

51 *Ibid.*

tion to the "hard" faction in the Soviet leadership than a general expression of Italian disagreement with the Soviet handling of Poland. In the struggle for power in the USSR at that moment, Poland was as important an issue as Yugoslavia, for it dramatized the contention of the neo-Stalinists that Khrushchev's policies had caused a dramatic decline in Soviet political and moral authority. The Italian party was prepared to reaffirm, by its favorable appraisal of Polish developments, its support for Khrushchev's policy.

The attitude of the PCI leadership toward the Polish road was complicated, however, by political considerations at home. It was tempting to speak favorably of the innovative quality of Polish discussions on domestic policy—the stress on broader mass participation in economic life through workers' councils and other such devices, on full liberty of expression, on social justice, on greater democracy in party life. These represented precisely the kinds of internal reforms likely to brighten the tarnished image of communism in action held by the Italian electorate and by many disillusioned members of the Communist and Socialist parties.

The problem was, however, that many of the ideas that blossomed in Poland during 1956 and early 1957, above all those advocating greater freedom of expression and fewer bureaucratic restrictions in party life and enlarged participation of the worker rank and file in party and government affairs, were being adopted by Togliatti's opponents in the party and by his Socialist critics as well. The party leaders were concerned about the impact of Polish views. Spano revealed this in the article just mentioned, when he said that "certain of his [Gomułka's] political attitudes are today being adopted by some of our Italian comrades, in a rather summary fashion, as positions of principle" and chided these unnamed comrades for accepting all Gomułka's positions as uncritically as Stalin's had been accepted in the past.

Concern over Polish influence was further revealed at the PCI's Eighth Congress, when Togliatti had to face the challenge of the small but vigorous "revisionist" minority represented principally by Antonio Giolitti. The speeches made by Togliatti and the other top party leaders contained no reference whatever to Gomułka or to Polish events. This official reticence, in itself a sign of coolness, was commented on by Aldo Natoli, Secretary of the Roman federation and no revisionist, who noted discreetly and without amplification that the party view tended to underplay the positive aspects of the Yugoslav and Polish events; "these might have found a more ample place in the first part of Comrade Togliatti's report."[52]

[52] *VIII Congresso*, p. 456.

The only substantive references to the *via polacca,* in fact, were those made by such men as Giolitti, Furio Diaz, and Giuseppe Di Vittorio, the most outspoken critics of the official party line. Despite his earlier retraction, Di Vittorio now reiterated his original view on Poznań, arguing that if one accepted the view that the riots were caused essentially by the actions of fascist provocateurs and imperialist agents, the only logical conclusion would be to reinforce the police. He went on to say that whereas he would hesitate to approve unreservedly everything the Polish party had done in the recent dramatic months, its actions were nevertheless "clearly positive." It was of particular importance that the party had succeeded in accomplishing "a great change that has allowed it to establish anew warm and live ties with the whole working class and with the people of its own country. . . ."[53] And Renzo Trivelli, Secretary General of the Communist Youth Federation, went out of his way to praise and encourage Polish youth for their contributions to the "renewal" under way, noting that Italian young people had much to learn from the Polish experience.

No doubt gratified by these signs of sympathy, the Polish delegation to the Congress appeared to lend its moral support to the outnumbered "revisionist" elements present. By repeating forcefully his party's views on Poznań, which coincided closely with Di Vittorio's, Jerzy Morawski, head of the Polish delegation, was implicitly intervening in PCI affairs and giving aid and comfort to Togliatti's critics.[54] The Poles, in need of allies in their effort to influence the Soviets, perhaps hoped to help shift the center of gravity in the Italian party to the right. "Certain circles in Warsaw" had already been accused the previous month of meddling in the affairs of the French party by writing letters to French journals criticizing the PCF.[55]

Despite these minor tensions, however, the Italian attitude toward the Poles did not revolve around questions relating to the domestic policies of either country. The critical issue was that of Poland's behavior toward the Soviet Union and the Communist movement as a whole. The article by Velio Spano referred to earlier had singled out three specific dangers in Gomułka's thought: (1) his failure to comprehend that the class enemy and the imperialist

---

53 *Ibid.,* pp. 432–433.

54 *Ibid.,* p. 689. It may well not have been accidental that the loudspeaker system evidently failed unaccountably during the translation of Morawski's speech from the Polish. A. Dormont, "Le Huitième Congrès du P. C. Italien," *Est & Ouest,* IX, 166 (January 16–31, 1957), p. 19.

55 See *L'Unità,* report from Paris, November 22, 1956, quoting Raymond Guyot's speech to the Central Committee.

agent had played a major role at Poznań and in Hungary; (2) his mistaken assertion that communism might under some circumstances be built without Communists acting as the guide and leading force; and (3) his view that the personality cult had been not just a personal aberration but a system for the exercise of power.[56]

Spano was criticizing Gomułka's questionable attitudes toward the Soviet Union, toward the basic ideological principle of the dictatorship of the proletariat, and toward the imperialist threat—not his attitudes on domestic affairs. These same tendencies in Polish thought were also being frequently criticized in the Soviet press at the time. Gomułka himself was not attacked, presumably because the Soviets were confident of winning him back to the fold without further direct tests of strength, but arguments insisting on the need to respect the principles of proletarian internationalism and the universal laws of socialist construction were certainly directed his way.[57] The Italian Communist press generally reported such Soviet criticism without editorial comment, implying at least acquiescence in the Soviet line.

Soviet-Polish relations began to improve in the early spring of 1957, as the Poles, following the reassuring electoral victory in January, began to retreat from their exposed ideological positions. Gomułka, his power in the party and the country consolidated, quickly moved to control the revisionists.[58] The Soviet-Polish rapprochement paralleled that achieved with the Yugoslavs and coincided in time with the reassertion of Khrushchev's power at the February meeting of the Central Committee. Once the Soviets had concluded that Gomułka was "safe" and that the peril of a Polish "national communism" could be avoided, much of the reason for Italian concern also vanished. If the Poles could now be counted on to respect the basic discipline of the movement, they ceased to be a potential threat to Togliatti's regime at home. From this time on, the Italian and Polish parties began slowly to manifest an implicit *entente*, rooted in similar interests concerning the organization and mode of operations of the Communist movement. In particular, the PCI firmly supported the Poles in resisting the idea being promoted by certain other parties, including the French, that a new organization along the lines of the Cominform was required to restore discipline and unity to the movement. This point will be examined more fully later on, in connection with the November 1957 Moscow meeting.

[56] *L'Unità*, November 27, 1956.
[57] See Brzezinski, *The Soviet Bloc*, pp. 274–278.
[58] *Ibid.*, pp. 351–358.

In Defense of the Italian Road

The uncertain blend of sympathy and suspicion characterizing the Italian party's response to the revisionist currents flowing from Belgrade and Warsaw can be put in sharper perspective by contrasting it with the strong hostility manifested between the French and Italian parties during the same period. A preliminary word or two of background may be helpful here, for it would be out of focus to attribute the open hostility between these parties exclusively to their divergent responses to the events of 1956 and 1957.

There had been a history of personal rivalry between Thorez and Togliatti since the early years of the Comintern, apparently based on a combination of temperamental incompatibility and an almost inevitable competition for Soviet favor. The French Communist party had been the undisputed leader of European communism in the prewar years; after the war the Italian leaders succeeded in building a party stronger in numbers, more flexible in tactics, and more imaginative in the pursuit of power. Although the PCF remained the leading Communist party in the West, primarily by virtue of France's central role in the power structure of Europe, the balance had begun to shift toward Rome. The pronouncements of the Twentieth Congress, implying the need for each party to rely essentially on its own political resources in the struggle for socialism rather than on direct Soviet assistance, were better adapted to the talents and operating style of a Togliatti than of a Thorez. They were better fitted, too, to the Italian political and social configuration which for a number of reasons seemed more suited to a strategy of parliamentary advance toward socialism. The conflicts of 1956 and subsequent years should be seen in the context of this long personal and political rivalry.[59]

In many respects Thorez and Togliatti reacted similarly to the destruction of the Stalin myth: each tried to protect his personal reputation by insisting on the essential correctness of the general line of the past and by shifting some of Stalin's responsibility onto other Soviet leaders.[60] At the start the two might have reached an explicit agreement on how to handle the situation, which was certainly discussed when Thorez visited Rome in the spring of 1956

---

59 On this subject see, *inter alia*, Serge Mallet, "The Thorez-Togliatti Quarrel," *France Observateur*, XII, 12 (November 30, 1961), translation in *Joint Publications Research Service*, No. 11,581, December 19, 1961, pp. 28–33; and Claude Harmel, "Thorez et Togliatti," *Est & Ouest*, XVI, 326 (September 16–30, 1964), pp. 1–5.

60 "Session du Comité central (Arcueil, 9–10 mai 1956): Intervention de Maurice Thorez," *Cahiers du Communisme*, XXXII, 6 (June 1956), pp. 760–768.

during an ostensible vacation trip with his family.[61] But if agreement had been reached, publication of Khrushchev's secret speech rendered it irrelevant. The French Politburo's resolution of June 18 echoed Togliatti's call for a Marxist analysis of the causes of Stalin's errors, but declined to suggest even the rudimentary elements of one, referring vaguely only to "the whole atmosphere" of the Stalin era. The resolution made not the slightest concession to the idea that the Soviet system might have either caused or been affected by Stalin's excesses, nor did it draw Togliatti's conclusion that the Communist movement would henceforth move in the direction of greater autonomy for the parties.[62] The French were rewarded for their faithfulness by being specifically commended in that same Soviet resolution of June 30 in which Togliatti's views were singled out for attack.

Similar differences of emphasis were revealed over Poland and Hungary, the French accepting Moscow's interpretation of these events and backing both Soviet military interventions without a trace of the hesitations and half-regrets expressed in varying degree by the Italians, Poles, and Yugoslavs. By the third week in November the PCF had in fact begun to criticize these three parties harshly. Party Secretary Raymond Guyot insultingly accused Tito of taking positions that were not only close to those of Pietro Nenni but capable of pleasing even the reactionaries Admiral Horthy and Cardinal Mindszenty. The Poles were implicitly charged with seeking to destroy the unity of the Communist world and explicitly accused of interference in the PCF's internal affairs. The Italians too were blamed for indirectly encouraging the spread of intellectual dissent in France: "Certain hesitations of Italian intellectuals and certain concessions made to them by the leadership of our brother party in Italy have fed this opposition group."[63]

A later article lumped Togliatti and Tito together ("Those who speak of 'multiple centers' or who propose to divide arbitrarily the forces of the Communist movement into 'Stalinists' and 'non-Stalinists' . . .") as violators of Lenin's principles of proletarian internationalism.[64] The PCI defended itself in an editorial article critical of the Yugoslavs as well as the French for the sharp tone of their polemics:

[61] *L'Unità*, March 30–April 2, 1956.
[62] "Déclaration du Bureau politique du Parti communiste français," *Cahiers du Communisme*, XXXII, 8–9 (August–September 1956), pp. 926–927.
[63] Quoted in *L'Unità*, November 22, 1956.
[64] Pierre Villon, "Nationalisme et internationalisme," *Cahiers du Communisme*, XXXIII, 2 (February 1957), p. 239.

To judge the political line of a party too sharply and to accuse it of opportunism only because certain intellectual comrades have, in the first moment, expressed divergent opinions on the facts of Hungary means without doubt to exaggerate the sense of things. The French comrade who made this criticism even lacked information. The Hungarian facts were so grave that it was legitimate that perplexity and even uncertainty should have been aroused not only among some intellectuals but also among other militants of the party.[65]

These were minor frictions, however, compared with the dispute that came into the open shortly after the Eighth Congress, when Roger Garaudy published a long and critical review of the Italian party's basic strategy. The main thrust of Garaudy's argument was that the whole concept of the "Italian road to socialism," as articulated before and during the Congress, tended to violate the crucial distinction between a reformist and a revolutionary perspective. Openly revisionist notions such as Giolitti's, Garaudy argued, were not being fought with sufficient vigor because of "certain confusions" in the PCI's official line. The first such "confusion" lay in the PCI's tendency to underestimate the Communist party's role in the construction of socialism. Togliatti was explicitly criticized on two grounds: for having placed excessive emphasis on the tendency of capitalist productive forces themselves to create an inevitable and objective pressure toward socialism, and for having suggested that even in a socialist society one might envisage the continued existence of several political parties. These ideas were labeled as concessions to spontaneity and to the reformist attitudes manifested by the Yugoslav leader Kardelj; their effect was to blur the distinction between the party of scientific socialism and other socialist and social democratic parties which had proved themselves incapable of representing the true interests of the proletariat.[66] The French were, here again, attempting to link Togliatti with the Yugoslav deviationists.

These comments were delivered with somewhat the air of debaters' points, however; the core of the argument dealt with the PCI's basic assumption that a program of structural economic and social reform implemented by parliamentary action could lead directly to the creation of a socialist society. Garaudy strongly rejected Togliatti's open refutation of Lenin's belief in the necessity of destroying parliament along with the rest of the machinery of the

[65] *L'Unità*, November 25, 1956.

[66] "A propos de la 'Voie Italienne vers le socialisme,'" *Cahiers du Communisme*, XXXIII, 1 (January 1957), pp. 33–56. Garaudy, it should be noted, did not indefinitely play this role of defender of the faith; a decade later he would distinguish himself as one of the most vigorous and convincing proponents within the French party of "Italian" ideas and attitudes, particularly as regards Communist relations with the Catholic world.

bourgeois state. In his June 24 address to the Central Committee Togliatti had said, referring to Lenin's thesis: "When we, in fact, affirm that a method of advance toward socialism is possible not only on democratic terrain, but also making use of parliamentary forms, it is evident that we are correcting something in this position, taking into account the transformations that have taken place and are still occurring in the world."[67] Garaudy acknowledged that under certain conditions parliamentary institutions might be used to weaken other instruments of the bourgeoisie, but he insisted that they nevertheless remained a part of the state machinery and would thus ultimately have to be destroyed. Similarly, he contended that the PCI's emphasis on structural reforms and land reform in agriculture merely helped create the dangerous illusion that capitalist institutions could be transformed from within in such a way as to benefit the working class and damage the bourgeoisie. To foster illusions on this score was to risk disarming the workers, destroying their revolutionary consciousness and their capacity for decisive class action. As a whole, Garaudy's article represented nothing more or less than a classical polemic against revisionism in the name of Marxist-Leninist orthodoxy.

The Italians quickly confronted this challenge.[68] They defended themselves against the specific charges levied by Garaudy and counterattacked by asserting that the French appeared to have missed all the essential implications of the Twentieth Congress for the Western European parties. The idea of different roads to socialism did not represent, as the French seemed to believe, merely an up-to-date version of the Popular Front, a slogan around which to build a temporary alliance structure. It implied, rather, an effort to come to grips with an essentially new international and domestic reality that necessitated rethinking of many traditional ideas and methods of action. Each party now had to decide whether "to remain a party of propagandists," merely trumpeting the traditional slogans and objectives of the working class, or whether to confront reality boldly and adapt the values and doctrines of communism to the new demands.[69]

Communist doctrine must not become dogma, the Italians insisted. Even the most sacred formulas must be looked at afresh to see how they can be applied in the conditions of the day:

[67] "La via italiana al socialismo" in Togliatti, *Problemi del movimento*, p. 150.
[68] See the unsigned editorial appearing both in *L'Unità*, January 20, 1957, and in *Rinascita*, XIII, 12 (December 1956), pp. 680–683; also, for a fuller reply, Velio Spano, "Origini e lineamenti della nostra politica," *Rinascita*, XIV, 1–2 (January–February 1957), pp. 47–52.
[69] See Spano, *ibid.*, p. 48.

Even the general political statements made by the great teachers, the classics of our movement, must always be considered in relation to the real situation if we are to grasp their meaning properly, if we do not wish to lose the correct understanding of our doctrine as a method and a guide for action, not as a compendium of universally valid rules, which it is not and does not wish to be.[70]

The Marxist principle of the absolute and relative pauperization of the working class, for example, is not a "categorical, immutable law" as the French comrades maintain but rather a tendency of capitalist economics that can be slowed down or reversed by the action of the workers. Likewise, nationalization of industry, while not in itself a socialist measure, can nevertheless help weaken the monopolies and strengthen the power of workers and their allies to control the course of economic and social development. The logic of the struggle, argued the PCI, requires mobilization of the proletariat and the productive middle class behind a program of economic reforms that will gradually strip monopoly capital of its powers and privileges, thus preparing the ground for an eventual political transformation. The French party, by contrast,

. . . seems to say that the logic of this struggle resides in the practical demonstration of the laws of relative and absolute impoverishment of the proletarians under capitalism. When the workers are convinced of this truth they will rebel against capitalism, and everything will be over.[71]

Maurice Thorez himself now came to his party's defense, linking Spano's arguments with those employed long ago by Bernstein and other revisionist and anti-Marxist thinkers.[72] Pauperization of the proletariat was a fact, he insisted, providing data to demonstrate that Italy could in no way be regarded as an exception to the rule. Furthermore, he noted, citing West German and American Communist documents supporting his view, it was only the Italians who seemed to have become confused on this score. Thorez quoted an explicit and unqualified endorsement of the French view by the Soviet economist Arzumanyan in an article in *Kommunist* which "rebuffed all the reformist attempts to establish heaven knows what sort of divergence between his point of view and that expressed by our party."[73] Thorez was alluding here to the fact that Velio Spano had, it turned out incautiously, appended to his discussion of pauperization a footnote inviting the reader to contrast Arzumanyan's written views on the subject with those of Thorez. One may

70 *L'Unità*, January 20, 1957.
71 *Ibid.*
72 M. Thorez, "Encore une Fois la Paupérization!," *Cahiers du Communisme*, XXXIII, 5 (May 1957), pp. 657–686.
73 *Ibid.*, p. 666.

suspect, whatever the relative merits of the rival interpretations of the Soviet economist's argument, that Thorez had persuaded someone in high place in Moscow of the need for an explicit endorsement of the orthodox position he defended.

This series of exchanges reflected the deep divergences between the strategies and styles of the two parties, one dedicated largely to disruption of the economic and political system by mobilization of working-class forces, the other oriented toward acceptance of the system and its gradual transformation through structural reforms and new political alliances. But these differences had existed for some years and would continue to smoulder beneath the surface after a truce in the public polemics had been worked out. How does one explain, then, the sudden French onslaught following the Eighth Congress? One reason, no doubt, was the PCF's concern over Italian influence in its ranks, especially among the intellectuals attracted by Togliatti's ideological and tactical flexibility. French party officials felt obliged to demonstrate unequivocally that they would not tolerate any trace of Italian revisionist poison in the system. Just as the Soviets (and, as we have seen, even the Italians) were fearful of Polish influence on sections of the party and on the younger generation as a whole, so the French wished to minimize the risks of contamination from their unorthodox rivals to the south.

Would Thorez, however, have unleashed such a broad offensive against the *via italiana* had he not been encouraged to do so by Moscow? Revisionism in the French party was not so acute a threat as to require an attack on the PCI. It is plausible to suppose that the French move was part of the larger antirevisionist campaign inspired from Moscow and directed principally against the Yugoslavs and the Poles. Such verbal aggression by proxy is certainly not unknown in the history of the Communist movement, as the surrogate roles of Albania and Yugoslavia at a certain stage of the Sino-Soviet conflict remind us. French and Italian Communist relations in both party and trade union spheres in the years since 1956 reveal other occasions, some of which will be mentioned later on, when the French clearly appeared to be carrying the torch for the Soviet leadership.[74]

If, in this instance, the French were in fact serving Soviet interests as well as their own, they were undoubtedly doing so in the context of the political battle then under way in Moscow. The resur-

[74] In the course of conversations with Communist party and trade union officials in Italy the observation was more than once volunteered to me that arguments with the French often indicated disagreements with the Soviets as well.

gence of the conservative faction led by Molotov was based above all on the disasters to which Khrushchev's policies of liberalization in Eastern Europe and rapprochement with Yugoslavia appeared to have led. The campaign to discredit revisionism in Yugoslavia, Poland, and Italy was also in part a campaign to discredit Nikita Khrushchev. There can be little doubt that Thorez hoped for, and perhaps anticipated, a Molotov victory; in June 1957 he had apparently already prepared a message congratulating Molotov on his victory.[75] The open quarrel between the two great Communist parties of Europe was tied in with still unresolved succession crises in the Soviet Union.

The November 1957 Moscow Meeting

The fortieth anniversay of the October Revolution afforded the Soviets an appropriate occasion on which to bring together the Communist parties of the world for a review of grand strategy and a reaffirmation of the unity and strength of the movement. The results were embodied in a declaration of common principles, signed by all the ruling parties but the Yugoslav and including an explicit restating of the Soviet Union's leading position as "first and mightiest" among socialist states.[76] Unity appeared to be restored and the challenge implicit in the Polish October contained. If the Yugoslavs had not been induced to pay the price required to rejoin the socialist bloc, they had at any rate been quarantined, and revisionism had been proclaimed the "greatest danger" to the movement.

The nature of Sino-Soviet relations during the 1957 meeting is in some measure still a matter for conjecture. The Chinese themselves, in subsequent accounts of the history of the dispute, have emphasized their differences with the Russians, especially over the question of the peaceful transition to socialism. On other apparently more sensitive issues, however, such as recognition of Soviet hegemony over the movement and condemnation of revisionism, Mao and Khrushchev apparently saw eye to eye.[77] What is perfectly

75 François Fejtö, *Chine-U.R.S.S.: La fin d'une hégémonie: Les origines du grand schisme communiste, 1950–1957* (Paris: Librairie Plon, 1964), p. 190.

76 "The 1957 Moscow Declaration," translated in G. F. Hudson, Richard Lowenthal, and Roderick MacFarquhar, eds., *The Sino-Soviet Dispute* (New York: Praeger, 1961), pp. 46–56.

77 No full analysis of the 1957 meeting has yet appeared taking into account the information acquired since 1963 concerning the early stages of the Sino-Soviet controversy. See William E. Griffith, *The Sino-Soviet Rift* (Cambridge, Mass.: The M.I.T. Press, 1963), p. 16, footnotes 8 and 9, for a listing of the major relevant

clear, in any event, is that China's central role in the Moscow meeting marked the beginning of a new stage in the history of the international Communist movement.

As a nonruling party, the PCI did not have an important part to play in Moscow. Its views were apparently conveyed through consultation, but it took no part in the decisive conferences of ruling parties at which the Declaration was prepared. Togliatti did deliver a speech at the gathering of 64 parties that followed immediately thereafter; not published until two years later, it reveals some interesting contrasts between the PCI's positions and those contained in the Moscow Declaration. No issue was made of these differences at the time, however, and the Italian party was quick to endorse both the Declaration and the Peace Appeal signed by the 64 parties as "integral parts of the party's general orientation and a guide to its work and its struggles."[78] For the PCI, the three most sensitive issues confronted at Moscow can be summed up under the headings of revisionism, national roads to socialism, and the organization and leadership of the Communist movement.

REVISIONISM. Among the most important results of the meeting was the designation of revisionism as "the main danger at present" for the Communist movement, a pronouncement qualified in response to pressure from the Poles and the Italians by the acknowledgment that dogmatism and sectarianism might at certain times also become the greater threat to one or another party. The PCI dutifully adopted the slogan in its official pronouncements on the Moscow meetings.[79] It was clear, however, that the Italian party would have preferred a different formula. Togliatti's speech to the 64-party gathering in Moscow, delivered at a time when the Declaration's wording on this point was already known, referred instead to "the struggle against reformism and sectarianism, which are today the principal danger of the working-class movement."[80]

---

documents. Griffith, along with other analysts, believes that the meeting "saw a serious and essentially indecisive Sino-Soviet confrontation" over basic issues of policy; *ibid.*, p. 17. Other observers have stressed the collaboration between the two in resisting Polish and Yugoslav attempts to weaken the discipline and unity of the bloc; see Crankshaw, *The New Cold War*, pp. 62–73. This emphasis is shared by Frank J. Rendall, who is writing a history of the early years of the dispute.

[78] "Pieno accordo con la Dichiarazione e con l'Appello di pace dei partiti comunisti e operai," Risoluzione del CC e della CCC del PCI, December 11, 1957, in *Documenti politici e direttive del Partito comunista italiano dall' VIII al IX Congresso* (Rome: A cura della segreteria del Partito Comunista Italiano, 1960), pp. 205–207, at p. 205.

[79] *Ibid.*, p. 206.

[80] "Sugli orientamenti politici del nostro partito," *Rinascita*, XVI, 11 (November 1959), p. 758.

This formulation coincided, it will be recalled, with the one Togliatti had offered a year earlier at the PCI's Eighth Congress. Although it might appear at first glance that he was according equal weight to the two dangers threatening the Communist movement, this was not the point. Togliatti's comment carefully referred not to the Communist parties alone, but to the "working-class movement" as a whole. In his Congress speech Togliatti had made it plain that he regarded the reformist threat as pertaining primarily to the socialist and social democratic sections of the workers' movement in its broadest sense. Within the Italian party, on the other hand, the main danger was sectarianism. At Moscow Togliatti affirmed that in his view this distinction applied not to the Italian scene alone but to European communism in general:

> Our action for many years and the decisions of our Eighth Congress reflect the effort to conduct a decisive struggle to liquidate every form of sectarianism. We believe that if all the parties had acted in this way, they would have been able to liquidate that old sectarianism that has prevented them from becoming mass parties.[81]

At this and other points during his speech Togliatti thus let it be known that as far as the Italian party was concerned, the essential obstacle to progress in Europe lay in the widespread failure of the Communist parties to understand and accept the realities of contemporary capitalism: dogmatism, not revisionism, was in fact the main danger for European communism. Although Togliatti appeared to have the smaller parties primarily in mind, there was little room for doubt that the French party was intended to be a principal target. Jacques Duclos, at any rate, is said to have taken violent exception to the tenor of Togliatti's remarks, accusing him of assuming revisionist and anti-Leninist positions.[82]

Although Togliatti's opinion in the matter was clear, the moment was hardly opportune to insist upon it. The issue before the house was not rejuvenation of the Western European parties but restoration of the unity of the parties already in power, a question on which Italian views did not count for much. Under the circumstances, no politician in Togliatti's position would have set himself in open opposition to the principles enunciated at Moscow,

81 *Ibid.*, p. 759.

82 According to reports from several sources, a sharp verbal battle erupted between Togliatti and Duclos at some point during the Moscow deliberations. Togliatti apparently reported this to the Central Committee upon his return, though no mention was made in the text published by *L'Unità*. See Norman Kogan, "National Communism vs. the National Way to Communism—an Italian Interpretation," *Western Political Quarterly*, XI, 3 (September 1958), pp. 660–667.

among which the declaration of struggle against revisionism was particularly crucial. The antirevisionist campaign, with all the complications it implied for the PCI's pursuit of a vigorous program of party renewal and domestic reform, was simply part of the price to be paid for belonging to the international Communist fraternity.

NATIONAL ROADS TO SOCIALISM.   The struggle against revisionism concerned the Italians especially insofar as it appeared to threaten the critical principle of each party's right to develop its own independent road to socialism. Well before the November meeting the PCI had revealed its concern with the renewed Soviet emphasis on the absolute validity of certain universal laws of socialist construction. In July 1957 an Italian delegation led by Luigi Longo, Mario Alicata, and Emilio Sereni, all members of the *Direzione,* had gone to the USSR for three weeks of travel and consultation; they met with Khrushchev, Mikoyan, Suslov, and other top political leaders as well as with the Secretariat and Central Committee officials directly responsible for dealings with the Italian party.[83] Some aspects of these talks provide more insight than the November meeting itself into the relations between the Soviet and Italian parties.

An allegedly accurate transcript of a discussion between the Italians and a group of officials in the agitation and propaganda section of the Soviet Central Committee quotes the visitors as saying that recent Soviet propaganda against national communism was causing two sorts of difficulties in Italy and other European countries because it failed to make clear the vital distinction between out-and-out nationalist deviations and the search for new forms and methods of building socialism. First, as Mario Alicata observed, the bourgeois press was being given an excuse to claim that the Italian Communists were being "repudiated by Moscow" for their efforts to pursue an independent strategy.[84] Second, and more important, the European Communist parties were themselves being inhibited in pursuing their own roads to socialism by the fear of being accused of nationalist deviations. As Emilio Sereni put it:

The danger in the capitalist countries is insufficient research into national roads, not national communism. I understand that in the countries of the socialist camp the principal danger is the other. But with us, no. There are in fact Communist parties in the capitalist countries who do

[83] Longo's report to the Central Committee on his talks was printed in *L'Unità,* September 26, 1957, and the discussion of it on September 28. The full report of the delegation was published as *Problemi e realtà dell'URSS.*
[84] *Ibid.,* p. 66.

not go beyond the level of propaganda. From the propaganda standpoint everything is perfect, but from the standpoint of political action, no.[85]

The Soviet officials professed surprise at the idea that the struggle against nationalist deviations could possibly have been construed as a repudiation of efforts to adapt the general laws of development to particular national conditions, assuring the Italians effusively of their support for an independent Italian road to socialism. One of them added, by way of clarification: "We repeat, our criticism of national communism is not directed against research on national peculiarities but against the affirmation that these are more important than the general laws."[86]

At such a level of discourse it was difficult to disagree. It would hardly have been possible for a Communist leader to maintain, in the abstract, that the universal Marxist laws of development were of lesser importance than differing national circumstances, and Longo accordingly reassured his colleagues in the Central Committee that there was absolutely no controversy with the Soviets over this issue.[87] Subsequent speakers also blandly reiterated in one way or another that it was only necessary to ensure that these essential universal principles be put into effect in such a way as to reflect accurately the realities of national life.

Despite these reassurances, an issue of real substance did exist, one that was hardly going to be resolved by manipulation of empty formulas. In raising the subject with the Soviets themselves, the PCI leadership ensured that the question would be publicly discussed in language that did not seem to contradict the PCI's claims to autonomy. But underneath this public relations aspect lay a serious issue reaching close to the heart of relationships between the parties. Soviet insistence on the validity of certain general laws of socialist development was to some degree only another—but more acceptable—way of asserting the continued ideological authority and political supremacy of the CPSU. As long as general laws were regarded as being in principle superior to national circumstances, then the Soviet party, as the interpreter of these laws, would be justified in denouncing aspects of the PCI's domestic program that seemed to go too far toward revisionism in adapting to the realities of Italian life. That the PCI had such concerns could not be admitted publicly in 1957, but four years later Mario Alicata would

85 *Ibid.*, pp. 68–69.

86 *Ibid.*, p. 67.

87 *L'Unità*, September 26, 1957. Kogan has given substantial excerpts from Longo's speech and a less extensive résumé of the ensuing debate; *Western Political Quarterly*, XI, 3, p. 671.

observe with reference to the new Soviet party Program that to insist on general laws of development and a single road to socialism was to put into jeopardy the very essence of the principle of national roads.[88]

In his discussion of this issue, both during the July talks in Moscow and upon his return home, Longo tried to suggest a rather different yardstick for defining nationalist deviations from the one being offered by the Soviets: "The difference between national communism and national roads is that the latter recognize the need for international unity and common action, whereas the former denies it."[89] The relevant criterion for judging a party's actions, Longo implied, was not the degree to which its program appeared to correspond to the Soviet interpretation of the Marxist laws of social development. For a party out of power, imposition of tactical and strategic prescriptions from the outside was likely to result in sectarian, propagandistic behavior, divorced from real needs. In Longo's view, a party should be judged by its attitude toward the USSR and toward the movement as a whole, by its readiness to accept the discipline of proletarian internationalism. The PCI, having proven its loyalty in the dark days of Hungary, should be trusted to steer its own course at home.

The November 1957 Moscow Declaration gave the PCI little comfort on this score. Although it several times repeated the usual qualifications concerning the need to respect national conditions and avoid mechanical imitation of other parties, the Declaration gave greater weight to the thesis that "the processes of the socialist revolution and the building of socialism are governed by a number of basic laws applicable in all countries embarking on a socialist course."[90] While this formulation was designed with the socialist countries in mind, it was intended to apply to the nonruling parties as well, and was dutifully repeated in the PCI's postconference statements.[91]

Togliatti's own speech at Moscow, by contrast, nowhere alluded to universal laws. The emphasis was entirely on such elements of the PCI's domestic program as relations with the Church, alliances with the rural and urban middle classes, and the need for autonomy of the trade unions and other mass organizations—in short, on

[88] L'Unità, November 12, 1961.
[89] Problemi e realtà dell'URSS, pp. 67–68; L'Unità, September 26, 1957.
[90] "The 1957 Moscow Declaration" in Hudson et al., The Sino-Soviet Dispute, p. 51.
[91] "Per la unità e la compattezza del movimento comunista," Rinascita, XIV, 10–11 (October–November 1957), p. 500.

matters not likely to be included in anyone's listing of universally valid Marxist laws. By way of clarification and theoretical justification of these positions, Togliatti made the following point:

And this brings up the last question I intend to raise, one that concerns our whole movement. In the past we have always maintained that slogans of a transitory character can be used only in periods of acute revolutionary crisis. Today we have modified this position. We have reached the conclusion that in the present period of transition from capitalism to socialism, above all where the mass movement has gone far along on the road of democratic conquests and possesses great strength, it is possible even in a situation like the present one to employ slogans of a transitory character, of both an economic and a political nature.[92]

As would be indicated more explicitly on other occasions, Togliatti was here referring obliquely to Lenin's use of transitional slogans between April and November 1917, when program demands of a nonsocialist character were justified as a means of stimulating an imminent revolutionary crisis. In the advanced capitalist countries, Togliatti was arguing, we too find ourselves in a transitional phase between capitalism and socialism, and the content of our program must reflect this fact if we are to win the support we need from democratic forces outside the socialist camp. If our program appears to contain elements of revisionism, he implied, this is but a passing phenomenon, a necessary tactical adjustment to our situation.

If the Italians were concerned about potential interference with domestic strategy, the Soviet Union was not the only source of worry. Togliatti certainly knew, as the outside world was not to be told for another five years, that one of the major points of controversy at Moscow had concerned Chinese resistance to the new theory of peaceful transition from capitalism to socialism. Acknowledging the tactical utility for parties in capitalist countries of the slogan of peaceful transition through parliamentary means, the Chinese insisted that Communists should all the same not delude themselves: "To the best of our knowledge, there is still not a single country where this possibility is of any practical significance." To put excessive emphasis on the idea, even for tactical reasons, would be a grave error: far from serving to weaken or deceive the bourgeoisie, it would on the contrary disarm the working class, rendering it impotent for the task of destroying the machinery of the state and smashing the inevitable armed resistance of the bourgeoisie.[93] Here, in its crudest form, was a stubborn and open

92 *Ibid.*, XVI, 11, p. 760.
93 "The Origin and Development of the Differences between the Leadership of the CPSU and Ourselves," *People's Daily* and *Red Flag*, September 6, 1963, in *The Polemic on the General Line of the International Communist Movement* (Peking: Foreign Languages Press, 1965), pp. 55–114, at p. 106.

reassertion of the sectarian attitudes the Italians had been fighting within their own and the French party. The Chinese theses, besides representing an assault on the premises of the Soviet peaceful coexistence line, challenged the most basic principles of the Italian road to socialism.

The necessity for Italian support of the Soviets over this issue was obvious. Differences there were between the CPSU and the PCI, but they were differences of degree rather than kind. Particularly with Khrushchev, the author of the Twentieth Congress line, once more firmly in power after the defeat of the antiparty group in June, the basic interests of the Italian and Soviet parties appeared to coincide. They were agreed on the broad outlines of an international strategy; they both desired the restoration of a united international movement and were prepared to accept the verbal compromises necessary to achieve it; and the Soviets, whatever doubts they may have entertained about the Italian party's operating style and domestic policies, had not actually attempted to interfere in the PCI's domestic affairs. The logic of the situation left the Italian party no choice but to entrust to Soviet hands the defense of the doctrines of peaceful coexistence and nonviolent transition to socialism.

ORGANIZATION OF THE COMMUNIST MOVEMENT. Restoration of unity in the Communist world could not be achieved solely by the definition of general ideological principles acceptable to all parties. An organizational solution would also have to be found as a framework for inter-Communist relationships. Throughout 1957 this issue had been discussed, though not publicly, in the Communist world. Togliatti, referring to the new "polycentric system" of the international movement, had declared that a system based on full autonomy and bilateral relations would, in addition to enhancing the unity of the movement, also permit Communist parties more easily to establish ties with socialist, social democratic, and national liberation movements, thereby facilitating united action among the progressive forces of the world.

Bilateralism being the official Soviet solution as well, the major parties had promptly begun exchanging delegations and issuing joint communiqués. It had soon become obvious that bilateral relations could not effectively coordinate the actions and policies of the parties, and pressure apparently began to be exerted in some quarters for creation of a new organization to take the place of the Cominform, though no such proposal was ever made public. The French party appears to have been among the chief proponents of the idea. Raymond Guyot, for example, commenting on the PCF's development of interparty ties on both a bilateral and a multilateral basis, added: "We realize, however, that in the long run that will not suffice."[94] Another official French commentator alluding to the outmoded organizational forms of the Comintern (but making no reference at all in this connection to the Cominform) observed that "to renounce organizational forms and outmoded methods of work does not, however, mean to renounce all effective organizational forms for the international solidarity of the Communist movement."[95]

Such veiled allusions as these by the French and other "Stalinist" parties in Eastern Europe may well have reflected the preferences of the Soviet leadership, especially of the Molotov group, but there is no evidence that official Soviet endorsement was ever given the idea of a new Communist international organization. An indication to the contrary is suggested by the fact that in December 1956 *Pravda* did not delete from its heavily abridged version of Togliatti's Eighth Congress speech the flat assertion that "we are against restoration of any kind of centralized organization whatsoever."[96] The PCI's objection to a new organization was confirmed two months later, again with apparent Soviet backing, in the PCI's statement summarizing the results of a meeting in Moscow between top Soviet officials and an Italian delegation consisting of Longo and Spano.[97] By contrast, the declaration resulting from a similar meeting late the following month between Italian and Czech party leaders failed even to mention the question of bilateral or multilateral relations, a sure sign of failure to reach agreement.[98] The French had similarly declined to endorse bilateralism in their joint declaration with the Poles.[99]

The central reason for Soviet unwillingness to press for a new international organization was undoubtedly unyielding Polish and Yugoslav resistance. Though Yugoslavia could be regarded as expendable to a consolidated socialist bloc, Poland was not, and Gomułka was determined that his return to the fold would not entail a fresh acceptance of the humiliations a united international

94 *L'Humanité*, February 16, 1957.

95 Victor Joannes, "L'internationalisme prolétarien," *Cahiers du Communisme*, XXXIII, 7–8 (July–August 1957), p. 1187.

96 *Pravda*, December 11, 1956.

97 "Contatti del PCI con i partiti fratelli," Comunicato della Direzione del PCI, February 15, 1957, in *Documenti politici e direttive*, p. 28.

98 "Fraterna solidarietà fra il PCI e il PC cecoslovacco," Dichiarazione comune delle delegazioni del PCI e del PCC, Prague, April 1, 1957, in *Documenti politici e direttive*, pp. 49–53.

99 Brzezinski, *The Soviet Bloc*, p. 295.

organization could impose. He had proven to his own satisfaction, as had Tito before him, that a determined nation could successfully defend its deepest interests even against overwhelming Soviet political and military superiority. Poland would be better protected under a system of bilateral relations formally based on the principle of equality than in an international grouping operating under the unanimity rule, in which she would be isolated and easily outvoted. Gomułka thus insisted throughout 1957 on the bilateral principle, even declining to take part in the January meeting of the Communist states in Budapest.[100] The Soviet solution was to urge consultative multilateral party meetings, a formula proposed late in 1956 and put to the first real test in November 1957. It proved successful as a means of bringing Gomułka back into the mainstream of the movement and as a device for arriving at compromises capable of temporarily maintaining at least formal unity among the parties.

The Italians, while firmly in agreement with the Poles and Yugoslavs on the impossibility of restoring an international organization, quickly moved from support of pure bilateralism toward an acceptance of the need for multilateral meetings. By December 1956 Togliatti had endorsed their usefulness "in order to examine particularly important problems and to compare the different roads that are being followed in solving them, in different situations."[101] He showed his continuing reservations, however, by adding two significant qualifications. First, such meetings should not attempt to reach decisions binding for all, but should rather serve essentially informational purposes, "to make each other's position clear to everybody, thus strengthening the unity of the movement." Second, non-Communist organizations might be invited to take part; "this would be a step, even though small, toward overcoming the present division in the international workers' movement, or toward at least creating the conditions in which it might be overcome in the future." While bowing to the necessity for multiparty gatherings, Togliatti appears to have been hoping that they could become forums for discussion rather than for decision, a positive device to help overcome the isolation of the Communist parties from other working-class forces rather than an instrument for imposing Soviet policy. Under the circumstances these ideas were hardly realistic and were not mentioned again.

The delicate issue of Soviet authority was being expressed in another form as well in a muted controversy over the way in which

100 See *ibid.*, pp. 273–298, for details of the Polish position during this period.
101 *Eighth Congress*, p. 175.

the Soviet Union's undisputed supremacy in the Communist world should be acknowledged. The Chinese, insisting on the absolute necessity for unity, were vigorously urging explicit recognition of Soviet leadership. Most of the other ruling parties had similarly during 1957 employed various formulas affirming Soviet leadership of the Communist camp. The Poles, however, had carefully avoided that connotation, preferring instead vague phrases such as "the first and mightiest socialist power." The Italian party too had consistently employed circumlocutions—"decisive force," "axis of the socialist camp," "the Communist party that opened the road to all." The formulation agreed upon at Moscow for inclusion in the Declaration went further than Gomułka or Togliatti had wanted in its reference to "the invincible camp of the socialist countries headed by the Soviet Union."[102] The PCI demonstrated its lack of enthusiasm for this solution by omitting it from the Central Committee resolution approving the Moscow Declaration.[103]

The pronouncements of the November 1957 meeting were intended to be binding, as we have seen, although the nonruling parties were granted the courtesy of being told they should "assess and themselves decide what action they should take on the considerations expressed in the declaration."[104] The Moscow meeting nevertheless marked a significant shift in the organizational principles of the Communist world. The era of the single arbiter, manipulating general principles to suit its own exclusive needs, had given way to an era in which all the parties, at least all the ruling parties, had an actual or potential voice. Among the ruling parties Gomułka could be counted on to defend the principle of autonomous national roads to socialism, thus protecting the most basic interest of the PCI. The locus of authority had begun to shift, in principle if not yet in political reality, away from the Soviet Union toward the Communist movement in its entirety.

[102] "The 1957 Moscow Declaration" in Hudson et al., The Sino-Soviet Dispute, p. 49.

[103] "Pieno accordo con la Dichiarazione" in Documenti politici e direttive, pp. 205–207. By Zagoria's estimate, only Kardelj, Gomułka, and Togliatti failed to use the approved formulation in their declarations immediately after the conference; Zagoria, The Sino-Soviet Conflict, 1956–1961, p. 147. Wolfgang Leonhard adds Kádár to the list of those opposing its use in the Moscow Declaration; The Kremlin since Stalin (New York: Praeger, 1962), p. 262.

[104] "The 1957 Moscow Declaration" in Hudson et al., The Sino-Soviet Dispute, p. 47.

CHAPTER FIVE

THE BRIEF REIGN OF "FICTITIOUS UNANIMITY," 1958–1960

The international Communist movement, and the Italian party with it, entered a new stage with the signing of the 1957 Moscow Declaration. In Amendola's later phrase, it was a period of "fictitious unanimity,"[1] in which deep differences of interest were hidden beneath a veneer of formal adherence to the newly established general line of the movement.

During these years the distinguishing mark of the PCI's behavior was its conformity. Showing little outward trace of the special sensitivities aroused by the Twentieth Congress, the party appeared to revert substantially to its former posture of unquestioning endorsement of Soviet domestic and international policies. The PCI image that had been created in 1956 and kept alive during the controversies of the succeeding year began to grow dim: neither the Italian party nor its leader seemed any longer to be straining against the bonds of Soviet authority in the movement.

For the PCI to slip back into attitudes of conformity in the late 1950's was in every respect the natural and easy thing for it to do. If the crisis of 1956–1957 had proved anything, it was that weakening of Soviet prestige and open conflict within the Communist movement had a disruptive impact on the party, deepening internal tensions and threatening its strategy of alliances. This was inevitable, moreover, so long as the party avoided the painful responsibility of working out a genuinely independent domestic strategy. Only if the PCI could overcome the constraints imposed by an increasingly irrelevant ideology and by the priorities of Soviet international policy would it begin to be shielded from the damaging effects of weakness and conflict within the Communist world. A particular combination of domestic and international circumstances would be required to move the party to a point where it could begin not merely to indicate its preferences concerning

1 *L'Unità,* November 12, 1961.

141

international Communist affairs, but to take such action to further its interests as the narrow limits of its influence allowed. It would not be until after the Twenty-Second Congress in 1961, when issues much like those that had arisen in 1956 presented themselves in more acute and more permanent fashion, that the pressure for a qualitatively new posture would become strong enough to have a major effect on the party's behavior. In the interim, as this chapter will illustrate in several ways, events favored a return to more conventional modes of action.

Revisionism, the Main Danger

The consequences of the reassertion of Soviet authority at the November 1957 meeting were quickly brought home to the Italian leadership when a high-level Soviet delegation arrived for a three-week visit, ostensibly in reciprocation for the Italian mission to the Soviet Union the previous summer.[2] Although the delegation spent a good part of its time visiting party organizations in the North and in Sicily, the main business was transacted in a series of top-level meetings in Rome. The results of these discussions were summed up in a communiqué whose main purpose was to reiterate the validity and significance of the Moscow conference and of the "decisions" reached on that occasion.[3]

The term "decisions" in itself implied acknowledgment of the binding character of the Declaration, whose central principles were then uncompromisingly asserted. The "universal validity of the fundamental laws of the struggle for socialism" was proclaimed, with only a bow in passing to the relevance of "national peculiarities." The "particular importance" of "conducting a decisive struggle against revisionism was recognized as the principal danger in the ranks of the international Communist movement." The PCI's earlier reservations on all these points could no longer be upheld; an unambiguous proclamation of adherence to the new line was now required. Relations between the two parties were to be governed, it was declared, by Marxist-Leninist doctrine, by the

[2] The delegation, in Italy from February 13 to March 4, 1958, was headed by P. N. Pospelov, party Secretary and candidate member of the Presidium since July, and included Central Committee members Ponomarev and Rumyantsev, the former then in over-all charge of relations with Western parties, the latter editor of *Kommunist* and soon to take over direction of the new international Communist journal *World Marxist Review*. Also present were D. Shevlyagin and A. Dyakov, Central Committee officials responsible for Italian affairs.

[3] "Comunicato sulla visita in Italia della delegazione del PC dell' URSS" in *Documenti politici e direttive*, pp. 268–272.

principles of proletarian internationalism, and, almost as an after-thought, by considerations of equality and mutual respect.

On one point alone the PCI did not yet commit itself to the formulations of the Moscow Declaration. The Soviet Union was still described as continuing "to march in the advance guard of the great movement for socialist transformation of the world." Togliatti may quite reasonably have justified this omission on the ground that the Moscow formulation was out of place in a document concerning Soviet relations with a nonruling party; the claim to Soviet leadership did in fact formally apply to state relationships within the socialist bloc, not to party relations within the movement as a whole. Whatever the explanation, it is of no more than academic importance, for the PCI did not boycott the approved formula for long: Luigi Longo, the man who so frequently during these years conveyed the signals from Moscow, would employ it a few weeks thereafter.[4]

Though the communiqué did not mention the subject, Yugoslavia was a prime topic of discussion between the delegations. The Yugoslav refusal to sign the Moscow Declaration had marked the temporary defeat of Khrushchev's effort to bring Tito back into the fold. An antirevisionist campaign had quickly been launched, not at first indicting the Yugoslavs by name but clearly aimed their way; Shevlyagin, one of the chief members in the CPSU delegation to Rome, had himself written a major contribution to this effort.[5] Although it was not until April that the Soviets opened a frontal attack on the new Draft Program of the Yugoslav party, removing all doubt that it was indeed Tito and his associates who represented the "main danger" to the movement, the shape of things to come must already have been clear by the time the Soviet officials arrived in Rome. Prominent among their objectives, it may be presumed, was to ensure that the PCI would play its part in the campaign against the Yugoslavs.

The Italian leaders would certainly have preferred not to make a renewed excommunication of Tito the price for the restoration of unity. They made this clear by their action in 1960, at the Moscow meeting, when the PCI formally urged the Soviet party to avoid a renewed condemnation of the Yugoslavs, citing the difficulties this would create for the PCI at home. Perhaps they did the same in

4 "La realtà e l'attualità della prospettiva socialista," *Rinascita*, XV, 3 (March 1958), p. 149.
5 D. Shevlyagin, "The Fraternal Communist Parties' Struggle against Present-Day Opportunism," *Kommunist*, No. 18 (December 1957), pp. 27–44; translation in *CDSP*, X, 7, pp. 3–9.

1957, but there is no evidence of it. Publicly they went no further than to express regret at the differences that prevented the Yugoslavs from signing the Declaration and hope that through fraternal discussion these could be overcome.[6]

Publication of the Yugoslav Draft Program soon put an end to this bit of wishful thinking, for it signaled a world-wide onslaught against the Yugoslav revisionists, led off in relatively restrained fashion by the Soviets in mid-April and raised to a more intense level by the Chinese in May. It was apparent that the Yugoslav issue, like the question of Poznań and of Hungary before it, had become another proving ground of Communist loyalty. No party which itself wished to avoid being branded as revisionist—and the PCI was certainly vulnerable to the charge—could afford not to play its part. As a *Pravda* editorial bluntly put it:

> The most important question for every Communist and Workers' party in the present circumstances is the question of its relation to the whole international Communist movement, toward those program documents which publicize their experience on the basis of Marxism-Leninism and outline the tasks of the struggle for the cause of peace, democracy, and socialism. . . . In these conditions, the slightest deviation from the principles of Marxist-Leninism, any manifestation of disassociation or sectarianism, inevitably leads to the quagmire of revisionism, which, as the main danger, is being resolutely combatted by all Marxist-Leninist parties.[7]

By the end of May *Rinascita* had come out with the required statement, though it was neither as comprehensive a criticism as the Soviet nor as sharp as the Chinese.[8] The article dealt with two main themes, the lesser of which concerned the Yugoslav view of state capitalism. On this question the PCI was on difficult ground, for the program document presented at its own recent Congress had proclaimed theses on the role of state capitalism in the transition to socialism that were very close to the Yugoslav formulation. The PCI had maintained that state capitalism "can pave the way to socialism when it is accompanied by a democratic struggle that assures the working classes access to the leadership of the state and allows them to exercise an effective control over the management of public wealth."[9]

---

[6] "Per la unità e la compattezza del movimento comunista," *Rinascita*, XIV, 10–11 (October–November 1957), p. 500.

[7] *Pravda*, May 9, 1958; translation in Vaclav L. Benes, Robert F. Byrnes, and Nicolas Spulber, eds., *The Second Soviet-Yugoslav Dispute* (Bloomington: Indiana University Press, 1959), p. 155.

[8] V. Gerratana and A. Reichlin, "Contro la dottrina marxista-leninista e l'unità del movimento comunista," *Rinascita*, XV, 5 (May 1958), pp. 321–332.

[9] *Eighth Congress*, p. 119.

The Yugoslav program appeared to come to the same conclusions, including the affirmation that the positive effects of state intervention are conditional on forceful and conscious political action by the working class. The PCI argued, however, that there was a critical difference: the Yugoslavs merely paid lip service to the need for mass political struggle while in reality believing that state capitalism invariably represented a step in the direction of socialism. This positive attitude rested on their acceptance of the revisionist idea that the capitalist state could under some circumstances acquire an autonomous social function and serve as mediator between conflicting classes rather than defender of the interests of the bourgeoisie.

The Italian critique of Yugoslav theories of state capitalism was neither more nor less convincing than the French criticism of Togliatti following the Eighth Congress, nor, for that matter, than the Chinese attack on the PCI would be five years later. The Italian formulations were almost as vulnerable as the Yugoslav to the rigid interpretations being offered in 1958 by Soviet spokesmen, who declined to concede that state ownership or control of the economy in a capitalist system could actually serve to weaken the economic power of monopoly capital.[10] And yet there were contradictions in the dogmatic French and Soviet arguments as well, for they conceded that state monopoly capitalism helped objectively "to enhance the material requisites for the emergence of socialism."[11] Furthermore, it was acknowledged to be correct tactics to fight for nationalization of industry and expansion of the state capitalist sector: "The working class demands the most far-reaching nationalization, regarding it as a measure that, to a certain degree, undermines the 'sanctity' of private ownership and facilitates the subsequent socialization of production which the socialist revolution renders inevitable."[12]

The distinction between the authorized view and the revisionist view thus tended to boil down to the wholly subjective question of whether state capitalism was being regarded positively as a phenomenon valuable in its own right, thus implying acceptance of the capitalist system, or simply instrumentally, as a marginal means of weakening monopoly power. The Italian party, on this as on so

10 See P. Fedoseev, I. Pomelov, V. Cheprakov, "On the Draft Program of the League of Communists of Yugoslavia," *Kommunist*, April 15, 1958; translation in Benes *et al., The Second Soviet-Yugoslav Dispute*, pp. 96–100.

11 *Ibid.*, p. 97.

12 Y. Ostrovitianov and V. Cheprakov, "State-Monopoly Capitalism in the Distorting Mirror of Revisionism," *World Marxist Review*, I, 2 (October 1958), pp. 43–50.

many other issues, was obliged to walk a narrow path between the two versions: for the domestic audience it had to be persuasive enough in support of the virtues of state capitalism as an anti-monopoly weapon to pick up support from other leftist forces, while for the external audience it had to demonstrate its under-standing and acceptance of the traditional Marxist-Leninist case. In late 1956 and 1957, when Soviet ideological and political guidance was weak and uncertain and the international movement divided, the PCI could and did emphasize the "revisionist" side of the argument in open debate with the French. In 1958, with Soviet authority restored and the Communist world reunited on an ideo-logical and political platform of opposition to Yugoslav revisionism, the Italians found it convenient to show the other side of the coin.

Nevertheless, the PCI consistently held to the view that the prime criterion of proletarian internationalism for a Western Communist party was not rigid alignment of its domestic practice and doctrine to Soviet institutions and ideologies, but loyalty to Communist international goals and tactics as defined by the movement under Soviet guidance. The main thrust of the PCI's argument with the Yugoslavs, accordingly, concerned their "profoundly mistaken" understanding of the world scene. Having lost the class perspective, the Yugoslavs were failing to grasp the essential fact that the goal of reaching socialism by different roads and in an environment of peace was conceivable only in the context of an expanding and united international system of socialist states. By attacking the USSR and putting the blame on Stalin rather than the imperialists for having divided the world into opposed military blocs, Tito was only helping to perpetuate the cold war and to delay the progress of socialism. Rather than supporting the Soviet Union and the other socialist states, the Yugoslavs were vainly attempting to reinterpret the concept of proletarian internationalism so as to include a broader alliance of working-class and progressive forces around the world. This flies in the face of political reality, argued the Italians, and defies the true relation of forces in the world:

No, we believe concretely [in Soviet policy], basing our views on a clear vision of the relations of force on the international level and on the conviction that it is possible to give birth to a new, more advanced revolutionary strategy precisely because socialism in the world today is not a vaguely defined "universe," but rather a very precisely defined force. Based on the existence of a political, economic, and military system, this force extends out to the international workers' movement and to its allies and is in a position to have direct influence over the internal structure of the capitalist world. We believe in it, in a word, because the existence of the socialist system is one of the essential conditions for providing a revolu-

tionary thrust and therefore for making concretely possible the struggle
for peace, the Bandung policy, or the search for national roads and new
democratic and revolutionary alliances in the capitalist West.[13]

This statement, one of the more forthright explanations of PCI
allegiance to Soviet foreign policy, has the ring of conviction about
it. While the Italian leaders were battling within their party to
overcome the "sectarian" illusion retained by many from the early
postwar days that power would ultimately be won at the point of
Soviet bayonets, they nevertheless clung firmly to the belief that
the prospects for Communist success in the West depended heavily
on the entire international balance of power, and above all on
Soviet military and political might. The Western Communist
parties might assist in the revolutionary process by gradually weakening the economic strength and the will to resist of the capitalist
foe, but the critical factor in the struggle against imperialism, at
moments of offense and defense alike, was the united force of
international communism under Soviet leadership. Alone, the
Italian or the Yugoslav party could count for little in the world
balance; by joining with the rest under Soviet leadership, their
small weight could help swing the scales. The PCI's attitude toward
Tito's international pretensions, toward his effort to build up an
effective moral and political "third force" of neutralist states,
revealed with unusual clarity the essential premises of Italian Communist international policy.

The Soviet Union, Builder of Communism

One of the more important factors favoring the Italian party's
return to conventional patterns of action within the Communist
movement was the rapid restoration of Soviet prestige after the
Hungarian debacle. One should not suppose that any conscious
sacrifice was required for the PCI in the late 1950's to reaffirm its
unqualified solidarity with the USSR. Nor did the Italian party's
confidence in the USSR's ability to lead the Communist offensive
against the West, gradually transforming the world balance of
power, rest merely on an ideologically motivated faith or on a
disciplined acceptance of the Soviet line. The simple fact was that
during these years the Soviet Union was enjoying a string of
domestic and international successes that seemed to many in the
West, let alone in the Soviet orbit, to betoken a steady trend of
Communist advance.

[13] Gerratana and Reichlin, *Rinascita*, XV, 5, p. 328.

These were the years of stunning triumphs in space, of a supposed Western missile gap, of constant pressure against Berlin, of mounting and apparently effective Soviet political and economic action in the Middle East and Africa. They were also the years in which the Soviet economy appeared to be moving forward at an unprecedented rate, in sharp contrast with slow American growth rates, affected particularly by the 1958–1959 recession. The Soviets appeared, too, to have decisively broken from the Stalinist pattern in matters of social and economic administration: far-reaching reforms of the industrial system, of agriculture, of schools and legal procedures; growing though still uncertain freedom for writers and artists; fresh attention to the trade unions, the local soviets, and other instruments of popular participation in economic and social affairs.

These and similar developments, heavily publicized by the Russians themselves and by all the Communist parties, seemed to justify a renewed and strengthened faith in the power and virtue of the socialist system. Things did indeed appear to be changing in the Soviet Union, and changing fast, under the erratic but indefatigable personal command of the First Secretary of the CPSU. This brief "golden age" reached its climax in 1959, at the Twenty-First Congress, with the presentation of a grandiose seven-year plan designed to surpass the capitalist countries in per capita production, accompanied by the pronouncement that the USSR had now entered on the final stage of the construction of a communist society under which Soviet man would achieve both a new morality and a level of personal welfare never before imagined. A glorious vision indeed, until its luster gradually began to fade under the combined weight of economic difficulties at home and serious setbacks abroad.[14]

14 Detailed citation and illustration from some of the many articles glorifying the USSR would make unnecessarily tedious reading. One of the most consistent Italian boosters of the Soviet Union, whether by conviction or in consequence of an occupational hazard, was Giuseppe Boffa, the PCI's leading Moscow correspondent. See, for example, his articles in *Rinascita* of May 1958 lauding the third sputnik as "the most audacious scientific achievement of our times," and of January and March 1959 elaborating on the Twenty-First Congress. Of the party leaders, Luigi Longo continued to be the most frequent and most ardent defender of things Soviet and of the PCI's adherence to the USSR. A classic example of his rhetoric is the speech delivered in November 1957, in celebration of the fortieth anniversary of the October Revolution; the PCI's fidelity to the USSR, he explained, "has not been only an act of faith; it has been proof of political wisdom, of an exact evaluation of the political and social forces operating in the world. . . ." See the introduction to *Problemi e realtà dell'URSS*, p. 30.

Enthusiasm was not limited to Communists alone. Lelio Basso, a prominent left-wing Socialist intellectual who was in no sense a Soviet mouthpiece, wrote glowingly after a trip to the USSR of "the change in the public spirit, the overcoming of the old dogmatism, an extraordinary capacity for renewal of both men

As long as the bloom stayed on the rose, the PCI made the most of it, pointing incessantly both to the tangible material successes of the Soviet system, whether measured in units of steel, grain, or missiles, and to the full restoration of "Leninist" democratic norms. These Soviet accomplishments, real or imagined, were useful to the PCI in rebutting the continued charges from the Socialist right wing and other quarters that the evils of Stalin's day were those not of a paranoic individual but of an entire social system. Relying on the shortness of memory that so often seems able to wipe away the effects of the most shocking revelations, Togliatti began to distort the meaning of de-Stalinization, implicitly renouncing even his own cautious opinions of 1956. In response to Nenni's insistence on the need for greater political liberty under socialism, for example, Togliatti maintained that Khrushchev's attack on Stalin had to do not with matters of politics, legality, or human rights, but simply with the administration of the economy. The liberty of Soviet citizens has never been in question, he argued, and it is therefore absurd of the Socialists to suppose that Soviet economic growth might lead to greater political liberty of the bourgeois variety:

Whoever created that interpretation has not observed that the criticism against Stalin concerned above all negligence and errors in the management of the economy, which led in consequence to a certain stagnation in the development of productive forces. And the correction consists, as we have already noted, not so much in the restoration of Soviet democratic legality as in the introduction of several economic reforms which have given a new impulse to industrial and agricultural production.[15]

In short, the Stalinist system had been wrong not because it deprived people of their liberties but because it had not produced enough; now that production had risen and was being organized on a less centralized basis, the decisive test had been successfully met.

The leaders of the PCI were apparently persuaded, and with good reason, that they had nothing to lose by making the most of their ties to the USSR. Togliatti meant it when he said that "as far as we are concerned, solidarity with the socialist countries, and informing people of the realities of their progress, are elements of prestige and of strength for our party."[16] As long as the Soviet Union was manifestly strong and successful, at home and abroad, why should

and institutions, an intense participation of the masses in discussions concerning public affairs, a more mature awareness of political problems." "Alternativa democratica, massimalismo e frontismo," *Problemi del socialismo*, II, 8 (August 1959), p. 627.

[15] "Le decisioni del XX Congresso e il partito socialista italiano," *Rinascita*, XV, 10 (October 1958), p. 615.

[16] "Ancora su socialismo e democrazia," *Rinascita*, XVIII, 5 (May 1961), p. 433.

the PCI not identify with it as closely as possible? Whereas for a time in 1956, and then again after the Twenty-Second Congress, Italian Communists eagerly sought to demonstrate their autonomy and to dissociate themselves from the USSR by refusing to accept responsibility for what went on there, quite the opposite practice prevailed as long as things were going well. That the effort probably paid off is suggested in the following observation by an intelligent commentator from the non-Communist left seeking to explain the PCI's success in the November 1960 elections:

At one time, for many [intellectuals], a vote for the Communists was justified "despite the USSR" as a declaration of faith in the validity and possibility of an internal opposition within the Communist world, of an autonomous elaboration of an "Italian road." In the changed political situation, paradoxically, the same people seem today to find the opposite motivation for their vote: a vote "more for the USSR than for the PCI," . . . that is, an act implying lack of confidence with respect to the Italian situation, but at the same time a compensatory faith in an evolutionary process of the Soviet world, in the capacity of the USSR to introduce on the international plane those perspectives of "change and movement" that people do not believe the PCI capable of producing on the Italian scene.[17]

WESTERN EUROPE: FASCIST REACTION AND MONOPOLY RULE. The attitudes of the PCI toward political and economic developments in Europe offer another good illustration, especially by contrast with the positions assumed in subsequent years, of the generally conservative and conventional tendency of its policies during the late 1950's. And just as the strained relations between the French and Italian parties in 1956–1957, and again in 1961–1962, highlight the reformist aspect of the PCI's "personality," so their collaboration and relative cordiality in the intervening years are measures of the conformist dimension.

The temporary rapprochement was possible essentially because a variety of circumstances favored the characteristic attitudes of the French rather than the Italian party. The first factor was the restoration of the formal unity of the Communist movement on terms distinctly favorable to the PCF. Despite Khrushchev's victory over the Molotov group, desired by the Italians and feared by the French, Soviet ideological positions in the struggle against revisionism had swung back toward those defended by Thorez. Although by no means renouncing the principles of the *via italiana*, the PCI had, in accepting the mandate to fight revisionism, tacitly conceded the French a temporary victory in the ideological debate. For the

17 Franco Momigliano, "Paradossi nel voto a sinistra," *Passato e presente*, No. 18 (November–December 1960), p. 2365.

moment, at least, the argument could be set aside and an environment fostered more conducive to collaboration. An early tangible sign of the change was a meeting held in Rome "in an atmosphere of great fraternal spirit" at the end of February 1958 between leading intellectuals of both parties.[18]

Events in Europe also seemed to favor the more intransigent style of the French party. During 1958 and well into 1959 both parties took up the cry that a resurgent neofascist reaction posed a political and economic threat to all progressive forces. For the French party in particular it was in truth a time of danger. The right seemed triumphant in France: despite the PCF's efforts to bolster the Pflimlin government and muster support for its opposition to de Gaulle, the Fourth Republic had fallen, and along with it the constitutional system that had given large powers to the National Assembly and thus to its strong Communist minority. In the November election for the new Assembly the Communists had not only dropped from 25.7 per cent to 18.9 per cent of the popular vote since the elections of 1956, but through the introduction of single-member constituencies had gone from 140 seats in the Assembly to a mere 10.[19] The dramatic events in France and Algeria were viewed by both parties as evidence of an all-out attack on democratic liberties, a blow by the bourgeoisie against the parliamentary system, a threat to the entire democratic and socialist movement in the capitalist countries. In an issue of the party monthly devoted exclusively to "France in torment," dark reference was made to "a vast reactionary plan" conceived on a world scale by the most rabid imperialist groups, and the French Communists were assured of the PCI's full support in their hour of need.[20]

The political situation in Italy hardly justified such a grim picture. Both Communists and Socialists had emerged strengthened from the May 1958 elections, in which the Christian Democrats had failed to obtain a majority permitting establishment of a one-party government. The political configuration had for some time, nevertheless, been shifting to the right. The Christian Democratic party, having lost the backing of Saragat's Social Democrats, had been obliged to bargain for monarchist and neofascist support,

18 See "Collaborazione tra PCF e PCI nella battaglia culturale," Comunicato del PCI e del PCF, March 5, 1958, in Documenti politici e direttive, pp. 266–267.

19 See Edgar S. Furniss, Jr., France, Troubled Ally: De Gaulle's Heritage and Prospects (New York: Praeger, 1960), pp. 391–394, for electoral data.

20 See, inter alia, "No a de Gaulle," Rinascita, XV, 6–7 (June–July 1958), pp. 353–355; and Mario Montagnana, "Solidi legami de lotta comune fra comunisti francesi e italiani," ibid., pp. 471–472. See also Togliatti's report to the Central Committee, L'Unità, October 16, 1958.

eliciting from the PCI the judgment that "the foundations are being laid for a new regime of a totalitarian type, a permanent clerical tyranny masked by electoral forms."[21] Any excuse to highlight the dangers of attack from the far right was welcomed by a party grown powerful during the anti-Fascist Resistance; and at this moment such an emphasis particularly suited the party's desire to stem the rightward drift of Nenni's Socialists and, more generally, to create the conditions for a new alliance of leftist forces.[22]

Both French and Italian Communists were prepared, therefore, to collaborate in an international appeal for unity of the left against the resurgent neofascist threat. This was the main content of the joint declaration issued after a five-day meeting in Rome at the end of December 1958. The document was markedly defensive in tone, urging the need for vigorous working-class defense against the attacks of the reactionary big bourgeoisie on democratic liberties and on the living standards of the people. The American recession, the collapse of colonial empires, and the great advances of the socialist countries had combined, it was asserted, to create a situation of grave threat to monopoly capital, which was striking back in a coordinated offensive against the deepest interests of the working and middle classes.[23]

Chief among the manifestations of the reactionary offensive denounced at the December 1958 meeting was the European Economic Community. This institution had been the target for attack since early 1957, in an apparent effort to prevent or slow down ratification and implementation of the Treaty of Rome, signed in March of that year. In the main, the argument of the two parties was the same: the Common Market, an aggressive instrument of the United States and its faithful ally, West Germany, was aimed at consolidating monopoly control over the Western

---

21 "Prospettive di una lotta aspra," *Rinascita*, XIV, 6 (June 1957), p. 266.

22 See Palmiro Togliatti, "Per una sinistra europea," *Rinascita*, XVI, 3 (March 1959), for a major statement of this theme.

23 "Déclaration commune des delegations," *Cahiers du Communisme*, XXXV, 1–2 (January–February 1959), pp. 134–140, at p. 135. The Italians did not neglect to see that the joint declaration included reference to the need to struggle "for a series of economic and social transformations that would tend to limit the power of the monopolies," including the nationalization of certain sectors of industry. This was certainly a French concession to the standard Italian line, but the document as a whole did not emphasize such positive perspectives for action. The head of the French delegation reported on the meeting and on the PCI's activities in highly complimentary terms but referred exclusively to political and economic crisis, strikes, and mass action; not a word about economic and social reforms. Raymond Guyot, "Le Peuple Italien en lutte pour un changement radicale de l'orientation politique du pays," *Cahiers du Communisme*, XXXV, 4 (April 1959), pp. 318–333.

European economy, reinforcing the Atlantic Pact, and weakening the Soviet Union. Not only was its motivation essentially political, but its economic impact, far from being positive, would gravely damage the national economies of the weaker member countries for the benefit of international monopoly capital: the PCI warned against "the grave and real danger that the whole Italian economy, except for certain large monopolistic sectors, would be transformed into a great depressed area, with grave consequences for an important part of our population."[24] The very sovereignty of the weaker countries, France and Italy among them, would be threatened by the creation of supranational institutions designed to remove vital economic and social decisions from the hands of national parliaments. This latter theme, an appeal to traditional nationalist and anti-German sentiment, was particularly prominent in French propaganda, which attempted to mobilize the extremes on both left and right of the political spectrum against the Common Market.[25]

In these general lines of the campaign against the Common Market, both parties, but especially the French, were following the Soviet lead in attributing primarily political motivations to the Market. Until the early 1960's Soviet analysts largely ignored the economic purposes and potential economic impact of the Market, focusing their attention first on American intent to dominate Europe, then increasingly on the German and Franco-German threat.[26] Despite the PCI's basic acceptance of the Soviet line and its continued denunciation of the Market, however, its analysis did have some distinctive features. The difference lay essentially in the Italian readiness to acknowledge, indeed to insist, that the Common Market, despite its political purposes, might be economically significant. This idea was expressed in two ways. First, the PCI acknowledged that economic arrangements transcending national boundaries did in principle have validity:

The tendency to overcome the present situation and to prepare for a better future through an enlargement of restricted national markets and new forms of international collaboration in the economic field is there-

---

[24] "Sul Mercato comune europeo," Comunicato della Direzione del PCI, March 24, 1957, in *Documenti politici e direttive*, pp. 44–49, at p. 47.

[25] For a strong Italian statement of the political motivations alleged to be behind the EEC, see Celeste Negarville, "I trattati 'europeistici' nel quadro dell' attuale politica dell' imperialismo," *Rinascita*, XIV, 3 (March 1957), pp. 79–82. For the PCF view, see, *inter alia*, Georges Cogniot, "Les Nouveaux Pièges 'Européens,'" *Cahiers du Communisme*, XXXIII, 2 (February 1957), pp. 178–194.

[26] See Chapter Nine for a fuller summary of the Soviet position.

fore understandable and also correct. The workers and the laboring classes cannot be hostile in principle to this tendency. . . .[27]

The stated basis for this acceptance of the integration principle was the recognition that economically backward Europe faced a serious problem of competition with the Soviet Union and the United States; if the European nations could overcome national barriers, it was implied, there might result a weakening of American economic and political influence in Europe. Here was the germ of a more positive view of the Common Market as a potentially disruptive force within the Western alliance. Although by 1960 Soviet analysts would themselves arrive at similar conclusions, in the spring of 1959 an authoritative "Observer" writing in the *World Marxist Review* was still able to declare dogmatically in reference to the Common Market:

> *The Bonn-Paris axis policy does not signify greater freedom to maneuver vis-à-vis the United States.* This "European bloc" is not a neutral force between the East and West: in any circumstances, and on all major issues, it is but a *subsidiary of American strategy.*[28]

The second sense in which the PCI took seriously the economic aspect of the Common Market was in the repeated insistence that real harm would result to all but the large monopolistic sectors of the economy. Italy, the Communists insisted, would bear a greater burden than any other country because of its generally low wages and high unemployment, technical backwardness, and above all its underdeveloped and impoverished South. Long before the provisions of the Common Market treaty even went into effect, the PCI was hammering away at the dire consequences already evident as the monopolies prepared to meet the foreign competition.[29] The European Economic Community being an instrument of monopoly capital, the industrial working class and the smaller capitalists were bound to suffer, the former through reduced wages, poorer working conditions, and growing unemployment, the latter through competitive weakness resulting from the end of tariff protection and the inefficiency of their obsolescent equipment. Even harder hit would be the landless peasants and the small independent farmers, inevitably driven out of business as monopoly capital penetrated the countryside.[30]

---

27 "Sul Mercato comune europeo" in *Documenti politici e direttive,* p. 45.

28 "The Bonn-Paris Axis," *World Marxist Review,* II, 4 (April 1959), p. 25.

29 See, for example, Bruzio Manzocchi, "Le prime dannose conseguenze del MEC sull' economia italiana," *Rinascita,* XV, 8 (August 1958), pp. 515–519.

30 For a convenient summary of the argument, see Bruzio Manzocchi, "Unity of the People and Anti-Monopoly Forces against European 'Integration,'" *World Marxist Review,* II, 2 (November 1959), pp. 79–84.

The PCI's heavy stress on these economic arguments against the Common Market must be viewed in the context of its over-all political line. The emphasis was on gaining the sympathy and support of all groups, especially among the rural and urban middle classes, who could be presumed to have grievances against the big monopolies. The economic dislocations inevitably resulting from introduction of the Common Market provisions undoubtedly appeared to offer fertile ground for Communist campaigns against monopoly capital and its allies in the Church and the right wing of the Christian Democratic party.

Another more specific consideration reinforced this strategy of playing on economic discontent: during 1958 and early 1959 Italy, along with the rest of Europe, was feeling the pinch of the American recession, which had resulted in reduced industrial production, a drop in foreign trade, and other indicators of a generally depressed economic situation. Furthermore, the recession was being treated by the most prominent Communist economic theoreticians as something serious and probably continuing. The Soviet thesis, backed by the dean of Soviet economists, Varga, and by his heir-apparent, Arzumanyan, was that the American recession signaled the start of a major world crisis of overproduction. At a meeting in Prague attended by several of the Italian party's economists, Arzumanyan forecast the likelihood of "a serious depression in the U.S. economy," stating that even if the economic situation did not continue to worsen, it could not be expected to show notable improvement in the near future.[31] With such authoritative prognoses as these before them, it is hardly surprising that the PCI tried to capitalize on what seemed to be a highly promising opportunity for propaganda and action.

As it turned out, Communist expectations were grossly mistaken. By the middle of 1959 it began to be recognized that economic indexes were moving rapidly upward, that an "economic miracle" attributable in good part precisely to the beneficial effects of the Common Market was taking place in Italy. Loud opposition to the Common Market suddenly became not only unprofitable but downright foolish, and the PCI ceased making a major issue of it. It was not for some time, however, that the party leadership could begin explicitly to acknowledge, as did Amendola early in 1962, that the PCI's position had been wrong: "The coincidence of the entry into effect of the EEC with the American recession created a particular situation that led us to attribute to the EEC economic dif-

31 "Special Features of the Post-war Cycle and the Current Crisis," *World Marxist Review*, I, 1 (September 1958), pp. 61–62.

ficulties that were, instead, a consequence of the phase of the international economic cycle."[32]

The consequences of this reappraisal will be the subject of a later chapter, at which point we will also look at the CGIL's position toward the Common Market, which in many respects anticipated the party's revised appraisal. The central point to keep in mind with respect to the party's early policies toward the Common Market is that they did not represent simply a reflex action in response to the demands of Soviet policy, though this consideration played a part, but a tactical line that suited the needs of the PCI's domestic situation. There appeared to be, in short, a coincidence of interests uniting the Italian, French, and Soviet parties around the same basic position.

PEACEFUL COEXISTENCE. The coincidence of Soviet foreign and Italian Communist interests emerges with particular clarity and lack of ambiguity in relation to "the struggle for peace." The PCI, like many another Communist party, has devoted much effort over the years to linking the Soviet Union not only with military might, scientific prowess, and industrial achievement but also and most particularly with the cause of peace. The Communist "peace offensive" is an unusually flexible instrument of foreign policy, suitable for defensive action at times of external threat and weakness, for offensive action at times when the military and political balance seems relatively favorable. Its fundamental and constant purpose, whatever the circumstances, is to divide and weaken the enemy, whether by directly disrupting his military potential or by splitting off the "reactionary" and "militaristic" elements of the bourgeoisie from the "progressive" forces. Maintenance of world peace certainly also has intrinsic validity in the thermonuclear age, for the Soviets as for the West, but this fact does not cancel—indeed, may even enhance—the potential of the peace issue as a multipurpose instrument of Soviet policy.[33]

Not the least of the incidental virtues of the peace campaign is that, unlike many other techniques of foreign policy, it generally serves the interests of Western Communist parties as well as of the USSR. In the postwar period the cause of peace has performed a function for the European parties analogous to that served by anti-

---

[32] "Lotta de classe e sviluppo economico dopo la liberazione," *Tendenze del capitalismo italiano: Atti del Convegno di Roma, 23–25 marzo 1962*, Vol. I (Rome: Editori Riuniti, 1962), p. 200.

[33] A particularly lucid analysis and illustration of Soviet "peace policy" is to be found in Shulman, *Stalin's Foreign Policy Reappraised*, especially chaps. 4 and 9.

fascism during and immediately after the war, though more syn-
thetically and far less successfully: a rallying point around which
men of good will from all sectors of society could unite under the
leadership of the Communist party, directly and through its affiliated organizations. (Not that antifascism was ever wholly abandoned
as a slogan for rallying the masses and the intellectuals against the
government, especially when an artificial national crisis could be
stimulated as in Italy in July 1960; but as an issue capable of
commanding support under anything but exceptional circumstances
antifascism had lost most of its appeal by the mid-1950's.) The PCI
saw the peace issue as ideally suited both for overcoming the strong
anti-Communist sentiments of left-wing lay and Catholic groups,
softening them up for alliances in other areas of political action,
and for strengthening the militancy and political consciousness
of the working class. Here is a characteristic expression of this view,
made in reference to the PCI's efforts to stir up the Italian people
against Anglo-American actions in Lebanon and Jordan in the
summer of 1958:

> The peace movement could not help but emerge strengthened from this
> situation, in which all the conditions existed for providing an impulse to
> a renewed and still broader movement, capable of organizing and winning
> over . . . new forces from every social stratum and every political sector,
> and in particular from among the ranks of the workers and the Catholic
> intellectuals. In the atmosphere of this new phase of political struggle for
> peace, moreover, the consciousness of the working class, of Communist and
> Socialist militants, is also heightened and tempered.[34]

The peace campaign was often also intended to serve immediate
interests of Soviet foreign policy. In 1958 and early 1959 the PCI
contributed to that end by agitating in the name of peace against
installation of missile and other military bases in Italy and by
protesting loudly during the 1958 Mid-East crisis. In both instances,
mass demonstrations were organized in Rome and other major
cities, brief protest strikes called, signatures for petitions collected
from door to door, delegations of local officials dispatched to provincial and national government offices. The use of Italian airfields
to transport troops to the Middle East tied the two specific causes
together, creating the more general issue of Italian assistance to
imperialist aggression against the Arab peoples.[35]

[34] Enrico Bonazzi, "Nella lotta per la pace si e rafforzata l'unità del movimento
operaio," Rinascita, XV, 8 (August 1958), p. 495.
[35] For a sample of detailed reports of these actions, see L'Unità of July 1958;
for a summary intended for a Communist audience, see Alberto Cellini, "In the
Front Line," World Marxist Review, I, 3 (November 1958), pp. 66–68; and Velio

Campaigns of this sort, however, employing techniques of mass agitation on specific policy issues, had important limitations. To the extent that they could be readily identified with specific interests of Soviet foreign policy, the effectiveness of such efforts in mobilizing support in non-Communist working- and middle-class circles was seriously compromised. Indeed, an aggressive peace campaign aimed at thwarting Western military or political action could not be primarily intended as a means of extending Communist influence outside its own ranks; the central purposes were rather to mobilize direct mass pressure on the government and in the process to deepen the political consciousness and commitment of the working-class militant or sympathizer.

Aggressive in tone, the peace campaigns of 1958 based on protest against specific Western actions were essentially defensive in purpose, aimed more at inhibiting Italian support of the Atlantic alliance than at promoting a broad alliance of forces under Communist leadership. Instead of extending its influence, the PCI often found itself accused of being alarmist, of artificially manufacturing grave crises where none in fact existed. The Communists, on the other hand, berated others, especially the right-wing Socialists, for taking peaceful coexistence too seriously and falling into the "unscientific and un-Leninist" view that the process of international détente was irreversible and that an active peace movement was therefore unnecessary; this dangerous illusion was explained as the reason for the Socialist party's formal withdrawal from the Communist-sponsored peace partisans' movement.[36] The growing difficulty of winning Socialist collaboration for Communist-initiated peace actions must have given the party's leaders food for thought: was it not possible that mass action of the old style, linked too obviously to Soviet interests, was serving to retard rather than promote unity of action with the Socialists on other issues as well?

During 1959 the quality of the PCI's use of the peace issue began to change in response to a shift in the Soviet line. The dominant emphasis of Soviet policy shifted from what we might call the peace "struggle," understood as a defensive rear-guard action against Western military capability, toward the peace "offensive," implying a longer-term strategy of disarmament and summit negotiations aimed at creating the conditions for gradual erosion of Western economic and political strength. This approach was given its ideological basis by Khrushchev's pronouncement at the Twenty-

Spano, "The Italian People Protest Against Rocket-Launching Installations," ibid., II, 3 (March 1959), pp. 93–95.
[36] See, inter alia, Bonazzi, Rinascita, XV, 8, p. 495.

First Congress that a real possibility now existed of eliminating war, even before the complete victory of socialism.

Intensive efforts ensued to reduce international tensions and thus lay the groundwork for serious negotiations with the West on such issues as Berlin and disarmament. Soviet and Western statesmen exchanged visits—Macmillan, Gronchi, and Nixon to Moscow; Mikoyan, Kozlov, and then Khrushchev himself to the United States—and Soviet doctrinal pronouncements came increasingly to stress the importance of distinguishing between the militant and the more peacefully inclined elements of the bourgeoisie and of accepting the necessity of compromise as a way of advancing the cause. The death of Secretary of State Dulles in the spring of 1959 and the subsequent meetings at Camp David allowed President Eisenhower himself to be ranked among the proponents of peace. These demonstrations of Khrushchev's intent to promote a significant détente with the West had the critical byproduct of speeding the deterioration of Sino-Soviet relations. Soviet efforts to exert pressure on the Chinese by abrogating the agreement to provide nuclear weapons and, it appears, by making contact with Mao's domestic opponents were countered by Chinese provocation of border incidents with India, challenges to Soviet control of Communist-front organizations, and other moves.[37]

The PCI enthusiastically took up the cause of international détente, using it not only to further Soviet aims but as an increasingly promising weapon in its own campaign, then going into high gear, to capitalize on the divisions within the Christian Democratic party. The DC right, under the Pella government, was accused of collaborating with intransigent forces in the Vatican in an effort to sabotage the détente by interfering with President Gronchi's state visit to Moscow and more generally by spreading the notion that to support the cause of peace was tantamount to supporting the Communist party.[38]

We will examine more carefully in a subsequent chapter the PCI's efforts to advance its political fortunes by using the peace issue to assert and promote an identity of interest among all left-of-

[37] For an exposition of the Soviet policy of détente, see J. M. Mackintosh, *Strategy and Tactics of Soviet Foreign Policy* (New York: Oxford University Press, 1962), chap. 17, and J. M. Mackintosh, "Three Détentes, 1955–1964," in Eleanor L. Dulles and Robert D. Crane, eds., *Détente: Cold War Strategies in Transition* (New York: Praeger, 1965), especially pp. 107–111. For an analysis of Sino-Soviet relations at this time see Zagoria, *The Sino-Soviet Conflict, 1956–1961*, chaps. 8–14, and Lowenthal, *World Communism*, chap. 7.

[38] See Palmiro Togliatti, "L'Italia e la distensione," *Rinascita*, XVI, 10 (October 1959), pp. 145–148.

center forces. At this point we need only note that the search for effective grounds for collaboration with non-Communist groups clearly came to prevail over the more militant potentialities of the peace issue. In the international movement the PCI came to be one of the most active opponents of the narrow and militant view that saw in the peace offensive only an instrument for mobilizing the workers against their government. The head of the PCI's peace organization, the Partisans of Peace, wrote in the *World Marxist Review* in the spring of 1959 that the success of the peace movement depended above all on achieving successful collaboration with other forces, an impossible goal unless the Communists could overcome a narrowly instrumental conception of their own activities: "First and foremost, the other peace forces should realize that for the Communists, defense of peace is not at all an instrument in the struggle for power."[39] The Communists must not insist, he argued, that their collaborators in the peace movement accept their views on such major international questions as where responsibility rested for the origin of the cold war; otherwise it would be impossible to construct a broad front of the forces for peace.

The PCI was active in promoting support for Soviet détente strategy on an international scale as well as in Italy itself. Toward the end of November 1959 a gathering of representatives of all the European Communist parties took place in Rome on the initiative of the Gramsci Institute, the PCI's research establishment, but undoubtedly with Moscow's strong encouragement. The text of the "Appeal to All Workers and Democrats" issued after the meeting suggests a dual purpose from the Soviet standpoint.[40] It was, first, to be a sounding board for the Soviet campaign for relaxation of tensions, then at its peak following Khrushchev's trip to the United States, and for such other specific interests as a German peace treaty. It was also probably intended as a demonstration to the Chinese of the solidarity of the European parties behind the USSR, as was suggested not only by the content of the document issued but by the strong affirmation that the European parties' strength derived "from the indestructible solidarity of the Communist parties of the world, above all, with the great Communist Party of the Soviet Union."[41]

The Rome meeting, and the détente strategy as a whole, provided

[39] Velio Spano, "Some Problems of the World Peace Movement," *World Marxist Review*, II, 5 (May 1959), p. 16.

[40] "Appello di 17 partiti comunisti dei paesi capitalistici d'Europa," in *Documenti politici e direttive*, pp. 499–508; English text in *World Marxist Review*, III, 1 (January 1960), pp. 46–50.

[41] *Ibid.*, p. 50.

opportunities for the PCI to begin asserting once again its own special perspectives for Communist action in Europe. The "fascist threat" so loudly trumpeted by the French and Italian parties in their meeting the year before had been dropped from the agenda; the time was now ripe to appeal to the working class and the petty bourgeoisie for unity with the Communists, not in defense of their democratic liberties but in pursuit of a positive policy of peace and antimonopoly economic reforms. The strategy of international détente required as its natural corollary a "soft" domestic policy designed to break down anti-Communist prejudice and promote faster collaboration with other groups—an Italian reformist policy, in short, not a French sectarian one.

It is revealing to compare the articles on the meeting written for the *World Marxist Review* by Alicata on the Italian side and Figuieres on the French; while Alicata stressed the need for structural reforms and cooperation with Social Democrats and Catholics, Figuieres highlighted the need for action by the masses to defend democratic gains against the fascists. In the tug of war between the two parties, the Rome document was not an unqualified victory for the Italian line, for it contained some clearly French orientations as well. On balance, however, the document reflected the Italian perspective, as is suggested by Alicata's reference to it as "a policy document of considerable importance"; the French spokesman did not similarly highlight its significance.[42]

Italian Response to the Chinese Offensive

The Soviet Union's intensive pursuit of a peaceful coexistence strategy may have been creating conditions favorable to Italian Communist interests at home and in Europe, but it was having precisely the opposite effect to the East. As Soviet relations with the West improved, those with China suffered increasing deterioration. In the spring of 1960, the shooting down of the U-2 and the subsequent collapse of the summit meeting in Paris gave the Chinese an opportunity to launch a counterattack. Khrushchev appeared determined not to allow the incidents to wreck his policy toward the West; Soviet words and actions toward the United States grew tougher for a time, as considerations of prestige both within and outside the movement demanded, but the long-term strategy continued to be defended against Chinese attack.

[42] Mario Alicata, "Solidarity between the Communist Parties," *World Marxist Review*, III, 4 (April 1960), pp. 50–52, and Leo Figuieres, "Defend and Develop Democracy," *ibid.*, pp. 52–55.

Given the substantial coincidence of Soviet and Italian Communist interests with respect to the West, it is not surprising that the PCI strongly endorsed the Khrushchev line. While U.S. political and military circles were to be condemned for their aggressive actions, and the Socialists berated for trying to divide the blame for events equally between the two big powers, the PCI argued that the process of détente was based on the objective reality of the relationship of forces and could not be disturbed by rash unilateral actions of the imperialists.[43] That this was anything but the Chinese view was made unmistakably plain to the Italians and the rest of the Communist movement at the General Council meeting of the World Federation of Trade Unions (WFTU) held in Peking in early June. The meeting seemed to offer the Chinese an ideal opportunity to profit from the apparent bankruptcy of Soviet policy and to challenge its basic premises before an international audience of Communists and other leftist forces from the underdeveloped world.[44]

The Chinese acted by organizing separate meetings of the Communists who were attending the WFTU meeting in their trade union capacity so as to put forward more bluntly than was possible in the general sessions their antirevisionist arguments. For this they would subsequently be accused of "fractionalism." Chinese resistance to Soviet hegemony was moving from the ideological to the organizational plane, a fact whose significance was certainly not lost on those present. The CGIL delegation, including both Communists and Socialists, was at the forefront of the battle, defending Soviet policy and resisting the Chinese contention that the trade unions, instead of misleading the workers about the illusory possibilities for disarmament and peace as long as imperialism still existed, should be leading a frontal assault on the capitalist system.[45]

---

[43] "I compiti attuali nella lotta per la pace," Risoluzione della Direzione, May 26, 1960, in *Documenti politici dal IX al X Congresso* (Rome: A cura della Sezione Stampa e Propaganda della Direzione del Partito Comunista Italiano, 1962), pp. 76–84.

[44] For further comment on this meeting see Zagoria, *The Sino-Soviet Conflict, 1956–1961*, pp. 320–323, and William E. Griffith, *Albania and the Sino-Soviet Rift* (Cambridge, Mass.: The M.I.T. Press, 1963), pp. 37–38. The fullest documentation is in "Current Background" (U.S. Consulate General, Hong Kong), No. 620, June 22, 1960, and No. 621, June 27, 1960. The most extensive open criticism within the Communist movement of Chinese behavior at Peking is that contained in Maurice Thorez' speech at the Moscow conference in November 1960 and in the memorandum submitted by the PCF; see "Déclaration de la délégation" and "Interventions de Maurice Thorez," *Problèmes du mouvement communiste international* (Paris: Edité par le Comité Central du Parti Communiste Français, 1963), pp. 36 and 44–45.

[45] See the summary of the Chinese position by the Socialist CGIL leader Vittorio Foa, who attended the meeting: *Avanti!*, June 14, 1960.

It was wholly logical that the Italians should have been one of the most vigorous antagonists of the Chinese line. The PCI was, as we have seen, fully committed to the peaceful coexistence strategy. On the trade union front, moreover, the CGIL had long been a proponent of measures to promote united action with other unions, in Italy and in all of Europe; the Chinese position threatened to undermine completely the CGIL's efforts to turn the WFTU away from its traditionally sectarian behavior in this and other respects. Furthermore, the Chinese went well beyond the trade union sphere and challenged the Italian party's broader European strategy, explicitly rejecting the resolutions of the December 1959 Rome meeting as a concession to revisionism.[46] At Peking the Italians were engaged therefore in defending their own and not merely Soviet interests.

This first direct clash with the Chinese gives us an initial opportunity to ask how the Italian party viewed the state of affairs created in the Communist movement by the now semipublic Sino-Soviet confrontation. Did they regard it as a threat to their own interests or as an opportunity for gain? In discussing the Peking meeting, William Griffith has suggested that the Italians, along with the Poles, tended to welcome the situation, seeing in it an opportunity for enhancing their own autonomy:

The most important reason for this "rightist" tendency, however, was the increased possibility for maneuver which the public emergence of Sino-Soviet differences gave to smaller Communist parties. China needed Albania; the Soviet Union needed the Polish and Italian Communists, both of whom could hope to exact a certain increased freedom of expression of their genuinely rightist views as a price for their support against China. Not surprisingly, therefore, the Italian Communists made particularly clear, as did, albeit less so, the Poles, their strong opposition to the Chinese.[47]

It is beyond dispute, as the events of recent years have abundantly shown, that many of the smaller parties did gain an increased measure of autonomy from the Soviet Union in consequence of the Sino-Soviet split. Whether they confidently anticipated this result as early as 1960, however, is open to question. Although the evidence is scanty, there are indications to suggest that the Italian party feared exactly the contrary, that its freedom of action might actually be restricted as a result of the Chinese challenge.

The PCI appears to have been concerned that the Soviet Union, in rallying its forces to meet the Chinese threat, might in effect declare a state of emergency in the movement, applying strong

[46] "Interventions de Maurice Thorez," *Problèmes du mouvement*, p. 36.
[47] Griffith, *Albania*, p. 38.

pressure on all its allies to hew the Soviet line. The Italians had been through such a situation more than once, most recently during the antirevisionist campaign against the Yugoslavs following the November 1957 meeting. Soviet pressures to conform might be manifested in different ways. One possibility was for the sake of unity that the Soviets might be led to make verbal concessions to the Chinese, resulting in pronouncements unsatisfactory from the Italian point of view. This did in fact happen at Peking, where compromises had to be made in the final resolution which, in the words of the Socialist leader, Vittorio Foa, was "far from satisfying, especially to European trade union people."[48] It would happen again at Moscow the following November, where the PCI was obliged to swallow a fresh condemnation of Yugoslav revisionism.

A related possibility was that the PCI itself would be inhibited from raising controversial issues out of a reluctance to cause the Soviets additional trouble. There is some evidence that this mechanism was also at work at the WFTU meeting. According to Foa, the Italian delegation at Peking had planned to raise on that occasion many of the basic issues about WFTU policies and procedures that did not finally come to light until its Fifth Congress, a year and a half later; they did not do so because they found it impossible to embarrass the Russians by challenging the WFTU leadership in the face of such a flagrant Chinese assault.[49]

It took only a few days after the close of the WFTU meeting for the Soviets to begin brandishing their double-edged ideological weapons—aimed primarily against the Chinese, but pointed also at others who might be tempted to stray from the narrow road of truth. N. Matkovsky, writing in *Pravda* to mark the fortieth anniversary of Lenin's *Left-Wing Communism—An Infantile Disorder,* quoted both Lenin and Khrushchev to the effect that the Soviet model, the path of the October Revolution, was valid for all Communist parties: "The search for a separate path to socialism for each country, individually, the desire to build socialism on the basis of imperialist handouts or attempts to skip entire historic stages serve only the enemies of the working class interested in weakening socialism."[50] The primary targets in this case were of course Yugoslavia and China, but Italian sensitivities could hardly

48 *Avanti!,* June 14, 1960.

49 Interview, Rome, June 1964. Foa was a member of the Italian delegation. The Socialist members of the delegation were doubtless more eager to raise the issues than their Communist colleagues, who quite likely welcomed an excuse to postpone the confrontation.

50 *Pravda,* June 12, 1956; quoted from *CDSP,* XII, 24, p. 4.

help but be aroused by a generalized indictment that branded the principle of separate roads to socialism as embracing "false, anti-Marxist views."[51]

It seems hardly coincidental that Togliatti decided at this time to publish a long article on Lenin reviewing his writings about Italy and his attitudes toward capitalism and the socialist revolution. The largest part of the article expounded Lenin's dedication to the principle of peaceful coexistence and his struggles against left extremists as well as opportunists. But this contribution to the anti-Chinese campaign, undoubtedly the chief purpose of the article, was accompanied by a lengthy exegesis of Lenin's belief in the necessity of adapting basic revolutionary principles to the needs of individual countries. "The revolution in Italy," Lenin is quoted as saying, "will not develop as it did in Russia," to which observation Togliatti added his own suggestive comment:

I do not know whether there is anyone who will be surprised at this clarity of reference to the peculiarities of individual countries, made precisely at the moment in which a common task had been placed on the order of the day for all. It will not surprise anyone having a familiarity with Lenin's work, in which this idea is never forgotten. It is clear, however, that the awareness of the truth that it contains was somewhat obscured in successive periods and had to be re-established, not without a certain effort.[52]

This pointed reference to national peculiarities was beyond much doubt intended for Soviet eyes. By including a defense of the principle of national autonomy in a document intended primarily to support the Soviet case against the Chinese, Togliatti was showing that while he accepted responsibility to share in the "common task," he was uneasy about the direction of the Soviet counterattack. The Italian party would object, he implied, if the Chinese or any other party were to be condemned for having developed its own special path to socialism. The legitimacy of this principle, understood by Lenin and recognized afresh after the Twentieth Congress, could not now be denied.

Togliatti's affirmation could conceivably be interpreted as an effort to seize an opportunity presented by the Sino-Soviet split to assert the PCI's claim to greater autonomy. In my judgment, the value to be put on the statement is more defensive than self-assertive. The general context suggests that Togliatti was concerned more to protect his party from a new wave of Moscow-enforced

51 *Ibid.*
52 "Lenin e il nostro partito," *Rinascita*, XVII, 5 (May 1960), p. 329.

orthodoxy than to assert the need for a greater measure of autonomy. At least, there is no positive evidence to suggest that Togliatti and his party greeted the outbreak of open Soviet-Chinese hostility with enthusiasm, as an opportunity to promote Italian interests in the movement. It is more likely that they felt concerned and wary, unsure of the consequences of the split and aware that the PCI, as a relatively minor player in the game, would have little to say about its outcome.

The Moscow Conference of Eighty-One Parties

The Chinese challenge at the WFTU meeting in Peking did not go unanswered. The Soviet leaders responded with a series of articles in *Pravda* following which, on the occasion of the Rumanian party Congress in late June, Khrushchev personally carried the fight to the enemy, defending all the basic tenets of the Soviet line against the attacks of Mao's representative, P'eng Chen. The Italian party, after discussing the situation in its July Central Committee meeting, issued statements approving the decisions made at Bucharest.[53]

Togliatti made a speech on that occasion which, while basically in full accord with the Soviet line of the moment, contained some interesting differences of emphasis, highlighted by *Pravda*'s deletion of certain sensitive passages in its version of the speech.[54] Whereas some of the cuts doubtless reflected the usual shortage of space, others indicated unwillingness to endorse the positions involved. The first deletion was of Togliatti's mild but unmistakable acknowledgment that the intransigent Chinese attitude toward the United States was, after all, understandable:

One should add that the aggressiveness of American imperialism is manifested in particularly violent ways against People's China. . . . The situation in the Far East on the periphery of the Chinese border has shown itself to be particularly acute, and we cannot fail to take this fact into account in discussing the problems that now concern us.[55]

By eliminating this point entirely from Togliatti's listing of the factors influencing the current international situation, the Soviet leaders showed their unwillingness to excuse Chinese behavior as

53 "Approvate le decisioni di Bucarest," in *Documenti politici dal IX al X Congresso*, pp. 96–97; "Il Congresso di Bucarest," *Rinascita*, XVII, 7–8 (July–August 1960), pp. 497–498. See *L'Unità*, July 19 and 22, 1960, for speeches by Luigi Longo and Giuliano Pajetta, respectively, both strongly supporting the Soviet line.

54 *L'Unità*, July 24, 1960. *Pravda*'s summary appeared on July 28.

55 *Ibid.*

a natural response to the direct military danger of imperialist action in the Far East. To do so would be to concede implicitly the difficulty of developing a united general line for the entire movement.

Togliatti, for his part, presumably felt it necessary to provide his party with some sort of explanation of the reasons for Sino-Soviet conflict on basic strategic issues. The one offered was consistent with the general position developed in 1956–1957 to the effect that differences in the objective situations and phases of development of the various Communist states and parties would inevitably require greater flexibility and permissible variety in the policy responses of individual parties. This was, in Togliatti's view, one of the inescapable consequences of a polycentric system. Such a note of cautious sympathy for the Chinese attitude would be expressed on other later occasions by members of the PCI, the sentiment generally being that although the Chinese were dangerously wrong in their conclusions, one could all the same understand their reactions. By taking such a line Togliatti could assume his favorite posture of reasonable mediator between opposed tendencies, conciliating such pro-Chinese sentiments as there were in the party without at the same time seriously compromising the PCI's pro-Soviet position on the substantive issues.

The second interesting deletion from Togliatti's text illustrates a different but equally characteristic tendency. In discussing the characteristics of modern war, Togliatti made some observations that *Pravda* reported with unusual selectivity. The old distinction between troops on the front line and the civilian population, he argued, is no longer tenable:

> *Even the population of nations not directly involved in war are on that line because of the deadly nature of atomic clouds.* In the second place, the present military instruments of mass destruction are such that their use is destined to cause total destruction of *all* centers of human civilization *as well as of human, animal, and vegetable life, making it impossible to resume any human activity whatsoever for a length of time we cannot today calculate.* In the third place, since both sides possess these weapons of mass destruction, it is impossible for the initiator of a war to calculate the consequences to himself under any circumstance. . . . *If one side suffers total destruction, the other will suffer it too* [italics added].[56]

The italicized passages, deleted by *Pravda*'s editors, were a bit stronger than Soviet pronouncements had yet become concerning the destructive characteristics of modern war, although Khrushchev had by then gone so far as to declare that "millions of people

[56] *Ibid.*

might burn in the conflagration of hydrogen explosions, and for some states a nuclear war would be literally a catastrophe."[57] In addition to the tactical consideration of not wishing to appear excessively fearful of nuclear war, and thus "soft" by Chinese standards, Khrushchev was undoubtedly constrained by the fact that this issue had played a prominent part in his own accusations against Malenkov in 1955. At that time, Togliatti had weighed in on Malenkov's side of the argument with a speech warning of the universal destructiveness of nuclear war.

From the PCI's vantage point, the desirability of playing upon popular fear of nuclear war was obvious, just as it had been five years before, but Soviet propagandists were evidently not yet authorized to go quite that far. Within the next few weeks, however, an article in *Kommunist* took the plunge, asserting that thermonuclear war "would lead to the complete destruction of the main centers of civilization and the wiping out of whole nations. . . ."[58] What had appeared at first to be an Italian deviation from the Soviet line turned out to be only an anticipation of it.[59] Togliatti may or may not have been aware when he spoke that the "destruction of world civilization" line was about to be rehabilitated; it hardly matters, for the main direction of Soviet thought on the question was clear enough. More interesting is the light the episode sheds on one of the broader consequences for the PCI of the Soviet dispute with the Chinese: as ideological weapons on both sides were sharpened, the Russians began to articulate and defend positions previously implicit only in their general line, thus bringing them closer in many respects to the preferred positions of the PCI.

[57] Nikita S. Khrushchev, speech to Rumanian party Congress, June 21, 1960; quoted in Hudson *et al.*, *The Sino-Soviet Dispute*, pp. 132–139, at p. 133.

[58] A. Belyakov and F. Burlatsky, *Kommunist*, No. 13, 1960; translation in Hudson *et al.*, *The Sino-Soviet Dispute*, p. 154.

[59] This is an instance that appears to lend support to the hypothesis put forward by Giorgio Galli (see Chapter One, pp. 2–3) that until late 1963 a general division of labor existed between the Soviet and Italian parties whereby the PCI was permitted on occasion to anticipate positions only later publicly assumed by the Soviet Union. Galli's suggestion, however, that such anticipation occurred in response to an agreed-upon "distribution of roles" seems to me to attribute an unduly mechanical and apolitical quality to relations between the two parties. There may have been occasions on which the PCI has clearly floated trial balloons for the USSR, although no convincing cases come to mind. A more likely possibility is that Togliatti, relying on political intuition, had to judge for himself when he could get away with voicing an attitude at variance with the current Soviet line. Often he succeeded; at other times, as in June 1956 when other considerations were paramount, he evidently failed.

It having been agreed at Bucharest that a fresh gesture should be made toward reaching a détente in the Communist world, a summit meeting of the parties was called. Intensive preparatory discussions on a draft declaration got under way in September, and the meeting itself, attended by representatives of 81 Communist parties, convened in Moscow in November and early December. The conference resolved no issues, although it may have clarified them for the parties hitherto only marginally involved; it ended with a compromise declaration structured basically along Soviet lines but containing qualifications at every juncture reflecting the Chinese position.[60]

On the major questions of international strategy debated at the Moscow meeting little need be added to what has already been said. The majority of parties, including the Italian, firmly supported the Soviet positions as they had emerged in the Twentieth and Twenty-First Congresses and the 1957 Moscow Declaration. Despite certain concessions of phrasing and emphasis, peaceful coexistence was confirmed as the basic general line of the movement, and the possibility of preventing war was strongly reasserted. Longo, as head of the PCI delegation, assisted the anti-Chinese campaign by lauding Khrushchev and by making special reference to the great value of international détente for the class struggle in capitalist countries: "During the year the Italian Communist Party has carried out a major supporting action to the Soviet initiative for easing of tensions and has drawn from it great assistance for its own political action."[61] The disastrous consequences of war were not dramatized in the final declaration as strongly as Togliatti had done in July, but a step forward, from the PCI's perspective, was taken in the recognition that there was no more pressing task for the Communist

[60] See "Statement, Meeting of Representatives of Communist and Workers' Parties, Moscow, 1960," *World Marxist Review*, III, 12 (December 1960). For an analysis of the meeting see Zagoria, *The Sino-Soviet Conflict, 1956–1961*, chap. 15, based on the evidence at hand through 1961; and William E. Griffith, "The November 1960 Moscow Meeting: A Preliminary Reconstruction," *The China Quarterly*, No. 11 (July–September 1962), pp. 38–57, which takes advantage of the materials that became available during the following year. More recent sources are listed in Griffith, *The Sino-Soviet Rift*, p. 19, footnote 14.

[61] "Primo intervento del compagno Luigi Longo a nome della delegazione del PCI," *Interventi della delegazione del Partito Comunista Italiano alla Conferenza degli 81 Partiti comunisti ed operai* (Rome: A cura della Sezione centrale di Stampa e propaganda della Direzione del PCI, January 15, 1962), p. 52. In addition to Longo's two speeches, this pamphlet contains the lengthy memorandum submitted by the PCI to the conference preparatory commission and a letter addressed to Khrushchev by the PCI delegation urging certain changes in the draft declaration then still under negotiation.

movement than "safeguarding humanity against a global thermonuclear disaster" which might "reduce key centers of world industry and culture to ruins."[62]

An advance toward the position advocated by the Italian party
also appeared to have been taken with respect to the issue about
which so much had been heard in 1956–1957, the extent of permissible diversity in pursuing separate national roads toward a
socialist society. It is true that the argument with the Chinese over
the possibility of peaceful transition was not resolved; precisely the
same equivocal language as had been agreed upon for the 1957
Declaration was again employed, demonstrating the existence of a
stalemate on that question. Nevertheless, on a more general level,
the emphasis of the Statement did visibly shift several degrees away
from the earlier assertion of the universal character of the passage
from capitalism to socialism. Whereas in 1957 it had been stated
dogmatically that every socialist revolution was "governed by a
number of basic laws applicable in all countries," nine of which
had been specified, the Moscow Statement of 1960 merely referred in
general terms to "the universal truth of Marxism-Leninism regarding the socialist revolution and socialist construction" and
warned against "undue emphasis on the role of national peculiarities." The weight of the document came down more strongly than
before on the need for all parties to be independent and equal and
to "shape their policies according to the specific conditions in their
respective countries."[63]

This shift of emphasis probably reflected both an attempt to
reassure other parties of Soviet tolerance and a belated Soviet recognition that significant institutional diversity did in fact exist in the
socialist countries and was if anything likely to increase. Neither
the Poles nor the Chinese, to take perhaps the most striking example, were about to reorganize their agricultural systems after the
Soviet model. As in 1957, the Polish, Hungarian, and Italian parties
were in the forefront of those stressing the importance of adapting
"universal laws" to the special situation of each country.

It has been suggested that the Chinese "almost certainly" joined
those favoring an emphasis on "national peculiarities" out of a
desire to protect their domestic autonomy from attacks such as the
Soviets had been making on the Commune program and the policies
of the Great Leap Forward.[64] Although plausible on the face of it,
it seems to me questionable to assume that the Chinese would have

62 "Statement," *World Marxist Review*, III, 12, p. 11.
63 *Ibid.*, p. 10.
64 Zagoria, *The Sino-Soviet Conflict, 1956–1961*, p. 364.

gone far to defend the *principle* of stressing national differences as against generally applicable laws. The entire character of their strategy within the movement—insistence on formal Soviet headship, constant stress on unity based on ideological principle, attacks on Communist tactics in Europe designed to respond to the special circumstances of the capitalist world—rested on an assumption of the need for monolithic unity. As a party seeking ultimately to replace the Soviet general line with its own, the Chinese party could not consistently have moved far toward weakening the entire concept of a general line.[65] The Chinese attitude must, therefore, be clearly distinguished from that of the Poles, Hungarians, and Italians. These smaller parties, having no pretensions about the eventual possibility of substituting their own general line for that of the USSR, were in the first instance concerned to secure themselves against the imposition of unsuitable doctrines and institutional practices from whatever quarter.

The results of the Moscow conference, despite the increased acknowledgment of the importance of local conditions, were by no means wholly satisfactory to the Italian party. It was evident, for example, that the Soviet leadership, despite its defense of the principle, did not yet fully accept the possibility of a parliamentary, peaceful transition to socialism for a country such as Italy. In his January report on the Moscow conference, Khrushchev repeated the qualification he had made at the Twentieth Congress that a violent transition to power would be inevitable in countries "where capitalism is still strong and still commands a huge military and police apparatus."[66] The PCI leadership, whatever its own estimate of the probabilities, would doubtless have preferred that such opinions, directly at odds with its own domestic line, be kept within the Communist family. More disturbing than such ambiguous pronouncements about the future, however, was the position taken at Moscow with respect to the tangible case that most mattered to the PCI, that of Yugoslavia.

The Italian non-Communist left had since 1957, and with good

[65] Premier Ulbricht in a postconference speech indicated that the perennial issue of "universal laws" had again been a subject of controversy. By implication he accused the Chinese of two quite incompatible heresies: "Someone," he said, had objected to the very concept of a general line, and "someone" had raised the question of "who it is who determines what is truth and what complies with the principles of Marxist-Leninist doctrine." *Neues Deutschland,* December 18, 1960; quoted in Zagoria, *The Sino-Soviet Conflict, 1956–1961,* p. 345. The second of the two charges would seem to jibe better with the CCP's subsequent attitudes.

[66] "For New Victories for the World Communist Movement," *World Marxist Review,* IV, 1 (January 1961), p. 22. This report appears to have been substantially identical to Khrushchev's speech to the Moscow conference itself.

reason, fastened upon Yugoslavia as the most important test of Soviet policy toward the Communist parties. As long as the Yugoslav effort to develop an independent and original brand of socialism continued to be greeted with hostility, the PCI would not find it easy to persuade even a potentially sympathetic audience of the genuineness of its own pretensions to an autonomous policy responsive to Italian rather than Soviet priorities.[67] How could the PCI, furthermore, convincingly argue for unity and collaboration between Communist and other left-wing groups, a policy presumably responsive to Soviet European interests as well as to Italian needs, in the face of a continuing Communist repudiation of Yugoslavia, the country best fitted to serve as a bridge between the two worlds?

The Italian delegation at Moscow pointed out these considerations in a letter proposing amendments to the draft statement on Yugoslavia:

We cannot take a position toward the Yugoslav Communist League that conflicts so radically with our attitude toward the social democrats in general, the left-wing socialist parties, the labor and working-class organizations of many countries, and even many of their leaders.

We should like here to point out a fact that often escapes some comrades who do not work in capitalist countries. The tone in which we speak of our quarrel with the Yugoslav Communist League is one of the yardsticks by which the social democratic parties and unions, and public opinion in general, evaluate the sincerity of our unity policies and our capacity for collaboration with groups ideologically and politically remote from us.[68]

The Italian amendments were said to include a "severe condemnation" of Yugoslav positions, but "in a less bitter and offensive tone, such as not to create any irremediable break with Yugoslav public opinion. . . ."[69] They also "tried to reduce to more accurate proportions the influence of Yugoslav revisionism today within the international Communist movement" and proposed to eliminate entirely the thesis that one of the basic tasks of the Communist parties was to "isolate Yugoslavia from the workers' movement."[70] To what extent, if any, the final Statement reflected the Italian view on this

---

[67] For an illustration of the way in which the outcome of the Yugoslav issue at the Moscow conference was used against the PCI, see Pietro Nenni in *Avanti!*, December 11, 1960. The PCI insisted in reply to such criticism that attacks on Yugoslavia in no way implied a rejection of the principle of national roads to socialism. See, for example, the rebuttal to Ferruccio Parri's comments in the January 1961 issue of *Il Ponte,* and Fausto Gullo, "Parri e gli 81," *Rinascita,* XVIII, 4 (April 1961), pp. 369–371.

[68] "Lettera della delegazione del PCI al compagno N. S. Krusciov e alla delegazione del PCUS," *Interventi della delegazione,* p. 76.

[69] *Ibid.,* p. 75.

[70] *Ibid.,* p. 76.

point is unclear, for we lack the text of either their proposed amendment or the draft to which they were objecting. The Statement does not contain an explicit proposal in so many words for "isolating" the Yugoslavs, but it comes very close by accusing them of "subversion" and calling for "an active struggle to shield the Communist and workers' movement from the anti-Leninist ideas of the Yugoslav revisionists. . . ." Longo subsequently professed to be satisfied with the outcome, but at the same time violated its spirit by assuring the PCI Central Committee that the Statement did not prohibit "meeting of the minds and common actions on given problems" with Yugoslav organizations.[71]

The Italians made an effort at Moscow to do more than simply ensure their domestic autonomy. The most interesting and original aspect of their position was the theme that capitalist Europe was not being given sufficiently high priority in the Communist scheme of things. The PCI's memorandum to the conference preparatory commission stressed in various ways the potentially "decisive role of the European working class in the current world situation":

We think the conference should indicate that capitalist Europe constitutes a key position of the organized forces of the world-wide working class, even though it also represents one of the key bastions of world imperialism, and even though recent years have brought an increase in the reactionary movements and in the inclination of its leading capitalist circles toward cold war policies.

It seems to us that the action of the Communist parties can suffer seriously as a result of underestimating the role of the working class and the other strata—intellectual and worker strata—in capitalist Europe in the struggle for peace, democracy, and socialism.[72]

The basic premise for this assertion was the conviction that lay at the root of the polycentrist idea: that the differences between the socialist, capitalist, and underdeveloped regions of the world were

[71] L'Unità, December 19, 1960. There is insufficient evidence to permit an unambiguous interpretation of the interplay between the Italian and Soviet parties on this issue. It does seem reasonably clear that the Soviets would, all things being equal, have preferred to take a less intransigent stand toward the Yugoslavs but felt obliged to concede something to Chinese pressure on this score. On this assumption, the Italian amendment could possibly have been a Soviet-inspired maneuver intended to strengthen their hand in the negotiations. Griffith interprets it in this light; see The China Quarterly, No. 11, p. 54. It is also possible, and seems to me more likely, that the Italians may have been expressing an independently felt concern at Soviet readiness to concede too much to the Chinese, with the further motive that at some future date it might prove useful to them at home to have gone on record in favor of a more liberal position.

[72] "Promemoria della delegazione italiana alla commissione preparatoria," Interventi della delegazione, p. 36.

so great as to require a new flexibility and variety in the Communist response. This conviction had been acquiring new and more threatening meaning as a result of the increasingly assertive Chinese view, expressed so clearly at Peking a few months before, that the center of world revolution lay in the underdeveloped world and that Communist resources, political and ideological, should be allocated accordingly. It was not only the Chinese, furthermore, who were turning their faces toward the less developed nations. The Soviet Union too seemed to be shifting its energies toward the diplomatic and revolutionary possibilities inherent in the independence movement sweeping the globe. The PCI appeared to feel it necessary to reassert Europe's traditionally dominant place in world revolutionary strategy and to remind the Soviets that it was in the capitalist West that their most vital interests lay.

Communist action in the West has not lived up to its potential, the PCI insisted: the campaign for united action with other groups "is meeting with great difficulty"[73] and "the political influence of the Communist parties is inferior to the influence they have in the trade union movement. . . ."[74] In the Italian view, the failure was to be attributed basically to the inability of the parties to move beyond sectarian attacks against the social democrats onto more positive ground, developing the points of common interest that would permit collaboration in the struggle for peace and democratic social reforms. The Communist appeal "to the workers and democrats" of Europe elaborated at the Rome conference the year before would be nothing but ineffectual propaganda, the PCI maintained, unless the parties learned to act in such a way as to destroy anti-Communist prejudice and participate in serious debate with social democratic circles. In sum, while the PCI explicitly and modestly disclaimed any intent to offer the Italian experience as "a model for all to follow," it was in fact urging a European strategy paralleling the one being applied in its own political domain.

These arguments were familiar, having been advanced consistently, though quietly, since 1956. Togliatti had said similar things at the 1957 conference. The Italian presentation at Moscow did, however, contain one new and important line of thought strongly reinforcing its contention that Europe merited higher priority. Although the conclusions of the Rome conference were basically correct, the PCI's position paper maintained, the problem of Communist strategy in Europe should be re-examined in the light of an

---

[73] *Ibid.*, p. 25.
[74] *Ibid.*, p. 30.

important new fact: the recent and remarkable economic progress of Europe. The success of the European economy in resisting the effects of the American recession of 1957–1958 and the subsequent high growth rate of production in Europe as compared to the United States "permit us to state that capitalist Europe today is economically independent and that it is capable of and needs competition with the other imperialist countries such as has not been true for the past 20 years."[75]

This picture of a capitalist Europe "which is expanding and demonstrating its vitality and energy" not only clashed with the standard Marxist image of a decaying, crisis-ridden economic system; by explicitly pointing to the growing independence of Europe from the United States, it also provided the basic premise for a new assessment of Europe's role in Communist world strategy.[76] As long as Europe could be regarded as a mere appendage of the United States, economically and politically dependent, then the role of the European parties was logically of secondary importance: a direct assault on American imperialism, *à la Chinoise,* was the order of the day. But if Europe were beginning to acquire an independent role in world politics, successfully competing with the United States, the Communist effort should be to encourage the process, deepening the contradictions between the European nations and the center of world capitalism. These conclusions were not explicitly drawn in the PCI's memorandum, but the implications were clear.

The Italians did draw one specific policy conclusion from their analysis of European economic progress. They argued that the increasingly close collaboration among the European monopolies required revision of Communist attitudes and action toward international bodies such as the Common Market. They acknowledged that the very nature of monopolies and the law of uneven development of capitalism tended to make agreements between the big monopolies rather fragile, but they maintained that the Communist parties must nevertheless accept the fact that agreements had been made and institutions created. The Communist position could no longer be limited to simple protest; the parties and their labor unions had to meet the united capitalist front with a united front and integrated strategy of their own. Among other things, the Communist forces should fight to achieve representation within the European organizations: "The very act of denouncing the activities

75 *Ibid.*, p. 33.
76 *Ibid.*, pp. 33–34.

of the monopolies and mobilizing the masses of the workers can be facilitated by the presence of the legitimate representatives of the working class in these organizations."[77] As we shall see in a later chapter, the attitudes and tactics suggested here had been part of the stock in trade of the CGIL for several years; now the PCI itself was beginning to argue a case that would by early 1962 develop into a full-fledged controversy in the Communist world.

As mentioned earlier in the chapter, the PCI's basic premise of growing European economic independence from the United States had by this time been accepted as the official Soviet view. Nevertheless, Soviet doctrine and policy on the issue of European integration was still hesitant and ambivalent concerning both de Gaulle's potential role in world politics and the possibility of Britain's entry into the Common Market. Given this uncertain and evolving orientation, the Italian Communists saw the possibility of influencing the course of debate and political action.

The main foe, on this issue as on so many others, was Thorez, who continued stubbornly to insist on the original Communist treatment of the Common Market as an instrument of U.S. imperialism. At the Moscow conference Thorez maintained that "the dependence of certain fundamental branches of the [French] economy on the United States is worsening," and that de Gaulle's "whims for independence" could not cover up his firm attachment to the "aggressive Atlantic bloc coalition."[78] The appeal to French nationalism was still directed against de Gaulle's capitulation to American and German monopoly capitalism. At Moscow, therefore, the French and Italian parties joined in backing the Soviets against the Chinese challenge, but contended with each other for influence over the direction of Communist strategy in Europe.

The PCI's efforts to shift Communist priorities somewhat toward the European scene were not notably successful. The conference Statement dealt with European strategy only perfunctorily and in traditional terms, and both Longo's report to the PCI Central Committee and Togliatti's assessment of the conference reflected positive dissatisfaction with its results.[79] They urged renewed discussion of these questions, particularly economic problems, by the Communist parties of Europe, thereby serving notice to the French in particular that the Italian line would continue to be pressed when the occasion arose.

[77] *Ibid.*, pp. 39–40.

[78] "Interventions de Maurice Thorez," *Problèmes du mouvement*, p. 24.

[79] See Palmiro Togliatti, "Commenti alla conferenza di Mosca," *Rinascita*, XVIII, 1 (January 1961), p. 22.

These various issues of international Communist strategy gave tangible expression to the question of organization and power that lay just beneath the surface and in reality dominated the Moscow conference. The key issue at Moscow, given urgency by Chinese "subversive" tactics at the Peking WFTU meeting, was the classic one of "fractionalism": could the Chinese be made to accept a ban against factional activity, against persistent efforts by a minority to pursue its own course in the face of decisions reached collectively by all the fraternal parties?[80]

The European parties gave the Russians their unanimous backing against the Chinese contention, justified by reference to Lenin's behavior in pre-Revolutionary days, that a minority need not be bound by the decisions of a majority when these were wrong and would be proven so by the course of history. There was, however, a characteristic difference between the French and the Italian position on this question. Thorez argued in favor of the draft the Soviets had originally presented to the preparatory commission, which had contained an explicit ban on factionalism in the movement.[81] Although this formulation had been adamantly rejected by the Chinese during the preparatory meeting, the question had been reintroduced at the conference itself through an amendment proposed jointly by the Cuban and Brazilian parties. The Italian delegation, while agreeing "wholeheartedly that the Statement should exclude any possibility of factional subversion by one party toward the fraternal parties or within the international organizations," nevertheless maintained that an explicit admonition against such activity was unnecessary. Longo urged instead a more positive statement of the criteria governing relations between the parties and submitted an amendment to this effect.[82] Since the Soviets were not ready to accept the probable consequence of a Chinese walkout over the issue, they had to accept a compromise such as the Italians were urging. The final Statement did not explicitly refer to the binding character of the decisions reached, although Khrushchev tried to interpret the results of the meeting in that sense when he insisted in his speech after the conference that "each party will strictly and undeviatingly abide by these decisions in everything it does."[83]

80 For amplification of this point see Griffith, *The China Quarterly*, No. 11, especially pp. 41–45 and 55–57.

81 "Interventions de Maurice Thorez," *Problèmes du mouvement*, p. 35.

82 "Lettera della delegazione," *Interventi della delegazione*, p. 77.

83 "For New Victories in the World Communist Movement," *World Marxist Review*, IV, 1, p. 26. The Moscow Statement contained only general assertions regarding the need to maintain inviolate the unity of the movement. Thorez

The Chinese attempted to blunt the charge of factionalism by making two proposals that appeared on the surface intended to strengthen rather than disrupt the unity of the movement. The first was to urge the creation of a secretariat or other permanent co-ordinating body, presumably as a means of introducing a permanent Chinese veto into international Communist affairs. The proposal was rejected, and the Italian party, long an opponent of such a device, was understandably gratified to have the issue settled "with the utmost clarity and without any possibility of misunderstanding."[84] The second Chinese proposal was that the Soviet party be formally designated as head of the Communist world. The Russians, who had not urged this formula even in 1957, were by now firmly set against it.[85] Not only did such a slogan render virtually impossible an eventual reconciliation with Tito, but it was now clearly being used as a backhanded Chinese weapon against the Soviet party. As Thorez said in Moscow, "under the cover of such a formula attempts are being made at injuring the prestige of the Soviet Communist party and the authority of its leadership, in particular that of Comrade Khrushchev."[86]

The terms in which Thorez presented the issue, however, made it perfectly plain that from his standpoint, and presumably that of the Soviets as well, rejection of the form was not intended to imply repudiation of the substance. He called for "concrete recognition of the pre-eminent role" of the CPSU, adding that "the unity we need is the voluntary but real unity of all the detachments of our movement about the Soviet Communist party. This unity is not and cannot be formal."[87] Longo, on the other hand, chose to treat the issue at face value, as a confirmation of the impossibility of a single world leadership of a movement whose member parties were operating under "historical and political conditions at great variance with each other."[88] In contrast to Thorez' call for unity under Soviet leadership and to Khrushchev's insistence on strict adherence to the

later revealed that language explicitly prohibiting "action by a faction or group" had been dropped from the original text; he insisted that this in no wise weakened the intent. "Rapport au Comité Central," *Problèmes du mouvement*, p. 53.

84 Luigi Longo, *L'Unità*, December 19, 1960.

85 Khrushchev personally stated his objection in a speech during the banquet that opened the conference. Suggesting the term "vanguard" rather than "head," he asked the delegates in apparent jest: "What do you want a head for—so you can chop it off?" Elizabeth Gurley Flynn, "Recollections of the 1960 Conferences," *Political Affairs*, XLII, 11 (November 1963), p. 29.

86 "Interventions de Maurice Thorez," *Problèmes du mouvement*, p. 34.

87 *Ibid.*, pp. 24–25.

88 *L'Unità*, December 19, 1960.

decisions reached, Longo went no further than to ask that "an acknowledgment be made of common general tasks and a common action developed against imperialism and in favor of peace, democracy, and socialism on the basis of commonly accepted evaluations and a political and ideological unity."[89]

As in 1957, the PCI's position did not entail repudiation of the need for ideological and political unity. The essential point was that unity could no longer be enforced but would have to be the freely accepted result of collective deliberations. Formal rejection by the CPSU of its leadership role in the movement, while perhaps essential to counter the Chinese maneuver, also inevitably implied a genuine loss of authority. By refusing to accept formal responsibility for directing the movement, the USSR not only laid itself open to Chinese taunts and eventual counterclaims to leadership, but also tacitly conceded its inability to keep the Chinese and Albanians in line. A phrase of Longo's seems to suggest the core of the Soviet dilemma: to adopt the slogan of Soviet leadership, he said, "would serve only to cause trouble for the Communist parties and to make the CPSU responsible for the political line of each individual party, for which only the respective leading bodies can be responsible."[90]

But if the movement were to be without a head, the implication was that unity could be achieved only at the most general and long-range level. Differences of opinion and of action on current questions, in the realm of international as well as of domestic affairs, would have to be accepted as an inevitable part of the game if harmony were to be preserved among the parties. In 1960, this understanding of the situation was only implicit in the PCI's position, as it had been at the 1957 conference and in Togliatti's original conception of polycentrism. The PCI's proposed amendments toning down both the criticism of Yugoslav revisionism and the attack on Chinese factionalism were characteristic of the party's desire to smooth over rough edges and avoid confrontations that might irreparably damage the prospects for unity. It would take some time, however, and further disintegration of Sino-Soviet relations, for the Italian party to begin to translate this consistent but rather passive preference into a more active effort to influence the course of affairs.

[89] *Ibid.*
[90] "Primo intervento," *Interventi della delegazione*, p. 69.

CHAPTER SIX

THE IMPACT OF THE
TWENTY-SECOND CONGRESS

It had been anticipated that the Soviet Twenty-Second party Congress, which met in Moscow during the second half of October 1961, would be a relatively tranquil affair. On the agenda were a review of the substantial Soviet accomplishments of recent years and a formal presentation of the new party Program that was to launch the USSR on the "construction of communism." Although Soviet-Albanian relations had been deteriorating steadily since the Moscow meeting of the previous November, the controversy had been largely kept from view; there was no reason to anticipate the violent denunciation of the Albanians that quickly precipitated a fresh and open rupture in the Communist world.[1]

Still less reason was there to suppose that the Congress would become a forum for renewed charges against Stalin, buttressed by grim revelations not before made part of the public record and coupled with slashing attacks on Khrushchev's already discredited party enemies. These assaults in fact dominated the proceedings, reawakening in the Italian party all the bitter emotions of the traumatic days of June 1956. The political impact was, if anything, even stronger. Many had found it difficult indeed to cast aside the Stalin myth, but there had been another to take its place: the carefully cultivated image of a powerful and increasingly wealthy socialist system that had never been corrupted in its essentials by Stalin's errors and whose institutions represented, when all was said and done, the best available model of the future socialist society. Now that myth too was falling to the ground. The hard fact to be faced, as the outspoken Terracini declared to the PCI Central Committee, was that Stalin himself had not been solely to blame:

From Stalin, responsibility is now broadened to all the old ruling group of the Stalin era. Actually, that could have been understood from the

---

1 See Griffith, *Albania*, chap. 3.

day after the Twentieth Congress, since it was absurd to believe that the monstrous degenerative process unexpectedly unveiled at that time had had a single and exclusive author and actor. And it was a mistake to accept, even if not inwardly, this absurd hypothesis. . . . Hence the rebellious state of mind in the face of the new denunciations.[2]

If the entire ruling group shared responsibility for the tragedy, then the system itself could not be exonerated. And if the system was at fault, how much of it still remained intact, and how could there be guaranteed no repetition of the disasters of Stalinism? (Note that the term "Stalinism," angrily rejected in 1956 precisely because of these implications, was unabashedly used in 1961 by many of the party's senior figures without public rebuke.) From here the questioning led to the PCI itself. Had it also been affected by the "degeneration" of the Soviet system, how could it protect itself in the future, what bearing did all this have on its ties with the international movement? These and other such questions, the focus of agitated discussion everywhere in the party, boiled into public view at a dramatic session of the Central Committee and the Central Control Commission on the tenth and eleventh of November.

This was an unprecedented occasion, not only because so many sentiments bordering on heresy were expressed, but because Palmiro Togliatti, the master tactician, had for once misjudged the situation. The day after his return from Moscow (where, before the Congress opened, he had borne a wreath to Stalin's tomb), Togliatti had let his party know in indirect fashion how the Twenty-Second Congress was to be handled. A strongly worded article in *L'Unità* had deplored the "violent anti-Communist campaign" that had erupted in the bourgeois press against both the Soviet Union and the PCI, accusing the latter of complicity in the crimes of the Stalin era.[3] Criticism of the USSR, the article implied, would "objectively" aid the cause of the party's domestic enemies; appropriate limits to the critical comment were then suggested by printing long excerpts from Togliatti's *Nuovi argomenti* interview.

This effort to keep the party debate from going beyond the high-water mark of 1956 was more clearly seen in Togliatti's opening address to the Central Committee a few days later. While not altogether ignoring controversial issues, he tried to steer the debate into harmless channels by dwelling at length on such major "neutral" and anticipated themes of the Congress as the reaffirmation of the possibilities of peaceful coexistence and the "democratiza-

2 *L'Unità*, November 12, 1961.
3 *Ibid.*, November 5, 1961.

tion" of Soviet life through the gradual reduction of state functions. Togliatti repeated his opinion of five years before that further research was needed on the causes of Stalinism, but insisted that "the question of guarantees against a repetition of what took place in Stalin's time has been amply and convincingly dealt with by the Congress."[4]

In this comforting contention the party leader found himself virtually alone. All but a handful of the 31 speakers, some more bluntly than others, insisted that all was not well in the Soviet party and state, that the errors of the past had been neither fully analyzed nor overcome, that the very style of Khrushchev's denunciations at the Congress demonstrated that Soviet political life had not yet wholly transcended the Stalin era. There was, in short, an unprecedented, almost unanimous rejection of the limits Togliatti was attempting to impose. The criticism came, moreover, from all the party's most powerful figures except the faithful Deputy Secretary General Luigi Longo; Giorgio Amendola, Pietro Ingrao, and Gian Carlo Pajetta, the other powers in the Secretariat, were among the most outspoken.

Although there may be some risk of distortion in giving disproportionate emphasis to a single dramatic moment in the party's life, the debate over the Twenty-Second Congress merits fairly detailed analysis. Psychologically and politically, it came as close to being a watershed in the PCI's relations with the international movement as any other single event.

The Central Committee Debate on the Twenty-Second Congress

Even if the Twenty-Second Congress had not proved to be something of a turning point in the PCI's relations with the Soviet party, its immediate impact as reflected in the Central Committee's debate could hardly be ignored by any student of recent international Communist affairs. One contemporary observer, with good reason, termed L'Unità's summary of the debate "perhaps the most remarkable document of official European communism since the war," a judgment that would probably stand until the posthumous publication of Palmiro Togliatti's famous "Testament" three years later.[5]

4 Ibid., November 11, 1961.
5 Perry Anderson, "Debate of the Central Committee of the Italian Communist Party on the 22nd Congress of the C.P.S.U.," supplement to the New Left Review, Nos. 13–14 (January–April 1962), pp. 152–191, at p. 154. This

One of the most notable aspects of the debate was the constantly reiterated criticism of Soviet institutions and practices. A number of speakers took up the refrain that even in socialist societies, institutional and legal safeguards against abuse of power were required: in Gian Carlo Pajetta's words, "institutional problems have a definite importance, and the value of legal guarantees cannot be denied."[6] This was a delicate point for the PCI, not only because it flouted all the conventions concerning Soviet democracy, but because it came close to conceding the legitimacy of one of the key arguments propounded by the Socialists and Social Democrats in their perpetual assault on Communist positions.[7] It was obligatory for those raising the issue to insist, as did Alicata, that "the process of development of Soviet democracy certainly does not mean a revision of the system such as is indicated by Social Democrats, traditionalists, and Comrade Nenni." But he added that whereas traditional democratic procedures were indeed "pure institutional formalism" in the context of bourgeois society, they could and should acquire real substance once class exploitation had been abolished.

The critics were, it is true, reticent about suggesting specific reforms. The closest approach to a concrete proposal concerned the relatively insensitive cultural field; one of the PCI's leading art critics, Anatello Trombadori, is reported as having cited examples (not given in the summary) of the ways in which "the false idea of the merely pedagogical and instrumental function of art can give rise to institutional limitations objectively harmful to liberty of research, experiment, and creation. . . ."

These neorevisionist approaches to the problem of democracy in a socialist society were supplemented by criticism from a different perspective. Several Central Committee members, representing most often the youth and trade union movements, put their emphasis not on institutional guarantees but on the need to enhance the quality and quantity of participation by the masses in the life of society. Sergio Garavini, for example, CGIL secretary in Turin,

---

supplement contains a full translation of the summary of the debate that appeared in *L'Unità*, November 12, 1961. Selected excerpts from the debate have also been translated in Alexander Dallin, with Jonathan Harris and Gray Hodnett, eds., *Diversity in International Communism: A Documentary Record, 1961–1963* (New York: Columbia University Press, 1963), pp. 421–451.

[6] *L'Unità*, November 12, 1961; see also the remarks of Alicata, Alinovi, Trombadori, Luporini. Further quotations from speeches at the Central Committee meeting come from this same source; the citation will not be repeated on each occasion.

[7] See Chapter Seven for a discussion of PSI-PCI polemics on this score.

complained that the Twenty-Second Congress had paid excessive attention to quantitative economic data, ignoring the need for a more fully developed "political balance sheet" on the progress of socialist democracy and for a qualitative appraisal of the economic system: "Alongside figures for the expansion of productive forces, there must be found solutions to qualitative problems: besides the plan and its quantitative objectives, there must be participation by the workers in the drafting of the plan and in the control of production, in all sectors of economic, social, and political life."

Pietro Ingrao, a party Secretary and widely regarded as one of the most brilliant younger leaders, similarly stressed this theme of enlarging mass participation in social and economic life and in the party itself through enrichment of its internal democracy.[8] Ingrao would later emerge as the leading spokesman of the so-called PCI "new left"; the tendency to criticize the USSR for failing to involve the working masses adequately in the procedures of socialist democracy was a characteristic criticism from the left, in contrast to the concern for institutional guarantees typical of Amendola and his supporters.[9]

These cautious and generalized criticisms of the quality of Soviet society did not cut as close to the bone as did the efforts to explain how the degeneration could have taken place. Violations of democratic life in the Soviet party were repeatedly cited as the critical factor in understanding the origins of Stalinism. Mario Fabiani, an ally of Amendola, fixed upon the problem of unanimity in the party: "The degeneration of socialist legality began in the USSR when the myth of unanimity, of monolithism, was created: a myth theoretically mistaken and false in reality because there can be no unanimity when facing problems as great as the construction of a socialist society." Gian Carlo Pajetta explained the origins of the personality cult in the same terms: "The moment in which it is

8 Ingrao's views on this point emerge more clearly in his article in *L'Unità*, November 6, 1961, and in "L'origine degli errori," *Rinascita*, XVIII, 12 (December 1961), pp. 921–928.

9 As will be observed in the following, the "left" tendency was strongest in the Communist youth movement and is reflected most clearly in its weekly journal, *Nuova generazione*. Ingrao's sympathy for the left became plain in subsequent months, but in late 1961 it was still a matter for speculation.

The same distinction between institutional guarantees and mass participation was being debated in the Socialist party as well. Vittorio Foa, a leading trade unionist and representative of the Socialist left, commented in a round-table discussion of the Twenty-Second Congress: "We cannot, in my opinion, think of socialist democracy as a system of guarantees of the individual vis-à-vis society; we must regard it as a process of participation of the masses in decisions. . . ." *Avanti!*, December 3, 1961.

formed is that in which the party believes that every revolutionary transformation is necessarily linked to the elimination of every type of opposition and internal dissent, when monolithism becomes a doctrine and the dissenter becomes enemy number one, almost more dangerous than the class enemy."

There were inescapable implications here for the Italian party as well as the Soviet. While internal discussion in the PCI had always been relatively open, by Communist standards, the vital principle of the unanimity rule had never been questioned except by dissidents on the road to resignation or expulsion. But if the principle of monolithic unity was thought to be the root cause of the gross violations of legality in the USSR, what of the PCI itself? A number of Central Committee members raised the question, but it was Giorgio Amendola who argued most vigorously for a renewal of democratic practice within the party as the heart of a strategy of "renewal":

In our party as well, debate should be developed, if necessary right up to the formation from time to time, on various problems, of minorities and majorities: this does not mean formation of factions [correnti], which would crystallize the debate and dry it up, as happens in other parties; it means the progressively fuller development of an internal democratic dialectic. . . . This development of democracy is a necessary condition for achieving clarity, for furthering the renewal and strengthening of the party, and thus for opening new perspectives for a renewed advance of the Italian people toward democracy and socialism.

Even with all the necessary qualifications about the inadmissibility of factions, this call for an open recognition of temporary minorities in the party was a radical suggestion, especially coming from a member of the Secretariat. In part, as has often been the case in the history of the Communist movement, the demand for greater freedom of debate represented one leader's effort to legitimize his struggle to regain a voice in party policy. Amendola's influence in the hierarchy had for some time been declining, especially since the Ninth Congress in early 1960, when responsibility for organizational matters had been taken from him.[10] But the element of personal power was in this case, as in others, closely related to issues of policy. Amendola and the other proponents of "renewal" on the party's right wing were fighting for changes in the party's policies on a wide front, having become increasingly aware that the transformations of Italian society were outstripping the party's

[10] See "Modificazioni strutturale e politiche del partito comunista italiano al suo 9 congresso," *Tempi moderni*, New Series, No. 1 (April–June 1960), pp. 25–26.

capacity to respond to them. These aspects of the situation will be discussed in the next chapter. Here it is important only to note that the events of the Twenty-Second Congress gave to all who wanted a renewal, in whatever direction, an ideal opportunity to strike out against the tight discipline exercised by Togliatti.

Just as the Twenty-Second Congress raised disturbing questions about the validity of unanimity as a principle of internal party life, so it demonstrated beyond much doubt that what Amendola called "the formula of fictitious unanimity" in the international movement could no longer be upheld. The single really new fact of political importance to emerge at the Soviet Congress had been the tacit recognition that the compromises of 1957 and 1960 had utterly failed to re-establish unity under Soviet leadership. If the idea of polycentrism could appear in 1956 to be a bold declaration of how things ought to be, by late 1961 it was no longer anything more than a factual description of the status quo.

The refrain repeated over and over at the Central Committee session was the urgent necessity of going beyond "de facto polycentrism" and working out new organizational forms and methods of coordinating policy and resolving disputes. "Fictitious unanimity" had to be replaced by a new kind of unity, one respectful of differing views. In Pajetta's formulation, which expresses in brief compass the essence of what was later to become the PCI's official position:

It is not even worth asking whether unanimity would be better than diversity if it were a question of fictitious and mythical unanimity. And starting from an affirmation of the necessary diversity of orientations, judgments, and political lines, we shall necessarily move steadily forward, within a framework which can all the same remain one of basic unity. It will be necessary to proceed taking into account the concrete reality of the ideas, situations, and needs of others, without believing in the possibility of always being able to agree on everything or of always attaining definitive results. Hence a new problem is posed: how to coordinate the international workers' movement in diversity, in autonomy, in reciprocal respect, but also in critical, open, frank debate without reticences, because it is not true that "everyone is right in his own house. . . ." It is necessary to affirm the legitimacy of dissent, which will take the drama out of differences and at the same time avoid useless splits.

The demand for a "new look" in the Communist movement was not based solely on the pragmatic realization that deep divergences existed and had somehow to be coped with, although this was certainly an important part of the argument. The impetus stemmed also from a belief that the development of the PCI itself had been negatively affected by the necessity of remaining within the framework imposed by the unanimity rule. Reference was made by Amendola and several others to the approval in 1957 and 1960—as "a conscious act of self-discipline freely decided upon by us" so as to safeguard the unity of the socialist world—of documents which did not adequately reflect the PCI's positions:

This defense of international unity was correct. We have, however, paid the price of inhibiting creative research, not only on the topics of socialist democracy and criticism of Stalinism, but also on the analysis and elaboration of polycentrism, national roads, the economic development of the capitalist world, and the new possibilities of moving toward socialism even where no Communist party exists. We are proud of the themes of our Eighth Congress, but we recognize frankly that to a certain extent these themes were later set aside.

Mario Alicata, a member of the *Direzione* in charge of the party's cultural work, made the same point in specific reference to the old question of national roads to socialism. Even the new Soviet party Program, he observed, seems to misunderstand the significance of the Twentieth Congress on this score: "When this Program states that because the general laws of development of socialist construction are always and everywhere the same, there is a single path of transition to socialism, then the very substance of national roads is put in doubt." Here was an open reassertion of the view that Alicata, Longo, and others had discreetly urged upon the Soviets during their conversations in Moscow in July 1957.

But the problem was not limited to that of an Italian road to socialism, narrowly construed. Many felt the need for a new and strong affirmation, already evident in embryo in the PCI's confidential memorandum for the 1960 Moscow conference, of a potential Italian Communist contribution to the whole of capitalist Europe. Luciano Barca, for example, suggested that the party had done itself a disservice by too often defending its position on the grounds of Italy's particular national situation: "It could thus appear that it was a question of making particular concessions, whereas in fact needs and positions were involved to which we Italian Communists attribute general validity in the conditions of the present era, in the conditions of Europe. . . ." In the same vein, Alfredo Reichlin, editor of *L'Unità*, stated that for the PCI autonomy did not mean "a parochial self-containment but, on the contrary, must be an original contribution to the elaboration of a revolutionary strategy for the capitalist West, to be linked dialectically with the struggles of the socialist and underdeveloped countries." Reichlin later enlarged on this theme in an editorial claiming that the PCI "first and with greatest clarity" posed the problem of a new revolutionary strategy for the West; party autonomy, he added, means the struggle *for* this new strategy, not against something.[11]

The importance of the debate prompted by the Twenty-Second Congress lay above all in this affirmative, almost aggressive tone. "Our party wants to play its part in the international debate," Amendola proclaimed, and others echoed the sentiment. Far more than in 1956 the PCI felt itself to be engaged internationally. Togliatti had led the way after the Twentieth Congress by developing the outlines of an Italian position toward the international movement, but the initiative had not been followed up. Now, in the opinion of many, it was high time to do so.

THE BALANCE WITHIN THE PARTY.   It is important to note, though the subject cannot at this point be pursued fully, that the agitated mood of the Central Committee debate was not a consequence of the Twenty-Second Congress alone. This event was certainly the catalyst, but the reaction to it stemmed in good measure from a growing restiveness among many of the party's leaders about the situation at home. As Fausto Gullo observed in a speech to the Central Committee the following month, the party reacted with such intensity to the Twenty-Second Congress because the denunciation of the past had "taken place at a time when a degree of restlessness had already been noted in the party, which therefore turned into an open explosion of feelings that has at times violated the need for self-control and given a defensive flavor to our polemic with the enemy."[12]

The factors involved will be explored more adequately in the next chapter, but the essence of the situation was that the environment in which the party had to work was changing fast and in important ways, raising serious questions about the need for a new and revitalized Communist strategy. Strengthened by unprecedented economic progress, the capitalist enemy—from the factory owner to the Christian Democratic politician to the ecclesiastical hierarch—had been evolving a more flexible response to national problems, threatening by a more enlightened attitude and by partial reforms to weaken the PCI in a way that repression had never been able to do. These developments were coming to a climax in the maneuvering toward a Socialist-supported Center-Left government that was

11 *L'Unità*, December 3, 1961.
12 *Ibid.*, December 22, 1961.

to become a reality a few months hence, opening a new phase in the nation's political history.

By the end of 1961, in response to this situation, there had begun once again to emerge within the party the perennially latent tendencies that we may label, for want of better terms, "reformist" and "leftist." In their diagnoses of Italian reality and their prescriptions for action the proponents of these tendencies disagreed. The former, by far the stronger and represented at the party summit by Giorgio Amendola and his supporters, were inclined to commit the party definitively to a gradualist policy of adaptation to economic and social reality in the hope of eventually gaining political positions from which national policy could be decisively influenced; retention of a working alliance with the Socialist party was the key political dimension of their strategy. The new PCI left, on the other hand, at that time based largely in the Communist youth movement, was proposing a more radical "proletarian strategy" of direct confrontation with the bourgeois order, the front line being the factory and the trade union rather than the national parliament and municipal governments.[13]

These differences would grow more marked during the following years as the Center-Left experiment took shape and, by 1965, would be the source of serious and open dissent within the party.[14] In November 1961, however, the most relevant fact was not the divergence between the two groups but their shared conviction that the time was ripe to relax some of the inhibitions blocking the party's forward movement. Each wanted, in its own way, to invigorate the party and move it off the carefully balanced center position favored by Togliatti.

To do so, whether in a revisionist or a leftist direction, meant among other things loosening the political and psychological bonds

13 See Giorgio Galli, "Italy," *Survey*, No. 42 (June 1962), pp. 111–113, for a brief discussion of the various trends in the PCI at the time of the November Central Committee meeting. Galli's longer essay, "Italian Communism," in Griffith, *Communism in Europe*, Vol. 1, pp. 301–383, contains a fuller analysis of the revisionist and leftist trends as they developed during 1962; see especially pp. 316–321 and 327–338.

14 The existence of these two groupings became definitely confirmed after Togliatti's death, most dramatically in the open fight over the Theses for the party's Eleventh Congress in January 1966. By this time one would be entitled to speak unhesitatingly in terms of factionalism in the party, whereas earlier, as long as Togliatti was present as mediator and final authority, the rivalries were kept under control. The differences in evaluation and policy were, all the same, not difficult for experienced observers to see, especially on such burning issues as the Center-Left.

that linked the party to Soviet doctrine, Soviet priorities for action, the myth of Soviet socialism—for internal reasons, because it was difficult to galvanize a party whose cadres could not quite overcome the habit of "sterile waiting for a liberation that would come from outside,"[15] and for external reasons, in order to alter the view of outsiders that the PCI was bound to the USSR and to the Soviet model of a socialist state.

The central fact of the party's situation in late 1961, then, was the convergence of these two tendencies in opposition both to a greatly weakened conservative group (the "old" or "Stalinist" left), and to the narrow oligarchy of Togliatti and Longo that held the balance of power in the party. In contrast to 1956, Togliatti and his centrist allies could not rely on a strong "Stalinist" faction as a counterweight to the revisionists and the "new left." Although still strongly represented in the Central Control Commission, the power of the conservatives had steadily been whittled away by personnel shifts at the Eighth and Ninth Congresses. During the November meeting the conservatives remained silent, their spokesman Mauro Scoccimarro rising only to object to the character of the debate and to urge that it be resumed within the more restricted circles of the *Direzione*. Only once again, at the subsequent Central Committee meeting in December, was Togliatti able to use the conservative group against his opponents; afterward it disappeared as an effective political force.[16]

As in 1956, the objective of the critics was not to unseat Togliatti but to shift the party's center of gravity away from the conservative pole, thus requiring him to move toward positions of renewal in order to maintain his dominant position. Togliatti's personal authority was so great that a direct challenge by any other party leader would have been suicidal; during and after the November meeting, in fact, the other party Secretaries went to some lengths to insist upon the complete inadmissibility of factional activities and to reiterate in various ways their loyalty to Togliatti. (Gian Carlo Pajetta, for example, opened an unprecedented press conference staged by the PCI in the aftermath of the Twenty-Second Congress by twitting the bourgeois press about its sensational interpretations of a split in Communist ranks: "My Mama wrote to me, 'Gian

15 Giorgio Amendola, "Le nostre corresponsabilità," *Rinascita*, XVIII, 12 (December 1961), p. 940.

16 See Galli in Griffith, *Communism in Europe*, Vol. 1, p. 327: "The PCI old guard, sentimentally Stalinist and represented by such men as Mauro Scoccimarro, after being used by Togliatti against Amendola's followers at the end of 1961, began in fact to dissolve and was deprived of any positions of power in the PCI federations."

Carlo, is it true that you have set yourself against Togliatti?' ")[17] Disruption of the party's unity was then as always a capital offense, and Togliatti was the unchallengeable symbol of that unity.

The November meeting nevertheless produced unmistakable signs of sharp conflict within the leadership. The tone and substance of many of the speeches had beyond any question represented a challenge to Togliatti, brought home most sharply by Amendola's unprecedented defense of minority rights in the party and by the request of his supporters for an extraordinary party congress to debate the issues arising from the Twenty-Second Congress. Togliatti's initial response was anything but conciliatory. His concluding speech to the Central Committee (unpublished even in summary form, for the first time in the PCI's postwar history) was "apparently very sharp and brutal, in particular to G. Amendola."[18] A sure sign of its harshness is the regret at its not being published expressed by Mauro Scoccimarro and Vittorio Vidali at the next Central Committee meeting in December; these two unreconstructed leaders of the "Stalinist" left, bitterly opposed to the renovating spirit that dominated the November meeting, maintained that publication would have helped steer the subsequent party debate into "safer" channels.[19]

Togliatti persisted in his effort to smother the critical voices by issuing a brief statement in the name of the Central Committee and the Central Control Commission approving the decisions of the Twenty-Second Congress. The resolution, apparently put out on his own initiative without consulting other party leaders, was little more than a barefaced summary of his opening speech and contained no echo of the criticisms that had been expressed.[20] Upon its publication, a two-day meeting of the *Direzione* was convened, after which it was announced that the Secretariat had been asked to prepare a public document providing a fuller analysis of the controversial issues raised by the Central Committee.[21] Togliatti's hand had been forced, leading him to concede that the issues could not be swept under the rug without risking serious disaffection within the party. His tactic then became to control and limit the scope of discussion rather than to stifle it.

The resulting document, drafted by Togliatti with the help of

[17] *Avanti!*, December 2, 1961.
[18] "Crisi al vertice del PCI dopo il 22° congresso sovietico," *Tempi moderni*, New Series, No. 8 (January–March 1962), p. 183. Galli in *Survey*, No. 42, p. 113, repeats this appraisal.
[19] *L'Unità*, December 22, 1961.
[20] "Il XXII Congresso e i compiti del PCI," *L'Unità*, November 14, 1961.
[21] *L'Unità*, November 19, 1961.

the two junior members of the Secretariat, Berlinguer and Bufalini, then modified and approved by the whole of the Secretariat, was an ambiguous compromise weighted toward Togliatti's position.[22] Carefully balancing both sides of every question and entirely lacking the incisiveness that marked much of the Central Committee debate, it nevertheless went in several respects beyond Togliatti's original stand. After being approved by the Central Committee, the document became in effect the party's new platform on the major questions aroused by the Soviet Congress.[23]

It is important, first, to correct the impression that the debate on the Twenty-Second Congress was restricted to the upper circles of the party. The differences of outlook expressed in the Central Committee were reflected among the rank and file as well, and an intensive and relatively uninhibited debate was in progress among Communists throughout the country. Enrico Berlinguer, the man responsible for party organizational matters, estimated that up to 80 or 90 per cent of those enrolled were present at meetings of certain party cells and sections; this was not true everywhere, but for a brief period there was an almost unprecedented participation of the rank and file.[24] The discussions were, in Berlinguer's words, "impassioned and lively." Amendola's more graphic description refers to "the violence of the reactions, the impassioned debates, the crowded sections, the sleepless nights. . . ."[25]

As within the Central Committee, the conservatives in the rank and file had been put at a disadvantage by the events of the Twenty-Second Congress and largely kept their silence.[26] The pre-

[22] "Documento del PCI sul XXII Congresso," *L'Unità*, November 28, 1961.

[23] Michele Pellicani, in a small book prompted by the repercussions of the Congress, argues that since the Secretariat's document contained the essential points Togliatti had made in his opening Central Committee speech, it represented a victory for him and a defeat for the Amendola group. In some respects this was true, but the author's comparative analysis of the two texts bypasses some of the most interesting points of comparison to be discussed below. Pellicani, a former PCI member who then gained prominence in the Social Democratic party, was rightly concerned to rebut certain exaggerated appraisals of the press to the effect that Togliatti had been repudiated by the Secretariat and that the Amendola group had won a complete victory. He particularly objected to a journalist in *La Stampa* who suggested that the PCI might be turning toward "the methods and traditional principles of liberal democracy"; verbal acknowledgment of freedom of dissent, Pellicani correctly observed, has always been accepted by the PCI and is meaningless as long as the basic Leninist principles of party life continue to be accepted. Michele Pellicani, *La tragedia della classe operaia* (Milan: Edizioni Azione Comune, 1964), pp. 49–54.

[24] *L'Unità*, November 30, 1961.

[25] Amendola, *Rinascita*, XVIII, 12, p. 935.

[26] See Laura Conti, "Orientamenti nella base del PCI," *Problemi del socialismo*, IV–V, 12–1 (December–January 1961–1962), pp. 1262–1265, for a dis-

vailing accent of the debate in the party cells and sections, therefore, was critical: of the USSR for its violations of democratic principles, of the PCI leadership for its failure to keep the party informed of the realities of Soviet life and the causes and consequences of the divisions within the Communist movement. Particularly strong and widespread was the demand for greater democracy and participation by the rank and file in party affairs. A summary account of a series of party meetings in Rome reported the frequently expressed desire that the sections be more involved in matters of policy and the "insistent request" for a form of internal party democracy allowing formation of majorities and minorities.[27]

These demands for greater democracy and fuller involvement in party affairs can be assessed in many ways. Certainly they were in part a reflection of genuine grass-roots sentiment, always latent in the PCI and springing to life whenever events occurred to engage the intellect and emotions of the rank and file. From this perspective they were, however inconvenient for the leadership in some respects, at least an indication of vitality and of energies to be tapped. In part, they were also a response to the conflicting orientations among the party's leaders; Amendola and others desired and encouraged the debate as a means of demonstrating the widespread sentiment in favor of party renewal on all fronts. Considerable publicity was given the question of party democracy, to which the leadership responded by confirming the need for "increasingly more conscious participation by the party members in the party's political life, a free manifestation and expression of the opinions and even contrasts during debates and votes. . . ."[28]

Such a verbal concession, always set in the context of a reaffirmation of the absolute inadmissibility of organized factional activity, served two purposes: it relieved the pressure from the rank and file, and it encouraged the Socialists and others on the left to hope for

cussion of the reactions of the conservative party activists. Abdon Alinovi, Secretary of the Naples PCI federation and an ally of Amendola, did, however, make a point of stressing the strong emotional reactions of many, especially in the South, to the fresh attacks on Stalin; these "revealed the existence of notable residues of a mythical conception of socialism, of the Soviet Union, and of the relations among the Communist parties, a conception of which Stalin was when living a sort of incarnation and even after his death a particular type of inspiration." *L'Unità,* December 20, 1961.

27 *Ibid.,* November 30, 1961, pp. 1 and 9. The same issue contains a similar summary of the discussions in a group of Milan party sections.

28 "Documento del PCI sul XXII Congresso," *L'Unità,* November 28, 1961. See also the articles by Aldo Tortorella in *L'Unità,* December 10, 1961, and by Gian Carlo Pajetta and Alessandro Natta, "Considerazioni sulla democrazia nel partito," *Rinascita,* XVIII, 12 (December 1961), pp. 929–934, for further typical illustrations of the way the issue was being handled.

an evolution of the PCI toward a genuine internal liberalization. The phenomenon need not, however, be viewed exclusively in this instrumental light. The fact was—and this is the main reason for mentioning it here—that the PCI was gradually being confronted with one of the more serious long-run consequences of de-Staliniza- tion and the declining international authority of the Soviet Union. The principle of monolithic unity had been challenged—both for its effects on Soviet domestic life and for its increasingly evident inapplicability to the international movement. It would become difficult for a party to criticize aspects of Soviet life and to argue for greater tolerance of conflicting points of view within the move- ment while clinging at the same time to a traditional interpretation of democratic centralism as applied to its own internal arrange- ments. It cannot be said that the discussions of late 1961 represented a crisis in this regard, for the impulse toward greater internal free- dom was easily kept under control, and no notable change took place in the party's way of doing business. The issue was a prime symptom, however, of the dilemma confronting a party endeavoring to overcome the damaging heritage of "monolithism" without sacrificing one of its greatest strengths, the absence of open faction- alism and the tradition of united action.

International Repercussions of the Debate

The PCI's Central Committee debate aroused interest, not to say concern, in international Communist circles. One disturbing element of the discussion, understandably, had been the critical references to the Soviet Union. The summary document of the PCI Secretariat, while a good deal more cautious than some of the speeches, nevertheless went further than any but the Yugoslav party had ever gone in proclaiming the need for institutional change in the USSR. The transition to communism, it was stated, could not take place without revising the structures and practices of the trade unions, the soviets, and above all of the party. Existing bureaucratic methods should be denounced and changed "in order to break the fetters which are jeopardizing the process of development of Soviet society." Thorough historical research would have to be under- taken to obtain more satisfactory explanations than had yet been offered of the origins of the "errors and distortions," which could not by any means be justified as the inevitable result of a harsh time of revolutionary construction. The problem of institutional guarantees of socialist legality and the development of democracy would have to be examined afresh.[29]

These remarks were carefully worded to offer partial satisfaction to internal critics while not stepping unduly hard on Soviet toes. As the document was being drafted, Moscow had in fact manifested its displeasure at the resurgence of a line of thought it had protested back in 1956; an editorial appeared in *Pravda* refuting all those who continued to propound the bourgeois thesis that the cult of the individual was related to some presumed "degeneration" of the Soviet system.[30] Although the Italian Communist critics were not named, they were clearly the main target of the reference to "even some honest persons abroad who have failed to analyze deeply the essence of the matter, the nature of Soviet socialist society," and therefore echoed the slanders of bourgeois ideologists and their Menshevik and Trotskyite henchmen. This was not, as in 1956, a rebuke to Togliatti personally, although the Soviets could hardly have been pleased by his strong reassertion of the correctness of the views expressed in his *Nuovi argomenti* interview.[31] The most serious offenders had been the leftist elements in the Italian Federation of Communist Youth who had had the temerity to publish an article entitled "Bureaucratic Degeneration in the Socialist State" and to call for a critical reassessment of all Soviet history, including particularly the role played by Trotsky.[32] Maurice Thorez quickly echoed the Soviet complaint, pointing a finger directly at the scandalous behavior of an unnamed but perfectly identifiable "national Communist youth organization."[33]

The Soviet protest sounded *pro forma*, however. Although the Russians could not simply ignore such criticism, it was hardly their intention to stir up trouble for Palmiro Togliatti, then under fire from both left and right in his party; his support would be needed

[29] "Documento del PCI sul XXII Congresso," *L'Unità*, November 28, 1961, pp. 1 and 9–10.

[30] *Pravda*, November 21, 1961.

[31] A Yugoslav analyst flatly asserted that through its editorial "*Pravda* again rejected Togliatti's views on the need for a deeper analysis of the roots of Stalinism. . . ." This was in the context of a general review of the state of world communism after the Twenty-Second Congress in which only the Italians were congratulated for their willingness to examine the causes of the "degeneration" in the USSR and the international movement. Zvonimir Kristl, "The Disturbed Balance," *Vjesnik* (Zagreb), December 24, 1961; translation in Dallin *et al.*, *Diversity in International Communism*, pp. 590–594.

[32] Michelangelo Notarianni, "La degenerazione burocratica dello Stato socialista," *Nuova generazione*, November 17, 1961, pp. 3–4.

[33] *L'Humanité*, November 31, 1961.

in the struggle with the Sino-Albanian axis. The intervention may even have been intended to strengthen Togliatti's hand by invoking Soviet prestige against his left-wing critics while putting on record once again the official interpretation of the personality cult as "an alien excrescence on the healthy body of Soviet socialist society." *L'Unità*'s Moscow correspondent, reporting the *Pravda* article, noted dryly that "it appears to respond only in part to the demands that have emerged in the workers' movement . . . for a deeper analysis of the historical and political causes that led to that phenomenon."[34] On this issue, Togliatti was left in the desirable position, for his domestic purposes, of appearing as in 1956 to be in the vanguard of those taking a more independent stance toward Moscow, while at the same time not getting himself into difficulty with the Soviet comrades.

MORE ON POLYCENTRISM.   Even more alarming to the Communist world than the sensitive question of the Soviet system was the sudden revival of the concept of polycentrism. As we have seen, the term cropped up repeatedly in the Central Committee debate, and Togliatti himself, though not mentioning the word, used the apparently synonymous phrase "a multiplicity of leadership centers."[35] Over the next several weeks authoritative criticisms of polycentrism were made at Central Committee meetings of the Czech, Polish, East German, and French parties.[36]

The Czech, East German, and French statements were similar in tone and substance. (Gomułka's remarks took a rather different tack and are discussed separately below.) All interpreted polycentrism to mean the establishment of several centers of direction for the Communist movement and all flatly condemned the idea as concealing a tendency toward factionalism (Thorez), showing a lack of confidence in the correctness of Soviet policy (Koucký), or failing to comprehend the growing role of the CPSU as the center of the revolutionary movement (Axen). The theory of polycentrism, it was argued, only served to encourage the divisive forces of nationalism by denying the universal validity of the Marxist-Leninist theory of

---

34 *L'Unità*, November 21, 1961.

35 *Ibid.*, November 11, 1961.

36 For Czechoslovakia, see the speech of Vladimir Koucký, *Rudé Právo*, November 24, 1961, in Dallin *et al., Diversity in International Communism*, pp. 314–315; also Miloslav Tyller, *Tvorba*, November 30, 1961. For Poland, see the speech of Władysław Gomułka, *Trybuna Ludu*, November 24, 1961, in Dallin, p. 331. For East Germany, see the speech of Hermann Axen, *Neues Deutschland*, December 2, 1961. For France, see the speeches of Waldeck Rochet, *L'Humanité*, November 27, 1961, and of Maurice Thorez, *L'Humanité*, November 30, 1961.

revolution. National peculiarities and concrete historical conditions should be stressed "within legitimate bounds," said Thorez, but not to the detriment of the great laws enunciated in the 1957 Moscow Declaration; revisionism was still the principal danger to the Communist movement.

Polycentrism was never explicitly criticized by Soviet writers, presumably to spare the PCI the embarrassment of a public rebuke, but the Soviet leaders had other ways of showing their endorsement of the views being expressed by Communist leaders elsewhere. *Pravda,* for example, published excerpts from Gomułka's speech in which polycentrism was rejected as a *modus operandi* for the Communist movement.[37] And at the very moment polycentrism was coming under fire at Central Committee meetings in Paris, Warsaw, and Berlin, Luigi Longo and Giorgio Napolitano were in Moscow, ostensibly on a routine visit set up at the time of the Twenty-Second Congress.[38] They undoubtedly brought with them for discussion the text of the Secretariat's statement on the Twenty-Second Congress, which would be published before they had left Moscow; whether the text was revised in response to Soviet suggestions is not known.

In any event, the Secretariat's statement made no explicit reference to polycentrism. It sought, however, to combine its traditional insistence on autonomy with a quiet repudiation of the interpretation of polycentrism on which the criticism of the other parties was based. In the present stage of the movement's development, the statement maintained, "there does not exist and cannot exist either a directing party or state or one or more instances of centralized direction of the international Communist movement."[39] And when Longo later reported to the Central Committee on his conversations in the Soviet Union, he formally "recommended" that because of the confusion and ambiguity surrounding the term, polycentrism be dropped from the PCI's political lexicon.[40]

There was other evidence that Moscow was not enthusiastic about the idea. Moscow's overriding interest after the Twenty-Second Congress was to isolate the Albanians and Chinese and re-establish Soviet ideological and political authority in the movement. Its major statements thus strongly stressed the need for monolithic

[37] *Pravda,* November 25, 1961.
[38] *L'Unità,* November 30, 1961, reported their departure from Moscow on November 29; the length of their stay was not mentioned and *L'Unità* had not announced their departure from Rome.
[39] "Documento del PCI sul XXII Congresso," *L'Unità,* November 28, 1961.
[40] *L'Unità,* December 23, 1961.

unity and strict observance of the collective decisions reached in 1957 and 1960.[41] Not only was the PCI out of step with this campaign, but it was possible that the notion of polycentrism might encourage Chinese pretensions to a share in the leadership of the Communist movement. Czech party Secretary Koucký came close to making this point explicit when he said that polycentrism would inevitably tend to weaken internationalism; it could lead to the conclusion that "the European parties, for example, ought to leave the solution of Asian problems exclusively to the Asian Communist parties. . . ."[42] Acceptance of a separate and recognized Chinese sphere of influence was hardly part of the Soviet international design.

The PCI did not take official notice of the Czech and Polish comments on polycentrism, both of which were published on November 24.[43] The remarks of the PCF's Deputy Secretary General Waldeck Rochet, published in *L'Humanité* three days later, could not, however, be ignored. Although not mentioning polycentrism by name, Waldeck Rochet, unlike the Polish and Czech spokesmen, referred bluntly to "certain opportunist and revisionist elements" in the Italian party who apparently did not believe in the need for unity in the international movement.[44] Polycentrism was clearly the target, and the PCI quickly tried to set the record straight by printing an explanatory statement ahead of its Paris correspondent's report of Waldeck Rochet's remarks. The Secretariat's resolution, stated *L'Unità,*

. . . leaves no doubt as to the decisive importance that is attributed to the unity of the movement nor permits any interpretation of "polycentrism" as a multiplicity of centers of regional direction. The term is useful to underline the necessary and indispensable autonomy of each party in the framework of international proletarianism and the importance this autonomy assumes today.[45]

A few days later *L'Humanité* published Maurice Thorez' speech sharply condemning the PCI's revisionist tendencies and charging the thesis of polycentrism with concealing factionalist tendencies.

41 See, for example, Yuri Andropov, "The XXII Congress and the Development of the World Socialist System," *Pravda,* December 2, 1961; translation in *CDSP,* XIII, 48, pp. 8–10.

42 *Rudé Právo,* November 24, 1961; quoted in *L'Unità,* December 3, 1961, and in Dallin *et al., Diversity in International Communism,* p. 315.

43 Gomułka's speech was reported in *L'Unità* on November 23, even before its text appeared in *Trybuna Ludu,* but the Italian summary skips over the critical passage on polycentrism.

44 *L'Humanité,* November 27, 1961.

45 *L'Unità,* November 28, 1961.

Togliatti himself replied, repeating that polycentrism was intended only to underline the absence of a single center and the necessity for full autonomy of all parties, both of which Thorez had endorsed. He stated that the concept had never included the idea of different regional centers, and added:

It must be remembered, however, that in 1956, during the Twentieth CPSU Congress, in the course of a meeting attended by representatives of all the parties belonging to the Information Bureau, a proposal was made to try a certain type of "regional" organization based on a closer exchange of information among parties operating in similar situations. *It was not, however, made by our party.* The proposal was accepted, on an experimental basis and not without perplexity. Some effort to implement it was also made, especially by the French comrades and us, but no useful result was achieved; the approach was abandoned and has not been spoken of again on any occasion.[46]

Should the contention that polycentrism was never intended to suggest more than autonomy for individual parties and the absence of a single directing center be taken at face value? Or was the Italian party, in officially relinquishing the term and disavowing any intent to suggest a regional concept, retreating from its original position in response to pressures from the Russians and their more conventionally minded allies? At least one foreign Communist spokesman, an Austrian delegate to the Twenty-Second Congress, reported to his Central Committee that "our fraternal Italian Party later *changed its attitude* and declared itself, too, against any directing centers in the world Communist movement. . . ."[47] It is uncertain whether the interpretation given by other Communist leaders was based on inside knowledge of Togliatti's true intentions or was a conscious distortion of his idea as a take-off point for a general refutation of his whole conception of international Communist relationships. The evidence is incomplete, and the answer may lie somewhere between the two alternatives.

There is not enough in the written record to support the argument that Togliatti explicitly desired and proposed the establishment of regional centers. His remark in late 1961 about the need for "a multiplicity of leadership centers" (*molteplicità di centri di direzione*) is open to this interpretation, but in context it can also legitimately be read simply as an affirmation of independence for

[46] *Ibid.,* December 2, 1961. Italics in the original. The substance of this statement was repeated as a footnote to Palmiro Togliatti, "Diversità e unità nel movimento operaio e comunista internazionale," *Rinascita,* XVIII, 12 (December 1961), p. 913.

[47] Franz Muhri, *Volksstimme,* December 28–29, 1961; translated in Dallin *et al., Diversity in International Communism,* p. 528. [Italics added.]

all parties rather than as an organizational proposal for a regional arrangement.[48] Togliatti's rebuttal to Thorez and other critics rested essentially on his contention that the regional idea had already been proposed in 1956 by some other party (presumably the Soviets themselves), tentatively put into practice, and then dropped by mutual consent. The point gains conviction in light of the fact that Togliatti had already in 1956, in his report to the Eighth Congress, alluded to this sequence of events: "As there is no longer a single organization, and thus a single center of leadership, some thought was given to a system of groups and manifold centers; but even this form of organization seemed incompatible with full autonomy for each party, besides burdening one or another of them with excessive responsibility."[49]

In the absence of adequate evidence as to Togliatti's intentions, we are reduced to speculation. Conceivably he might in 1956 have welcomed the idea of a regional European center, coined the term polycentrism to describe the new organizational format that seemed to be evolving, then backed away later in the year in the face of Soviet efforts to recentralize and the evident impossibility of effective cooperation between the French and Italian parties. (In his report to the Eighth Congress Togliatti had used the word only once, in explicit reference to differences in the imperialist camp rather than to relations among the Communist parties: "The world has become polycentric.")[50] After the Twenty-Second Congress, according to this interpretation, he would have tried the idea out once more, feeling that the balance of forces within the Communist movement now favored a regional orientation for Europe in which the Italian party could play the leading role: the French, inevitably the PCI's rival in such an arrangement, had been weakened both domestically and within the movement, the international environment favored the preferred Italian tactics of gradualism and conciliation, and the worsening dispute with China seemed sure to push the Soviet party toward a more consistent application of rightist policies. Togliatti's remarks in 1961 about the "great success" of the meeting of European parties held in Rome in November 1959 could be taken to suggest a sense of confidence that the PCI was gradually emerging as the leader of an increasingly autonomous and differentiated European Communist movement.[51]

48 *L'Unità*, November 11, 1961.
49 "Togliatti's Report to the Congress," *Eighth Congress*, p. 173.
50 *Ibid.*, p. 164.
51 The text of Togliatti's speech in *L'Unità*, November 11, 1961, refers to the meeting "organized in 1958 by us together with our French comrades." The date

Against this interpretation stand two main considerations, aside from Togliatti's own disavowal that regional centers were ever intended. First, the PCI had since 1956 consistently maintained its firm opposition to the idea of re-creating any centralized organization whatever to replace the Cominform. Although such a position would not automatically exclude participation in a loose, regional organization of some sort, it does suggest the probability of strong resistance to any organizational form threatening to diminish the party's freedom of action by obliging it to endorse conclusions arrived at by compromise between competing outlooks. A second, related consideration concerns the ever present possibility of the PCI's subordination to the French party in any European regional organization. The international importance of France plus the utter reliability and orthodoxy of Thorez and his party would have gone far to assure that the burden of "excessive responsibility" would be borne by the French rather than the Italian party. It was plain, in any event, that a European organizational scheme could not be imposed on the French against their will; the idea would be feasible and effective only if a necessary minimum of collaboration could be achieved. Thorez made it plain in November 1961, and not for the first time, that that day was a long way off.

Whatever Togliatti's attitude toward the specific question of regional organizational arrangements, the main point is that the idea of regionalism, in whatever form it might be expressed, was clearly implicit in his perennial emphasis on the great diversity in the circumstances of the three main groups of Communist parties and in the consequent necessity for tactical differences in policy. Togliatti had emphasized all this in 1956, and events since then had only reinforced the obvious fact that the domestic and international priorities of Soviet communism were radically different from those of Asia and of Eastern and Western Europe. Whether this realization had led Togliatti explicitly to favor a corresponding organizational arrangement is a secondary matter, of greater tactical than strategic interest.

Togliatti's polycentrism should probably not be subjected to too rigorous an analysis. It is quite possible that Togliatti himself did not have anything very precise in mind when he invented the

appears to represent either a typographical slip or a lapse of memory. There was a bilateral meeting in Rome in December 1958 between the PCI and the PCF, but no other parties were involved and no "platform" of consequence resulted. Togliatti is obviously referring to the meeting of November 1959 that was later attacked by the Chinese. The *World Marxist Review*, III, 1 (January 1960), p. 46, describes it as organized "on the initiative of the Gramsci Institute" of the PCI, with no reference to joint sponsorship by the French.

word; it would have been wholly in character for him to express his ideas in an ambiguous fashion that suggested something and yet could be renounced, explained away, or further amplified according to the circumstances. Like so many of the PCI's domestic slogans, it seems to have reflected the innate opportunism and ambiguity of the man. An idea, like a political strategy, generally had its maximum and its minimum dimensions, to be stretched or shrunk as the occasion required. In this case the maximum meaning may have been that of regional organizations, the minimum that of autonomy for all parties and the absence of a guiding center. If this interpretation is correct, Togliatti simply retreated to the latter formula when the going got rough.[52]

THE PCI AND THE CHINESE QUESTION.   Whereas Thorez may have reacted as sharply as he did to polycentrism out of fear of Togliatti's ambitions in Europe, this was hardly the main concern in Moscow. A more salient fact was that polycentrism in its most general sense implied an attitude toward the Sino-Soviet quarrel not fully consistent with Soviet interests. The point should not be overdone. On the substantive issues of the dispute the Italians were among the most vocal and most convinced supporters of the Russian position and would continue to be so; as Togliatti had been among the first to denounce the Albanians publicly, so he would be one of the main

[52] At least one observer accepted at face value the assertion that polycentrism was intended to imply separate regional centers. An unsigned article in *Tempi moderni* interprets Togliatti's reply to Thorez as indicating that Togliatti favored regionalism even though it was not his own idea. The article suggests that from the remarks made at the November Central Committee meeting "we can reasonably conjecture that significant disagreement was expressed as to the limits and the content of the 'region' that ought to belong to Italy in the polycentric Communist system." Togliatti, it is suggested, had in mind a region embracing the Mediterranean basin and including France, Yugoslavia, and Albania, while Amendola and others had Western Europe in view; the European regional concept was premised on a long-range political strategy in a world without war, whereas Togliatti's idea was in essence a military one, based on the presumption of eventual war. "Il PCI e alcune questioni aperte dal 22 congresso del PCUS," *Tempi moderni*, New Series, No. 8 (January–March 1962), pp. 113–120, at p. 116.

I have found no evidence to support the conjecture that Togliatti favored a military-oriented strategy centered on the Mediterranean basin; indeed his interest in North Africa and the Middle East appeared to be minimal. It is true that the PCI was developing a more active interest in this area, as well as in Europe, and there may have been differences of opinion within the Central Committee as to the relative priority the two should be given. They cannot be sharply distinguished, however, if only because both approaches involved competition with the PCF for influence over other smaller parties. In general it does not appear that the question of polycentrism was being debated within the party in terms as concrete as those suggested by *Tempi moderni*'s author.

targets of attack by the Chinese once the split became public.[53] Nevertheless, on the issue of how the dispute should be handled, and how the movement should be organized to cope with the new situation, the tendency of the PCI's approach was worrisome.

Of all the issues arising from the Twenty-Second Congress, the one dealt with least fully and least candidly by the PCI leadership was the Soviet-Chinese split. Following the Soviet lead, the PCI declined to confront the issue squarely: the Chinese were either ignored, as in the document prepared by the Secretariat, or referred to in passing as partially backing the Albanian positions.[54] Such reticence might have gone unchallenged at other times, but not when the non-Communist press was speculating almost daily on the subject and when so many members of the PCI itself were in no mood to be put off easily with superficial explanations—or none. What was being demanded above all from the leadership was candor: about the Soviet past, about the PCI's own mistakes, about the relationships among the parties. No one who thought about the matter could take seriously the notion that Soviet differences with the Chinese stemmed only from a disagreement over Albania.

Those in the PCI with leftist inclinations and thus a natural sympathy for Chinese radicalism were particularly inclined to push the party leaders into a fuller explanation of the causes of the dispute. An interesting illustration of this is an article written by Laura Conti, an intellectual described as a "Communist militant," for Lelio Basso's left-wing Socialist review:

The Soviet-Chinese quarrel must have much more important reasons [than Albania], and the very fact that these are not being deeply explored makes them worrisome. The rank and file are very concerned over this,

[53] A reference to the "erroneous and dangerous" manner in which the Albanian party discussed its internal situation was included in Togliatti, "A proposito di socialismo e democrazia," *Rinascita*, XVIII, 4 (April 1961), pp. 353–363, at p. 361. As Griffith has noted, only Ulbricht had previously openly criticized the Albanians; *Albania*, pp. 79–80. Griffith goes on to comment that by stating his lack of responsibility for what the Albanians were doing, "Togliatti for the first time implicitly recognized the potential organizational community of interest between all small Communist parties, be they rightist or leftist in policies, which do not wish to be totally subservient to Moscow." The line of reasoning here is not clear or convincing to me; it perhaps illustrates the difficulty of interpreting a party leader's statements on international issues without full awareness of the domestic context. The article in question was primarily intended as a rebuttal of Pietro Nenni's charge that the PCI could be judged not by what it said or did in Italy, but by how socialism was practiced where it had taken power. I doubt that Togliatti was making an esoteric comment about the international Communist movement. See Chapter Seven for more on the context.

[54] See Togliatti's report to the Central Committee, *L'Unità*, November 11, 1961.

and it is not enough to reassure them with declarations to the effect that the basic reasons for unity and solidarity of the Communist movement on a world scale have not been weakened. That the Chinese, precisely during the Twenty-Second Congress, have reaffirmed their consideration for Stalin in a way so different from the judgment offered by the Soviets is a fact that gives Sino-Albanian solidarity a grave and obscure meaning. The rank and file are aware of this gravity and obscurity, but the official documents of the party pass over the question in silence.[55]

It is entirely possible that Conti's purpose in writing as well as the nature of her personal contacts in the party led her to overstate the extent to which ordinary party members were concerned about the issue and looking for explanations. Among students and intellectuals, however, the question was clearly being hotly discussed. In an attempt to penetrate beneath the ideological cover to the heart of the matter, and at the same time to understand why the Twenty-Second Congress had been the occasion for a sudden worsening of the dispute, many Italian Communists and Socialists turned to the new Soviet party Program, wondering whether the conflict related to the Soviet decision to announce the start of the building of communism in the USSR. Particularly at a moment when critical attention was being directed toward Stalin's role in the early years of the revolution, the implications of that decision could not go unexamined: "A party having vivid memories of the bitter struggle that accompanied the theoretical formulation of the building of socialism in a single country cannot accept without reflection and without discussion the theory of communism in a single country."[56]

Having got so far, one could hardly ignore Trotsky. Had he been right, after all, not only in his condemnation of the bureaucratic degeneration of Soviet socialism but also in his contention that the theory of socialism in one country was a betrayal of the world revolution? Perhaps the Soviet decision to proceed alone to the building of communism was yet another indication of a parochial perspective, of a failure to understand and act creatively upon the new opportunities for expansion of socialism in the underdeveloped countries and in Western Europe. Trotsky suddenly became, as Giuseppe Boffa acknowledged, a fashionable subject: "Besides, any bookseller can say how the sale of Trotsky's works increased after the Twenty-Second Congress of the CPSU."[57] The young intellec-

---

55 Conti, *Problemi del socialismo*, IV–V, 12–1, p. 1274.
56 *Ibid.*
57 "*Nuova generazione* e il XXII Congresso," *Rinascita*, XIX, 2 (February 1962), p. 130. The Socialists helped stimulate this interest by publishing articles such as the one in *Avanti!*, November 5, 1961, provocatively entitled "Was Trotsky Right, Then?"

tuals shocked the Communist world by printing Trotsky's picture in the Youth Federation's weekly newspaper with a caption labeling him "one of the most original figures of the October Revolution," a man whose thought was once again being discussed and who had written one of the most interesting histories of the Revolution and some of the best pages on Lenin. The accompanying article called for a fresh look at the Soviet ideological and political struggles of the 1920's and of the views of such men as Trotsky.[58]

These remarks stirred up a violent storm in Italy and abroad. The editors of *Nuova generazione,* while apologizing for their failure to take into account "the extreme delicacy of the subject," especially for older Communists who had lived through the Trotsky era, nevertheless refused to accept the accusations leveled by Thorez and echoed in the bourgeois press that they wished to "rehabilitate" Trotsky: "We are not Trotskyites nor have we the least sympathy for Trotskyism."[59] Trotsky had been quite wrong, they insisted, in assuming that the objective processes of economic and social development would soon lead Western Europe to a socialist revolution; Stalin had correctly grasped the fact that revolution in the West could not occur unless the power of the proletariat had been consolidated elsewhere in the world. But while Stalin had in practice been right in his choice of strategies, the ultimate failure of Stalinism lay in having failed to perceive the link between the Soviet and the world revolution, "in having, in short, made a theory out of the self-sufficiency of the Bolshevik Revolution":

Here, then, is the present political value of the Trotsky problem. Today it is possible to reject and defeat Trotskyism as could not be done in the past. But it is also possible, even necessary, to understand the positive element that lies within it, that of affirming the irreplaceable value, the qualitative contribution of the Western revolution. And all this runs counter to an always possible tendency toward self-sufficiency and "productivism" in Soviet society; and above all counter to an Afro-Asian deformation of Marxism as the revolutionary doctrine of the backward countries.[60]

Stalin's policy of concentrating resources on strengthening the USSR as a base for an eventual international socialist system was not hard to justify even to those on the left: it had, after all, succeeded, and it was in any event a revolutionary policy demanding bitter sacrifice and struggle of the Russian people. It was not so

[58] Elio Mercuri, "Sviluppo economico e libertà socialista," *Nuova generazione,* November 17, 1961, p. 5. The photograph was actually one of Lenin addressing a meeting, with Trotsky barely distinguishable in the background.

[59] "Perchè non siamo trotzkisti," *Nuova generazione,* December 15, 1961, pp. 10–11.

[60] *Ibid.,* p. 10.

easy, though, to construe Khrushchev's decision in a similarly favorable light. The question inescapably arose whether the USSR was really justified, given its already great military and economic strength, in concentrating its resources so exclusively on its own advanced domestic goals, at the expense of other socialist societies badly in need of economic assistance. It began to be suggested that the Soviet decision to strive above all for economic growth and peaceful coexistence implied a weakening of its obligation to aid other parties seeking to make their own revolution. The Secretary of the Youth Federation addressing his Central Committee found it necessary to answer those young Communists who saw the Soviet program as a "manifestation of nationalism."[61] Laura Conti mentions the "dissatisfactions and perplexity" arising from the leadership's failure to refute the "suspicion of isolationism" stirred up in many by the Soviet decision to move to the stage of building communism.[62]

These speculations merited careful refutation not just because they were offensive to the Soviet Union. If the USSR had in fact no serious interest in advancing the cause of revolution outside its own borders, then the PCI's entire past would be suspect and the logic of its continued adherence to Soviet policy would become tenuous indeed. Probably the most careful rebuttal was that provided by Valentino Gerratana in a lengthy theoretical analysis of the wisdom both of Stalin's original choice (which "many people still do not understand") and of the Soviet decision to move forward at its own pace toward a communist society. The alternative of delaying Soviet progress in order to bring other socialist countries up to the same level and thus permit a simultaneous march to communism had to be rejected: such a strategy rested on the implicit Stalinist assumption that the capitalist economic system was in such dire straits as to collapse of its own weight, whereas in reality its decline could be guaranteed only by steady competitive pressure from an economically powerful socialist system led by the USSR.[63]

Gerratana made no explicit reference to the Chinese, although he did acknowledge in passing that his analysis might be less convincing to those socialist countries who happened to be having major domestic economic difficulties. A few days later, however, Luigi Longo, returned from his round of conversations in Moscow, explicitly attributed to the Chinese the theory of simultaneous

61 Rino Serri, *L'Unità*, December 6, 1961.
62 Conti, *Problemi del socialismo*, IV–V, 12–1, p. 1274.
63 *L'Unità*, December 12 and 13, 1961.

progression to communism. The disagreement between the Soviet and Chinese parties, he suggested, went deeper than the questions of peaceful coexistence, inevitability of war, and the personality cult:

At the root of this disagreement there is perhaps a different conception of the march toward socialism and communism of the countries of the socialist system. This march, according to a certain conception, should occur as a united whole; the more advanced countries ought to regulate their pace by that of the more backward countries, putting all their material advantage at the disposal of the latter so as to accelerate their progress.[64]

The Chinese view, Longo added, was obviously incompatible not only with the basic premises of Soviet foreign policy—the economic challenge to capitalism, peaceful coexistence, and economic aid to the underdeveloped countries—but also with the program of transition to communism and the substitution of a state of all the people for the dictatorship of the proletariat.

It seems curious at first glance that Longo should tentatively offer as the semiofficial view of the party the same general explanation of the Sino-Soviet dispute as was being propounded by intellectuals on the party's left wing. Several explanations are possible. For one thing, Longo's thesis tended to cut the ground out from under the critics by accepting their analytical framework but reversing the blame: his conception made it the Chinese, not the Russians, who were acting from a narrowly nationalistic and materialistic standpoint, insisting that the advance of socialism on a world scale be retarded in order to satisfy more rapidly their own needs. Furthermore, Longo was thereby able to suggest that those who questioned Soviet policy in this regard were not only directly supporting the Chinese cause but also weakening the opportunities for revolution in the West. The PCI's future, he was reminding the party, depended on the power and prestige of Russian, not Asian, communism: only an economically powerful USSR "can offer perspectives of a very advanced society, nearer to the sensibilities and aspirations of the peoples of the technically more advanced countries of the capitalist world, and for this very reason, can accelerate their march toward socialism."[65]

The most interesting aspect of Longo's explanation is its implicit de-emphasis of ideological issues—its interpretation of Sino-Soviet differences as in part a conflict between states defending separate

[64] *Ibid.,* December 23, 1961.
[65] *Ibid.*

national interests rather than exclusively an ideological quarrel between Communist parties. This explanation had the advantages of making the dispute seem somehow more susceptible to negotiation and of draining some of its explosive potential for the Italian party. The threat of serious factionalism in the PCI might not have been intense at that moment, but the impassioned debates over the Twenty-Second Congress had given legitimate cause for future alarm. The strong leftist inclinations among the young Communists were particularly worrisome, giving rise to the possibility of pro-Chinese factions in the party.

In order to avoid bringing these latent conflicts to the surface, open confrontation of competing ideological perspectives was something to be avoided. The PCI therefore followed a policy of minimizing the implications of the dispute, incorporating into the document prepared by the Secretariat statements that were shortly to prove no more than wishful thinking:

> It would be profoundly mistaken to conclude from such disagreements and from other differences that have occurred or may occur on other occasions between the Communist and workers' parties that the basic reasons for unity and solidarity of the Communist movement on a world scale have become less compelling and that we confront the prospect of a period of serious conflicts and splits.
>
> Beyond the differences and disagreements, even serious ones on important problems of evaluating the international situation and on the strategy and tactics of the workers' movement, there exists a broad basis of general shared objectives and of common ideal principles. This basis could not break up without grave consequences for the movement as a whole and for the development of its individual parties.[66]

This posture was entirely consistent with the perception on which polycentrism was based: that the objective differences in the circumstances of Communist parties and states around the world were so great as to necessitate variation in their tactics and strategies. Of all the party leaders who commented on the subject of polycentrism, only Władysław Gomułka explicitly attacked this point and its critical implications:

> The differences in the political activity and working methods of the various Communist and workers parties do not always stem from objective conditions, from the specific conditions of the country in which a given party is active. They can also be an expression of dogmatic or revisionist tendencies influencing their policy. For example, the present policy of the leaders of the Albanian Party of Labor, the methods they employ in Albania's domestic life, do not stem from objective conditions, they stem from dogmatism, sectarianism, and adventurism; whereas in the League

---

[66] "Documento del PCI sul XXII Congresso," *L'Unità*, November 28, 1961.

of Communists of Yugoslavia, a country neighboring on Albania, revisionism has triumphed. Consequently, it is not only objective conditions that dictate the policy of a given party.[67]

From this perspective, polycentrism seemed to encourage a sympathetic attitude toward ideological deviation: the Chinese position, instead of a heresy to be fought to the end and uprooted, became something to be viewed in terms of national interest, mistaken but nonetheless comprehensible.

This accent did in fact occasionally appear in PCI literature. For example, an article summarizing attitudes expressed in the meetings of party organizations in Milan after the Twenty-Second Congress supported the Soviet foreign policy line but added the following observation about China:

Every militant was able to understand how the Chinese people can at this moment feel that different requirements are pre-eminent, respectable but regional ones related to the expectations of the underdeveloped countries, to the concrete conditions of imperialist aggressiveness, to the very material necessities that require hasty and scattered assistance.[68]

Togliatti himself had shown traces of such an attitude, as we noted earlier, and now after the Twenty-Second Congress, referring to the idea that war cannot be avoided because imperialism has not changed, he wrote: "It is a mistaken conception, yet one understands how it can be accepted in those parts of the workers' movement that find themselves directly and immediately faced with the continual pressure and provocation of an aggressive and insolent imperialism, like that of the United States, for example, with regard to the great Chinese People's Republic."[69] To a Soviet leader engaged in mortal combat with the Chinese over the correct strategy for the international movement, such talk might sound all too much like apologetics for the Chinese position. In one sense, Togliatti was in fact being soft on China. It was his hope, which he maintained despite repeated discouragement until his death, that the problem could somehow be resolved without a confrontation that would split the movement and perhaps his own party. One begins to sense quite clearly his preference and that of his party for a *modus vivendi* based on tolerant acceptance of the inevitable fact that Soviet and Chinese strategic priorities were not and could not be the same.

This attitude did not imply endorsement of the procedures em-

[67] Władysław Gomułka, *Trybuna Ludu*, November 24, 1961; quoted in Dallin et al., *Diversity in International Communism*, p. 331.

[68] *L'Unità*, November 30, 1961.

[69] Togliatti, *Rinascita*, XVIII, 12 (December 1961), p. 915.

ployed in 1957 and 1960 to reach a formal agreement that concealed irreconcilable differences. Although in his opening address to the Central Committee Togliatti had asserted that these meetings had provided "an unshakable basis for the ideological and political unity of our entire movement,"[70] by the time the Secretariat's statement had emerged from the process of compromise at the party summit this judgment had been reversed: the PCI went on record with the view that the meetings had not "fully satisfied the need for a further development of theoretical and political positions." Such general conferences might "under certain circumstances" usefully supplement bilateral contacts and regional meetings, but not too much should be expected from them:

> We believe, however, that one should not always on all problems expect to reach an agreement that could turn out to be merely formal. On the contrary, within certain limits, the expression of different views should be allowed, without this resulting in irreparable conflicts and political splits.[71]

The similar position expressed in 1956 and early 1957 had been quietly abandoned in the face of Soviet pressures to restore the unity of the movement around an antirevisionist platform. Was the same experience to be lived through again, with the parties now mobilized against the sectarian outposts of the Communist movement? Many of the leaders of the PCI, bolder than in 1956 and beginning to develop and articulate a more independent sense of their party's interests, wished to avoid such a repetition, with its stultifying effect on the vitality and flexibility of the party. It remained to be seen whether they could, or dared, begin to act in accordance with their desires.

THE RESPONSE FROM POLAND AND YUGOSLAVIA.   Alone, the PCI could not hope to exercise much influence over the course of events in the movement. One consequence of the Twenty-Second Congress, however, was to revive and consolidate the affinities that had appeared in 1956–1957 between the Italian, Polish, and Yugoslav parties. From this time on, despite some differences over tactics, there came to exist a common understanding among the three on the major issues in international Communist affairs.

The proceedings at the PCI's Central Committee meeting in November were followed with intense interest in Warsaw.[72] On

70 L'Unità, November 11, 1961.
71 "Documento del PCI sul XXII Congresso," L'Unità, November 28, 1961.
72 "It can be said without fear of exaggeration that, especially this time, there has been notable interest in the work of the Central Committee of the Italian

the issues relating to de-Stalinization, the Polish position was close to that of the PCI: an editorial in the party weekly implicitly accepted the contention that the personality cult was a manifestation of a "whole system" that had to be destroyed and rejected the view that this system had been the inevitable result of the process of modernization.[73]

But while many in the Polish party welcomed the PCI's bold attitude toward the Soviet past, Gomułka and his colleagues appear to have been somewhat concerned lest the demands of the Italian reformists for greater freedom of discussion and action within the party cause repercussions in Polish circles. As Hansjakob Stehle has observed, Gomułka was worried that the Twenty-Second Congress might stir up once again the intellectual ferment of 1956–1957, disturbing the precarious ideological basis for his position.[74] There was thus in some respects a curious reversal of the situation of 1956, when the liberal winds blowing strongly from Warsaw had aroused Togliatti's concern by lending moral support to those who wished to enhance the democracy and autonomy of the PCI. In 1961, however, there was little cause for friction between the leaders of the two parties, both of whom were seeking to control and contain the reformist impulses by a blend of firmness and conciliation.

A similarity of views existed with respect to international Communist affairs as well. None stressed more frequently than the Poles the principles of autonomy and equality; and in no other quarter was there more clearly echoed the Italian thesis that the false unanimity of the past was both wrong and unattainable for the future:

It is a new unity, qualitatively different from that of the past era, which was to a large degree illusory unity. Because, in point of fact, the premise that there may exist a total unanimity in every matter and at every moment among various parties, as well as among members of each of

Communist party, both in leadership circles of the Polish United Workers' Party and other parties of the national front, and in the general public." *L'Unità,* November 18, 1961; the article reported in detail which Polish newspapers devoted how much space to Togliatti's speech. The party weekly *Polityka* on November 18 quoted from the Central Committee discussion, and *Nowe Drogi,* February 1962, printed ten pages of excerpts from the articles in the December issue of *Rinascita.* Between November and February both *Polityka* and *Argumenty* ran a series of articles containing excerpts from the speeches and articles of PCI officials and appraisals of the work of various Italian Communist intellectuals, from Antonio Gramsci to Cesare Luporini.

[73] "The Direction of Renewal and the March Toward Communism," *Nowe Drogi,* December 1961, excerpted in Dallin *et al., Diversity in International Communism,* pp. 342–343.

[74] Stehle, "Polish Communism," in Griffith, *Communism in Europe,* Vol. 1, pp. 125–126.

these parties acting in different and frequently in completely dissimilar conditions, faced by variable problems, was profoundly undialectical. Such a unity resulted in reality from the fact that the views and opinions of one party . . . were being imposed on all parties.[75]

The logical corollary of such a rejection of the old-time monolithic unity was a desire to conciliate the Sino-Soviet dispute and minimize its ideological aspects.

Despite this basic similarity of interest between the two parties, there remained the difference in emphasis implied in Gomułka's rejection of the polycentrism idea. Gomułka seemed to be warning the Italians, and perhaps some in his own party as well, that it would be a mistake to go too far in the direction of explaining Communist differences as the product only of divergent circumstances. Ideology too was important, and political errors must be fought, not excused or justified on pragmatic grounds.[76]

Such issues as these were undoubtedly discussed when Longo and Napolitano passed through Warsaw late in November on their way home from Moscow, and the PCI's subsequent "clarification" of the meaning of polycentrism may have been influenced as much by Gomułka's as by Khrushchev's opinions. Longo and Togliatti, indeed, probably felt that polycentrism had acquired connotations they did not wish to endorse. In an article that in effect summed up the party's debate on the issue of international Communist unity, Togliatti went out of his way to emphasize that autonomy was not the whole answer:

The system of autonomy of individual parties has, however, negative aspects and even serious dangers. It would be a mistake not to recognize it. First of all there is the danger of isolation, of shutting every party up within itself, in a blind provincialism of its own. . . .

There are, in fact, general objectives of struggle, directions and perspectives of action strictly dependent on the very character of the historical period in which we live. They must be common to the whole workers' movement and to all Communist parties, because if they were not, we should leave the field of autonomy to enter that of disorder, bewilderment, and confusion.[77]

75 "The Direction of Renewal and the March Toward Communism," *Nowe Drogi*, December 1961; excerpted in Dallin *et al.*, *Diversity in International Communism*, p. 344.

76 See Stehle in Griffith, *Communism in Europe*, Vol 1, p. 127. Stressing the similarities, Stehle interprets Gomułka's statement as only a "seeming sideswipe at Togliatti" intended "to efface the impression that he supported the Italian rightist position." This seems to me to overlook the real differences of view discussed above.

77 Togliatti, *Rinascita*, XVIII, 12, p. 914. In this article Togliatti made his remark about the "mistaken and catastrophic decision" of the Comintern in dissolving the Polish party. This was Togliatti's public apology to Gomułka for his part in the affair, an act necessary for future collaboration.

Gomułka and Togliatti were accustomed to slanting their remarks to the particular situation confronting them, and both appear to have felt, after the confusion stirred up by the Twenty-Second Congress, that the theme of unity should be given particular play. Their basic positions, as subsequent months would demonstrate, were similar and in principle straightforward: they wished to see the unity of the movement retained, under terms allowing the maximum possible degree of autonomy to each of the parties. They were both, therefore, opposed in principle to the centralizing tendencies of the Soviet Union and of China alike, while fully backing the former on the substantive issues of the dispute. The Polish and Italians had by late 1961 begun a tacit collaboration to this end.

As for the Yugoslavs, they responded with even greater warmth and encouragement to the innovators in the Italian party. The debate on Stalinism and on its consequences for the PCI was seen as a wholly positive development, marred only by the continued Soviet unwillingness to adopt an adequately self-critical reappraisal. A sympathetic analysis of polycentrism, more extended than anything attempted by the Italians themselves, appeared in a leading Yugoslav journal. In words very close to those of the *Nowe Drogi* editorial quoted before—but in implicit contrast to Gomułka's stress on the ideological roots of Communist differences—the writer insisted that "it is impossible to achieve perfect ideological unity among so many and such different parties and movements." A sufficient though not perfect degree of unity could be achieved only by respecting the different circumstances in which the parties had to work, by encouraging free discussion and social research, and by rejecting "ideological monopoly and pretensions to the absolute correctness of individual views." The article concluded with the regret that the Italian Communists had felt obliged to renounce their support of polycentrism after being criticized by the dogmatists: "this is yet another indication of the times in which we live."[78]

To be praised by the Yugoslavs was of course hardly something to enhance one's influence in international Communist circles. Nevertheless, the trend of Soviet policy was manifestly toward a second rapprochement with Tito, and it became possible for the PCI once again to lead the way. There developed a community of interests between the Italian and Yugoslav parties that first manifested itself on the trade union front, at the Fifth Congress of the WFTU in December 1961.

---

[78] Puniša Perović, "Discussion on 'Polycentrism,'" *Review of International Affairs*, XIII, 289 (April 21, 1962), pp. 10–12.

CHAPTER SEVEN

THE PARTY'S DOMESTIC STRATEGY

The Italian party's relations with the international Communist movement cannot be fully understood without some appreciation of its domestic circumstances and strategy. This contention would require little amplification save for the fact that it has not always been self-evident. When Stalinism was at its height, and for some time thereafter, one could often correctly assume that a nonruling party almost invariably subordinated its domestic requirements to those of the USSR. As a working model of reality, this premise no longer suffices, even though in specific instances it may still hold true.

With the decline of Soviet authority in the movement and the collapse of monolithic unity, it began to be possible for parties out of power to give their domestic needs priority over those of the Soviet Union. But they were not automatically led to do so, if only because Communist leaders were strongly biased toward identifying their own and their parties' interests with Moscow's. Although we have in recent years sometimes professed admiration for the growing "boldness" of the nonruling parties, perhaps we should rather have been wondering why the process of emancipation has been so slow and gradual, for the nonruling parties have lagged far behind many of the parties in power.

The basic reason for this comparative backwardness is probably the relatively more tenuous connection between their domestic and international interests. A ruling party can readily perceive how national economic or political interests may be damaged by Soviet actions, and it can weigh the injury against the advantages of Soviet protection or the threat of Soviet attack. It can, furthermore, rely on the nationalist sentiments of its people as a compensating source of strength. In short, however complex its calculations, they are based on fairly straightforward principles of nationalism. The nonruling party has no comparably clear standard of measurement.

The classic dilemma of Communist parties in the West has been that their access to power seemed to depend, in one degree or another, on Soviet support (whether by force of arms, as after the Second World War, or by gradual reversal of the international balance of power, as at present). To the extent this premise has seemed true, a party's own long-run interests have tended to keep it in the Soviet camp. To the extent, however, that a party has felt it possible to make its own way, the reasons—logical as well as psychological—for dependence on the USSR have been correspondingly reduced. Here the Italian party has been in the vanguard, however timidly, precisely because it has taken relatively seriously its prospects for advancing toward power through its own efforts and has thus created a "party interest" analogous to the national interest perceived by a party in power.

What, then, makes up this "party interest"? To explain this fully would require a separate book. Alternatively, one might limit the discussion to a few general observations about the nature and domestic problems of the party and their effects on international behavior, leaving elaboration to others. I have looked for a middle road, believing that the analysis of international matters would carry greater conviction if certain aspects of the party's domestic role were explored. This does not imply a well-rounded summary evaluation of all major aspects of party life and strategy; the aim has been rather to select and illustrate, dwelling on those points that seem to be most relevant to the PCI's relations with the international movement.

The more general purpose of this review is to illustrate the nature of the party's over-all domestic strategy by exploring its dealings with the Christian Democratic and Socialist parties and its response to Italy's economic modernization. This strategy has, in its essence, remained the same throughout the postwar period. Its substance, and equally important its style, go some distance toward explaining the party's characteristic behavior on the international front. A second and parallel purpose is to investigate the specific effects of the domestic changes occurring at the end of the 1950's and the early 1960's—hopefully, so as to understand the circumstances conditioning the party's response to the international movement during the crisis caused by the challenge of the Chinese party and the corresponding decline of Soviet authority.

The years 1956–1964 were dynamic ones for Italy. The two related phenomena that dominated the period, the *apertura a sinistra* and the *miracolo economico,* together seemed to be pushing the country forward into a new era. Despite the enormous handicap of a still backward South, Italy was fast acquiring the economic characteristics of an advanced industrial society: steady growth of output, greater social mobility, shift of labor from agriculture to industry, modernization of economic structures, high living standards, a mass culture. Her economic output had been expanding since 1948 at an over-all rate unequaled elsewhere in Europe, but appreciation of this rapid advance had been obscured and its political impact muffled by many factors, including particularly the recession of 1958. The Communists, conditioned to look for the worst in the economic picture, were slow to grasp the importance of the trend. By the early 1960's, however, with all economic indicators pointing sharply upward, they were obliged to recognize openly that their classical expectations about capitalist economics might have to be thought through afresh.

A similar transformation, equally important but with far less apparent "inevitability" about it, was brewing on the political front. Ever since 1956, Italian politics had been in active pursuit of a new equilibrium: the Soviet and East European events provided the catalyst necessary to break the *immobilismo* of previous years, permitting Pietro Nenni to begin the precarious operation of disengaging his party definitively from the Communist sphere. This was the essential prerequisite for a shift of the power balance from right to left within the Christian Democratic party and for an eventual realignment of the entire structure of politics.

The payoff began to come four years later, after the decisive defeat of the Christian Democratic attempt to restore a conservative coalition supported by the Liberal party and the neofascist Movimento Sociale Italiano (MSI). The collapse of rightist hopes in the dramatic "July days" of 1960, which demonstrated the continued potency of the Communist slogan of the unity of the left against the Fascist danger, seemed to leave open for the middle run but one viable formula: a government of the Center-Left based on the Christian Democrats but supported by the two socialist parties of Nenni and Saragat. The drama of recent Italian political life has lain in the high tensions and vicissitudes of the search to implement what seemed both inevitable and yet almost impossible.

The sense of inevitability came from the rational perception that, once a coalition of the Center-Right had been discredited, a move to the left was the only remaining alternative for a Christian Democracy that lacked the strength to govern alone. The sense of impossibility arose from the fact that each of the two parties principally involved was itself deeply divided, with a large minority fiercely opposed to the compromises that would be required to consummate the contemplated unholy alliance. Those working for the new coalition had to face the constant threat of a split or of a reversal of the balance within the party. This endemic factionalism gives to Italian politics its special flavor; the interparty battle can be understood only in terms of the far more intense struggle within each of the major parties.

Its relatively passive role and its greatly superior discipline enabled the PCI for some time to present a more united front to the world than the other parties. From its secure position as the major opposition party, the PCI could afford to delay a commitment, stressing now the favorable, now the unfavorable sides of the situation. As the Center-Left grew closer to realization, however, it became more difficult to equivocate. Basic decisions were clearly going to be required, and the competing orientations within the party began to make themselves more clearly heard.

There was no mistaking the nature of the threat. If Pietro Nenni were to follow Saragat and lead the Socialist party into near-permanent participation in a reformist coalition led by Christian Democracy and a consequent ideological and political competition with the Communists for allegiance of the working class, one of the keystones of the PCI's strategy would be shattered. A Communist party alone on the left, in an environment of growing national prosperity and social reforms, might manage to hang onto its existing electoral strength by keeping alive old voting habits and drawing on new pockets of discontent, but the prospects for a significant improvement of its fortunes would be dim. Lacking prospective allies, and unable on its own to poll more than a quarter or perhaps a third of the votes, it might have to resign itself to playing the exclusively disruptive game of the French Communist party. At the local level, too, its control of many town and provincial governments, in itself a major element in assuring a large Communist vote, would be weakened or lost if the Socialists should break off their traditional collaboration.

Such a gloomy prognosis, however, logically calling for a strategy of unmitigated opposition to Socialist collaboration with Christian Democracy, was not altogether compelling. It rested on many dubious assumptions, most notably that a coalition of the Center-Left in which the Christian Democratic right and their Vatican supporters would remain a powerful minority could actually accomplish serious reforms. If not, it would have been demonstrated to all those on the left, of whatever party, that the Communists were indeed, as they always maintained, indispensable to a program of national "renewal." The threat that the Socialist party might be "captured" by the conservatives and transformed into an obliging partner in a neocapitalist middle-class government could be balanced off against the vulnerability of both Socialists and Christian Democrats to pressures from the left. A Socialist entente with Christian Democracy could thus be viewed as the first step toward creation of a "new majority" that included the entire "lay left" and a significant portion of Christian Democratic strength.

Communists, Christian Democrats, and the Catholic Church

The Communists have long professed to believe that Italy's fate would in the end be decided by the outcome of a contest between two powerful political and ideological movements, communism and Catholicism. And the similarities between them are striking. Only they among Italian political movements have been able to attract widespread support from the masses, to control powerful political, social, and trade union organizations reaching into all levels of the society, to articulate ideologies aspiring to universal validity. Each is attached, moreover, to one of the two competing international power systems, thus linking the conflict in Italy to the outcome of the international struggle.

The PCI's bipolar view of the Italian political scene is reflected in constant references to the necessary meeting of the "Communist and Catholic worlds," an encounter that seems to be understood both as collaboration and as confrontation. The party, inspired in this as in other matters by Togliatti, pretends to a serene confidence that it, along with the Church, represents something permanent in Italian and world history. The lesser parties are viewed in a largely "instrumental" light, as subject to manipulation by the big two. Those on the right, representing outmoded ideas and social groups, will soon disappear entirely. Those on the lay left, caught squarely between the two protagonists, will sooner or later be obliged to choose definitively between them. Nenni's Socialist party in particular is seen as facing an inevitable decision between its Marxist principles and the lures of the capitalist establishment upheld by the Christian Democrats.

VULNERABILITIES OF CHRISTIAN DEMOCRACY. While the course of history may have given the Christian Democratic party advantages in the competition, it is not, in the Communist view, anything like an impregnable monolith. The PCI's political strategy has banked on the assumption that certain vulnerabilities of the DC could be exploited by correct Communist action. From a Marxist standpoint the "inherent contradictions" of the DC are indeed formidable: here is a party long dominated by a reactionary alliance of the Church hierarchy and of big capital which yet also pretends to represent the interests of the lesser bourgeoisie and of the proletariat, relying on their votes to stay in power. Elementary Marxist analysis shows up the weaknesses of such *interclassismo*, demonstrating that the interests of conflicting classes cannot be served by a single party so long as capitalism continues to reign.[1]

What holds the Christian Democratic party together despite the disruptive tendencies induced by its interclass character? For the Communists, the answer lies principally in the pull of Catholic tradition and the strength of the anti-Communist ideology so assiduously cultivated by the ecclesiastical hierarchy, the industrial and financial elite, and the politicians of Christian Democracy. In a characteristic analysis, Togliatti once explained the Italian political formula of the 1950's as based on a "union of the ruling forces of the Catholic camp with the economic right, hence with the most reactionary and conservative groups of Italian society. An obsession with anticommunism was its ideal foundation and justification."[2] The PCI has known all along that to play successfully upon the weaknesses of Christian Democracy requires wearing down the official insistence of the Catholic movement that for Catholics to collaborate with communism in any form is tantamount to a religious offense.[3]

The enormous secular power of the Vatican and the logic of democratic politics in a country nominally 99 per cent Catholic strongly encouraged the Communists to adopt an attitude of religious tolerance. This decision was manifested in two striking ways in the immediate postwar years. The PCI statutes then adopted were unique in the Communist movement in specifying that any citizen, independent of race, religious faith, and philosophical conviction, might be accepted into the party so long as he accepted its political program.[4] This departure from Marxist-Leninist orthodoxy

[1] On this theme see, *inter alia*, Pietro Ingrao, "Questioni della politica verso i cattolici," *Rinascita*, XVIII, 1–2 (January–February 1961), pp. 23–28.

[2] Report to the Central Committee, *L'Unità*, December 4, 1960.

[3] As Norman Kogan has put it, the Christian Democratic party "prefers to define the voter's choice as one between virtue and evil, between Rome and Moscow, between Christ and anti-Christ." *The Government of Italy* (New York: Crowell, 1962), p. 178. Kogan notes in another spot that about one-third of the voters "will vote the way the Church tells it to vote"; *ibid.*, p. 72. This is notoriously true of Italian women, who make up an unusually high percentage of the DC electorate: one pre-1956 analysis calculates that about two-thirds of DC voters are women, whereas the ratio in the PCI and the PSI is approximately reversed; see table reproduced in Joseph LaPalombara, "Political Party Systems and Crisis Government: French and Italian Contrasts," *Midwest Journal of Political Science*, II, 2 (May 1958), p. 139.

[4] Kogan writes that the PCI "asserted and maintained, against strong pressure

not only made it possible for some faithful communicants to become party members, but allowed the party to present itself to the voters as having no ideological hostility to the Church.[5]

The second such conciliatory move was the famous occasion in 1947 when the Communists parted company with the Socialists and other leftist parties to vote in favor of Article 7 of the Italian Constitution confirming the Lateran Pacts and thus perpetuating the Church's special official position in Italian society. Then and subsequently the PCI eschewed the anticlericalism of the other lay parties. In 1957, for example, Togliatti sharply attacked the proposal made by a group of Liberals and Radicals for abolition of the Concordat governing Church-State relations, arguing that such a "maximalist" approach would only exacerbate relations with the Church and sabotage the patient application of a policy designed gradually to break down the barriers between the Catholic masses and the parties of the left.[6]

A principal aim of the PCI's postwar strategy, then, has been to overcome Catholic anticommunism and disrupt the unity of the Christian Democratic party by demonstrating to a portion of its membership and its electorate that they have a greater community of interests with the Communists than with the intransigent right wing of their own party. The tactics by which this goal has been pursued have varied according to the PCI's estimate of where, at any given moment, the greatest opportunities were to be found.

Through the 1950's the dominant emphasis tended to fall on the basic class conflict between the Christian Democratic masses and the capitalists who controlled the party. At the Eighth party Congress in 1956, for example, Togliatti discussed the problem of contact with Catholicism primarily in terms of seeking "contact, agreement, and collaboration" with the Catholic masses.[7] As one critical analyst on the Socialist left summed it up, the hope was to accomplish "the gradual erosion of the ecclesiastical armies right up to the point of achieving an absolute majority for the workers' parties."[8] This

---

from Stalin, the clause in the Party's constitution that opens Party membership to all adult Italians no matter what they believe." *The Politics of Italian Foreign Policy* (New York: Praeger, 1963), p. 124. No evidence is given to support this report on Stalin's attitude.

[5] For a discussion of this point see Luciano Gruppi, "I rapporti con i cattolici nella storia del PCI," Mario Gozzini, ed., *Il dialogo alla prova: Cattolici e comunisti italiani* (Florence: Vallecchi editore, 1964), p. 170.

[6] "Una Proposta massimalista: abolire il Concordato," *Rinascita*, XIV, 5 (May 1957), pp. 206–209.

[7] *Eighth Congress*, p. 201.

[8] Domenico Settembrini, "Stato e chiesa nella politica delle opposizioni oggi in Italia," *Problemi del socialismo*, III, 6 (June 1960), p. 503.

aspect of Catholic-Communist relationships has always retained its importance, as is suggested by a party spokesman's endorsement in 1964 of the continuing validity of the observation made by Togliatti ten years before that "there are many more points of contact between the Communist and Socialist masses and the masses on whom the organized Catholic world is based than between the cadres that lead them and especially between the summits of the two worlds."[9]

By the time of the Ninth Congress, four years later, stress on this classic strategy "from below" had been replaced by a dominant, though not exclusive, emphasis on contradictions within the bourgeoisie itself. All "democratic" elements of society—the individual peasant landowner, the small industrialist, the intellectual, the white-collar technician—were now presumed to have a common interest with the industrial proletariat and the landless farm worker in the fight against monopoly capital. The goal was now the creation of a "new majority" of democratic forces constructed around a minimal reform program and ranged against the entire economic and clerical right.[10]

The shift of emphasis ratified at the Ninth Congress was primarily in response to what the PCI regarded as a highly encouraging development, a confirmation of the general expectations concerning the fragility of Christian Democratic unity. Ever since the Segni government's fall in the spring of 1957, the Christian Democratic party had been struggling in vain to produce a stable political coalition. Coalition partners were available on either left or right, but the party was so deeply divided that no solution had more than temporary effect.[11] Amintore Fanfani, as party Secretary and leader of the largest left-wing faction, tried in 1958 to construct a Center-

[9] Ignazio Delogu, "Impegno comune per la pace," in Gozzini, *Il dialogo alla prova*, p. 335, quoting Togliatti speech of April 12, 1954.

[10] See "La risoluzione politica," *IX Congresso del Partito Comunista Italiano: atti e risoluzioni*, Vol. 1 (Rome: Editori Riuniti, 1960), pp. 539–542. Togliatti's address to the Congress, *ibid.*, pp. 23–83, also develops the theme at length. The PCI's reform program included the same basic points that were eventually included in the agreement arrived at between the Socialists and the Christian Democrats in 1962: establishment of regional governments, nationalization of electric power, planned economic development, democratic school reform, aid to small farmers.

[11] For a brief survey of political developments of the period see Hughes, *The United States and Italy*, pp. 209–214. A useful analysis of the DC's factional struggles between 1946 and 1963 is to be found in Raphael Zariski, "Intra-party Conflict in a Dominant Party: The Experience of Italian Christian Democracy," *The Journal of Politics*, XXVII, 1 (February 1965), pp. 3–34. The ideological and political history of the several factions of the Christian Democratic left is studied in Giorgio Galli and Paolo Facchi, *La sinistra democristiana: storia e ideologia* (Milan: Feltrinelli, 1962).

Left government only to be shot down after a few months by dissidents within his own party. Openly supported by the Vatican, the DC right wing was unyielding in its resistance to any move to the left that might open the door to eventual Socialist participation in the government: "We will never collaborate with a socialism that collaborates with the Communists. On that we will be inflexible. . . ."[12] The deadlock was so severe and the frustrations of the DC left so intense that a split in the party, while never probable, could not be ruled out entirely.

The Communists were already benefiting from this situation in several tangible ways. On the labor front a wave of strikes during the spring and summer of 1959 showed the two competing union federations far more than usually willing to collaborate with the CGIL as a means of demonstrating their hostility to the forces of the right.[13] Another hopeful sign was the dissolution of Christian Democratic coalitions in the autonomous regions of Val d'Aosta and Sicily and their replacement by coalitions that included the Communists. The Sicilian case was especially noteworthy, for the crisis had resulted from a split within the Christian Democratic party, leading to the formation of a competing Catholic party, the Sicilian Christian Social Union, under the leadership of Silvio Milazzo. Despite threats of excommunication against Catholics voting for a party prepared to enter an unholy alliance with the Communists, Milazzo triumphed in the June 1959 elections and the PCI entered his government. As one observer noted, "one had the impression that the old deterrent constituted by the natural anticommunism of the Catholics was no longer operating."[14]

The DC's internal crisis came to a climax in the spring and summer of 1960 when a government was formed under Tambroni to which a majority of his own party was opposed and which depended for support on the votes of the neofascist MSI. Tambroni's decision to allow the MSI to hold a party Congress in Genoa, and his use of armed force against the ensuing popular wave of antifascist strikes and demonstrations in Genoa and many other cities led to a clamorous collapse of his wholly discredited government, and with it, an end of right-wing domination of Christian Democracy. The Communists hailed this episode as signaling a revival of the spirit of Resistance days, uniting the parties of the left once more against the threat of authoritarian rule.[15]

12 Guido Gonella at the DC Congress in 1962, quoted by Vittorio Gorresio, *L'Italia a sinistra* (Milan: Rizzoli editore, 1963), p. 160.

13 Galli and Facchi, *La sinistra democristiana,* p. 261.

14 Gorresio, *L'Italia a sinistra,* p. 81.

15 A typical statement is this one by Togliatti: "At this point I wish to under-

In its effort to capitalize on the crisis of Christian Democracy the PCI met with considerable internal resistance from the old left, necessitating "a battle against the sectarian positions that hinder us from understanding and influencing the new ferments being manifested in the Catholic movement and in other political groups."[16] The Communists were, all the same, careful not to attribute decisive short-run significance to the signs of weakness in the Catholic camp. Even at the height of the crisis, in the spring of 1960, Togliatti made a special point of using the term "differentiation" rather than the more decisive "split" in referring to the disagreements in the Catholic camp.[17] Later, when a relative degree of harmony had been restored by the defeat of the extreme right, the party's assessment became even more cautious. A comment in *Rinascita* reflects rather well the basic ambivalence of the Communists toward the cohesion of the Christian Democratic party:

A unity that, no doubt, has deep fissures under the surface and that can also, perhaps, enter rapidly into crisis if confronted by an energetic and resolute opposition on the left; but a unity that is all the same, for the moment, a real fact.[18]

INTERNATIONAL DÉTENTE AND CHRISTIAN DEMOCRACY. As one of the principal means of demonstrating a community of interests with Catholic as well as lay forces on the left, the PCI used not only a moderate program of democratic social reforms but also the struggle for peace, which, as Togliatti once observed, "becomes effective and successful whenever there is collaboration to this end among men and parties of diverse origins, tastes, and aims."[19] Manipulation of the peace issue was intended, in addition to encouraging neutralist sentiments destructive of Italy's commitment to the Atlantic alliance,

---

score the great political value of what happened then. . . . During the fervent weeks of June and July all the lay democratic forces—and also a part of the Catholic forces—admitted that in the face of an open threat of a return to fascism, it is necessary that the same democratic and anti-Fascist unity that existed during the Resistance and the struggle against fascism be re-created." *L'Unità*, December 4, 1960.

[16] "Chiarezza di una linea politica e capacità di realizzarla," *Rinascita*, XVII, 2 (February 1960), p. 85. One illustration of such sectarianism is the criticism levied by a left Socialist, Roberto Barzanti, against the PCI's efforts to collaborate with leftist Catholic intellectuals. Instead of seeking common ground with a generic Catholic "left," the party's central goal should be to extract the worker and peasant masses from the influence of the DC; "Lettere al Direttore," *Rinascita*, XVII, 10 (October 1960), pp. 805–808. Barzanti was undoubtedly expressing sentiments shared by many in the PCI whose misgivings could not be so openly conveyed.

[17] Report to the Central Committee, *L'Unità*, December 4, 1960.

[18] Giuseppe Chiarante, "Il trasformismo d.c. e il giuoco di Fanfani," *Rinascita*, XVII, 9 (September 1960), p. 705.

[19] *L'Unità*, August 1, 1961.

to lay the grounds for such collaboration. The appeal was of course suitable for "men of good will" of any political affiliation since, as one party member crudely stated, it "played on the instinct of self-preservation."[20] Togliatti's insistence in 1954 and again after the summer of 1960 upon the universally destructive effects of nuclear war was but one indication of the high priority the PCI placed on heightening the awareness of the entire Italian people of the possibility and the dangers of war.

The campaign for peaceful coexistence was directed particularly toward the Christian Democratic party and its voters. The apparent simplicity of the issue was in itself an advantage in appealing to a party whose members came from all social classes and included an unusually high proportion of women: peace was an easily understood and universally desired goal, lacking the technicalities and the conflicting class interests surrounding the most important social and economic questions. The pursuit of international détente was thus admirably suited to undermine the cold war psychology and dissolve the anti-Communist sentiment that had made the Communists "untouchables" for all those whose political opinions were influenced by the Church. The following characteristic passage conveys the significance the party attached to the peace campaign in breaking down Catholic resistance to communism:

The process of international détente now in progress can aid the formation in Italy of a new political unity of democratic forces. . . . The affirmation of the Soviet Union's will to peace, the demonstrations of the scientific and cultural superiority of the socialist system, the development of commercial and cultural exchanges between capitalist and socialist countries all signify liquidation of the lies nourished during the cold war. They therefore make a precious contribution to breaking down the anti-Communist prejudices and discriminatory barriers that have until now prevented a meeting between the popular forces of the left and the democratic Catholic forces for the purpose of achieving a minimum program based on implementation of the Constitution and of economic development.[21]

Others outside the Communist camp shared this view of the effects of détente on Italian politics. Referring to the difficulties confronted by Christian Democracy in developing a reform program while maintaining its distance from the Communists, one observer commented:

In this framework détente is bothersome, not because there is anyone among the Christian Democrats who loves tension for its own sake, but

20 Luigi Conte, *ibid.,* October 7, 1961.
21 Giorgio Amendola, "La nostra funzione unitaria," *Rinascita,* XVI, 12 (December 1959), pp. 835–836.

because international policy is felt to be something remote, of concern to others, while détente, especially in its sensational aspects, transforms the untouchables into almost normal interlocutors and thus brings still closer those who have always maintained that it is possible to deal with Russia and that no sin is being committed if, in a local government or a trade union, reasonable and limited things are being decided together, just as, moreover, Eisenhower will be able to decide and resolve questions together with Russia.[22]

Important though the goal of influencing general public opinion may have been, this was not the primary aim of the PCI's posture as resolute supporter of international détente. More important, especially in the late 1950's and early 1960's, was the specific objective of supporting the Christian Democratic left in its battle with the conservatives in the party and the ecclesiastical hierarchy. Norman Kogan has made the significant observation that "the principal issue in Italian foreign policy is whether to preserve or change the domestic social structure."[23] Certainly neither Italian Communists nor Christian Democrats would deny that their foreign policy preferences, their almost equally rigid adherence to Soviet and American positions, respectively, had something to do with their need for great-power support in the effort to transform or uphold the existing social, political, and economic order. A Communist analyst has expressed in this way his party's understanding of this connection as it pertains to Christian Democracy:

The other condition for an effective and suitable utilization of actions for peace in the general movement for a turn to the left is that precisely the link between a foreign policy of peace and an internal policy of structural reform be made clear and unequivocal. The masses must become aware that if the leadership group of Christian Democracy insists so much on "loyalty to Atlanticism" it is because through this "loyalty" it wishes to guarantee itself the connection with the international system of monopolies necessary to ensure that no domestic innovation will damage the system of monopolies within the country.[24]

The power of the Christian Democratic right had indeed traditionally rested heavily on its undisputed claim to be the most uncompromising proponent of a rigid anticommunism and the staunchest defender of American foreign policy. But this, rather than the conservative economic ideologies and interests it represented, would seem to have been the principal factor determining the support it received during the first postwar decade from both the Vatican and

---

22 E.E.A. [Enzo Enriques Agnoletti], "Sconfitta non necessaria," *Il Ponte*, XV, 12 (December 1959), pp. 1498–1499.

23 *The Politics of Italian Foreign Policy*, p. 50.

24 Franco Calamandrei, "Le questioni della pace nel dibattito e nel movimento per la svolta a sinistra," *Rinascita*, XIX, 2 (February 1962), p. 110.

the United States.[25] With a relaxation of the international climate and a desire for détente on the part of these two powerful supporters, the DC right wing was increasingly becoming more of a nuisance than an asset, an embarrassing residue of the intransigent attitudes of the days when John Foster Dulles and Claire Booth Luce set the tone for United States policy in Italy.

There had in fact never been complete unanimity among Christian Democrats on the commitment to the Atlantic alliance. As the cold war was developing in 1947, some important figures on the left, centered around Giuseppe Dossetti, favored détente and Italian neutralism rather than association with NATO, fearing the strengthening of their opponents in the party.[26] Although rendered largely inconsequential by the realities of domestic and international politics, such sentiments never entirely disappeared. Traces of them re-emerged, for example, through the election to the Italian presidency in 1955 of Giovanni Gronchi, a leader of the Christian Democratic left with "a reputation for neutralist leanings and for being 'soft' toward Communism. . . ."[27] The controversy occasioned by an initiative of Gronchi's, five years later, illustrates both the tensions existing in the Catholic world and the value the Communists saw in manipulating them.

Desiring to contribute to the détente and to enhance Italy's international prestige, President Gronchi resolved to pay an official state visit to the Soviet Union early in 1960.[28] Strong resistance was put up within the government and the Vatican, whose newspaper, *L'Osservatore Romano,* had been openly critical of Khrushchev's trip to the United States. Cardinal Ottaviani, the most outspoken opponent of international relaxation and an opening to the left, ventured to attack "men of high responsibility in the West . . . who say that they are Christians . . . [but] shake the hand that slapped

25 See Kogan, *The Politics of Italian Foreign Policy,* pp. 80–83 and 126–127.

26 One of Italy's leading commentators on the Church and its politics writes about this group, which then included Amintore Fanfani and Giorgio La Pira: "They were opposed to any sharp division between the political blocs, whether in foreign or internal policy, and disliked purely sterile and demagogic manifestations of anti-Communism. Instead, they continued to maintain the usefulness of a coalition government with the Communists and Socialists even after the three-party coalition between these parties and the Christian Democrats had come to an end. . . ." Carlo Falconi, *Pope John and His Council* (London: Weidenfeld and Nicolson, 1964), p. 78.

27 Hughes, *The United States and Italy,* pp. 203–204.

28 According to Falconi, *Pope John,* p. 119, the trip was negotiated by Giorgio La Pira, as part of his long-time campaign to improve East-West relations; in Falconi's view, it marked "a historic turning point" in relations between Moscow and the Vatican.

Christ in the face."[29] When Gronchi's trip finally went through, after some delay, the PCI considered it "a grave defeat for the right-wing forces."[30] The party's broader appraisal does not seem too wide of the mark, namely, that "one of the key elements" affecting the balance of forces within the ruling party was the fact that "just at this time there fell on the heads of the Christian Democratic leaders and on their equilibrium policy the brick of détente, of the international turnabout, of the change in that European and world framework that had in the past represented the most solid and definite support of the internal Italian regime."[31]

THE IMPACT OF POPE JOHN XXIII. By the early 1960's the Communist party's perennial effort to encourage a "dialogue" with the Catholic Church suddenly seemed to be bearing fruit, as Togliatti found in Pope John XXIII a worthy interlocutor. The last few years before his death in 1963 saw the culmination of the Pope's quiet but determined attempt to adapt his Church to the realities of contemporary Italian and international life. The extent to which he succeeded in doing so was both astonishing and gratifying to the PCI, for the effect was virtually to reverse the official Vatican attitude on the two issues of primary importance to the party, the *apertura a sinistra* and relations between communism and the Church.

The Communists appeared wary for a time of attributing particular significance to the efforts of the papacy. In the fall of 1961, for example, one of the party's leading commentators on Catholic affairs reviewed at length the papal Encyclical *Mater et Magistra* in a disparaging vein, depicting it as an attempt to win over the Catholic masses to support of neocapitalism by making minimal adjustments in the Church's social philosophy. Although apparently impressed by the unusually nonideological tone of the Encyclical, the writer denied that the Church could, as some might hope, serve as a mediator between East and West or between socialism and capitalism.[32]

29 Quoted in Kogan, *The Politics of Italian Foreign Policy*, p. 83.
30 "Survey of the Italian political situation," *Foreign Bulletin of the PCI*, February–March 1960, p. 5.
31 Alfredo Reichlin, "Crisi di governo e crisi di una politica," *Rinascita*, XVII, 3 (March 1960), p. 165.
32 Alberto Cecchi, "Il neocapitalismo nella nuova enciclica," *Rinascita*, XVIII, 9 (September 1961), pp. 687–695. Perhaps the most interesting aspect of the article was Cecchi's highlighting as an "extremely important point" a passage urging Catholics in their social and economic activities to display "a spirit of understanding and disinterestedness" toward those not sharing their views. This appeal for tolerance was promptly qualified by the admonition not to make compromises on religion and morals and to obey absolutely the decisions of the Church hierarchy concerning the specific application of general ethical and spiritual princi-

During the following two years, however, the PCI became fully persuaded that a revolution was stirring in the Vatican and that the party's tactics should be revised accordingly. The clearest sign of the change as far as domestic politics were concerned was the Church's abstention from the political battle in early 1962 when the Christian Democrats at their Naples Congress approved a Center-Left government—to be supported by Socialist votes. Two years before precisely such a development had been blocked by the Vatican's public reminder that collaboration with Marxists was inadmissable; this time, despite Cardinal Ottaviani's attempts to discredit the move, the Vatican declined to intervene.[33]

From the PCI's standpoint, however, the critical change in the posture of the Church was a new attitude toward the Communist world. By 1962 it began to be evident that the Pope genuinely hoped, as one non-Communist observer expressed it, "to establish a bridge between the West and the East on a basis of coexistence that would eliminate forever the slow suicide of the cold war and the dangers of a fresh world conflict."[34] While thus serving the cause of peace, the Pope saw an opportunity at the same time of improving the Church's position in Eastern Europe, especially in Poland, Hungary, and Czechoslovakia where the majority of the population remains Catholic.[35]

One tangible sign of change was the presence of thirty Catholic bishops as well as two observers from the Russian Orthodox Church at the Vatican Council that opened in Rome in October 1962. Pope John went out of his way to pay special attention to the Hungarians[36] and Poles, even stirring up a diplomatic hornet's nest by making a remark that appeared to represent endorsement of the Oder-Neisse line and thus a reversal of long-standing Vatican policy;

---

ples. Rarely is one offered such a fascinating glimpse of the similarity between the policy dilemmas of the Vatican and the Communist movement in attempting to relax obsolescent authoritarian and sectarian attitudes without sacrificing the necessary degree of central control.

[33] The 1960 intervention was through an article in *L'Osservatore Romano*, May 18, 1960. The article's insistence on the Church's right to determine when collaboration with those not accepting religious principles was morally lawful aroused widespread international concern in Catholic and lay circles, embarrassing presidential candidate Kennedy, among others; for a review of these reactions see " 'Punti fermi' e reazioni cattoliche nel mondo," *Tempi moderni*, New Series, No. 3 (October–November 1960), pp. 143–148. For reference to Cardinal Ottaviani's opposition to the Center-Left in 1962 and the general expectation of Vatican intervention, see Gorresio, *L'Italia a sinistra*, p. 175.

[34] Falconi, *Pope John*, p. 111.

[35] Miklos Vetö, "Kremlin and Vatican," *Survey*, No. 48 (July 1963), pp. 163–172, reviews the status of the Church in the Eastern European countries and notes some of the moves made by Moscow and Rome to improve relations.

[36] *Ibid.*, p. 165.

a formal protest by the German ambassador was required to set the matter straight.[37] Shortly thereafter the Communists had another opportunity to associate papal views with their own: following the Cuban missile crisis of November 1962, "the decisions taken by the Soviet government in order to avoid a world holocaust received an almost explicit approval on the part of Pope John XXIII. . . ."[38] The following March Pope John gave further evidence of his open-mindedness by giving a private audience to Khrushchev's daughter and son-in-law, Alexei Adzhubei.

The PCI's enthusiasm for the spirit of the Pope John era reached its climax with publication in April 1963 of the famous Encyclical *Pacem in Terris*, which lent the full force of papal authority to the search for peace and the overcoming of ideological barriers. In Stuart Hughes's estimation, "the endorsement of the new tendencies in Italian politics could scarcely have been more explicit; Pope John seemed to be saying that the unbridgeable separation between Catholicism and Marxism, Pius XII's excommunication of the Communists, and the old injunction against voting Socialist, perhaps the very ideological division of the world, were being relegated to an unhappy past."[39]

Well before the appearance of *Pacem in Terris* the party had determined to exploit as fully as possible the breakthrough in the Vatican. The advent of a vigorous campaign to demonstrate a new and more enlightened Communist attitude toward religion was signaled in the Theses for the Tenth Party Congress, issued in September 1962. "It is difficult to exaggerate their novelty and importance," commented the party's most prominent advocate of the new stance.[40] The key passage reads as follows:

The new social attitudes of a section of the Catholic movement—despite the fact that an important section is still anchored to conservative, reactionary views—show that important forward steps are possible even in this direction. Today it is no longer merely a question of overcoming the prejudices and sectarianism that hinder collaboration between socialist and Catholic forces in an effort to achieve immediate political and economic results. It is a matter of understanding not only that the aspiration

[37] Falconi, *Pope John*, pp. 133 and 178–179.

[38] Alberto Cecchi, "Prospettive di possibili intese," in Gozzini, *Il dialogo alla prova*, p. 234; see also Ignazio Delogu, "Impegno comune per la pace," *ibid.*, especially p. 345.

[39] Hughes, *The United States and Italy*, p. 217.

[40] Lucio Lombardo Radice, "Un marxista di fronte a fatti nuovi nel pensiero e nella coscienza religiosa," in Gozzini, *Il dialogo alla prova*, p. 90. Lombardo Radice adds that the theses on religion were among the most controversial and had met with considerable resistance, which suggests that their novelty was recognized within the party.

to establish a socialist society can arise in men who have religious faith, but that such an aspiration can find a stimulus in a tormented religious conscience confronted with the dramatic problems of the contemporary world. Thus the problem of respect for religious rights also arises in a new way in a new society.[41]

The statement goes well beyond the passive tolerance of religion that had heretofore represented the limit of the PCI's conciliatory attitude. The religious conscience is presented as a potentially positive force, capable of contributing to the revolutionary impulse toward a socialist society. The classical Marxist-Leninist view of religion as a wholly reactionary force, an instrument of the exploiting capitalist class, has been explicitly rejected.[42] The PCI maintains that its experience has shown that people with a predominantly religious motivation can play an effective part in the major struggles of the day: the resistance movement, the anticolonial fight, the peace movement, even (as in Poland) in the construction of socialism itself.[43]

Pacem in Terris seemed to some in the Communist party to mark a decisive turning point in that the Church first reciprocated the party's long-standing insistence that collaboration between the two movements for practical earthly goals was possible, despite continued ideological opposition. Had not the papal letter stated clearly that cooperation with historical movements, which change over time in response to their environments, may now "be considered opportune and useful" even though the original false teachings of these movements had not undergone a corresponding change?[44] Here was the Pope himself sanctioning the principle underlying the party's simple message to its potential allies among the Christian Democrats: let us maintain our doctrinal differences but not allow them to interfere with the work there is to be accomplished in common.[45]

The PCI, the Socialist Party, and the Center-Left

While the long-term "forward strategy" of the Communist party has rested heavily on the possibility of developing an entente with middle- and working-class forces presently controlled by Christian

[41] "Tesi approvate dal X Congresso," *X Congresso del Partito Comunista Italiano: Atti e risoluzioni* (Rome: Editori Riuniti, 1963), p. 668.

[42] Lombardo Radice, "Un marxista di fronte a fatti nuovi," in Gozzini, *Il dialogo alla prova*, pp. 87–88.

[43] *Ibid.*, pp. 90–91.

[44] *Pacem in Terris*, paragraphs 159–160; English translation edited by William J. Gibbons, S.J. (New York: Paulist Press, 1963).

[45] See Togliatti, "Il destino dell'uomo," *Rinascita*, March 30, 1963, for an extended discussion of this same theme; reprinted in Togliatti, *Comunisti e cattolici* (Rome: Editori Riuniti, 1966) along with a 1954 speech.

Democracy, an even more critical role in the shorter run has been assigned to the Socialists.

If the Socialists continued to collaborate with the Communists and to fight for basic economic and social reforms inside a coalition of the Center-Left, it could serve as an instrument for splitting the Christian Democrats, softening the prejudices of anticommunism, and ultimately allowing the Communists to move from sterile opposition to participation in a reform coalition. In principle, therefore, the Communists have favored the idea of Catholic-Socialist cooperation. It was natural, as Togliatti has said, that Catholics should seek contact with Socialists first, for the barriers built up over the years against the Marxist left could not be overcome easily and all at once. We realize, he added confidently, "that party jealousy would be out of place in this regard, precisely because it is with the Communist movement as such, through what it represents in the world, that the most intelligent men of the Catholic movement will inevitably be led, if they understand the course of events, to seek reciprocal understanding and possible collaboration."[46] Under the right circumstances, then, the Socialists could serve to break the ice, eroding away the political and psychological barriers that had so firmly blocked the way to further Communist progress.[47]

This essentially optimistic view about the utility of Socialist collaboration with Christian Democracy represented, however, but one side of the picture. It was an essential prerequisite of any future Communist advance to hold firmly to present positions of power, positions inevitably threatened by the PSI's movement to the right. If the Socialists, in the process of making themselves sufficiently respectable as coalition partners, were to cut their ties with the PCI in the trade unions, cooperatives, and local governments, renounce their class ideology and the last remnants of proletarian internationalism—in short, abandon themselves to a posture of outright hostility to communism—then not only would the prospects of Communist participation in a coalition of the left recede impossibly far

---

[46] *L'Unità,* October 6, 1961.

[47] This strategy, based on an approach to the Catholic left through the medium of the Socialists, has been the dominant party line, represented in clearest form by Amendola. This justifies, I believe, my reference to it as *the* PCI strategy. Another approach, supported by Ingrao among the leadership, envisages more direct access to the Catholic movement and even, although this is never more than hinted at ambiguously, an eventual accord between the PCI and the DC itself, at the expense of the non-Communist lay left. Although by 1965 this strategy became increasingly clearly presented as an alternative, it has for the most part been less a competing than a corollary approach. The party has wanted to keep both lines open, varying the emphasis as tactical considerations of the moment seemed to warrant.

into the future, but the PCI's considerable strength at the grass-roots level would be seriously compromised.

The risks inherent in the *apertura a sinistra* were thus consider-able. To minimize them, the PCI did its best to salvage what it could from the early postwar relationship expressed in the unity of action pact that had for a time made the PSI a virtual Communist satellite. The limited consultation pact agreed upon as a substitute in 1956 had never been implemented, and the PSI had declared at its 1957 Congress that future collaboration could not be between the parties but only in such mass organizations as the CGIL and in the town and provincial governments.[48] The Communists had no choice but to accept this fact and to strive to maintain a working alliance at these levels, for they represented its most significant source of real power in the society. Relations between the two parties in the CGIL were one critically important aspect of the picture, but since the topic will be reviewed at some length in the next chapter it will be bypassed here. The question of cooperation in local governments will serve as an equally useful illustration.

The Communist party, in alliance with the Socialists and other parties of the lay left, has controlled local government bodies in about 20 per cent of the nation's smaller cities and towns, and about 30 per cent of the larger cities and provinces, primarily in Northern and Central Italy.[49] Although the responsibilities and financial re-sources of local governments are sharply limited in Italy, control nevertheless brings with it patronage in the form of jobs and con-tracts for construction and public works. Far more important, it brings the opportunity to demonstrate in tangible ways that Com-munists can operate successfully, and in many instances a good deal more efficiently than other parties, within the existing administra-tive structure of the state. In this way the Communists have managed to become part of the establishment, benefiting from prosperity and developing vested interests in the status quo.[50] As Giorgio Galli has pointed out, the PCI right wing has found its strongest support in

[48] See Giorgio Amendola, "Cause e pericoli dell' allentamento dei legami uni-tari tra comunisti e socialisti," *Rinascita*, XV, 1 (January 1958), pp. 14–20.

[49] In September 1960, according to Togliatti, there were PCI-PSI majority coalitions in 248 towns of over 10,000 inhabitants, 1,410 towns of less than 10,000 (out of a total of almost 8,000 municipalities), and in 24 of the 92 provinces; *L'Unità*, September 25, 1960.

[50] See Ruggero Rinaldi, "Communists in Local Government Bodies," *World Marxist Review*, II, 4 (April 1959), pp. 74–76, for a useful discussion of the ways in which the Communists attempt to utilize the opportunities provided by con-trol of municipal and provincial councils. A general review of the structure and functions of local government can be found in Kogan, *The Government of Italy*, pp. 149–164.

Emilia and Tuscany not only because the Communists there have been participating in power, thus leading them to adopt more gradualist positions, "but also and above all because they see their control threatened by dissolution of their alliance with the Socialists (PSI) which alone enables them to control the communes and provinces of Emilia and of Central Italy."[51]

It is hardly surprising, then, that the Communists were concerned that the first concrete move toward realization of an opening to the left on a national scale should have been the creation of local government coalitions between the Socialist, Christian Democratic, and Social Democratic parties following the administrative elections of November 1960. By March of the following year Center-Left administrations had been formed in three provinces and thirty-six large towns, including Milan, Florence, and Genoa,[52] Even though the PSI-PCI administrative alliance remained intact in the nearly two hundred large towns where the two parties could combine to form a clear majority and in the many smaller towns where they had won with a common electoral slate, the Communists saw the rapprochement between the PSI and the DC as a serious potential threat to their local positions of power.[53]

COMPETITIVE COEXISTENCE.   The inherent ambiguity of the situation assured that relations between the PCI and the PSI would be a curious and unstable blend of sharp competition and mistrustful collaboration. At the electoral level the two parties continued to present joint voting lists in the smaller communities where a simple majority of the votes was required and to form coalitions in many larger communities where proportional representation was in effect. At the same time, Socialists and Communists competed strenuously for the working-class vote. Because of the difficulties of 1956–1957, some Communist support swung over to the PSI, but in the 1958

51 "Italian Communism" in Griffith, Communism in Europe, Vol. 1, p. 316. For background on Communist policies and internal politics in Emilia, see Gianluigi Degli Esposti, Bologna PCI (Bologna: Il Mulino, 1966), passim.

52 "Situazione giunte comunali e provinciale," Tempi moderni, New Series, No. 5 (April–June 1961), pp. 115–118, gives a tabulation of the political structure of town and provincial administrations formed by March 1961.

53 As usual the judgment rendered was ambivalent. It was acknowledged that the PSI-DC entente occasions "contrasts and differentiations within the bourgeoisie and the Catholic world and entails some minor concessions by Christian Democracy," but the price paid by the Socialists was too high and the dangers too great; on balance, therefore, "the operation has a negative character." "La lotta per una svolta a sinistra," Rinascita, XVIII, 2 (February 1961), p. 85. The party may have been surprised and concerned that the DC right had proven willing to endorse local alliances with the Socialists on any terms short of a complete break with the PCI.

elections, although the Socialists made over-all gains, they lost perhaps half a million votes to the PCI in the industrial North.[54]

In the 1960 administrative elections the Communist vote had increased more than 1 per cent above 1958 and almost 4 per cent above the previous local elections of 1956; the Socialists not only failed to advance but lost most heavily in the Northern and Central provinces where the Communists had done particularly well.[55] The voting trend was a real asset to the PCI, for it demonstrated vividly the Socialists' continuing heavy reliance on participation in the CGIL and in local governments for prestige and contacts among the working class. The PSI's failure to increase its share of the vote, confirmed once again in the 1963 elections, was presumed to create difficulties for Nenni and to strengthen the Socialist left.

On the level of programs and ideologies, too, a similar mixture of antagonism and cooperation was evident. When it came to specific domestic reform proposals, the PCI played down its differences with the Socialists, stressing the objective necessity of solidarity based on proletarian principles.[56] In early 1962, for example, the PCI endorsed the Socialist demands for nationalization of the electric power industry, establishment of the regional governments promised in the Constitution, and for industrialization of the South and abolition of sharecropping.[57] Such demonstrations of basic identity of interest were invariably accompanied by an insistence that the goals could never be achieved by parliamentary combinations alone; powerful mass pressure generated by joint PSI-PCI action was a vital pre-

[54] For analysis of the election returns, see Paolo Vittorelli, "Le elezioni politiche del 1958," *Il Ponte*, XIV, 5 (May 1958), pp. 658–666; also "Dopo le elezioni," *Il Mulino*, VII, 6 (June 1958), pp. 418–426. The PCI used the results to demonstrate the need for united action, arguing that the Socialists had done best wherever the electorate had been least aware of differences between the positions of the two parties. See Gian Carlo Pajetta, "Il successo di una chiara posizione unitaria e comunista in Lombardia," *Rinascita*, XV, 5 (May 1958), pp. 297–301, and Pietro Ingrao, "Il problema dell' unità della classe operaia nell' attuale situazione politica," *ibid.*, pp. 333–338.

[55] For the PSI's own appraisal, see "Risultati elettorali e prospettiva politica," *Mondo Operaio*, XIII, 10–11 (October–November 1960), pp. 1–3. As Togliatti pointed out, the results were hardly encouraging to Nenni, who had set his party the goal of taking away a million votes from the Communists; *L'Unità*, December 4, 1960. Over-all analyses of the voting can be found in "Elezioni 1956–58–60: legge e percentuali nazionali," *Tempi moderni*, New Series, No. 4 (January–March 1961), pp. 125–138; and in "Prima analisi dei risultati del 6 novembre," *Rinascita*, XVII, 11 (November 1960), pp. 862–872.

[56] See, for example, Luciano Gruppi, "For Communist-Socialist Cooperation," *World Marxist Review*, I, 2 (October 1958), pp. 33–42, in which it is urged that ideological differences be minimized and "special attention paid to the slightest possibility of establishing an alliance between the Communist and Socialist Parties."

[57] Togliatti, report to the Central Committee, *L'Unità*, February 13, 1962.

requisite. Unless the PSI could bring the force of the working class to bear behind its proposals, the Communists maintained, its leverage on the Christian Democrats would be negligible.[58]

Whatever solidarity was maintained on programmatic questions, an almost incessant and at times quite unrestrained polemic persisted on basic issues of political orientation. The Communists found themselves under attack from Nenni and his supporters on various grounds, but especially on the issue of the PCI's continuing close identification with the Soviet Union in ideological and foreign policy matters.

From 1956 on the leaders of the two parties had kept up a running debate on the nature of democracy and of socialism, and on the relationship between them. The Socialist argument was premised, in Nenni's words, on a "recognition of the inalienable and permanent value of democracy and liberty, without which even a revolution that transforms capitalist property into state or communal property results in re-establishing, in different forms, oppression and even exploitation of the workers."[59] Democracy, he added, implies commitment both to a method of nonviolent resolution of problems and to a set of basic institutions including universal suffrage, a parliament, and a plurality of parties. Although the Communist party had given formal endorsement to these democratic principles and institutions, it had never done so unambiguously. Moreover, and this was the core of the Socialist argument, verbal declarations of support for democracy were meaningless in the face of the PCI's persistent acceptance of the principles and practice of "democracy" as understood in the Soviet Union. Not only had the Communists continued to insist that democracy and the dictatorship of the proletariat were essentially one and the same, but they had also stubbornly refused to concede, despite the overwhelming evidence of the Twentieth Congress, that Soviet political institutions deprived the ordinary citizen of democratic liberties with respect to state authority.

The PCI's continued allegiance after 1956 to what Nenni called "the inflexible logic of the Communist authoritarian system" definitively placed the two parties in "radically opposed camps":

It was inevitable, therefore, that from that moment on every appraisal of the Communists should be based less on this or that Congress thesis than on the context and totality of Communist action in the countries

[58] See Togliatti and Longo reports to the Central Committee, *ibid.*, July 19, 1960, for characteristic expressions of this theme.

[59] "Come è stato possibile che queste cose avvenissero?," report to PSI Thirty-Second Congress, February 1957, in *Le prospettive del socalismo dopo la destalinizzazione*, p. 78.

where they hold power. It was inevitable from that moment that whatever might be the day-to-day motives for agreement on joint demands of the workers, there would be less said about a general political alliance between the two parties, and a joint struggle for power would become unthinkable.[60]

Such direct attacks as these, presumably reflecting Nenni's revised personal convictions as well as the political necessity of establishing his credentials as a democrat by repudiating his own former ties with communism, put the Communists on the defensive. It was not enough to reiterate, as they did, the standard Marxist distinctions between "bourgeois" and "socialist" democracy, between a set of formally democratic institutions that in reality concealed a minority dictatorship of the capitalist class and a genuinely democratic rule of the majority under socialist institutions. They had also to face squarely the fact that the PCI would be judged by Soviet actions as well as its own.

Unable to repudiate the method and content of Soviet democracy, the PCI could publicly concede little more than that the state of affairs in the international movement had regrettably made it more difficult for Italian communism to display its distinctive qualities. In response to Nenni's taunts that the renewed condemnation of the Yugoslavs at the November 1960 meeting hardly justified great confidence in the principle of different roads to socialism,[61] Togliatti lamely acknowledged that "the Communist leaders holding power in the various countries have probably made and continue to make the mistake of stressing above all the common features of their actions rather than what differentiates them, even in very important fields."[62] The Italian Communists, he maintained, could not be held responsible for the mistakes made by other parties, even though the movement as a whole would have to bear their consequences. (The allusion was not to the Soviet party but to the "dangerous and mistaken" line being followed by the Albanians.)[63] As for the USSR, Togliatti unhesitatingly affirmed his party's readiness to stand on the Soviet record:

And let us say straight off that it does not bother us in the least to be judged, as Communists, on the basis of the "context" and the "complex" of Communist action in the countries where the Communist parties hold power. In that context and complex, in fact, the positive attributes clearly

60 "Dalla polemica all' azione," *Avanti!*, April 9, 1961.
61 *Avanti!*, December 11, 1960.
62 "A proposito di socialismo e democrazia," *Rinascita*, XVIII, 4 (April 1961), p. 360.
63 *Ibid.*, p. 361.

prevail and overshadow, if they do not entirely cancel out, the negative or doubtful elements. . . .[64]

It was this running debate on socialism and democracy that gave the Soviet Twenty-Second Congress much of its special significance for the Italian left. Although the startling new revelations about Stalin's crimes and the injustices of Soviet society gave Nenni and his associates fresh justification for the wisdom of the Socialist party's break with communism at home and abroad,[65] the anguished response of many of the PCI's leaders to Soviet failings raised hopes that Italian communism might finally be discarding its leading strings. The revisionist wing of the PCI saw the possibility of transforming what loomed as a major loss of prestige and a blow to the possibility of collaboration with the non-Communist left into a positive opportunity to demonstrate the autonomy and the democratic credentials of their party. It was thus natural that the Communist leader most committed to maintaining the Socialist alliance, Giorgio Amendola, should also have been the one to speak out most insistently at the PCI's Central Committee meeting in November 1961 against the traditional automatic acceptance of the virtue of everything Soviet.

The PSI right wing, committed almost irrevocably to the formula of the Center-Left, made more of Communist antidemocratic traditions and past performance than of the apparently more liberal tendencies of the moment. The Socialist left, equally certain to oppose the Center-Left if it meant a final break with the Communists, took the position that "a process is beginning which makes collaboration more possible."

An end is coming to what used to be the essential element of the Communist movement, the uncritical acceptance and mechanical transposition of Soviet experience that is being denounced today by the PCI expressly as something to be abandoned. Thus, in my opinion, much more favorable possibilities than in the past are opening up for encounters and collaboration with the Communist movement, on an international scale and in particular with the PCI. . . .[66]

The more cautious but still hopeful opinion of Riccardo Lombardi, representing a middle position in the Socialist spectrum, must have been especially encouraging to the PCI:

[64] "Ancora su socialismo e democrazia," *Rinascita*, XVIII, 5 (May 1961), p. 433.
[65] See Nenni, "I problemi lasciati aperti dal XXII Congresso di Mosca," *Mondo Operaio*, XIV, 10–11 (October–November 1961), pp. 1–11.
[66] Lelio Basso, "I socialisti discutono sul XXII Congresso del PCUS," *Avanti!*, December 3, 1961. (Round-table discussion.)

It is also necessary for the Communist parties to realize that as long as they had the closest possible mutual ties—even if we do not wish to speak of subordination to the aims of the Soviet state—the possibility of the alliances essential for the reform of society were limited. The transitory quality of such alliances is due to the constant practical principle prevailing in the Communist parties, the principle of judging the actions of other political forces more according to the possibility of dominating them than on their merits. This is also a direct consequence of adherence to the principle of the hegemony of the USSR over the labor movement. If a process of thorough review is carried out by the working class, things will change, and there may also be a change in the relations among their parties. I do not say that this will happen, but I do say that this is a historic opportunity because it can happen.[67]

If the majority of the Socialist party's leadership could be brought to believe in the genuine possibility of a fundamental change in the relations between Italian communism and the Soviet Union, the PCI would have relatively little to fear from the opening to the left.

QUESTIONS OF FOREIGN POLICY.   The growing overtones of reserve and defensiveness that marked Communist attitudes toward Soviet socialist democracy were nowhere in evidence when it came to international matters. Except for such differences of emphasis as have already been mentioned concerning the struggle for peace and international Communist relationships, the PCI's identification with Soviet foreign policy was complete. The Italians may have gone a bit too far in highlighting the menace of nuclear war, and conversely not pushed quite hard enough on such questions as Berlin, relatively remote for an Italian audience, but there was no issue of major importance on which the PCI did not associate itself with the Soviets.[68]

In foreign policy matters, there was no attempt to develop a doctrine analogous to that of the *via italiana* in domestic affairs. On the contrary, the PCI openly justified its international positions by affirming the necessity for solidarity among working-class parties and by identifying the interests of the international proletariat in the struggle against imperialism with those of the Soviet state.[69] Since capitalism had organized itself for concerted action on an international scale, anyone who professed to believe in the class struggle could not but follow suit, under the natural leadership of the Soviet Union. To accept the principle of neutralist autonomy, as the So-

67 Riccardo Lombardi, *ibid.*

68 Kogan, *The Politics of Italian Foreign Policy*, pp. 59–60, illustrates this point.

69 See Togliatti, "Le decisioni del XX Congresso e il partito socialista italiano," *Rinascita*, XV, 10 (October 1958), p. 616, for a characteristic defense of this position in rebuttal to Nenni.

cialists had done, was to forsake the class struggle, abandon oneself to exclusively nationalistic positions, and cast aside the one valid criterion by which international affairs could be judged.[70] Togliatti expressed his party's position with utter clarity in a reply to one of Nenni's attacks when he said that although there might be "a period of temporary incomprehension" of Soviet policy on the part of the working class, "there is no contradiction between the original de- velopment of each country toward socialism and the advance of socialism in the world. . . . The workers are 'in favor of the Soviet Union and of China' in the same way they are against the employers and the employers' parties."[71]

The Socialist party, consistent with its historical traditions and with its desire to find an autonomous middle ground between left and right in domestic politics, tried to define and uphold an interna- tional position of neutralism or, as it was often termed, *equidistanza* between the two military blocs. Within this general framework, however, on which all Socialist factions were formally agreed, there has been a steady drift from a neutralism favoring the Soviets toward a neutralism favoring the Atlantic alliance. NATO, opposed by the PSI in 1949, came to be accepted as a fact of life by the Socialist majority in 1958, on the grounds that Italy was irrevocably com- mitted to it, that it had come to be a factor maintaining the interna- tional equilibrium, and that it was, in any case, losing its importance along with the waning of the cold war.[72] The explanation for the policy shift did not lie so much in an evaluation of the international scene as in the requirements of domestic politics: the PSI could not expect to be accepted as an ally by the Christian Democrats (or by the Vatican) unless it renounced its opposition to the Atlantic alliance.

While the Socialists could lend passive support to a pro-Western foreign policy, ideological considerations and internal party pres- sures kept them far from enthusiastic about many aspects of Ameri- can and Italian policy. They have, for example, fought against American missile bases in Italy and against nuclear proliferation in Europe. For several years after 1956 they rested their hopes on the emergence of a viable "third force" in international politics, based on the nonaligned underdeveloped countries and including promi- nently the Yugoslavs. There seemed, indeed, to be a marked affinity

[70] Rossana Rossanda, "Come si evolve l'ideologia del PSI," *Rinascita*, XVIII, 6 (June 1961), p. 530.

[71] *L'Unità*, June 18, 1960.

[72] See Nenni, "Where the Italian Socialists Stand," *Foreign Affairs*, XL, 2 (January 1962), pp. 213–223.

between the position of Yugoslavia and that of the PSI, both uncomfortably perched with a foot in each of the two great camps.[73]

The basic belief governing the PSI's international position was that the process of détente on both sides was rapidly rendering obsolete "the logic of blocs," thereby making it increasingly possible for Italy to decide each issue on its merits rather than by semiautomatic allegiance to the Atlantic alliance. The PSI itself accordingly attempted to play the part of an "active neutralist," defining its own positions and generally declining to make common cause with the Communists even when their views on specific issues coincided. A typical statement of the principle was made in rejecting the PCI's appeal for joint action in July 1961:

> To safeguard the peace, according to the fundamental principle of independence from opposing military blocs, the *Direzione* believes it essential that mass pressure and mobilization take place in a completely autonomous fashion, so that the objectives of such action might not be confused and obscured by the needs and aims of other political parties which do not share our policy of neutrality or the PSI's position of independence from the blocs.[74]

In accord with this attitude, the Socialists resigned in 1957 from the Communist-controlled peace partisans' movement and in 1959 from the World Federation of Democratic Youth.

The Communists insisted that the Socialist outlook rested on a gross misreading of the international power structure. Like it or not, the world was divided into two camps, one of which was steadily shifting the military and economic balance in its favor, while the other was being rendered increasingly impotent through loss of its one-time military superiority and its colonial empire. "Two roads are open," Togliatti maintained in a neo-Stalinist vein, one based on stubborn defense of the capitalist world and leading to the grave possibility of war and atomic extinction, the other involving collaboration with the Communist world and leading toward peace: "One

[73] The Socialist left, seeing in Yugoslavia a model for a nontotalitarian brand of socialism in which the working class actually appeared to play a leading role, was particularly struck by the similarities between the international situations of the PSI and Yugoslavia. See, *inter alia*, Vittorio Orilia, "Osservazioni sulla politica estera italiana," *Problemi del socialismo*, I, 4 (April 1958), pp. 285–295. It has been asserted that the Socialists received financial support from Yugoslavia during this period; this is not improbable, but I have no evidence on the point.

[74] *Avanti!*, July 28, 1961. The Socialists could not always hold the line against members of the party who wished to join with the PCI in protest movements and other actions. In June 1960, for example, many Socialists in Brindisi, including the town's mayor, joined in a Communist-sponsored demonstration against the construction of missile bases despite an official ban by the local party organization. See *L'Unità*, June 13, 1960.

must therefore make a choice, and in so doing one must not forget that it is very difficult, if not impossible, to find a middle road that does not boil down to a series of compromises, without principle or prospects. . . ."[75]

SOCIALISTS, COMMUNISTS, AND THE CENTER-LEFT. The PCI's ambivalence toward the Socialist party was reflected equally clearly in its attitude toward the Center-Left. The situation was, of course, ambiguous by its very nature, the outcome depending on a whole series of imponderables hardly susceptible to Marxist or any other "scientific" method of analysis. The PCI could neither simply endorse nor oppose Socialist participation in a Center-Left government: everything would depend on the precise terms of the coalition agreement and on the extent to which they were put into effect—in short, on the exact balance of forces at any given moment within the two parties principally concerned.

In the broadest terms, the Communists could perceive two possible final outcomes of the political battle focused around the formula of the Center-Left. The most favorable result would be the establishment of a Center-Left coalition that the PCI could encourage and support with the aim of gradually wearing down anti-Communist prejudices to the point of rendering the party ultimately acceptable as a governmental partner. This was the outcome "predicted" by the Christian Democratic right as part of its campaign to discredit the Center-Left formula by treating the PSI as nothing more or less than a Communist Trojan horse. At the other extreme lay the disastrous possibility that the Center-Left might prove stable and successful enough to exclude the Communists indefinitely from a major role in the political game by depriving them both of potential allies and of politically effective issues.

Between these two polar extremes, each unlikely in its pure form except as the end product of a long period of gradual evolution, there lay a broad middle range of acceptable possibilities that were, in effect, only variations on the status quo. The Communists need not regard themselves as having suffered a serious defeat as long as the possibility of alliances with the Socialist party and/or the left Catholics had not been foreclosed. Whether the entente with the Socialists was maintained while the latter were participants in a

[75] "Sinistra e comunisti," *Rinascita,* XVI, 4 (April 1959), pp. 228–229. The analogy is obvious between this opinion and the PCI's more general view of the impossibility of the Socialists' finding a permanent place midway between the dominant political forces in Italy. As Ingrao once put it, "this is a frankly mistaken and unacceptable position"; "Il problema dell' unità della classe operaia nell' attuale situazione politica," *ibid.,* XV, 5 (May 1958), p. 334.

Center-Left coalition (difficult, but correspondingly more open to future PCI advance) or while the two parties were together in opposition (a safer but more defensive position) was a secondary issue. What mattered most, as the majority of the PCI leaders saw it, was to avoid any irrevocable break between the parties, however sharp the differences between them might become. Since the PSI had a similar interest, in order to safeguard the party's unity and maintain its bargaining power with the far stronger Christian Democrats, mutual compromises could be expected.

Within this general perspective, the Communists had blown alternately hot and cold toward the Center-Left idea since it first began to be seriously discussed in 1958. Until the "July days" of 1960 a substantially positive appreciation prevailed, largely because of the highly favorable situation presented by the crisis within the Christian Democratic party described earlier.[76] The Center-Left did not in fact appear politically possible during this period because of the fierce resistance of the Christian Democratic right and the Church; or, to put it differently, it could only have taken place under the highly favorable circumstances of a split in the Catholic party. Under those conditions the PCI had nothing to lose by appearing to support the idea.[77]

This pseudo support for the Center-Left turned into outright opposition by the fall of 1960, when it became clear that the Christian Democrats had temporarily patched up their internal difficulties and that the hoped-for revival of a united opposition on the left was not yet in the cards. From that time on the Socialists rather than the Christian Democrats became the key to the PCI's appraisal. The "Center-Left operation" was between late 1960 and early 1962 described predominantly as a political maneuver designed only to absorb the Socialists into a centrist political formation without actually undertaking any of the reforms demanded by the masses.[78] As mentioned earlier, the creation of Center-Left administrations in a number of important cities served particularly to heighten the

[76] See Togliatti, *L'Unità*, May 12, 1960.

[77] Gian Carlo Pajetta said in the spring of 1962, "there was a time recently when a Center-Left government seemed impossible," *L'Unità*, April 26, 1962. A reliable clue that the PCI was not at the time seriously anticipating the possibility of the Center-Left can be seen in the stress it gave to the urgent need for "a powerful and effective mass movement." Mass pressure, not political negotiations among the parties, was named as the "decisive factor" in the situation in Togliatti's speech of May 1960; *ibid.*, May 12, 1960. The "instrumental character" of the PCI's support of the Center-Left was pointed out in "Schede politiche," *Tempi moderni*, New Series, No. 2 (July–September 1960), p. 110.

[78] See *L'Unità*, December 4, 1960, for a typical analysis by Togliatti along these lines.

PCI's concern over the readiness of the Nenni Socialist majority to collaborate with the Christian Democrats without imposing a sufficiently stiff price in return.

Until their eventual secession from the PSI in early 1964, the Socialist left was a key factor in Communist calculations about the Center-Left. However much Nenni's betrayals of Marxist principles might be reviled, the Communists continued to maintain that the Socialist party should on no account be written off as long as there remained "a strong left-wing minority actively fighting to safeguard the party's class, Marxist, and international character."[79] Just as the intransigence of the DC right had earlier seemed sure to block realization of the Center-Left, now the loyalty to class principles of the Socialist left appeared the best available guarantee that the PSI would not be seduced too far along the treacherous road of social democracy.[80]

Communist support of the left was especially in evidence whenever Nenni's majority position appeared particularly shaky, as for example just before the PSI's Thirty-Third Congress at Naples in January 1959.[81] Although Nenni succeeded through his great personal popularity in regaining control at the Congress, the left

[79] "La lotta per una svolta a sinistra," *Rinascita*, XVIII, 2, p. 86.

[80] To speak of "the Socialist left" grossly simplifies a complicated factional situation, for there have been many different "lefts" in the postwar Socialist party. Nenni himself was until 1953 a leftist leader, before beginning his steady march toward social democracy. After 1956 there were three leftist factions: a group led by former party Secretary Lelio Basso; a group of party bureaucrats associated with the late Rodolfo Morandi; and a group of strong pro-Communists labeled *carristi*, tank drivers, because of their refusal to condemn Soviet military intervention in Hungary. By 1958 the latter two groups had united under Tullio Vecchietti's leadership and had the backing of about one-third of the party; Basso's faction was supported by an additional 7 or 8 per cent. It is often alleged that some members of the PSI left were controlled and financed by the PCI, that they were in fact clandestine members of the party. While this may have been true in some individual cases, the Socialist left as a whole did not behave as an agent of the PCI; when the extreme left seceded to form the PSIUP in 1964 it was apparently against Communist wishes. The best summary and analysis in English of postwar PSI factional history is Raphael Zariski, "The Italian Socialist Party: A Case Study in Factional Conflict," *American Political Science Review*, LVI, 2 (June 1962), pp. 372–390.

[81] Togliatti was, for example, plainly attempting to influence the voting for delegates to the forthcoming Congress in an article that accused Nenni of "social democratic deviation" and "slanderous distortion of the truth" and defended in the most rigid terms Soviet institutions and the necessity for solidarity between socialist parties and the Soviet state: "Le decisioni del XX Congresso e il partito socialista italiano," *Rinascita*, XV, 10 (October 1958), pp. 609–617. Nenni had been put in the minority at a recent Central Committee meeting and there seemed a good chance that the Congress might ratify his defeat. For a detailed review, see A. Dormont, "Le XXXIII Congrès du Parti Socialiste italien (P.S.I.)," *Est & Ouest*, No. 211 (March 1–15, 1959), pp. 10–17.

remained sufficiently strong, with about 42 per cent of the votes, for the Communists to continue to hope for the eventual defeat of reformism. Luigi Longo expressed his party's attitude in his speech at the Moscow conference of November 1960:

> We should point out and criticize the shortcomings, the mistakes, and even the betrayals of the leaders of these [Socialist] parties whenever this is justified. We must do so, however, bearing constantly in mind the common goals and the real identity existing between us and the better part of the rank-and-file members of these parties so as to influence them and win them over to united action, even encouraging them to fight within their own organization to change this attitude and orientation.[82]

The results of the PSI's next Congress, in March 1961, showed the continuing strength of the left wing. Nenni's already slim majority in the Central Committee was narrowed by 2 votes down to 45 out of 81, and the left regained the representation it had lost on the party's executive body, receiving a third of the 21 posts. Nenni's control seemed further threatened, moreover, by the emergence of significant differences between himself and Riccardo Lombardi, who took up a mediating position between the two factions and appeared to many to hold the balance of power in the party.[83] The PCI claimed, with reason, to be much encouraged by this evidence that the left remained a factor to be reckoned with.[84]

The Communist position continued through 1961 to be on balance suspicious and hostile toward the Center-Left. The issue was, however, an increasingly open source of discord within the party, as became evident during the Central Committee meetings of October and December, just before and after the heated debates on the Soviet party Congress. The extreme positions were represented by such old-line conservatives as Mauro Scoccimarro, openly hostile to the Center-Left, and the group led by Giorgio Amendola, who insisted that outright opposition would play perfectly into the enemy's hands and ensure realization of his malicious designs. Togliatti, as was his custom before an issue had been resolved, produced a carefully balanced appraisal that did not close the door on future moves in either direction; for the time, however, it was weighted against the Amendola position.[85]

82 "Primo intervento," *Interventi della delegazione,* p. 66.

83 Zariski, *American Political Science Review,* LVI, 2, p. 380.

84 See, *inter alia,* Ingrao, *L'Unità,* March 21, 1961, and Aldo Tortorella, "Il Congresso socialista di Milano," *Rinascita,* XVIII, 4 (April 1961), pp. 339–345.

85 The October Central Committee debate was reported in *L'Unità* on October 6, 7, and 8, 1961, the December debate on December 21, 22, and 23, 1961. One of the sharpest manifestations of the Amendola-Togliatti differences can be seen in the contrast between Amendola's editorial, *L'Unità,* December 17, 1961, reacting enthusiastically to the new economic program worked out by Lombardi as the basis for a Center-Left government, and Togliatti's speech reported the following

By the following February the situation had changed, and along with it Togliatti's position. The Socialists and Christian Democrats had produced what Togliatti was willing to call "a fairly precise outline of an antimonopoly economic policy," thus putting the Center-Left into the reform context necessary to justify Communist support.[86] While the economic platform provided the doctrinal basis for the more favorable Communist view, its political basis was the decision taken by the Christian Democrats at their January Congress to accept Socialist external support for a Center-Left government. Despite the last-ditch efforts of Cardinal Ottaviani and the DC right-wingers, the Vatican had remained neutral, declining to veto this first major step toward eventual direct Socialist participation in the government. The left Socialists had also agreed, although with much skepticism, to give the formula a try so as to test the intentions and ability of the DC to carry through on their reform promises.

From the standpoint of the Socialist left and the Communists alike, the experiment proved to be a failure. Although some reforms (notably, nationalization of the electric industry) had been undertaken, the net result was not seen as justifying the decision taken by the PSI at the end of 1963 to enter Moro's government; the PSI left, regarding the party's drift toward social democracy as inexorable, soon seceded to form the Italian Socialist Party of Proletarian Unity (PSIUP). The Communists understandably regretted the loss in leverage this gave them and apparently did their best to persuade the left to continue the fight from within. The new government was condemned in a resolution of the Central Committee as a "transformist" maneuver that would only shift the PSI to the right rather than the country to the left.[87] The party nevertheless continued to insist on the necessity of upholding the essential principle of the Socialist alliance, for despite the PSI's capitulation of the moment, it would be wrong "to consider that the process of degeneration of the Socialist party toward social democratic positions is under present conditions something fatal and irresistible."[88] Pressures from below, the abiding class nature of the party, the emergence of a new left to replace the old—such permanent factors

---

day, which continued to give a predominantly negative appraisal of the prospects. Differences had long been simmering between the two over the correct strategy toward the Center-Left; Amendola's leadership in repudiating Togliatti's response to the Soviet Congress is certainly explained in part by his hope of using the emotion generated by the events in Moscow to turn the tide in favor of his position.

[86] *L'Unità*, February 13, 1961.
[87] *Ibid.*, December 8, 1963.
[88] Togliatti, "Dialettica unitaria," *Rinascita*, January 4, 1964, p. 2.

were cited as justifying continued faith in the possibility of collaboration between Socialists and Communists for a true national turn to the left. No matter how reformist the PSI became, it seemed, the Communists would adjust, for they were unwilling to relinquish the alliance that both multiplied the PCI's own strength at the local level and gave the best hope of moving closer to the centers of power.

We shall not pursue the story further, into the phase of full Socialist participation in the Center-Left government. Once it had joined the majority, thereby gaining access to patronage at the national level, the PSI's dependence on its ties to the Communists began to decline. Tensions between Socialists and Communists were accordingly heightened and the competitive aspects of their relations intensified, especially in local governments and in the CGIL. To all the old grounds for controversy were added those deriving from the necessity for official Socialist support of a governmental performance that was anything but brilliantly successful. Nevertheless, precisely because the Center-Left could legitimately be viewed as at least a partial failure, leading those now at the PSI's left to keep up pressure for the party's withdrawal unless its conditions were met, the Communists had continued reason to hope for restoration of closer collaboration.

By the fall of 1964, under Amendola's prodding, the PCI had begun to debate what seemed at first to be the most far-reaching political proposal of its history: the dissolution of the PCI itself in order to create a new united socialist party capable of winning a majority. Although the proposal was ambiguous and unrealistic, and subsequently "clarified" to destroy much of its content, that it could be taken with some seriousness by the Italian political world was in itself a measure of the distance the party had traveled in its quest for respectability and acceptance. The idea confirmed, moreover, the PCI's persistent interest in keeping alive its ties with the Socialist party in a political context that appeared to be growing increasingly disadvantageous for the future of Italian communism.[89]

The Italian "Economic Miracle" and the Strategy of the Working Class

It seems surprising, at first glance, that Italy's unusual economic progress did not begin to make much of a dent on the political

[89] For an analysis of Amendola's proposal and of the political context in which it emerged, see Norman Kogan, "Italian Communism, The Working Class and Organized Catholicism," paper prepared for delivery at the 1965 Annual Meeting of the American Political Science Association.

scene until the late 1950's. Ever since 1948 the Italian economy had been turning in an impressive performance, building the base for what would later be recognized as a transformation of major dimensions.[90] From 1948 to 1961 there were regular substantial gains in such categories as real gross domestic product and industrial output, the cumulative gain in these categories totaling about 120 per cent and 214 per cent, respectively.[91] As these data suggest, progress was most dramatic in the advanced sectors of big industry, where output per worker hour increased at the "extremely high compound annual rate of 8.3 per cent."[92] As a whole, the Italian growth rate in the decade after 1950 was well above the Western European average.[93]

This impressive statistical progress could in good measure be explained, to be sure, by Italy's relative backwardness and by the consequent short-term gains to be derived from modernization of plant and adoption of new techniques. There was little reason for confidence that the upward trend would continue as long or as strongly as it did. The significance of the advance was further obscured by the all too visible evidence of the gross deficiencies remaining in the country's economic structure and performance. The gap between North and South was large and continuing to grow, despite government efforts to redress the balance: between 1950 and 1958 agricultural output increased by an average annual rate of 3.3 per cent as compared with 9 per cent for industry, and the South's share of per capita income, 48.2 per cent in 1951, had dropped by 1960 to 42.3 per cent.[94] Even in the favored industrial sector serious problems existed. Employment, for example, especially in the technologically advanced industries, was rising far too slowly to make a dent on the dangerously high unemployment figure.[95] Consumption too, although rising, was by no means keep-

[90] For a good over-all review and analysis of the postwar boom, see George H. Hildebrand, *Growth and Structure in the Economy of Modern Italy* (Cambridge, Mass.: Harvard University Press, 1965), chaps. 1–4. For the period up to 1961, see Vera Lutz, *Italy, a Study in Economic Development* (London: Oxford University Press, 1962); also Giuseppe Scimone, "The Italian 'Miracle,'" in Jossleyn Hennessy, Vera Lutz, and Giuseppe Scimone, *Economic 'Miracles': Studies in the resurgence of the French, German and Italian economies since the Second World War* (London: André Deutsch for the Institute of Economic Affairs, 1964).

[91] Hildebrand, *Growth and Structure*, p. 47.

[92] *Ibid.*, p. 61.

[93] Hughes, *The United States and Italy*, p. 227.

[94] Scimone in Hennessy *et al.*, *Economic 'Miracles,'* p. 167; Hildebrand, *Growth and Structure*, p. 70.

[95] Hildebrand, *Growth and Structure*, pp. 151–188, examining the great discrepancies among the available data on unemployment, concludes that no precise quantitative estimate is possible. The trend seems clear, however: after reaching a peak in 1956 of close to two million, unemployment declined slowly through 1959, then began to drop off more rapidly.

ing pace with the growth of over-all output.[96] Add to these politically potent factors the recession of 1958, which slowed down the
economy all along the line, and it becomes understandable why the
economic advance of the first postwar decade was slow to have a
strong impact on the political scene.

Beginning in 1959, however, the upswing took on such notable
proportions as to predominate over the remaining dark spots in the
economy. Gross national product, which had increased by only 1.6
per cent in 1958, rose by 10 per cent in 1959 and 20.3 per cent in
1960.[97] Growth of industrial gross product in the same years went
from 3.1 to 10.9 to 15.3 per cent, with the iron and steel industry
growing in 1960 by a stunning 25.4 per cent.[98] Imports and exports
showed similar dramatic rises, especially within the European Economic Community, where Italy's gains in these respects far out-
stripped those of any other country.[99] Consumer goods became more
widely accessible to large sections of the population, including the
industrial working class, aided by the introduction of consumer
credit on a substantial scale. In virtually all respects save agriculture, the 1959–1961 period was an exceptionally favorable one.[100]

Important structural changes were occurring as well, most notably
a steady shift of the population from the countryside to urban
centers and from agricultural to industrial pursuits. Between 1950–
1960 the net reduction of the agricultural work force amounted to
over a million persons. The rate of migration increased even faster
thereafter, as industrial expansion began at last to create a demand
for labor, and the old legislation limiting movement to the cities
was revoked.[101] While this movement was advantageous from any
long-range economic standpoint, it came far too fast for Italy's in-
efficient political and administrative machinery to handle. Housing,
transportation, and other facilities were grossly inadequate to the
demands of urban populations that had grown by well over a third
in a single decade, as was the case in Milan and Turin.[102]

96 *Ibid.*, p. 47.
97 Scimone in Hennessy *et al.*, *Economic 'Miracles,'* p. 176, from annual
report of the Banca Commerciale Italiana.
98 Antonio Pesenti and Vincenzo Vitello, "Tendenze attuali del capitalismo
italiano," *Tendenze del capitalismo italiano*, Tables 2 and 3, Vol. I, pp. 74–75.
99 Scimone in Hennessy *et al.*, *Economic 'Miracles,'* p. 198, from European
Economic Community, *Bulletin*, February 1964.
100 Hildebrand, *Growth and Structure*, pp. 47–64, gives data demonstrating
the sharp rise in a number of important economic indexes during these years.
101 Pesenti and Vitello, "Tendenze attuali," *Tendenze del capitalismo italiano*,
Vol. I, p. 51.
102 Enrico Berlinguer, report to the Central Committee, *L'Unità*, January
20, 1961.

The Communist party was not in the vanguard when it came to taking official notice of the economic transformation. Mesmerized by the 1958 recession, which the PCI's analysts, along with their Soviet mentors, treated as a confirmation of the deepening crisis of capitalism, the party was slow to accept the significance of the economic upturn. The first recognition of important change concerned not expansion of output but structural changes in the composition and geographical location of the working class. The party had good reason to take seriously the organizational problems raised by the large-scale movement from agriculture to the cities and by shifts within the industrial work force itself that were tending to reduce the relative weight of the proletarian component.[103]

One basic problem was simply that a new generation of workers was coming to the fore, gradually displacing the old guard of factory militants who had joined the party during and just after the war. The new wave of women, former peasants, and young workers did not bring with them the dedication, loyalty, and class consciousness of the old timers.[104] Many of the younger ones, indeed, were displaying tendencies a good deal more worrisome than a mere lack of interest in the party's activities and slogans: they were often radical and impatient in their mood, mistrustful of the party's habitual compromising, reformist stance. The party press, from 1961 on, began regularly to expose the "neomaximalist" and "anarchosyndicalist" outlooks of those who saw the labor struggle and the trade union rather than parliament and the party as the heart of a working-class strategy for socialism.[105]

Though it had to confront certain of the social effects of economic development insofar as they impinged directly on its operations, the party was understandably reluctant to acknowledge that a qualitatively significant change could be taking place in the capitalist economy. Dramatic economic progress under capitalism represented a serious challenge, both ideologically and politically, since the party's appeal to the Italian masses rested so heavily on bread-and-

[103] Amendola noted in May 1961 at a national conference of Communist factory workers that the number of "workers" in a certain group of plants had dropped by 3 per cent despite an over-all increase of about 10 per cent in the number of employees; the clerks and technicians had increased by 27 per cent, the number of women employees by 22 per cent. *L'Unità*, May 6, 1961.

[104] Amendola pointed to the difficulties of "ripening the class consciousness of the new strata of workers," noting that more than 50 per cent of the workers were under thirty years old. *Ibid.*

[105] See Amendola, *ibid.*; Berlinguer, "Dibattito politico e tesseramento al partito," *Rinascita*, XVIII, 5 (May 1961), pp. 478–479; and Adalberto Minucci, "Aspetti della spinta operaia a Torino," *ibid.*, p. 449.

butter issues. However much they denied it and presented them-selves as champions of popular welfare, the Communist leaders were surely aware that a prolonged rise in living standards might cut the ground out from under their voting strength.

As late as October 1961, therefore, Togliatti could still refer disparagingly to the "so-called economic miracle," calling attention not to the industrial expansion itself (which, he noted, could always occur for brief periods "even in the present phase of general crisis and decadence of the capitalist world") but to its inability to solve the country's basic problems. Some workers might now be living better, he said, but only because they were working longer and harder: "On the whole, I believe it can be affirmed that the cost of the miracle has been paid for by a more intensive exploitation and a relative impoverishment of the working class, by the decay and crisis of agriculture, and by the permanent depression of the Southern regions and the islands."[106] But while the party could never be expected to grant that capitalism could definitely resolve Italy's economic and social ills, neither could it continue indefinitely acting as though the "economic miracle," so much at the forefront of popular attention, were somehow only a mirage.

It was Giorgio Amendola, in September 1961, who gave the signal for the opening of a debate on these economic developments and their political significance. Acknowledging that the party's Ninth Congress the year before "did not provide an adequate evaluation of the results attained by the economic expansion," he noted that "the influence exercised by the miracle is succeeding in penetrating widely into the working-class movement and even into the ranks of the party itself."[107] The last phrase was probably the crucial one. A direct confrontation of the issues posed by the economic boom was necessitated not so much by concrete signs that the party's relations with the masses had already begun to deteriorate as by a growing feeling among influential groups in both Communist and Socialist parties that continued rapid economic progress would require a substantially new strategy in the fight against capitalism.

The economic "miracle," together with its political counterpart, the Center-Left, was bringing into the open once again the ten-dencies toward rightist and leftist deviations perennially latent within Marxist parties. The two deviations, although appearing to be polar opposites, are generally ascribed by Communist leaders (them-

106 *L'Unità,* October 6, 1961.
107 "Il 'miracolo' e l'alternativa democratica," *Rinascita,* XVIII, 9 (September 1961), p. 673.

selves by definition in the center) to the same basic error, in this instance to a gross overestimation of the duration and success of the current capitalistic expansion. The difference was that whereas the "revisionists" (i.e., Nenni and his supporters) were adopting "opportunistic positions of yielding to capitalist influence" on the hopeful assumption that the monopolies would be able to solve the major problems of contemporary Italy in a progessive fashion, the "sectarians" of the Socialist and Communist left, fearing precisely such an outcome, were urging a frontal assault on the monopolies by the industrial working class before all opportunities had been irrevocably lost. "In order to fight these positions effectively," Amendola maintained, "it is necessary to make a thorough analysis of the basic trends of contemporary Italian capitalism . . . [and] to arrive in the clearest manner possible at a judgment on the limits and the political consequences of the 'economic miracle.' "[108]

The main terms of the debate can be seen from the arguments presented at the PCI Central Committee meetings in late 1961 and early 1962,[109] but most particularly in a conference on "Tendencies in Italian Capitalism" organized by the party's Gramsci Institute in March.[110] Three related questions dominated the discussion. First, what are the impulses behind the Center-Left and how great are the dangers associated with it? Second, how much can the new capitalist order in Italy accomplish and what are the basic "contradictions" limiting its effectiveness? Third, in the light of these considerations, what should working-class strategy be?

APPRAISAL OF THE CENTER-LEFT. The PCI's official position by early 1962, as we noted earlier, was that despite the intent of its creators to use the Center-Left as a device to destroy working-class unity and isolate the Communist party, the over-all situation was not conducive to a realization of that design. Similarly, the fact that notable economic development had occurred under the direction of the monopolies was not to be taken simplistically as a political vic-

---

[108] *Ibid.*, p. 674.

[109] See especially *L'Unità*, February 14–15, 1962.

[110] The written contributions for the conference and the speeches made there were subsequently reproduced in two large volumes entitled *Tendenze del capitalismo italiano: Atti del Convegno di Roma 23–25 marzo 1962* (Rome: Editori Riuniti, 1962). As one of the participants complained, the conference appeared designed primarily to ratify and buttress the political decision already taken; "Intervento di Lucio Magri," *ibid.*, Vol. I, pp. 323–324. It was nominally, however, a "scientific" rather than a political gathering and included leading representatives of the Socialist left; the discussion was therefore a good deal less reticent than would have been the case in an official PCI meeting.

tory for capitalism and a setback for the revolutionary struggle of the proletariat.[111] Such mistaken and defeatist views, the party insisted, overlooked the fact that both the Center-Left and economic development were in large part results of unrelenting and effective mass pressure, and thus reflected the party's steadily growing ability to influence the course of events.

The dissenters on the left did not accede to this comfortable myth of the party's pre-eminent role in conditioning Christian Democratic acceptance of the new situation. Pietro Ingrao, for example, the lone member of the Secretariat to manifest a degree of sympathy for the leftist positions, formally granted the importance of mass pressure but put his primary emphasis on the needs arising from within the bourgeoisie itself. In his view, the need for planning, for control of the monopolies, for greater mass consumption, for more civilized labor practices were all to be understood largely as an inescapable aspect of the modernization of industrial techniques.[112] Lucio Magri at the Gramsci Institute conference stated the case for the left more fully, arguing that agricultural reform, industrialization of the South, school reform, administrative decentralization, expansion of mass consumption, state intervention in the economy were all part of a complex strategic plan of the capitalist class, undertaken for the purpose of making capitalism more efficient and permitting its uninhibited further expansion.[113] To accept passively this process, to try, indeed, to take credit for it as the party was doing, only played into the enemy's hands by underrating and misunderstanding the dynamism and internal pressures of the capitalist system.

THE "CONTRADICTIONS" OF CAPITALISM. The left tended toward the view not only that the capitalists were setting out in their own interest consciously to solve these problems, but that they could in time actually succeed in doing so. The conflicts between North and South, between agriculture and industry, between consumer and producer—the "secondary contradictions" of the Marxist frame of reference—were on their way to being surpassed in consequence of advanced capitalist development.[114] In other countries modern capitalism had already demonstrated its capacity to raise standards of living and overcome many of the basic injustices of the early

---

111 Amendola, "Lotta di classe e sviluppo economico dopo la liberazione," *Tendenze del capitalismo italiano*, Vol. I, p. 146.

112 *L'Unità*, February 14, 1962.

113 "Intervento di Lucio Magri," *Tendenze del capitalismo italiano*, Vol. I, p. 146.

114 *Ibid.*, p. 326; "Intervento di Rodolfo Banfi," *ibid.*, p. 350; "Intervento di Lucio Libertini," *ibid.*, pp. 354–358.

stages of its development. As one critic of the party line put it, the problem is that capitalism itself, "by extending the consumer market, is attempting and tending to develop, not just in the middle class but among the working class as well, a petty bourgeois attitude, in order to dull the edge of revolutionary consciousness and assuage the thirst for a violent overthrow of the very foundations of bourgeois society."[115]

What capitalism could never do, however, was to resolve the "primary contradiction" between capital and exploited labor, inherent in the capitalist system itself. It was not a question of denying that the "old, historical contradictions" of Italian society were still present, but that they were radically changing their character, becoming subsumed under the more basic labor-capital confrontation that was now emerging with greater intensity than ever before. The peasant landowner, for example, increasingly caught up in capitalist market relationships, was becoming more exploited and more proletarianized.[116] The working-class parties ought, therefore, to shift their attention from the old social problems originating in precapitalist days to the characteristic issue of advanced capitalist society.

Amendola ridiculed these views in his closing speech at the Gramsci Institute conference. They were wrong economically because they were premised on "a fatalistic acceptance of the continuation of monopolistic expansion, an extrapolation from the data of recent economic progress as though it were fatally destined to continue until 1970 at the same rate." They were wrong politically because the party had to deal with the needs of today, not those of tomorrow: Italy was as yet far from being an "affluent society," and the party's political support derived from its concern with the classical problems of the Italian South and with the newer issues being created by the expanding industrialization and urbanization of the country.[117] The special and original character of the Italian situation, he argued, lay in the stubborn persistence of so many precapitalist phenomena in the midst of modernity, creating an "explosive interlacing" of old and new contradictions.

STRATEGIC ALTERNATIVES.   This apparently abstract and artificial debate over the economic and social vulnerabilities of the capitalist system had a direct bearing on the party's strategy. When the leader-

[115] Armando Borelli, *L'Unità*, November 3, 1962.
[116] "Intervento di Vittorio Foa," *Tendenze del capitalismo italiano*, Vol. I, pp. 230–231.
[117] "Le conclusioni di Giorgio Amendola," *ibid.*, p. 427.

ship stressed the continuing saliency of "secondary contradictions," it was in effect announcing its intention to continue along the traditional path of developing broad alliances with nonproletarian sections of the population and with the parties representing them. The peasantry and the nonmonopolistic elements of the middle class would continue to be prime targets of the party's efforts, collaboration would continue to be sought with the Socialists and the Christian Democratic left, the party's program would continue to be dominated by "democratic" rather than specifically "socialist" objectives. In its parliamentary activity the PCI would attempt to introduce a greater degree of democratic control over national economic life, influencing economic planning, investment policy, the conduct of state monopolies. The PCI would serve, in short, as the "interpreter of national needs," defending the general interest of the nation as the bourgeois parties no longer could.[118]

This reassertion of the PCI's standard approach was countered from the left by an insistence that the moment was ripe to shift to a strategy more consonant with the social and economic conditions of modern capitalism. The party's traditional position, it was argued, had reached a dead end because it was tending increasingly to defend obsolescent institutions and social groups destined shortly to disappear from the scene: technologically backward small industries, discontented shopkeepers, small peasant landholders. The leftist critics apparently concurred in Stuart Hughes's judgment that the party appeared to have lost its impetus: "With so much of its intelligence and its moral fervor gone, it ran the deadly danger of being reduced to a protest party of the economically desperate and the 'sub-proletariat'—the unemployed, the pensioners, and agrarian labor."[119] To avoid degenerating into a force for preservation of the status quo, the left wing argued, the party should associate itself with technical and economic progress, concentrating its attention on the vital industrial sector of society and seeking to exploit the tensions arising there in consequence of monopoly expansion.[120]

Instead of a strategy of political alliances elaborated primarily at the level of parliament and political parties, the left urged an emphasis on the unity of the proletariat and an alliance with other worker elements realized at the level of the productive enterprise,

---

118 *Ibid.*, p. 429.

119 Hughes, *The United States and Italy*, p. 208.

120 For a useful discussion of the debate in Communist circles over these issues, see G. Tamburrano, "Lo sviluppo del capitalismo e la crisi teorica dei comunisti italiani," *Tempi moderni*, New Series, No. 10 (July–September 1962), pp. 5–36, especially pp. 22–25.

above all the factory. Although developed in its most extreme form by the Socialist rather than the Communist left, echoes of this position existed within the PCI as well, especially among some trade union leaders. Bruno Trentin, a leading Communist CGIL official, put great emphasis on the need to arrive at more rigorous distinctions among the various components of the "middle class" according to the economic function they performed; a link could be forged, for example, between the proletariat and the growing army of industrial clerks and technicians, not as in the past by stressing the economic dimensions of the exploitation of the white-collar workers, but rather the subordination of their creative professional instincts to the logic of the production process.[121] The emphasis of the left on the confrontation at the factory level, with its corresponding enhancement of the union's role, evoked charges of sectarianism and anarchosyndicalism from the PCI leadership. In Amendola's words, "the 'working-class alternative' or other similarly formulated positions are not ours because they isolate the working class, destroy its system of alliances, and prevent it from performing a national ruling-class function in which it can interpret the general needs of the nation."[122]

The Relevance of Domestic to International Strategy: Some Preliminary Observations

Although no sudden or radical transformation occurred in the Italian party's orientation toward the Soviet Union and the international movement in consequence of the various domestic developments that have been described, a significant evolution was gradually taking place that amounted, in the end, to a qualitative change.[123] Many of the party's fundamental attitudes toward international Communist affairs had already been articulated in 1956,

[121] "Le dottrine neocapitalistiche e l'ideologia delle forze dominanti nella politica economica italiana," *Tendenze del capitalismo italiano*, Vol. I, p. 142.

[122] "Una svolta obbligata nella lotta politica," *Rinascita*, XIX, 2 (February 1962), pp. 97–98. See also Luciano Barca, "Per una giusta linea del partito," *ibid.*, XIX, 3 (March 1962), pp. 177–180, and Lucio Libertini, "Che vuole e dove va la sinistra socialista," *ibid.*, pp. 181–186. The latter was a direct reply to Amendola's article of the previous month attacking the Socialist left. Libertini vigorously denied repudiating an alliance policy or assuming that capitalism had solved such problems as agriculture; the issue was only that of finding the *decisive* weak links in the system.

[123] The following comments are not intended as a full discussion of the relations between the PCI's domestic and international behavior. This would be in some respects redundant, in others premature. The objective is rather to tie together some of the threads of the present chapter and to flag briefly some of the considerations that will emerge more clearly in later chapters.

and in some respects even earlier. In part, the evolution of its policies after that time reflected the changing environment within international communism itself, which permitted the party a greater freedom to express its preferences and to act accordingly. Equally important, however, was the fact that the course of domestic events was such as to reinforce and deepen these preferences. The PCI's distinctive position in the Communist movement was confirmed, and new dimensions added, by the need to articulate an international stance as consistent as possible with the party's domestic strategy.

Italy's economic and political development of the late fifties and early sixties had one general consequence for the PCI that was, in a sense, a premise for all the rest: it forced the party to recognize the need to rethink old assumptions. The realities of Italian life were changing, everything was in motion, no one could be certain where it would all end. A sense of uncertainty, of difficulty in getting a firm grasp of essentials, emerges from beneath the superficial confidence of Communist dialogue. Gian Carlo Pajetta once felt it necessary, in not unsympathetic tones, to reassure those comrades who were manifesting "indecision or even discouragement" in the face of so much that was new and threatening.[124]

The controversies that arose within the party with respect to the Center-Left and the new capitalism were visible reflections of the fact that the old guideposts were no longer reliable. No one denied that the party had to change to keep pace with reality—in dispute was only the question of what was required: a minor shift in course, or an entirely new direction. Togliatti, in rejecting the "doctrinaire" approach of those on the left who called for a purer proletarian strategy, granted that the right road was difficult to find and that not much help could be gotten either from the Marxist classics or from history: "In reality, there is as yet no experience as to how the struggle for socialism can and should be waged in a regime of advanced state monopoly capitalism."[125] The *via italiana*, which in the mid-fifties had still seemed little more than a propaganda slogan, now had to be taken a good deal more seriously. The course of international events had given decisive proof that the road to power was not through revolution and Soviet arms: the party was on its own, more deeply aware than at any time in the past that success or failure hinged on its capacity to understand and influence the world around it.

124 *L'Unità*, February 15, 1962.
125 *Ibid.*, February 13, 1962.

Neither a pragmatic orientation toward politics nor a more sophisticated appreciation of economic matters could in themselves automatically determine the party's strategic choices. Both leftist and rightist elements in the party could justify their intuitive policy preferences by analyses of existing reality and projections of the likely future course of events. The point is, rather, that the need to confront the uncertainties of a new situation tended to bring out with increasing sharpness latent differences of orientation.

In the broadest terms, two roads were open. The party could move with the tide, accommodating itself as necessary to the new political and economic terrain and seeking to influence events from within through cooperative action with the Socialists and other allies on the left. Or it could take up a more aggressive, less "reasonable" stance, using parliamentary and grass-roots pressure for radical reform as a means of weakening and finally destroying the Center-Left coalition, thereby laying the groundwork for a more decisive turn to the left.[126]

In choosing the first of these roads, the PCI was in effect confirming its previous strategy and implicitly committing itself to further steps in a reformist direction. It was showing itself more willing to accept the long-run dangers of social democratic degeneration than the more immediate threat of becoming politically isolated by losing the Socialist alliance and sacrificing its aspirations to support from middle- as well as working-class sections of the electorate. This prudent and undramatic choice had certain implications for the party's international position.

The most important general consequence was to confirm the PCI's support for the basic orientation of Soviet foreign policy. As long as the Italian party was placing a premium on making itself respectable and acceptable as a potential political ally, it naturally had a strong preference for an international Communist strategy aiming at relaxation of tensions. The last thing the PCI wanted was a revival of the cold war and a consequent rebirth of the anti-Communist psychology

126 It is an oversimplification to present the alternatives this crudely. As compared with the conservative centrist position, advocates of left and right tendencies agreed on some important points, including the desirability of greater and more public autonomy from the Soviet Union. Moreover, the party would obviously never make an irrevocable choice for one or the other approach; the door would always be kept open for a subsequent reversal if conditions were to change. Nevertheless, a basic difference in emphasis existed, hinging essentially on a conflicting appraisal of the viability of the Center-Left formula. If it could be expected to collapse of its own weight, then the PCI could afford to play a relatively cautious waiting game. If, on the other hand, strong external pressure would be required to bring it down, the more aggressive tactics of the left might seem more appropriate.

that had made its life so difficult after 1948. Too much effort had gone into breaking down the barriers between the PCI and the Catholic society in which it lived to contemplate with equanimity a return to the state of hostility that would almost certainly have followed from resumption of an intransigent Soviet line. It was thus characteristic of the party to appear a bit apologetic in its defense of such unpopular Soviet acts as the nuclear bomb tests during the fall of 1961, and correspondingly enthusiastic in its support of the Soviet retreat from Cuba a year later.

The implication is not intended that the PCI left, had it found itself in a majority position, would have thrown peaceful coexistence overboard and jumped aboard the Chinese bandwagon. China's international strategy was far too aggressive and too patently irrelevant to the European scene to have attracted genuine support from any but the PCI's lunatic fringe and the remnants of the Stalinist old guard. Nevertheless, the party's "new left" showed a certain undercurrent of dissatisfaction with the passive, self-satisfied quality of Soviet foreign and domestic policies. Peaceful coexistence appeared to some of these critics as little more than a Soviet effort to buy time while pursuing the material objectives of an affluent society of the bourgeois type. The depth of Soviet commitment to international revolution seemed to them about as questionable as the PCI's commitment to revolution at home. Such attitudes as these would become more evident in later years and will be referred to again.[127] At this point it need only be noted that the partial and muted sympathy of some party members for certain aspects of Chinese criticism of the Soviets tended, if anything, to reinforce the PCI leadership's loyalty to the Soviet policy line of peaceful coexistence.

Although in this basic respect the PCI's domestic strategy was compatible with Soviet policy, the correspondence between Italian interests and international Communist policy was hardly complete. One source of tension arose from the fact that the Italians increasingly came to perceive their interests in a European context. They felt not only that the PCI's strategy of alliances and structural reforms was valid, actually or potentially, for Communist parties elsewhere in Europe, but that the domestic success of their own party depended to some extent on bringing other parties around to this view. The barriers of anticommunism could not be expected to fall in Italy unless they were simultaneously being weakened elsewhere, which meant that both the USSR itself, in its dealings with Europe, and other parties such as the French should adopt the flexible and relatively conciliatory tactics of the Italians.

127 Chapter Ten, pp. 350–354.

It was on the trade union front that this Italian interest came to be most clearly and consistently expressed, and the resistance of the French and the Soviets correspondingly most evident. The trade unions seemed potentially better suited than the parties themselves to develop collaborative relationships with non-Communist forces, especially in the context of European unification. The growing power of international monopoly capital, expressed above all in the Common Market, created the possibility of and the necessity for comparable coordinated action by the trade unions. But in the Italian view the Common Market, like its domestic counterpart state capitalism, could not be overcome by direct assault. Here too the situation required a gradual policy of infiltration and reform, buttressed by judicious application of mass pressure through strikes and other forms of action.

The PCI may in fact have been less impressed with prospects for the success of this strategy than with the domestic benefits to be derived from the image it conveyed. The PCI's case to the other Communist parties had to be put in terms of the real possibilities of weakening international capitalism, but the prime interest of the Italians was probably in the effects of their advocacy on the domestic audience. To the extent that other European parties adopted the Italian style and tactics, it would be that much easier for the PCI to demonstrate convincingly that communism as a whole had indeed "really changed" and that to continue trying to isolate, contain, and repress it was anachronistic. The PCI could then present itself as the prime "liberalizing" force of a movement gradually coming around to its own views. If the effort to swing other parties into line behind it should fail, the Italians could of course still reap the considerable benefits of appearing to be the maverick, a Communist party unlike all the rest and therefore more to be trusted.

This need either to see modified or to repudiate traditional Communist principles and practices in other countries has been most clearly evident with respect to the vexing question of freedom in socialist society. From this perspective, the PCI's identification with the USSR has beyond doubt been the single greatest impediment to its strategy of alliances. For the Nenni Socialists, the key issue has been political freedom, for the Catholics, religious and cultural freedom. As Longo once remarked, discussing "the reasons that keep [the Catholics] away from us":

The problem of freedom is one of the basic questions. This problem is related to the guarantees of respect for religion and for the Church. Concerning this problem, our positions are clear and well defined, and our actions have rigorously respected these positions. They imply an absolute respect for religion and a full acknowledgment of its rights and needs.

Nevertheless, Catholic diffidence toward us persists and centers on the problem of liberty. Evidently, the problem overcomes the limits of our actions and of our country and becomes a world-wide problem.[128]

In that last sentence, Longo only hinted at the question that every intelligent Italian Communist had to ask himself and that some were beginning to express in public: international solidarity was desirable, even necessary, but at what cost? As one left-leaning party member expressed it in a letter to L'Unità: "Up to just what point does the need for solidarity with the socialist countries—where socialism had to take on certain forms in order to establish itself in a backward country that had never had the liberal bourgeois experience—constitute an obstacle to the continuing growth of our party?"[129]

That such questions could be posed in the party press was but one of many indications of a significant change in the party's psychology. The spell of dependence on the USSR had been broken by the Twentieth and Twenty-Second Congresses, but more was involved than mere disenchantment with the Soviet workers' paradise. The course of Italian politics made it increasingly imperative for the PCI to associate itself less and less with Soviet domestic practice. What appeared to be predominantly emotional outbursts in 1956 and 1961, following the Soviet Congresses, gradually became a matter of conscious policy, particularly with respect to cultural affairs. After the Pasternak affair, for example, Togliatti declared on several occasions that he considered the Soviet decision not to publish Dr. Zhivago a mistake.[130] During 1963 and 1964, in reaction to the Soviet campaigns against intellectual, artistic, and religious freedom, such critical attitudes came to be expressed with increasing frequency and forthrightness.[131] The quality of other aspects of Soviet democracy was also criticized especially by Communists of the "new left" particularly concerned with the participation of the working masses in the management of the state.

The demands of domestic matters also influenced the PCI's attitude toward the split in the international movement. Italian Communist strategy at home called for the party to support Soviet coexistence strategy and the "revisionist" wing of the movement. Despite these strong preferences, and despite the Chinese party's public attacks on the PCI which would begin in 1963, the Italian posture never became one of unqualified support for the Russians and outright hostility for the Chinese.

128 L'Unità, April 27, 1962.
129 Ibid., November 3, 1962.
130 Ibid., April 12, 1962.
131 See Chapter Ten. pp. 341–349.

The Italian party did not desire a decisive break in the movement nor feel that such a break was inevitable, particularly because it assumed quite correctly that the international movement as a whole could only be damaged by such a rupture. But domestic factors also influenced this attitude: notably, the concern that a formal rupture would lead to a strengthening of the leftist forces inside the party. By the summer of 1962 the existence of some pro-Chinese sentiment in the party had become evident, and several Paduan comrades had been expelled for publishing a left-wing pamphlet with the provocative title of "Long Live Leninism." The danger was not so much that a Chinese faction in or out of the party could itself develop sufficient strength to challenge the party leadership as that the existence of an ideological alternative to the extreme left could be a constant source of irritation to a party steadily moving to the right. Chinese inspiration and funds, supplied on a substantial enough scale, could conceivably provoke dissension and cause some party members of the old-guard Stalinist left to defect. A more subtle danger was that the party's "new left," without itself embracing the Chinese line, might acquire greater respectability and persuasiveness by contrast to the pro-Chinese extremists. We shall return to this theme again. For now, the relevant point is only that a decisive Sino-Soviet rupture, because it would tend to complicate the party's factional situation, was looked upon with apprehension by the PCI.

The Italians not only wished to avoid a split but appeared to feel this to be a realistic possibility. A good deal of sheer wishful thinking doubtless entered into this calculation: if one ceases to believe that one's goals are attainable, they lose their influence over action. But there is also good reason to suppose that the PCI's hopes in this regard may have been strongly affected by its domestic experience. Far more than most Communist parties, the PCI had learned to live in a permanent state of ambiguity, of tension between its own goals and beliefs and those of other Italain parties that were, simultaneously, both opponents and potential or actual collaborators. Tolerance was more than a virtue for the PCI: it had become a necessity. The party had lived with compromise so long it was now an instinctive reflex; nothing was so sacred as to be above discussion, and in areas where disagreement could not be overcome, it was always possible to point to some broader common interest as the basis for an eventual accord. For Togliatti and his party the essence of political wisdom seemed to lie in taking no irrevocable steps that would foreclose a possible future avenue of advance or retreat. No provocation could be so grave as to exclude the possibility of compromise.

This mentality the Italians seem instinctively to have applied to international Communist affairs as well. There is continuity between their attempts in 1956–1957 to tone down the polemics that burst out after the Hungarian revolution and their insistence after 1963 on doing everything possible to avoid or mitigate a Sino-Soviet split. Doctrinal differences, the PCI maintained in both instances, need not be magnified to the point of preventing collaboration toward shared ends. And precisely the same contention was being made concerning the party's relationships with Socialists and Christian Democrats at home. A party ideologist writing about *Pacem in Terris* remarked on the similarities between the basic premises of the papal Encyclical and those held by the party: "There is nothing new in the notion that the ideological conflict itself need not necessarily result in reciprocal excommunication, that it may be dealt with on a basis of tolerance and of critical comparison, that it cannot rule out all understanding on aims vital to all humanity."[132] This lesson, the party seemed to feel, was valid for relations among Communists as well as between the competing ideologies of Catholicism and communism.

[132] Alessandro Natta, "Socialismo e coscienza religiosa," *Rinascita*, September 19, 1964, p. 2.

CHAPTER EIGHT

AN ITALIAN CHALLENGE
ON THE TRADE UNION FRONT

The critical mood of many Italian Communists after the events of the Twenty-Second Congress was first translated into effective international action in the context of trade union rather than party relations. At the Fifth Congress of the World Federation of Trade Unions (WFTU) early in December 1961 the Italian point of view was put forward with clarity and vigor in a serious effort to modify that organization's strategy and style. The Moscow Congress of the WFTU thus offered an early and solid indication of the growing conviction of the Italian Communists that they had something of value to contribute to the evolution of the movement.

We are concerned here, of course, with trade unions rather than parties. For the CGIL to challenge the WFTU, even though that organization was firmly under Soviet control, was not as though the PCI had challenged the Soviet party directly. Proletarian internationalism was still the accepted criterion of loyalty for Italian Communists, but in this context it could be interpreted less rigidly. The WFTU itself acknowledged the special qualities inherent in a mass organization whose membership was not in principle (though it was nearly so in fact) exclusively Communist. Although in reality its central function was to promote Soviet foreign policy, the WFTU purported to be seeking broader goals, such as the economic well-being and unity of the working class in the struggle for peace and socialism. For the CGIL to advocate a more flexible structure and a less rigid allegiance to Soviet goals was thus in part legitimized by the formal purposes of the organization.

Equally relevant, the CGIL itself was and remains a nonparty organization of the working class in which Communists are dominant but are not in exclusive control. CGIL policies must to some extent take into account the interests of the Socialist as well as the Communist party. The degree and nature of this influence are discussed more fully in the following; but we note here that the major importance of the Socialist presence has lain in its ability to push the Communists in the CGIL into taking certain positions sooner and more forcefully than they might otherwise have done. The PSI's pressure has in fact enabled innovators among the CGIL's Communist leadership to get away with things their party would under other circumstances have found it difficult to accept. In the same way the CGIL itself certainly found it easier to take up critical positions in the WFTU than if the Communists had been in exclusive control. The PSI presence served as a justification as well as an inspiration for unconventional behavior on the CGIL's part.

A further circumstance played some part in causing the Italian Communists to express certain of their ideas sooner and with greater clarity in the WFTU than elsewhere. The Communist labor movement, unlike the parties, still operated within a formal organizational structure, with a secretariat, regular meetings, and official program documents. Although the Communist parties had found it necessary to re-create some of the attributes of an organization through the pronouncements of the 1957 and 1960 Moscow meetings, they were not controlled by a secretarial hierarchy whose job it was to ensure that the Soviet line was reflected in the propaganda and other activities of a centralized organization and its affiliates. It was partly the existence of such a Secretariat that made the WFTU notoriously the most rigid and sectarian of all the Communist international organizations.[1] This organizational rigidity and dogmatic approach tended to stimulate resistance by the Italians and at the same time made it possible, even necessary, for their opposition to manifest itself formally, by challenging the Secretariat and proposing amendments to the WFTU Program. This tended to enhance the visibility and the precision of the Italian position.

The special character of both the CGIL and the WFTU thus operated in such a way as to bring Italian Communist opinions out into the open sooner and with greater clarity in the sphere of trade union than of party relations. In this sense the CGIL acted as the

---

[1] Several of the CGIL officials with whom I talked readily agreed that the WFTU often seemed to take a more dogmatic line than the Soviet party itself. This may in part reflect the personal style of Secretary General Louis Saillant, brought up through the ranks of the doctrinaire French labor movement; one CGIL Communist remarked scathingly to me that Saillant, who had never been a party member, was a typically hard-line front organization man. WFTU dogmatism may also reflect, as another CGIL official suggested, the particularly narrow and insular outlook of the Soviet trade unionist: Viktor Grishin, the leading trade union official, was clearly not regarded with particular esteem in Rome.

PCI's spearhead in the effort to influence the evolution of international Communist policies.

The CGIL: Crisis and Recovery

Italian unionism is basically political. Ever since 1948, when the effort to maintain the CGIL as the sole trade union federation collapsed, the union scene has been dominated by the existence of two major rival federations, the CGIL and the CISL (Confederazione italiana sindacati lavoratori), each largely responsive to the interests of a political party, the PCI and the DC respectively. The third federation to emerge from the split, the UIL (Unione italiana del lavoro), has professed to socialist in orientation but completely independent from parties and thus more single-minded in its pursuit of the workers' welfare; it has, however, remained in a distinctly minority position.[2]

After the 1948 split, the CGIL continued to dominate the labor scene, successfully exploiting its superior size and wealth, its organizational strength, and its ideological claim to be the only genuine representative of the working class and proponent of socialism. In addition to its economic and trade union demands, during these years its Communist leaders repeatedly used the federation as a political weapon. Demonstrations, brief strikes, and other forms of agitation were employed in protest against Italian involvement in European defense and economic integration matters and on other major foreign policy issues. The CGIL seemed to be steadily in the ascendancy through 1953, when it was able to call two effective general strikes in support of nation-wide wage demands.[3]

But by 1954 there were growing indications that the CGIL was in

[2] Independent estimates of union membership invariably stress the unreliability of official statistics and membership claims. Arthur Ross, preferring to accept "the educated guesses of careful observers," has suggested figures of between 2,750,000 to 3,000,000 for the CGIL; 1,750,000 to 1,850,000 for the CISL; 250,000 to 350,000 for the UIL. Arthur M. Ross, "Prosperity and Labor Relations in Western Europe: Italy and France," *Industrial and Labor Relations Review*, XVI, 1 (October 1962), p. 74. Union claims run much higher. See Daniel L. Horowitz, *The Italian Labor Movement* (Cambridge, Mass.: Harvard University Press, 1963), p. 303, for the official claims for 1958.

[3] Horowitz, *The Italian Labor Movement*, pp. 237–243, provides a good politically oriented summary of trade union activities between 1948 and 1953; the book covers the entire period through early 1962, though not in as great detail on the later years as might be wished. The first half of the book is an excellent historical study of the prewar period. For a listing of major PCI sources on trade union questions between 1953 and 1959, see Alberto Merola, "Appunti bibliografici sulla politica operaia del P.C.I.," *Passato e presente*, No. 14 (March–April 1960), pp. 1868–1877.

serious trouble. Its main rival, the CISL, had gained strength both in the factories and at the national political level, while the CGIL's power had begun to wane. Elections to the Internal Commissions, the arena of trade union competition at the factory level, were resulting in a steady decline for the CGIL, which was, moreover, finding it increasingly difficult to mobilize support for politically oriented strikes and demonstrations. In the spring of 1955 the negative trend was verified in a stunning upset in the elections at the Fiat plants in Turin, long a Communist stronghold: CGIL support, which had been running at around 65 per cent of the total, suddenly declined to 36 per cent.[4] The opinion was widespread, and shared by many in the union itself, that the CGIL's relative neglect of worker problems and of organizational activities at the plant level had at last caught up with it, and that an era had begun in which blatantly political trade unionism would no longer work.

A vigorous internal debate got under way, first clearly reflected at the CGIL's Fourth Congress in late February 1956. Some, especially the Communist members of the CGIL leadership, continued to favor the traditional emphasis on action influencing the national political and economic scene: mobilization of the working classes behind parliamentary programs of large-scale structural changes such as land reform and nationalization of industry. Others, including most of the Socialists and many Communists as well, were convinced that the union's energies had to be turned primarily and urgently to the factory level in an effort to improve the worker's daily lot and strengthen the union's contractual power against the employers. This approach, already adopted by the other unions, required detailed research on economic, social, and technical questions of a sort neither the CGIL nor the PCI had previously undertaken on any serious scale. Technical articles now began appearing with great frequency in *Rinascita* and other journals, and the Gramsci Institute organized a study conference on changes in labor relationships and in the technical and organizational aspects of production.[5]

---

4 See "Les élections syndicales de la Fiat," *Est & Ouest,* IX, 174 (May 16–31, 1957), p. 10, for a convenient tabulation of Internal Commission elections at the Fiat plants between 1948 and 1957. For the country as a whole it has been estimated that from 1953 the GGIL had suffered an average annual decline in Internal Commission elections of about 14 per cent; Maurice F. Neufeld, "Il movimento sindacale italiano: panorama di una crisi," *Il Mulino,* VI, 4 (April 1957), footnote on p. 244.

5 See Merola, *Passato e presente,* No. 14, pp. 1873–1874, for references to the PCI literature pertaining to these subjects. For analysis of the CGIL Fourth

The CGIL had not yet recovered from the Fiat elections when it was dealt a blow from a different quarter: the Soviet party's Twentieth Congress and the upheavals in Eastern Europe threatened to undermine the prestige of the CGIL along with that of the party. Just as serious were the potential consequences for the CGIL's unity and its relations with the party. Giuseppe Di Vittorio, the CGIL's Secretary General, at first violated party discipline by expressing sympathy with the Poznań workers and the Hungarian rebels, then bowed to pressure and acknowledged the necessity of Soviet military intervention. This reversal occurred, however, only after the CGIL had for the first time in its history taken an official stand on a major international issue (Soviet military intervention in Hungary) contrary to that of the PCI. The internal tensions aroused by these events were so great that the CGIL found it expedient to adopt a resolution declaring that it would not in the future necessarily take an official position on every great international event; if unanimity could not be achieved between the Socialist and Communist factions, each would henceforth be free to express its own views.[6]

One effect of these international and domestic difficulties was a sharp drop in CGIL membership; between 1956 and 1958, by the union's own certainly conservative estimates, it lost almost a million members, many of whom simply transferred their allegiance to CISL and UIL.[7] Joseph LaPalombara, an experienced observer of the Italian labor scene, could refer in the spring of 1957 to "the gradual decline of CGIL," and to "certain signs that the balance of power in the Italian labor movement is shifting."[8]

A crisis it was, but not a mortal one. Over the next several years the CGIL managed to regain much of its earlier vigor, playing a leading role in the widespread strike actions of the late 1950's and developing a set of new policies more responsive to the changing environment. The "renewal" of which CGIL officials liked to speak took three main directions. First, the CGIL began consciously to

---

Congress by non-Communist sources, see, *inter alia,* Giuseppe Canavese, "Una promessa da mantenere," *Il Ponte,* XII, 3 (March 1956), pp. 339–341; Pino Tagliazucchi, "Note sul IV Congresso della CGIL," *ibid.,* XII, 4 (April 1956), pp. 559–563; Fidia Sassano, "Il Congresso della CGIL," *Mondo Operaio,* XIII, 4–5 (April–May 1960), pp. 29–36; and Piero Boni, "Per un dibattito sul V Congresso della C.G.I.L.," *ibid.,* XIII, 6 (June 1960), pp. 12–15.

6 For a summary of the resolution of November 20, 1956, see "La politica della CGIL del IV al V Congresso," *Rassegna sindacale,* No. 28 (April 1960), p. 17.

7 Horowitz, *The Italian Labor Movement,* pp. 298–299.

8 Joseph LaPalombara, *The Italian Labor Movement: Problems and Prospects* (Ithaca: Cornell University Press, 1957), pp. xv–xvi.

define a new role for itself in Italian economic and political life: this meant above all concentrating its energies more intensively on contractual problems within specific plants and industries, while searching for ways to integrate this grass-roots activity more effectively with a long-range attempt to influence economic policies and plans on the national level. Second, the CGIL made a considerable effort to demonstrate that it could perform as a genuinely independent union, not merely as an instrument of the Communist party. Third, it assumed a commitment to play a more vigorous international role, in European trade union affairs and in the Communist labor movement. Each of these requires some elaboration.

A NEW DOMESTIC STRATEGY. The most evident manifestation of the CGIL's "new look" was a sharp decline in blatantly political activity, the one notable exception being the general strike called to protest the deaths that occurred in the "anti-Fascist" riots against the Tambroni government in the summer of 1960. This was a case, however, of using the union as a political weapon on a domestic issue of great popular appeal rather than on a foreign policy question involving obvious Soviet interests. Political militancy of this sort suited the CGIL and the PCI perfectly, for it allowed them to be in the vanguard of the left-of-center forces against the extreme right and its allies in the Christian Democratic right wing.[9]

One positive corollary of this decline in the overtly political content of the CGIL's activities was a new attention to union organization and demands at the factory level. The trend toward bargaining for plant-level rather than industry-wide agreements on such issues as incentive payment systems, job evaluations, and productivity bonuses had been introduced by CISL and UIL several years before and had begun to pay off in terms of increased bargaining power, more votes in plant committees, and stronger local trade union organization. Although the CGIL endorsed this trend in principle at its Fourth Congress in 1956, the idea was still resisted at many levels, and not until the early 1960's did the union definitely accept a plant-level bargaining policy similar to that inaugurated by its rivals.[10]

[9] The episode is a useful reminder that the CGIL's change of strategy does not at all imply a reluctance to use the union for political purposes, only a desire not to associate itself with political causes, above all in the foreign policy realm, that are both obviously Communist sponsored and only marginally related to legitimate trade union functions.

[10] Luciano Lama, then head of the CGIL's federation of metalworking unions (FIOM), has pinpointed the spring of 1960 as the time when the unions

Resistance to the new approach was understandable. To many old-line trade unionists, masters at organization and political agitation, the new techniques represented a personal threat, for they required a technical competence in details of production, wage rates, and the like that they had never been called upon to acquire.[11] Beyond that, there were also ideological resistances to adopting techniques of trade union action that seemed to imply an acceptance of the whole capitalist framework and way of thinking about problems. Franco Momigliano, in commenting favorably on the "themes" developed for the CGIL's Fifth Congress in 1960, observed that the union had finally come to accept the arguments of the left-wing intellectuals and technicians against the traditional political orientations and schematic notions of the union's role:

> In those days [1952–1953], to present in such a way the problems of contracting, salary structures, job evaluation, incentives, relations with employees and technicians, action at the plant level, insufficiency of the organizational structure of the category unions—this was often regarded by the leaders as an intellectual exercise, or as heresy, or even worse, as a "sign of enslavement to advancing neocapitalist ideologies."[12]

It was an affront to old preconceptions, for example, that the new approach involved the practice of negotiating wage increases and other benefits according to the relative economic success of individual plants and the relative productivity of their work force. This seemed to violate the principle of class solidarity, for it meant seeking special advantage for the already relatively affluent workers in the more productive industries rather than fighting for across-the-board increases for all the workers. Was this not simply playing into the hands of the capitalists by allowing them to buy off with higher wages and benefits the most advanced sections of the working class? To traditionalists in the Communist labor movement, in short, the whole trend implied tacit acceptance of the capitalist system rather than a stubborn fight against it. And to a degree they were right, for the CGIL's "new look" was only the trade union reflection of a more general Communist strategy of seeking not to

---

under his command first became seriously involved in detailed bargaining at a level below the traditionally accepted nation-wide contracts. Within the CGIL, Lama and his successor at FIOM, Bruno Trentin, have been among the leaders in promoting the new trend. See Lama, "Sviluppo e motivi delle lotte operaie," *Rinascita*, XVIII, 1 (January 1961), pp. 30–35. See also Horowitz, *The Italian Labor Movement*, p. 320.

11 Ross notes that this response occurred in the non-Communist unions as well; *Industrial and Labor Relations Review*, XVI, 1, p. 73.

12 "Una tematica sindacale moderna," *Passato e presente*, No. 13 (January–February 1960), p. 1638.

overthrow but to reform and influence from within the structure of the Italian economic and social system.

Structural reform being the medium-term goal, the CGIL's shift of tactics did not in any sense imply acceptance of a narrow, welfare-oriented understanding of the union's role in society. On the contrary, the CGIL justified its new tactics with the argument that only by enhancing its over-all contractual power could it gain a greater voice in national policy as well as improve the daily lot of the worker. The CGIL's basic objective was, as it had always been, political: by mobilizing the working class, it sought to intervene decisively in the major issues of national economic policy, and thereby to achieve "a permanent increase in its power in society."[13]

During the early 1960's the CGIL's attention, along with that of the other unions, came increasingly to focus on problems of economic planning. Whether the union should participate actively in the planning process, thus tacitly accepting responsibility to respect the contours of a plan even if the immediate interests of the workers should suffer, was a difficult issue. The CGIL did not wish to restrict its freedom of action by accepting a national wage policy, but it had to recognize that participation in the planning process was one of the major ways in which influence could be exerted on the nation's economic structure. By 1964 this issue had become the central focus of a more general debate within the CGIL concerning the extent to which it should participate responsibly and constructively in the modification of a system it was ideologically committed to destroy.[14]

COMMUNISTS AND SOCIALISTS IN THE CGIL. Along with the trend away from direct political action went an effort to modify the CGIL's traditional strong subordination to the Communist party. This was a goal consistent with enhancing the CGIL's effectiveness on the national scene and it was desired by many of the union's Communist leaders; it was the presence of the Socialists, however,

13 Vittorio Foa, "I problemi del V Congresso della CGIL," Rinascita, XVII, 3 (March 1960), p. 175. (Round-table discussion.)

14 The Communist left tended to resist having the CGIL assume a responsibility to respect the guidelines of an economic plan. See, for example, the discussion of Ingrao's views as presented at the Fourteenth FIOM Congress in March 1964, in Fidia Sassano, "Il Congresso della FIOM e la programmazione," Mondo Operaio, XVII, 2–3 (February–March 1964), p. 9. For a collection of the basic CGIL documents on the planning question, see CGIL e programmazione economica (Rome: Editrice Sindacale Italiana, 1964). For a good analysis of the politics of planning in Italy, including a brief discussion of the response of the trade unions to the question, see Joseph LaPalombara, Italy: The Politics of Planning.

that forced the issue. Once the PSI had chosen to break its political alliance with the Communists, continued Socialist participation in the CGIL came to depend on giving the principle of autonomy a greater degree of real substance. This was a political necessity welcomed by all those, of whichever party affiliation, whose prime loyalty and responsibility were toward the union and who felt the need for a maximum degree of flexibility in pursuing their objectives.

The need for decisive action in this regard had been brought home to Secretary General Di Vittorio by the events of 1956, prompting him at the party's Eighth Congress to urge the "definitive liquidation of the famous theory of the 'transmission belt'" that had traditionally governed trade union–party relations in the Communist world.[15] Although the Theses issued before the Congress had called for union autonomy and an end to the "transmission belt" theory, the party had not yet moved far enough for Di Vittorio; he expressed his regret that these principles had not been given greater precision and incorporated into the Political Resolution of the Congress.[16] In the years after 1956, however, the Communist line moved steadily in the direction urged by Di Vittorio. It was essential to the face-lifting operation being performed by the CGIL that the "transmission belt" concept be formally and unequivocally rejected so as to permit an unqualified insistence on the necessity for complete autonomy on the part of all the trade unions from political parties. Gradually, over the next half-dozen years, the CGIL managed to transform its stance on this question from the early largely defensive one, in which the primary concern was to refute criticisms about the CGIL's subordination to the PCI, into a partially offensive weapon against the CISL, which was itself liable to the charge of being an instrument of the Christian Democrats. Trade union unity, the *summum bonum* of the labor world, could be achieved—so the CGIL was arguing—only when all the union federations had abandoned their ideological preconceptions and their links with political parties and agreed to col-

15 *VIII Congresso,* p. 437.
16 *Ibid.,* p. 630. Di Vittorio's remarks were made at the very end of the Congress when several participants were indicating their reservations about the contents of the political document, then about to be put to a vote. Di Vittorio's complaint was symptomatic of the tension between party and trade union leaders over the question of autonomy for the CGIL. In his comments on the "transmission belt" issue, Horowitz does not do justice to this aspect of the matter, referring to the party as undergoing only a "showcase cleansing of methods" in response to public pressure and to Di Vittorio as having "played the role of innovator" on the party's behalf; Horowitz, *The Italian Labor Movement,* p. 297.

laborate in pursuit of social and economic gains in the interest of the working class.

It is unlikely that the goal of unity (or of full autonomy, for that matter) was taken seriously by either side; certainly the prospect of its realization was and has remained remote. Trade union unity resembles the question of German reunification in that its political potency bears little direct relation to its feasibility; everyone appears to feel that the aspiration, or the myth, is either so attractive or so traditional a feature of political discourse that it cannot safely be abandoned. The Communists have played on the unity theme with particular fervor for many reasons, but particularly because it is the main ideological justification for continued adherence by the Socialist party to a union in which their representatives are bound to remain a small minority. The Communist effort to bury the theory of the "transmission belt" and to insist that the CGIL is the only nonideological, nonparty, and thus genuinely "unitary" union has been directed above all toward countering the potential threat of a Socialist walkout. This threat, and thus the need to counter it, has mounted steadily since the late 1950's, as the Center-Left experiment has evolved from possibility into reality.

For the PCI to relinquish even as hallowed a symbol as the theory of the "transmission belt" did not of course automatically enhance the level of participation by the Socialists in CGIL decision-making. Nor did the answer lie primarily in the direction of strengthening Socialist representation in CGIL executive bodies. Some steps could be taken in that direction (as was done at the Fifth Congress in 1960 with respect to the composition of CGIL bodies at the national level), but the basic fact of overwhelming Communist predominance, especially at the middle and lower levels, could not be changed by marginal shifts at the top.[17]

More significant than their numerical strength was the increased leverage acquired by the Socialists in consequence of the PCI's need to assure that they remained in the organization. Compromises and bargaining have been a constant aspect of the situation at the

17 See Giorgio Benvenuto and Fidia Sassano, "Il corrente socialista nella CGIL," *Tempi moderni*, New Series, No. 14 (July–September 1963), pp. 145–146, for interesting data on the composition of CGIL bodies at all levels. Whereas, for example, at the national level Socialists made up 37 per cent of the 181 member steering committee and 41 per cent of the 48 member executive committee, an analysis of 1,831 CGIL secretaries at all levels of the union federation revealed that about 76 per cent were Communists, 14 per cent left-wing Socialists, and only 8 per cent "autonomous" Socialists of the Nenni faction. See also "Dirigenti socialisti e comunisti nella CGIL," *ibid.*, New Series, No. 3 (October–December 1960), pp. 171–172.

policy-making level, and the necessarily confidential nature of the interplay between the two party interests has made it virtually impossible for an outsider to arrive at a precise calculation of the degree of Socialist influence. The general consensus is that the Socialists have played a major role in pushing the CGIL toward new positions on such issues as the Common Market, the WFTU, and economic planning—and this can be supported by comparing the respective party positions on the issues with those adopted by the CGIL—but without detailed case studies it would be difficult to provide a much more refined estimate of the extent of Socialist influence.[18]

To put the question simply in terms of a contest for influence between Communists and Socialists in the CGIL would in any case seriously distort reality, for party members were themselves not generally of a single mind. In the first years of rebuilding after the 1954–1957 decline, the significant struggle was between innovators and conservatives on both sides of the party fence. In the words of one close analyst of CGIL affairs:

> The dividing line in the confrontation with sectarian, Stalinist, instrumental, antidemocratic positions in the CGIL does not separate schematically the Socialists from the Communists. . . . There are innovators and conservatives among Socialists and Communists alike, not only in politics but also in the trade union, in the cooperatives, in the local bodies. And often the most static and closed positions are those that appear to be the most "revolutionary," while the bolder ones are held by men of prudence and gradualism, whose "feet are on the ground."[19]

The innovators among the Communists, led by such men as Luciano Lama, Luciano Romagnoli, and Bruno Trentin (and generally supported by Agostino Novella, who became Secretary General after Di Vittorio's death in 1957), shared with many Socialists the

18 Even Socialist analysts of the CGIL, while generally stressing the PSI's role in the innovations of recent years, do not attempt to provide a precise measure of the contributions made by their party. Giorgio Lauzi, for example, referring to the CGIL's new outlook toward economic planning, concludes: "To a certain extent, it was acquired by the CGIL as a result of the decisive, although perhaps not exclusive, impetus of the Socialist group . . ."; Giorgio Lauzi, "La politica sindacale del PSI," *Tempi moderni*, New Series, No. 14 (July–September 1963), p. 142. See also Alfredo Livi, "Per una politica della corrente sindacale socialista," *Mondo Operaio*, XVII, 4 (April 1964), pp. 21–25. Most analysts seem agreed that whatever the PSI contribution to general policy, its real weakness has lain in its inadequate organizational strength at lower levels, where Communists have always been dominant.

19 Fidia Sassano, *Mondo Operaio*, XIII, 4–5, p. 31. Sassano was writing after the Fifth Congress in 1960. A similar view of the situation, at an earlier stage, is found in Canavese, *Il Ponte*, XII, 3, p. 339, and Tagliazucchi, *ibid.*, XII, 4, p. 560.

conviction that the union had to adapt to the new political and economic facts of Italian life. Often referred to as *sindacalisti,* or trade union men, to distinguish them from those presumed to regard the union's function in a primarily instrumental light as an agent of the party, they genuinely believed in the need for fuller union autonomy and for the greatest possible concentration on the economic and technical issues of primary legitimate concern to a trade union.

The work of the innovators, as well as the larger task of maintaining the CGIL's unity, was substantially eased by the deep divisions within Socialist ranks. The left-wing Socialists, although consistently a minority in the party as a whole, were in the majority among Socialists in the CGIL.[20] Vittorio Foa, a Secretary of the CGIL and a leader in the faction that later broke away to form the PSIUP in protest at the PSI's entry into the government, was the intellectual leader of the group. The point is not that Foa and other left Socialists in the PSI generally supported Communist positions. As was observed in the previous chapter, they in fact disagreed with the PCI on domestic problems from a left-wing perspective about as strongly as they disagreed with their Socialist colleagues. The strength of the PSI left did mean, however, that within the CGIL the Socialists could not bring to bear the weight they might otherwise have exerted in consequence of the political situation between the two parties. Had the Socialist minority in the CGIL been united and thus able to argue consistently for the official positions of their party, its leverage would have been greater, and collaboration between the Socialist and Communist factions would have been markedly more difficult.[21]

A NEW INTERNATIONAL ORIENTATION. The CGIL's "new look" had an international dimension as well. In the process of rebuilding the union's strength after the difficulties of the mid-1950's, domestic problems took priority, so that in late 1961 one of the CGIL secretaries could still admit that "for many years in the past we have given short weight to our international work. . . . We have been cultivating our own garden, not always well, without thinking

20 See Benvenuto and Sassano, *Tempi moderni,* New Series, No. 14, pp. 145–146.
21 Concerning the CGIL's relations with the WFTU, for example, the right-wing Socialists urged actions tending toward a complete break, whereas the left-wing group shared the PCI's desire to use their influence to transform the organization. The single negative vote at the WFTU's Fifth Congress was cast by a right-wing Socialist. The effects of this situation became clearer after the creation of the PSIUP, when three distinct currents began to operate in the CGIL; those on the right now pushed more strongly than before for a break with the WFTU, as in the debate preceding the WFTU Sixth Congress in 1965.

much about the gardens of our neighbors. . . ."[22] It was only at the WFTU's Fifth Congress in December 1961 that the CGIL began seriously to worry about these things, a development that proved disturbing to its nearest neighbor, the French CGT (Confédération Générale du Travail), and to the WFTU itself.

This new interest in international matters was motivated by the same general factors that determined the two aspects of the CGIL's evolution already discussed. Internationally as well as domestically the CGIL was attempting to set aside its traditional reactions in order to respond more effectively to a world in rapid change. It had to do so sooner and more decisively than it might otherwise have done because of pressure from the Socialists within its midst, but this was not the dominant consideration. The most important aspect of the new reality to which the CGIL had to adjust in its international dealings was the emergence of an economically integrated Europe. The CGIL was not slow to understand that the Common Market would have an important impact on Italy, even though it misinterpreted the nature of that impact, expecting an economic disaster for the working class and all but the largest and most competitive of the monopolies. Whatever the economic prognosis, the Market appeared to the CGIL certain to strengthen the industrial and managerial class relative to the workers by creating a united front of European capitalism.

It has been characteristic of Italian communism when faced with a threatening but powerful aspect of reality—the Catholic Church, Parliament, economic planning—to respond not by ignoring or attacking it but by accepting its existence, to a degree even collaborating with it, so as to remove or moderate its sting. Every menace also contains the opportunity to influence the course of national policy and to build alliances with those outside the Communist ranks. So it was with respect to the Common Market, which might be influenced from within its own bodies and through its member governments provided—and it was a big proviso—some unity of aim and action could be achieved with other European labor organizations. And if collaboration could be achieved with regard to the Market, the larger goal would have been advanced of breaking down the barriers between the Communist unions and the rest of the European labor movement.

A brief review of the CGIL's early response to the Common Market will illustrate these points and show how it was that the Italian

---

[22] "La relazione di Luciano Romagnoli," *Rassegna sindacale*, No. 47–48 (November–December 1961), pp. 2433–2434.

response came almost automatically to conflict with that of the French CGT and of the WFTU itself. It was not until July 1957, three months after the Rome Treaty had been signed, that the CGIL issued an official resolution on the Common Market.[23] Although similar in some respects to the PCI's statement, it was certain meaningful differences of emphasis that attracted attention, encouraging the CGIL to point proudly to the document as "courageous, serious, and responsible," as the best possible proof of its autonomy from the Communist party.[24] The Common Market issue was the first significant test since Hungary of the CGIL's capacity to elaborate a united position in the face of contrasting party positions. (The PCI had voted against the Treaty of Rome, while the PSI had abstained, expressing reservations about certain aspects.) The test was successfully passed and a workable compromise achieved.

Two main points distinguished the PCI statement from that of the CGIL. The first involved the emphasis given to the positive value of economic integration: the CGIL made this the leading theme, treating the Common Market more as a legitimate economic institution than as an instrument of the Atlantic Pact. Like the party, the CGIL insisted that the economic consequences of an integration policy sponsored and controlled by the European ruling class could not help but damage working-class interests: in a European-wide labor market, the unions, if they remained divided, would be helpless before a powerful coalition of monopolies and governments controlling wage and investment policies. But this challenge was not to be met, as in the PCI's prescription, by frontal attack and verbal denunciation. The CGIL argued instead the urgent need for joint action by unions of all political affiliations, in each country and on an international scale, to prevent the monopolies from exploiting the workers through this new device.

That this line was not meant solely for domestic consumption became clear at the Fourth Congress of the WFTU, held in Leipzig in October 1957. Giuseppe Di Vittorio, from his position as CGIL Secretary General and WFTU President, presented his union's case against the official WFTU line enunciated by its Secretary General, Louis Saillant, and by the head of the French delegation, Benoît Frachon. Di Vittorio complained that the WFTU was seriously underestimating the seriousness of the problems the Common Market would create for European workers and their unions;

23 *L'Unità*, July 20, 1957.
24 "Il MEC e noi," *Lavoro*, July 28, 1957.

Saillant's "very summary review of the subject," he argued, was "not adequate." Second, he insisted that the WFTU and its member unions accept the existence of the Common Market, which was "in process of becoming a reality," and begin to work to transform it rather than simply denounce its establishment. Third, and here was the main thrust of his argument, he urged that the Common Market afforded a perfect opportunity for the WFTU to work concretely toward what had always been one of its central declared goals, the re-establishment of unity among all the trade unions of Europe. "Is it really not possible," he asked, "when we are confronted by this type of coalition on the part of the big employers, to achieve agreement, at least for united action, among all the workers' trade unions?"[25] It appears from the objections registered that Di Vittorio also argued, although the point does not appear in published versions of his speech, for making a serious effort to have the Communist unions included among those participating in the work of the Common Market's Economic and Social Committee, a move which would have entailed a degree of implicit acceptance of the institution itself.

Opposition to this approach was led by Benoît Frachon, Di Vittorio's counterpart in the French CGT. Frachon insisted in a militant speech that approval of the Common Market by the several parliaments was no reason "for abandoning the struggle for its liquidation"; the workers must continue "to fight for its destruction" and "not withdraw before the *fait accompli*." Implicitly ridiculing Di Vittorio's plea for united action with non-Communist unions as "a vague, sentimental ideal for the working class," he contrasted it with the only true unity, that won by fierce struggle against the opponent. As for the suggestion that the Communist unions might effectively resist the Common Market by boring from within, this was a dangerous reformist illusion that could only strengthen the enemy. A few sentences from his speech give the flavor of the French polemic against both the Common Market and their Italian colleagues:

A place has been reserved for trade union representatives in the bodies of the Common Market by the monopolies and their governments; not for all unions but only for those supporting the Market, which shows that they are not at all keen on seeing authentic working-class representatives in their learned gatherings, condemning their contrivances and informing the workers of the real facts. . . .
But the monopolies need workers' representatives in their nefarious

25 "We are a Great World Force," *World Trade Union Movement* (hereafter cited as *WTUM*), November 1957, p. 28.

undertakings merely to pull the wool over people's eyes and serve as a front, nothing more. Naïve indeed are those who believe that the monopolies will embarrass themselves by allowing the advice of union representatives to be heard in the Common Market, in this gathering of vultures. . . .

But we are not harbouring the dangerous illusion of being able to tame this infernal machine forged by the monopolies at the instigation of the American monopolies—the Common Market.[26]

The dispute over the Common Market was only one aspect of an almost irreconcilable difference of policy and style between the CGIL and the CGT. Since the latter invariably mirrored in its attitudes those of the WFTU, whose Secretary General had come from the CGT's ranks, there can be seen in this conflict the essence of that between the CGIL and the WFTU as well. The gulf between the two unions was similar to that which divided the respective Communist parties, but it ran even deeper, for the reformist tendencies that aggravated the French in the PCI were magnified in the CGIL. At the Leipzig Congress of the WFTU Di Vittorio repeated many of the standard Italian attitudes against which the French had protested not long before in the famous article by Garaudy: the wages of the proletariat were not inexorably declining, technical progress would not inevitably bring disaster to the working class, relations with other unions should not be limited to "sterile and harmful polemics."[27] The CGIL's attitude toward its brother union had already been unmistakably revealed in the condescending tone in which its delegates to the CGT Congress in July had described their impressions: the CGT was fortunately freeing itself from some aspects of its sectarianism, they reported, but it remained "backward" in many respects; and "it was strange for us to note the almost total lack of criticism and self-criticism" in the debate.[28]

Soon after the Leipzig Congress efforts were made to heal the breach between the two unions. Early in February 1958 their representatives met at WFTU headquarters in Prague to try to work out a compromise approach to Common Market problems. They failed to do so (the official communiqué lacks any general characterization of the Common Market) but agreed to the desirability of further discussion.[29] By September a follow-up meeting had been arranged in Paris, at which all the WFTU unions of

26 "Unity is a Battle," *ibid.*, p. 42.
27 "The Fourth World Trade Union Congress will open up new possibilities for Working Class Unity," *ibid.*, September 1957, pp. 16–19.
28 "Dibattito sull' unità," *Lavoro*, July 7, 1957.
29 "Un' azione in comune nel MEC concordata fra CGIL e CGT," *Avanti!*, March 1, 1958.

Western Europe as well as several French African unions were represented. The principal result was the creation of a standing Coordination and Action Committee charged with the task of analyzing the economic and social problems resulting from the Common Market and recommending appropriate action.[30]

The Committee for Coordination and Action, which the CGIL took credit for having initiated, convened four or five times during the next three years before quietly fading from the scene. Given the difference in orientation of its two dominant members, it is not surprising that the committee failed to accomplish anything more striking than the issuance of formal statements decrying the increased pressure of European and American monopoly capital on the working class and urging working-class unity around a common program of traditional trade union demands.[31] As usual under such circumstances, the least common denominator prevailed: the CGIL could prevent inclusion of such denunciations of the Common Market's political origins and purposes as had marked Frachon's Leipzig speech as well as subsequent CGT and WFTU statements and could see to it that the theme of united action with non-WFTU unions figured prominently in the declarations. The CGT, on the other hand, could block reference to participation in Common Market bodies and frustrate any serious attempt to make the search for unity among European unions anything more than a subject for propaganda.

The CGIL did manage to achieve one trivial success along these lines, not through the WFTU committee but in direct collaboration with the CGT. In January 1959 the two unions met in Rome and agreed on a letter to be sent to all unions in the Common Market countries, proposing a meeting at which coordinated action against the monopolies could be worked out.[32] But while the appeal may in itself have represented a small victory for the CGIL, the total lack of positive response could only have reinforced the French view that appeals for unity, while marginally useful for propaganda purposes, could not be expected to produce tangible results.[33]

30 "The Common Market and Unity," *WTUM*, November 1958, pp. 35–36.
31 See, for example, "Trade Unions Face the European Common Market by Drawing Up Their Demands," *ibid.*, June 1959, pp. 29–32; "Remarks on the European Common Market," *ibid.*, December 1959, pp. 17–19; "Working Class Unity and the Common Market," *ibid.*, July 1960, pp. 24–28.
32 "Danger of Common Market: C.G.T. and C.G.I.L. Propose a Meeting," *ibid.*, March 1959, pp. 36–37.
33 For a revealing indication of the contrasting styles of the CGIL and the CGT in this matter of unity, see the letters written by the heads of the French and Italian metalworkers' unions to their counterpart organization in Belgium, an affiliate of the ICFTU. In reply to a proposal for reunification of the

This review makes it apparent that the CGIL, well before the Fifth Congress of the WFTU, had reason to be dissatisfied with an organization that appeared neither interested in nor capable of furthering the Italian interest in playing a larger role in European affairs. This problem alone, however, was hardly grave enough to have aroused the spirited opposition displayed by the CGIL's delegation at the Moscow Congress, to which occasion we shall now turn.

The CGIL at the WFTU Moscow Congress

A combination of circumstances in the fall of 1961 led the CGIL to generalize its long-standing dissatisfactions with the WFTU into a coherent expression of opposition to many of that organization's basic principles of policy and action. First, the CGIL needed to prepare a basic platform statement in response to the Draft Program of Trade Union Action issued by the WFTU for its Fifth Congress in December.[34] This occasion gave those who felt most strongly the negative weight of the WFTU's policies, above all the Socialist minority in the CGIL, an opportunity to insist on a direct confrontation of issues that other CGIL leaders, all things being equal, might have preferred to pass over in silence. The influence of the Socialists, moreover, was at that moment enhanced by the general expectation that the slow movement toward an opening to the left was almost certain to result, before many more months had passed, in a Christian Democratic government supported by the Socialists. For the PCI, concerned that this development could result in a rupture between the two working-class parties, it was hardly the moment to make a dogmatic stand in favor of proletarian internationalism and unconditional loyalty to the WFTU.

Into the midst of the already complicated political situation dropped the bombshell of the Twenty-Second Congress. Officials of the CGIL have made a point of refuting the "propagandists" in the bourgeois press who attempted to explain the behavior of the Italian delegation at the WFTU Congress as simply a reflection of

---

European unions, the French letter stubbornly reiterated the CGT's standard views, referring to the Common Market as "a great operation designed to deceive the working class." Luciano Lama, on the Italian side, played down the differences, terming them of "minor importance" compared to the basic similarity of views, and called for mutual concessions and abandonment of suspicion for the sake of unity. See "In the Interests of the Workers . . . YES!," *ibid.*, April 1959, pp. 32–35.

34 *Draft Programme of Trade Union Action*, supplement to *WTUM*, August 1961.

the turmoil in Communist ranks caused by the Soviet party Congress and effectively exploited by the Socialists.[35] To attribute the CGIL's action to such circumstances of the moment, they have argued, grossly understates its significance and fails to recognize its relation to the broader process of renewal in which the union had for some time been engaged. In the main, the reproach is justified; the CGIL's position at Moscow was not only coherently related to the broader patterns of change sketched out above, but proved to be a permanent feature of CGIL policy. All the same, while one can rule out the Twenty-Second Congress as the exclusive or principal motivating factor, it cannot be dismissed altogether.

We must rely largely on inference in deciding how much weight to give to the effects of the Twenty-Second Congress. A prolonged and intense debate over the contents of an "orientation statement" for the WFTU Congress reached its climax in the first two weeks of November 1961, immediately following the Soviet Congress; the statement was finally published, with apologies for its long delay, two days after the conclusion of the dramatic November meeting of the PCI Central Committee.[36] We know also that the Socialists, less inhibited by a particular sense of loyalty to Moscow, were strongly and openly critical of the WFTU's Draft Program. Both before and after the appearance of the CGIL's "orientation statement," the columns of *Avanti!* frequently contained articles and letters on the WFTU, many urging the need for fundamental change in its policies and modes of operation.[37] Nothing of the sort appeared in *L'Unità*.

The Twenty-Second Congress certainly did much to strengthen the hand of the CGIL's Socialists and of those Communists favoring a critical attitude toward the WFTU. We are entitled to assume that the criticisms of the USSR expressed at the November Central Committee meeting were shared by the Communist CGIL leaders, even though those who were Central Committee members had discreetly not spoken at the PCI meeting, probably so as not to

[35] See, for example, Luciano Romagnoli, "Significato e motivi del dibattito nella FSM," *Rinascita*, XIX, 1 (January 1962), p. 23.

[36] *L'Unità*, November 16, 1961, contains excerpts from the text of the statement along with an explanatory statement by Secretary General Novella.

[37] See, *inter alia*, "Dalla FSM si deve esprimere una politica più unitaria," *Avanti!*, November 8, 1961; "Colmare le lacune del documento CGIL," *ibid.*, November 21; "La politica internazionale del sindacato," *ibid.*, November 22. See also the pamphlet, *Sulle questioni e sulle iniziative di politica internazionale della C.G.I.L.* (no author, no date), apparently prepared in late 1965 by the Socialist current of the CGIL since it has an introduction by Giovanni Mosca, Socialist member of the CGIL Secretariat; pp. 14–15 summarize the Socialist contribution to the pre-Congress debate in the fall of 1961.

complicate their delicate bargaining position at the forthcoming WFTU Congress. The defiant mood of that meeting very likely influenced the CGIL's deliberations as well, encouraging a more determined stand against the WFTU than would otherwise have been made.

A clear distinction should be made here between the substance of the CGIL's attitude and the decision to express it with some vigor at the Moscow Congress. The CGIL's behavior before and more particularly after the WFTU Congress makes it clear that the Communists genuinely endorsed the positions they assumed there; they were not merely catering to Socialist and public opinion. The issue was one of expediency: how far could the CGIL safely go in fighting the hierarchy of a Soviet-controlled front organization without causing difficulties for the PCI? Since all other considerations (e.g., CGIL European interests, PSI pressure, desire to establish an image of autonomy) favored a tough stand, a restraining hand could come only from the PCI. And at this particular moment the PCI's capacity to restrain the CGIL was, for psychological and political reasons, uncommonly low.

An additional consideration undoubtedly played a part in the decision to stand up to the WFTU, although this too cannot be supported by direct evidence. The PCI and the CGIL could not have helped but try to calculate the consequences for the WFTU and for themselves of the Sino-Soviet dispute. In the spring of 1960 the open Chinese attack on the Soviet line at the Peking meeting of the WFTU General Council had made it plain that the rivalry would affect trade union as well as party relationships. The Chinese action had, moreover, apparently inhibited the CGIL's intention of raising some of the issues that finally came to light at the Moscow Congress.[38]

The actions of the Italians at Moscow indicated, however, that their experience at Peking and their general evaluation of the state of affairs in the international Communist movement had aroused the conviction that the WFTU could be held together only if it could learn to live with the new reality of profound differences among its leading members. If it were to become a battleground for competing national strategies, its usefulness as a trade union international would be totally destroyed. Objectively, therefore, the Italian interest in greater national and regional autonomy was in the interest of the organization as a whole. Here was, in effect, a testing ground for the idea of polycentrism, of a new kind of unity in diversity.

38 See Chapter Five.

None of this was ever explicitly stated or even hinted at by CGIL officials in their public statements at the time of the Moscow Congress; no reference at all was made, in fact, to Sino-Soviet rivalry. These considerations were clearly implicit, however, in the CGIL's proposals at Moscow and must have been taken into account in private deliberations. In December 1961, just after Khrushchev's denunciations of Albania at the Twenty-Second Congress, a Communist leader could hardly have failed to include them in his calculations, and it would not be long before such obvious facts of life would receive public mention.[39] In sum, by the end of 1961 the Chinese challenge appears to have become an additional motive for the CGIL's opposition to the traditional WFTU line rather than a reason for suppressing it. The further fact of Soviet need for support from such strongly anti-Chinese unions as the CGIL made it all the easier to undertake the campaign.

The "orientation statement" issued by the CGIL two weeks before the Congress differed in many significant respects from the WFTU Draft Program circulated several months previously. These differences were noted and discussed by Communists and Socialists alike. Elio Capodaglio, for example, an important Socialist trade union official, observed that the contrasts between the two "are quite noticeable and reveal a noteworthy divergence in conceptions concerning the nature and functions of unions." The essential problem, in his view, was that the WFTU "calls the ideologically engaged trade union the only really valid kind of union"—a union, that is, that considers its primary duty the struggle on behalf of the "socialist camp"—whereas the CGIL, while emphasizing its class character, "also stresses the specific function of the union and its autonomy with respect to governments and parties." Capodaglio did not hesitate to make a choice between the two conceptions:

It seems to me that the alternative chosen by the CGIL is certainly the only possible one, the only way to conceive of a trade union, a real trade union, at any rate. This is to say that a real union is neither a wheel in the gears of the "capitalist" system, nor an accessory of the party or the government in the "socialist" system; in either case it lays claim to broad functions that are definitely not of a subordinate nature.[40]

Similar observations were made by Communist members of the

39 See, for example, Secretary General Novella's remarks at a CGIL press conference a year later; L'Unità, January 23, 1963. My conversations with CGIL officials in the summer of 1964 also revealed how central an element the Sino-Soviet split had become in their thinking about the WFTU.

40 "Due diverse concezione del sindacato," Avanti!, November 19, 1961. The Poznań crisis in 1956 had first brought into the open Socialist objections to the subordinate role of the trade unions in the USSR and the WFTU's failure to address itself to this question; see Fernando Santi, ibid., July 11, 1956.

CGIL, most notably by Luciano Romagnoli in a speech to a meeting of the Executive Committee.[41]

Shortly thereafter, in an unprecedented display of constructive opposition, the CGIL presented its views before the WFTU Congress, summing up its case in twenty-eight amendments to the Draft Program and to the WFTU's constitution.[42] Although some changes were made in parts of the Program in response to the Italian amendments, the CGIL's subsequent claims that they were "largely accepted"[43] and the Program "modified substantially"[44] are certainly exaggerated. The spokesman for the committee charged with drafting the final version of the Program correctly reported back to the Congress that some amendments had been introduced, but "without changing the fundamental orientation of the Draft Program."[45] These inflated claims were presumably intended both to impress the Italian audience with the CGIL's effectiveness and to justify the fact that the members of the delegation, with one exception, voted to accept the Congress resolutions.[46] Perhaps the most appropriate judgment was the one made in the press release issued by Agostino Novella and Fernando Santi, the CGIL's top officials, upon their return to Rome: "Our delegation has, by its activities and remarks, started a democratic debate within the Congress and the international workers' movement such as has never been seen before. . . ."[47] Fundamental issues had been brought into the open which it would be impossible for the WFTU leadership subsequently to ignore.

Although it agreed to endorse the Program, in recognition of the modifications introduced in response to its objections, the CGIL delegation qualified its vote with a statement of the major points

41 "La relazione di Luciano Romagnoli," *Rassegna sindacale*, No. 47–48, pp. 2433–2436.

42 *L'Unità*, December 16, 1961.

43 *Ibid.*, January 6, 1962.

44 *Avanti!*, December 19, 1961.

45 *Ibid.*, December 16, 1961.

46 The lone dissenter, Socialist Bruno Di Pol from Milan, continued stoutly to insist after the Congress that since the CGIL's most important points had been ignored, a vote of approval could not be justified (*Avanti!*, December 30, 1961). When I happened to comment on this episode in a conversation with a leading Communist CGIL official, he replied scathingly that Di Pol may have been right about the limited acceptance of the CGIL's points but that he had behaved irresponsibly and foolishly; a negative vote by the delegation would simply have destroyed any future chance for the CGIL to exercise influence in the WFTU. The comment helps to bring home the obvious but crucial fact that a strategy of influencing the movement from within, in a posture of loyal opposition, imposes sharp limits on the extent and nature of a challenge.

47 *Ibid.*, December 19, 1961.

on which it continued to find the Program inadequate. On the last day of the Congress, CGIL Secretary Luciano Lama summarized the three main reservations: first, the Program did not express "the decisive importance of working out national programs for the trade union organizations" corresponding to their particular domestic circumstances; second, it gave a "wholly inadequate" evaluation of the search for new autonomous, regionally based trade union organizations in Africa and elsewhere; third, it adopted a sterile, purely polemical attitude toward the problem of unity with unions outside the WFTU.[48] These complaints, and other related ones Lama did not mention, amounted to nothing less than a general challenge both to the essential elements of WFTU strategy and to the quality of its relations with its affiliated organizations in the non-Communist countries. Lama's points merit analysis, for they reveal a good deal about the Italian Communists' perceptions of the outside world and of the state of affairs within the international movement.

THE ROAD TO INTERNATIONAL TRADE UNION UNITY. The Italian position at the WFTU Congress implicitly challenged the traditional role of that organization as an auxiliary arm of the international Communist movement. In effect, the CGIL was challenging the WFTU to act as though it really wished to achieve what it had always proclaimed to be its fundamental goal: unification of the international labor movement around a platform of class struggle against capitalism and imperialism.

The WFTU maintained, both before and after the labor schism of 1948–1949, that, as the only union based on class principles, it alone could represent and articulate the true interests and aspirations of the working class of the entire world. This pretension was, in a general sense, only an application to the trade union movement of the traditional claim of the USSR, as the leader of world communism, to represent the interests of the international proletariat. Thus, the WFTU Congress was always officially designated as a "World Trade Union Congress" and its program described by the Secretary General as "a practical basis for unity of action which can embrace all trades and all countries."[49]

To maintain the fiction, periodic gestures toward collaboration have been made toward the International Confederation of Free

[48] "Dichiarazione di voto della delegazione italiana presentata da Luciano Lama," *Mondo Operaio*, XVI, 12 (December 1961), p. 50.
[49] Louis Saillant, *The W.F.T.U. and the Tasks of the Trade Union Movement* (London: W.F.T.U. Publications Ltd., [1962]), p. 78.

Trade Unions (ICFTU), gestures wholly empty of content in view of
the WFTU's transparent unwillingness to envisage the least compromise in its ideological and political positions or in its traditionally
aggressive attitude toward its rival.[50] It has been perfectly clear that
unity could be achieved only on the WFTU's own terms, and that
the slogan has been manipulated purely for propaganda purposes,
or as a means of mobilizing support behind Communist leadership
on particular issues of domestic or international concern. In Communist terms these have been tactical rather than strategic moves,
intended to take temporary advantage of favorable situations rather
than to form longer-term alliances capable of significantly influencing the political situation. Aside from this purely instrumental
and short-term use of the "unity of action" theme, the WFTU has
been interested in unity only in the ultimate sense of absorbing
other organizations, or their members, into the WFTU itself. True
unity, like peace, is in the traditional Communist view something
to be achieved only when the enemy has been overcome.

It was this sectarian view of trade union unity that the CGIL
chose to fight within the WFTU, just as the PCI had for years been
doing within its own ranks. Italian Communist strategy at home, as
we have seen, was deeply rooted in the premise that the goal of
united action with labor and left-wing forces in the Socialist and
Catholic camps was something to be taken seriously, not just talked
about. Any long-run strategy that was not purely defensive and
oriented toward the *status quo* demanded that bridges be built to
the non-Marxist labor world. This principle held true, so the CGIL
believed, in the realm of international labor as well: old barriers
had to be broken down, new uncommitted forces won over, dogmatic ideological prescriptions and outmoded policies modified.

The CGIL had been uncomfortable with the WFTU unity line
for many years. At least as far back as 1957, during the preparations
for the Fourth WFTU Congress in Leipzig, Di Vittorio had
registered misgivings on this score.[51] His insistence on the need to
overcome the grave damage caused by disunity, especially in the

50 In his Congress report, for example, Saillant cited a 1959 proposal that
the two organizations meet to work out an "economic and social program geared
to universal and complete disarmament." How, he asked, could anyone allege,
"as some are doing" (the Yugoslavs were intended), that neither side is willing
to make a first move? *Ibid.*, p. 74. See "W.F.T.U. Concrete Proposals for 1960,"
WTUM, February 1960, pp. 3–4, for the text of an open letter sent to the
individual ICFTU unions as a follow-up to the earlier proposal that had been
transmitted to the ICFTU Congress.

51 "The Fourth World Trade Union Congress will open up new possibilities
for Working Class Unity," *WTUM*, September 1957, pp. 16–19.

face of the growing internationalization of monopoly capital, was as unusual an argument in WFTU circles as his moderate tone toward the ICFTU. At the Congress itself Di Vittorio had further developed his theme, arguing that "it is pointless and even harmful to the cause of united action to engage in sterile polemics with other unions on issues which are only too familiar causes of dissension. To become bogged down in endless polemics on such points can only result in deepening the gulf between us."[52] When this is contrasted with the contemporary remarks of other leading WFTU figures, consisting of little but those same "sterile polemics," it is evident that the Italian position was even then out of step with that of the WFTU as a whole. Not until the Moscow Congress, however, was the issue again brought up, this time in a more serious way.

The CGIL did not quarrel with the WFTU's ambition to represent the interests and objectives of the whole working class. It did, however, take strenuous objection to the presumption that the WFTU's Program provided anything like a realistic basis for this aspiration. From the rostrum of the Moscow Congress Novella labeled as "completely mistaken" Saillant's statement to this effect and pointed out that there were many progressive organizations belonging to the ICFTU which could never collaborate with the WFTU on the basis of its Draft Program.[53] The WFTU's persistent habit of attacking the leaders of the ICFTU actually set back the cause of unity.[54]

The attack was taken up again a few days later by Fernando Santi, top-ranking PSI member in the CGIL. Noting that Novella's remarks "had occasioned a certain surprise and perplexity," he pointed out that whereas the Soviet policy of peaceful coexistence had made considerable progress over the past five years, relations between the WFTU and the other unions had not improved since the split a dozen years before.[55] The Italian spokesmen did not get a sympathetic hearing on this point from the majority of the Congress delegations.[56] A Yugoslav observer at the Congress noted

52 "We are a Great World Force," *ibid.*, November 1957, p. 28.

53 "Discorso di Agostino Novella," *Mondo Operaio*, XVI, 12 (December 1961), pp. 41–45, at p. 44. Novella's speech, and that of Fernando Santi, are also to be found along with other congress materials in *Rassegna sindacale*, No. 49 (January 1962), pp. 2493–2517. See also the detailed reporting in *L'Unità* and *Avanti!* during the Congress.

54 "Discorso di Agostino Novella," *Mondo Operaio*, XVI, 12, p. 43.

55 "Discorso di Fernando Santi," *ibid.*, p. 46.

56 According to the *Avanti!* correspondent, Santi was greeted by "a glacial silence, broken only by applause from the Italians and the Poles." *Avanti!*, December 13, 1961.

the manner in which Novella's remarks on unity had been handled by subsequent speakers:

> For some days his attitudes were not mentioned. They were ignored in a special way. Unity was discussed, but from factionalist positions. The motto was: Whoever is not in our organization is against us.[57]

As would be expected, the sharpest voice on the other side was that of Novella's counterpart in the CGT, Benoît Frachon, who called for "pitiless denunciation" of the ICFTU splitters, "the agents of the monopolies and of imperialism."[58] At the end of his speech, it was reported, there was a standing ovation during which the entire Italian, Polish, Yugoslav, and Cypriote delegations remained in their seats.[59]

Despite the prevailing hostility, the Italians continued to fight for their views down to the last minute in the committees charged with preparing the final text of the Program; during the last two days of the Congress the drafting committee remained in session virtually around the clock trying to deal with the Italian amendments.[60] In the battle of words over the unity issue, the CGIL came off better than on any other point of criticism. One particularly objectionable passage about the ICFTU leadership's "disruptive attitude" was eliminated entirely,[61] and several positive paragraphs were added to the effect that both in the ICFTU and in autonomous trade unions there were forces ready to collaborate with the WFTU.[62] Particularly valuable was the acknowledgment that even certain trade union *leaders* could be counted in this category, a departure from the standard argument that the leadership had sold out to the enemy and that only action from below had any prospect of success. This admission, plus the recognition that unity policies had to take the special circumstances of each country into account, adequately legitimized the CGIL's own pursuit of the reunification of the Italian labor movement.

These additions and deletions to the WFTU Program were significant enough to enable Lama in his concluding statement to associate the CGIL "with almost the whole part of the document dealing with union unity."[63] He expressed continued regret, how-

---

57 Risto Bajalski, "How to Achieve Unity," *Borba*, December 24, 1961.

58 *L'Unità*, December 12, 1961.

59 *Ibid.*

60 *Avanti!*, December 15, 1961.

61 *Draft Programme*, p. 14, paragraph 114.

62 "Programme of Trade Union Action," *Texts and Decisions of the Fifth World Trade Union Congress* (London: W.F.T.U. Publications Ltd., [1962]), pp. 30–32.

63 "Dichiarazione di voto," *Mondo Operaio*, XVI, 12, p. 50.

ever, at the evident persistence of the intent to debate with the ICFTU over responsibility for the split rather than seek a serious dialogue on issues of present concern to the working class. He and his colleagues were aware that their modest success in the drafting committee had made only the smallest dent in the theory and practice of the WFTU. As far as the Program was concerned, the Italian formulations were merely piled on top of the contradictory statements of the original version, making for the sort of ineffectual verbal compromise which had become the style in the Communist movement. The WFTU was not about to launch a serious effort to break the ice in the international labor movement. If the CGIL had gained something from its effort beyond a valuable demonstration to an Italian audience of its growing independence of mind and action, it lay in having opened up the issue for debate within the hitherto monolithic structure of the WFTU.

THE IMPORTANCE OF NATIONAL AUTONOMY.   The reason why the unity issue tended to dominate the debate was that the CGIL's approach hampered performance of the WFTU's central obligation, that of lending support to Soviet short-term foreign policy goals. As Bernard Morris wrote some years ago in an appraisal that has not lost its validity, "it is probably more accurate to characterize the WFTU as an international propaganda agency operating in the field of labor than as an international trade union organization."[64] Acting essentially as a militant auxiliary of the peace movement and as a mobilizer of Communist labor organizations everywhere behind specific Soviet political objectives, the WFTU's task has been to propagate a "general line" for the Communist labor movement and to command allegiance to that line. Its focus has basically been turned inward, toward its own membership, not toward those whom it could not hope to control. Despite its rhetoric, therefore, the WFTU has never seriously sought influence over or collaboration with non-Communist labor forces unable to accept the essential ideological and foreign policy premises of the Communist movement: those who were clearly in the enemy camp were to be fought, those who appeared to be uncommitted were to be manipulated and eventually won over.

The Italians, with strong support only from the Yugoslavs (present at the Moscow Congress as observers, for the first time since quitting the WFTU in 1950), were attempting to overthrow this conception of the WFTU's role. They wished to direct its energies

64 Bernard S. Morris, "Communist International Front Organizations," *World Politics*, IX, 1 (October 1956), p. 81.

outward, to transform it into an instrument for advancing the Communist cause into new territory by breaking down barriers and winning fresh allies. The necessary corollary was to stop using the organization as a short-term weapon of propaganda and policy and to encourage its members to develop their own approaches toward collaboration with other trade unions.

The WFTU had already, at its 1960 General Council meeting in Peking, confronted an outright challenge from China to the automatic priority of Soviet positions. The Chinese, however, had merely been using the occasion to make public, in what seemed to them highly favorable circumstances, their fundamental opposition to Soviet policy; it was the line itself they wished to change, not the WFTU's right to impose it on its members. The CGIL, on the other hand, was objecting not only to the content of the general line but also, although not entirely explicitly, to the very existence of such a line, except at a high level of generality. In this sense, despite the more sensational quality of the Chinese attack, Italian "revisionism" presented "the greater danger" to the WFTU's principles of operation. The CGIL was in effect arguing for polycentrism in the international Communist labor movement.

The essential premise of the CGIL's entire position at the Congress, as Novella expressed it, lay in the fact that the member unions of the WFTU were operating in "three great groups of countries developing amidst very different economic and social conditions," leading them necessarily to adopt policies so "profoundly different" that genuine unity could not be achieved unless its Program took these national differences centrally into account.[65] This was not primarily an assertion of the right to develop independent domestic trade union programs. As Luciano Romagnoli had remarked in his pre-Congress speech, autonomy in this sense was not at issue and to demand its formal recognition would be merely "to burst through an open door."[66] The WFTU had in fact never made any pretense of controlling the domestic behavior of its members; this was the party's responsibility.

The CGIL was arguing, on the contrary, for the principle that the national interests of member unions had to be respected even where the WFTU's *international* program was concerned. When Novella and Santi returned from Moscow, they issued a statement referring to national goals as "the basic element" of trade union activity "even with regard to the international activities and pro-

65 "Discorso di Agostino Novella," *Mondo Operaio*, XVI, 12, p. 44.
66 "La relazione di Luciano Romagnoli," *Rassegna sindacale*, No. 47–48, p. 2434.

grams of the trade union movement."[67] In certain respects the CGIL's understanding of an effective international role did not at all coincide with that of the WFTU.

A case in point concerned the CGIL's responsibility as an agent in the "struggle for peace." The Italians, unlike the Chinese, did not object to the general principle that one of the most urgent tasks of the labor movement was the fight for peaceful coexistence. They did maintain, however, as Novella delicately told the Congress delegates, that in so doing the unions should not "mechanically assume slogans and goals that are also correct and necessary, but that belong to other movements or repeat diplomatic positions which, as experience has shown, are necessarily changeable."[68] Efforts should rather be made to develop what the CGIL had in its "orientation statement" called "an autonomous and original peace policy" free of any taint of international power politics.[69]

In these statements the CGIL was resisting the WFTU's habit of mirroring in its policies and day-to-day pronouncements the latest turns of Soviet policy. The Italians had been considerably embarrassed a few months earlier by the WFTU's unqualified endorsement of the unilateral Soviet decision to resume nuclear testing in the atmosphere, since the WFTU had not long before proclaimed itself opposed to all testing whatsoever. The CGIL, and the PCI as well, although expressing their understanding of the Soviet Union's need to defend itself, continued to proclaim a principled opposition to testing by either side.[70]

Flexibility of this sort, the Italians believed, was essential if the WFTU's long-range goal of breaking down the barriers of anti-communism and cold war attitudes was to be realized. From the CGIL's provincial standpoint, moreover, uncritical adherence to Soviet positions had become an impossibility as long as continued Socialist participation in the organization was desired. The WFTU could not directly dictate the formulation of CGIL positions on such major international issues, but it was not without important means of influence. It could, for example, with great fanfare convene an international labor conference, as had been done in Sep-

[67] *Avanti!*, December 19, 1961.

[68] "Discorso di Agostino Novella," *Mondo Operaio*, XVI, 12, p. 43.

[69] *L'Unità*, November 16, 1961.

[70] See, for example, Ando Gilardi, "Hanno scoperto la bomba atomica!," *Lavoro*, September 24, 1961, pp. 6–7. Togliatti managed to straddle the fence by taking the attitude that he "regretted" the Soviet decision but recognized that no other choice was open; see his statement during a national television interview, *L'Unità*, April 2, 1962. This was reminiscent of the way in which he had regretted but nonetheless supported Soviet armed intervention in Hungary.

tember 1961 in Berlin as part of the Soviet offensive on the German question. The CGIL would then be obliged either to take part, and thus associate itself with the resulting proclamations, or to create something of an international incident by failing to attend. A third alternative was in fact often followed: in the context of general support for the Soviet and WFTU position, the CGIL could issue its own statement with different emphases and shades of meaning.[71]

Such incidents as these were minor irritations, however, compared to the growing divergence between the CGIL and the WFTU concerning the appropriate trade union strategy for Europe. The CGIL had become sharply aware of the increasing need and opportunity for the European labor movement to unite in opposition to the international front of monopolies and governments organized in the European Economic Community. If the Communist unions in Europe could not somehow forsake their doctrinaire rigidity sufficiently to appreciate the realities of modern capitalism and to cooperate with the non-Communist labor movement, they risked becoming more and more isolated and ineffectual, at home as well as on a continental scale. This realization gave particular urgency to the CGIL's effort to introduce some of its own perspectives into the WFTU's general platform.[72]

The CGIL had virtually no success in persuading the WFTU to acknowledge that differing national interests should be reflected more generously in its action program. A token gesture was made in this direction by including in the final Program a statement qualifying the usual assertion that the WFTU represented the common interests of all workers everywhere: "In fighting for these common aims and drawing inspiration from this Programme, trade union organizations will naturally bear in mind the precise national, social and political conditions in which they have to conduct their

---

[71] See "La conferenza sindacale internazionale di Berlino per un trattato di pace tedesco," *Lavoro*, October 8, 1961, pp. 5–6, for the CGIL's report on the Berlin conference. While going along in all essentials with the conference line, the CGIL expressed its distinctive view on the question of nuclear testing.

[72] It is somewhat surprising, in view of its importance and of the long history of controversy on the question, that the Common Market was apparently not a central point of concern at the Moscow Congress. The WFTU Program referred to it only once, in passing, and the CGIL spokesmen did not include it among the specific issues in dispute. This may have represented a prior agreement not to raise publicly a topic on which the deep differences between the CGT and the CGIL had already been fully explored and found to be beyond resolution. The Soviet attitude, moreover, was far from firm, as subsequent months would reveal. In any event, if a bargain had been struck, it had only temporary effect, for at the next Executive Committee meeting of the WFTU, in the spring of 1962, the Common Market became the center of a major controversy.

activities."[73] Even this limited acquiescence to the principle of local autonomy was further watered down by the phrase legitimizing only those actions which could be construed as "drawing inspiration from this Program." Moreover, and this is the main point, the formula even in its most liberal interpretation pertained only to the right of national unions to adapt their own domestic policies to local situations; it conceded such unions no right to a voice in developing the general strategies and policy lines of the WFTU itself.

One further dimension of the CGIL's effort to reduce the overwhelming priority given by the WFTU to Soviet policy and propaganda was revealed in the Italian delegation's attempt to get modifications of those paragraphs in the Draft Program describing in characteristically inflated terms the democratic rights and responsibilities of the unions.[74] Although it was likely to have been the Socialists who pressed particularly hard on this point, we know from the debate in the PCI Central Committee meeting that many Communists as well had begun to express openly serious misgivings about the extreme centralization of Soviet life and the low degree and quality of participation by the masses in economic and social matters. Luciano Romagnoli, in his pre-Congress speech to the CGIL Executive Committee, had referred to a "diffuse dissatisfaction . . . with the way the WFTU document deals with the problems of the trade unions in the socialist countries." He explained that the workers of the world deserved to know something of how the Soviet and other socialist unions were solving their problems and contributing to the development of their societies, but that the WFTU had "almost kept this experience from us."[75]

Neither Novella nor Santi was impolite enough to hint even this cautiously in their Congress speeches at any possible deficiencies in the operations of unions in the socialist countries. But it was almost certainly as a result of Italian prodding that a vague sentence about the constantly growing rights of the unions[76] was replaced by a far stronger one stating that "the enlargement of the functions and rights of the trade unions, the increase in the direct participation of the workers in drawing up production plans and in the administration of the national economy and national affairs, are an integral part of the development of socialist democracy."[77]

[73] "Programme of Trade Union Action," *Texts and Decisions*, pp. 4–5.
[74] Bruno Di Pol, *Avanti!*, December 30, 1961.
[75] "La relazione di Luciano Romagnoli," *Rassegna sindacale*, No. 47–48, p. 2436.
[76] *Draft Programme*, p. 10, paragraph 72.
[77] "Programme of Trade Union Action," *Texts and Decisions*, p. 21.

In the context, however, this appeared to be a statement of existing reality rather than an aspiration for the future, as was certainly intended by the CGIL critics.

Although this particular item was not one of the more important in the catalogue of Italian complaints, it was symptomatic of the way in which the ground rules were changing. Little by little, and still at this stage extremely cautiously, old taboos were being overcome; one could at last begin to hint that the emperor was not quite fully clothed. The Italians could not have hoped to have any influence on the evolution of Soviet trade unions. They could, however, attempt to avoid having to endorse patently utopian descriptions of a system whose actual operation they could hardly support any more enthusiastically than could their trade union colleagues outside the CGIL. The widespread awareness that the trade unions in the socialist countries served only as handmaidens of the state and transmission belts for the party certainly did not do the CGIL's image any good. But beneath this pragmatic consideration there almost certainly also lurked a genuine disdain for the pretensions of a trade unionism that claimed much and in fact counted for little in Soviet society. Within their world, Italian trade union leaders played a far more vital role than Soviet unionists did in theirs; and had they been transposed suddenly into the Soviet system, they would surely have fought as hard for the autonomy of their organizations as had the Soviet trade union leaders of the 1920's.

One need not make overmuch of this. If such scornful attitudes did in fact exist, however, they would not have been without political significance. It could well be that a touch of self-righteousness would have been just the ingredient needed to transform the "diffuse dissatisfaction" of which Romagnoli spoke into a decision to stand up in defense of one's principles. These considerations, valid for trade union relationships in the Communist world in a way they could not be for relations among the parties, where the balance of power and responsibility was so clearly on the Soviet side, may be some part of the reason why Italian resistance to Soviet leadership first manifested itself within the WFTU.

AUTONOMY AND UNITY OF AFRICAN TRADE UNIONS. One of the chief Italian objections to the final WFTU Program was its "absolutely inadequate evaluation" of the importance of the recently established All-African Trade Union Federation (AATUF), which represented for the CGIL "the first significant experience of searching for and establishing trade union unity at the regional and continental level."[78] A positive attitude toward this organization, it was argued, and above all a recognition of its full autonomy, was an essential aspect of the WFTU's efforts to further international unity, gain the support of labor in the underdeveloped countries, and weaken the hitherto dominant influence in Africa of the ICFTU.

The WFTU Program to which the CGIL objected described the creation of AATUF as "a great victory of the forces fighting for unity of the African trade union movement."[79] The CGIL's implication to the contrary, this was hardly a negative appraisal; the WFTU's support for the new African organization had, moreover, been frequently reiterated in official pronouncements.[80] The CGIL's complaint was rather that the WFTU was all too closely tied to AATUF, that it was treating the organization essentially as a pawn in the international trade union battle. Despite the CGIL's considerable efforts during the Congress, the final text of the Program failed to give explicit recognition to the necessity of autonomy for AATUF and the general value of such independent regional labor federations. AATUF's founding was seen strictly in terms of a battle won over "the splitting elements represented by imperialism and the ICFTU."[81]

The CGIL failed to get this provision altered—in contrast to its partial successes in revising the Program's provisions on unity because not verbal formulas but immediate and serious issues of policy were at stake. Although this is not the place for a review of the complex history of Communist involvement in the African labor movement in the late 1950's and early 1960's, a few words of background will be helpful in establishing the context.[82]

---

78 "Dichiarazione di voto," *Mondo Operaio*, XVI, 12, p. 50.
79 "Programme of Trade Union Action," *Texts and Decisions*, p. 16.
80 See, for example, "African Unity and International Solidarity," *WTUM*, August 1961, pp. 13–15, and Ibrahim Zakaria, "Trade Union Unity will Triumph," *WTUM*, May 1962, pp. 4–7.
81 "Programme of Trade Union Action," *Texts and Decisions*, p. 16.
82 See George E. Lichtblau, "The Communist Labor Offensive in Former Colonial Countries," *Industrial and Labor Relations Review*, XV, 3 (April 1962), pp. 376–401, for a good general review of the WFTU's role in the underdeveloped countries as a whole. Zbigniew Brzezinski, ed., *Africa and the Communist World* (Stanford: Stanford University Press, 1963), provides much useful political and economic analysis and refers to some aspects of WFTU activity; see especially Alexander Dallin, "The Soviet Union: Political Activity," pp. 26–30, for the WFTU attitude to AATUF, and Robert and Elizabeth Bass, "Eastern Europe," pp. 105–108, for East European financial and training assistance to African unions. A useful review of efforts to establish a Pan-African trade union federation between 1958 and 1961 is contained in Colin Legum, *Pan-Africanism: A Short Political Guide* (New York: Praeger, 1962), pp. 81–91; the appendix, pp. 221–222, contains extracts from the charter of AATUF adopted at Casablanca in May 1961.

Ever since the formation of the short-lived Union Générale des Travailleurs d'Afrique Noire (UGTAN) under Guinean leadership in early 1957, the WFTU had lent its backing to the drive toward a Pan-African labor federation capable of overcoming the dominance of the ICFTU on the African scene. The rise of the Casablanca group of African states during 1960 provided a new opportunity to establish a parallel trade union federation, uniting, it was hoped, all African labor around an anti-imperialist platform. The effort was greatly complicated by personal and national rivalries and by international maneuvering between the WFTU and the two Western internationals (the International Federation of Christian Trade Unions, IFCTU, played a minor role in former French Africa), but the founding conference of AATUF was eventually held in Casablanca in May 1961.

From the standpoint of those genuinely desiring unification of African unions under a single federation, the Casablanca conference was a total failure. Before it ended, about a third of the delegations had left in protest against the extreme militancy of the Casablanca group unions and their successful efforts to pack the conference by controlling accreditation and other procedures.[83] The major issue at the conference was whether the members should be required to disaffiliate from other international organizations. This meant principally from the ICFTU and the IFCTU, since the WFTU had some time ago ceased trying to recruit new members in Africa and no longer had affiliates of any real consequence on the continent.[84] When the anti-Western majority prevailed, the dissenters, led by the Tunisians, Kenyans, and Senegalese, walked out of the meeting and shortly thereafter declared their intention of establishing a competing organization; in January 1962 the African Trade Union Confederation (ATUC) came into existence with headquarters at Dakar.

The exact role of the WFTU in setting up AATUF and guiding its early course is not a matter of public record, but it is assumed to have been considerable. Several of its prime movers, including former WFTU Vice-President Diallo Abdoulaye, at the time Secretary General of the All-African Peoples' Organization, were closely linked to the WFTU. The militant ideological line adopted at

[83] "Pan Africanism and the ICFTU," *Free Labour World*, July 1961, pp. 273–275 (the monthly journal of the ICFTU), described how the Casablanca conference was packed and controlled by its organizers. See also Legum, *Pan-Africanism*, pp. 88–90.

[84] See Lichtblau, *Industrial and Labor Relations Review*, XV, 3, p. 388, for a listing of WFTU affiliates in Africa.

Casablanca gave every indication of Moscow's influence behind the scenes, as did the tactical decision to press for the principle of international disaffiliation, even though this meant sacrificing the hope of a more broadly representative organization. It seems virtually certain that AATUF received extensive financial support from the WFTU as well as assistance in training cadres.

The WFTU appeared to be torn between two incompatible goals. At a minimum, it hoped to destroy the influence of the ICFTU in Africa by creating an ostensibly nonaligned labor movement; this is why it endorsed and probably inspired the insistence on disaffiliation from international organizations at the founding session of AATUF. If this had been the only goal, however, it would have been logical to support autonomy and nonalignment in a genuine way, encouraging creation of an organization whose neutralist ideological credentials were impeccable enough to win support away from the ICFTU.

The ultimate objective went well beyond this. The point was not to weaken the other side by creating a third force, but to win the temporarily nonaligned unions as fully and quickly as possible to the Communist side: in short, to control, then to absorb. This goal showed itself in various indirect ways. A revealing appraisal of AATUF appeared in the *World Marxist Review* just after the WFTU Congress adjourned under the signature of Ali Yata, Secretary General of the outlawed Moroccan Communist Party. The article contained the expected attacks on the ICFTU and ritual praise for AATUF's independence, but it also conveyed perfectly clearly, in its criticism of certain "shortcomings," that complete independence and neutrality were not appropriate attitudes with respect to the Communist world. Fraternal ties with the WFTU should be maintained and strengthened and greater emphasis given to fighting colonialism and to condemning union leaders who failed to grasp the vital difference between the foreign policies of the imperialist and the socialist camps. A firm solidarity based on proletarian internationalism existed between the two organizations, said Ali Yata, and AATUF might one day join the WFTU, "but we are realists and we know that the moment for this is not yet ripe. . . ."[85]

The CGIL's attitude toward AATUF contained no such dualism.

[85] "New Weapon for Embattled Africa," *World Marxist Review*, IV, 12 (December 1961), p. 19. See also Dallin, "The Soviet Union: Political Activity," in Brzezinski, *Africa and the Communist World*, pp. 28–29, for reference to the "suspicion," "resentment," and "concern" evident in the WFTU toward AATUF, despite the public expressions of friendship and support.

The comments offered at the time of its founding had invariably stressed the vital importance of autonomy and unity of the African labor movement.[86] One guarded comment urged that solidarity with the international working class (i.e., the WFTU), although necessary, should not be expressed in the "negative and paternalistic form" of "financial aid" or "advice." (The latter terms, *"aiuti"* and *"consigli,"* were set in quotation marks as a sign that they were being used euphemistically in place of other stronger and more accurate expressions.)[87]

At the Moscow Congress itself, as far as the public record reveals, the CGIL did not give a full explanation of its critical attitude. It would hardly have been politic to accuse the WFTU publicly, at a moment of particularly sharp competition for the allegiance of African labor, of an insufficient regard for the autonomy of the new organization. It is perfectly clear, however, that this was the chief burden of the Italian charge, which may well have been pressed in closed-door sessions of the drafting committees. Several years later, in a retrospective review of the CGIL's position at the Moscow Congress prepared by the Socialist wing, the substance of the CGIL's complaint at the Congress was brought out into the open: after AATUF was formed "the WFTU sought, however, to dictate the political and trade union line that it was supposed to follow."[88] And just a few months after the Congress, at a meeting of the WFTU Executive Committee, the Italian Communist press had come close to a blunt statement of the issues at stake. On that occasion the CGIL had argued that autonomy, coupled with "a rigorous anticapitalistic and anticolonialist orientation," was a necessary condition for union unification in both Africa and Latin America:

> It is significant that the ICFTU has created a counterorganization to the All-African Federation of Casablanca. The position of the WFTU ought to be clear: it is impossible at the same time to defend "Casablanca" and to put in doubt the genuineness of the autonomy on the basis of which this organization has emerged. . . .
> Clarity is needed with respect to Latin America as well. We maintain that unitary tendencies of struggle can be reinforced in a large autono-

---

[86] See, for example, Renzo Rosso, "L'Africa sindacale," *Lavoro,* June 25, 1961, p. 12.

[87] Pino Tagliazucchi and Renzo Rosso, "Unità e autonomia cardini della politica della Federazione sindacale panafricana," *Rassegna sindacale,* No. 43–44 (July–August 1961), p. 2154. The article as a whole provides one of the fullest expressions of the background of the CGIL's attitude toward the African labor movement. Tagliazucchi was the ranking Socialist official in the CGIL's international office.

[88] *Sulle questioni e sulle iniziative,* p. 3.

mous organization which fights actively to liberate the South American continent from the economic and political imperialism of the United States. We must say this openly and act accordingly, leaving to the unions of the countries in question the most complete freedom as to the form, the methods, and the pace of building trade union unity in Latin America.[89]

The issue had by no means been entirely ignored at the Congress itself, for both Svetozar Vukmanović-Tempo, head of the Yugoslav trade union federation, and Fernando Santi for the CGIL had undertaken to raise the question. Vukmanović praised the creation of AATUF as a promising step toward breaking down the polarization of the international labor movement, stating that the question of "membership or nonmembership in international organizations can no longer be of decisive importance to international cooperation."[90] On the next day Santi followed with a similar plea that the WFTU recognize that in many countries and continents the road to trade union unity was through autonomy rather than participation in any of the existing international organizations. We should, he added, not simply accept this fact passively, but rather set our policies consciously toward the goal of encouraging unity through autonomy: "This is, we believe, the best way to throw the ICFTU into crisis and to expel its collaborationist ideology and organizational forms from entire regions and continents."[91]

These implied criticisms of the WFTU's policies in the developing world did not go unchallenged. In rebuttal to Vukmanović even before Santi had spoken, the Secretary General of the All-India Trade Union Congress, S. A. Dange, drew a pointed distinction between state policies and trade union policies. Nonalignment of nations such as those at the Belgrade Conference was acceptable, he said, because support of peace, disarmament, and anticolonialism objectively united countries with the camp of socialism. The same did not hold, however, for class organizations such as unions, for if they defended such positions they would "inevitably join WFTU and no longer be neutral." Formation of an autonomous "third bloc" of unions would, far from facilitating the achievement of unity, only retard its formation around the WFTU.[92]

89 *L'Unità*, June 6, 1962.
90 *Borba*, December 12, 1961.
91 "Discorso di Fernando Santi," *Mondo Operaio*, XVI, 12, p. 48.
92 *Pravda*, December 12, 1961. This issue carried almost a half page of excerpts from Dange's speech, an honor accorded to no other speaker save Khrushchev, the head of the Soviet trade unions, Grishin, and those who presented the major reports for the WFTU Secretariat. The Soviets apparently felt it necessary to go on record against the Yugoslav view and had presumably asked Dange to be their spokesman.

The Yugoslav-Italian point of view was particularly offensive, one may assume, by virtue of the fact that the Yugoslavs had begun to translate their general sympathy for nonalignment in the labor world into a specific organizational initiative, a campaign to muster support for an international trade union meeting paralleling the Belgrade Conference.[93] Preliminary soundings to this end were already well under way, and even at the Congress itself the Yugoslav delegates had done some lobbying among the delegations of autonomous trade unions.[94] A serious suspicion may have arisen that the Yugoslavs were aiming not at a single labor conference but at the creation of a third, neutralist international, although they pointedly and repeatedly denied this intention. (The Chinese later made the charge explicit and with Indonesian help set about organizing a rival trade union conference which many believed represented their threat to create an Afro-Asian counterpart to the WFTU.)

The Yugoslav activities represented a challenge not only to the WFTU's ideological monopoly and its ability to attract support from the unions of the underdeveloped world, but to Soviet policy in a broader sense. Many WFTU members may have felt that the CGIL, by arguing in favor of autonomous regional organizations in the developing world, was objectively assisting the Yugoslav effort. Some collusion might legitimately have been suspected, for an Italian delegation headed by Novella had spent twelve days in Belgrade a few weeks before the Congress began; the joint communiqué previewed the concern both unions expressed at Moscow for the need to overcome the disunity of the labor movement by respecting fully the independence of each union and its need to adapt to its own national circumstances. The positions of the two had evidently been explored and to some extent coordinated in advance.[95]

Why was it that the CGIL should have taken on the cause of

93 See, for example, Aser Deleon, "The Trade Union Movement and the Conference," *Rad*, September 2, 1961. The article deplores the fact that the union internationals base their policies on those of the existing political blocs and suggests that the success of the Belgrade Conference could encourage "progressive" union forces to work for an autonomous international policy of the working class. Such hints as these became progressively stronger until in February 1962 Vukmanović made a major address, later published as a pamphlet, that concludes with an open call for conferences of autonomous unions; see S. Vukmanović-Tempo, *Topical Problems of the International Trade Union Movement* (Belgrade: Yugoslav Trade Unions, 1962).

94 G. E. Lynd, "Workers Disunite," *Problems of Communism*, XI, 2 (March–April 1962), p. 21.

95 "Joint Statement by the General Confederation of Italian Labor and the Yugoslav Federation of Trade Unions," *Borba*, October 23, 1961. See also *Avanti!*, October 22–23, 1961.

unity and autonomy for the African trade union movement? The Italians no doubt wished to use the African case to advance their own flexible, regionally oriented conception of the WFTU's entire strategy and mode of operation, but this objective was linked to a more particular interest in creating a significant international position for the CGIL in the Mediterranean basin. In 1959 and 1960 unmistakable signs had emerged of an active Italian effort to promote a new and closer relationship between the North African unions and those of Europe and the Communist world. Italy's historical ties with Somalia facilitated a special link with the labor movement there, but the main thrust was toward two far more important unions, the Union Marocaine du Travail (UMT) and the Union Générale des Travailleurs Algériens (UGTA).

These two federations, being affiliates of the ICFTU as well as founding members of AATUF, represented a potential bridge not only between the WFTU and the ICFTU, but between Europe, the Arab world, and Africa south of the Sahara. Beginning in 1959 the CGIL had undertaken an energetic diplomatic operation in Africa, exchanging official delegations on a number of occasions with the UMT and the UGTA, as well as with other African unions.[96] The CGIL had also taken the initiative in planning, together with the Yugoslav and Moroccan unions, a Conference of the Agricultural Workers' Unions and Peasants' Organizations of the Mediterranean Basin, held at Palermo in October 1962 after two years of preparation.[97] By such activities as these the CGIL evidently hoped to extend its own influence in the region and at the same time, by assuring the African unions of respect for their autonomy, to translate their natural anti-imperialist bias into closer cooperation with the Communist trade union movement as a whole.

The CGIL, in sum, was trying simultaneously to promote certain special international interests of its own and those of the Communist movement at large. Its vision of Communist interests, however, was not at all that of the WFTU. The CGIL's view, resting on the premise of a general identity of interest between Communist and nonaligned unions in the fight against capitalism and imperialism, called for tactics of tolerance, respect for independent opinions, and a pattern of loose cooperation. But the WFTU, like the Soviet

[96] For examples of the joint communiqués issued after such meetings see *Rassegna sindacale*, No. 40 (April 1961), pp. 2007–2008 (Somalia); No. 43–44 (July–August 1961), p. 2159 (Tunisia); No. 47–48 (November–December 1961), pp. 2347 and 2354 (Algeria); and No. 53 (May 1962), pp. 2810–2811 (Morocco).

[97] A report on the Palermo Conference is given in "The Conference of the Mediterranean Basin," *CGIL News Bulletin*, No. 6 (November 1962), pp. 21–30.

Union itself, was less prepared to take the long view and to sacrifice the immediate advantage of dominating ostensibly neutralist organizations for the sake of possible future alliances of a looser sort with people who, if left to their own devices, could never be fully trusted. Not being burdened with responsibilities of state, the CGIL was not in the best position to appreciate the nature of Soviet priorities.

There was another aspect of the CGIL's concern with unions in the underdeveloped countries more directly linked to its European strategy. In his concluding speech at Moscow Luciano Lama had complained that the WFTU Program "does not sufficiently emphasize the sharp limits of the actions taken by the unions of the capitalist countries in direct assistance to the peoples who are struggling today against all forms, old and new, of colonial exploitation. . . ."[98] The Program had, in fact, barely mentioned at all that the European unions might have something to contribute to the anticolonial struggle; the emphasis lay overwhelmingly on the decisive value of "the generous, unconditional, moral and material assistance given by the socialist countries and their trade union organizations."[99]

The emphasis of the CGIL's own "orientation statement" had been entirely different. In discussing the wave of national independence it recognized three significant factors of assistance—the peaceful coexistence policy, support from socialist countries, and the struggles of workers in capitalist countries. The first two were mentioned only in passing, while the third was the subject of ten out of the fourteen paragraphs in the section on colonialism. The main thrust of imperialism today, the statement argued—aside from "furious attempts to preserve colonial remnants"—consisted in the attempt to expand economically into the underdeveloped countries in order to conquer new markets for its goods and capital. This being so, the battle against imperialism had to be fought at the source, within the imperialist countries themselves:

The struggle against neocolonialist trends is therefore an integral and essential part of a trade union action intended to attack the basic structures and monopoly control of society in its various aspects and, therefore, in its very patterns of development.[100]

Ordinary trade union action against the monopolies is not enough, the statement continued. The unions must concentrate their atten-

98 "Dichiarazione di voto," *Mondo Operaio*, XVI, 12, p. 50.
99 "Programme of Trade Union Action," *Texts and Decisions*, pp. 15–17.
100 *L'Unità*, November 16, 1961.

tion specifically on Italy's economic relations with the new countries, working in particular to force state economic agencies such as IRI and ENI to adopt "a policy that will foster the autonomous and independent development of underdeveloped and newly independent countries on the level of both financial aid and investment and of commercial relations."[101]

At the Congress itself Novella reiterated these concerns, saying that with respect to the Program "what leaves us dissatisfied is the absence of a specific and substantial convergence of our aims and those of the peoples struggling for their political and economic liberation." He also added a significant new note when he said that "this is a commitment which should be seen on the international level, especially on the European level, but which we do not see adequately treated in the document which is the basis for the Congress preparation. . . . In fact, this is one of our most serious criticisms."[102]

These were not altogether new themes for Italian Communists—the PCI's memorandum for the November 1960 Moscow conference, for example, had raised the whole question of European relations with the underdeveloped countries—but they had not previously been discussed quite this explicitly and in such critical terms. As had been revealed during the Central Committee debates following the Twenty-Second Congress, the Italians were becoming increasingly articulate about their conviction that Europe's contribution to world revolution was being underrated both generally and with particular reference to the struggle for independence from imperialism and neocolonialism. International communism could be strengthened and the case against the Chinese bolstered if the European parties and unions could be brought more vigorously into the game as opponents of modern imperialism at its source. Through economic and political action, they maintained, the maneuverability of the monopolies and their governments with respect to the "third world" could be significantly reduced.[103]

Such attitudes toward general international Communist strategy were supplemented by more parochial considerations. The Italians believed that the colonial issue could be used as a means of promoting their European strategy. If properly exploited, it might serve as a unifying factor for the whole European left, something which the conservative approach of the WFTU and the French

101 *Ibid.*
102 "Discorso di Agostino Novella," *Mondo Operaio,* XVI, 12, p. 42.
103 See Chapter Ten for a fuller discussion of this question.

Communists had wholly failed to do. The colonial question tied in, moreover, with the CGIL's insistence on the need for united action by European labor against the international front of the monopolies expressed in the Common Market. The CGIL was arguing that the Common Market was proving to be a significant weapon of colonialism, especially with regard to Africa, and should, therefore, be taken more seriously by the WFTU: the campaign against it should be elevated from the level of propaganda and denunciation to that of effective action, in concert with other labor forces. This point of view would soon lead to a bitter fight between the CGIL and the WFTU, a controversy reflecting the larger divergences between the interests of Italian communism and those of the movement at large.

CHAPTER NINE

THE COMMON MARKET CONTROVERSY

Just as the Italian economic boom had, by early 1962, obliged the PCI to re-examine its understanding of the capitalist system, so at about the same time the unexpected success of the Common Market forced the Communist world to take a fresh look at the effects of European economic integration. We have earlier observed how the Italian party, while sharing prevailing Communist expectations about the disastrous economic consequences of the Common Market, had from the start expressed relatively greater sympathy for the principle of economic integration and had tended to treat the EEC more as an economic than a political-military phenomenon. By March 1962 the party and trade union leaders had taken the further step of openly acknowledging that, in Luigi Longo's words, "we failed to predict accurately the consequences of integration provisions on the Italian economic situation. . . . It is a fact that European integration has been a fundamental factor in Italy's economic leap forward."[1] This belated recognition of the Common Market's positive impact on economic growth, one aspect of the PCI's persistent pragmatic effort to come to grips with its environment, was the basis for a new policy line that would in several respects be out of harmony with the priorities of Soviet foreign policy.

An obviously coordinated series of articles that appeared during the spring of 1962 made it clear that a reappraisal of the Common Market was also under way in the Soviet Union.[2] In sharp contrast

---

[1] Report to Central Committee, *L'Unità*, April 27, 1962. See also Agostino Novella's similar remarks at the meeting of the CGIL's National Executive Council, *Rassegna sindacale*, No. 51 (March 1962), p. 78, and the previously cited comments by Giorgio Amendola at the Gramsci Institute conference on modern capitalism.

[2] See, *inter alia*, the full-page coverage in *Trud*, May 22, 1962, and *Pravda*, May 23, 1962; and the two-part article by I. Lemin, "European Integration: Some Results and Prospects," *Mirovaya ekonomika i mezhdunarodnye otnosheniya*, Nos. 4 and 5 (April and May 1962). Khrushchev himself strongly attacked the Common Market for the first time in a speech on May 30 welcoming an African delegation; *Pravda*, May 31, 1962.

to the PCI's qualified recognition of the Market's contribution to the European economy, the Soviet response was entirely negative. Whereas the Italian comrades, perennially prepared to come to terms with apparently irreversible realities, were seeking to exploit whatever positive opportunities might be latent in the Common Market, the Soviets saw it purely and simply as a threat against which all available resources should be mobilized.

The prime circumstance that had triggered the Soviet reaction was the British government's decision in the summer of 1961 to seek membership in the European Economic Community. The importance of this decision, in itself a striking indication of the Common Market's success, was enhanced by Britain's statement that her entry was dependent on her six allies in the European Free Trade Association being offered full or associate membership. This prospect conjured up in Soviet minds the disturbing vision of a strong and prosperous Europe united economically and politically on a continental scale around a Franco-German entente. Such a development would not only challenge Communist ideological preconceptions concerning the viability of capitalist economies and the possibility of cooperation among imperialist states; it would strike at the heart of the basic Soviet strategy of dividing the enemy by manipulating the internal and external "contradictions" of the capitalist world.[3]

It was true, as Soviet spokesmen increasingly came to observe, that a united and strengthened Europe seemed to imply a decline of American influence on the continent. But even this apparently desirable outcome might have destabilizing political and military consequences if it led to a corresponding increase in German power over European affairs. Soviet assessments of the Common Market were then and have remained more ambivalent than confident about the potential political consequences of one or another course of action. What counts for our purposes is that the net Soviet response was consistently hostile.[4]

---

[3] For useful analyses of the Soviet response to the Common Market see Zbigniew Brzezinski, "Russia and Europe," *Foreign Affairs*, XLII, 3 (April 1964), pp. 428–444; and Marshall D. Shulman, "The Communist States and Western Integration," *Problems of Communism*, XII, 5 (September–October 1963), pp. 47–54.

[4] The emphasis of the Soviet line has periodically changed in response to the shifting tides of influence within the Atlantic community. Early assertions that the Common Market was little more than a reflection of American power on the continent yielded during the late 1950's to a stress on German-American domination, then to an insistence on the threat of a Franco-German alliance. Although there was some ambivalence about the possibility of Britain's entry into the Common Market, which it was thought might dilute the Franco-German entente, the dominant Soviet line was opposed to such expansion.

The Russians saw the Common Market, moreover, as affecting adversely their interests not only in Europe but in the underdeveloped areas as well. Many colonial and trusteeship territories in Africa had been given associate membership in the Community, entitling them to tariff preferences and access to aid from the European Development Fund. This arrangement was scheduled to expire at the end of 1962, and negotiations had long been in progress over the terms of a new five-year association with the now-independent African countries.[5] Britain's request for membership made the issue even more salient, for it raised the larger question of the attitude of the Commonwealth countries to the EEC. Soviet economic relations with such countries as India, Nigeria, and Ghana, highly valued as a means of political access, might be seriously weakened if their economies became more closely linked to Europe through the Common Market. Fortunately for the USSR, the leading Commonwealth countries had considerable sympathy for the Soviet contention that the powerful and wealthy industrial states were seeking through the Common Market to perpetuate colonial economic ties and oblige the developing countries to remain as suppliers of raw materials for Western factories.[6] It was not surprising that Khrushchev singled out this aspect of the Common Market for attack in his first personal involvement with the issue in the spring of 1962.[7]

Soviet strategic concerns were reinforced by straightforward economic considerations. An integrated European market, even on the existing limited scale, posed potentially serious economic difficulties for the Communists, particularly for the Eastern European states dependent on trade with Common Market countries for a significant amount of their machinery, industrial raw materials, foodstuffs, and foreign currency.[8] Yugoslavia's position was particularly vulnerable, caught as it was between the two discriminatory trading areas of West and East Europe. Expansion of the Common Market would not only threaten to disturb the Yugoslav

[5] See U. W. Kitzinger, *The Politics and Economics of European Integration: Britain, Europe, and the United States* (New York: Praeger, 1963), pp. 97–119, for a review of the Common Market's association with Africa through 1962.

[6] See Rupert Emerson, "The Atlantic Community and the Emerging Countries," *International Organization*, XVII, 3 (Summer 1963), pp. 628–648, for a review of African and Asian attitudes toward the Common Market.

[7] *Pravda*, May 31, 1962.

[8] To quote Marshall Shulman: "The rise of the Common Market tariffs threatens the countries of Eastern Europe with diminished trade, with serious economic shortages, with the loss of an intangible sense of contact with the West, and with an enforced increase of dependence on the Soviet Union," *Problems of Communism*, XII, 5, p. 53.

export market in Europe, but would restrict its economically and politically profitable trade with the nonaligned countries in Africa. These factors led Yugoslavia to adopt a particularly strong stance against the Common Market.[9]

Even this hasty a review allows us to establish that the Soviet and East European reaction to the Common Market did not have any of the overtones of reluctant acceptance of the inevitable that characterized the Italian Communist response. An early measure of the difference came to light during a meeting of the WFTU Executive Committee in Budapest at the end of May 1962, when the CGIL representatives openly clashed with WFTU Secretary General Louis Saillant, with his former colleagues from the French CGT, and above all with Viktor Grishin, head of the Soviet trade union federation. The Common Market question had not been on the announced agenda for the meeting but Grishin took advantage of the occasion to further the Soviet Union's recently launched campaign against the EEC.

Describing the Common Market as a "kind of Holy Alliance of the imperialists" whose real aim was the political and military subordination of Europe to the great powers and the economic exploitation of the people by the monopolies, Grishin demanded an all-out fight to defeat it:

> Progressive trade unions must increase their struggle against state-monopolist associations, particularly against the Common Market, and resolutely unmask it as a plot of a handful of monopolies against the vital interests of the masses in the capitalist countries, as a weapon of the imperialists against the working people and against nations which have emancipated themselves from colonial slavery.[10]

There has, he acknowledged, been "a temporary improvement" in the economy of certain European countries which the bourgeoisie, attributing the gains to the Common Market, was trying to exploit so as to bribe the elite of the working class, spread reformist illusions, and weaken the struggle against the monopolies. But economic progress was a passing phenomenon, he assured his listeners, for "the crises of capitalism are sure to follow in quick succession"; attempts at economic "cooperation" would in the end only aggravate class conflicts. This being so, it was the task of the trade unions to "help mobilize public opinion against the entrance of new countries into the Common Market and support the struggle of the working

9 See William E. Griffith, "Yugoslavia," in Brzezinski, *Africa and the Communist World*, pp. 116–141, at pp. 129–132.

10 *Trud*, June 1, 1962.

people against the difficult economic and social consequences connected with entrance into this imperialist association."[11]

Grishin's call to arms was not greeted with enthusiasm by the CGIL delegation. It was not only that his argument ran counter to the Italian approach to the Common Market. More important, it implicitly challenged the CGIL's conception of the proper role of the WFTU's affiliates as well as certain basic principles of the CGIL's domestic strategy. Fernando Santi's reply dealt particularly with Grishin's implication that the economic gains of the working class might weaken their militancy and class consciousness and lead them toward a passive reformism. Just as the Italian workers, he implied, were successfully advancing their interests in an environment of growing prosperity through a strategy of structural reforms, so the European workers' movement now had to contend in a similar manner with the indisputable reality of the Common Market.[12] Rather than frontally attacking an institution that was here to stay, the WFTU affiliates in Europe should seek to break down the barriers that kept them from participating in its affairs.[13]

Neither the CGIL's resistance to a purely denunciatory posture nor its advocacy of consequential efforts to influence the Common Market from within were new; such arguments had already been advanced, though less forthrightly, at the WFTU's Leipzig Congress in 1957. The novelty of the CGIL's position in 1962 derived from two developments that appeared to strengthen both the substance of its case concerning the EEC and its readiness to challenge the over-all rationale and operational style of the WFTU.

The first factor was of course the Common Market's economic success. The Soviet Union conceded this, but as a temporary though dangerous phenomenon. The Italian Communists, however, were persuaded of the need to accept the premise that modern capitalism, assisted by integration of the European economies, was able to overcome many of the classic weaknesses that had previously been thought to prevent a continuing expansion of productivity. The PCI and the CGIL considered it foolish and dangerous to mount a stubborn rear-guard resistance against an institution that Italian opinion regarded as having contributed in substantial measure to the country's rising prosperity. Although the Communists were, for reasons of both doctrine and foreign policy, a good deal more an-

---

11 *Ibid.*

12 For excerpts from his speech, see "Presenza e lotta sindacale nel MEC," *Lavoro*, June 14, 1962, pp. 5–6.

13 See *L'Unità,* June 8, 1962, for the statement made by the CGIL delegates Santi and Lama upon their return from Budapest.

tagonistic in principle to the Common Market than their Socialist colleagues, their deepest instincts nevertheless rebelled against the prospect of a virtually hopeless propaganda campaign that could only isolate them further from the political mainstream and weaken their efforts to maintain working relations with the Socialists in the CGIL and elsewhere.

The second determining factor behind the CGIL's position at Budapest was the knowledge that much more was at issue than WFTU policy toward the Common Market alone. The Soviet effort to gear the WFTU into its campaign against the EEC was a classic illustration of precisely what the CGIL had been objecting to at the Moscow Congress a few months before. The WFTU was once more to be used as an instrument of Soviet policy, regardless of the damage this might do to the domestic interests of certain of its members. And not only would the CGIL itself be set back by an aggressive WFTU-sponsored attack on the Common Market, but the larger interests of the Communist movement in Europe, as the Italians perceived them, would be equally seriously offended.

The potential influence of the Communists within the European working-class movement and thereby on European political and economic affairs as a whole depended in the Italian view on creating a new spirit of unity and cooperation with unions outside the WFTU. If a Communist trade union campaign against the Common Market were to have any effect at all, the CGIL reasoned, it would be to reduce to a minimum the prospects of collaboration with other working-class organizations, long since committed to the EEC and participating in its institutions. At the Budapest meeting, therefore, the CGIL coupled its resistance to Soviet Common Market policy with a reassertion of the principles put forward at Moscow regarding the proper relationship between the WFTU and its affiliates. It took the further step, indeed, of proposing to that end a series of amendments to the WFTU constitution, the precise contents of which were not made public.[14]

The CGIL's concern was compounded by yet another factor. The tone of Grishin's entire speech, and of other "official" contributions to the debate, was notable for its aggressive and uncompromising character. In Stalinist accents reminiscent of cold war days,

---

[14] As a further demonstration of their unwillingness to appear to be a direct instrument of Soviet policy, the CGIL objected to the WFTU's involvement in the World Peace Congress planned for the coming summer. Individual trade union figures should attend, Santi maintained, but the WFTU as an organization should not help to promote and sponsor an initiative of this sort (*L'Unità*, June 6, 1962).

Grishin called upon the WFTU to unite behind an intransigently anti-imperialist line:

Under these conditions, the most important task of the working class and its trade unions consists in all-out activization of the struggle against imperialism, in unmasking its antinational essence, in mobilizing the masses for the struggle against the armaments race and the preparation of a new war, in acting more resolutely in support of the people's national liberation movements, the liquidation of military bases in other people's territory, and the withdrawal of U.S. forces from other countries.

It is the duty of progressive trade unions to help people realize what a serious danger to the fate of the world and to all mankind modern imperialism and its predatory policy represent. There are still quite a few people in the capitalist countries who underestimate this danger. . . . The pernicious policy of imperialism must be continually laid bare.[15]

The aggressiveness of these and other references to the need for renewed "vigilance" in order to counter the "savage resistance" and "dangerous intrigues" of the imperialists was particularly striking by its contrast with the relatively dispassionate tone of Soviet foreign policy pronouncements made in other contexts during the same period.[16]

It seems apparent in retrospect, as it may well also have appeared to those in attendance at Budapest, that the USSR was expounding a notably more belligerent foreign policy line for the WFTU than on other fronts. In part this verbal intransigence undoubtedly reflected the fact that the WFTU (like its Western counterpart, the ICFTU) had been notoriously reluctant to abandon the cold war attitudes that had persisted since the split in the international trade union movement in the dark days of 1948–1949.[17] But there seemed more to Grishin's intransigence in the spring of 1962 than a simple carry-over of the psychology of the cold war. The central aim may well have been that of restoring the unity the WFTU had so patently lacked over the past two years, ever since the General Council meeting in Peking in the spring of 1960. By adopting an unusually tough and uncompromising line Grishin may have hoped

---

15 *Trud,* June 1, 1962.

16 For an echo of Grishin's remarks, see the editorial by P. Pimenov, Soviet representative on the WFTU Secretariat, *WTUM,* July 1962, pp. 1–3. Compare these with Gromyko's report to the Supreme Soviet on the Geneva disarmament talks, *Pravda,* April 25, 1962, or with Khrushchev's speeches in Bulgaria, *Pravda,* May 17, 19, and 20, 1962.

17 It is difficult not to agree with the observation made about that time by one of the more astute Italian Socialist analysts of Italian and international trade union affairs; of the WFTU and the ICFTU he writes that "there is nothing in the world more objectively reactionary than these Internationals." Fidia Sassano, "Panorama sindacale degli anni sessanta," *Il Ponte,* XVIII, 8–9 (August–September 1962), p. 1122.

on the one hand to appease the Chinese and on the other to intimidate the Italians and force them back into line.

It seems relevant that there occurred, just at this time, a definite
but short-lived "surface improvement in Sino-Soviet-Albanian relations," presumably reflecting a mutual desire of the Russians and
the Chinese to take some of the heat out of their quarrel.[18] The
Soviets may have been attempting at Budapest to demonstrate their
good faith during this period of temporary détente, or perhaps to
deter Chinese assaults in the WFTU by giving assurance that their
policy line would be adequately reflected there. It seems more
likely that the Soviets saw the WFTU meeting as a suitable occasion
on which to demonstrate to potential supporters of the Chinese in
the Communist movement, but without attracting diplomatic
attention and thus complicating relations with the West, that the
USSR still knew how to manipulate the old revolutionary symbols.
In any event, the Chinese representative endorsed Saillant's report,
which followed along the lines of Grishin's speech, as providing "a
correct analysis of the international situation."[19]

If, by artificially creating an atmosphere of international crisis,
the Soviets were also attempting to intimidate the Italians into a
disciplined loyalty to proletarian internationalism, they certainly
failed. The day had long since passed for techniques such as these,
which seemed if anything only designed to make the Italians more
stubborn than before. Experiences such as the CGIL's at Budapest
go some distance toward explaining the Italian Communists' concern that the Russians, in order to restore unity and discipline to
the movement, might be prepared to appease the Chinese and to
fall back on the language and the political tactics of Stalinist times.
Of all possible outcomes of the confused state of affairs in the
Communist movement, this was the one the Italians feared the most.

The Moscow Conference on Contemporary Capitalism

The new urgency of the Common Market question and the realization that Communist theory had not adequately assimilated the
recent progress of the European economies prompted Moscow to
organize a conference of Marxist scholars to discuss the evolution
of modern capitalism.[20] Ostensibly only a scholarly gathering con-

18 Griffith, *Albania*, pp. 143–145.

19 New China News Agency, in English, from Budapest, June 5, 1962.

20 According to one Yugoslav report, it was a lecture given in Moscow by
Giorgio Amendola in the spring of 1962 that persuaded the Soviets of the need to
agree on a common line on capitalism and on the EEC; Frane Barbieri, *Vjesnik*
(Zagreb), October 7 and 8, 1962, cited in "Yugoslavs and the Common Market,"
Radio Free Europe analysis, October 18, 1962.

vened jointly by the Institute of World Economy and International Relations and by the *World Marxist Review,* the meeting was clearly intended, as Academician Arzumanyan later confirmed, to elaborate a definitive ideological line and to lay down the guidelines for Communist action in Europe.[21]

The Italian party was just then attempting to formulate its position on modern capitalism and other equally basic aspects of its program in the Theses to be presented at its forthcoming Tenth party Congress. What gave this theoretical exercise particular international meaning was the PCI's conviction that the Italian road to socialism was valid not just for the PCI alone but for the Communist parties of all highly developed capitalist countries. The "leading idea" of the Theses, it was claimed in an authoritative article written for an international Communist audience, was its "realistic perspective of the struggle for democracy and socialism in countries at the monopoly-capitalist stage." The article observed that it was precisely this breadth of perspective that made the Theses "a step forward" compared with earlier interpretations of the Italian road, "a still bigger contribution to the general strategy of the struggle for socialism in capitalist countries."[22] The Moscow conference, which convened toward the end of August 1962, was an important occasion for the PCI: the international relevance and Marxist orthodoxy of its strategy would have been difficult to insist upon if the conference had arrived at conclusions incompatible with the main lines of the Italian approach.[23]

The first topic on the agenda concerned the nature and origins of state monopoly capitalism. The Italians, viewing the extension of the state's role in the economy as essentially a capitalist response to technological progress and to the increasing pressure of the working class, took a generally positive attitude toward the phenomenon. The Communist parties, in the Italian view, should not be working to prevent the emergence or expansion of state monopoly capitalism, which represented a necessary stage in the evolution and general

---

[21] *Pravda,* September 3, 1962.

[22] Alessandro Natta and Giuliano Pajetta, "The Struggle for Socialism in Italy," *World Marxist Review,* V, 11 (November 1962), pp. 19–20.

[23] For the PCI's coverage of the conference see the daily reporting in *L'Unità,* August 27–September 4, 1962; also Eugenio Peggio, "Capitalismo di Stato e MEC al Convegno di Mosca," *Rinascita,* September 8, 1962, pp. 12–13; and Peggio, "Elementi di una alternativa al Mercato comune europeo," *ibid.,* September 29, 1962, pp. 12–13. For the basic position paper of the Italian delegation, see "Le posizioni della delegazione italiana alla conferenza economica di Mosca," *ibid.,* October 6, 1962, pp. 17–21.

crisis of the capitalist system. They should, rather, be attempting to take advantage of the fact that capitalism now required government intervention to solve its inherent economic and social problems; through parliamentary and mass action the working class could now steadily improve its power to control the economic policies of the state.[24]

The Italian Theses were opposed at Moscow, as one would expect, by the French representatives, who insisted on the doctrinaire view that as long as the bourgeoisie held state power, state ownership of industry and other similar structural reforms could not possibly benefit the working class. Indeed, they argued, state control could well be harmful, insofar as it tended to foster illusions that genuine progress was being made toward socialism. Nationalization could serve to undermine the economic domination of the monopolies only if it was accompanied by "the simultaneous transfer of power into the hands of an antimonopoly government. . . ."[25]

For once, when an issue of Marxist orthodoxy was involved, Russians and Italians seemed to find themselves on the same side, criticizing the purely "formal logic" of the analysis offered by the French delegate, Henri Claude. The problem had to be viewed dialectically, they agreed, in full recognition of all the genuine contradictions of life: whereas state ownership of industry under a capitalist system might indeed seem to reinforce monopoly control, the struggle for nationalization and other "democratic" reforms was at the same time one of the most effective ways of mobilizing the masses against the monopolies. But the Italian victory was only partial. While the Russians rejected the sterile orthodoxy upheld by the French, they stated their own case essentially on tactical grounds: their statements appeared carefully phrased so as to defend not nationalization itself as a valuable step in the direction of socialism, but only the instrumental value of the slogan in mobilizing the workers. Thus interpreted, the French too were entirely willing to accept the demand for nationalization. The Italians, however, continued to believe in "the significance and value of structural

[24] For a characteristic statement of this theme see "Tesi approvate dal X Congresso," X *Congresso*, pp. 678–684.

[25] Maurice Thorez, "Epoch of Great Revolutionary Change," *World Marxist Review*, V, 11 (November 1962), p. 17. The French party's attitude toward economic planning was essentially the same. As Benoît Frachon said at the CGT Thirty-Fourth Congress in May 1963, to hold that planning may benefit the working class "presupposes that democracy has already led to the socialization of the means of production and the existence of a State entirely free from capitalist influence." Quoted in R. Telliez, "The 34th Congress of the French C.G.T.," *WTUM*, July–August 1963, p. 28,

reforms and the expansion of state-monopoly capitalism as potential conditions for the transition to socialism."[26]

The Italians did not appear troubled by this essentially tactical Soviet interpretation of Communist reformist efforts. What mattered far more was the strong emphasis placed by the Soviets on the necessity to vary tactics according to national circumstances, to work out "varied and flexible forms of class struggle" aiming at the formation of large antimonopoly coalitions.[27] Such positive stress on the need for tactical diversity was a far cry from the halfhearted acknowledgment of former times that the operation of the "fundamental laws" of the transition to socialism would be modified according to differing national circumstances. Soviet dogmatism was evidently yielding to a pragmatic opportunism that concealed an absence of theoretical conviction behind a veil of "dialectical" reasoning. (Was it helpful to a Communist policy maker in Western Europe to know that state monopoly capitalism, "while adding to the power of monopolies over society, . . . also generates contradictions which shatter the very foundations of capitalism . . . ?")[28] The new flexibility of official Soviet doctrine, in effect giving each party free rein to pursue its own path, was in itself perhaps enough to justify the claim of one of the PCI's delegates that the Moscow conference was of "notable political significance," a "decisive step forward in superseding somewhat unilateral opinions."[29]

The conclusions reached at the Moscow conference on the second topic on the agenda, the Common Market, were a similarly ambivalent blend of new and old, but on the whole constituted a cautious advance toward the Italian position. The day before the conference opened there appeared in *Pravda* a set of "Theses" on the Common Market prepared by the Institute of World Economy and International Relations under the direction of the prominent economist Anushavan Arzumanyan.[30] Although the Common

[26] Natta and Pajetta, *World Marxist Review*, V, 11, p. 22. The fullest account of the Moscow conference discussions on this score is to be found in "Problems of Modern Capitalism," *ibid.*, pp. 69–86; the Soviet view on nationalization emerges most clearly in the excerpts from Arzumanyan's paper, p. 72, and in the remarks by V. Cheprakov, p. 81.

[27] A. Mileikovsky, *ibid.*, p. 81.

[28] *Ibid.*, p. 80.

[29] Peggio, *Rinascita*, September 8, 1962, p. 12; see also *L'Unità*, September 1, 1962. Henri Jourdain, one of the French delegates, offers a defensive but unrepentant summary of his party's position on this point in *L'Humanité*, September 17, 1962, asserting that the conclusions of the Moscow conference "confirm those expressed for more than ten years by the PCF."

[30] "Concerning Imperialist 'Integration' in Western Europe (The Common Market)—Theses," *Pravda*, August 26, 1962; translation in *CDSP*, XIV, 34, pp. 9–16.

Market continued to be described in the Theses and at the conference itself in the usual terms as "a weapon of the imperialist 'cold war' policy," the emphasis of the Soviet line had shifted somewhat on both political and economic planes. The Italians were pleased to discover that the Russians had discarded the idea, still upheld by the French, that the European monopolies were completely subordinated to United States monopoly capital. Recognition that the balance of economic power had shifted in favor of Europe and that European economic integration was thus assisting in the weakening of American leadership was an important part of the Italian argument in favor of a more balanced view of the Common Market.

On the economic side, the Soviets had similarly arrived at a more rational perception of the situation. The Common Market was seen not simply as a plot, but as "a new phenomenon in the development of the capitalist economy" arising from an objective economic need to create larger markets and greater international specialization of production.[31] The European Economic Community had been created as an economic weapon against the socialist states and the underdeveloped countries, a substitute for the unrestrained competition and naked colonial aggression no longer possible under contemporary political conditions. While the Common Market was certainly still seen as serving the military and political interests of the NATO alliance, it was thus no longer regarded as merely a direct expression of the foreign policy of the imperialist governments, but as a response to the economic requirements of international monopoly capital in the present stage of its development.

One significant corollary of this analysis was that the Common Market, although by no means the basic cause of recent European economic progress, had in some measure contributed to it. This conclusion, expressed in the formula that "the Common Market is not simply the arithmetical sum" of the various national markets,[32] was contested at the Moscow conference by the elderly but still prestigious Soviet economist Eugene Varga, who argued that economic integration had had little to do with capitalist progress and would not result in a permanent expansion of production. The conclusion implicit in Varga's analysis, which rested on the standard interpretation of the cyclical expansion and contraction of the capitalist economy, was that the Common Market, instead of being an "objective" and relatively permanent phenomenon with which

31 *Ibid.*, p. 9.
32 *Ibid.*, p. 10.

the Communist movement would have to contend, was only an association of state monopolies subject to the usual laws of capitalist contradictions and decay which would eventually fall of its own weight (a denouement that could be hastened, no doubt, by appropriately vigorous Communist action). In the opinion of the Italians and the majority of the Soviet economists, the "excessive theoretical abstraction" of Varga's approach dangerously underestimated the effectiveness of the Market and the likelihood of its further expansion.[33]

It should be noted that the Soviets did not go nearly so far as the Italians had done in recognizing the Common Market's contribution to European prosperity; whereas the PCI was prepared to grant that working-class standards of living had advanced, in part because of the Market's effect, the Soviets continued to stress in the Theses and elsewhere the ruinous economic consequences for all but the monopoly groups. This had always been, and would remain, a cardinal point of the French party's position as well, a logical corollary of its refusal to join the PCI in dropping the "pauperization" slogan from its vocabulary.[34] Since one of the prime motives behind the sudden Soviet surge of interest in the Common Market was to mobilize opposition to Britain's entry into the Community, it was necessary to propagate the argument that membership "would have a ruinous effect on the standard of living of British workers, would do serious harm to the country's agriculture, and would impede the struggle of the working people for full employment and expansion of the social security system."[35]

The Italians had a quite different perspective on the possible expansion of the Common Market. Since the tendency toward economic integration and transcendence of national barriers was rooted in the logic of capitalism's evolution, it had to be regarded as an objective, even progressive, process. As one of the PCI's leading economists would a few months later conclude, on the premise that integration was a "progressive and hence irreversible" tendency: "For this reason, a struggle against this tendency would be a struggle without prospects, doomed to fail insofar as it took on the dimensions of a pure and simple fight to retain national barriers or to return to historically outmoded organizational forms of social

[33] See "Problems of Modern Capitalism," *World Marxist Review,* V, 12 (December 1962), pp. 52–54, for the official summary of this aspect of the conference discussion.
[34] See *L'Humanité,* September 17, 1962, for Henri Jourdain's reiteration of this point.
[35] "Theses," *CDSP,* XIV, 34, p. 12.

life."[36] Rather than fight to keep the Common Market a closed corporation, with strong protectionist instincts, the course of wisdom would be to encourage its enlargement while at the same time working to overcome its discriminatory features with respect to the African and the socialist countries alike.[37] Italian Communist prescriptions with respect to the Common Market exactly paralleled their approach to domestic economic and political affairs: do not stand in the way of the inevitable, but seek to mold it to your purposes.

The PCI was primarily interested not in preventing the further expansion of the Common Market or in protecting Communist trade with the West, but in dealing effectively with the Market as an operating institution that seemed likely for the foreseeable future to exert a powerful influence on European political and economic life. The Soviet Union, being concerned least of all with this aspect of the problem, could not view it in so simple a perspective. Opposing pressures almost inevitably led to ambivalence in Moscow, such that openly hostile efforts to hinder the integration process were combined with a partial and tacit acceptance of the Common Market as an operational reality. Fulminations against the military and political objectives of the EEC and its disastrous economic consequences for the masses represented the negative, purely hostile side of its policy, the aspect most congenial to the French comrades. Recognition of the Market's contributions to productivity and of the validity of the whole process of economic integration represented the other, "Italian" side of the coin. So also did the hint thrown out by Khrushchev himself at about the time of the Moscow meeting in an important article dealing with the need to revitalize the Communist equivalent to the EEC, the Council of Mutual Economic Aid. Pointing to the "objective trend toward internationalization of production," Khrushchev mentioned "the possibility of economic cooperation and peaceful economic competition not only between the separate countries with differing social systems, but also between their economic amalgamations."[38] We may not like the Common Market, he was implying, but we must all the same in our own interest learn to deal with it.

[36] Amedeo Grano, "Linee di un' alternativa al Mercato comune europeo," *Rinascita,* May 4, 1963, p. 21.

[37] For a concise expression of this view see the statement issued by the CGIL Executive Committee on January 23, 1963, following the WFTU Leipzig meeting on the Common Market: *Rassegna sindacale,* New Series, No. 5 (February 9, 1963), p. 22; also *Avanti!,* January 24, 1963.

[38] "Vital Questions of the Development of the Socialist World System," *World Marxist Review,* V, 9 (September 1962), p. 7.

Faced with a situation that was both highly unpredictable and largely outside the realm of their influence, Soviet policy makers were trying to play it both ways. They would continue the old tactic of attacking the Market in an attempt to weaken its internal cohesion and slow down its expansion. But they would at the same time—and this was the essential innovation introduced by Khrushchev's speech and at the Moscow conference—begin hesitantly to deal with it as though it were a permanent feature of the European scene. The Soviet Theses on the Common Market thus contained, in a stiff and unenthusiastic form, the favorite Italian theme that in Western Europe the existence "of common problems born of 'integration' creates objective opportunities for working out and agreeing upon concerted actions by the national detachments of the working class."[39] This formulation, hinting at the "democratic alternative" to the Common Market that the PCI and the CGIL wished to promote in concert with non-Communist elements of the European working-class movement, was welcomed by the Italians along with the other "positive" features of the new Soviet position. The trend of official thinking in Moscow appeared to be moving in the right direction, toward an increasing acceptance of the realities of Western European life.

The Leipzig Meeting of the WFTU

If the Moscow conference had given the Italians legitimate grounds for hope of a more constructive Soviet policy toward the Common Market, it soon began to seem either that they had overestimated the extent of the change or that word of a new orientation had failed to reach the Secretary General of the WFTU. The WFTU Secretariat had announced during the summer that an international trade union conference on the Common Market would be held in Leipzig at the end of October; the objective, it was presumed, would be to unite the trade unions behind the conclusions of the forthcoming Moscow conference and in so doing heal the breach opened up at the Executive Committee session in Budapest. A few weeks after the Moscow meeting Louis Saillant held a press conference at WFTU headquarters in Prague confirming the convocation of the Leipzig conference and making it clear by the proposals he advanced for action against the Market that he, at least, saw no reason for a change in policy.

The Italian reaction to Saillant's declaration was one of open

---

[39] "Theses," *CDSP*, XIV, 34, p. 15.

irritation. The Socialist daily found it "astonishing" (*L'Unità* more politely expressed "a certain surprise") that Saillant should virtually have attempted to determine the conclusions of the conference in advance rather than await the results of the intensive debate necessary to overcome the differences among the WFTU's affiliates.[40] It was observed that Saillant, by declining to grant the existence of an objective tendency toward economic integration, was virtually advocating "the restoration of old customs barriers and a return to outmoded concepts of economic nationalism. . . ." Only because he resorted to the use of "partial and unilateral data" could he continue to defend the unrealistic and erroneous view that the workers in the Common Market countries were in general worse off than in the past.[41]

Shortly thereafter the CGIL Executive Committee met to approve a document confirming its positions on the Common Market and flatly rejecting two of the three specific proposals made by Saillant. His recommendation to establish a world-wide trade union committee to coordinate action against the monopolies was dismissed as "too ambitious," unless it was to be regarded as "predominantly propagandistic in function and without an effective grasp on reality." Rather than put before the workers an "exclusively negative orientation," the WFTU should present a positive program of economic cooperation that might protect the interests of the less developed countries. Saillant's proposal for a meeting of what he called the five "most important" European trade unions to work out a plan of resistance to monopoly control was given equally short shrift. What sense would there be, the CGIL asked, in discriminating against all the other European unions, especially those in Italy and France that did not belong to the WFTU? Moreover, since the object of such a meeting was presumably to further unity among the European unions, care should be taken to formulate the agenda in such a way as to avoid sensitive political issues such as the link between NATO and the Common Market on which disagreements would inevitably arise. As it stood, the CGIL implied, Saillant's invitation was all too obviously only a propaganda gesture, certain to be rejected out of hand. Saillant's third proposal, that African unions be encouraged to promote establishment of an African Common Market independent of the EEC, was supported by the CGIL so long as African economic integration did not imply

40 *Avanti!*, September 28, 1962; *L'Unità*, September 29, 1962.
41 *L'Unità*, September 29, 1962.

a tendency toward a closed market system and isolation from other economic groupings.[42]

The CGIL's position paper was made public on October 14, two weeks before the Leipzig conference was scheduled to begin. The East German press, which had been regularly reporting the conference preparations, did not make further reference to it after October 18, nor apparently did any other Communist source.[43] It became evident, when the announced opening date passed by without comment, that the conference had been quietly, though as it turned out temporarily, put on the shelf. It is tempting to suppose that the delay was occasioned primarily by the intransigence of the Italians, who were clearly intending to make a public issue of their quarrel with Saillant. While this was undoubtedly a contributing factor, a more critical role was probably played by the simultaneous eruption of the Cuban and Sino-Indian crises, which damaged Soviet prestige and caused an open rupture with the Chinese of vastly greater consequence for the movement than the CGIL's quarrelsome attitude. It was by any measure an inauspicious moment for an international Communist conference.

After a six-week delay the conference finally got under way, opening on December 14 with an all-day speech by Louis Saillant that revealed nothing by way of concession to the Italian views. The CGIL's delegates, once again Santi and Lama, restated their union's opposition to both Saillant's analysis of the Common Market's economic consequences and his recommendations for action against it. Despite the apparent victory at Moscow of the more liberal Arzumanyan, Saillant forcefully repeated the essence of the position that had been upheld by Varga: the so-called economic "miracles" of Western Europe reflected a cyclical advance rather than a long-term trend, such wage increases as had been won were only transitory, employment levels had in fact already begun to decline.[44]

The Italians countered with their now familiar argument that such a schematic and partial view of reality was dangerous, not merely because it was factually wrong but because it logically implied a struggle not against "the real enemy," the employers and

[42] *Ibid.*, October 14, 1962; also "La CGIL per la Conferenza sul MEC," *Rassegna sindacale*, No. 57–60 (September–December 1962), pp. 93–96.

[43] "The Mystery of the Missing Conference," Radio Free Europe research report, November 16, 1962, quoting Otto Frey, *Neue Zürcher Zeitung*, same date. Also Arthur Olsen, "World Red Labor Parley Cancelled to Avoid Rift," *The New York Times*, November 23, 1962.

[44] "Extracts from the Report of Louis Saillant," *WTUM*, February 1963, pp. 4–24, at pp. 6–7.

the monopolies, but against the principle of economic integration as such, which on the contrary could actually represent "a fact of progress and development of progressive forces."[45] The point should be to fight against monopolistic distortions of the principle of integration by means both of a coordinated struggle to achieve traditional trade union goals and broader democratic structural reforms in individual countries and of a united effort to influence the plans and policies of the Common Market institutions themselves. To further both these objectives, the CGIL now formally proposed what it had suggested in Budapest, that the WFTU establish in Brussels "an office of representation and coordination" concerned with Common Market affairs. As Santi explained it, "this will not automatically open the door to representation in the organisms of the EEC, but it will satisfy a necessary condition for facilitating contacts with the other trade union organizations and will serve as a point of departure for the development of unity of action."[46]

In marked contrast to what had occurred at the Moscow economists' conference, the Italian position aroused very little sympathy indeed. The point of the Leipzig exercise was not at all to conduct a more or less objective, scholarly appraisal of the nature of capitalism and the effects of economic integration; it was to help set in motion as vigorous and extensive an international propaganda campaign as could be mustered against the Common Market and in favor of Soviet initiatives for expansion of trade. Saillant's proposal for a world trade union conference on economic and trade relations was nothing but the WFTU counterpart to the recent Soviet request for an international trade meeting under United Nations auspices. And the effort to agitate for an African Common Market and for an international trade union committee for action against the monopolies was designed to stimulate pressures against the EEC at just the moment when the representatives of the African countries associated with the Common Market were assembled in Brussels negotiating a revision of the terms of the agreement. As Saillant had made plain in an interview before the conference began, its central purpose was to transform the Common Market from a narrowly European to a truly international issue. The fight against monopolies, he had proclaimed, must be shown to be a universal problem: "This is why trade unions from Africa, Asia, and America have been invited to Leipzig. Our task will be to show,

---

45 Speech of Fernando Santi, *L'Unità*, December 17, 1962.
46 *Ibid.* For a summary of the full CGIL position at Leipzig, see "La Conferenza di Lipsia," *Rassegna sindacale*, New Series, No. 3 (January 12, 1963), p. 18.

especially to delegates of African countries, the urgent need for a united front against West European capitalism."[47]

Given such ground rules as these, the CGIL's concerns were bound to appear largely irrelevant. The correspondent for *L'Unità*, putting the best face on the situation, maintained that the CGIL's was not at all "an isolated voice." By way of evidence he noted that the Polish and Yugoslav representation shared the Italians' analytical approach toward the impact of the Common Market in Europe.[48] They too appeared able to regard the European economic situation in a reasonably objective light, acknowledging that economic integration had produced certain positive results and proposing to attack not the principle itself but its distortion by the monopolies.[49]

Their sympathy for the Italian perspective on European affairs was not sufficient, however, to lead the Poles and Yugoslavs to support the CGIL proposals, which appeared too parochial for their purposes. Yugoslavia had much at stake in the fight against Common Market trade restrictions, both as they affected Yugoslav trade with Europe and as they influenced the underdeveloped "neutralist" countries that played such a large role in Yugoslav foreign policy. The Italian strategy might be appropriate for the long run, but it promised little as a way of bringing immediate political pressure to bear against the damaging international consequences of the Common Market. As the Polish delegate observed, in implicit criticism of the CGIL, it was important to avoid a "unilateral and local approach" to the Common Market, since its effects were felt not only by the workers of Western Europe but by peoples the world around.[50]

In bringing the Leipzig conference to a close after four days of discussion, Louis Saillant claimed to appreciate the diversity of views expressed, but maintained, not very persuasively, that there had nonetheless been achieved "a sort of unanimity on principles." The WFTU had, he contended, once more lived up to its responsibility as "a sort of healing agent," and had inoculated itself against the dread diseases of dogmatism, sectarianism, opportunism, and class collaboration.[51]

[47] Czechoslovak News Agency, November 23, 1962.
[48] *L'Unità*, December 18, 1962.
[49] For the Yugoslav position, see "Interest Is Focused on the Process of Integration," *Rad*, December 22, 1962.
[50] Polish Press Agency, December 17, 1962.
[51] "Extracts from the Conclusions Presented by Louis Saillant," *WTUM*, February 1963, p. 25.

The fact was that of his four proposals, only the recommendation for assistance to African unions in establishing an African Common Market emerged unscathed. The proposal for a world trade union conference to promote expansion of international trade was opposed by the Chinese on the grounds that it implied collaboration with the imperialists in maintaining their neocolonial ties with the underdeveloped countries.[52] The suggestion for a meeting of five leading European unions was rejected by the CGIL on the ground that it was discriminatory, and the Italians also objected to the proposal for an antimonopoly trade union committee because it appeared certain only to serve propaganda purposes and not to further unity of action among the European unions.[53]

The Leipzig conference being of a consultative character, with many delegations present from outside the WFTU, no formal resolutions were passed. The following month, however, Saillant's proposals were formally brought before the WFTU's Executive Committee meeting in Prague. All were passed, but for what may well have been the first time in the organization's history, the vote was not unanimous: the CGIL, repeating its various objections to the proposals and to the WFTU's approach to the Common Market, made a point of abstaining from the vote. This step was taken so as to make an organizational as well as a substantive point: the CGIL intended to establish the legitimacy of dissent, to challenge the old rituals of "fictitious unanimity." A step forward had been made, a CGIL official observed, when Saillant had been obliged to admit "that it was necessary to take account of the diversity of positions existing in the trade union movement and that he therefore regarded it as an inevitable and positive fact that the existence of disagreement was expressed even up to the point of minority and majority voting."[54]

The CGIL also believed it had gained an important victory for

[52] Diamante Limiti, "Aperto dibattito a Lipsia sui sindacati nel MEC," *Rinascita*, December 29, 1962, p. 13. This theme was further developed in the Chinese broadside against the PCI that appeared a few days later, in response to the debate at the PCI Tenth Congress: "Even more astounding is the fact that Togliatti and certain other people extend their idea of class collaboration in the international arena to cover 'joint intervention' in the underdeveloped areas." "The Differences between Comrade Togliatti and Us," *Peking Review*, VI, 1 (January 4, 1963), pp. 9–21.

[53] Limiti, *Rinascita*, December 29, 1962, p. 13. Without mentioning the CGIL by name, Saillant referred caustically in his concluding address to the "skepticism" that had been expressed about the usefulness of an antimonopoly committee: "Skepticism in itself is not a theory. One could even say that it is not a normal attitude for a class organization." "Extracts from the Conclusions," *WTUM*, February 1963, p. 27.

[54] "Unità e autonomia dei sindacati su scala europea e mondiale: intervista con Mario Dido," *Rassegna sindacale*, New Series, No. 5 (February 9, 1963), p. 24.

its Common Market policy at the Executive Committee session. The delegation returned from Prague declaring that a favorable decision had been reached "in principle" on the CGIL's proposal for establishment of a WFTU office in Brussels.[55] This positive result seemed to be confirmed by the WFTU's own subsequent announcement that a meeting had been arranged between representatives of the WFTU's three affiliates in the Common Market countries (the CGIL, the CGT, and the FLA of Luxembourg) "with a view to examining ways and means" of setting up an information bureau.[56] But if the French had in fact agreed to this move, they shortly thereafter changed their minds. By the time the three unions met in Paris the following month, the CGIL found itself isolated. The only compromise possible was for the CGIL to proceed on its own, with the WFTU reluctantly endorsing what it could no longer prevent. In announcing the decision to establish its own information office in Brussels, Luciano Lama observed that the primary purpose was not to exert influence directly on the EEC itself but to break down barriers between the Communist unions and the rest, already represented in the Common Market's Economic and Social Committee:

> The main aim of our initiative is not in fact to provide for exchanges of information with the High Authority and the top bureaucracy of the EEC, or to win posts in this or that commission. All this is necessary, if it goes along with an opening up of relations and a search for common ground between the various trade unions represented in Brussels. The point is for all the unions to escape from the absurd isolationism in which they have so far been voluntarily confined, even the ones belonging to the same international organization.[57]

The establishment of the CGIL's Brussels office, which had appeared to signal the start of an aggressive effort to play a larger role in European trade union affairs, turned out to be more a gesture of principle than an effective policy move. The Brussels office, staffed by one Socialist and one Communist CGIL official, limited itself essentially to observing the activities of the EEC and of the trade unions accredited to it and sending back reports to the CGIL's international office.[58] Neither the non-Communist Italian unions already represented at the EEC nor the ICFTU secretariat showed any inclination to soften their attitude toward the CGIL;

[55] *Ibid.;* also *L'Unità,* February 3, 1961.
[56] "Decisions adopted by the 26th Session of the W.F.T.U. Executive Committee," *WTUM,* March 1963, p. 3.
[57] Luciano Lama, "Per una intesa tra i sindacati dei paesi del MEC," *Rassegna sindacale,* New Series, No. 7 (March 9, 1963), p. 24.
[58] Fidia Sassano, "L'esame di coscienza dei sindacati europei," *Avanti!,* August 1, 1964.

they saw no point in rewarding the CGIL's partial concessions and thus reducing tensions between the Socialist and Communist wings of the organization. They took the position, therefore, that as long as it remained part of an international trade union body that continued to denounce the EEC on principle, the CGIL could hardly expect to be admitted into Community deliberations.[59]

This situation illustrates well the point the CGIL had been making ever since the WFTU Moscow Congress, that its own full autonomy required not merely a free hand at home but an influential voice in formulating the WFTU's international line. As it tried to demonstrate in setting up the Brussels office, the CGIL could attempt to go it alone, but this was rather an empty gesture. As long as it remained affiliated with a centralized international organization whose prime interests and policies conflicted with its own needs, the CGIL's statements and actions, however conciliatory and reformist they may have appeared, could safely be discounted by those to whom they were intended to appeal.

For the Italian Communists, the Common Market represented essentially one of those institutions of the existing order with which, since they lacked the strength to destroy it, they would have to come to terms. Like other institutions and techniques of the capitalist system, from parliament to economic planning, it was seen as being susceptible to Communist influence: as long as one appeared to accept the *principle* of parliamentary democracy, of planning, of economic integration, then one could logically fight not the institution itself, but rather the presumed distortion of those principles imposed by the monopolist elite.

When it came to applying this view of things specifically to the Common Market, the trade union appeared to have a special opportunity that the party lacked. At the European level it was the CGIL, not the PCI, that had potential leverage to exert. "A special function belongs to the unions," observed one of the PCI's main analysts of Common Market affairs, because they "represent an outstanding force in every one of the countries of 'little Europe' and because under the present structure of the Community organizations they are the only forces that can exert leverage for a democratic alternative to the EEC."[60] A political party out of power had no mode of access to the EEC and thus no role outside its own country but that of propagandist. The EEC's Social and Economic Committee was only an advisory body without great influence, but

---

[59] Sassano, "Il Belgio rifiuta la 'guerra fredda,'" *ibid.*, July 29, 1964. I have also benefited from conversations in the summer of 1964 with officials in the international offices of the CGIL and the CISL.

[60] Grano, *Rinascita*, May 4, 1963, p. 22.

it did give the unions represented there some formal voice in Community affairs.

The CGIL's interest in the Common Market did not, however, rest essentially on the belief that under existing circumstances the unions could actually exert significant direct influence on Community affairs.[61] Trade union representation in the EEC was important primarily because it established the presumption of a legitimate union involvement in Community matters; and this, in turn, laid the basis for the CGIL's insistence on the need for united action among unions of all ideological and political persuasions. The establishment of working-class unity, as was observed in the previous chapter, was more than just a propaganda slogan for the PCI. Maintenance of Communist-Socialist collaboration in the CGIL, as well as any longer-run hope of a broader alliance of left-wing forces in Italy, demanded convincing demonstrations of Communist sincerity in the pursuit of unity. The CGIL's European policy was thus useful in part as one more demonstration of Communist readiness to adapt to existing institutions and to collaborate for reform purposes with other working-class forces.

The importance of united action extended beyond the domestic level. Italian Communist policy toward the EEC was also motivated by the conviction that European communism as a whole would grow increasingly ineffectual unless it managed to break out of national boundaries and to unite with other left-wing forces at an international level. The growth of international economic integration under monopoly domination had created an imperative necessity for a corresponding unification of antimonopoly forces: "At the present stage of high monopoly concentration, with an international alliance of the monopolies the order of the day, *the struggle waged by the working people at national levels in the different sectors of the economy cannot produce the desired effect unless it is elevated onto the international plane.*"[62] Coordination of the trade union struggle, the CGIL maintained, is perfectly possible, so long as emphasis is placed not on propaganda but on specific actions based on a careful analysis of the real situation: "Such vigorous action would help to inflict an ideological and practical defeat on the rigid ideological anachronism which still divides the international trade union movement."[63]

The Common Market question was the most important concrete

[61] Lama, *Rassegna sindacale,* New Series, No. 7, p. 24.

[62] Umberto Scalia, "Current Problems of the Trade Union Movement in the Common Market Countries," *World Marxist Review,* VI, 9 (September 1963), p. 40.

[63] *Ibid.,* p. 41.

case in which the WFTU's function as international propagandist for the Soviet foreign policy line conflicted with the Italian interest in influencing in more tangible ways the European economic and political scene. Looked at more broadly, the CGIL's insistence on the importance of the Common Market was but one manifestation of the Italian conviction that Europe and European communism were entitled to receive a higher priority in the calculations of the international movement. Given the predominant weight in the WFTU of the Soviet Union and the other socialist states, it was clear that this could only be achieved through a loosely structured movement that could combine adherence to a common set of general principles with maximum flexibility and autonomy.

The organizational answer to this problem, the CGIL came to feel, lay in the principle of regionalism. The CGIL therefore began to advocate, as one of the principal planks of its platform, the creation of a West European branch of the WFTU that could coordinate the activities of the WFTU affiliates there and more energetically pursue whatever opportunities emerged to collaborate with other unions.[64] By advocating the establishment of a semi-autonomous regional organization the Communists in the CGIL hoped to achieve the best of both worlds: to maintain solidarity with the Communist trade union world while at the same time developing a program of action suited to the specific requirements of the Western European trade union situation. Such a solution might also serve the purpose of fending off the increasingly open demands from many in the Socialist party for outright secession from the WFTU, whose principles and mode of operation appeared increasingly irrelevant to European needs.[65]

But the idea of regionalism, appealing as it seemed in principle, ran afoul of one critical snag. It was not only the WFTU's sectarianism and attachment to Soviet interests that blocked the CGIL's efforts to coordinate Communist trade union action in Europe and to promote cooperation with non-Communist trade union forces. The WFTU's line was solidly supported by the CGIL's nemesis, the French CGT. Had the Communist parties and unions in Europe themselves been united in their view of the situation, to swing the WFTU into line behind them would have been much less of a problem. But they were not, and would not be so long as Thorez lived. The CGT, as in the past, liked to talk of the need to create a

[64] See the speech by Agostino Novella at the WFTU General Council meeting in Budapest in October 1964, "Documentazione," *Rassegna sindacale,* New Series, No. 47 (November 14, 1964), pp. 1–6.

[65] By the time of the Sixth WFTU Congress in the fall of 1965 the Socialist current in the CGIL had formally raised this demand.

common front of trade unionists, but since it would join hands only with those who believed that the Common Market had brought "bitter fruits" for all but the monopolies, its appeals found no takers.[66] As for the Italian position, Thorez summarily dismissed it: "The revisionists have proposed an allegedly positive policy calling for the 'insertion' of the working class and its organizations in the Common Market."[67]

There is a certain irony in the fact that in March 1963, at just the time the CGIL was announcing its decision to break solidarity with the CGT by opening a Brussels office on its own initiative, the PCI was meeting in Brussels with the five other Communist parties of the Common Market countries. In view of its repeated insistence on the importance of a united Communist front in Europe, the PCI had little choice other than to accept a compromise declaration that inadequately reflected its own position. In exchange for a strongly worded appeal for united action between Communist, Socialist, and Catholic forces, the PCI accepted a characterization of the Common Market that stressed its disastrous economic consequences and its linkage with the menacing and militaristic Bonn-Paris axis.[68] The fact was, as L'Unità took no pains to conceal in its reporting of the event, the PCI had been outvoted, receiving support only from its Belgian allies.[69]

Missing from the declaration was any reference to the main point the PCI wanted to include, a proposal for united action to revise the EEC treaties in such a way as to modify the character and direction of the economic integration process. This had been the keynote of a long statement issued by the PCI Direzione two weeks before, constituting its platform for the Brussels meeting.[70] The Italian proposal, with its reformist implications, was of no interest to the French, and as long as French Communist policy remained unchanged, the CGIL could not realistically hope to accomplish much by a regional approach.

[66] Telliez, WTUM, July–August 1963, p. 27.

[67] Maurice Thorez, quoted in Henri Jourdain, "Sur la Rencontre de Moscou," Cahiers du Communisme, XXXIX, 1–2 (January–February 1963), p. 30. See also the special section devoted to the Common Market in France Nouvelle, No. 905 (February 2–26, 1963), pp. 11–24.

[68] "Dichiarazione dei partiti comunisti dei paesi del MEC," L'Unità, March 9, 1963.

[69] Ibid., March 8, 1963. See also Luca Pavolini, "L'azione e la critica dei partiti comunisti verso la 'piccola Europa,'" Rinascita, March 16, 1963, pp. 10–11, for an account of the "lively and animated" debate. The entente between the Belgian and Italian parties had been evident since their meeting in Rome in May 1962; see the joint declaration, L'Unità, May 18, 1962.

[70] "Per una iniziativa democratica europea e una revisione dei trattati del MEC," L'Unità, February 23, 1963.

CHAPTER TEN

ITALIAN COMMUNISM AND THE
INTERNATIONAL MOVEMENT, 1962 – 1964

In August 1964, while in Yalta awaiting a meeting with First Secretary Khrushchev, Palmiro Togliatti was stricken with a fatal illness. Only a few hours before, he had finished writing a memorandum for the Soviet leader in which he set forth more fully and in many respects more bluntly than ever before his views on the problems besetting the international Communist movement.[1] Togliatti's Testament, as it came to be called, contained nothing that he or his party had not said before in one form or another on one or another occasion. Why then did it so shake the political world?

Its impact stemmed partly from the fact that it was intended for Soviet eyes alone as a recapitulation of Italian disagreements with Moscow, and therefore lacked the careful balance that characterized most official PCI statements on international Communist affairs. Absent, because irrelevant in this context, were the usual criticisms of the Chinese and reaffirmations of Italian support for basic Soviet strategic positions. But the impact stemmed also from the incidental circumstance of Togliatti's sudden death, followed by the decision of his successors to publish his last Testament despite apparent Soviet protests.[2] By this act the PCI leadership committed itself, psychologically and politically, to follow Togliatti's lead.

Our story began in the spring of 1956 and gave prominence to Togliatti's *Nuovi argomenti* article, that early and apparently bold declaration of principle concerning the nature of Soviet society and the organization of the international Communist movement. Although the perspectives of that article were reinforced over time

1 "Promemoria sulle questione del movimento operaio internazionale e della sua unità," *Rinascita*, September 5, 1964, p. 4. A complete translation of the document (not used here) can be found in William E. Griffith, *Sino-Soviet Relations, 1964–1965*, pp. 373–383.

2 It was widely rumored that Brezhnev had urged at Togliatti's funeral that the document not be published. See *La Stampa*, September 6, 1964, and "L'Ultima lettera di Togliatti a Kruscev," *L'Espresso*, September 6, 1964, p. 3.

330

and gradually incorporated into the basic outlook of the Italian party, their realization in practice had been inhibited by many factors, including particularly Togliatti's own unwillingness to isolate his party from the mainstream of international Communist affairs. Despite the sometimes unorthodox quality of his thought, at least by Moscow standards, Togliatti had in action proven more of a conformist than a rebel. There is some irony, then, in the fact that the last year of his life found him leading his party in open and active resistance to some aspects of Soviet policy. The purpose of this chapter will be to explain how and why this conflict came about, largely in response to the steadily deepening split between the Russians and the Chinese.

For nearly a year after the excitement generated by the Twenty-Second Congress had died down, the Italian Communists found their attention captured primarily by domestic political and economic problems and, on the international front, by the controversy over the Common Market. As long as the state of affairs in the Communist movement would permit, the PCI appeared content to remain immersed in predominantly domestic concerns and to stay on the sidelines in the still developing Sino-Soviet struggle.

Through the summer of 1962, therefore, the Italian party participated in the dispute only to the extent of occasionally lending a hand to the Soviet campaign against the Albanians, upbraiding Enver Hoxha and the other Albanian "leaders" ("comrades" no longer) for their insulting and intemperate charges against the USSR.[3] Although the Italians doubtless welcomed the détente that occurred in Sino-Soviet relations during the spring and summer of 1962, they appear to have played no part in the mediating efforts of a group of Asian and European parties, whose proposal for discussions leading toward a new international conference was accepted in principle by both the Chinese and the Soviet parties.[4]

By fall, this temporary détente came to an abrupt end. The steady

[3] See the unsigned editorial, "Ingiurie in luogo di discussione," *Rinascita*, XIX, 4 (April 1962), pp. 297-298. There is a sharp contrast, present also in the Soviet literature of the period, between the vituperative tone of this anti-Albanian editorial and the calmly reasoned approach to the "Chinese comrades" in the article immediately preceding; Giuliano Pajetta, "Disarmo, pace e lotta rivoluzionaria," *ibid.*, pp. 293-296. See Griffith, *Albania*, pp. 129-158, for a full account of the ups and downs of Soviet-Albanian relations between the Twenty-Second Congress and the fall of 1962.

[4] See Dallin *et al.*, *Diversity in International Communism*, p. 651, for an account of this initiative by the Communist parties of North Vietnam, Indonesia, New Zealand, Sweden, and Great Britain. Neither the Italians' consistent opposition to the idea of another international meeting nor their well-known "revisionist" stance equipped them to play a mediator's role.

Soviet rapprochement with Yugoslavia, capped by Brezhnev's official visit to Belgrade in September, aroused the Albanians and Chinese to renewed and strengthened expressions of hostility. The nearly simultaneous eruption of the Cuban and Sino-Indian border crises then suddenly shifted the conflict onto a more intense and more open level. There was no question where the Italian party would stand on these questions. The PCI, long favoring a rapprochement between the Soviet Union and Yugoslavia, vigorously defended Tito against the threatening charge of the Chinese that he was aiming toward a restoration of capitalism.[5] Soviet actions in the Caribbean crisis were also unreservedly supported on the ground that Cuban independence had been safeguarded and peace preserved in the face of imperialist aggression.[6]

With regard to the Sino-Indian conflict, Togliatti's initial response was to minimize its importance, dismissing it as essentially a complex border dispute "on which we are not even remotely tempted to venture an opinion, any more than we are inclined to meddle in border disputes all over the world that do not concern our country."[7] But this hands-off attitude, consistent with Moscow's initial uncertain response, fell into line with the revised Soviet stance of implicit criticism of the Chinese for trying to disrupt the peaceful coexistence policy and sabotage Communist relations with the nonaligned countries.[8]

This sudden intensification of the Sino-Soviet conflict made the PCI's policy of minimizing its importance increasingly untenable. The party was obliged to declare itself, not only out of elementary considerations of loyalty to the USSR, but also because of mounting pressures within the PCI itself. Preparations were already far advanced for the party's Tenth Congress, scheduled to convene in December, and the opinions of the rank and file were being voiced in preparatory meetings at lower levels of the party and in letters and articles concerning the Theses for the Congress.

Beginning in early November complaints began appearing in *L'Unità* and *Rinascita* that the party was not abiding by its own oft-repeated counsel to seek unity in the movement through open debate of divergent positions. The Theses themselves, it was pointed

[5] p.t. [Palmiro Togliatti], "A proposito della 'cricca di Tito,'" *Rinascita*, October 13, 1962, p. 15.

[6] Togliatti, "Potenza socialista, potenza di pace," *Rinascita*, November 3, 1962, pp. 1–2.

[7] *L'Unità*, November 5, 1962. See also Silvia Ridolfi, "La vertenza di frontiera tra la Cina e l'India," *Rinascita*, November 3, 1962, pp. 12–13.

[8] See *L'Unità*, November 22, 1964, for an acknowledgment that "something much more important is at stake than the drawing of a boundary line. . . ."

out, gave only a few lines to international Communist affairs, sharply condemning the Albanians but ignoring entirely the obvious deep dissent between the Russians and the Chinese. Many in the party were said to be disturbed by the recent course of events and in need of guidance: "At a time when the press of the two countries are hurling at each other reciprocal accusations of deviationism, dogmatism, and revisionism, it is obvious that comrades must become disturbed about the differences and clashes. . . ." Was it not time, they asked, for the party to provide more information on the dispute and to state its position clearly?[9]

For such criticisms to have been given prominent public expression suggests that they were both fairly widespread and shared by at least some major figures in the party. To some extent the complaints probably represented the honest bewilderment and concern of Communists left prey to their own doubts and to the jibes and sensational interpretations of nonparty channels of information; party members were not used to being left without an official explanation of major events. But the pressures for clarification stemmed in part from another, more dangerous source, from the small but increasingly vocal band of Chinese supporters within the PCI.

The previous September a pro-Chinese pamphlet provocatively entitled *Viva il Leninismo* had been issued by a small group of local PCI leaders in Padua, all of whom were promptly expelled.[10] After the same group had produced a second document the following month, their action was emulated in November by some young Communists belonging to Roman sections of the party's youth organization. Even more disturbing than these evidences of sympathy for Chinese positions was the realization that internal dissent was being abetted by interference from the outside. Togliatti revealed at a press conference and later repeated at the Tenth Congress that the Albanian party had begun to distribute polemical literature within the PCI.[11]

The PCI's need to combat such subversive efforts by open con-

---

[9] Domenico Coggiola, "Maggiore chiarezza nei rapporti tra partiti comunisti," *L'Unità*, December 1, 1962. For a similar view, see Licio Lecchini, "Favorire il confronto tra le posizioni dei partiti comunisti," *ibid.*, November 24, 1962. See also Ezio Ferrero, "La rivoluzione coloniale," *Rinascita*, November 3, 1962, p. 7, for quotations from a resolution of the PCI's Turin federation complaining of a "certain timidity or lack of clarity" in the Theses on various aspects of Soviet international policy such as nuclear testing, relations with the "third world," and international Communist relationships.

[10] *Viva il Leninismo* has been reprinted in *Corrispondenza socialista*, III, 11 (November 1962), pp. 573–584.

[11] *L'Unità*, November 13, 1962.

demnation of the Sino-Albanian positions corresponded with Soviet requirements. As became evident during a series of five party Congresses in November and December, the internal dynamic of the dispute was leading inexorably toward an open expression of hostility between the Soviets and the Chinese. The PCI's Tenth Congress itself represented a step in this evolution. Togliatti's opening address politely ("We have great respect for the Chinese comrades") but firmly criticized the Chinese party for its renewed efforts to discredit the 1960 Moscow Statement's position on peaceful coexistence and for its support of the Albanians.[12] Except for Poland, the other pro-Soviet parties represented in Rome echoed the latter charge, which had already been voiced the month before at Sofia. The Chinese delegate, Chao Yi-min, countered with a refutation of the PCI's reformist domestic strategy and a defense of the fraternal Albanian party. Furthermore, reacting to the presence of a Yugoslav delegation at a Commmunist Congress for the first time since 1957 and to Tito's arrival in Moscow on that very day, Chao delivered a tirade against the "Tito gang" that was restoring capitalism to Yugoslavia.

The Italian rebuttal was offered the next day by Gian Carlo Pajetta, who took a further step toward formal acknowledgment of the controversy. Prefacing his remarks with an approving reference to the demands expressed at the provincial congresses for fuller information about the dispute, Pajetta declared that the PCI was the kind of party in which "when we mean China, we cannot say Albania."[13] Our party, he went on, intended to assume responsibility for conducting a debate on the differences in a fraternal but open fashion; he then proceeded to rebut the Chinese criticisms point by point. Togliatti repeated these arguments in his concluding speech but adopted a more conciliatory tone, again stressing the PCI's esteem for the Chinese party and affection for its leaders, and inviting the Chinese to send a delegation to Italy for first-hand observation and a direct exchange of views. He also revealed that he personally had insisted that the political resolution adopted by the Congress not criticize the Chinese by name in order to avoid a further deterioration of relations.[14]

These conciliatory gestures could hardly have been intended to do more than demonstrate to friend and foe, in the party and

---

12 "Relazione di Palmiro Togliatti," X Congresso, pp. 41, 45, and 56.
13 X Congresso, p. 278. This remark, implicitly critical of the still prevailing convention of using Albania as a surrogate for China, was not included in the summary of his speech provided in L'Unità, December 6, 1962.
14 X Congresso, pp. 619–620.

outside, the "reasonableness" of Togliatti's attitude. What the Italians appeared to want, at this stage, was to bring the dispute increasingly out into the open so as to make the Chinese position easier to refute and, at the same time, force both sides to eschew the particularly offensive and slanderous verbal assaults that polemic-by-proxy permitted. Togliatti appears to have believed what he and his colleagues so persistently maintained, that the eventual restoration of Communist unity would be possible only through open discussion and greatly enlarged tolerance of divergent opinions. In the short run, however, it must have been evident that to clarify the issues and address the Chinese directly rather than through their Albanian proxies meant in fact to intensify the dispute.

The Chinese at any rate thought so, and on the last day of December published an article amplifying their critique of Italian revisionism; it proved to be the first in a series aimed at the main "revisionist" parties.[15] This move was almost certainly welcomed by the PCI leaders, for it permitted them at last to mount a more open counterattack against the pro-Chinese in the party and to satisfy the appetite for information about the dispute that the Tenth Congress had only further stimulated.[16]

The Chinese attack was therefore promptly reprinted and answered in a series of articles by the PCI's chief spokesmen on international Communist matters.[17] Togliatti's own reply is the most interesting, for in two respects it confirms the impression that he was seeking to make the terms of the quarrel more explicit than the Soviets were yet willing to do. For one thing, he deplored the fact that the Chinese were still hiding behind the screen of attacking "certain people," not specified by name, whereas everyone knew that their target was Comrade Khrushchev and the Soviet leaders; if this were to be made explicit, he argued, they might be compelled to speak in a less offensive manner.[18] The observation, of course, applied equally as much to the Soviet leadership itself: although *Pravda* had on January 7 for the first time criticized the Chinese by name for their support of the Albanians, the Soviets continued for several months to direct their substantive arguments to the

[15] "The Differences between Comrade Togliatti and Us," *Peking Review*, VI, 1, pp. 9–21.
[16] See "Come discute e come lavora il partito dopo il X Congresso," *Rinascita*, January 12, 1963, pp. 29–30.
[17] See, *inter alia*, the articles by Longo, *L'Unità*, January 4 and 16, and by Gian Carlo Pajetta, *ibid.*, January 12, 1963.
[18] "Riconduciamo la discussione ai suoi termini reali," *Rinascita*, January 12, 1963, p. 13.

Albanian party alone. Second, Togliatti went on record in favor of an explicit revision of the Moscow Statement's negative judgment on Yugoslavia, "because on this point it was mistaken."[19] *Pravda*'s omission of these two points in its otherwise extensive summary of Togliatti's article[20] confirmed Soviet unwillingness to take the substantial steps of escalation these suggestions implied.

At the East German party Congress in mid-January, Khrushchev made a notably conciliatory speech, in sharp contrast to the provocative anti-Chinese demonstration that showed the true temper of the meeting. He urged that polemics be suspended to permit tempers to cool, saying that socialist countries, even if one did not agree with the policies of their current leaders, could not simply be excommunicated from the movement like heretics from a church. He further observed that a meeting of all the parties, while desirable in principle, was not opportune, since it "would not lead to a calm and sensible settlement of differences but to their aggravation and the danger of a split."[21]

This kind of talk was exactly what the Italians liked to hear. In his own speech at the Berlin Congress Luigi Longo also urged an end to polemics and, repeating the PCI's invitation to the Chinese to send a delegation to Italy, expressed the hope that through various such contacts the way would be paved for the reconciliation of divergent views.[22] A similarly conciliatory speech was made by Gomułka, who had used his opportunity as Khrushchev's host in Warsaw just before the Congress opened to urge patient discussions and proposals for compromise.[23] The following month, as a further sign that the Italian and Soviet parties were then on much the same wavelength, *Pravda* reprinted verbatim an interview with Longo concerning international Communist affairs. Longo again stressed, as had Khrushchev in Berlin, that unity could eventually be achieved through frank exchanges of opinion because the universal ideals and objectives linking the parties were far stronger than the issues dividing them. An international meeting should be convened, he said, but only after careful preparation through a series of preliminary bilateral and multilateral meetings had shown that real possibilities for agreement existed.[24]

19 *Ibid.*, p. 14.
20 *Pravda*, January 15, 1963.
21 *Ibid.*, January 17, 1963.
22 *L'Unità*, January 19, 1963. Khrushchev's conciliatory attitude was given particular prominence in PCI editorial comment on the event; see "Sul dibattito tra i partiti al congresso di Berlino," *Rinascita*, January 26, 1963, pp. 9–10.
23 Stehle in Griffith, *Communism in Europe*, Vol. 1, pp. 148–149.
24 *L'Unità*, February 24, 1963; *Pravda*, February 25, 1963.

The next several months produced a complex and in some respects contradictory pattern of events in the Communist movement.
The Sino-Soviet feud grew increasingly bitter, with the Chinese
bearing the major responsibility for steadily raising the ante.[25] At
the same time, however, negotiations were undertaken for a direct
Soviet-Chinese confrontation, finally scheduled for early July. Public polemics were accordingly suspended in mid-March, but relations
in fact continued to deteriorate. Any last hope for the success of
the bilateral meeting was shattered before it even began, when, on
June 14, the Chinese delivered and then made public a wholly uncompromising letter setting forth "twenty-five points" which should
govern the general line of the international movement. By the
timing and the content of their letter the Chinese had made it plain
that they were now prepared to split the movement. A month later,
with the meeting still in progress, the Soviets published the letter
together with their reply, revealing to all that chances of a reconciliation, or even of a cooling-down period, had vanished.

From this time on Soviet tactics appear to have been essentially
aimed at mobilizing support for precisely the "excommunication"
of the Chinese that Khrushchev had declared a few months before
to be an unacceptable method of dealing with conflict in the
Communist world. The Soviets were apparently convinced that
"speedy 'political isolation' of the Chinese was necessary, that is,
that there must be a formal split whereby neutrals and recalcitrants
could be forced into line and the decline of Soviet influence thereby
halted if not reversed."[26] They believed, moreover, that the tactical
need for a conciliatory stance had ended: the Chinese had by this
time so clearly demonstrated their utter intransigence that even the
moderate pro-Soviet parties might be expected to comprehend the
futility of continued appeasement.

This was not a line of reasoning to which the Italians were
prepared to subscribe. For a variety of reasons, the PCI continued
to defend the principle that the unity of the movement could and
must be preserved. Despite the Chinese lack of interest in reaching
a compromise, a fact which the Italians acknowledged and condemned, they continued to feel that a showdown should be avoided.
Somehow, they felt, the passage of time would alter circumstances
sufficiently to permit a reconciliation. In the meanwhile, the parties
directly concerned and the movement as a whole had to learn to
live with the differences, accepting them as inevitable and thus

25 See Griffith, *The Sino-Soviet Rift*, pp. 104–142, for a detailed review of the
period between March and June 1963.

26 Griffith, *Sino-Soviet Relations, 1964–1965*, p. 12.

perforce tolerable in the short run, but reconcilable over a longer perspective. Precipitous action in the heat of the moment leading to a break on both party and state levels would sharply reduce and perhaps destroy forever the prospects for Communist unity in the fight against imperialism.

The Chinese, for their part, reversing their field just as the Soviets had done, now evidently also wished to avoid a formal and definitive split. With the tide of events for the moment flowing their way, they intended to continue disrupting the unity of the movement from within. By such a tactic they could hope not only to win and consolidate the allegiance of their natural allies, the radically minded parties in the underdeveloped countries, but also to profit from the cautious, middle-of-the-road attitude of parties which, for one or another motive of their own, were opposed to a definitive split.

Even though it was one of the prime Chinese targets, the Italian party fell into this latter category. The Italians, who had obligingly followed the Soviet lead as long as the emphasis remained on bilateral talks, suspension of polemics, and other proposals intended to lower the temperature of the dispute, were reluctant to endorse the tougher Soviet stand that emerged during and after the summer of 1963. In particular, as we shall shortly review in some detail, the PCI declined to support Soviet efforts to convene a new international Communist conference, which under the circumstances could only have led to a decisive rupture in the movement. Italian resistance to this move represented something more than a disagreement over Soviet techniques for handling the dispute. It reflected a more pervasive loss of confidence in Soviet foreign and domestic policy, and a growing willingness to articulate differences of view. The Italian attitude toward certain aspects of Soviet "socialist democracy" serves as a useful case in point.

Socialist Democracy and Soviet Cultural Policy

Ever since 1956 the Italian party had been asserting the need for a deeper analysis of the causes and consequences of Stalinism and a more vigorous effort to overcome its continuing effects on Soviet life. Two developments in 1963 had the effect of bringing the issue once more into prominence: the increasingly open Sino-Soviet breach, and the CPSU's campaigns against certain Soviet artists and writers and against what were called "religious survivals."

It was the Chinese, in their letter of June 14, who introduced the issue into the dispute by charging that the Soviet battle against the "cult of the individual" was no less than an "erroneous and harmful" violation of Lenin's teachings about the role of the leader in a proletarian party.[27] The Soviets, no doubt pleased at the chance to brand the Chinese as Stalinists, retorted that they had succeeded through these efforts in wholly overcoming "the atmosphere of fear, suspicion and uncertainty" and in thereby liberating the Soviet people for rapid progress along the road toward communism.[28]

The Italians found the Chinese position intolerable, implying as it did a renunciation of the sacred principles adopted at the Twentieth Congress. But neither was the Russian attitude entirely satisfactory, for it asssumed that far greater progress had been made than the Italians believed to be the case, implying that the battle against Stalinism was over. If the issue were to be reopened, the PCI maintained, it could only be so as to improve upon "the sometimes inadequate analyses" hitherto made of such issues, and in particular to shed more light on such vague formulas as the "personality cult," which could not adequately explain the complex reality of the Stalin era nor give new impetus to the search for new forms of socialist democracy.[29] Each of the PCI's major statements on international Communist affairs after this time called pointedly in one way or another for "the overcoming and total liquidation of those illegitimate restrictions and violations of democratic principles and of socialist legality that have for too long a time tarnished the socialist ideal and injured economic construction and democratic growth, both in the Soviet Union and in other socialist countries."[30]

The PCI suggested, moreover, that the Soviet Union bore the responsibility to itself and to the entire movement of going beyond a mere repudiation of the past and a restoration of legality. It must lead the way in a creative search for new forms of socialist democracy that might ensure "the most secure and direct participation of the workers and the masses in the leadership of economic, social, and cultural life": the old socialist aspiration toward "the complete liberation of man" had to be given fresh and vital content.[31] As had been the case in 1961, the most insistent voices on this subject

[27] "A Proposal Concerning the General Line of the International Communist Movement," *People's Daily*, June 17, 1963; translation in Griffith, *The Sino-Soviet Rift*, pp. 259–288, at p. 280.

[28] "Open Letter from the CPSU Central Committee to Party Organisations and All Communists of the Soviet Union," *Pravda*, July 14, 1963; translation in Griffith, *The Sino-Soviet Rift*, pp. 289–325, at pp. 307–311.

[29] "Necessità della discussione," *Rinascita*, July 20, 1963, p. 2.

[30] "Per una nuova avanzata e per l'unità del movimento comunista internazionale," Documento del Comitato centrale, *L'Unità*, October 26, 1963, pp. 3–5, at p. 5.

[31] "Problemi del dibattito tra i partiti comunisti," *Critica marxista*, I, 4 (July–August 1963), pp. 15–16.

tended to be those of the young Communists, generally oriented toward the party's left wing. The Secretary of the Italian Communist Youth Federation, Achille Occhetto, was thus often more outspoken than his older colleagues in the party about the need to "see beyond the negative mythology of the personality cult" in order to discover "what has failed to function in the social and political organization and in the democratic life of the Soviet Union, what has impeded the development of active forms of socialist democracy in which the masses could take their part in the control and direction of the entire economic and social organism."[32]

Even Palmiro Togliatti was becoming more outspoken. In his Yalta memorandum he explained to the Soviet leaders how it was that their domestic style and policies created problems for the Communist parties in the West. He stressed the difficulty of explaining the contradictions and setbacks that even socialist countries were bound to face, but which they always preferred to hide: "the worst thing is to give the impression that everything is always going well, while we then suddenly find ourselves faced with the necessity of talking about and explaining difficult situations." Reports of economic and political successes in the Communist countries, he noted, tended to be received with "a certain dose of skepticism" in the West. He made what a Soviet party boss would regard as the radical suggestion that occasional open debates on current problems in which the leaders themselves took part might help clarify the situation for people in the West and "contribute to a growth in the authority and prestige of the socialist regime itself." He saw the chief need, however, as that of overcoming "the regime of restrictions and suppressions of democratic and personal liberties introduced by Stalin."

The general impression is of a slowness and resistance in returning to the Leninist norms that ensured, within the party and outside it, a wide freedom of expression and debate, in the field of culture and art and in the political field as well. This slowness and resistance are difficult for us to explain, especially considering present circumstances when capitalist encirclement no longer exists and economic construction has had tremendous successes. We always start from the idea that socialism is the regime in which there is the fullest freedom for the workers and that they genuinely participate, in an organized manner, in management of the entire social life. We therefore salute all positions of principle and all facts showing us that such is true in all the socialist countries, and not only in the Soviet Union. However, facts that sometimes show us the contrary do damage to the entire movement.[33]

[32] "For a New Unity in the International Communist Movement," *Nuova generazione*, November 3, 1963, pp. 3–6; translation in *Joint Publications Research Service*, No. 22,440, December 24, 1963, pp. 5–6.

[33] "Promemoria," *Rinascita*, September 5, 1964, p. 4.

For reasons that are not hard to fathom, Italian criticism focused most sharply on Soviet cultural policy. This was not only a realm in which the tensions between liberal and conservative forces in Soviet society were particularly strong and particularly evident to the outside world. It was also a realm in which Italian Communists had unusually important interests to defend. Many Italians from the worlds of literature, the arts, and the cinema had been attracted to the PCI both because it was the prime symbol of opposition to the existing social order and because it took creative intellectuals seriously, catering to their tastes and interests in its various journals and often using their prestige in its political appeals. The PCI has probably been unique among Communist parties in the extent to which it has carefully cultivated a highbrow image as a defender of creative freedom and progressive trends in literature and the arts.[34]

Cultural questions were regarded by the PCI as falling within the range of its proper concern, for the instruments of culture were admirably fitted to reveal the disintegration of the bourgeois ethical system and to promote the values of socialism. This mission could not be achieved, however, as long as one held to "a rigidly authoritarian and pedagogical conception of a party that thinks and decides for the entire social body."[35] A Communist party's function, so the Tenth Congress Theses solemnly proclaimed, was not "to propose solutions for problems of scientific and artistic research or to rule on the scientific or artistic validity of this or that solution."[36] Such bureaucratic intervention could only serve to stifle the experimentation and clash of opposing views necessary not just for cultural progress itself but for the effective use of art and literature as instruments of social change. Precisely because culture had been viewed by the Soviet authorities largely in terms of propaganda, the PCI maintained, the USSR had produced not only poor art but poor propaganda as well.[37]

[34] An interesting discussion of this point is to be found in the forthcoming study, *Political Participation in Italy*, conducted at the Carlo Cattaneo Research Institute, Bologna. See also Italo Martinazzi, "Crisi della cultura del disgelo," *Il Mulino*, XII, 7 (July 1963), pp. 645–658, which refers at p. 657 to the "Communist cultural hegemony" in Italy.

[35] Rossana Rossanda, "Il dibattito culturale in URSS e la funzione del partito," *Rinascita*, March 23, 1963, p. 25.

[36] "Tesi approvate dal X Congresso," *X Congresso*, p. 725.

[37] See Rossana Rossanda, *Rinascita*, March 23, 1963, pp. 25–26, and Alessandro Natta, "Cultura e ideologia," *Critica marxista*, I, 2 (March–April 1963), pp. 96–101, for characteristic expressions of this view. Giuseppe Boffa, "Il 'lavoro ideologico,'" *Rinascita*, June 1, 1963, p. 8, gives an unusually forthright criticism of Soviet ideological efforts; of the Soviet press he writes that "since their orientation remains primarily propagandistic, they sacrifice information, ignore the problems raised by their readers, and are therefore less effective precisely for propaganda purposes."

The glaring contradictions between the PCI's relatively tolerant and progressive stance and the traditional Soviet concepts of rigid party control over the arts became manifest whenever the turn of the wheel led to a renewed effort by the Soviet authorities to maintain control over its increasingly emancipated literary and artistic community. When the Pasternak case shocked the Western world, for example, Togliatti did not hesitate to affirm that he regarded censorship of *Dr. Zhivago* to have been a mistake.[38] That episode was trivial, however, compared to the storm that blew up during the early months of 1963, just as the PCI was deeply engaged in a national election campaign that rendered it more than usually vulnerable to attack.

In December 1962, at a particularly delicate moment in its domestic and international affairs, the Soviet Union had suddenly reversed what had appeared to be the prevailing liberal trend in its handling of the intellectuals and artists and launched an all-out campaign against certain leading representatives of the cultural avant-garde. Beginning with abstract painting and sculpture, the authorities quickly took the writers, especially the younger Western-oriented ones, as their main target. The particular crudeness and venom of the attack by the cultural bureaucrats and their allies among the intellectuals, as well as its obvious political implications, assured it of prominent attention in the Western press. The PCI's opponents in the forthcoming election seemed to have been handed a thoroughly exploitable issue.

It was, however, an issue the PCI could turn to its own advantage. Italian Communist sympathies definitely lay with the hard-pressed artists and writers in the USSR and nothing was to be gained by concealing the fact. Open expressions of dissent from Soviet views and actions were no longer so rare as to be a source of scandal likely to weaken the party at the polls. On the contrary, an episode that would have occasioned the party acute discomfort in past years now provided an opportunity to demonstrate not only the party's sincere dedication to intellectual and artistic freedom but also its independence of Soviet control. Such a manifestation of autonomy was useful, moreover, as a signal to the Russian leaders themselves that Italian responsiveness to Moscow's lead was not unconditional, that Soviet authority in any given instance would henceforth depend on the substance of the positions assumed. By its partisan reporting of the controversy and by the personal participation of Communist literary and film figures at certain stages

38 *L'Unità*, April 12, 1962.

of the debate, the PCI gave tangible evidence of its intention to do what it could to influence the outcome.

To a greater extent than any other area of Soviet life, the cultural field was in fact subject to outside intervention. For once, therefore, the PCI was in a position to take an active though marginal part in the controversy, to do more than merely reiterate sterile expressions of concern over the course of events. The Soviet leaders were caught in a dilemma of their own making. They wished to insulate Soviet intellectuals from Western ideas and artistic styles, and yet they also wished to practice cultural diplomacy as an instrument of a peaceful coexistence policy, sending selected individuals as cultural ambassadors to the West and receiving delegations of "progressive" intellectuals in return. The possibility of infection from foreign diseases was a risk that had to be run. Viktor Nekrasov, for example, whose travel diary on Italy and the United States became one of the first targets of official criticism early in 1963, wrote of the astonishment with which Italian Communists learned that he had never seen a film by Bergman, Antonioni, or Fellini, and that translations of Faulkner and Kafka were not to be had in the USSR.[39]

Italian Communist intellectuals also traveled in delegations to the Soviet Union, where they did not hesitate to make known their unorthodox views. In early April 1963, at what proved to be a critical moment in the culture controversy, a delegation of left-wing Italian film makers headed by Paolo Alatri, Communist historian and Secretary General of the Italy-USSR Association, held a two-day debate in Moscow with a group of their Soviet counterparts. The detailed reports of the exchanges published in *L'Unità* and *Paese sera* show, by their sharpness of tone as well as their content, that the debate was in effect only a continuation of the controversy then raging within the Soviet intellectual world. The Russian participants, with the notable exception of the film director Grigory Chukhrai, expounded the official line. The Italians, with Alatri in the lead, countered with appeals for freedom of expression, for an art not limited to satisfying the average popular taste, for courage in portraying the gray sides of Soviet life.[40]

Three months later an episode occurred that revealed even more acutely the shape of the Soviet dilemma. The international jury

[39] *Rinascita* ran excerpts from Nekrasov's account as published in *Novy Mir* shortly before it was attacked in *Izvestia;* "Dal diario del viaggio in Italia dello scrittore sovietico pubblicato dalla rivista *Novi Mir*," *Rinascita,* January 5, 1963, p. 32.

[40] *L'Unità,* April 14, 1963; *Paese sera,* April 14, 1963.

344 THE INTERNATIONAL MOVEMENT, 1962-1964

choosing the best film at the Third International Film Festival in Moscow found itself deadlocked when the nine members from Communist countries refused to award the prize to Federico Fellini's film *8 1/2,* considered by the six other judges (including an Italian Communist, Sergio Amidei) far and away the superior entry. After a demonstrative walkout of the dissident minority, who knew that at least some of the Communist judges privately agreed with them, the Soviet authorities gave in, and the prize was unanimously awarded to the Fellini film. Soviet officials hastened to make plain that the vote did not constitute an endorsement on their part of a film with such a pessimistic and unhealthy outlook, only a recognition of Fellini's skill as a director. It was, nonetheless, a striking defeat for the Soviets in the cultural battle. As Priscilla Johnson has written of the episode, "What better illustrates [Soviet] vulnerability to pressure from Westerners whose good opinion they covet, especially when those Westerners happen, like the Italian directors at the festival, to be bona fide Communists as well?"[41]

It would be impossible to do more than assess impressionistically the weight that the intervention of Italian and other foreign Communists may have carried in the Soviet cultural battle. One may certainly agree with the conclusion that the resistance of several parties to the wave of reaction in early 1963 "may well have given a strong argument to moderates among the Soviet comrades who wanted it to go no further."[42] The critical condition implied in this assessment was the existence of a delicately balanced political situation in the USSR, within both the intellectual community and the political elite. Under such circumstances, where the party's policy was essentially that of maintaining control by playing off the liberals and the conservatives against each other, outside influences could enter that would otherwise have had little room for maneuver.

The potential influence of a foreign party like the PCI under such conditions is difficult to distinguish from the diffuse pressure exerted by the "progressive" Western European intellectual community as a whole. The Soviet Union, for reasons of cultural pride as well as foreign policy, had good reason to avoid alienating this

41 Priscilla Johnson, *Khrushchev and the Arts: The Politics of Soviet Culture, 1962–1964* (Cambridge, Mass.: The M.I.T. Press, 1965), p. 64. For the critical Italian reaction to the subsequent Soviet attacks on the Fellini film, see Augusto Pancaldi's dispatches from Moscow, *L'Unità,* July 28 and 30, 1963. See Johnson, pp. 62–70, for an excellent documented account of the film festival as well as of the conference between writers of East and West held in Leningrad early in August where cultural diplomacy once again complicated the politics of the Soviet literary controversy.
42 *Ibid.,* p. 45.

group. This Soviet interest, however, confronted as it was by conflicting domestic interests of far higher priority, was not nearly as strong as that of the PCI. The Italian Communists, identifying themselves with the cause of the Western intellectuals whose support they solicited, acted in effect as their most influential spokesmen in Moscow.

The "contradiction" between Soviet domestic and foreign interests in the cultural sphere was manifested in the repeated Soviet assertion that peaceful coexistence among nations could not be taken to imply coexistence among competing ideologies or forms of art.[43] The PCI objected vigorously to this way of putting the matter. To transfer the concept of peaceful coexistence from its legitimate frame of reference to that of art and ideology led to absurd conclusions, maintained Luciano Gruppi, one of the party's leading theoreticians. For one thing, it tended to cast doubt on the very principle of peaceful coexistence among nations, "as though this could mean the end or a relaxation of the political struggle, of the struggle for hegemony among different social and political systems." It only played into the hands of the Chinese to foster such a notion.[44] Furthermore, Gruppi maintained, ideological and artistic differences could only be resolved through open confrontation of ideas: to attempt to settle the issue by administrative measures was to renounce the ideological struggle, to concede that the socialist countries could not compete on even terms with the products of bourgeois culture. Instead of facing the real problem, which was that of "overcoming tastes and mentalities tied to the past," the USSR was tending to close itself off from all that was new under the pretext of defending itself from Western bourgeois pressure in the cultural field.[45]

Soviet diatribes against the "enemies of communism" who were attempting to introduce the idea of peaceful coexistence into the ideological realm were just as applicable to the Italian Communists, with their appeals for complete tolerance and freedom of artistic expression, as to the Soviet writers against whom they were directed. The PCI may have been particularly disturbed at the possibility that the Soviets might attempt to extend their campaign against ideological coexistence into Western Europe itself. This concern

[43] For a typical statement, see the speech by Leonid Ilyichev, *Pravda*, December 22, 1962; translation in Johnson, *Khrushchev and the Arts*, pp. 105–120, especially pp. 113–115.

[44] Luciano Gruppi, "Coesistenza pacifica e lotta ideale," *Rinascita*, June 22, 1963, p. 24.

[45] *Ibid.*

may have partly motivated Cesare Luporini's rebuttal of a French Communist attack on Jean-Paul Sartre as a political and ideological foe of Marxism and the Communist world. Observing that he was answering the French article only because its appearance in the *World Marxist Review* indicated that it was addressed to the whole Communist world, Luporini strongly objected to treating Sartre as an enemy of the working class. Whatever the merit and apparent intent of his ideas, he argued, Sartre must surely be seen, "objectively," as an opponent of the imperialists: one must always keep in mind the "objective class significance that a given position of thought can assume even in contradiction to the political and human ideals of the person expressing it. . . ." While Marxism must not "compromise" with other ideologies, he added, neither can it afford to remain shut up within itself; it must be constantly exposed to other schools of modern thought, from which it may learn how to deal more effectively with the real world.[46]

The PCI's defense of cultural liberty was expressed with respect not only to literature and the arts but to religion as well. The discrepancy between the PCI's attitude toward religion and that of the Soviet party became strikingly evident when Moscow attempted, toward the end of 1963, to reinvigorate its campaign against "religious survivals" in the USSR.

As with broader cultural questions, it was all too easy for the PCI's opponents to accuse it of *tatticismo* pure and simple, of appearing to endorse religious liberty solely for tactical political purposes. To blunt this charge the PCI began to make explicit its rejection of the Soviet approach. Lucio Lombardo Radice, the party's most frequent and most liberal spokesman on religious questions, wrote an article explicitly registering his dissent from the views presented by the Soviet ideologist Ilyichev in his November 1963 report to the Soviet Central Committee's Ideological Commission. Ilyichev's insistence that religion could not help but constitute "a brake on scientific progress and on social progress in general," and that religious morality was "diametrically opposed to the principles of the moral code of the builders of communism" ran directly counter to the PCI's acknowledgment of the value of Christian morality and its affinity with certain socialist principles.

Lombardo Radice dissented from the opinions of those Marxists

---

46 Cesare Luporini, "Sartre e i comunisti," *Critica marxista*, I, 2 (March–April 1963), pp. 102–110. As though to underline its total rejection of the sectarian view, the PCI later published an interview with Sartre precisely on the question of ideological coexistence; "Intervista con Sartre: coesistenza pacifica e confronto tra le idee," *Rinascita*, September 7, 1963, pp. 25–26.

who believed that religion in the modern world was "necessarily an opiate of the people, an instrument of conservative domination or of reactionary counteroffensive," and that recent changes in the Church represented nothing but a tactical and defensive response to the growing influence of socialism among the masses.[47] Traditional Marxist atheistic propaganda, he added, was useless not just in the West, but in the Soviet Union itself: "The fact is that if one wants to confront the problem of the survival or the revival of religion in a socialist society like the Soviet one, it is necessary to examine what elements and motives of alienation persist or may arise in a socialist society."[48] Here again the Italians were advising their Soviet comrades to stop looking to outside influences as the source of their domestic difficulties and to delve more deeply into the limitations of their own society.[49]

The Italian party's reaction to Soviet cultural and religious policies well illustrates the changed quality of relations between the two parties. As late as December 1961, in the crisis that followed the Twenty-Second Congress, Italian Communist criticism of Soviet society had had a strongly emotional quality about it. Latent antagonism to the Soviet way of doing things had erupted openly in the Central Committee and elsewhere only under the stimulus of a fresh evocation of the disasters of the Stalin era, in a context complicated by the increasingly evident disruption of international Communist unity. Because it was still rare and illicit, the Italian criticism had then been regarded within and outside the Communist world as something of a scandal. By 1963, PCI resistance to certain aspects of Soviet life was no longer being expressed in emotion-laden individual declarations or in heavily qualified official pronouncements that seemed determined to avoid upsetting the party militants or unduly irritating the Soviet leaders. Criticism of the Soviet Union had at last been accepted as a matter of policy, as a positive aspect of the party's life rather than a distasteful but occasionally necessary act.

[47] Lucio Lombardo Radice, "Libertà religiosa e via italiana al socialismo," *Rinascita*, July 4, 1963, p. 20.

[48] *Ibid.*, p. 22.

[49] The Lombardo Radice article was only one of many PCI efforts to stimulate a constructive "dialogue" between Communists and Catholics in Italy. See also, for example, "Marxismo contro di me?," *Rinascita*, August 1, 1964, p. 27, in which Lombardo Radice answers critics of his earlier article; Alberto Cecchi, "Compiti storici concreti per comunisti e cattolici," *ibid.*, October 3, 1964, pp. 20–21; and especially Gozzini, *Il dialogo alla prova*, a collection of essays by Catholics and Communists dealing with the points of contact and difference between the two. For an excellent recent review of the efforts of both the French and the Italian parties to deal with this issue, see Kevin Devlin, "The

Criticism was kept within judicious bounds because of the continued necessity to defend the historical significance of the October Revolution and to avoid feeding the fires of anticommunism. But PCI discussions of the USSR now regularly acknowledged, though often only vaguely, the existence of negative aspects and of shortcomings, explaining them in terms of the economically backward and undemocratic society inherited by the Bolsheviks and the extreme pressures of civil war and revolutionary transformation. Of the socialist paradise of former days few traces remained; the stress was now on Soviet striving to achieve the original democratic impulse of Lenin's model of socialist society.[50]

The Soviet Union's special aura of primacy and prestige was largely gone. This intangible but precious asset had been dissipated, bit by bit, by the original attack on Stalin in 1956 and by subsequent failures to move vigorously enough to correct the errors of the past, by domestic and international setbacks, by the bold and subversive attack of the Chinese. The Soviet Union was now officially recognized to be fallible and its policies subject to open criticism by other parties. The principles of equality and mutuality of interest ostensibly governing relations within the Communist world were beginning to acquire real content, and Moscow could no longer expect the automatic allegiance even of closely allied parties unless it assumed a reciprocal obligation to respect their interests.

The Italian Communists did not believe that their advocacy of more liberal Soviet cultural and religious policies represented a narrow or provincial interest, dictated only by their special sensitivity to Italian intellectuals and Catholics. Soviet policy in these regards was seen as only one aspect of a deeper problem, that of overcoming Stalinist methods of leadership. As party Secretary Alessandro Natta put it, the cultural controversy in the USSR arose from "a contradiction between the character and democratic foundations of the new [Soviet] society and a leadership that is to a great extent authoritarian, a situation bound to hinder the development of socialist democracy and to have particularly serious repercussions in the field of ideological and cultural creativity."[51]

Catholic-Communist 'Dialogue,'" *Problems of Communism,* XV, 3 (May–June 1966), pp. 31–38.

50 See Togliatti, "Ancora sulla libertà," *Rinascita,* June 8, 1963, pp. 1–2, for a typical statement along these lines.

51 *Critica marxista,* I, 2, p. 97. See also Alberto Carocci, "Partiticità della cultura," *Rinascita,* April 13, 1963, p. 32, for a similar but more explicit statement.

It was this vision of the problem that led the PCI to connect it with the broader issue of international Communist unity. There was some feeling in the party that the reversal in early 1963 of the previous liberal trend in the arts may have had something to do with the state of affairs within the movement. Rossana Rossanda, head of the party's cultural office, suggested that Khrushchev may have felt a need to demonstrate, to the Russian people and to Communists elsewhere, that the Soviet commitment to coexistence did not, as some appeared to believe, imply "renunciation of ideological and revolutionary rigor."[52] Alberto Carocci put forward the more explicit proposition that "the motives of Khrushchev's speech of March 8 are perhaps to be sought in the need for finding harmony in the debate with China, by making concessions to the Chinese way of viewing Communist policy and ideology."[53] Remarks such as these suggest once more the PCI's concern that the Sino-Soviet dispute might lead the Soviets, whether to appease the Chinese or to demonstrate their revolutionary virility, back along Stalinist paths.

This above all the Italian Communist party was determined to prevent. The party's ambitions went well beyond the short-term credit it knew it might acquire in Italy by adopting a critical attitude to Soviet dogmatism and authoritarianism, in the cultural or any other field. The PCI knew that its long-term prospects for achieving power depended in some measure on the Soviet Union's gradually becoming a more open and democratic society, once more capable of casting a positive image among the workers and intellectuals of Western Europe. By persistently raising the issues of cultural freedom and socialist democracy in its policy statements dealing with the international Communist movement, the PCI was informing the Soviet leaders of part of the price they might have to pay if they wished the full support of their Italian allies.

Questions of International Communist Strategy

More directly relevant to the Sino-Soviet conflict than its views about Soviet domestic policies was the Italian party's attitude toward certain broad issues of international Communist strategy. Fundamentally, the interests of the Russian and Italian parties converged. On most of the central issues of the dispute, the PCI not only backed the Soviets against the Chinese but took up posi-

[52] *Rinascita*, March 23, 1963, p. 25.
[53] *Ibid.*, April 13, 1963, p. 32.

tions somewhat farther to the right, endorsing the allegedly "revisionist" doctrines of the Twentieth Congress more strongly and consistently than the Soviets themselves had done. The Italians were necessarily more deeply committed in words and especially in practice to the possibility of a peaceful, parliamentary road to socialism. They had also committed themselves earlier and more decisively than the Soviets to the absolute necessity of avoiding nuclear war, and they accordingly gave their unhesitating support to the Soviet decision not to supply China with nuclear weapons.[54] One can imagine the Chinese reaction to the PCI's near pacifist declaration, intended especially for Catholic ears, that "the salvation of peace acquires the universal and categorical value of a supreme good."[55] And on the touchstone issue of Stalin, the PCI again found itself on the Soviet side against the Chinese, although always urging the Russians to move farther and faster than they were prepared to go along the trail blazed at the Twentieth Congress.

It would oversimplify the picture, however, to suppose that this basic correspondence between Soviet and Italian positions, as well as the generally reformist tendencies of the PCI's domestic strategy, implied that Italian sympathies were invariably on the side of the Russians. Alongside the basic Italian commitment to the Soviet line there coexisted a distinct but only partially articulated current of dissatisfaction over certain aspects of Soviet international strategy and action. It was, in the PCI's view, "obviously essential to keep the door open for dialogue and discussion" concerning such broad questions as the transformation of the underdeveloped world, the new forms of capitalism, and the increasingly complex relationship among the different revolutionary movements at work in the world. "In these areas," it was said, "the Communist movement frequently lacks adequate experience to formulate generalizations that are valid beyond specific and particular situations."[56] The truth was not to be found, in other words, exclusively on the Soviet side. To propose continued discussion implied that there was something left to discuss, that mutual concessions and compromises might be made that would permit differences to be resolved or contained within a higher unity.

Although it was never expressed unequivocally, the crux of Italian dissatisfaction seemed to be that the Soviet party had too often allowed its international actions and its relations with the

54 Togliatti, "Sull' accordo pel divieto delle esplosioni atomiche," *Rinascita,* August 24, 1963, pp. 1–2.

55 "Per una nuova avanzata," *L'Unità,* October 26, 1963, p. 3.

56 *Rinascita,* July 20, 1963, p. 2.

Communist movement to be guided by the narrow perspectives of the Soviet state. The predominance of Soviet national interests over the larger requirements of the world revolutionary movement had, in the judgment of some in the PCI, led to an insufficiently well-coordinated and vigorous resistance to imperialism.

It was not that the PCI had any sympathy for the Chinese contention that the heart of the contemporary world revolution lay in the struggle for independence of the former colonial countries. Formally at least, the Soviet and Italian parties were entirely agreed that the advancement of the socialist revolution depended on the effective interaction of three distinct revolutionary forces: the system of socialist states, the Communist parties in the capitalist world, and the national liberation movement in the developing countries. But the apparent agreement on this point concealed a significant difference of emphasis. The PCI, feeling that the European parties were being denied their rightful role in the movement, strongly disputed every tendency to assert the primacy of any one of the three revolutionary streams: "Events are demonstrating the inadequacy and error of all the concepts that seek to entrust the defeat of imperialism to any single one of the driving forces of world revolution."[57]

While such statements were aimed above all at the Chinese, many Italian Communists felt that the Soviets as well had fallen into the error of overestimating the value of their own particular contribution to the advance of socialism. In a variety of ways the Soviets had repeatedly affirmed their belief that, in the words of Suslov's February 1964 report, "the prime role in the world revolutionary process belongs to the socialist countries."[58]

There were objections in the Italian party not just to the excessive Soviet emphasis on the role of the socialist countries, but more particularly to the increasingly evident priority being given economic competition over political and military forms of struggle in the battle with imperialism.[59] Rossana Rossanda, a prominent intellectual on the left wing of the party, referred in a speech to the Central Committee to the "general theoretical and strategic inadequacy" of international Communist strategy. She pointed in

57 "Per una nuova avanzata," *L'Unità*, October 26, 1963, p. 4.

58 *Pravda*, April 3, 1964; quoted from *CDSP*, XVI, 13, pp. 5–16, at p. 7. For other typical statements defining the USSR and the "socialist world system" as "the decisive international factor" in assuring the victory of the national liberation movement, see "The Socialist World System and the National Liberation Movement," *World Marxist Review*, VI, 3 (March 1963), pp. 52–73.

59 See Boffa's report of Soviet articles on the subject and their relevance to the Sino-Soviet conflict, *L'Unità*, July 19, 1963.

particular to that part of Suslov's report "according to which the
ability of the USSR to achieve a competitive level with the capitalist
system is posed as a necessary and sufficient condition for the development of revolutionary movements in all countries." This attitude,
she maintained, evades the need for careful analysis of the revolutionary situation in individual countries and reduces international
strategy to the pragmatic fact of "the presence and strength of the
USSR."[60]

Similarly, a lengthy theoretical discussion of the underdeveloped
countries in the weekly journal of the PCI youth organization, also
known for its leftist leanings, complained about the gross theoretical
inadequacies of the Soviet concept of "national democracy" and
maintained that Soviet economic aid to India and other countries
had neither helped promote a radical transformation of society nor
done anything to counter "the absolutely precarious, unstable, and
illusory character of neutralism."[61] Another commentator, while
refuting the Chinese belief that armed struggle was the invariable
recipe for victory, reproached certain Soviet analysts for their
"timid attitude" in avoiding open acknowledgment of the importance of armed insurrection in the postwar period:

> In other quarters there exist worries about the risks that armed struggle
> involves. It seems that peaceful coexistence is being confused with the
> political status quo, that any recourse to armed struggle is accused of being
> adventurism, that efforts are being made to minimize, if not to "excuse,"
> the importance of armed insurrection.[62]

Togliatti's writings and other fully authoritative party pronouncements do not contain equally explicit adverse judgments about
Soviet international strategy. One does find, however, frequent if
muted echoes of comments like the above, leading one to believe
that the party leadership, while generally sympathetic with the
complexity of the problems faced by the Soviet Union, was attempting to present its views on certain matters in such a way as to
establish a bridge between the Soviet and the Chinese positions.
PCI declarations, for example, frequently insisted on the need to
define peaceful coexistence in terms of a struggle:

60 *L'Unità*, April 24, 1964.

61 Michele Figurelli and Franco Petrona, "The Colonial Revolution," *Nuova
generazione*, November 3, 1963, pp. 28–30; translation in *Joint Publications Research Service*, No. 22,440, December 24, 1963. See also a similar analysis objecting to the tendency of Soviet analysts to rate economic over political struggle
in the underdeveloped countries; Lisa Foa, "La *Pravda* e le *Izvestia* sui movi-
menti di liberazione," *Rinascita*, July 27, 1963, pp. 10–11.

62 Asiaticus, "Lotta politica e lotta armata," *Rinascita*, May 25, 1963, p. 14.

Peaceful coexistence is a competitive arrangement. . . . We reject and fight against the do-nothing, lazy diplomatic approach to coexistence formulated in the imperialist camp according to which coexistence amounts to nothing more than an understanding among the great powers for the maintenance of the status quo, for the partition of spheres of influence between the two camps in such a way as to establish a static equilibrium and, in the last analysis, a system of defense and of guarantees for imperialism's present sphere of control.[63]

Also often reiterated was the belief that it would be a grave error "if one entrusted the fate of world revolution . . . solely to the victory of the socialist over the imperialist camp in economic competition." The economic development of the socialist states was naturally of vital importance, "but only a schematic and erroneous evaluation of capitalism and a decisive underestimation of the subjective aspects of the actions of the working-class movement could lead to the belief that a victory of the socialist camp in economic competition would automatically and objectively determine the definitive crisis and collapse of the capitalist system. . . ."[64]

Although the origin of these fallacious views was either unspecified or assigned to the imperialists, their similarity to the earlier cited explicit criticisms of the USSR is apparent. Togliatti himself was not willing publicly to go beyond the general observation that Communist doctrine and practice had not yet adequately resolved the problem of relations with the developing countries: ". . . I believe we must honestly recognize that in this field there exist problems that ought to be examined more thoroughly."[65] Behind such vaguely critical observations there appeared to lie a feeling that the Soviets were somehow lagging in the competition with the Chinese for the allegiance of the underdeveloped world. In his Yalta memorandum Togliatti made the point that the Chinese could be defeated not by "an ideological and propagandistic polemic" but only by achieving "real and important victories" of a tangible sort, citing the nuclear test ban and Khrushchev's recent trip to Egypt as illustrations.

Khrushchev's Egyptian trip had already been hailed by Togliatti in rather extravagant terms as a prime example of an international policy designed to encourage and assist newly liberated democratic states, a model of the sort of "convincing and effective" action that could, better than words, demonstrate the errors of the Chinese

---

[63] "Per una nuova avanzata," *L'Unità,* October 26, 1963, p. 3.

[64] "Problemi del dibattito," *Critica marxista,* I, 4, p. 14.

[65] "Per l'unità del movimento operaio e comunista internazionale" in Togliatti, *Sul movimento operaio internazionale* (Rome: Editori Riuniti, 1964), p. 348. Originally in *L'Unità,* April 24, 1964.

position.[66] His particular enthusiasm for this initiative is revealing, for the Egyptian visit was one of the high points of a gradual shift in Soviet policy toward the countries of the Middle East and Africa. The change was regarded with favor by the PCI leaders, for it corresponded to their own attitude toward the newly independent states.

During 1963 and 1964, in response to the Chinese challenge and to an increasingly anti-Western mood in many of the key underdeveloped nations, the Soviets had begun to adopt a distinctly more positive attitude toward the radical nationalist movements of such countries as Egypt and Algeria.[67] The chief symptoms of the policy shift were a more favorable attitude toward such "revolutionary democrats" as Ben Bella and Nasser and a more confident expression of faith in their ability to lead their countries from the bourgeois democratic to the socialist stage of the national revolution. The Soviet Union appeared to have reached the conclusion that its own immediate strategic interests as well as the longer run prospects for advancing the Communist cause could best be served by cooperating more closely with ruling nationalist movements and eventually infiltrating their ranks, even if this meant disregarding the immediate needs of the local Communist parties, many of which had been persecuted and declared illegal.

This trend entirely suited the PCI. Ever since Togliatti's first vague reference in 1956 to the polycentric nature of the world revolutionary movement it had been evident that the Italian party favored developing as close relationships as possible between the Communist parties and the new national movements of the "third world." This attitude, which the PCI shared with the Yugoslavs, had met conservative resistance from the Soviet, French, and other parties. In the spring of 1964, despite the encouraging trend of Soviet policy, Togliatti was evidently not yet persuaded that "dogmatism" in this regard had been entirely overcome:

It is a great success of our doctrine and a great hope for the future that peoples and governments of newly liberated states are openly proclaiming their desire to build socialist economies and societies. But here also we must fear dogmatism and superficiality. We must learn how to understand

[66] "Krusciov in Egitto," *Rinascita*, May 23, 1964, p. 2.

[67] For a useful series of articles analyzing this shift and giving references to the Soviet literature see *The Mizan Newsletter*, VI, especially Nos. 2, 5, 6, and 8 (February, May, June, and September 1964). Uri Ra'anan, "Moscow and the 'Third World,'" *Problems of Communism*, XIV, 1 (January–February 1965), pp. 22–31, analyzes the dispute over this issue among different factions of the Soviet political and intellectual elite, with particular reference to Khrushchev's visit to the United Arab Republic.

that the advance toward socialism in countries that were colonial until yesterday and remain backward even today will be an original and different thing from what it has been until now.[68]

The major complaint of the PCI, however, concerned not Soviet policy directly, but the marginal role assigned the European Communist parties in the struggle against imperialist oppression and the "serious errors" committed by some of them in their dealings with the developing countries. Many Italian Communists believed, with Togliatti, that the workers' movement in the West "has not accomplished well its proper task in the struggle against colonial oppression and in support of the movement of the oppressed peoples." Expressions of solidarity there had always been, he said, but not enough genuine understanding or effective mutual assistance.[69]

The Italians were particularly disturbed by what they regarded as the gross mishandling by the French and Soviet parties of the Algerian revolution. The French Communists, committed to a satellite Algerian Communist party composed largely of Europeans, had in the Italian view utterly failed to comprehend the potentialities of the Algerian insurrection in 1954, even opposing the use of armed force.[70] The French party's subsequent support of the FLN had been severely inhibited by considerations of domestic and international politics—above all, by the desire not to alienate the nationalist sentiments of those who opposed German rearmament but supported a French Algeria—and by the Soviet diplomatic interest in maintaining friendly relations with de Gaulle. The Italians, unconstrained by these special factors, had developed a special sympathy for the FLN as well as for other nationalist, non-Communist independence movements.

The PCI was convinced that the Communist movement, not only in Algeria but in much of the rest of North Africa and the Middle East as well, had suffered incalculable losses by allowing the revolutionary wave to pass it by. Instead of taking a leading part in the new national and anti-imperial ferment, Communist parties everywhere had found themselves persecuted, outlawed, and devoid of influence. Mario Alicata, referring enthusiastically to the "historic event" of the establishment of the Algerian FLN as a political party, drew this lesson for the Communist movement:

We see included among the Theses of this party an affirmation of the

68 "Per l'unità del movimento" in Togliatti, *Sul movimento*, pp. 348–349.
69 *Ibid.*, p. 348.
70 See François Fejtö, *The French Communist Party and the Crisis of International Communism* (Cambridge, Mass.: The M.I.T. Press, 1967), chaps. 4 and 8, for a discussion of the PCF and the Algerian question.

will to build socialism, but we find at the same time a series of ideological elements that are not reconcilable with Marxism-Leninism. . . . It would be a true disaster if, after having hindered—through obvious errors especially on the part of certain sectors of the European Communist movement—the development of Marxist-Leninist parties in Algeria and other African countries, we were to begin to evaluate the socialist inspiration and revolutionary nature of the new party on the basis of preconceived ideas.[71]

This Italian attitude certainly contained a grain of sympathy for the Chinese reproaches to Khrushchev for delaying to the last moment recognition of the Algerian Provisional Government, and to Thorez for his servile acquiescence to Soviet needs and his chauvinist and neocolonialist attitudes toward national liberation movements in the former French colonies. As far as the Italians were concerned, however, the point was not to boost the priority of national liberation movements themselves but to insist that the European parties' contribution to world revolution was being underrated, both generally and with particular respect to the struggle for independence from imperialism and neocolonialism.

The PCI had been playing on this theme since at least the end of 1961. Enrico Berlinguer, summing up the party debate in the weeks following the Twenty-Second Congress, had stated the official view this way:

This [debate] demonstrates that there exists today, more widely than in the past, the realization that the defeat of imperialism and of capitalism cannot be achieved solely on the basis of the successes that the USSR and the other socialist countries have already attained—and that will become steadily more evident with the development of socialist construction—nor on the sole basis of the victories of the liberation movement of the peoples. These factors are of decisive importance, but imperialism and capitalism cannot be vanquished without the intervention of an equally decisive third factor: the struggle of the working class of the West, the advance of a democratic and revolutionary movement which strikes imperialism and capitalism in the heart, in the vital centers of its force and its power.[72]

From that time on, the Italian party had been increasingly insistent about the need to establish collaborative relationships between the Communist parties of the capitalist countries and progressive forces in the developing countries. These relations, Togliatti stressed, "must be created not only with the Communist parties of these countries, but with all the forces struggling for independence and against imperialism and also, insofar as possible,

71 L'Unità, April 24, 1964.
72 Ibid., December 21, 1961.

with governmental circles of newly liberated countries having progressive governments."[73]

The PCI had already begun to engage in vigorous diplomatic efforts to this end. During January 1964, in addition to Togliatti's trip to Belgrade where this issue was discussed, high-ranking PCI representatives visited Algeria and Cuba, two of the developing countries of greatest current importance to the Communist world. Upon his return from Algeria Luigi Longo made much of the FLN's commitment to develop a socialist society and proclaimed that the PCI and the FLN felt themselves to belong to "a single movement conducting a single struggle for liberty, for social progress, against colonialism and neocolonialism." He was pleased to second Ben Bella's remark that the PCI's visit "opened a new page in the relations between the Algerian revolution and the workers' movement of Italy and of all Western Europe."[74] Pietro Ingrao took much the same line regarding Cuba, in this case contrasting the solid help given by the socialist countries with the "gaps, limits, and errors" in the Western parties' relations with the liberation movements. He stressed that the recent travels of the PCI leadership should not be thought of as "casual" but rather as reflecting a firm policy orientation.[75]

The PCI's attitude toward the national liberation movement is perhaps best seen as one more dimension of the increasing assertiveness we have observed in other contexts. The ideological and political battle between the Russians and the Chinese for hegemony over the revolutionary upheavals of the underdeveloped countries was disturbing to the PCI not only because it threatened the unity of the Communist movement but because it betokened a decline in the relative influence of the Western parties. The leaders of the PCI could hardly have imagined that the Communist parties of Europe, weak and ineffectual as most of them were, could actually come to play what anyone might be willing to regard as an "equally decisive" role in Communist world strategy. By no conceivable reckoning could Western Europe of the 1960's be considered ripe for revolution. It was, all the same, indisputably a strong point of world imperialism, a center of big monopoly capital and of Western military might. The PCI could legitimately argue that the Communist parties of the West could play a vital auxiliary role by

---

[73] "Promemoria," *Rinascita*, September 5, 1964, p. 4.

[74] *L'Unità*, January 15, 1964.

[75] *Ibid.*, January 22, 1964. The PCI's diplomatic activities were continued in 1965 after Togliatti's death, with Gian Carlo Pajetta leading missions to Cairo and Hanoi, and Mario Alicata heading a delegation to Cuba.

attacking imperialism at the roots. We must make clear, said Togliatti, "the very intimate and real link between the way in which big monopoly capital works to dominate the more advanced countries and the way it works to maintain its own dominion, in forms old or new, over the entire world."[76]

The PCI's recipe for enhancing the effectiveness of the European Communist parties was, in general terms, clear enough. Insofar as possible, they should adopt the main attributes of the Italian road to socialism, becoming better integrated parts of their own societies and thus ultimately able to exert greater influence over them, through alliances with other parties and participation in economic planning and other activities on a national scale. But beyond this, European communism needed to develop a common, coordinated line of attack against the monopolies, which themselves had already gone some way toward pooling their resources in pursuit of a common strategy. The CGIL's policy toward the Common Market was one reflection of this need. Another was Togliatti's proposal that the European parties organize an international conference with wide representation from the progressive movements of the developing countries in order to work out concrete forms of assistance and cooperation.[77]

Both the Common Market question and the problem of relations with the developing countries seemed to the PCI to provide issues on which the European left, Socialist and Communist alike, might find grounds for united action. And if they succeeded in so doing, this would not only contribute to the over-all strength of world communism but would boost the prestige of the European sector of the Communist movement as well. As the Italian party declared in its statement of October 1963: "At the heart of our participation in the debate among the Communist parties and of every move we make on the international plane, we shall place the great idea of the role that the working class of Western Europe can and must play within the great world strategic plan in the struggle for peace, democracy, and socialism."[78]

The Saga of the International Conference

To meet or not to meet? For the Communist world in 1963 and 1964 that was indeed the question; and each party's answer revealed better than any other single indicator its entire attitude toward the

[76] "L'unità e il dibattito," *Rinascita*, August 3, 1964, p. 3.
[77] "Promemoria," *ibid.*, September 5, 1964, p. 2.
[78] "Per una nuova avanzata," *L'Unità*, October 26, 1963, p. 5.

Sino-Soviet split. When the idea of a new international meeting of all the parties had first been broached, late in 1962, it had been accepted by the Chinese and opposed by the Russians, who then favored bilateral Sino-Soviet talks. By September 1963 these positions had been reversed. The Soviets now began to promote the convocation of an all-party meeting at which they believed the Chinese would be decisively outvoted and thus forced into silence or open defiance of the majority; the Chinese, profiting from the state of instability and uncertainty in the movement, were attempting to delay the Soviet drive for a showdown.[79]

The Soviet campaign became visible in September and October 1963 with *Pravda*'s republication of resolutions by various pro-Soviet parties calling for convocation of an all-party international conference. It was evident from the language of the resolutions that the conference question was already a controversial one. The particularly outspoken Paraguayan statement included a rebuke to "certain honest comrades" who declined to take a stand in the ideological struggle against the splitters and who believed it possible, in the name of unity, to play the role of judge or mediator in the conflict. "There can be no justification," the resolution read, "for any vacillation or hesitation in the principled struggle, any 'neutralist' position or any position of passive contemplation."[80]

Among those "honest comrades," Togliatti and his associates were in the front rank. Almost two months earlier, at the beginning of August, Togliatti had gone on record with the view that "it is neither feasible nor desirable to call a great international conclave to consider all the issues facing our movement today in all the countries in the world and to provide an adequate solution for all of them. This form of unity received from on high is no longer suited to present circumstances."[81] Although expressly qualified as "only my personal opinion" so as to leave room for a graceful retreat, Togliatti's statement was clearly intended to be an authoritative indication of the PCI's answer to a Soviet campaign evidently launched well before signs of it had appeared in the press. The entire article, moreover, exemplified the attitude the Paraguayan resolution would later deplore: it stressed that unity of the movement was "indispensable," that debate could be harmful unless it

[79] For a detailed account of the maneuvering on this issue, see Griffith, *The Sino-Soviet Rift*, pp. 207–223, for the period up to November 1963, and *Sino-Soviet Relations, 1964–1965*, pp. 11–48, for the period up to September 1964.

[80] *Pravda*, September 30, 1963; see Griffith, *The Sino-Soviet Rift*, p. 213, for translation of the key passages.

[81] *Rinascita*, August 3, 1961, p. 3.

strengthened mutual understanding, that some of the issues raised by the Chinese "unquestionably require further attention." From Moscow's vantage point this sort of talk would understandably look all too much like "vacillation or hesitation in the principled struggle."

September and October saw an intense and only partially visible sequence of maneuvers on the conference question, with the USSR refraining from committing its own prestige irrevocably to the idea in the face of resistance by the Italian and other parties. Contradictory signs in the Soviet press revealed the delicacy and uncertainty of the situation, but by early November the signals all began to point in the same direction: the Soviet party had decided that it would not, at least for the time being, insist on its plan for a conference. Opposition to the scheme by the Italian and other pro-Soviet parties was certainly a major factor, and probably the decisive one, in halting the Soviet initiative. Toward the end of October, at about the moment when the Soviet decision appears to have been made, the PCI Central Committee issued a formal position paper on international Communist affairs. After noting that the party had no objection in principle to international meetings, provided they could be properly prepared so as to permit real discussion of important issues, the statement went on to confirm Togliatti's earlier "personal" view:

> Our party feels called upon to express its reservations about the advisability of calling another international conference of the Communist and workers' parties. . . . Such a conference might well, if it were summoned today, find itself confronted with a choice between two solutions equally prejudicial to the Communist movement: either a heightening of the present differences, with a possible split, or a completely formal and unsatisfactory compromise. It would almost certainly prove impossible to confront in an objective fashion the new problems of analysis and elaboration that are before us today and to achieve even a partial but effective step toward closer political and ideological unity for our movement.[82]

82 "Per una nuova avanzata," *L'Unità*, October 26, 1963, p. 5. It is uncertain how the timing of this statement related to that of the Soviet decision to cease pushing for a conference. The PCI statement may have been intended to bring pressure to bear on the Soviet leadership at a moment of uncertainty. It seems more likely that by October 26 the Soviet decision had already been made. The previous day Khrushchev had delivered a speech (*Pravda*, October 27, 1963) noticeably more moderate in tone toward the Chinese than the tough party statements issued during the preceding weeks; this appears to have been the first sign of a tactical retreat. If so, the PCI may have published its statement only after learning of the Soviet decision. As long as the USSR could be privately induced to refrain from what the Italians regarded as rash steps certain to worsen the dispute, the PCI would have preferred not to make public its differences with the Soviet party.

Shortly after the Soviet tactical retreat on the conference issue, there appeared in *Pravda* an esoteric expression of irritation at the PCI's position in the form of an article by O. V. Kuusinen, member of the Presidium and Secretariat and an old-time Comintern official.[83] Primarily an attack on Chinese positions, the article went out of its way to report an episode in 1921 when the German, Austrian, and Italian delegations attempted to "correct" the Theses prepared for the Third Comintern Congress. Singled out for special mention was Umberto Terracini, in 1921 as in 1963 a leading figure in the Italian party. The burden of the changes proposed by Terracini and the others was to exclude from the Theses everything sharply criticizing the "impatient and politically immature" leftist elements in the movement. Lenin, reported Kuusinen, reacted impatiently to this call for moderation, saying that "if the Congress does not decisively condemn these mistakes and such leftist stupidities, then the whole movement will be condemned to destruction." Comrade Terracini, confronted by this valid Leninist criticism, thereupon realized the error of attempting to shield the unprincipled, antiparty, anti-Soviet splitters and ceased his opposition. The moral for Comrade Togliatti-Terracini, more than forty years later, was plain. One only wonders whether the PCI leadership reacted with indignation or amusement to this anachronistic attempt to recall the discipline and spirit of those long-gone Comintern days.

During the fall of 1963 and on into 1964 the PCI undertook an extensive diplomatic campaign to explain its position to other Communist parties. In July 1963 Gian Carlo Pajetta visited Hungary, Yugoslavia, Bulgaria, and Rumania for talks with party leaders. At the end of September an Italian delegation went to Holland; in October Polish and Cypriote delegations were in Rome and a PCI delegation traveled to Israel; in November a meeting was held in Stockholm with the leaders of the Swedish party.[84] In January Pietro Ingrao was sent to Havana,[85] and Palmiro Togliatti, for the first time since June 1956, met with Marshal Tito for a week of talks in Belgrade.

Of these meetings, the last was far and away the most important.

[83] O. Kuusinen, "How Lenin Cured in the Comintern the Infantile Disease of Left-Wing Communism," *Pravda*, November 7, 1963. I am indebted to a Radio Free Europe analysis that brought Kuusinen's article to my attention; R. C. [Richard Cook], "Esoteric Attack on Togliatti?," November 6, 1963.

[84] See *L'Unità*, October 2, 24, 30, November 1, and December 10, 1963, for the joint declarations with the Dutch, Cypriote, Israeli, Polish, and Swedish parties, in that order.

[85] *Ibid.*, January 22, 1964.

The Yugoslavs had up to this time remained publicly uncommitted on the conference issue, apparently caught between a desire for a complete rupture with the Chinese so as to ensure against a possible Soviet capitulation, and an opposite concern that the Russians might attempt to use a split to reinvoke strict discipline on its allies in the movement.[86] The text of the long communiqué on the meeting revealed a close understanding on international matters but did not refer specifically to the touchy conference question.[87] In a meeting with the press, however, Togliatti had referred to the PCI's "reservations" about the conference and stated that these were shared by the Yugoslavs.[88] Since the Poles and the Rumanians as well, although for different reasons and in different degrees, were also resisting a conference of "excommunication," the Italians were not alone in their opposition to the Soviet plan.[89]

The Soviet decision not to press for an early international meeting was followed by several ostensibly conciliatory moves, both public and private, including a letter from Khrushchev to Mao at the end of November calling for an end to polemics and an improvement of relations for the sake of the movement as a whole. The call for an all-party conference was repeated, but with the "Italian" qualification that it should lead to "genuine unity and solidarity" rather than a split.[90] The Soviets were evidently seeking once more to demonstrate their moderation to those parties opposed to a split. When the Chinese responded to these gestures with renewed factional activities and open polemics, the Soviets early in February sent a letter to all but the pro-Chinese parties announcing that the time had arrived when it was imperative to take action against the splitters. Suslov's report to the Central Committee two days later condemned the Chinese in the strongest fashion yet, proclaiming them to be "the chief danger to the world Communist movement" and calling for a meeting of the parties that, given the context, could only have been intended to read the Chinese out of the movement. The report remained unpublished for some time, primarily in deference to a last-minute Rumanian mediation attempt, but when the Chinese attitude remained wholly unyielding, the text of the report was, on April 3, finally made public.

86 See the exchange of views on this score between Leopold Labedz, William Griffith, and others in Leopold Labedz and G. R. Urban, eds., *The Sino-Soviet Conflict: Eleven Radio Discussions* (London: Bodley Head, 1964), pp. 54–55 and 132–133.

87 *L'Unità*, January 23, 1964.

88 *Ibid.*, January 22, 1964.

89 Stehle in Griffith, *Communism in Europe*, Vol. 1, pp. 155–156, discusses the Polish attitude toward the conference question.

90 Griffith, *Sino-Soviet Relations, 1964–1965*, p. 15.

The showdown was at hand. Confronted now with a direct contradiction between its own consistent opposition to an international meeting and the Soviet determination to force the issue by convening one, the PCI did not equivocate. Within a few days, in response to questions raised "in various quarters," Longo reaffirmed the party's reservations about the conference.[91] Togliatti's first public response to the crisis, an article implicitly critical of the Soviets as well as the Chinese, revealed his determination not to retreat. Addressing himself in *Rinascita*'s lead article to "A Challenge We Accept," he defined that challenge not as a matter of defeating the Chinese, but rather of setting the whole Communist movement solidly on the course launched at the Twentieth Congress. Only by revising doctrine and action to suit the conditions of modern times, he insisted, could the movement achieve the political successes in the struggle against imperialism that alone could succeed in restoring unity, by proving which side was right. Unity would not result from joint resolutions or from "repeating the rosary of quotations": history has shown that "in the great clash of opposing factions in the workers' movement, the decisive factor has always been success in action."[92]

On April 22 Togliatti went before the Central Committee to offer the fullest explanation yet of his views. On the conference question, crucial because the entire manner of dealing with the Chinese was at stake, Togliatti repeated his opposition to any gathering that might end by excommunicating the Chinese. The Yugoslav experience, he insisted, had proven decisively that reasoned discussion of differences, not excommunication, was the only possible path to unity. And had not Khrushchev himself, at the East German party Congress, declared it unthinkable to read any socialist party out of the movement? "The technique of the solemn excommunication," Togliatti argued, leads back to the errors of Stalin's time in that it "contains the danger of a resurgence of authoritarian and sectarian systems in the leadership of individual parties." It also threatens the effectiveness, even the very existence, of the international mass organizations, which can only survive if they permit "the coexistence of opposed currents of opinion." The method of excommunication, he argued finally, would turn the Communist movement inward, forcing it to exhaust its energies "in an organized struggle between these two centers, with little splinter parties of a Chinese stamp that would almost inevitably emerge in every country." The creative search for new strategies would be

91 *L'Unità*, April 8, 1964.
92 "Una sfida che accettiamo," *Rinascita*, April 11, 1964, pp. 1–2.

abandoned and parties on both sides would become encased in "forms of organization and discipline unsuited to present situations and necessities."[93]

Rather than a new international conference, Togliatti urged a series of bilateral and group meetings in which constructive debate could be held. The PCI had in fact already begun to promote the idea of a regional meeting of the West European parties: a recommendation favoring such a conference had been included in the joint declaration of the Italian and Swedish parties.[94] The point was, Togliatti maintained, "to continue to discuss and to work for a correct political line and for unity of the international movement in the present conditions, using methods that, as I have indicated, may give some hope of attenuating the harshness of the polemics, establishing positive contacts, and gradually restoring full unity."[95]

During the ensuing months the PCI held firmly to this position. A three-man delegation headed by Pietro Ingrao was dispatched to Moscow to explain the party's stand, but it was clear from the statements subsequently issued that no progress toward reconciliation had been made.[96] Soon thereafter, as though in reluctant acceptance of the impasse, *Pravda* belatedly printed excerpts from Togliatti's April report to the Central Committee, including the passage disputing the utility of the international conference.[97] At the end of May Togliatti found an oblique but unmistakable way of reaffirming to the Russians his objections to their handling of the dispute. Answering Kuusinen's earlier indirect criticism with an esoteric historical reminder of his own, he published an exchange of letters between himself and Antonio Gramsci in 1926 concerning the factional struggle then raging in the Bolshevik party.[98]

Gramsci's letter, addressed from the PCI Central Committee to that of the Bolshevik party, had been sent for transmittal to Togliatti, then serving as the Italian party's representative to the Comintern. In essence, the letter appealed to the Soviet comrades to recognize the great damage that would be done the movement if the dispute within the Soviet party were permitted to reach the point of an open and irreparable breach. A split in the party, Gramsci maintained, would quickly result in the creation of left and right factions in all the other parties of the International.

93 "Per l'unità del movimento" in Togliatti, *Sul movimento*, pp. 352-355.
94 *L'Unità*, December 10, 1963.
95 "Per l'unità del movimento" in Togliatti, *Sul movimento*, p. 357.
96 *L'Unità*, May 6, 1964.
97 *Pravda*, May 13, 1964.
98 "1926: sulla rottura nel gruppo dirigente del partito Bolscevico," *Rinascita*, May 30, 1964, pp. 17-20.

Moreover, by revealing its inability to place the interests of the international movement as a whole above its own factional struggles, the Soviet party would forfeit its claim to leadership of the International, a claim acknowledged by the Western European masses only to the extent that the Soviet party appeared to be acting as a united force for the advancement of socialism. The Italian party, Gramsci went on, while agreeing with the policy of the Soviet majority and accepting the need to refute the opposition's line, had become greatly concerned about the methods being adopted in the struggle:

> But unity and discipline in this instance cannot be mechanical and coerced. . . . Comrades Zinoviev, Trotsky, and Kamenev have contributed greatly to educating us for revolution, they have several times most energetically and severely corrected us, they have been our teachers. . . . We want to be certain that the majority of the Central Committee of the USSR does not intend to abuse its victory and is disposed to avoid excessive measures. The unity of our brother party in Russia is necessary for the development and triumph of the world's revolutionary forces, and to this necessity every Communist and internationalist should be prepared to make the greatest sacrifices. The costs of an error made by a united party can easily be overcome; the damage done by a split or by a prolonged state of latent rupture can be irreparable and mortal.[99]

The parallel between Gramsci's views in 1926 and Togliatti's in 1964 is obvious. From an internationalist as well as a strictly Italian perspective, each in his time feared the damaging consequences both of a split in the movement and of drastic actions taken against a defeated opposition. The irony is that Togliatti, after consulting with his ally Bukharin, had brusquely rejected Gramsci's arguments, on much the same grounds as the Soviet leaders in the spring of 1964 must have used against Togliatti. The essential point, Togliatti had insisted, was the correctness of the majority view; once this was clear, "the best way to contribute to overcoming the crisis is to endorse this line without reservation." He had chided Gramsci for implying that some of the fault might lie with the majority, an attitude that "cannot help but end in *totally* benefiting the opposition," and for hinting that Stalin might possibly be tempted to abuse his victory.[100]

In 1964 it was hardly necessary for Togliatti to make it explicit that he, not Gramsci, had been wrong about Stalin. Events had shown all too clearly that the enforced unity of the 1920's had been bought at too dear a price. Togliatti could, however, issue a reminder

99 *Ibid.*, p. 19.
100 *Ibid.*, p. 20.

that he had at least been relatively quick to learn his lesson and to recognize the dangers of repression within the Soviet party. Six weeks after publication of his exchange with Gramsci, Togliatti again resorted to history to make a point by publishing the speech he had prepared for the Sixth Comintern Congress in 1928. In an introductory note it is explained that although Stalin had already begun to turn against Bukharin and his rightist policies, Togliatti's speech had expressed "open resistance to extremist left-wing positions," for which reason he was prevented, on pretext of time, from delivering the last part of his prepared remarks.[101] These included a warning, ostensibly pointed to the PCI alone, against "unprincipled factional struggle" resulting in "certain organizational measures" that could lead by a process of internal logic, even against the will of those involved, "to the disruption and atomization of a party's leadership forces."[102] Seeing that Stalin was repudiating the views he shared with Bukharin, Togliatti had perhaps come to appreciate the legitimacy of Gramsci's concern. In 1964, at any rate, when he exhumed these documents from the distant but still relevant past, he appeared to be saying to Moscow that he would not again retreat from the conviction that internecine quarrels should not be resolved by coercive means.

The Soviet leaders were not prepared to abandon their plan for a conference, and at the end of July they formally invited the twenty-six members of the preparatory committee for the 1960 Moscow meeting to a similar planning session, to convene in Moscow the following December. They did reiterate, however, in an obvious effort to meet the objections of the Italians, Rumanians, and others who shared their views, that "the meeting will not be called to condemn anybody, to 'excommunicate' anybody from the Communist movement and the socialist camp, to attach insulting labels, or to throw irresponsible charges."[103] The Italians were not reassured. Enrico Berlinguer explained, several weeks later, why the PCI continued to maintain its "preoccupations and reservations":

There are even those who say that in so doing we are demonstrating a certain lack of faith in the assurances and the intentions of other parties. We reply that our doubts, our worries, derive not only from certain formulations that tend in an opposite direction to the one mentioned, but also from the fact that we believe the logic of events themselves, above and beyond intentions, may push the conference toward a negative result.[104]

101 "Il discorso di Ercoli al VI Congresso dell' Internazionale," *Rinascita*, July 11, 1964, p. 15.
102 *Ibid.*, p. 20.
103 Soviet circular letter, quoted in Griffith, *Sino-Soviet Relations, 1964–1965*, p. 44.
104 *L'Unità*, October 15, 1964.

Shortly after receiving the invitation to the preparatory meeting, Togliatti departed on his previously scheduled trip to the Soviet Union. He summed up in his Yalta memorandum the PCI's objections to the conference, agreeing to send a delegation to a preparatory meeting only for the purpose of propounding the party's already well-known views. By publishing the memorandum and reaffirming its conclusions, the party committed itself virtually beyond recall to opposing the Soviet plan.

It should be added that the PCI's objection to Moscow's handling of the dispute concerned the whole Soviet style of argumentation as much as it did the conference itself. As it had done in 1956 and 1957, the PCI insisted that the traditional methods of Communist discourse would have to change if unity were to be preserved. Differences of view might be inevitable but they need not be irreconcilable. If the parties could learn to refrain from hurling invectives at each other, thereby creating an atmosphere of mutual recrimination, the possibility of reconciliation would always remain open. Equally culpable, in the Italian view, was the habit of arguing from scripture and from general ideological principle rather than applying rational processes of thought. The Italians regularly condemned the Chinese for using such methods, as in this comment by Togliatti:

In dealing with any issue they in fact depart not from an examination of the real circumstances confronting us today, in such large measure new, but from certain schematic affirmations of principle, at least alleged to be such, that they set up like primitive idols outside time and space. They then proceed on the basis of these statements to stir up a mad commotion that is provoking beyond all measure. All semblance to the real state of affairs vanishes, hidden behind a fog of verbiage or willfully distorted and falsified, ending in thundering condemnations or excommunications without appeal, resounding, however, in the void.[105]

Although directed principally against the Chinese, who were assuredly the earliest and gravest offenders of his sense of propriety, Togliatti's remarks were also aimed at the Soviet style of argumentation. While the Soviet polemics never quite managed to achieve the superlative heights of the Chinese taunts and anathemas, they were fully as barren intellectually in their reliance on Communist scripture and fully as determined in their resolve to excommunicate the heretic. The Italians warned against "the serious danger our movement is facing of being pushed onto the terrain chosen by the Chinese comrades . . . and of returning to the epoch in which it was thought possible to solve political and ideological differences . . . by seeking the necessary support for 'excommunicat-

[105] *Rinascita*, April 11, 1964, p. 1.

ing' the party or the state with which one disagrees in order to 'expel' it from the movement or from the family of socialist states, accusing it of objective or subjective 'complicity' with imperialism."[106]

The Italians professed to believe that reasoned discussion and careful research could heal all wounds: "The right way to go about it is to become fully conscious of the totality of the problems within the socialist camp, of their roots and interconnections, and then to work toward eliminating their causes in a farseeing spirit and with short-range, realistic action."[107] The Soviets, and such loyal supporters as the French, were no longer in a mood to take a good, long look at the roots of the dispute. They knew they were in a fight to the finish and were already mobilizing their forces for a showdown, accusing the Chinese of factionalism, of promoting Trotskyite positions, of contradicting the essence of Marxism-Leninism.[108] The stated preference of the Italian party for reasoned discussion over slanderous polemic was one additional indicator of its continued faith in the possibility of compromise, an attitude in itself implying clearly that truth and wisdom did not lie exclusively on the Soviet side.

The Italian "Chinese"

We should not leave the question of the PCI's attitude toward the Sino-Soviet dispute without making some reference to the existence within and outside the party of a small but vocal pro-Chinese minority. Detailed examination of the activities and program of the "Chinese" left is not required, if only because its influence was marginal. It is important, however, to try to measure in a rough way the extent to which the actions and the potential of this radical minority may have influenced the PCI's position toward the Sino-Soviet dispute up to the time of Togliatti's death in 1964.

By mid-1963 it had become clear that the Chinese were energetically encouraging factional activities within the PCI. An Italy-China Friendship Association had been established in Perugia, publishing a pro-Chinese bulletin called *Italia-Cina* and organizing a national convention in Rome reportedly attended by seventy

106 Mario Alicata, *L'Unità*, April 1, 1964.
107 "Per una nuova avanzata," *L'Unità*, October 26, 1963, p. 4.
108 See, for example, "Marxism-Leninism Is the Basis for the Unity of the Communist Movement," *Kommunist*, No. 15 (October 1963), pp. 13–47; report of Waldeck Rochet to the French Central Committee, *L'Humanité*, October 8, 1963.

delegates representing leftist groups from twenty cities.[109] A new publishing house, Edizione Oriente, had been created in Milan by Mario Geymonat, a prominent member of the Communist youth organization, with the primary purpose of publishing documents translated from the Chinese.[110] In early July, party members in Bologna received an anonymous five-page document mailed from Rome (apparently by a Chinese news agency) enjoining them to send telegrams to Moscow backing the Chinese position in the bilateral conference then in progress.[111] Small dissident groups were appearing in other cities as well, polemical literature was being distributed attacking the PCI for its revisionism, and slogans like "Long Live Mao" were appearing on the walls of factories and apartment buildings.[112]

The non-Communist press naturally made the most of every manifestation of pro-Chinese activity. As the Socialist daily observed, "All over Italy news editors' desks are being piled high with reports from every part of the country about pro-Chinese activities within the PCI and about the disciplinary countermeasures taken by party leadership bodies against such goings on."[113] The furor was too great to be ignored, especially during the month of July, and the party found it necessary on more than one occasion to issue an explicit refutation of the rumors of serious dissent within the ranks. It ridiculed, for example, the "absurd campaign" undertaken by certain bourgeois papers to prove the existence of a "rank-and-file revolt" among the young Communists of Milan, quoting with approval the judgment of the left Socialist journal *Mondo nuovo* that the presumption of a "strong Chinese movement" in Milan was wholly unrealistic.[114] Mario Alicata had earlier held a press conference to assure reporters eager for confirmation of cracks in the party's monolithic structure that "the problem of a Chinese wing in the PCI does not exist."[115]

Taken literally, Alicata's remark was justified. The number of outright Chinese sympathizers within the PCI, while difficult to measure precisely, was certainly too small to represent a significant

109 *Times* (London), July 5, 1963; "Commenti del mese: Parri e le due 'Italia-Cina,' " *Corrispondenza socialista*, IV, 4 (April 1963), p. 195.

110 *Avanti!*, July 19, 1963.

111 *Ibid.*, July 6, 1963.

112 *Ibid.*, July 16, 1963.

113 *Ibid.*, July 20, 1963.

114 m.n., "Perchè i giovani sono irrequieti," *Rinascita*, August 10, 1963, p. 2.

115 *L'Unità*, July 18, 1963; see *ibid.*, July 5 and July 20, 1963, for additional refutations of speculations concerning pro-Chinese sentiment among leaders and rank and file.

and cohesive opposition. Open dissenters, whether in the party or the youth federation, could easily be isolated and expelled for violations of party discipline.[116] Expulsion, however, only shifted the locus of the problem. The party could not afford to ignore entirely the potential threat inherent in the possibility that dissidents expelled from its own ranks might merge with other pro-Chinese extremists to create a new party supported and financed by the Chinese Communists. To be sure, the repeated past failures of leftist splinter groups to overcome ideological and personal rivalries and organize an effective political movement gave good reason to presume that the new thrust from the left would again dissolve into ineffectual agitation. The situation had been made qualitatively different, however, by the fact of Chinese intervention, both in Italy and on an international scale.

Since the spring of 1963, when the Chinese had given official recognition to a Brazilian anti-Soviet splinter party, evidence had been mounting of a concerted attempt to establish dissident parties wherever the opportunity presented itself.[117] By the spring of 1964 the main "Chinese" groups in Italy had come together for a conference in Milan under the leadership of the editors of *Nuova unità*, a new monthly review envisioned by its founders as the organizational center of a "truly Marxist-Leninist revolutionary party" that would take over the proud but tainted inheritance of Italian communism.[118] The possibility that this or some other group might one day formally declare itself a rival party, recognized by Peking as the legitimate heir to the Communist mantle, had to be recognized by the PCI's leaders. Such a rival ideological center, however inconsequential it might be on the national political scene, could function as a sounding board for antirevisionist propaganda and a potential pole of attraction for disaffected left-wingers in the PCI.

The prospect of a "Chinese" party belonging to a new Chinese International was thus bound to be a disquieting one, although in the party's domestic propaganda the potential threat from the left was consistently minimized. Togliatti's Yalta memorandum, however, addressed to the Soviet leaders rather than to an Italian audience, referred to this as one argument among others for avoiding a decisive split in the movement. We are concerned, Togliatti de-

---

116 Some of the more prominent cases are discussed in *Avanti!*, July 20, 1963; also *L'Espresso*, July 14, 1963, p. 5, and December 29, 1963, p. 5.

117 For a comprehensive review of these efforts see Kevin Devlin, "Schism and Secession," *Survey*, No. 54 (January 1965), pp. 29–49.

118 See *Nuova unità*, I, 1 (March 1964), and subsequent issues.

clared, that an all-out struggle against the Chinese would lead the Communist parties in the capitalist countries in precisely the wrong direction, away from constructive action with non-Communist forces and toward "internal polemics of a purely ideological nature, far removed from reality."

The danger would become particularly serious if one were to arrive at a declared break within the movement, with the formation of an international Chinese center which would create its "sections" in all countries. All the parties, especially the weaker ones, would be forced to devote a large part of their activity to the polemic and the battle against these so-called "sections" of a new "International." This would cause discouragement among the masses, and the development of our movement would be gravely impaired. It is true that the splitting efforts of the Chinese are already in full swing in almost all countries. One must prevent the quantity of these efforts from becoming qualitative, that is, a true, general, and consolidated split.[119]

The PCI would doubtless have been less concerned on this score had there not been evident in certain party circles what the Socialist newspaper with some exaggeration termed "a general state of unrest and alarm."[120] The existence of a diffuse anxiety over the implications of the Sino-Soviet split, a mood often associated with vaguely radical sentiments, was noted by Gian Carlo Pajetta at the Central Committee meeting in July 1963, where the Sino-Soviet problem received its first serious examination. Insisting that the party debate was "certainly not aiming at the Italian 'Chinese' or the 'Chinese' in Italy, no matter what you may read in the columns of those who have so often been so egregiously wrong about us," Pajetta made the following revealing comment:

Insofar as it lies within our power, we intend to accomplish a careful job of political clarification, aware of the existence of zones of elementary radicalism, of sectarianism, of dogmatic positions, which even result from objective causes. We shall also work to counter every kind of demoralization, every bit of alarmist pessimism that the international polemic may occasion among groups of workers or in certain comrades who do not accept the Chinese positions and maintain that they support the party line.[121]

Togliatti confirmed the existence of sympathy for the Chinese in his Yalta memorandum, referring specifically to the poor Italian peasants "among whom the Chinese revolution had become rather popular as a peasant revolution."[122] Such pro-Chinese sentiments

---

[119] "Promemoria," *Rinascita*, September 5, 1964, p. 4.
[120] *Avanti!*, July 19, 1963.
[121] *L'Unità*, July 27, 1963.
[122] "Promemoria," *Rinascita*, September 5, 1964, p. 4.

obliged the party, he wrote, to make a particular effort to explain and refute the Chinese position.[123]

Emotional pro-Chinese sentiments among the working class, while imposing a need for caution and considerable "political clarification," were probably not seen as the most serious aspect of the problem. Potentially more significant from a political standpoint was the existence in Communist student and intellectual circles of latent and, in some instances, active sympathy for certain aspects of the Chinese line. We have discussed in an earlier chapter the growth in the PCI during 1962 of a small but articulate intellectual left wing, opposed to the party's compliant attitude toward both the Center-Left and the social and economic manifestations of modern monopoly capitalism. These radical and doctrinaire voices were louder than they were numerous or prestigious, and in themselves represented little more than a nuisance to the leadership. Nevertheless, even though the PCI left, as well as its more prominent counterpart in the PSI, repudiated the main lines of Chinese international policy, an indisputable kinship existed between the antirevisionist arguments of the Chinese and those of the Italian radical left. The Chinese challenge thus potentially enhanced the persuasive power and Marxist legitimacy of the PCI's internal opposition.

The party tacitly displayed its concern on this score by publishing in its new theoretical journal *Critica marxista* an exchange between Luigi Longo and one of the PCI left-wing intellectuals, Giorgio Tosi, on the time-worn issue of whether the economic and political power of the monopolies could be eliminated in a capitalist regime.[124] Appearing not long after the Chinese party had issued its second and most comprehensive attack on Italian revisionism,[125] the article was certainly intended as a simultaneous rebuttal of the party's internal and external critics. Tosi, like the Chinese, raised the familiar charge that since monopolies were an inseparable aspect of capitalism in its highest stage of development, it was absurd to suppose one could somehow destroy their power without destroying the roots of the capitalist system itself and instituting a socialist regime. If one took literally the PCI's insistence on the desirability of

123 For further discussion of what is described as the instinctively pro-Chinese orientation of a large part of the PCI rank and file, see Leone Iraci, "I comunisti 'di sinistra' e il PC cinese," *Corrispondenza socialista*, IV, 8–9 (August–September 1963), pp. 445–460.

124 Luigi Longo and Giorgio Tosi, "È possibile in regime capitalistico eliminare il potere economico e politico dei monopoli?," *Critica marxista*, I, 3 (May–June 1963), pp. 89–108.

125 "More on the Differences Between Comrade Togliatti and Us," *Peking Review*, VI, 10–11 (March 15, 1963), pp. 8–58.

promoting a nonmonopolistic capitalism, Tosi argued, one ended not only by violating the essence of Marxist-Leninist thought but by tending "to favor neocapitalism, that is, to integrate ourselves into the system so as to make it function better."[126]

Longo countered with all the standard arguments: we are interested in the concrete reality of today, not in debaters' points supported by the Communist classics of yesteryear; Marxist social and economic tenets must always be understood not as immutable "laws," but in a dialectical fashion as tendencies subject to reversal by the action of the working class. In any case, wrote Longo, Lenin had recognized even in his debate with Kautsky that a gradual and peaceful transition to socialism was entirely conceivable as an exception to the general rule postulating the need to destroy the bourgeois state machinery during the transition to socialism. These arguments were the standard stuff of the PCI's defense against revisionism. What made them interesting was not their intellectual novelty but the fact that the criticism of Tosi was implicitly associated with the PCI's rebuttal of the Chinese attack. Longo made frequent allusion to statements at Chinese party Congresses in 1945 and 1956 in which Mao had articulated the need for original national roads to socialism and spoken of the possibility of a gradual, peaceful transition to power. By invoking Mao as a witness against himself in the context of a rebuttal of the PCI left, Longo seemed to be subtly linking the two. His tactic appeared to be to discredit the domestic opposition by demonstrating its ideological affinity with the more comprehensive charges of the Chinese.

To give exact weight to the internal "Chinese" factor as an element in the PCI's position in the international movement is difficult. The similarity between Chinese criticisms of Italian revisionism and the dissatisfactions of a radical minority within the party itself, among intellectuals and workers alike, certainly reinforced the PCI's resistance to Chinese ideological and organizational efforts in Italy and other capitalist countries. But the party leaders did not at all desire to aggravate the situation inside the party or within the Italian left as a whole. They hoped to keep within their ranks all but the most extreme of the radicals and thus to isolate and minimize the effectiveness of those who chose to rebel. It behooved the party, therefore, to temper its basically pro-Soviet stance with some indications of sympathy for aspects of the Chinese position. Above all, it made sense to resist the Soviet effort for a showdown, for the danger of being outflanked to the left could become poten-

[126] *Critica marxista,* I, 3, p. 89.

tially serious only if a split in the international movement created the necessary preconditions for establishment of a rival Communist party.

Even then, the situation would certainly be more embarrassing than genuinely threatening to the party's position, for a new radical party could not hope to compete effectively with the PCI for popular support. Prudence nevertheless argued convincingly for an effort to minimize the risk by acting to reduce rather than enhance the possibility of a decisive Sino-Soviet split. This consideration thus reinforced others working in that same direction.

CHAPTER ELEVEN

INTERNATIONALISM, ITALIAN STYLE

In the typically dialectical slogan of "unity in diversity and autonomy" the Italian party summed up its belief in the possibility of reconciling the conflicting values it considered essential to the future of the international Communist movement. Despite steadily mounting evidence that neither the Russians nor the Chinese were about to compromise on issues they regarded as vital to their respective national interests, the PCI stubbornly persisted in affirming, in deed as well as word, the imperative need for unity of the movement. It did so not in the name of parochial party interests of its own, but under the flag of proletarian internationalism. From Moscow's vantage point, however, the Italian attitude was a breach of solidarity, a repudiation of the brand of internationalism purveyed for so many years by the Soviets themselves.

The PCI at every opportunity refuted the charge that it had forsaken its internationalist heritage for "an isolationist or neutralist or simply conciliatory line."[1] The PCI's verbal affirmations of loyalty to the principles of Communist internationalism, however, matter less than the special content the Italian party has given its internationalism in the attempt to reconcile the conflicting values and political practices implicit in the concept of unity, on the one hand, and of diversity and autonomy on the other.

Unity in Diversity and Autonomy

UNITÀ IN DIVERSITÀ. The slogan "unity in diversity" was the Italian party's way of emphasizing what it perceived to be the single most salient fact governing international Communist relations. Ever since 1956 the PCI had been asserting that the very success of the world revolutionary movement had imposed the absolute necessity of developing qualitatively different relationships among its component parts. In his *Nuovi argomenti* interview Togliatti had first

[1] Enrico Berlinguer, *L'Unità*, October 15, 1964.

pointed to the historic significance of the transition from an era of socialism in a single country to one in which there existed not only an international system of socialist states but a strong though diffuse movement toward socialism in countries all over the world. This qualitative change called for a corresponding shift in the style and content of relations among socialist parties and movements, in and out of power. Like it or not, Togliatti was suggesting, monolithic unity and the presumption of Soviet hegemony were things of the past. "Polycentrism" was the not entirely felicitous expression he coined to describe the new state of affairs. Revived briefly after the Twenty-Second Congress, the term was soon permanently erased from the PCI's vocabulary: not only had it aroused too great a stir of protest in the Communist world, but it failed to satisfy the PCI's own desire for a formula acknowledging the virtues of unity as well as of regional and national autonomy.

As the Sino-Soviet rift became increasingly open and bitter, threatening to destroy forever the international solidarity so central to the ideological appeal and political effectiveness of the Communist movement, the PCI became ever more strongly convinced that its vision of reality was the only possible correct one. By 1963 at the latest it had become clear that genuine unity could not possibly be restored unless the diversity of interests of the various parties could be acknowledged, tolerated, and somehow contained within a loosely structured framework of Communist state and party relationships. As Richard Lowenthal has put it, "The only way to maintain a modicum of unity within this new pluralistic constellation would have been a common effort to tolerate the inevitable political and doctrinal differences, to develop a looser form of international cooperation based on pragmatic compromise and ideological nonaggression."[2]

For different reasons and in different degrees, both the Soviets and the Chinese came to look upon such a solution as unrealistic and unresponsive to their vital state interests: in consequence they abandoned at least temporarily the very goal of unity. By 1964, as it pressed once again to convene an international meeting of the parties, the Soviet Union was striving to achieve unity *against*, not *with*, the Chinese. But for the Italians, this kind of unity was unacceptable. In Togliatti's unequivocal phrase, "one cannot imagine that China or the Chinese Communists could be excluded from this unity."[3]

2 "The Prospects for Pluralistic Communism" in Drachkovitch, *Marxism in the Modern World*, pp. 227–228.

3 "Promemoria," *Rinascita*, September 5, 1964, p. 2.

In this matter, as in others, the Italians believed themselves to be realists. Diversity of national experiences, stages of development, international interests, had become an undeniable fact of life in the Communist world. Like capitalist economic integration, the "reality" of which had determined the PCI's attitude toward the Common Market, diversity existed and would have to be coped with. It was worse than useless, in the Italian view, to fight rearguard actions against the inevitable, whether it be economic integration, the Center-Left, or divergences among Communist states and parties. Only by flexibly attuning strategy and tactics to new realities, and seeking to capitalize on their "progressive" aspects, could each apparent defeat become the terrain for new and greater victories. The Center-Left, from one perspective a blow because it weakened the Socialist alliance, was better seen as the necessary condition for a new and broader alliance of antimonopoly forces. Similarly, the fact of Communist diversity was most aptly to be regarded as an opportunity to endow the movement with a new, more flexible, and realistic approach to its environment. As Togliatti proclaimed, in a document otherwise marked by its pessimistic appraisal of international affairs:

Very favorable conditions exist for our advance in the working class, among the working masses and in social life in general. But it is necessary to know how to take advantage of, and exploit, these conditions. For this the Communists must have much political courage: they must overcome every form of dogmatism, face and resolve new problems in a new manner, work in ways that suit a continuously and rapidly changing political and social scene.[4]

The Italian party's entire attitude toward the Sino-Soviet dispute was thus strongly tinged by the same official optimism that governed its reaction to domestic affairs. If the PCI was subject to any particularly notable *déformation professionelle,* it lay in what Italians like to refer to as *possibilismo,* the sense that anything is possible, that any difficult situation can be coped with by bending just far enough, but not too far, before the prevailing wind. The instinct exists in politics everywhere, but in the PCI's case it has been accentuated not only by the Leninist tactical heritage but by having lived so long on the margins of power.

Lacking government responsibility at home and leadership responsibility in the international Communist movement, the PCI did not and could not have the same attitude toward events as a party in power. Since the PCI could not often significantly influence

4 *Ibid.*

the course of events, its dominant instinct was to temporize, to adapt, to compromise, but at all costs to stay in the game. Just as the party at home should strive above all to preserve its unity and its strength, so as to fight a future battle on some more favorable terrain, so the movement as a whole should remain united or risk being decisively weakened in the struggle against imperialism.

The PCI's awareness that it was only a lesser cog in the international Communist machine had strongly conditioned its response to the Moscow meetings of 1957 and 1960. Objecting to various aspects of the conclusions reached on these occasions, the party had nonetheless formally accepted them, expressing its dissent only privately or by indirection and contenting itself with defending the principle of each party's right to determine its own domestic policies. By 1963 a new stage had clearly been reached, expressed in a more assertive concept of what party autonomy should entail.

UNITÀ IN AUTONOMIA. If diversity was the great new fact with which the PCI believed the Communist movement had to contend, autonomy was the organizational principle that followed logically from it. The essential meaning of the term was self-evident: "It means, and ought to mean, full respect for the principle of non-interference by any party in the internal affairs of other parties, but allowing for necessary debate and confrontation of opinions."[5]

As a logical corollary to the principle of each party's full and final responsibility for its domestic affairs went the belief that no party ought to be blamed for the actions of others: "[Autonomy] means that every party is responsible before its own people only for its own policy and for the contribution it makes to the general orientation and advance of the whole movement; it cannot regard itself as sharing responsibility for every position or individual act of other parties in whose decisions it took no part and which may in any case conflict with the general principles that inspire our movement."[6] This corollary was important to the PCI as a basis for blunting the anti-Communist attacks directed against it in consequence of the actions of the Soviet Union and other Communist countries. Implied in this refutation of guilt by association, moreover, was the right to criticize the actions of the fraternal parties.

In addition to protecting itself against direct Soviet interference and against the damaging indirect effects of undemocratic or belligerent actions by the socialist states, the PCI needed to insulate itself from the pressures that could be brought to bear by the Com-

5 "Per una nuova avanzata," L'Unità, October 26, 1963, p. 5.
6 Ibid.

munist movement as a whole, whether through international organizations or through meetings and joint declarations of the assembled parties. The Italian party, along with many others, had made it clear that it was no longer prepared to submit to the discipline of accepting the decisions of an international body, even one in which expression of minority opinions was tolerated. As Luciano Gruppi bluntly stated before the Central Committee, "what we cannot accept is the principle of a majority that can oblige the minority to accept its decisions; this principle was valid when there was an international organization, but it can no longer be so today, when it would signify a limitation of the autonomy of the parties."[7]

These related points comprised what might be called the defensive side of the PCI's concept of autonomy, its irreducible minimum content. They had been part of the PCI's platform since 1956, but it had taken several years for them to be given real substance. The core of the party's relations with the Soviet Union between 1956 and 1961 had lain precisely in the struggle to realize these minimum objectives. This was the meaning of the PCI's uncompromising rejection of the idea of reconstituting a centralized international organization and of its more discreet efforts to defend "national roads to socialism" from the encroachments implicit in the "universal laws of socialist construction." This was the meaning, too, of the exasperated outburst following the Twenty-Second Congress, when Soviet institutions were criticized and the "fictitious unanimity" represented by the 1957 and 1960 Moscow meetings was thrown aside in favor of a renewed assertion of polycentrism and autonomy.

But by mid-1964, at the time of Togliatti's death, did not the battle over these issues seem to be resolved? The question of creating a new Communist international organization was no longer on anyone's agenda, nor did the domestic autonomy of the Italian party seem likely to be seriously threatened from the Soviet or any other quarter. The PCI had by that time demonstrated more forcefully than many had thought possible that it knew how to exercise its right to criticize certain aspects of Soviet life and to take up a minority position against the USSR in the international movement and, through the CGIL, in the WFTU as well. Soviet hegemony in the old sense had ended, and the political and psychological development of the PCI had passed the point of no return: one could no longer expect it to acquiesce for the sake of proletarian solidarity in Soviet actions damaging to the party's domestic fortunes and

[7] *L'Unità*, October 15, 1964.

disruptive of its internal stability. But while it may have been evident to the Italian Communists, and to outside observers as well, that the Russians no longer had the power to diminish PCI autonomy by restoring their former control over all or some portion of the international movement, was it all that clear to the Russians themselves? However dim his chances of success, might not Khrushchev take the gamble of trying to reimpose the discipline of old over what was left of a movement from which the Chinese and their allies had been expelled?

To Togliatti and his colleagues the possibility may not have seemed wholly remote. Their opposition to the proposed international conference was motivated not only by an unwillingness to see the Chinese drummed out of the movement but also by their concern lest Khrushchev attempt to use the conference precisely as a means of restoring the norms of the past. It is impossible to speak with assurance about Soviet organizational objectives, but there are some clues that Moscow's maximum goal went well beyond what the PCI could accept. One report quoted East European sources to the effect that the USSR had it in mind to establish "a loose association of world Communist parties to discuss and coordinate joint policies," a sort of consultative "ideological council."[8] With respect to East Europe, at least, Khrushchev himself had already advanced the thought that "it would be expedient to think jointly about those organizational forms that would make it possible to improve the constant exchange of opinions and the co-ordination of foreign policy between the member countries of the Council for Mutual Economic Aid, the participants in the Warsaw Pact."[9] Soviet ambitions to improve the coordination of Communist policies also apparently extended to the nonruling parties, as could be surmised from the contents of the Theses issued in celebration of the hundredth anniversary of the First International.

The Theses constituted an attempt to revive the faded doctrine of proletarian internationalism and to justify in ideological terms the Soviet pressure for an international party conference. The "supreme criterion" of internationalism, it was explained, was no longer defense of the USSR but a party's "attitudes toward the world socialist system and its unity."[10] Although the Communist

8 Theodore Shabad, The New York Times, September 12, 1964.

9 Pravda, April 4, 1964; cited in William E. Griffith, Sino-Soviet Relations, 1964–1965 (Cambridge, Mass.: The M.I.T. Press, 1967), p. 27.

10 Institute of Marxism-Leninism of the CPSU Central Committee, "100th Anniversary of the First International: 1864–1964 (Theses)," Pravda, September 11, 1964; quoted from CDSP, XVI, 37, pp. 3–11, at p. 3.

movement no longer possessed a central leadership, it was nevertheless "unthinkable as an entity without definite organizational principles strengthening the political solidarity of various national units
of the working class which are part of it."[11] The organizational
principles said to govern the activities of the First International,
and to "retain their importance in our time as well," were these:
acceptance of the organization's basic principles; adherence to its
decisions, with the minority subordinated to the will of the majority;
and the banning of factional schismatic activity.[12] The Theses also
once again explicitly confirmed that the statements issued at the
1957 and 1960 Moscow meetings incorporated the decisions and
principles to which all fraternal parties were expected to adhere.

There was, evidently, room for valid concern that the Soviet comrades had not yet reconciled themselves to the fact that a growing
number of parties, most notably the Rumanian in Eastern Europe
and the Italian in the West, were no longer willing automatically
to endorse Soviet decisions and compromise resolutions, even if
these should be supported by a majority of the parties. The touchstone here was the attitude of the various parties toward the 1957
and 1960 statements, of which Gian Carlo Pajetta was shortly to
say: "Our positive estimate of these documents, which we signed,
has not prevented us from seeing their limitations and negative
aspects; we have therefore reached the conclusion that it would be
impossible for us today simply to ratify them, thus preventing the
necessary corrections and additions."[13]

The new Soviet definition of proletarian internationalism, even
though it provided for collective rather than Soviet leadership of
the movement, remained too authoritarian, too little receptive to
the interests and positions of other parties. The PCI continued to
expound the need for international solidarity, but in the name of
principles and practices more protective of its own autonomy than
those put forward by the Soviet party.

During Togliatti's last years, the party was beginning to give a
more positive slant to the concept of autonomy. After 1961, emphasis had begun gradually to shift from autonomy as the right to
independence in domestic affairs, toward autonomy as a party's
active participation in the formulation of an international strategy
reflecting not only its own local interests but its conception of the
general interests of the movement as well. This claim, as we have
noted earlier, was first openly introduced by the CGIL at the

[11] *Ibid.*, p. 10.
[12] *Ibid.*
[13] "La politica del Ventesimo," *Rinascita,* October 24, 1964, p. 2.

WFTU Congress in December 1961: the centralized nature of the WFTU combined with Socialist pressures in the CGIL had brought the issue to a head sooner in that context than in the sphere of party relationships. The steady disintegration of Sino-Soviet relations, the parallel decline of Soviet authority, and the PCI's increasingly open disenchantment with aspects of Soviet domestic and foreign policy soon rendered the issue relevant for the party as well. By the fall of 1963 the party's definition of autonomy could include the following claim to a voice in international Communist strategy:

An integral and essential part of this search for the revolutionary line that every party must map out for itself is an over-all view of the necessities of the revolutionary battle being waged throughout the world against imperialism, an understanding of the need for loyalty to the principles of Marxism and of proletarian internationalism, for solidarity in the struggle with the socialist states, with the workers of every country, and with the oppressed people who are fighting for their liberation. This is and will always be the way in which we conceive of and work to achieve our autonomy.

Understood in this sense there is nothing in the concept of autonomy that could lead to a narrow nationalistic view. On the contrary, autonomy becomes the most effective channel through which each party can make the greatest possible contribution to the elaboration of the common general strategy, to the development of our doctrine, to the progress of our entire movement, and to the building of a sounder and higher unity.[14]

Although a trifle extravagant in their implied claim to a significant role in Communist policy making, such statements were not intended purely for rhetorical effect. The PCI had in fact begun to suggest certain modifications of Soviet international strategy—an expanded regional role for the West European parties, a more consistently positive attitude toward non-Communist radical nationalist movements, a greater tolerance of diversity in the international movement, above all avoidance of a final split with the Chinese. And more important, within the relatively meager limits of its resources the PCI was beginning to act in support of these goals. It was this more active sense of international commitment that most clearly distinguished the PCI's role in the international movement during the last years of Togliatti's life from what it had been in the 1956–1961 period. The groundwork had been laid in the earlier years, but the position had then been essentially a passive one.

More than anything else it was the Chinese challenge, and the Soviet response to it, that had transformed a latent sense of the right to a voice in common strategy into a conscious and active principle of policy. By the spring of 1964, when the PCI's resistance

14 "Per una nuova avanzata," *L'Unità*, October 26, 1963, p. 5.

to the Soviet party on the conference issue had become sharply delineated, the tone of the party leaders' comments concerning international Communist strategy had taken on a new aggressiveness. At the Central Committee meeting in April 1964 Gian Carlo Pajetta expressed the prevailing sentiment when he referred to the party's internationalism as a "refutation of every provincial concept," "an element of our strength," "a conscious awareness of our share in responsibility toward the entire international movement." "The strong points in our position," he added, "are the fact that we are taking part in the struggle and the fact that we are looking not for the road of 'prudence' but of effectiveness. We are not standing at the window looking in. . . ."[15]

International Solidarity or National Communism?

This study has been particularly concerned with conflict, with the increasing divergence between the interests of the Italian and the Soviet parties as a case study in the gradual collapse of international Communist unity. But this perspective, however amply justified by the dominant trend of events, should not be allowed to obscure entirely the other side of the coin. The fact is that for the Italian party at the time of Togliatti's death, solidarity with the international Communist movement was still something that mattered.

The PCI's internationalist perspective led it into a serious difference of opinion with the Soviet party over the preservation of Communist unity. This same internationalism, however, also meant that the PCI's newly asserted autonomy did not necessarily carry with it the implication of breaking solidarity with the Soviet Union. Palmiro Togliatti, sometimes thought of as an archtypical "independent" Communist, certainly believed what he said in 1963:

A workers' and socialist party must always maintain its solidarity with these [socialist] regimes. If, for any reason whatsoever, a workers' and socialist party breaks its solidarity with them, then it goes over to the other side, it forgets its own essential function, it forgets the objectives for which it is fighting.[16]

From Moscow's vantage point there must have appeared to be a large dash of hypocrisy in such a statement. Was not the PCI precisely breaking solidarity with the USSR by refusing to follow its

15 *L'Unità*, April 24, 1964. For other similar comments see the Central Committee debate the following October, including particularly the report by Berlinguer and the speeches by Ingrao and Alicata; *ibid.*, October 15, 1964.
16 *L'Unità*, July 26, 1963.

lead in dealing with the single most serious issue confronting the Communist movement, relations with the Chinese? Such skepticism would be partly warranted, for the PCI's continuing verbal allegiance to the principle of solidarity did in fact conceal a significant shift in the content of the idea. As late as the spring of 1962 Luigi Longo could still explicitly identify the concept of proletarian internationalism with support of the USSR:

The example and the policy of the Soviet Union and the socialist countries represent a strong point of the international workers' movement and of the Communist parties. Therefore the ideological and political bond, the solidarity with the Soviet Union, are permanent factors for the Italian workers' movement and for our party, factors which no campaign of denigration and slander has ever succeeded in weakening. Proletarian internationalism is and must remain one of the most valid tenets of our policy.[17]

But in later party statements direct references to the USSR as the focal point of proletarian solidarity tended to be replaced by more general expressions of allegiance to the international movement as a whole. It was, indeed, in the name of defending the unity of the entire movement that the PCI opposed the Soviet effort to convene an international conference.[18]

This shift in the meaning given to internationalism by the PCI represented essentially an attempt to preserve what was regarded as a vital aspect of the party's ideological heritage, while removing some of the damaging connotations the concept had acquired over the years. For a number of reasons, the PCI could not simply abandon or openly repudiate either its internationalist inheritance in general or its special ties with the Soviet Union. These principles were so deeply imbedded in the party's history and ideology and in the consciousness of at least the older generation of militants that the party's unity might well not have survived a repudiation of the principle of solidarity with the USSR. But this is so not merely because the weight of the past has impeded rational adjustment to the party's present needs. The PCI's ties with the USSR have remained important because of other considerations bearing more directly on

17 *Ibid.*, April 27, 1962.
18 Soviet ideologists, it might be noted, did not themselves lack ambivalence on this score. While the Theses celebrating the anniversary of the First International defined the criterion of internationalism as "the attitude toward the Socialist world system, toward its unity," other authoritative comments endorsed the older definition. Pyotr Pospelov, for example, quoted approvingly the passage from János Kádár's speech in Tashkent in July 1963 stating that proletarian internationalism today, as forty-five years ago, must be defined as solidarity with the Soviet Union; "The Working Men's International Association and the Triumph of Its Ideas," *Kommunist*, No. 13 (September 1964), pp. 24–34, at p. 33.

the party's current situation and its calculations for the future. Before exploring these factors further, it may be helpful to view the PCI's internationalism in the broader context of a more general dilemma the party has faced.

To appropriate a phrase currently fashionable in the discourse of the behavioral sciences, the Italian Communist party might be said to have been undergoing a latent and potentially severe identity crisis. All the pressures operating on the party from the Italian domestic scene have pushed it in a revisionist direction, that is, toward accommodation with the reality of a moderately successful existing social and political order. The longer Italian society has maintained its basic stability under a capitalist, parliamentary system and the further the prospects for revolutionary change have receded, the stronger have become the temptations for the PCI to relinquish the special attributes of an ostensibly Leninist, revolutionary party that have kept it from translating its considerable political strength into a share of government power. From a Communist perspective, this was essentially the temptation to which Pietro Nenni succumbed as he led the Italian Socialist party from principled but ineffectual opposition to unprincipled participation in an allegedly reformist but ineffective government. In Giorgio Amendola and other Italian right-wing Communists one can perhaps discern, though they would of course deny it, a confused and imperfectly articulated desire to walk the same path.

For the party as a whole and for each of its responsible leaders, the dilemma and the incipient crisis have resided in the fact that to move decisively in this direction—that is, far enough to make a significant difference politically—would have meant violating the party's integrity, its image of self. It might have meant giving up precisely those precious qualities upon which the party has most prided itself, those which it has regarded as the most vital attributes of its strength. Revisionist though its political behavior has in many respects become, the Italian party has nonetheless continued to prize and to preserve what it regards as the essential features of its Leninist patrimony. It is the tension between these conflicting demands—the clash between the revisionist and the Leninist halves of the party's personality—that has always, but never so sharply as in the 1960's, lent a special and dramatic quality to Italian communism.

The tension does not primarily have to do with the programmatic issues of classical revisionism. From an orthodox Marxist perspective, the PCI's program has for some years been decisively revisionist in character. The more orthodox parties have finally ceased their rear-guard actions against the PCI's revisionist economic views and its too easy accommodation to the political requirements of the Italian scene, in recognition not so much of the PCI's opposition as of the objective strength and stability of European capitalism, facts that the PCI had perceived earlier and more clearly than the rest.

The pressures of the PCI's environment have been focused principally on two other potential soft spots in the party's rusting Leninist armor. Probably the more significant of these for the future is one we cannot here pause to discuss, fascinating though it is—the strong pressure from both inside and outside the party for relaxation of the principles and practices of "democratic centralism." The PCI's efforts to persuade others to accept its democratic credentials and join with it in a new reformist coalition have been compromised above all by its authoritarian internal regime. As long as the PCI is unable to practice within its own house the democratic principles it professes to accept on the national political scene, its pretensions will not be taken seriously. Understanding this fact, the party's leaders must all the same fight to preserve the traditions of strong central control and united action, not just because their own positions are at stake but because they honestly and with good reason see the PCI's relative strength over other Italian parties as resting heavily on its capacity to avoid splits and to act in a united, monolithic way, even when serious dissent exists.[19]

The second point of tension relates directly to the internationalism of the PCI. The party's ties with the USSR, even though attenuated in recent years, have nevertheless remained one of the strongest obstacles to its acceptability as a legitimate participant in a government coalition. The problem is not only or even primarily that of being labeled as an "agent of a foreign power," although the PCI's loyal adherence to the Soviet foreign policy line has of course constituted a strong argument against it in many circles. The force of that particular objection has been weakened over the years, both by the declining aggressiveness of Soviet policy in Europe and by the recognition that given the present state of affairs in the Com-

---

[19] The demands for greater internal democracy in the party have been mounting steadily since, and in good part because of, Togliatti's death. The context, inevitably, has been the struggle for power among the potential successors of Luigi Longo, with Pietro Ingrao cast in the role of spokesman for the rights of minority groups. At a Central Committee meeting in June 1965, the final resolution was not approved unanimously for the first time in the party's postwar history, with four votes opposed and three abstentions; see *L'Unità*, June 6, 1965. The October meeting, preparatory to the Eleventh Congress, was equally marked by open dissent; see *ibid.*, October 27–31, 1965. Factionalism became only slightly muted during the January 1966 Congress itself and in subsequent months.

munist movement, even a Communist government in Italy need not automatically be assumed to act as a Soviet satellite. The fact that the PCI has represented the interests of one of the two great world powers may, on balance, have constituted more a point of strength than of weakness.

The more significant consideration, one to which we have made frequent allusion, is the almost inescapable identification of the PCI with the authoritarian nature of the Soviet party and state. Repeated assertions of the irrelevance for Italy of the "Soviet model" and the "Soviet road to socialism" are not enough to demonstrate convincingly that if the PCI actually came to power it would not exercise it in the same way as has occurred in Communist states everywhere. This is a problem of which the party has been very much aware, though it has not often been raised as frankly as by one contributor to the pre-Congress discussions in late 1962, who wondered "just how much of an obstacle" to the party's advance was created by its solidarity with the socialist countries. No one can even question the need for proletarian internationalism, he repeated ritualistically, but then went on to ask whether "the formula of national paths to socialism is enough to guarantee, in the eyes of the masses of the people, that in our country the party is fighting for a brand of socialism that will not repeat the errors, the tyranny, the barriers that have resulted elsewhere."[20]

The PCI's commitment to "scientific socialism" has imposed fairly stringent limits on how far it can go toward repudiating the essential features of the Soviet system. Even Giorgio Amendola, responding to the urging of a prominent intellectual of the non-Communist left that the PCI come out more strongly against Soviet authoritarianism, qualified his own rather sharp criticism of the USSR with the following comment:

But after having expressed our criticism and manifested our dissent for the delay with which efforts are made to overcome the contrast still existing today between the development of the socialist foundation of the Soviet system and the development of the democratic structures that should assure "respect for democratic and personal liberties" and "de facto participation of the workers in the direction of all social life," what should be done by us Communists, members of a party fighting in a capitalist country, to help the comrades of the socialist countries resolve these problems? Begin a campaign of agitation? Point out for those countries as models the democratic institutions of our capitalist countries . . . ? Nonsense! We Communists will never lend ourselves to a campaign of agitation and denigration of a country where capitalistic exploitation has

[20] Armando Borelli, "Come aderisce il PCI alla nuova realtà di oggi?," *L'Unità*, November 3, 1962.

been abolished and where the socialist character of the system is a guarantee that errors and delays that are being pointed out and criticized will be overcome, with the cooperation of the workers and through the economic and civic progress of the society![21]

Many in the Italian party may have lost much of their respect for the Soviet Union, they may often have wished they were not saddled with the burden of Soviet misdeeds, but there is rather little they have been able to do about it. Without repudiating their own past and the ideological and political heritage of their party, the PCI leaders have not been able to dissociate themselves or their party from the Soviet Union. They have been prisoners of their past just as Stalin's successors in the Kremlin have been constrained by the terrible legacy he left behind. The Italian party has managed to do little more than take comfort in whatever signs of liberalization have appeared in Soviet society, criticizing when necessary and even intervening on the fringes when possible, but basically waiting and hoping for things to improve.

It would distort the truth, however, to see only the negative side of the story. Dissatisfaction has certainly existed with the USSR, and there have doubtless been many in the PCI who have wished that the historical bonds did not exist as a constraint on the party's capacity to elaborate and pursue a fully autonomous and genuinely original road to power. Such wishful thinking aside, there have remained valid reasons, given the party's perception of its own interests, why basic solidarity with the Soviet Union still makes sense.

To begin at a pragmatic level, it is almost certainly the case that the PCI has derived some tangible political benefit from its image as a leading participant in an international movement headed by one of the two most powerful nations on earth. It is not just a question of capitalizing on the reflected glory of a Soviet space spectacular or other positive achievement of the Soviet state, although there have certainly been times when the PCI has profited thereby. More important is the sense that the Italian party's prestige and general significance have been enhanced by virtue of its connection with a major power, the first socialist state. As an Italian journalist has observed,

The PCI . . . was built on the myth of the Soviet Revolution, of the first socialist society in history. Its strength in its dealings with the socialist parties has always resided in the fact that it could tell them this: you have nothing to back you up, you do not have a society in which the means of production have been socialized; but we have such a society, for better

---

21 "Il socialismo in Occidente," *Rinascita*, November 7, 1964, p. 4.

or for worse. This has always been the essence of the strength of the PCI, the source of its large vote. Without the Soviet myth, the PCI could never have gained the authority it has in the Italian labor movement.[22]

Although somewhat overstated, the point is generally valid that the Communist party has been taken seriously not only because of its own considerable local strength, but because it has partaken of Soviet strength as well. To the extent that the PCI has been thought of not as just another party, but as somehow different from the rest, its international connection provides a good part of the explanation, just as the Christian Democratic party derives much of its special aura from its ties with the Vatican.

The weight this point deserves would be difficult to ascertain without careful study of the attitudes of those who have joined and voted for the Communist party. It seems evident, however, that the asset has been a declining one. For the PCI to belong to a powerful and monolithic international movement claiming with some persuasiveness to represent the revolutionary wave of the future is one thing, but for it to belong to a movement irreparably split into two major portions and a growing number of minor fractions, a movement whose former unchallenged leader has lost not only much of its authority over the movement itself but its revolutionary élan as well—this is quite another matter. While it may perhaps prove possible for the Soviet Union, given a few successes at home and abroad, to regain the international prestige it boasted until only a few years ago, it seems almost beyond imagining that the international Communist movement as a whole could ever be restored to its former glory. The PCI's efforts to salvage something of the unity of old against such heavy odds have surely reflected some concern over the effect on the party's prestige of a formal and final split.[23]

A second order of considerations pertains to the prospects for the party's eventual accession to power. All during the first postwar decade, and particularly after the Twentieth Congress, the party's leaders struggled to disabuse their more militant followers of the notion that revolution would come to Italy on Soviet bayonets.

[22] Alberto Ronchey, "Un dibattito sui problemi del PCI dopo la destituzione di Kruscev," *L'Espresso*, November 15, 1964, p. 6. (Round-table discussion.)

[23] For a stimulating discussion of the effects on the PCI of declining Soviet prestige and the Sino-Soviet split, see Giorgio Galli, "Unificazione socialista e il PCI," *Corrispondenza socialista*, VI, 11 (November 1965), pp. 544–545. Galli's argument, in brief, is that these factors, together with Italian domestic developments, have created the real possibility of splitting off from the PCI a substantial reformist group prepared to concede that the Communist model of socialism will not work for Italy. The case is made again in the last chapter of Galli's book *Il bipartitismo imperfetto* (Bologna: Il Mulino, 1966).

Rather than wait passively for this mythical "X-hour," the party was repeatedly told, it had to learn to rely on its own efforts, to achieve the victory of socialism through the peaceful road of parliamentary action. Revolution was ruled out for Italy, as seemed to be shown decisively in 1948 with the leadership's repudiation of the spontaneous uprising that followed the assassination attempt on Togliatti. And with revolution no longer a realistic prospect, the PCI's potential dependence on the USSR for assistance at some critical future moment seemed logically to be greatly reduced if not ended altogether.

But can one take this line of reasoning wholly at face value? The PCI has undoubtedly succeeded since 1956 in putting aside whatever last lingering hopes there may have been of a Soviet-sponsored revolution and in addressing its energies fully toward parliamentary forms of struggle. It does not necessarily follow, however, that the possibility of a violent revolutionary upheaval has been altogether excluded, or that the USSR might not under some circumstances still have a significant part to play in an Italian revolutionary crisis. The Italian Communists have for understandable reasons avoided drawing attention in recent years to the dictum laid down by the Soviets in 1956 that despite the possibility in certain cases of carrying out a socialist revolution by peaceful means, violence and civil war could by no means be ruled out, since the ruling classes would never relinquish their power voluntarily. But if the PCI's leaders have not chosen to publicize this bit of doctrine, neither have they repudiated it. In November 1963, in an article written for an international Communist audience, Longo explicitly confirmed the principle.[24]

Longo's endorsement was probably not intended only to affirm, as a theoretical possibility, that violent revolution could occur in some capitalist country other than his own. To the extent that the PCI leaders have thought seriously in recent years about the possibility of coming to power—which they may have done despite the remoteness of the prospect and their apparent satisfaction with the perquisites of the party's status as permanent parliamentary opposition—they could not have failed to recognize that such an event, or even its immediate prospect, would be bound to provoke a grave political crisis in Italy. The possibility would have arisen not only of a rightist *coup d'état* backed by armed force, but, in some conceivable circumstances, even of military intervention by Amer-

24 "The Historical Role and Significance of the Struggle of the Communist Party of the Soviet Union," *World Marxist Review*, VI, 11 (November 1963), p. 7.

ican or other outside forces in support of a non-Communist Italian regime.

There is no need to dwell on hypothetical scenarios of a political crisis verging on civil war. The contingency of such an acute crisis has seemed increasingly remote, vastly more so since 1956 than in the early postwar years when Togliatti was constrained by the knowledge that the Soviets would not and could not lift a finger in the event of American military intervention to thwart a Communist takeover attempt. But as long as the possibility of outside intervention in one form or another to prop up a non-Communist government could not be entirely ruled out, then neither could one dismiss the potential usefulness of Soviet power to neutralize and forestall such intervention. It is not intended to assert that the PCI leadership has actively or consciously been thinking in such terms as these; their attention has been fully focused on much more immediate and parochial problems. The point is only that even down into the 1960's there has remained, however attenuated it may have become, some strategic link between Soviet military and diplomatic strength and the prospects for Communist victory in Italy.

It may help to look at the situation in a broader context. The admittedly remote possibility that the USSR might be of specific assistance to the Italian party in the event of a major internal upheaval in Italy is less interesting than the more general consideration that the PCI has seen its political prospects as being in some way related to the over-all balance of international power. One of the strong points of the Leninist perspective is its insistence that revolutionary strategy be conceived in global terms. For Lenin and his followers, the struggle between socialism and imperialism was being fought on a world-wide scale, with the prospects in any given country closely tied to what was happening elsewhere. Despite the Stalinist corruption of this idea into an absolute priority for defending the interests of the first socialist state, the global perspective on revolution has remained one of the central principles underlying the whole notion of proletarian internationalism. Togliatti once expressed his faith in the principle this way:

> Finally, it must be underlined strongly that the struggle for socialism within a given national environment must always be linked to the international struggle against imperialism. Otherwise one would move around like a blind man, not knowing where the enemy is or else believing that he does not exist.[25]

The same point was made more recently by Romano Ledda, a member of the Central Committee, in an article taking Amendola

25 *L'Unità*, December 4, 1960.

to task for his controversial proposal that a new unified working-class party be created because neither the Social Democratic nor the Communist alternative had, in fifty years, proven itself capable of achieving a socialist transformation of society.[26] The starting point of Ledda's critique was that Amendola's proposal represented in effect a capitulation to reformism because it "separated, objectively speaking, the revolution in the West from the world revolutionary processes."[27] Reformism, he went on, was basically inferior to Leninism because it could not see beyond the local scene, could not "express a general strategic vision of the proletarian struggle in the world." The reformists wholly failed to understand that the PCI's support of the October Revolution and its continuing solidarity with the USSR had not been based on sentiment but on the rational awareness that the prospects for revolution everywhere were thereby being enhanced. Amendola's proposal, Ledda implied, partook of the same reformist fallacy by envisioning the prospects for socialism in the advanced capitalist countries as though they were entirely independent of socialist progress elsewhere in the world:

> This is one possible version of autonomy, but I contest its socialist character as well as its practical effectiveness because it loses sight of the basic contradiction of our epoch, cultivating the illusion that a third way is possible. . . . I want to say, therefore, with complete clarity, that autonomy is valid as an essential condition of socialist development in the world, and does not become a retreat into provincialism, only if the necessary discussion of the *diversity* of the nature of revolution and of socialist construction in the advanced capitalist countries takes account of the need for *unity* with the revolutionary experience of the past and with the world revolutionary action of the present.[28]

Ledda's resort to this particular argument in his case against Amendola is revealing. Above and beyond the general implication that the Soviet Union still very much matters to the PCI because it is the spearhead of socialist forces in the world, there is the explicit recognition that even the party's domestic choices must in the broadest sense be guided by a correct understanding of the international scene. If the party is to avoid behaving like Togliatti's blind man, groping at random for the enemy, it must keep alive its ties with international communism.

What this comes back to is essentially the same question with which we opened the discussion: how has the PCI believed it could

26 Ledda, "La riunificazione: come e per che cosa," *Rinascita*, December 5, 1964, pp. 8–9. He was objecting to Amendola, "Ipotesi sulla riunificazione," *ibid.*, November 28, 1964, p. 8.

27 Ledda, *ibid.*, December 5, 1964, p. 8.

28 *Ibid.*, p. 9.

continue to balance on the tightrope between revisionist capitulation to the pressures of its domestic situation on the one hand, and perennial political isolation on the other? The difficulty is that when it has come to making particular tactical choices, virtually any move could be justified within the framework of the remarkably flexible reformist strategy that has constituted the Italian road to socialism. In order to demonstrate that a given proposal such as that of Amendola for a new united working-class party goes beyond legitimate bounds and threatens to destroy the party's very identity, recourse must be had to the old faith in the link between the advance of socialism in the West and revolutionary forces elsewhere. One of the essential ways of avoiding a headlong fall into the abyss of revisionism has been continued solidarity with the international Communist movement and identification with the fundamental values implied in the October Revolution.

It seems that there is an important sense in which the Italian party, despite its having been in many respects the most overtly revisionist in practice of all the parties, may at the same time be considered to have been one of the last upholders of Leninist internationalism. This apparent paradox is understandable in terms of one essential difference between a nonruling party like the PCI and a Communist party in power. If the history of the Communist movement in recent years has proven anything, it is that the force of nationalism is greater than that of any international bond. National interest has proven in case after case to be the decisive criterion for action, in the Soviet Union itself, in China, Yugoslavia, Hungary, Poland, Albania, Rumania, and elsewhere. Long repressed and concealed by Soviet dominance and the domestic weakness of the fraternal parties, the nationalist impulse has now come fully into its own, tempered only by the Soviet Union's remaining capacity to provide economic assistance and military security to its allies.

The contrast in this respect with a nonruling party is striking. The PCI has, to be sure, made increasing demands that the Communist movement adapt its strategy to the needs of communism in Italy and in Western Europe as a whole. In this sense, and in its insistence on autonomy, its attitude could perhaps be described as nationalistic: a kinship obviously does exist between the positions of a Tito and of a Togliatti with regard to the need for each party and state in the Communist movement to be rid of the centralized control formerly exerted from Moscow. But a more important qualitative difference exists between the two points of view. A party in power has a relatively uncomplicated yardstick, that of national interest, by which it can determine its domestic and foreign policies; it has, moreover, every reason to adopt such a criterion, for in so doing it can mobilize its own people most effectively behind the government's policies. With the decline of terror, nationalism has become a ruling party's most potent domestic weapon, as Tito, Gomułka, Ceauçescu, and others have shown themselves to be supremely aware.

The Italian party has had no such criterion for its actions and no comparable profit to derive from its employment. The basic fact is that the PCI does not have a nation behind it. Able to gather only about a quarter of the vote, it has stood in explicit opposition to a majority of its country's people, to their government and its policies at home and abroad. Qualified though this opposition has always been by the party's opportunistic half-acceptance of the system, it has not been able in any but a latent sense to claim to represent the interests of the Italian nation. Rather than being governed by the relatively secure standards of national interest, the PCI has been a creature of ambivalence and ambiguity, its policies more often than not representing only tactical responses to the initiatives of others.

In this fundamental respect the PCI, as an international force, has been inherently weak. Its bargaining power in the Communist movement has been limited because it does not represent a nation and does not appear likely ever to do so. Tito succeeded in demonstrating the absolutely vital point that an independent Communist state was possible in Europe, and Khrushchev in the end virtually had to acknowledge that Yugoslavia might be more important to him than the Soviet Union appeared to be to Tito. For the Italian party such a demonstration would seem to be impossible. A fully independent nonruling Communist party, no longer affiliated with the USSR or defending Soviet foreign policies (or, alternatively, those of China), would seem to be virtually a contradiction in terms. At any rate, this is certainly what the leaders of the Italian party have professed strongly to believe. They have continued to perceive the identity of their party as being irrevocably bound up with the future of the Communist movement and of its original and most powerful member, the Soviet state.

THE PCI AFTER TOGLIATTI

The fall of 1964 can with good reason be taken as a watershed, the end of an era for the Italian party and the international movement alike. As both a symbol of the change and a contributing cause stands the fact that within the space of a few months, between July and October, there passed from the scene the three leaders who have dominated our story—not only Palmiro Togliatti and Maurice Thorez, long-time competitors for influence in the Communist world, but Nikita Khrushchev as well, in whose person and policies were summed up the tensions and frustrations of the Soviet state and party during a troubled time of transition.

Of the three, Togliatti has thus far been most gently dealt with by his heirs. At the same time that many of Khrushchev's programs and methods of operations were being harshly criticized, and Thorez' doctrinaire approach was being cast aside in favor of a flexible and surprisingly successful *communisme à l'italien,* Togliatti's successors were striving to be faithful implementers of his policies. There is particular irony in the contrast between the French and Italian parties. While pursuing a policy of basic continuity with the past, the PCI has suffered domestic setbacks and experienced something of a decline in its relative stature within the Communist movement, whereas the French party, by adopting wholesale Italian recipes for action, has regained international prestige and made dramatic forward strides at home. In the following pages we can provide only a rough outline of the recent developments most relevant to the themes we have pursued, concluding with some observations on the future of the PCI.

In its international actions, the Italian party has without major exception adhered to the principles and policies elaborated in the years since 1956 and summed up in Togliatti's Yalta Testament. An early and unexpected opportunity to reaffirm its autonomy and its right to criticize Soviet domestic institutions was provided by Khrushchev's dismissal, an event that caused the dispatch of a high-level delegation to Moscow to express the party's "perplexity and reservations" about the "development of democratic life and political debate" in the Soviet Union.[1] And when appropriate occasions arose, the PCI continued its practice of condemning Soviet and East European cultural and religious policies, most notably during the furor aroused in Western literary circles by the harsh verdict rendered against the writers Sinyavsky and Daniel early in 1966.[2] By this time, however, the Communist world had grown accustomed to such protests, regarding them as a regrettable but understandable response to the special conditions in which the Western parties were obliged to operate. Even the French party, through a strong statement by that long-time defender of Soviet interests, Louis Aragon, was now associating itself with the chorus of protest from the West.[3]

Of far greater moment to the new Soviet leadership than such irritating but ineffectual criticism was the Italians' persistence in opposing the plan to convene an international conference of the Communist parties. The PCI stubbornly continued to insist that a full-scale conference should not be held until a long period of careful preparation had gradually restored the grounds for cooperation. Only after the Soviets had agreed to regard the proposed gathering as a preliminary "consultative meeting," as Togliatti had urged, did the PCI decide to attend, primarily so as to continue lobbying against moves to lay the ideological or organizational groundwork for a subsequent larger conference with a clear anti-Chinese intent.[4]

The March 1965 Moscow conference was a triumph for the Italian position: nothing was done to cause further deterioration of relations among the parties, and the proposed international meeting was postponed indefinitely. The PCI's success resulted not from superior diplomatic skill but from the fact that it was acting as de facto spokesman for several parties, many of them not present in Moscow, which were by this time decisively set against the Soviet conference plan. The resistance of such important ruling parties as those of North Vietnam and Rumania was seconded by a growing number of European parties, including particularly the British, Swedish, and Dutch. Unlike some of these parties, the Italians were not seeking an abstentionist or neutralist role, which they felt would have left them without further influence in the movement. They intended to

[1] *L'Unità*, November 4, 1964.

[2] See *ibid.*, February 16, 1966.

[3] *L'Humanité*, February 16, 1966.

[4] See Enrico Berlinguer, "La posizione del PCI all' incontro di Mosca," *Rinascita*, March 13, 1965, pp. 3–5, for a partial text of the PCI delegate's speech at the Moscow meeting. A fuller summary of the Italian position and of the meeting as a whole is in Griffith, *Sino-Soviet Relations, 1964–1965*, pp. 79–91.

participate actively in international Communist diplomacy, restraining the Soviet party when possible from steps likely to cause further damage to the movement's unity, but remaining firmly within the Soviet wing of the movement.

The PCI's decision to play the delicate part of loyal opposition within the Soviet alliance was most clearly revealed in a vigorous campaign of bilateral diplomacy that reached a peak during the first half of 1965. Shortly after the Moscow meeting in March, the PCI dispatched two high-level delegations, one under Mario Alicata to Havana, the other under Gian Carlo Pajetta to Hanoi, with additional short stops at Prague, Moscow, Peking, and Djakarta. Discussions with the Cuban and North Vietnamese parties were regarded by the PCI as "two different aspects of a political initiative" whose essential purpose was to call attention to the urgent need for united action by the Communist world against American imperialist aggression in the Far East and in Latin America.[5] The Italians appear to have hoped that their own convictions about the need to replace polemics with concrete actions of mutual support against imperialism might find an echo in Hanoi and Havana. Pajetta noted encouragingly upon his return that the Vietnamese party had expressed its appreciation of Togliatti's slogan of "unity in diversity," considering it "a watchword that should be adopted by the whole Communist movement."[6]

The PCI's diplomatic campaign was primarily intended to advance its own policy of restraint in dealing with the Chinese, but once the conference plan had been shelved, it suited Soviet interests as well. Although undoubtedly frustrated by their failure to mobilize enough support for an anti-Chinese conference, and irritated by the Italian opposition, the Soviets were now presumably prepared to encourage the PCI's efforts to restore a climate of cooperation within the Communist world. For many months after the Moscow meeting, the Soviets played a cautious hand, limiting their pressure for a conference to the hopeful reiteration that the necessary conditions for it were "ripening." But by the fall of 1966, bolstered by the shocking excesses of the Cultural Revolution and other signs of Chinese weakness, they resumed the campaign for a conference.

For the first time, on the issue that more than any other had come to symbolize the party's position in the Communist movement, the PCI appeared to waver. Clearly contrary opinions on the conference issue emerged during a meeting of the Central Committee in Feb-

[5] *Rinascita,* May 15, 1965, p. 2.
[6] *L'Unità,* May 20, 1965.

ruary 1967. Speakers such as Zangheri and Cossutta urged the party to drop its reservations about the conference, to stop the futile debates over whether or not conditions for it were ripe, and to face the obvious fact that some of the parties would not attend. The risk of holding a conference that took a stand against the Chinese, they proclaimed, was less serious than the risk that the movement as a whole and the PCI itself might become paralyzed, rendered incapable of action by undue concern for an unattainable unity. Pietro Ingrao and his supporters, unwilling to back a Soviet offensive against Peking, insisted that unity be preserved at all costs and that the Chinese challenge could only be defeated by vigorous political and economic initiatives in the "third world" and in Europe.

As Togliatti would have done, Longo steered the party onto middle ground. On the one hand, taking refuge in the now sacred formula of "unity in diversity," he expressed the view that "at least for this year" no one believed that favorable conditions existed for a conference. The general tenor of his remarks, however, was noticeably less hostile to an eventual conference than before. He reminded his listeners that the party had never opposed multilateral meetings on principle and suggested that circumstances had greatly changed since the Yalta memorandum: first, the Chinese had repeatedly rejected out of hand all conciliatory overtures, and second, the worrisome trend toward provincial isolation of the parties was now more evident and more dangerous than ever before. It was time, Longo implied, for the PCI to put greater weight on the unity side of the delicate balance between unity and autonomy that had henceforth to be maintained in the Communist movement.[7]

If relations between the parties were not to deteriorate even further, a terrain for united action would have to be found that did not depend on either collaboration or excommunication of the Chinese and their allies. American aggression in Vietnam, for all its usefulness as a rallying cry to unite Communist and "progressive" forces against the imperialist threat, had its limitations as a political platform. Vietnam was itself a central dimension of the Sino-Soviet rivalry, too directly contingent on Russian and Chinese military and diplomatic action to permit other parties more than a subsidiary propaganda role in mobilizing international support for the Communist cause. Europe seemed to be the answer, both because it appeared to offer unusually promising opportunities for Soviet political and economic maneuver, and because it was the field of

7 See *ibid.*, February 25, 1967, for the Central Committee speeches.

primary concern for the East and West European parties that constituted the core of Soviet support in the movement.

This convergence of interest was reflected in the spring of 1967 in a regional conference of all the European parties held at Karlovy Vary, Czechoslovakia, following a preliminary conference in Warsaw and an intensive series of bilateral negotiations in which the PCI played a leading part. Toward the end of March, Longo had gone to Moscow for conversations with Brezhnev during which an understanding was reached: if the Russians would agree that propitious conditions did not exist for a general meeting of the parties, the Italians would pledge themselves to support a regional European conference and do their best to persuade reluctant parties to attend.[8] Longo had returned to Rome after a brief consultation in Paris with Waldeck Rochet only to depart the following day for Bucharest, where he apparently attempted to reverse the Rumanian refusal to attend the conference.[9] Perhaps the Italians, with their impeccable credentials as opponents of Soviet-sponsored party conferences, might manage to reassure the Rumanians that the forthcoming meeting would not be used either as an anti-Chinese forum or as an occasion for inducing the assembled parties to accept the Soviet policy line on European security matters. But the Rumanians insisted on upholding the form and substance of an independent, nationalist posture; along with the Yugoslavs, they declined to be moved by reassurances and appeals for unity. Having only recently broken solidarity with the Communist countries by establishing diplomatic relations with West Germany, the Rumanian party was not about to present itself for criticism at Karlovy Vary.

The substance of the conference itself, devoted to problems of European security, need not concern us in detail. The Soviets saw it as an opportunity to capitalize on resistance to the American presence in Europe and on the anti-American sentiments stimulated by Vietnam, and to rally the European Communist states and parties behind a program leading to eventual withdrawal of U.S. military forces and a further weakening of NATO. The Italians endorsed these objectives but put greater emphasis in their commentary on their favorite theme of collaboration with Socialists

[8] *L'Unità*, March 30, 1967, contains the joint communiqué affirming the importance of participation by all the European parties and acknowledging that further political and organizational preparation would be required for a larger conference; only three months before, the Soviets had announced that conditions were "favorable."

[9] See *ibid.*, April 6, 1967, for the joint communiqué.

and Catholics and on the positive implications of the conference for relations among the parties. A great step forward had been made, in the PCI's view, because differences of opinion had been openly and constructively discussed and because, despite the regrettable absence of several parties, the day of recrimination against those who chose to abstain or to disagree had passed forever.[10]

In another respect as well the Karlovy Vary meeting confirmed a favorable trend. After years of failure to collaborate effectively on European issues with their French colleagues, the Italians were finally rewarded during 1965 and 1966 by a rapid and far-reaching *volte face* on the part of the PCF. A preliminary step in this direction was taken only two months after the 1965 Moscow meeting, during which traditional French-Italian conflicts had still been much in evidence, when the leaders of the two parties met in Geneva for two days of "frank and friendly" talk.[11] Longo later announced that despite their serious past differences, the two parties were now converging in their analysis of the realities of Western European life. Especially encouraging to the Italians was the PCF's stated readiness, although still "without changing its own basic judgment about the EEC," to collaborate with socialist and other leftist forces in efforts to change the antisocial and antidemocratic character of the Common Market.[12]

The following week there convened in Brussels the first formal conference of the European parties since the 1959 Rome meeting. Italian enthusiasm at this manifestation of the regional cooperation they had so long urged was only slightly dampened by the fact that since the conference was a PCF initiative, its agenda bore a distinctly French cachet—the theme under discussion was "dangers to world peace," i.e., Vietnam, NATO, and European fascism. But for the sake of demonstrating that the two parties could, for once, act in concert the PCI was satisfied to postpone consideration of the internal European questions to which it gave priority.[13]

The PCI's Gramsci Institute shortly thereafter countered with an international conference more in the Italian style: two hundred Marxist economists and intellectuals from East and West, including a number of prominent non-Communists, gathered in Rome to discuss "the tendencies of European capitalism." For the PCI the con-

10 See Gian Carlo Pajetta, "Presenza comunista," *L'Unità*, April 30, 1967, and Carlo Galuzzi, "Apertura politica per la sicurezza europea," *Rinascita*, May 5, 1967, pp. 3–4.

11 *L'Unità*, May 27, 1965.

12 "Incontro a Ginevra," *Rinascita*, June 5, 1965, p. 3.

13 "Comunisti a Bruxelles," *Rinascita*, June 12, 1965.

ference was noteworthy primarily for the openness and variety of opinions expressed. Having long urged the need for research and exchange of views on contemporary European problems, the party was pleased to stress that the meeting "marked the end of a certain style of reasoning and of certain patterns of judgment that have for too long fettered Marxist economic debate."[14]

Once begun, the rapprochement between the two parties rapidly picked up speed. The PCI appears to have made one silent but important concession: it ceased its public criticisms of the PCF and its tacit support to the "revisionist" students and intellectuals who had since 1961 been relying on Italian backing in their battle against the French party leadership. During 1964 the PCF had been challenged by the National Bureau of the Union des Étudiants Communistes (UEC), then dominated by what was known as an "Italian faction." By the spring of 1965, however, the PCF had managed to bring the student rebellion under control by engineering the election of a new National Bureau in which the "Italians" were reduced to a small minority. This bureaucratic success ended the possibility of potentially dangerous Italian intervention in PCF affairs and permitted the reconciliation between the two parties to proceed.[15]

The essential condition, however, for the PCF's rapprochement with the PCI and with its own students was the fact that French Communist tactics began in 1965 to acquire a distinctly Italian look. A major source of antagonism between the two parties over the years had been the inability or unwillingness of the French to give priority to working toward a united front of the left, in France and on a European scale. Like other parties, the PCF had formally endorsed this objective, but the dangers of ideological revisionism and loss of internal discipline implicit in compromise with the socialists had in fact impressed the party far more seriously than the opportunities for political gain. Maneuvering on the French left during 1965 to select a presidential candidate to oppose de Gaulle at last created conditions in which the PCF saw the pos-

---

[14] Valentino Parlato, "La classe operaia e le tendenze del capitalismo europeo," *Rinascita*, July 3, 1965, p. 24. The entire proceedings of the conference were published as *Tendenze del capitalismo europeo: Atti del Convegno di Roma organizzato dall'Istituto Gramsci, 25–27 giugno 1965* (Rome: Editori Riuniti, 1966).

[15] For a fuller account of the PCF's struggle with the UEC see Fejtö, *The French Communist Party,* especially pp. 145, 165–166, and 201. Fejtö concludes, p. 196, that to liquidate the UEC opposition "the PCF seems to have requested and obtained from the 'fraternal' Italian party the abandonment of its French protégés."

sibility of emerging from the sterile isolation in which it had stagnated for so long. The relative success in December 1965 of François Mitterand's presidential candidacy, which the PCF supported, and the even more impressive victory against de Gaulle in March 1967 by the united front of the Communists and the newly created Fédération de la Gauche were proof that the new approach was paying off handsomely. The PCI responded by congratulating the French party for the skill and flexibility of its electoral tactics and by asserting, as it had until recently done on behalf of its own policies, that the French success in uniting the left was a great lesson for all of Europe.[16]

One of the most encouraging aspects for the PCI of the changes in France was its effect on the CGT, which in its own realm began industriously pursuing opportunities for collaboration. As the CGIL had long been saying, the search for united trade union action had international as well as domestic implications. The CGT's refusal to make ideological and practical compromises concerning the Common Market had deprived it of opportunities for fruitful contact with non-Communist unions and symbolized its inability to face squarely the conditions of contemporary European economic life. By the end of 1965 the CGT and the CGIL had decided to set up a joint Permanent Committee, later provided with a Secretariat in Brussels, whose mission it was to promote united action among European unions and to fight for Communist representation within the appropriate organs of the EEC.[17] A long way had been traveled since the spring of 1963, when the CGT and the WFTU had refused to join the CGIL in establishing a Common Market liaison office in Brussels.

Regional cooperation continued on the party level as well, especially through a third conference of West European parties held in Vienna in May 1966. Like its predecessor, the conference was prefaced by a Longo–Waldeck Rochet summit meeting, this time in San Remo. The Vienna conference, attended by representatives of fifteen parties, departed in style and content from all previous such gatherings. Questions of foreign policy were not on the agenda, American aggression in Vietnam and German imperialism being mentioned only in passing in the brief final communiqué. For the first time the parties concentrated their attention on the prospects

16 For a typical example of the many PCI commentaries on events in France see Giorgio Napolitano, "Una grande lezione," *Rinascita*, March 17, 1967, pp. 1–2. Fejtö, *The French Communist Party*, pp. 196–203, provides a convenient summary of developments through mid-1966.

17 *L'Unità*, December 11, 1965; *Rassegna sindacale*, February 19, 1967, p. 36.

and problems of building alliances with "other democratic antimonopoly forces," in particular the socialist parties, the trade
unions, and "a considerable part of the Catholic world." Notably
optimistic in tone and devoid of the usual shrill accusations, the
communiqué stressed that political and ideological differences need
not inhibit mutual understanding and constructive collaboration
for common goals.[18]

In both content and method, therefore, the Vienna conference
fulfilled the prescription for Communist relationships in Western
Europe that the Italians had been advocating for years—regional
meetings to discuss concrete problems of political action that would
result not in artificial declarations of a rigid general line but in a
common orientation within which individual differences could be
fully respected. As we have noted, the Karlovy Vary meeting a year
later extended this pattern of relations to include the East European
parties.

Since Togliatti's death, relations between the Italian and the
Soviet parties appear to have entered into a new era. In retrospect,
the Yalta memorandum and the March 1965 meeting in Moscow
seem to have marked the end of a turbulent and dynamic period
during which the Italian party, by challenging traditional Soviet
policies and premises, came to be widely regarded as the most
consistent and articulate proponent among the nonruling parties
of a new style of international Communist relations. This is not to
imply that there will be no further tensions or disagreements: Soviet
interests will never correspond completely to the domestic needs
of the PCI, which will doubtless continue to find good reason to
oppose the Russians on international matters and to criticize their
domestic policies.

The point is rather that the Soviets have finally, and it would
seem irrevocably, come to accept the fact that this is a normal state
of affairs, that it must be so. Reluctantly, they have had to acknowledge the reality and inevitability of a "polycentric" Communist universe, in which differences of opinion and policy, even with respect
to important international issues, must be accepted because they
cannot be suppressed. They have begun, though still partially and
awkwardly, to learn to tolerate dissent and to deal with allies whom
they can influence, but not control.

---

[18] "Communiqué of the conference of representatives of the Communist
parties of European capitalist countries," *World Marxist Review*, IX, 6 (June
1966), pp. 60–61. For the main speech of the Italian delegation, see Ugo Pecchioli,
"Le forze democratiche e l'Europa del MEC," *Critica marxista*, IV, 3, (May–
June 1966), pp. 3–20.

The Italians cannot take much of the credit for bringing home this lesson to Moscow: that honor belongs to parties with more power than the PCI could ever muster, to the Yugoslavs, the Poles, the Chinese, the Rumanians. But Palmiro Togliatti and his colleagues can and should be given the credit for having seen, earlier and more clearly than most, the direction in which events would move. Within the limits imposed by their basic fidelity to the principles of proletarian internationalism and their desire to preserve the unity of their own party, the Italian leaders did what they thought they could to give history a helping hand.

Almost equally important as a sign of the end of an era is the commitment of the Soviet and French parties to a strategy for European communism based on the premises that have characterized the "Italian road to socialism." At their Twentieth party Congress in 1956 the Soviets had of course already formally endorsed the essential doctrinal principles of a peaceful, parliamentary transition to socialism. But the new line, welcome though it was to the Italians as an official sanction of their reformist strategy, had not yet become an operational guideline for Communist strategy in Europe. Official Soviet preferences still lay more with the ideological orthodoxy of the French Communists and their intransigent opposition to European economic integration than with the Italian style of making the best even of unpleasant realities in order to lay the groundwork for alliances with other leftist groups.

Soviet foreign policy itself, moreover, had moved only slowly and intermittently in the decade after 1956 to accept the futility of direct political-military challenges to the status quo and to rely instead primarily on long-term economic and political initiatives to achieve its goals in Europe. By the mid-1960's, the USSR appeared to have understood that the way to enhance its own influence and prestige, to stimulate trade and credits, and to wear down American power on the continent was to make itself into a normal and acceptable feature of the European scene. The tensions of the cold war, which had invariably helped mend the cracks in the Western alliance structure, could be reinvoked only at a high cost. And in order to deal effectively with governments in power now and in the future, the USSR had to make efforts to cultivate those socialists, social democrats, left-wing Catholics, "progressive" intellectuals, and other forces likely to sympathize with Soviet policy initiatives, especially those relating to European security.

Recent Soviet writings on European politics and economics have reflected this trend, particularly in their stress on the decline of anticommunism and the corresponding new possibilities for united action between Communists and all but the extreme right wing of European social democracy (to which category Pietro Nenni has now been consigned). Especially in France and Italy, where communism as a political movement if not as an ideology remains a force to be reckoned with, the convergence between Soviet interests and the domestic needs of the European parties may be greater today than at any time since the immediate postwar years.

THE DOMESTIC OUTLOOK. It is ironical that just at the time European communism was beginning to acquire a consistent "Italian" look, the PCI itself was running into a political impasse more serious than any it had faced since 1956. The talk in Italy was once again of "crisis" and "isolation" for the PCI, of the possibility that Italian communism might at last be coming near the end of the road. As at earlier difficult moments for the party, such speculations have too great an element of wishful thinking about them to be taken at face value. If the PCI faces a crisis, it is not one of recent origin, nor is it such as to lead to an early collapse. Its present problems are essentially the ones it has been confronting for the past decade, ones that have grown more severe, however, as the party has failed to adapt rapidly enough to a political, economic, and social environment in which traditional Communist ideas and practices have become increasingly irrelevant.

We can only allude briefly to various symptoms of the difficulty. Despite vigorous efforts, party membership has continued its slow decline, by 1966 down to slightly more than 1.5 million. Particularly troublesome has been the reluctance of young people to commit themselves to the party: in 1966 only 300,000 party members were less than thirty years old, and membership in the Communist youth movement had slipped to a new low of 168,000. Party leaders, urging more energetic recruitment especially among young industrial and professional groups, have been openly concerned that the party might be losing its mass character and becoming what they disparagingly term an "opinion" or "electoral" party.

The party's much vaunted organizational machinery has also appeared to be running down. Communist cells and sections in the factories have become thinner and less effective, particularly ill adapted to reaching the important "new strata" of industrial society, the technicians and skilled workers. Party officials everywhere have been finding that the old appeals and slogans no longer serve to mobilize their members for traditional party duties and social activities. The deficiencies have even begun to show up in voting statistics, for the party's performance in recent local and regional elections has been below par, especially but not exclusively in the South, where emigration has cut heavily into the Communist vote. Southern radicalism has also resulted in a few noisy cases of dissidence and expulsion, involving in one instance a Communist senator and the mass defection of an entire party section. And the party has been subjected to continual loud harassment, more irritating than politically significant, from the bewildering assortment of "Marxist-Leninist" groups, each possessing a journal and a handful of members, that makes up the "Chinese left" in Italy.

Organizational and political difficulties such as these would be less disturbing if they were not symptomatic of a deeper weakness. The revolutionary perspective had long since been discarded, and now the prospect of the party's eventually coming to power by parliamentary means seemed to be receding, primarily because of the continued and perhaps irrevocable erosion of Communist ties with the Socialists.

Ever since 1956, a dominant concern of the Communists has been to keep within tolerable bounds the Socialist party's drift away from its former alliance with the PCI. Trying to make the best of a trend that it proved unable to reverse, the PCI continued to insist on the possibility of collaboration even after the PSI, minus its radical left, had joined the Center-Left government of the Christian Democrats. By the end of 1966, however, when Nenni and Saragat overcame their split of twenty years before and merged their parties in the new United Socialist party (PSU), Communist strategy seemed to many to have reached a dead end. All things considered, the Center-Left looked to be a rousing political success: by cementing all but the most radical socialists to their ruling coalition the Christian Democrats had consolidated their own position in power and left the Communists more isolated than ever before.

There were some among the Communist leadership who took this pessimistic a view of the situation. Ever since the debates of the early 1960's over the opening to the left, a minority had been arguing that the potential dangers of the Center-Left far outweighed the opportunities it presented for Communist advances. The PSI's alleged failure as a member of the governing coalition to push vigorously for reforms and above all its reunification with the despised Saragat party confirmed the Communist minority in its conviction that the PCI had to cut its losses and write off the right-wing Socialists and Social Democrats as potential allies. Instead of relying so heavily on parliamentary compromise with the ruling hierarchies of the governing parties, the PCI should appeal to the "real forces" of the country, to the genuinely socialist base of all the parties, including the Christian Democratic left. To do so, it would have to gain the intiative by formulating a strong and coherent reform program that faced up to the real problems of a modern industrial society in such a way as to appeal to all genuinely working-class and progressive forces in the country, regardless of party.[19]

During 1965, in meetings of the Central Committee and the special commissions assigned to prepare the programmatic texts for the forthcoming party Congress, a small group led by Pietro Ingrao openly challenged the party line, some even taking the unprecedented step of voting against the official document. The rebels were decisively defeated by a coalition of Longo and Amendola supporters and at the Eleventh Congress early in 1966 suffered the consequences. Several of the most articulate dissenters lost their jobs, and Ingrao, while remaining in the leadership, was isolated and weakened by a reorganization of the leading party bodies.

Their defeat was not attributable exclusively to bureaucratic weakness or to the difficulty of challenging the majority line in a party where factionalism remained the cardinal sin.[20] The fact was that the minority had not succeeded in articulating a clear and convincing strategic alternative for the party. Their appeal for a direct challenge to the class enemy on "more advanced terrain" was too easily dismissed as an abstract and schematic formula reflecting a mood of frustration rather than a specific program of political action. The implicit premises of the left did not seem realistic: social and economic conditions were not so bad that the Italian masses would eagerly embrace a program with radical overtones, nor was it likely that significant portions of the Socialist or Christian Democratic left could be detached from their parties and persuaded to join the Communists in the political wilderness.

[19] The platform of the PCI left has not been summed up in any single well argued statement, but its general tendency is evident in the articles and speeches of such Central Committee members as Ingrao, Reichlin, Pintor, Natoli, Rossanda, and Ledda. See especially *L'Unità*'s coverage of the Central Committee debates of June 3–5 and October 27–31, 1965, where the challenge of the left was most clearly expressed.

[20] One should not underestimate the difficulty a party minority faces in presenting its case. If it attempts to make an explicit and detailed public criticism of past party actions, it opens itself to the damaging charge of weakening the party by disrupting its unity at a time of crisis. But if it limits itself to general and implicit criticism by subtly stressing one or another side of a complex issue, the majority can easily absorb and blunt the attack by appearing to agree with its critics. The PCI leadership can refute its leftist critics by insisting, quite legitimately, that of course they too believe in developing contacts with the Catholics, in extending democracy within the party, in attacking the class enemy. In a party like the Italian, where the range of policy alternatives is inherently narrow, differences between one and another line generally come down to matters of emphasis which are hard for a minority to dramatize.

Unwilling to gamble with a new strategy, the PCI has in effect resolved to try harder with the old. Despite the discouraging trend of events, it has clung to the hope that the United Socialist Party would in the end be obliged by its need for mass support to remain loyal to class principles and avoid committing itself irrevocably to an anti-Communist and social democratic perspective. Although rejecting the most revisionist implications of Amendola's controversial proposal for a new unified working-class party that might transcend the failure of both social democracy and communism to bring about socialism, the PCI has accepted the essential thrust of the idea by continuing to regard collaboration with the Socialists as the party's main strategic goal. Action toward this end has gone forward on several fronts. Polemical exchanges in party publications have not prevented continued collaboration in a significant, though declining, number of local governments. The Communist youth movement has done its part by encouraging an exchange of views and united action at the student level, as for example through a national convention of the PCI, PSI, and PSIUP youth organizations in the spring of 1965 to debate the prospects of socialist unification.

The most serious and sustained effort, however, has been on the trade union front, where the opportunities have seemed greatest and the costs of failure most damaging. Unification of the PSI and the PSDI created an inherently unstable union situation: trade unionists in the new party could not be expected indefinitely to remain divided between the CGIL and the UIL, the Social Democratic union federation. To counter pressures for Socialist withdrawal, the Communist leadership in the CGIL has moved energetically and skillfully along two parallel lines.

First, significant concessions have been made to the Socialist minority in the CGIL itself, the most striking of which was the decision in March 1967 to allow Communist union leaders who were also parliamentary deputies to abstain from the voting on the government's five-year economic plan rather than join the PCI delegation in a negative vote. This move aroused strong resentment among a minority in both the PCI and the CGIL as an unprincipled capitulation to social democratic reformism, symbolized by the acceptance of such hitherto rejected formulas as the linking of wage increases to rising productivity. The party and the union justified the decision almost entirely as a necessary step in defense of the CGIL's unity.[21]

21 See Rinaldo Scheda, "La CGIL e il Piano," *L'Unità*, February 21, 1967;

The decision not to oppose the Pieraccini Plan was also intended to contribute to a second key dimension of CGIL strategy, the promotion of collaborative action leading to eventual reunification of the unions in a single federation. The vote on the economic plan was one way of demonstrating that ideological considerations would not inhibit the CGIL from joining other unions not only in strikes and other conventional modes of action, where cooperation in recent months had been unusually effective, but also on the "modern" and "constructive" terrain of influencing national economic planning. The vote also served to demonstrate that the CGIL had by now genuinely won its full autonomy from the party and that a unified union would thus no longer run the risk of being dominated by the Communists. The problem of autonomy was by this time fully as severe for the CISL and the UIL, with their ties to government parties, as for the CGIL, whose actions increasingly reflected the need for internal compromise among different union and party currents. The somewhat surprising receptivity of the CISL to the CGIL's initiatives is probably attributable not only to the expectation that a united union would acquire greater bargaining power, but also to the hope of increasing the influence of the labor group within the Christian Democratic party.

This last consideration introduces one of the most important political dimensions of the CGIL's campaign for union unity. For the Communist party, the campaign has been valued as a way of opening up paths of communication and common action with the Christian Democratic left. Communist strategy may have continued to place first priority on the Socialists, but by no means to the exclusion of a lively interest in all sectors of the Catholic left. The perennial "dialogue" between Marxist and Catholic intellectuals has gone forward, stimulated both by further liberalization in the Church and, on the Communist side, by Soviet encouragement and by the active participation of Communist intellectuals in other countries.[22] It is the trade unions, however, that have offered the best hope of tangible and politically useful collaboration between Catholics and Communists. Novella may be premature in declaring

Rassegna sindacale, March 26, 1967, pp. 3–13, contains a summary of the debate on the issue in the CGIL General Council and, pp. 15–18, the statements made in the Chamber of Deputies by Novella, Mosca, and Foa, representing the three party groupings in the CGIL. Foa did not join in the abstention.

22 See "La Chiesa, il marxismo, il dialogo," Il Contemporaneo, supplement to Rinascita, June 30, 1967, pp. 13–22, for a recent series of articles on the subject. Kevin Devlin has provided a good summary and analysis of this phenomenon in "The Catholic-Communist 'Dialogue,'" Problems of Communism, XV, 3 (May–June 1966), pp. 31–38.

that "trade union unity is on the way," but it is at least true that for the first time in two decades, the prospect is not wholly illusory.[23]

In summary, what emerges most clearly from this necessarily superficial review is that in its domestic policies the PCI has not significantly departed from the course along which we have followed it since 1956. The path has been a consistently conservative one. When its policies have seemed out of joint with the times, its style has been to seek a pragmatic reconciliation with reality. Rebutting those who claimed that Italian communism was in full crisis, Luigi Longo referred not long ago to "that continuous effort at renewal and adjustment that has been one of the secrets of our advance." "In reality," he said, "we face no ideological, political, or moral crisis for the simple reason that we have always made an effort to understand what Gramsci used to call the 'reality of history' and to play an active and vanguard part in all historical processes."[24] More crudely put, the PCI has been determined above all to remain in the political game.

Longo is right that one of the PCI's strengths has always been a great capacity to comprehend and adapt to forces more powerful than itself. Italian communism has not gone about tilting at windmills. But if one should assume, as Longo cannot, that the "reality of history" in Western Europe has no place in it for Communist parties as we have known them, then what? If staying in the game should require of the PCI a further weakening or redefinition of its class or international perspectives, the record suggests that the sacrifice will be made, reluctantly perhaps and gradually enough to soothe the more ideologically minded, but it will be made.

To suppose that the future can be read as an extrapolation of existing trends is often a gross mistake. It would in any case be presumptuous to speculate seriously about the future of Italian communism on the basis of the evidence related here, for many of the most critical variables have been wholly outside our ken. What happens to the PCI will depend above all on what happens to Italy as a whole, on the ability of that often ineffectual political system to meet the tremendous challenge of economic and social modernization, especially in the Italian South. The party's future will also rest heavily on the skills and attitudes of a new generation of Communist leaders, about whom we know relatively little. The transfer of power from Togliatti to Longo was skillfully managed, but the

23 *L'Unità*, March 23, 1966.
24 *Ibid.*, October 12, 1966.

battle for succession is already under way among Longo's lieu-
tenants. The next transition could result in grave damage to the
party's unity as well as, although this is less likely, a radical change
in its policies.

The generational shift may have particular relevance for the
party's internationalism. The PCI's profile has undeniably been
shaped by the personal histories and ideological commitments of
men like Palmiro Togliatti and Luigi Longo, whose most impres-
sionable years were spent outside of Italy in the service of the Soviet
Union and of international communism. Despite the degradations
to which Stalin submitted them, they emerged from the experiences
of the 1920's and 1930's still attached to a perspective of the world
that ranged far beyond the Italian scene. The same can be said,
although to a lesser degree, of such men as Giorgio Amendola and
Gian Carlo Pajetta, whose world outlook was shaped in the 1930's
when communism genuinely appeared to many Italian intellectuals
the only hope against fascism. It can be said far less of men in the
generation of Pietro Ingrao, who joined the party during or just
after the war, but who at least received their education and inspiration from those who had themselves been in Fascist jails, in exile,
in combat in the Spanish Civil War.

But what of the products of the postwar generation, those who
have known and served the party as a domestic political machine,
often as a vehicle for their own personal advancement? Whatever
revolutionary idealism there may be in these young people, it
surely has little by way of an international dimension beyond a
romantic—and slightly "Chinese"—tendency to identify with the
"revolutionary tide" in the developing countries. If the Soviet
Union had ever appealed to them as the heroic home of socialist
ideals, this naïve faith was certainly discarded in the years after
1956. More important, because they did not then hold positions
of responsibility in the party, such younger Communists are un-
tainted by complicity in the events of the Stalin era. They are thus
free to repudiate Stalinism in all its aspects without at the same
time disavowing a part of their own past.

These are men like Achille Occhetto, former Secretary of the
Italian Communist Youth Federation, who can bluntly proclaim
that "being revolutionary no longer necessarily means supporting
the Soviet Union." Like other Communists, Occhetto is concerned
about how to avoid "being engulfed by reformist opportunism."
But what a vast difference of perspective there is between his prescription and the one offered by Romano Ledda that we examined
a few pages ago. Ledda was insisting on a return to the values of

old, on the necessity of retaining ties with the international Communist movement as the prime guarantee that the party would remain on the track of scientific socialism at home. Occhetto is calling for a new system of values, based not on the classical precepts of a "formal and dogmatic internationalism" requiring automatic support for Soviet policy, but on the contemporary demands of a Western nation trying to build a socialist democracy.[25]

In one way or another the Italian Communist party will have to fight out the battle between these two perspectives. One cannot predict to what extent the older values of proletarian internationalism will manage to survive the pressures exerted by younger Communist leaders, increasingly free of the myths of the past and oriented more and more toward a parochial vision of the party's role as a domestic political force. It is tempting to assume that the perspective of the younger generation will over time inevitably prevail, and that Italian communism will in another decade or two become exclusively a national phenomenon, hardly more radical or international in its outlook than the European socialist parties of today.

In that event the PCI would have lost its last and greatest battle: it would have been absorbed by the society it sought to transform. But it is precisely this vision of the outcome that might conceivably prevent such an eventuality. Rather than betray its essence, the PCI might instead tacitly resign itself to playing a permanent and increasingly marginal opposition role in Italian politics, in effect perpetuating indefinitely its present ambivalent posture of half-accepting, half-rejecting the system of which it is a part.

The alternatives are of course not black and white. We are dealing in matters of degree about which differences of judgment are inevitable. A strong case can be made that even now, despite its professions of international solidarity and its continuing though weakened commitment to Leninist concepts of party organization and discipline, the PCI has in practice become a revisionist party, irrevocably linked to the existing system.[26] The PCI has indeed gone a long way in this direction, thus far with moderately little pain. It would be surprising, however, if greater traumas did not lie just over the horizon. In any case, the PCI must for the foreseeable future continue to struggle with the perhaps insoluble dilemma of preserving the minimal core of what it means to be a Communist

25 *La Città futura*, No. 6 (January 1965), pp. 3–6.
26 Sidney Tarrow implies as much when he writes of the "institutionalization" of the party's tactics and of its role within the system. See *Peasant Communism in Southern Italy* (New Haven: Yale University Press, 1967).

party, including a close tie with the Soviet Union and with whatever can be salvaged of the international Communist movement, without at the same time relinquishing forever its chance to mount to the seats of power.

BIBLIOGRAPHY

A List of the Principal Books, Journals, and Newspapers Consulted

I. ITALIAN COMMUNIST MATERIALS

A. *Books*

Amendola, Giorgio. *Classe operaia e programmazione democratica*. Rome: Editori Riuniti, 1966.

Boffa, Giuseppe. *Dopo Krusciov: L'eredità del decennio kruscioviano e le nuove prospettive della politica sovietica*. Turin: Einaudi editore, 1965.

———. *Inside the Khrushchev Era*. Translated by Carl Marzani. New York: Marzani & Munsell, 1959.

Confederazione Generale Italiana del Lavoro. *CGIL e programmazione economica*. Rome: Editrice Sindacale Italiana, 1964.

Di Vittorio, Giuseppe. *L'Unità dei lavoratori*. Rome: Editori Riuniti, 1957.

Ferrara, Marcella e Maurizio. *Conversando con Togliatti*. Rome: Edizioni di Cultura Sociale, 1953.

———. *Cronache di vita Italiana (1944–58)*. Rome: Editori Riuniti, 1960.

Istituto Gramsci. *Programmazione economica e rinnovamento democratico: Atti del convegno indetto dall'Istituto Gramsci, Roma, 14–15 marzo 1963*. Rome: Editori Riuniti, 1963.

———. *Tendenze del capitalismo europeo: Atti del Convegno di Roma organizzato dall'Istituto Gramsci, 25–27 giugno 1965*. Rome: Editori Riuniti, 1966.

———. *Tendenze del capitalismo italiano: Atti del Convegno di Roma, 23–25 marzo 1962*. Vols. I and II. Rome: Editori Riuniti, 1962.

Longo, Luigi. *Revisionismo nuovo e antico*. Turin: Einaudi editore, 1957.

Longo, Luigi e Gino. *Il Miracolo economico e l'analisi marxista*. Rome: Editori Riuniti, 1962.

Napolitano, Giorgio. *Movimento operaio e industria di stato*. Rome: Editori Riuniti, 1962.

Partito Comunista Italiano. *VIII Congresso del Partito Comunista Italiano: Atti e risoluzioni*. Rome: Editori Riuniti, 1957.

———. *The Eighth Congress of the Italian Communist Party, Rome, 8–14 December 1956*. Rome: Foreign Section of the Italian Communist Party, [1957].

414

————. *IX Congresso del Partito Comunista Italiano: Atti e risoluzioni.* Vols. I and II. Rome: Editori Riuniti, 1960.

————. *X Congresso del Partito Comunista Italiano: Atti e risoluzioni.* Rome: Editori Riuniti, 1963.

————. *XI Congresso del Partito Comunista Italiano: Atti e risoluzioni.* Rome: Editori Riuniti, 1966.

————. *Problemi e realtà dell'URSS: Relazione sul viaggio della delegazione del PCI nell'Unione Sovietica.* Rome: Editori Riuniti, 1958.

————. *Documenti politici e direttive del Partito comunista italiano dall' VIII al IX Congresso.* Rome: A cura della segreteria del Partito Comunista Italiano, 1960.

————. *Documenti politici dal IX al X Congresso.* Rome: A cura della Sezione Stampa e Propaganda della Direzione del Partito Comunista Italiano, 1962.

————. *Interventi della delegazione del Partito Comunista Italiano alla Conferenza degli 81 Partiti comunisti ed operai.* Rome: A cura della Sezione centrale di Stampa e propaganda della Direzione del Partito Comunista Italiano, 1962.

Ragionieri, Ernesto. *Palmiro Togliatti: Aspetti di una battaglia ideale e politica.* Rome: Editori Riuniti, 1966.

Scoccimarro, Mauro. *Nuova democrazia.* Rome: Editori Riuniti, 1958.

Strada, Vittorio. *Letteratura sovietica 1953–1963.* Rome: Editori Riuniti, 1964.

Togliatti, Palmiro. *Comunisti e cattolici.* Rome: Editori Riuniti, 1966.

————. *La formazione del gruppo dirigente del Partito comunista italiano.* Rome: Editori Riuniti, 1962.

————. *Il partito.* Rome: Editori Riuniti, 1964.

————. *Problemi del movimento operaio internazionale, 1956–1961.* Rome: Editori Riuniti, 1962.

————. *Sul movimento operaio internazionale.* Rome: Editori Riuniti, 1964.

B. *Periodicals and Newspapers*

Of the various publications of the Italian Communist party, two are indispensable for the researcher: *L'Unità,* the official party daily, and *Rinascita,* the party journal edited by Togliatti since its founding in 1944; until May 1962 the latter appeared monthly, then became a weekly. Also important for recent years is *Critica marxista,* a bimonthly journal established in 1963 to deal at greater length with theoretical, political, and economic questions.

Other useful party journals include *Il Contemporaneo* for cultural matters (in 1966 it became a monthly supplement to *Rinascita*); *Politica ed economia* for economic affairs (July 1957 to March 1962 only, then absorbed by *Rinascita*); *Cronache meridionale* for problems pertaining to the South; *Nuova generazione,* the official organ of the Italian Communist Youth Federation; and *Vie nuove,* the party's popular weekly magazine.

For trade union matters see two periodicals of the CGIL, *Lavoro,* the CGIL's weekly paper until it ceased publication in October 1962, and *Rassegna sindacale,* transformed from a monthly into a fortnightly the following month. Translations of some major articles and party documents are given in the *Foreign Bulletin of the Italian Communist Party,* a monthly published since 1960 by the Foreign Section of the PCI Central Committee.

II. NON-COMMUNIST MATERIALS ON ITALIAN AND EUROPEAN POLITICS AND ECONOMICS

A. *Books*

Almond, Gabriel A., and Verba, Sidney. *The Civic Culture: Political Attitudes and Democracy in Five Nations.* Princeton: Princeton University Press, 1963.

Basso, Lelio. *Da Stalin a Krusciov.* Milan: Edizioni Avanti!, 1962.

———. *Il Partito Socialista Italiano.* Milan: Nuova Accademia Editrice, 1958.

Braga, Giorgio. *Il comunismo fra gli Italiani: saggio di sociologia.* Milan: Edizioni di Comunità, 1956.

Brzezinski, Zbigniew. *Alternative to Partition: For a Broader Conception of America's Role in Europe.* New York: McGraw-Hill, 1965.

Cammett, John M. *Antonio Gramsci and the Origins of Italian Communism.* Stanford: Stanford University Press, 1967.

Carlyle, Margaret. *Modern Italy.* Rev. ed. New York: Praeger, 1965.

Crossman, Richard (ed.). *The God That Failed.* New York: Harper & Row, 1963.

Cucchi, Aldo. *Una delegazione italiana in Russia.* Florence: La Nuova Italia Editrice, 1951.

Delzell, Charles F. *Mussolini's Enemies: The Italian Anti-Fascist Resistance.* Princeton: Princeton University Press, 1961.

Einaudi, Mario, Domenach, Jean-Marie, and Garosci, Aldo. *Communism in Western Europe.* Ithaca: Cornell University Press, 1951.

Esposti, Gianluigi Degli. *Bologna PCI.* Bologna: Il Mulino, 1966.

Falconi, Carlo. *Pope John and His Council.* London: Weidenfeld and Nicolson, 1964.

Furniss, Edgar S., Jr. *France, Troubled Ally: De Gaulle's Heritage and Prospects.* New York: Praeger, 1960.

Galli, Giorgio. *Il bipartitismo imperfetto.* Bologna: Il Mulino, 1966.

———. *La sinistra italiana nel dopoguerra.* Bologna: Il Mulino, 1958.

———. *Storia del Partito comunista italiano.* Milan: Schwarz editore, 1958.

Galli, Giorgio, and Facchi, Paolo. *La sinistra democristiana: storia e ideologia.* Milan: Feltrinelli, 1962.

Giolitti, Antonio. *Riforme e rivoluzione.* Turin: Einaudi editore, 1957.

Gorresio, Vittorio. *L'Italia a sinistra.* Milan: Rizzoli editore, 1963.

Gozzini, Mario (ed.). *Il dialogo alla prova: Cattolici e comunisti italiani.* Florence: Vallecchi editore, 1964.

Grindrod, Muriel. *The Rebuilding of Italy.* London: Royal Institute of International Affairs, 1955.

Guiducci, Roberto. *Socialismo e verità.* Turin: Einaudi editore, 1956.

Guiducci, Roberto, and Onofri, Fabrizio (eds.). *Costituente aperta: Le nuove frontiere del socialismo in Italia.* Florence: Vallecchi editore, 1966.

Hennessy, Jossleyn, Lutz, Vera, and Scimone, Giuseppe. *Economic 'Miracles': Studies in the resurgence of the French, German, and Italian economies since the Second World War.* London: André Deutsch for the Institute of Economic Affairs, 1964.

Hildebrand, George Herbert. *Growth and Structure in the Economy of Modern Italy.* Cambridge, Mass.: Harvard University Press, 1965.

Hilton-Young, Wayland. *The Italian Left: A Short History of Political Socialism in Italy.* London: Longmans, Green, 1949.

Horowitz, Daniel L. *The Italian Labor Movement.* Cambridge, Mass.: Harvard University Press, 1963.

Hughes, H. Stuart. *The United States and Italy.* Rev. ed. Cambridge, Mass.: Harvard University Press, 1965.

Kaiser, Robert Blair. *Pope, Council, and World.* New York: Macmillan, 1963.

Kitzinger, U. W. *The Politics and Economics of European Integration: Britain, Europe, and the United States.* New York: Praeger, 1963.

Kogan, Norman. *The Government of Italy.* New York: Crowell, 1962.

————. *The Politics of Italian Foreign Policy.* New York: Praeger, 1963.

La Malfa, Ugo. *Il 1956: La crisi del comunismo e la via della democrazia.* Bologna: Il Mulino, 1957.

LaPalombara, Joseph. *Interest Groups in Italian Politics.* Princeton: Princeton University Press, 1965.

————. *Italy: The Politics of Planning.* Syracuse: Syracuse University Press, 1966.

————. *The Italian Labor Movement: Problems and Prospects.* Ithaca: Cornell University Press, 1957.

Lichtheim, George. *The New Europe: Today—and Tomorrow.* New York: Praeger, 1963.

Lutz, Vera. *Italy, A Study in Economic Development.* London: Oxford University Press, 1962.

Magnani, Valdo, and Cucchi, Aldo. *Crisi di una generazione.* Florence: La Nuova Italia, 1952.

————. *Dichiarazioni e documenti.* Bologna: Tip. Luigi Parma, 1951.

Maitan, Livio. *Teoria e politica comunista nel dopoguerra.* Schwarz editore, 1959.

Malfatti, Franco Maria. *La crisi del comunismo e la rivolta in Ungheria.* Rome: Edizione cinque lune, 1956.

Mieli, Renato. *Togliatti 1937.* Milan: Rizzoli editore, 1964.

Nenni, Pietro. *Le prospettive del socialismo dopo la destalinizzazione.* Turin: Einaudi editore, 1962.

Onofri, Fabrizio. *Classe operaia e partito.* Bari: Editori Laterza, 1957.

———. *Socialismo e potere.* Milan: Edizioni di Comunità, 1963.

Pellicani, Michele. *La tragedia della classe operaia.* Milan: Edizioni Azione Comune, 1964.

Perego, Angelo. *Dottrina e prassi del partito comunista italiano.* Rome: Società Grafica Romana, [1961?].

Pryce, Roy. *The Italian Local Elections, 1956.* (St. Anthony's Papers, No. 3.) London: Chatto and Windus, 1957.

Seniga, Giulio. *Togliatti e Stalin: Contributo alla biografia del segretario del PCI.* Milan: Sugar editore, 1961.

Shanks, Michael, and Lambert, John. *The Common Market Today—and Tomorrow.* New York: Praeger, 1962.

Spreafico, Alberto, and LaPalombara, Joseph (eds.). *Elezione e comportamento politico in Italia.* Milan: Edizioni di Comunità, 1963.

Tarrow, Sidney. *Peasant Communism in Southern Italy.* New Haven: Yale University Press, 1967.

Zaccaria, Guelfo. *Duecento comunisti italiani fra le vittime dello stalinismo.* Milan: Edizioni Azione Comune, 1964.

B. *Periodicals and Newspapers*

Italy abounds in newspapers and journals representing the entire spectrum of political opinion. For the purposes of this study the following have proven to be of greatest interest.

The various shades of opinion within the Socialist party are reflected principally in the daily *Avanti!* and the monthly *Mondo Operaio,* both representing generally, though not exclusively, the viewpoint of the Nenni majority wing of the party; and in the two left-wing monthly journals *Problemi del socialismo* and *Mondo nuovo,* edited by Lelio Basso and Tullio Vecchietti, respectively. The views of dissident Communist and other leftist factions are to be found in such journals as *Nuova unità, Bandiera rossa, Azione comunista,* and *Risorgimento socialista* (1951–1957).

Of the many journals dealing broadly with contemporary political, social, and cultural issues, and not formally associated with a political party, the following merit particular mention: the weeklies *L'Espresso* and *Il Mondo;* and the monthlies *Corrispondenza socialista, Il Mulino, Nord e Sud, Nuovi argomenti, Passato e presente* (1958–1960), *Il Ponte, Tempi moderni,* and *Tempo presente.*

III. MATERIALS ON SOVIET AND INTERNATIONAL COMMUNIST AFFAIRS

The listing below includes only non-Communist publications. Reference should also be made to the principal newspapers, journals, and other publications of the relevant Communist parties concerned: e.g., for the Soviet Union, *Pravda* and *Kommunist,* for France, *L'Humanité* and

Cahiers du Communisme. With regard to Communist international trade union affairs, see especially the monthly journal of the WFTU, *World Trade Union Movement,* and the materials resulting from WFTU Congresses and other meetings. The following Communist pamphlets have been cited in the text:

Parti Communiste Français. *Problèmes du mouvement communiste international.* Paris: Edité par le Comité Central du Parti Communiste Français, 1963.

Saillant Louis. *The WFTU and the Tasks of the Trade Union Movement.* London: WFTU Publications Ltd., [1962].

Vukmanović-Tempo, S. *Topical Problems of the International Trade Union Movement.* Belgrade: Yugoslav Trade Unions, 1962.

WFTU. *Texts and Decisions of the Fifth World Trade Union Congress.* London: WFTU Publications Ltd., [1962].

A. *Books*

Benes, Vaclav L., Byrnes, Robert F., and Spulber, Nicolas (eds.). *The Second Soviet-Yugoslav Dispute.* Bloomington, Ind.: Indiana University Press, 1959.

Bromke, Adam. *Poland's Politics: Idealism vs. Realism.* Cambridge, Mass.: Harvard University Press, 1967.

Brzezinski, Zbigniew (ed.). *Africa and the Communist World.* Stanford: Stanford University Press, 1963.

————. *The Soviet Bloc: Unity and Conflict.* Rev. ed. Cambridge, Mass.: Harvard University Press, 1967.

Cantril, Hadley. *The Politics of Despair.* New York: Collier Books, 1962.

Conquest, R. *Power and Policy in the U.S.S.R.: The Study of Soviet Dynastics.* New York: St. Martin's Press, 1961.

Crankshaw, Edward. *The New Cold War: Moscow v. Pekin.* Baltimore: Penguin Books, 1963.

Dallin, Alexander, with Harris, Jonathan, and Hodnett, Grey (eds.). *Diversity in International Communism: A Documentary Record, 1961–1963.* New York: Columbia University Press, 1963.

Drachkovitch, Milorad M. (ed.). *Marxism in the Modern World.* Stanford: Stanford University Press, 1965.

Dulles, Eleanor Lansing, and Crane, Robert Dickson (eds.). *Détente: Cold War Strategies in Transition.* New York: Praeger, 1965.

Fejtö, François. *Chine-U.R.S.S., la fin d'une hégémonie: Les origines du grand schisme communiste, 1950–1957.* Paris: Librairie Plon, 1964.

————. *The French Communist Party and the Crisis of International Communism.* Cambridge, Mass.: The M.I.T. Press, 1967.

Griffith, William E. *Albania and the Sino-Soviet Rift.* Cambridge, Mass.: The M.I.T. Press, 1963.

———— (ed.). *Communism in Europe: Continuity, Change, and the Sino-Soviet Dispute.* Vol. 1. Cambridge, Mass.: The M.I.T. Press, 1964.

————. *The Sino-Soviet Rift.* Cambridge, Mass.: The M.I.T. Press, 1963.

————. *Sino-Soviet Relations, 1964–1965*. Cambridge, Mass.: The M.I.T. Press, 1967.

Gruliow, Leo (ed.). *Current Soviet Policies—II: The Documentary Record of the 20th Communist Party Congress and Its Aftermath*. New York: Praeger, 1957.

Hudson, G. F., Lowenthal, Richard, and MacFarquhar, Roderick. *The Sino-Soviet Dispute*. New York: Praeger, 1961.

Johnson, Priscilla. *Khrushchev and the Arts: The Politics of Soviet Culture, 1962–1964*. Cambridge, Mass.: The M.I.T. Press, 1965.

Labedz, Leopold, and Urban, G. R. (eds.). *The Sino-Soviet Conflict: Eleven Radio Discussions*. London: Bodley Head, 1964.

Leonhard, Wolfgang. *The Kremlin since Stalin*. New York: Praeger, 1962.

Lowenthal, Richard. *World Communism: The Disintegration of a Secular Faith*. New York: Oxford University Press, 1964.

Mackintosh, J. M. *Strategy and Tactics of Soviet Foreign Policy*. New York: Oxford University Press, 1962.

Reale, Eugenio. *Nascità del Cominform*. Milan: Mondadori, 1958.

Rieber, Alfred J. *Stalin and the French Communist Party: 1941–1947*. New York: Columbia University Press, 1962.

Shulman, Marshall D. *Stalin's Foreign Policy Reappraised*. Cambridge, Mass.: Harvard University Press, 1963.

Zagoria, Donald S. *The Sino-Soviet Conflict, 1956–1961*. Princeton: Princeton University Press, 1962.

Zinner, Paul E. (ed.). *National Communism and Popular Revolt in Eastern Europe: A Selection of Documents on Events in Poland and Hungary, February–November, 1956*. New York: Columbia University Press, 1956.

B. *Periodicals and Newspapers*

Among the English-language journals dealing with Soviet and international Communist affairs, special mention should be made of *The China Quarterly,* of *Survey—A Journal of Soviet and East European Studies,* and of *Problems of Communism.* The French journal *Est & Ouest* is also useful, particularly on the French and to a lesser extent the Italian parties. Generally high-quality reporting and analysis of contemporary international Communist matters is to be found in the reports prepared by the Research Departments of Radio Free Europe.

Translations of many of the most important Soviet materials are provided in the *Current Digest of the Soviet Press.* The Joint Publications Research Service of the U.S. Department of Commerce provides in its series of "Translations on International Communist Developments" a useful and generally well-chosen selection of important material dealing with the principal nonruling Communist parties; the translations themselves, however, cannot be relied upon for accuracy.

INDEX

421

Chiarante, Giuseppe, 223n
Chinese Communist party (CCP), *see* Chinese People's Republic
Chinese People's Republic (CPR), and Albania, *see* Albania, and China antirevisionist campaign, 144, 162
and capitalism, 372–373
and CGIL, 283
Cominform 1953 meeting, 31–32
Commune Program, 170
Cultural Revolution, 397
and factionalism, 162, 177
Great Leap Forward, 170
international Communist movement, *see* International Communist movement
and national roads, *see* National roads to socialism
and PCI, 202, 206–209, 212–213, 261, 303, 332–339, 349, 351, 353–354, 359–360, 363, 367–374, 397
PCI 1965 visit to, 397
and PCI Tenth Congress, 324n
and peaceful coexistence, 136–137, 207, 291, 334
and peaceful transition to socialism, 136–137, 170–171, 373
and Poland, 163
and polycentrism, 66–67, 404
and revisionism, *see* Revisionism
and Soviet Union, *see* Sino-Soviet relations
and Stalin, 100
and Togliatti, 136n, 324n, 335n, 372n
and underdeveloped countries, 174, 338, 351, 353
and WFTU, 311–312, 324
and Yugoslavia, 332, 334
Christian Democrats, *see* DC
Chukhrai, Grigory, 343
CISL (Confederazione italiana sindacati lavoratori), 265–267, 271, 409
Claude, Henri, 314
Coggiola, Domenico, 33n
Cogniot, Georges, 153n
Colombi, Arturo, 100, 103n
Cominform, 15, 25, 31–32, 57, 59, 61, 65, 70, 74, 119, 123, 137–138, 201
July 1953 secret meeting, 31–32
Comintern, 7–8, 9–13, 23, 34, 60, 61, 65, 70, 119, 124, 138, 361, 364, 366
Commin, Pierre, 85
Common Market, CGIL and, 156, 273, 275–280, 292, 304, 309–310, 318n, 319–329, 358, 402
CGT and, 277–279, 292n, 328–329, 402

Economic and Social Committee of, 325–327
Great Britain and, 306, 317
Italy and, 248
PCF and, 152–153, 176, 317–318, 328–329, 400, 404
PCI and, 152–156, 175, 259, 276, 305–306, 316–319, 326, 329, 377
Poland and, 323
PSI and, 309–310
Soviet views on, 153–155, 176, 259, 292n, 305–308, 315–316, 318–319, 404–405
WFTU and, 292n, 308–310, 319–328, 402
Yugoslavia and, 307–308, 323
Communist youth movement, *see* Italian Communist Youth Federation
Conquest, R., 118n
Conte, Luigi, 224n
Il Contemporaneo, 36–37, 415
Conti, Laura, 192n, 203–204, 206
Cook, Richard [R.C.], 361n
Cossutta, Armando, 398
Council of Mutual Economic Aid, 318, 380
CPR, *see* Chinese People's Republic
CPSU (Communist party of the Soviet Union), *see* Soviet Union
Crane, Robert D., 159n
Crankshaw, Edward, 100n, 131n
Critica marxista, 372
Crossman, Richard, 11n, 12n
Cuba and PCI, 177, 332, 357, 361, 397
Cuban crisis, 321, 332
Cucchi, Aldo, 20
Cult of personality, *see* Stalin
Czechoslovakia, 138, 196, 198, 397

Dallin, Alexander, 183n, 195n, 196n, 198n, 199n, 209n, 211n, 212n, 295n, 297n, 331n
D'Amelio, Giuliana, 77n, 78n, 80n, 88n, 89n, 90n
Dange, S. A., 299
Daniel, Yuli, 396
DC (Democrazia Cristiana)
and Atlantic alliance, 226
and Center-Left, 216, 221–222, 241
and CISL, 271
elections of May *1958,* 151–152
electorate, 18–19, 219n, 224
factional differences, 155, 159, 217, 221n, 222, 225–226, 241–245
historical background, 15–16
internal crisis of *1960,* 216–223, 242

national roads to socialism, 134–135, 187, 373
and PCF, 400
PCI autonomy from USSR, 398
PCI's political style, 410
peace campaign, 169–170
peaceful coexistence, 207
peaceful transition to socialism, 373
polycentrism, 197
proletarian internationalism, 135, 384
proposed international conference, 336, 363, 398–399
and revisionism, 106, 107–108
and Rochet, Waldeck, 399, 402
role in PCI, 190, 386n
Sino-Soviet conflict, 206–208, 336
Stalin, 29
"unity in diversity," 398
unity of left, domestic, 244
and USSR, 133–135, 138, 148n, 166n
violent revolution, 390
on Yugoslavia, 79, 115–116, 173
Lowenthal, Richard, 2, 100n, 118n, 130n, 159n, 376
Luporini, Cesare, 183n, 211n, 346
Lutz, Vera, 247n
Lynd, G. E., 300n

MacFarquhar, Roderick, 130n
Mackintosh, J. M., 159n
Magnani, Valdo, 20–21
Magri, Lucio, 251n, 252
Maitan, Livio, 2n
Malenkov, Georgi, 32, 34, 57, 58, 168
Mallet, Serge, 124n
Manzocchi, Bruzio, 154n
Mao Tse-tung, 66–67, 130–131, 362, 373
Marchesi, Concetto, 43–44
Martinazzi, Italo, 341n
Marzani, Carl, 27n
Matkovsky, N., 164–165
Mercuri, Elio, 205n
Merola, Alberto, 265n, 266n
Mieli, Renato, 27n, 120n
Mikoyan, Anastas, 133, 159
Milazzo, Silvio, 222
Mileikovsky, A., 315n
Minucci, Adalberto, 249n
Mitterand, François, 402
Molotov, Vyacheslav, 32, 57, 113, 118, 130, 138, 150
Momigliano, Franco, 150n, 269
Mondo nuovo, 369
Montagnana, Mario, 151n
Morandi, Rodolfo, 243n
Morawski, Jerzy, 122

Moro, Aldo, 245
Morocco, 297, 301
Morris, Bernard S., 19, 289
Mosca, Giovanni, 281n, 409
Moscow Conference on Contemporary Capitalism (1962), 312–319
Moscow Declaration (November 1957), 131, 135, 140–144, 169, 170, 197, 198
Moscow November 1957, 1960 meetings, *see* International Communist conferences
Moscow Statement (November 1960), 169n, 170, 172, 176, 198, 264
MSI (Movimento Sociale Italiano), 216, 222
Muhri, Franz, 199n

Nagy, Imre, 84
Napolitano, Giorgio, 197, 212, 402n
Nasser, Gamal Abdel, 354
National communism, 99, 133–135, 393–394
National roads to socialism, CGIL, 88
CPR, 67n, 100, 136–137, 170–171, 373
Hungary, 170–171
Moscow meeting, November *1957*, 133–137
PCF, 150
PCI, 62–64, 96, 127, 133–137, 170–171, 187, 236, 358, 379, 387
Poland, 99, 118–123, 140, 170–171
Togliatti, 62–64, 135–136, 165, 236
USSR, 70, 133–137, 164–165, 170–171
Yugoslavia, 99, 115–116
NATO, 226, 239, 316, 320, 399, 400
Natoli, Aldo, 36, 121, 407n
Natolin group, 81
Natta, Alessandro, 117n, 193n, 262n, 313n, 315n, 341n, 348
Negarville, Celeste, 153n
Nekrasov, Viktor, 343
Nenni, Pietro, and "economic miracle," 250–251
left-wing PSI support, 235–236, 243–244, 385
and national roads, 172n, 236
on PCI, 203n
PCI-Soviet relations, 235, 238n, 239
on Poznań and Hungary, 87, 95, 125
and Saragat, 85, 87, 406
on Stalin and Soviet society, 47, 49, 53, 54, 149, 183, 235–237, 243n
and Suslov, 47–49
see also PSI
Neufeld, Maurice F., 266n
North Vietnam, 331n, 396–397

Tito, Josip Broz, excommunication of, 20, 143
national communism, 393–394
and PCI, 146, 332, 361–362
and polycentrism, 116–117
Pula speech, 112–114
and Soviet Union, 118, 143, 178, 334
and Togliatti, 116, 118, 361, 393
Togliatti, Palmiro, on Albania, 203n
attitude toward Soviet system, 50–58, 236–237, 260, 340
autonomy from Soviet Union, 23–24, 55–56, 61–66, 137, 200–202, 212–213, 236–237
and capitalism, 250–251, 256, 358
and Center-Left, 242n, 244–245
and "Chinese" left, 371–372
and Church, 218, 220–221, 230n
and Comintern, 212n, 364
and CPR, 165, 209–210, 324n, 334–335
"economic miracle," 250–251
and European communism, 358, 364
fidelity to Soviet line, 10, 168n
and Gramsci, 364–366
historical background, 7–20
and Hungary, 90, 96, 291n
international Communist movement, 55–56, 59–68, 138–140, 363–364
and Moscow November 1957 and 1960 meetings, 131–133, 135–136, 176
and national liberation movements, 353–355
and national roads, 62–64, 135–136, 165, 236
and Nenni, 243n
and nuclear war, 167–168, 291n, 350n
Nuovi argomenti interview, 41, 50–58, 71, 85, 181, 195, 330, 375–376
and PCF, 151n, 152n
PCI Eighth Congress, 138
and PCI factionalism, 190–191, 195–196
peace campaign of *1960*, 167–168
peaceful coexistence, 22–23, 165, 181–182, 240–241
peaceful transition to socialism, 136
and Poland, 71–74, 76, 81–82, 90, 119, 121, 210–213
political style, 10–12, 56, 96, 124, 190
and polycentrism, 55–56, 59–68, 137, 167, 179, 199–202, 212–213, 354, 375–376, 404
proletarian internationalism, 93–94, 383, 391

proposed international conference, 359–360, 363–367
and revisionism, 131–133
and sectarianism, 102, 117n, 131–133
and Sino-Soviet conflict, 166–171, 176–179, 209–210, 335–336, 359–360, 363–367, 370–372
and Stalin, 14, 25–27, 30–31, 34–41, 50–58, 71–72, 94n, 149, 182, 340, 363, 365–366
Testament, 182, 330, 340, 353, 367, 370–372, 395, 398, 403
and Thorez, 124–125
and Tito, 116, 118, 361, 393
"unity in diversity," 377, 397
and Yugoslavia, 113–118, 336, 361–362
Tortorella, Aldo, 193n, 244n
Tosi, Giorgio, 372–373
Trade unions, Italian, *see* CGIL, CISL, FIOM, UIL
Treaty of Rome, 152
Trentin, Bruno, 255, 269n, 273
Trieste, 62–63
Trivelli, Renzo, 122
Trombadori, Anatello, 183, 183n
Trotsky, Leon, 10, 11, 195, 204–205, 365
Twentieth Century Fund, 18n
Tyller, Miloslav, 196n

UIL (Unione Italiana del Lavoro), 265, 265n, 267, 408, 409
Ulam, Adam B., 29–30
Ulbricht, Walter, 171n, 203n
Underdeveloped countries, *see* National liberation movements
Union des Étudiants Communistes (UEC), 401
Union Générale des Travailleurs Algériens (UGTA), 301
Union Générale des Travailleurs d'Afrique Noire (UGTAN), 296
Union Marocaine du Travail (UMT), 301
United Socialist party (1966), *see* PSU
"Unity in diversity," 375–378, 397
Urban, G. R., 362n
Urban, Joan Barth, 9n

Varga, Eugene, 155, 316–317, 321
Vecchietti, Tullio, 243n
Vetö, Miklos, 228n
Vidali, Vittorio, 63, 191
Vie nuove, 42
Villon, Pierre, 125n
Vitello, Vincenzo, 248n